Principles of Marketing

Principles of Marketing

Adrian Palmer

Professor of Tourism Marketing, University of Ulster

OXFORD

UNIVERSITY PRESS

OXFORD
UNIVERSITY PRESS

Great Clarendon Street, Oxford OX2 6DP

Oxford University Press is a department of the University of Oxford.
It furthers the University's objective of excellence in research, scholarship,
and education by publishing worldwide in

Oxford New York

Athens Auckland Bangkok Bogotá Buenos Aires Calcutta
Cape Town Chennai Dar es Salaam Delhi Florence Hong Kong Istanbul
Karachi Kuala Lumpur Madrid Melbourne Mexico City Mumbai
Nairobi Paris São Paulo Singapore Taipei Tokyo Toronto Warsaw

with associated companies in Berlin Ibadan

Oxford is a registered trade mark of Oxford University Press
in the UK and in certain other countries

Published in the United States
by Oxford University Press Inc., New York

British Library Cataloguing in Publication Data

Data available

Library of Congress Cataloging in Publication Data

Data available

ISBN 0-19-877551-2

1 3 5 7 9 10 8 6 4 2

Typeset in Swift and Argo
by RefineCatch Limited, Bungay, Suffolk
Printed and bound in Italy by
Giunti Industrie Grafiche, Florence

Preface

THIS book is published at a time of great debate in marketing. As an academic discipline, marketing is relatively new, and some would still point to its insubstantial base in theory. Others would argue that marketing has lost its way and scientific approaches to the study of marketing lose the essential creative and interactive nature of marketing. This book provides an introduction to the principles of marketing, beginning from the underlying theoretical bases which are often borrowed from the discipline of economics, sociology, and psychology. Practical application of theory is provided through case studies and vignettes. These practical applications highlight shortcomings in the established frameworks for the study of marketing and the reader is encouraged to formulate alternative frameworks. This book tries not to present prescriptive solutions to marketing problems, but encourages debate about causes and effects. Underlying much of the discussion in this book is whether marketing should be considered a science or an art.

The book has necessarily been divided into a number of chapters in order to provide some form of structure. In the real world, marketing cannot be neatly compartmentalized in this way. With a holistic vision, it will be seen that any change in one aspect of marketing is likely to have consequences in other aspects. In an attempt to emphasize these linkages, each chapter closes with a summary of how that chapter relates to other chapters. Vignettes and case studies provide integrative perspectives.

To begin, a definition of marketing is provided and its essential characteristics identified. The marketing environment provides the stimulus for marketers to act and is explored in Chapter 2. Markets are not homogeneous and segmentation offers an opportunity to develop brands targeted at specific groups (Chapters 3 and 4). An opportunity is provided in Chapter 5 to reflect on the social responsibilities of marketing. Chapter 6 explores marketing research as a means of keeping in touch with a firm's operating environment. A study of buyer behaviour (Chapter 7) is closely linked to the development of ongoing buyer–seller relationships (Chapter 8). This can contribute to a firm's competitive advantage (Chapter 11). The following chapters explore the traditional marketing mix elements of product (Chapters 9 and 10); price (Chapters 12 and 13); place (Chapters 14 and 15); and promotion (Chapters 16–19). The growing importance of direct marketing as a distribution and communication medium is discussed in Chapter 20. Chapter 21 returns to integrative issues by discussing how marketing plans may look fine in theory, but only become effective with appropriate management implementation. The importance and distinctive characteristics of the services sector are discussed in Chapter 22. The final chapter moves the discussion of the previous chapters to a global stage with an analysis of how and why firms seek to exploit international marketing opportunities.

A.P.

The Author

Adrian Palmer is Professor of Tourism Marketing at the University of Ulster, Londonderry.

Contributors

The following have contributed to chapters in this book:

Tony Conway, University of Salford: chapters on Product Policy and New Product Development.
Nick Ellis, University of Derby: chapters on Intermediates and Physical Distribution Management.
Richard Mayer, University of Derby: chapters on Promotion Planning and Personal Selling.

Acknowledgements

Countless colleagues, reviewers, and organizations, too numerous to mention here, helped to bring this book to fruition, and their assistance is gratefully acknowledged. Many authors and organizations kindly granted permission to reproduce copyright material and this is specifically acknowledged throughout the book. The efforts of Sharon Ponsonby in co-ordinating much of this material are particularly acknowledged.

Contents

Detailed Contents

Part Two Understanding Customers

Part I

Marketing: The Fundamentals

Chapter 1
What is Marketing?

Chapter objectives

There is much misunderstanding about what marketing is. Many people equate it with promotion, or 'trying to sell things that people don't really want'. With higher levels of business education, this misperception is changing. This chapter sets out the foundations of marketing and distinguishes between marketing as a fundamental philosophy and as a set of techniques. While the techniques have now been widely adopted, many organizations still have a long way to go in developing a true customer focus which is at the heart of the marketing philosophy. This chapter discusses the relationship of marketing to other organization functions and reviews current debate about the nature of marketing. This is essentially a foundation chapter and many themes discussed will be returned to in more detail in later chapters. At the end of each subsequent chapter there is a summary section identifying specific linkages to other parts of the book. However, it may be a useful idea to return to this overview chapter to reaffirm a holistic view of marketing.

Introduction

MARKETING is essentially about marshalling the resources of an organization so that they meet the changing needs of customers on whom the organization depends. As a verb, marketing is all about how an organization addresses its markets.

There are many definitions of marketing which generally revolve around the primacy of customers as part of an exchange process. Customers' needs are the starting-point for all marketing activity. Marketing managers try to identify these needs and develop products which will satisfy customers' needs through an exchange process. The Chartered Institute of Marketing provides a typical definition of marketing:

Marketing is 'The management process which identifies, anticipates and supplies customer requirements efficiently and profitably'.

While customers may drive the activities of a marketing-oriented organization, the organization will only be able to continue serving its customers if it meets its own objectives. Most private sector organizations operate with some kind of profit-related objectives, and if an adequate level of profits cannot be earned from a particular group of customers, a firm will not normally wish to meet the needs of that group. Where an organization is able to meet its customers' needs effectively and efficiently, its ability to gain an advantage over its competitors will be increased (for example by allowing it to sell a higher volume and/or at a higher price than its competitors). It is consequently also more likely to be able to meet its profit objectives.

Even in fully marketing-oriented organizations, it is not just customers who are crucial to their continuing success. The availability of finance and labour inputs may be quite critical, and in times of shortage of either, an organization must adapt its production processes if it is to be able to continue meeting customers' needs. In addition, a whole range of internal and external pressures (such as government legislation and the emergence of new technologies) can affect its ability to meet customers' needs profitably. Organizations must adapt to a changing marketing environment if they are to survive and prosper.

Marketing as a fundamental business philosophy

As a **business philosophy**, marketing puts customers at the centre of all the organization's considerations. This is reflected in basic values such as the requirement to understand and respond to customer needs and the necessity to search constantly for new market opportunities. In a truly marketing-oriented organization, these values are instilled in all employees and should influence their behaviour without any need for prompting. For a fast food restaurant, for example, the training of serving staff would emphasize those items—such as the speed of service and friendliness of staff—which research had found to be most valued by existing and potential customers. The personnel manager would have a selection policy which recruited staff who could fulfil the needs of customers rather than simply minimizing the wage bill. The accountant would investigate the effects on customers before deciding to save money by cutting stock-holding levels. It is not sufficient for an organization simply to appoint a marketing manager or set up a marketing department—viewed as a philosophy, marketing is an attitude which pervades everybody who works for the organization.

To many people, marketing is simply associated with a set of **techniques**. As an example, market research is a technique for finding out about customers' needs and advertising is a technique to communicate the benefits of a product offer to potential customers. However, these techniques can be of little value if they are undertaken by an organization which has not fully taken on board the philosophy of marketing. The techniques of marketing also include—among other things—pricing, the design of channels of distribution, and new product development. Although many of the chapters of this book are arranged around specific techniques, it must never be forgotten that all of these techniques are interrelated and can only be effective if they are unified by a shared focus on customers.

Of course, the principles of marketing are not new. Some of the elements of marketing orientation can be traced far back to ancient Greece, the Phoenicians, and the Venetian traders. The bartering which still takes place in many eastern kasbahs is a form of marketing. In modern times, marketing orientation developed in the more affluent countries, especially for products where supply was outstripping demand and suppliers therefore faced high levels of competition for custom. Marketing became an important discipline in the United States from the 1930s and has since become dominant around the world. In a competitive business environment, an organization will only survive in the long term if it focuses on the needs of clearly defined groups in society and produces goods and services that satisfy their requirements efficiently and effectively. The emphasis is put on the customer wanting to buy rather than the producer needing to sell.

There have been many attempts to define just what is meant by marketing orientation. Among empirical attempts to measure marketing orientation, a study by Narver and Slater (1990) identified three important components (Fig. 1.1):

Companies that have wholly embraced the marketing philosophy put customers at the centre of everything they do. Being marketing oriented becomes a state of mind for all of a company's employees, who are aware that if they do not put customers first, somebody else will and win their profitable business. Here are some tell-tale signs of a company that may claim to be marketing oriented, but not all of whose employees have taken on board a genuine marketing orientation.

- In the car park, the prime parking spots are reserved for directors and senior staff rather than customers.
- Opening hours are geared towards meeting the social needs of staff rather than the purchasing preferences of customers.
- Management's attitudes towards lax staff is conditioned more by the need to keep internal peace than the need to provide a high standard of service to customers.
- When confronted with a problem from a customer, an employee will refer the customer on to another employee without trying to resolve the matter themselves ('it's not my job').
- The company listens to customers' comments and complaints, but has poorly defined procedures for acting on them.
- Advertising is based on what senior staff want to say, rather than a sound analysis of what prospective customers want to hear.
- Goods and services are distributed through channels which are easy for the company to set up, rather than what customers prefer.

Can you think of any more tell-tale signs?

- **Customer orientation**: An organization must have a thorough understanding of its target buyers, so that it can create superior value for them. Remember that value can only be defined by customers themselves, and can come about through increasing the benefits to the buyer in relation to the buyer's costs or by decreasing the buyer's costs in relation to the buyer's benefits. A customer orientation requires that a company understands value to the customer not only as it is today, but also how it is likely to evolve over time.

- **Competitor orientation**: As well a focusing on its customers, a firm should look at how well its competitors are able to satisfy buyers' needs. It should understand the short-term strengths and weaknesses and long-term capabilities and strategies of current and potential competitors.

- **Interfunctional co-ordination**: It is futile for marketing managers to develop marketing plans which are not acted upon by people who are capable of delivering promises made to customers. Many individuals within an organization have responsibility for creating value, not just marketing staff, and a marketing orientation requires that the organization draws upon and integrates its human and physical resources effectively and adapts them to meet customers' needs.

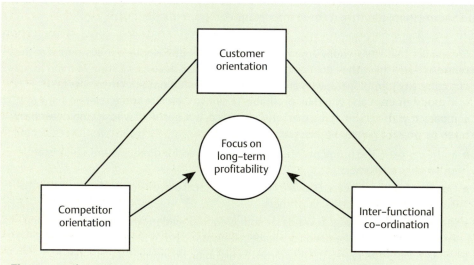

Figure 1.1 Elements of a firm's marketing orientation (based on Narver and Slater, 1990)

Is marketing a science or an art?

So far, marketing has been presented almost as a religion which should uncritically influence how people in an organization go about business. But is marketing based on a scientific method of enquiry, or is it essentially about an artistic process of creativity?

Attempts to study marketing empirically using scientific frameworks of the natural sciences have found favour with followers of the positivist school. The positivist approach holds that from observations of the real world, it is possible to deduce models which are of general applicability. On this basis, models have been developed to predict consumer behaviour, the profitability of retail locations, and price–volume relationships, among others. The great merit of the scientific approach is its claim to great objectivity, in that patterns and trends can be identified with greater confidence than if they were based on casual observation. Many marketers have appreciated the value of this scientific approach. Most major retailers rely heavily on models of retail location before deciding where to locate their next outlet. Armed with trading statistics from their existing network of stores and background information about their locations (e.g. the number of people living within twenty minutes' driving time, passing vehicle traffic per day, proximity to competitors, etc.), a regression model can be developed which shows the significance of each specified factor in explaining sales success.

To many people, marketing has no credibility if it does not take a rigorous, scientific method of enquiry. This implies that research should be carried out in a systematic manner and results should be replicable. So a model of buyer behaviour should be able to predict repeatedly consumers' actions correctly, based on a sound collection of data and analysis. In the scientific approach, data are assessed using tests of significance and models accepted or rejected accordingly.

To counter this view, it is argued that marketing cannot possibly emulate the natural sciences in its methodologies. Positivist approaches have frequently been accused of seeking meaning from quantitative data sets in an essentially subjective manner which is at variance with the scientific principles on which positivist approaches are based (Brown 1995). Experimental research in the natural sciences generally involves closed systems in which the researcher can hold all extraneous variables constant, thereby isolating the effects of changes in a variable which is of interest. For social sciences, experimental frameworks generally consist of complex social systems over which the researcher has no control. So a researcher investigating the effects of a price change in a product on demand from customers cannot realistically hold all factors other than price constant. Indeed, it may be difficult to identify just what the 'other factors' are that should be controlled for in an experiment, but they may typically include the price of competitors' products, consumer confidence levels, the effects of media reports about that product category, changes in consumer fashions and tastes, to name some of the more obvious. Contrast this with a physicist's laboratory experiment where heat, light, humidity, pressure, and most other extraneous variables can be controlled and the limitations of the scientific methodology in the social sciences become apparent.

The argument of post-positivist researchers is that while positivist approaches enhance reliability and replicability, they do so at the expense of validity, that is to say, the findings are not a mirror image of reality (e.g. Brown 1998; Gummesson 1993; Gronroos 1994). Post-positivists hold that the 'real' truth will never emerge in a research framework which is constrained by the need to operationalize variables in a watertight manner. In real-life marketing, the world cannot be divided into clearly defined variables which are capable of objective measurement. Constructs such as consumers' attitude and motivation may be very difficult to measure and model objectively. Furthermore, it is often the interaction between various phenomena which are of interest to researchers and it can be very difficult to develop models which correspond to respondents' holistic perceptions of the world.

Post-positivists place greater emphasis on exploring in depth the meaning of individual case studies rather than seeking objectivity and replicability through large sample sizes. Many would argue that such inductive approaches are much more customer focused in that they allow marketers to see the world from consumers' overall perspective, rather than through the mediating device of a series of isolated indicators.

There is another argument against the scientific approach to marketing which sees the process as essentially backward looking. The scientific approach is good at making sense of historic trends, but less so at predicting what will happen following periods of turbulent change. During the early 1990s, for example, models based in the scientific approach failed to predict accurately the change in consumer spending following changes in such variables as household income, taxation levels, and interest rates. These had traditionally been associated with changes in consumer spending. A more in-depth analysis of consumers' attitudes suggested that feelings of greater insecurity (brought about by the casualization of many jobs) and the memory of the fall in house prices had served as a warning to consumers which rendered many previously developed models of consumer spending obsolete.

There is a further argument that creativity combined with a scientific approach is essential for innovation. The scientific approach to marketing planning has a tendency to minimize risks, yet many major business successes have been based on entrepreneurs using their own judgement in preference to that of their professional advisers. Consider the following cases:

- A scientific analysis of the trans-Atlantic airline market in the 1980s would have concluded that the market was saturated and there was no opportunity for a new British operator. This did not stop the entrepreneur Richard Branson launching his own airline and, by using his own creative style, developing a distinctive and profitable style within the crowded market.

- Research had suggested that consumers would not want to purchase a miniaturized audio cassette player. Yet the Sony company persevered and launched its Walkman which became a great success.

- The reformulation of the taste of Coca-Cola in the late 1980s had followed the scientific process of conducting large-scale research into consumers preferences, and product testing. Nevertheless, when Coke was relaunched, it was a major failure, forcing the company to reinstate its original formulation as Classic Coke.

Marketing has to be seen as a combination of art and science. Treating it excessively as an art can lead to decisions which are poorly thought through in terms of cause and effect. Emphasizing the scientific approach can lead to a company losing sight of the holistic perceptions of its customers. Successful firms seek to use scientific and creative approaches in a complementary manner.

Is marketing an academic discipline?

IT has only been since the 1970s that Marketing has featured significantly on University syllabi. To some of the more traditional academic institutions, marketing has been seen as essentially a topic of application rather than a discipline in its own right.

Marketing has borrowed heavily from other discipline areas. Its antecedents can be traced back to industrial economics, but in the process of growth, it has drawn on the following discipline areas:

- Psychology has been central to many studies of buyer behaviour. Psychological theory in the fields of human motivation and perception has found ready application by marketers (e.g. Maslow 1943).

- Because of the importance of peer group pressures on many consumer and commercial purchases, a body of knowledge developed by sociologists has been used by marketers. As an example, social-psychologists have contributed an understanding of the processes by which interpersonal trust develops which has been applied to the study of long-term buyer–seller relationships (e.g. Dwyer, Schurr, and Oh 1987).

- In its claim to be a science, marketers are constantly borrowing statistical techniques. Large-scale empirical research into buyer behaviour, product design preferences, and pricing effectiveness draw heavily upon previously developed statistical techniques which have conceptual and empirical validity.

- The law represents an embodiment of a society's values and legal frameworks are becoming increasingly important to the study of marketing.

- Finally, economics remains an important discipline area which marketing draws on. As an example, marketers' pricing strategy has to be based on an understanding of the underlying theory of price determination in different market conditions.

Of course, as marketing has developed, the flow of theory has become more two-way. As well as borrowing from the discipline areas, marketers have developed theory and techniques which have been adopted by other discipline areas (for example, marketers contributed significantly to the development of conjoint analysis in the study of consumer preferences and this statistical methodology has now found widespread application elsewhere). In the world of academia, it can sometimes be difficult to identify who is a marketer. Indeed, the subject has benefited from multidisciplinary teams being brought together to develop new techniques which are appropriate to marketing. Unfortunately, the structure of many universities has a tendency to inhibit research between discipline areas which are based in different faculties.

As marketing seeks greater academic credibility for itself, there has been a desire by some marketing academics to prove itself with a rigorous scientific base. This is particularly evident in the approach adopted by US academics. Critics of this approach argue that preoccupation with methodology can obscure the benefits to business which can come from more subjective methodologies.

Foundations for success in business

So far, marketing has been presented as an indispensable approach to doing business. In fact, marketing is not appropriate to all firms at all times and in all places. Essentially, marketing assumes greatest importance where the main factor constraining a firm's survival and growth is the shortage of customers for its products. If a firm can be assured of selling all that it produces, it may consider marketing to be the least of its worries. Consider other factors which may be critical for success to some companies:

- Where raw materials and components which a company requires are scarce, but demand for its finished products is very strong, a company may consider that obtaining inputs to its production processes is its top priority. During the early 1990s, personal computers were selling very strongly, but following the Kobe earthquake, there was a worldwide shortage of memory chips. Faced with buoyant demand, computer manufacturers' priority was to obtain the inputs with which it could satisfy demand from prospective customers.

- For firms requiring high levels of skill among their employees, being able to recruit and retain the right personnel can be critical to business success. Firms in sectors as diverse as computer programming, direct marketing, specialist craft industries, and electrical engineering have had market-led growth held back by difficulties in filling key positions.

- Where a company is given a licence by government agencies to provide a monopoly service, its actions may be more motivated by the desire to keep the agency happy rather than its customers.

Modern marketing emerged in the 1930s at a time when the volume of goods supplied to markets was increasing faster than consumers' demand for them. Instead of taking markets as a given element of their business plan, firms now had actively to address the needs of their markets. If they did not, the market would slip into their competitors' hands.

It is common to talk about the production-oriented firm where production and not marketing is the focal point for business planning. However, when markets became more competitive, the first reaction of many companies has not been to take on board the full philosophy of marketing, but only the selling function. Eventually, firms have realized that rather than trying to sell products that buyers do not really want, it would be better to take on board the full philosophy of marketing which puts customers at the centre of all business planning.

A production or a sales orientation may be appropriate to firms at certain stages in the evolution of markets. Where the dominant business environment is based on the need for good production planning above all else, the company that does this best will achieve the greatest overall business success. Likewise, in competitive markets, the company that achieves the greatest business success is likely to be one that has the most effective marketing.

Because they are business environments which still occur in some markets in some places, production and selling orientation are described below. There has been an almost inevitable tendency for such business environments to progress to a full marketing orientation. Firms that have identified such trends and adapted have tended to survive, while those set in their traditional ways of doing business have fallen behind.

Production orientation

Marketing as a business discipline has much less significance where goods or services are scarce and considerable unsatisfied demand exists. If an organization is operating in a stable environment in which it can sell all that it can produce, why bother spending time and money trying to understand precisely what benefit a customer seeks from buying a product? If the market is stable, why take time trying to anticipate future requirements? Furthermore, if a company has significant monopoly power, it may have little interest in being more efficient in meeting customer requirements. The former state monopolies of eastern Europe are frequently cited as examples of organizations that produced what they imagined consumers wanted, rather than what they actually wanted. Planning for full utilization of capital equipment was often seen as more important than ensuring that the equipment was used

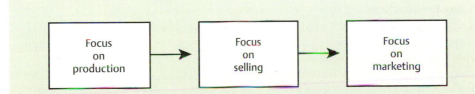

Figure 1.2 The development of the dominant business environment

to provide goods and services that people actually wanted. Production-oriented firms generally aim for efficiency in production rather than effectiveness in meeting customers' needs.

In the developed countries of America and Europe, production orientation was quite pervasive until the 1930s when a general shortage of goods relative to demand for them, and a lack of competition, resulted in a sellers' market. In many goods markets, the world depression of the 1920s and 1930s had the effect of tilting the balance of supply and demand more in favour of buyers, resulting in sellers having to address the needs of increasingly selective customers more seriously. Services markets in most countries have tended to retain a production orientation longer than most goods markets, reflecting the fact that many key services, such as postal services, telecommunications, electricity, gas, and water supply have been dominated by state or private monopolies which gave consumers very little choice of supplier. If the consumer did not like the service they received from their electricity supplier, they could not switch their business to another electricity company. Management in these circumstances would have greater freedom to satisfy their own interests rather than those of the consumer, and could increase their profits more effectively by keeping production costs down rather than applying effort and possibly taking greater risk through developing new services based on consumers' needs.

During periods of shortages, production orientation sometimes returns to an industry sector. The shortage could come about through supply limitations caused by strikes or bad weather or it could be the result of a sudden increase in demand relative to supply. For example, during a bus or train drivers' strike, taxi operators may realize that there is a temporary massive excess of demand relative to supply and so may be tempted to lower their standards of service to casual customers (for example by responding to requests much more slowly and doing so in a less friendly manner regular customers would have come to expect).

Sometimes, a company is just not able to be customer led when it faces acute problems of supply. The market for organic vegetables during the late 1990s illustrates this point. A combination of rising incomes, greater awareness of health issues, and a stream of food safety scares had led to rapid growth in demand for organic produce throughout Europe. But how can farmers grow organically on land which had been saturated by decades of artificial fertilizers? The Soil Association, which operates a widely recognized accreditation scheme for organic produce required that farmland should be free of artificial fertilizer for at least five years before any crops grown on it could be described as organic. So despite the rapid growth in demand and the price premiums that customers were prepared to pay, retailers found it difficult to satisfy demand. Furthermore, with a difficult and intermittent supply, could retailers risk their brand name by being seen as an unreliable supplier of second-rate produce? Marks & Spencer launched a range of organic vegetables in 1997, only to withdraw them soon afterwards, blaming the difficulty in obtaining regular and reliable supplies. In the short term, it was suppliers and not customers who guided the retailer's policy on organic produce.

Selling orientation

Faced with an increasingly competitive market, the natural reaction of many organizations has been to shout louder in order to attract customers to buy its products. Product policy was driven by the desire to produce those products which the company thought it was good at producing, rather than seriously asking what benefits customers sought from buying its products. In order to increase sales, the focal point of the business moved away from the production manager to the sales manager, who sought to increase effective demand by the use of various sales techniques. Advertising, sales promotion, and personal selling were used to emphasize product differentiation and branding.

A sales orientation was a move away from a strict product orientation, but it still did not focus on satisfying customer needs. Little effort was made to research customer needs and devise new product offerings which were customer led rather than production led.

A sales orientation has been characteristic of a number of business sectors. Package holiday companies have often grown by heavy advertising of their competitive price advantage, supported by aggressive sales promotion techniques, such as subsidized insurance and free child places. There are signs that this sales-led approach is now being replaced by a greater analysis of the diverse needs that customers seek to satisfy when buying a package holiday, such as the quality of airport check-in facilities, a reliable departure, and assurance about the standards of the booked hotel.

If a company had accurately identified consumer needs and offered a product which satisfied these needs, then consumers should want to buy the product, rather than the company having to rely on intensive sales techniques.

In the words of Peter Drucker:

The aim of marketing is to make selling superfluous. The aim of marketing is to know and understand the customer so well that the product or service fits him and sells itself. Ideally, marketing should result in a customer who is ready to buy. All that should be needed is to make the product or service available . . . (Drucker 1973)

What organizations undertake marketing?

MARKETING developed in competitive fast-moving goods sectors, followed by private-sector services. More recently, marketing has been adopted by various public-sector and not-for-profit organizations, reflecting the increasingly competitive environments in which they now operate. If an organization has a market which it needs to win over, then marketing has a role. But without markets, can marketing ever be a reality?

Many organizations claim to have introduced marketing when in fact their customers are captive, with no market-place within which they can choose competing goods or services. What passes for marketing may be little more than a laudable attempt to bring best practice to their operations in a selected area, for example in providing customer care programmes for front-line staff. But if customers have to come to the company anyway (as they do in the case of many local authority services), is this really marketing?

Within the public/not-for-profit sectors, financial objectives are often qualified by non-financial social objectives. An organization's desire to meet individual customers' needs must be further constrained by its requirement to meet these wider social objectives. In this way, a leisure centre may set an objective of providing a range of keep-fit programmes for disadvantaged members of the local community, knowing that it could have earned more money by opening its facilities to the larger group of full fee-paying visitors. Nevertheless, marketing can be employed to achieve a high take-up rate among this group, and persuading them to spend their time and money at the leisure centre rather than on other leisure activities.

Key marketing concepts

I**N** this section, the philosophy of marketing will be developed a little further by defining a number of key concepts which go to the heart of the philosophy. The concepts of needs, exchange, value, customers, and markets will be briefly introduced, but returned to in following chapters.

Customers

Customers provide payment to an organization in return for the delivery of goods and services and therefore form a focal point for an organization's marketing activity. Customers can be described by many terms, including client, passenger, subscriber, reader, guest, and student. The terminology can imply something about the relationship between a company and its customers, so the term patient implies a caring relationship, passenger implies an ongoing responsibility for the safety of the customer, and client implies that the relationship is governed by a code of ethics (formal or informal).

The customer is generally understood to be the person who makes the decision to purchase a product, and/or pays for it. In fact, products are often bought by one person for consumption by another, therefore the customer and consumer need not be the same person. For example, colleges must not only market themselves to prospective students, but also to their parents, careers counsellors, and local employers.

As a hospital patient, would you cringe at being referred to as a customer? Or what about the transformation of rail users from passengers to customers? Some universities now refer to their paying students as customers. The use of the word customer may sharpen minds within an organization, making everybody aware that they cannot take users for granted. Passenger, patient, and student are relatively static and passive terms, but customer provides a reminder that custom can be quite transient. But is the use of the term a double-edged sword? Does it raise consumers' expectations about standards of service which may be undeliverable? Can being a patient in an NHS hospital ever be likened to being a customer of Sainsbury's? And what about professional codes of ethics which put some groups of consumers in a very special, trusting relationship with their supplier? Does the use of the generic title of customer undermine this special relationship?

In these circumstances it can be difficult to identify on whom an organization's marketing effort should be focused. The role of influencers in the decision process is discussed further in Chapter 7.

For many public services, society as a whole benefits from an individual's consumption, and not just the immediate customer. In the case of health services, society can benefit from having a fit and healthy population in which the risk of contracting a contagious disease is minimized.

Different customers within a market have different needs which they seek to satisfy. To be fully marketing oriented, a company would have to adapt its offering to meet the needs of each individual. In fact, very few firms can justify aiming to meet the needs of each specific individual—instead, they target their product at a clearly defined group in society and position their product so that it meets the needs of that group. These subgroups are often referred to as segments and are explored in Chapter 3.

Needs

Consumers are motivated by the desire to satisfy complex needs, and these should be the starting-point for all marketing activity. We no longer live in a society in which the main motivation of individuals is to satisfy the basic needs for food and drink. Maslow (1943) recognized that once individuals have satisfied basic physiological needs, they may be motivated by higher order social and self-fulfilment needs. Needs as motivators are explored further in Chapter 7.

Need refers to something which is deep rooted in an individual's personality. How the individual goes about satisfying that need will be conditioned by the cultural values of the society to which they belong. So the need for self-fulfilment in some cultures may be satisfied by a religious penance, while others may seek it from developing their creative talents. It is useful to make a distinction between needs and

Nature of need	Likely sources of need satisfaction in primitive societies	Likely sources of need satisfaction in western Europe
Status	Ownership of animals Multiple wives	Make and model of car Type and location of house
Excitement	Hunting Inter-tribe rivalry	Fast car Adventure holiday
Identification with group	Body painting Adopting rituals of the group	Wearing branded clothing Patronizing 'cool' nightclubs and bars

Figure 1.3 Some basic human needs and how people in different societies may go about satisfying them

wants. Wants are culturally conditioned by the society in which an individual lives. Wants subsequently become effective demand for a product where there is both a willingness and an ability to pay for the product.

It must not be forgotten that commercial buyers of goods and services also have complex needs which they seek to satisfy when buying on behalf of their organization. Greater complexity occurs where the economic needs of the organization may not be entirely the same as the personal needs of individuals within the organization.

Value

For suppliers of goods and services, value is usually represented by payment received. For customers, value is represented by the ratio of perceived benefits to price paid. Customers will evaluate benefits according to the extent to which a product allows their needs to be satisfied. Customers also evaluate how well a product's benefits add to their own well-being as compared to the benefits provided by competitors' offerings.

$$\text{Customer Perceived Value} = \frac{\text{Benefits deriving from a product}}{\text{Cost of acquiring the product}}$$

Consumers often place a value on a product offer which is quite different from the value presumed by the supplier. Business organizations succeed by adding value at a faster rate than they add to their own production costs. Value can be added by better specifying a product offer in accordance with customers' expectations, for example by providing the reassurance of effective aftersales service.

Estimating customers' assessment of value is a difficult challenge for marketers. Chapter 13 deals with practical approaches to pricing which aim to set prices at a price which meets the needs of buyer and seller. Segmentation is crucial to this exercise, as some groups of buyers are likely to place significantly higher values on the firm's goods than others (Chapter 3). If the price of goods is set too high, no exchange may take place, or at least a one-off purchase which may be regarded by the buyer as a 'rip-off'. If the price is set too low, the supplier is failing to appropriate its share of the value of the exchange.

Exchange

Societies have different ways in which they arrange for goods and services to be acquired. In some less developed societies, hunting for food or begging may be the norm. In centrally planned economies, the goods and services may be allocated to individuals and firms by central government planners. In modern market-based economies, goods and services are acquired on the basis of exchange. Exchange implies that one party makes some sacrifice to another party in return for receiving something which it values. The other party similarly makes a sacrifice and receives something that it values. Of course, the sacrifices and valuations of goods received and given up are essentially based upon personal opinion and preferences, so there is no objective way of defining what is a 'fair' exchange, other than observing that both parties are happy with its outcomes. In market-based economies there is a presumption that each party can decide whether or not to enter into an exchange with the other. Each party is also free to choose between a number of alternative potential partners. Exchange usually takes the form of a product being exchanged for money, although the bartering of goods and services is common in some trading systems.

Can the concept of exchange be generalized to cover the provision of public services? Some have argued that the payment of taxes to the government in return for the provision of social services is a form of social marketing exchange. Within marketing frameworks, the problem with this approach to exchange is that it is difficult to identify what sovereignty consumers of government services have in determining the benefits that they receive.

Exchanges should not be seen in isolation from the preceding and the expected subsequent exchanges between parties. Marketers are increasingly focusing on analysing ongoing exchange relationships, rather than one-off and isolated exchanges (see Chapter 8)

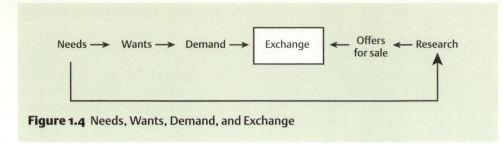

Figure 1.4 Needs, Wants, Demand, and Exchange

Markets

The term 'market' has traditionally been used to describe a place where buyers and sellers gather to exchange goods and services (for example, a fruit and vegetable market or a stock market). Economists define a market in terms of a more abstract concept of interaction between buyers and sellers, so that the 'UK cheese market' is defined in terms of all buyers and sellers of cheese in the UK. Markets are defined with reference to space and time, so marketers may talk about sales of a particular type of cheese in the north-west region of England per year. Various measures of the market are commonly used, including sales volumes, sales values, growth rate, and level of competitiveness.

Marketing management

Successful marketing does not generally come about by accident—it needs to be managed effectively (although there are nevertheless cases of successful marketing which occurred more by good luck than by judgement!). Three fundamental aspects of marketing management can be identified: processes, structures, and outcomes. Central to marketing management is the concept of the marketing mix. In this section, these are briefly introduced, but are returned to in more detail in following chapters.

The marketing management process

Some companies, as they emerge from a production orientation may think that they need only 'do some marketing' when trading conditions get tough. In fact, for well-managed businesses, marketing is an ongoing process which has no beginning or end. It is usual to identify four principal stages of the marketing management process which involve asking the following questions:

Analysis: Where are we now? How does the company's market share compare to its competitors? What are the strengths and weaknesses of the company and its products? What opportunities and threats does it face in its marketing environment?

Planning: Where do we want to be? What is the mission of the business? What objectives should be set for the next year? What strategy will be adopted in order to achieve those objectives? (e.g. should the company go for a high price/low volume strategy, or a low price/high volume one?).

Implementation: How are we going to put into effect the strategy which leads us to our objectives?

Control: Did we achieve our objectives? If not, why not? How can deficiencies be rectified? (in other words, go back to the beginning of the process and conduct further analysis).

Marketing management structures

Internally, the structure and politics of an organization affect the manner in which it can respond to changing customer needs. An organization which gives all marketing responsibilities to just a narrow group of people may in fact create tensions within the organization which make it less effective at responding to change, compared to an organization where the philosophy and practice of marketing are shared more widely. Marketing plans cannot be developed and implemented without a sound understanding of marketing managers' relationship to other members of their organization.

There are two aspects of management structures that particularly affect the role of marketers: firstly, the internal structure and processes of the marketing department itself (where one actually exists), and secondly, the relationship of the marketing functions to other business functions affect the marketing effectiveness of an organization. Issues of marketing management structures and processes are explored in Chapter 21.

Outcomes of the marketing management process

Ultimately, the aim of good marketing management is to allow a company to survive and produce an acceptable level of profits. In leading to this, a tangible outcome of the management process is the marketing plan. A plan should be distinguished from the process of planning—a plan is a statement fixed at one point in time, while planning refers to an ongoing process, of which the plan is just one outcome.

Companies typically produce a marketing plan for a five-year period. Over these

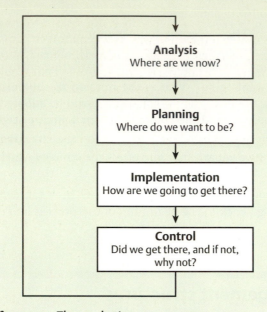

Figure 1.5 The marketing management process

time periods, projections can be subject to a lot of speculative estimation. Neverthe-less, a five year strategic plan can be vital to give a sense of direction to a company's marketing effort. Over the shorter term, companies usually produce an annual plan which gives more detail of how the strategy will be implemented over the forthcom-ing twelve-month period. Sometimes, where a marketing plan is based on a set of assumptions which are highly speculative, a company may choose to develop an additional contingency plan. This will give an alternative plan to use, should the assumptions on which the original plan was based turn out to be invalid.

There is continuing debate about the extent to which marketing plans should be flexible. If they are too flexible, they loose value in being able to act as a blueprint for all individuals in an organization to plan by. If the marketing department changes its sales targets half-way through the plan period, this might cause havoc in the produc-tion department which had geared up to meet the original budgeted level of sales. On the other hand, fixed plans may become an irrelevance when the company's market-ing environment has changed significantly.

The marketing mix

The marketing mix is not a theory of management which has been derived from scientific analysis, but a conceptual framework which highlights the principal decisions marketing managers make in configuring their offerings to suit customers' needs. The tools can be used both to develop long-term strategies and short-term tactical programmes.

A marketing manager can be seen as somebody who mixes a set of ingredients to achieve a desired outcome in much the same way as a cook mixes ingredients for a cake. At the end of the day, two cooks can meet a common objective of baking an edible cake, but use very different sets of ingredients to achieve their objective. Marketing managers are essentially mixers of ingredients, and, as with the cook, two marketers may each use broadly similar ingredients, but fashion them in different ways to end up with quite distinctive product offers. The nation's changing tastes result in bakers producing new types of cake, and so too the changing marketing environment results in marketing managers producing new goods and services to offer to their markets. The mixing of ingredients in both cases is a combination of a science—learning by a logical process from what has proved effective in the past—and an art form, in that both the cook and marketing manager frequently come across new situations where there is no direct experience to draw upon. Here, a creative decision must be made.

The concept of the marketing mix was first given prominence by Borden (1965) who described the marketing manager as :

... a mixer of ingredients, one who is constantly engaged in fashioning creatively a mix of marketing procedures and policies in his efforts to produce a profitable enterprise.

There has been debate about which tools should be included in the marketing mix. The traditional marketing mix has comprised the four elements of Product, Price,

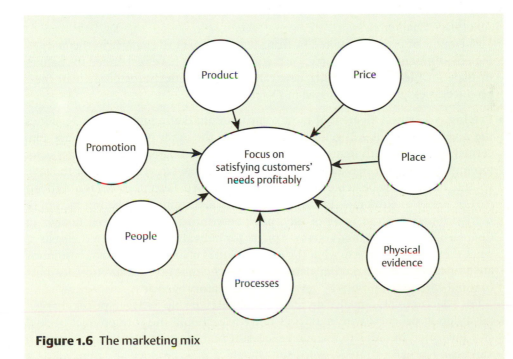

Figure 1.6 The marketing mix

Promotion, and Place. A number of authors have additionally suggested adding People, Process, and Physical evidence decisions. There is overlap between each of these headings and their precise definition is not particularly important. What matters is that marketing managers can identify the actions they can take which will produce a favourable response from customers. The marketing mix has merely become a convenient framework for analysing these decisions. A brief synopsis of each of the mix elements is given below, and returned to for a fuller discussion in the following chapters.

■ **Products** are the means by which organizations satisfy consumers' needs. A product in this sense is anything which an organization offers to potential customers which might satisfy a need, whether it be tangible or intangible. After initial hesitation, most marketing managers are now happy to talk about an intangible service as a product.

The elements of the product mix which the marketer can control include quality levels, styling, special design features, durability, packaging, range of sizes or options, warranties, after-sales service, and the brand image. Trade-offs are involved between these elements. For example, one firm may invest in quality control and high-grade materials to provide a durable, top quality product which would require a low level of after-sales service, while another company might offer lower quality but would ensure that a much more effective after-sales service did not make their customers any worse off than if they had bought the higher quality product. Brands are used by companies to help differentiate their product from those of their competitors. A brand is a name, term, symbol, or combination of these which is intended to differentiate the goods of one seller from all other sellers (see Chapter 4).

The range of products offered by firms needs to adapt to changes in the marketing environment. As an example, cosmetics companies have responded to changes in male attitudes by launching new ranges of cosmetics targeted at men (new product development is discussed in Chapter 10).

■ **Pricing** is a critical element of most companies' marketing mix, as it determines the revenue which it will generate. By contrast, the other mix elements are concerned essentially with items of expenditure. If the selling price of a product is set too high, a company may not achieve its sales volume targets. If it is set too low, volume targets may be achieved, but no profit earned. Setting prices is a difficult part of the marketing mix. In theory, prices are determined by the interaction of market forces and the bases of such price determination is explored further in Chapter 12. In practice, marketers set prices for individual products on the basis of what they cost to produce; what the competition is charging; and what customers are prepared to pay. Marketing managers in many public utilities additionally must contend with interventions by government regulatory agencies.

Price decisions also involve deciding on the relationship between prices charged for different products within a firm's range (e.g. should the core product be sold at a low price in order to encourage sales of highly profitable optional extras?) and also a pricing strategy over time (should a new product be launched as a prestige product, and its price gradually lowered as it becomes more common-place?)

- **Promotion** is used by companies to communicate the benefits of their products to their target markets. Promotional tools include advertising, personal selling, public relations, sales promotion, sponsorship, and—increasingly—direct marketing methods. Just as product ranges need to be kept up to date to reflect changing customer needs, so too promotional methods need to be responsive to changes in a firm's operating environment. Promotion decisions to be taken include: what message to use? which media? what timing of an advertising campaign? How much should be spent? How will this expenditure be evaluated? Promotional decisions are considered in more detail in Chapters 16–20.

- **Place** decisions really comprise two related areas of decisions. Companies usually make their goods and services in places which are convenient for production, but customers prefer to buy them where the purchase process is easiest. So place decisions involve determining how easy a company wishes to make it for customers to gain access to its goods and services. In the first place, this involves deciding which intermediaries to use in the process of transferring the product from the manufacturer to final consumer (usually referred to as designing a Channel of Distribution). Secondly, it involves deciding how to move and handle the product as it moves from manufacturer to final consumer (usually referred to as Logistics or Physical Distribution Management). Place decisions are considered in more detail in Chapters 15 and 16.

- **People** decisions are particularly important to the marketing of services. In the services sector, people planning can assume great importance where staff have a high level of contact with customers. Marketing effectiveness is likely to be critically affected by the actions of front-line employees who interact with customers. While a car manufacturer's employees may be unseen by its customers, a restaurant's waiters could make or break the benefits which visitors to the restaurant perceive. People decisions call for close involvement between marketing and human resource management functions to answer such questions as: what are the prerequisite skills for front-line employees?; how should staff be rewarded and motivated? The particular needs of services industries are discussed in Chapter 22.

- **Process** decisions are again of most importance to marketers in the services sector. Whereas the process of production is usually of little concern to the consumer of manufactured goods, it is often of critical concern to the consumer of 'high contact' services. A customer of a restaurant is deeply affected by the manner in which staff serve them. For busy customers, the speed at which a restaurant processes its customers may be just as important as the meal itself. Marketers must work closely with operations managers to design customer handling processes which are both cost efficient and effective in satisfying customers' needs.

- **Physical evidence** is important to guide buyers of intangible services through the choices available to them. This evidence can take a number of forms. At its simplest, a brochure can describe and give pictures of important elements of the service product—a vacation brochure gives pictorial evidence of hotels and resorts for this purpose. The appearance of staff can give evidence about the nature of a service—a tidily dressed ticket clerk for an airline gives some evidence that the airline operation as a whole is run with care and attention. A clean, bright environment used in a service outlet can help reassure potential customers at the point where they make a service purchase decision. For this reason, fast food and photo processing outlets often use red and yellow colour schemes to convey an image of speedy service.

The definition of the elements of the marketing mix is largely intuitive and semantic. However, dividing management responses into apparently discrete areas may lead to the interaction between elements being overlooked. Promotion mix decisions, for example, cannot be considered in insolation from decisions about product characteristics or pricing. Within conventional definitions of the marketing mix, important customer-focused issues such as quality of service can become lost. A growing body of opinion is therefore suggesting that a more holistic approach should be taken by marketing managers in responding to their customers' needs (Gronroos 1994). This view sees the marketing mix as a production-led approach to marketing in which the agenda for action is set by the seller and not by the customer. An alternative relationship marketing approach starts by asking what customers need from a company and then proceeds to develop a response which integrates all the functions of a business in a manner which evolves in response to customers' changing needs.

Marketing and its relationship to other business functions

COMPANIES are learning that their marketing departments cannot exist in isolation from the other functional departments of their organization. The importance attached to an organization's marketing activities is influenced by the nature of the environment in which the organization operates. In a production-oriented firm, a marketing department has little role to play, other than merely processing orders.

In a truly marketing-oriented company, marketing responsibilities cannot be confined to something called a marketing department. In the words of Drucker (1973):

Marketing is so basic that it cannot be considered to be a separate function. It is the whole business seen from the point of view of its final result, that is, from the customer's point of view

In marketing-oriented organizations, the customer should be the concern not just of the marketing department, but also all of the production and administrative personnel whose actions may directly or indirectly create value in the mind of customers. In a typical company, the activities of a number of functional departments can affect customer value:

■ The selection, training motivation, and control of staff by personnel managers cannot be considered in isolation from marketing objectives and strategies. Possible conflict between the personnel and marketing functions may arise where—for example—marketing demands highly trained and motivated front-line staff, but the personnel function pursues a policy which places cost reduction and uniform pay rates above all else.

- A marketing manager may seek to respond as closely as possible to customers' needs, only to find opposition from production managers who argue that a product of the required standard cannot be achieved. Production managers prefer long production runs of standardized products, but marketers increasingly try to satisfy market niches with specially adapted products.

- At a strategic and operational level, finance managers' actions in respect of the level of credit offered to customers, or towards stockholdings, can significantly affect the quality of service and the volume of customers with which the marketing department is able to do business.

Marketing orientation requires all of these departments to 'think customer' and to work together to satisfy customer needs and expectations. How you actually achieve such a company-wide customer focus is open to question. The concept of 'business process re-engineering' is currently popular and based on organizing the activities of a company around processes that create value as perceived by customers. However, there is a danger that as groups work collectively, individual responsibilities and accountabilities can diminish.

Marketing and social responsibility

Traditional definitions of marketing have stressed the supremacy of customers, but this is increasingly being challenged by the requirement to satisfy the needs of wider stakeholders in society. There have been many recent cases where companies have neglected the interests of this wider group with disastrous consequences. When it sought to dump the Brent Spar oil platform in the North Sea, Shell suffered at the hands of people who had probably never bought a gallon of petrol in their lives. Scenes of protesters outside Shell garages and newspaper coverage of the consequences of its actions took away from Shell something which its marketing department had spent years developing—its image. The opposite can be true where companies go out of their way to be good citizens. Cynics may describe the apparent benevolence of organizations such as the Body Shop as no more than a promotional strategy, and the financial benefits of addressing the needs of stakeholders can be difficult to quantify.

There are segments within most markets which place high priority on ensuring that the companies which they buy from are 'good citizens'. Examples can be found among consumers who prefer to pay a few pennies extra for 'dolphin friendly' tuna, or avoid buying from customers who test their products on animals.

Wider issues are raised about the effects of marketing practices on the values of a society. It has been argued that by promoting greater consumption, marketing is responsible for creating a greater feeling of isolation among those members of society who cannot afford to join the consumer society where an individual's status is judged by what they own, rather than their contribution to family and community life. Much advertising has been criticized as being unethical, as in the case of advertising for tobacco and alcohol which may appeal against an individual's better judgement and bring bad health to millions and the social costs of healthcare for sufferers.

Determining what should be the social responsibilities of organizations is a controversial subject and is discussed in more detail in Chapter 5.

What makes a good marketer?

FINALLY, what characteristics make for a good marketer? Are good marketers bred or born? To answer this question, it is necessary to have a clear understanding of just what marketing is about. The ability to identify, anticipate, and respond to customer needs puts a lot of onus on skills of observation and analysis. Outdated ideas that marketing is all about selling harder by shouting more loudly were probably never appropriate to even the most aggressive sales personnel, for whom listening to customers' needs has always been crucial to developing a winning sales pitch. The great emphasis on listening skills is one reason to explain the growing number of females who have made successful careers in marketing. Numerous studies have shown females to have much stronger traits of empathy and listening ability than males.

Of course, marketing as a business function is very broad and particular branches demand quite specific skills. Within the advertising sector, creativity is essential for successful copywriters, whereas a market analyst would be better equipped with patience and a rigorous methodical approach.

Can marketers be trained? There is a feeling among many employers that a little marketing knowledge by incoming employees may be quite dangerous. This idea holds that it may be better to take on staff who have an ability to think critically, communicate effectively, and show creativity. These abilities may have been developed in non-marketing environments, but the skills can be quite transferrable. Many engineers and biologists, to name but two science-based disciplines, have gone on to become very successful marketers, carried by their ability to approach any new problem with clear, critical thinking combined with creativity. This book seeks to cut through much of the jargon and mystique that has grown up around marketing and argues that many models are essentially based on straightforward critical analysis. By this argument, segmentation can be seen either as a specialist marketing technique, or more generally as a logical process of breaking down a large problem (how to serve a market) into a series of smaller problems (how to serve different parts of that market).

Recently, discussion about whether marketing is a free-standing discipline in its own right has added fuel to the debate about marketing education. Today, a rising number of new graduates are entering employment with at least some exposure to the principles of marketing. From being a specialist subject, marketing has now become mainstream. Michael Thomas eloquently summed up the state of marketing education at the 1994 Chartered Institute of Marketing Annual Conference when he stated that 'the ownership of the ideological resource, known as marketing knowledge, now extends beyond our specialism and threatens to dissolve its distinctiveness'.

Case study

Can Body Shop survive without marketing?

The Body Shop may have grown rapidly during the 1970s and 1980s, but its founder publicly dismissed the role of marketing. To Anita Roddick, marketers were ridiculed for putting the interests of shareholders before the needs of society. She had a similarly low opinion of the financial community, whom she referred to as 'merchant wankers'. While things were going well, nobody seemed to mind. Maybe she had found a new way of doing business, and if she had the results to prove it, who needed marketers? But how could even such an icon as Anita Roddick manage indefinitely without consulting the fundamental principles of marketing? By the end of the 1990s, the Body Shop was suffering bad times and the sceptics among the marketing and financial communities were quick to round on the folly of its founder's apparently idiosyncratic ways.

From a high of 370p in 1992, the Body Shop's share price fell to below 100p in 1999, despite the FTSE 100 index more than doubling during that period. Profits remained similarly depressed, with performance in the European market stagnant. An impressive performance in the Far East was more than offset by losses in the USA and near stagnation in the UK and Europe, but even this bright jewel was eclipsed by the economic turmoil of the Far East towards the end of the 1990s.

Roddick has been the dynamo behind the Body Shop. From a small single outlet, she has inspired the growth of the chain to some 1,500 familiar green-fronted shops in forty-six countries around the world. Yet until the late 1990s she boasted that the Body Shop had never had or needed marketing. Much of the company's success has been tied up with its campaigning approach to the pursuit of social and environmental issues. But while Roddick campaigned for everything from battered wives and Siberian tigers to the poverty stricken mining communities of southern Appalachia, the company was facing major problems in its key markets.

Part of the problem of the Body Shop was its failure to understand fully the dynamics of its market-place. Positioning on the basis of good causes may have been enough to launch the company into the public's mind in the 1970s, but how could this position be sustained? It soon became apparent that other companies had launched similar initiatives, for example the Boots company matched one of the Body Shop's earliest claims that it did not test its products on animals. Even the very feel of a Body Shop store—including its decor, staff, and product displays had been copied by competitors. How could the company stay one step ahead in terms of maintaining its distinctive positioning? Its causes seemed to become increasingly remote from the real concerns of shoppers. While most UK shoppers may have been swayed by a company's unique claim to protect animals, how many would be moved by its support for Appalachian miners? If there was a Boots or a Superdrug store next door, why should a buyer pay a premium price to buy from the Body Shop? The Body Shop may have pioneered a very clever retailing formula twenty years ago, but, just as the concept had been successfully copied by others, other companies had made enormous strides in terms of their social and environmental awareness.

Part of the company's problems has been blamed on the inability of Roddick to delegate. She is reported to have spent half of her time globetrotting in support of her good causes, but has had a problem in delegating marketing strategy and implementation. Numerous strong managers who have been brought in to try to implement professional management practices have given up in bewilderment at the lack of discretion that they have been given, and then left.

The Body Shop's experience in America has typified Roddick's pioneering style which frequently ignores sound marketing analysis. She sought a new way of doing business in America but in doing so dismissed the experience of older and more sophisticated retailers—such as Marks & Spencer and Sock Shop which came unstuck in what is a very difficult market. Body Shop decided to enter the US markets in 1988 not through a safe option such as a joint venture or a franchising agreement. Instead it chose to set up its own operation from scratch—fine according to Roddick's principles of changing the rule book and cutting out the greedy American business community, but dangerously risky. Her store format was based on the British town centre model, despite the fact that Americans spend most of their money in out-of-town malls. In 1996 the US operations lost £3.4 millions.

Roddick's critics claim that she has a naïve view of herself, her company, and business generally. She still argues that profits and principles don't mix, despite the fact that many of her financially successful competitors have been involved in major social initiatives.

The rift between Roddick's and others' view of the world was exemplified in the results of an innovative independent social audit commissioned by the Body Shop in 1996. The company was prompted to commission the report following media criticism that its social and environmental credentials might not actually be as good as the company claimed. The results highlighted shortcomings in virtually every one of the company's stakeholder relationships. The company scored well in areas such as promoting human and civil rights, pollution control, product information, wages and benefits, women's opportunities, and energy conservation. But it scored badly on corporate governance, relationships with shareholders, responsiveness to customer and franchise complaints, accuracy of promotional claims, communication, and their reaction to criticism.

Critics claim that had Roddick not dismissed the need for marketing for so long, Body Shop could have avoided future problems. But by the end of the 1990s it was paying the price for not devoting sufficient resources to new product development, to innovation, refreshing its ranges, and moving the business forward. It seems that heroes can change the rule book when the tide is flowing with them. But adopting the disciplines of marketing allows companies to anticipate and react when the tide begins to turn against them.

Case study review questions

1 In what ways could Anita Roddick have maintained her identification with social and environmental causes as a unique positioning feature?

2 To what extent are the pursuit of profit and meeting the needs of wider groups of stakeholders incompatible? Which companies, if any, have managed sustainably to reconcile these two aims?

3 What are the basic lessons in marketing that the Body Shop might have taken on board in its early years in order to improve its chances of long-term success?

Chapter review questions

1 Discuss how a car wash business might operate if management embraced a production orientation? A Sales orientation? A Marketing Orientation? A Societal marketing orientation?

2 Of what relevance is marketing to the public sector?

3 Of what value is the concept of an expanded marketing mix (as opposed to the traditional '4Ps')?

4 Why is it important for companies to segment their markets? Should providers of public services (e.g. city police forces) segment their markets?

5 Analyse the nature of the needs which may be satisfied by a household mortgage.

6 What is the difference between selling and marketing?

References

Borden, N. H. (1965), 'The Concept of the Marketing Mix', in G. Schwartz (ed.), *Science in Marketing* (New York: J. Wiley and Sons), pp. 386–97.

Brown, S. (1995), *Postmodern Marketing* (London: Routledge).

Brown, S. (1998), 'Romancing the Market: Sex, Shopping and Subjective Personal Introspection', *Journal of Marketing Management*, **14**, pp. 783–98.

Drucker, P. F. (1973), *Management: Tasks, Responsibilities and Practices* (New York: Harper & Row).

Dwyer F. R., Schurr, P. H., and Oh, S. (1987), 'Developing Buyer–Seller Relationships,' *Journal of Marketing*, **51**, Apr., pp. 11–27.

Gronroos, C. (1994), 'From Marketing Mix to Relationship Marketing', *Management Decision*, **32**, 1, pp. 4–20.

Gummesson, E. (1993), 'Relationship Marketing—A New Way of Doing Business', *European Business Report*, **30**, Autumn, pp. 52–6.

Maslow, A. (1943), 'A Theory of Human Motivation', *Psychological Review*, **50**, 4.

Narver, J. C., and Slater, S. F. (1990), 'The Effect of a Market Orientation on Business Profitability', *Journal of Marketing*, Oct., pp. 20–35.

Suggested further reading

This chapter has taken a very broad overview of marketing which sets the scene for the subsequent chapters. Further reading which relates to issues raised in this introductory chapter will be shown in chapters where introductory topics are returned to for a fuller discussion.

To review the debate about the nature of marketing, the following articles are significant contributors to the debate:

- Brown, S. (1995), *Postmodern Marketing* (London: Routledge).

- Brown, S. (1996), 'Art or Science?: Fifty Years of Marketing Debate', *Journal of Marketing Management*, **12**, pp. 243–67.

- Deng, S., and Dart, J. (1994), 'Measuring Marketing Orientation: A Multi-factor, Multi-item Approach', *Journal of Marketing Management*, **10**, pp. 725–42.

- Greenley, G. E. (1995), 'Market Orientation and Company Performance: Empirical Evidence from UK Companies', *British Journal of Management*, **6**, 1, pp. 1–13.

- Gronroos, C. (1989), 'Defining Marketing: A Market-Oriented Approach', *European Journal of Marketing*, **23**, 1, pp. 52–60.

- Gummesson, E. (1991), 'Marketing-Orientation Revisited: The Crucial Role of the Part-Time Marketer', *European Journal of Marketing*, **25**, 2, pp. 60–75.

- Houston, F. S. (1986), 'The Marketing Concept: What it is and What it is Not', *Journal of Marketing*, **50**, Apr., pp. 81–7.

- Kent, R. A. (1986), 'Faith in the Four Ps: An Alternative', *Journal of Marketing Management*, **2**, 2, pp. 145–54.

- Kohli, A. K., and Jaworski, B. J. (1990), 'Market Orientation: The Construct, Research Propositions and Management Implications', *Journal of Marketing*, **54**, Apr., pp. 1–18.

- O'Malley, L., and Patterson, M. (1998), 'Vanishing Point: The Mix Management Paradigm Reviewed', *Journal of Marketing Management*, **14**, 8, pp. 829–52.

Useful web links

Chartered Institute of Marketing: http://www.cim.co.uk/
American Marketing Association: http://www.ama.org/
Marketing magazine Online: http://www.marketing.haynet.com
Marketing Week online:http://www.marketing-week.co.uk/ OR
   http://mad.co.uk/mw/

Chapter 2
The Marketing Environment

Chapter objectives

The previous chapter established that marketing is essentially about being driven by the needs of customers as a means of achieving an organization's goals. This chapter explores how customers' needs are a product of an organization's marketing environment. The marketing environment can be defined as everything that surrounds an organization's marketing function and can impinge on it. Macro-environmental factors, such as a change in the birth rate, may seem inconsequential now, but could soon have a direct effect on a firm's micro-environment, expressed through demand for its products. This chapter explores the relationships between the different elements of a firm's environment and discusses ways in which it can respond effectively to environmental change, including how new production possibilities can be exploited. It also identifies situations where other forces may take precedence over customers as a means of ensuring the survival of an organization.

Introduction

In the previous chapter, marketing orientation was defined in terms of a firm's need to begin its business planning by looking outwardly at what its customers require, rather than inwardly at what it would prefer to produce. The firm must be aware of what is going on in its marketing environment and appreciate how change in its environment can lead to changing patterns of demand for its products.

An environment can be defined as everything which surrounds and impinges on a system. Systems of many kinds have environments with which they interact. A central heating system operates in an environment where key factors include the outside temperature and level of humidity. A good system will react to environmental change, for example by using a thermostat to increase the output of the system in response to a fall in the temperature of the external environment. The human body comprises numerous systems which constantly react to changes in the body's environment, for example the body perspires in response to a change in external temperature.

Marketing can be seen as a system which must respond to environmental change. Just as the human body may die if it fails to adjust to environmental change (for example by not compensating for very low temperatures), businesses may fail if they do not adapt to external changes such as new sources of competition or changes in consumers' preferences. An organization's marketing environment can be defined as:

the actors and forces external to the marketing management function of the firm that impinge on the marketing management's ability to develop and maintain successful transactions with its customers (Kotler 1997)

Naturally, some elements in a firm's marketing environment are more direct and immediate in their effects than others. Sometimes, parts of the marketing environment may seem quite nebulous and difficult to assess in terms of their likely impact on a company. It is therefore usual to talk about a number of different levels of the marketing environment.

■ The *micro-environment* describes those elements which impinge directly on a company. The micro-environment of an organization includes suppliers and distributors—it may deal directly with some of these, while others exist with whom there is currently no direct contact, but could nevertheless influence its policies. Similarly, an organization's competitors could have a direct effect on its market position and form part of its micro-environment.

■ The *macro-environment* describes things which are beyond the immediate environment but can nevertheless affect an organization. An organization may have no direct relationships with legislators as it does with suppliers, yet legislators' actions in passing new laws may have profound effects on the markets which the organization seeks to serve, as well as affecting its production costs. The macro-environmental factors cover a wide range of nebulous phenomena—they represent general forces and pressures rather than institutions with which the organization relates directly.

■ As well as looking to the outside world, marketing managers must also take account of factors within other functions of their own firm. This is often referred to as an organization's *internal marketing environment*.

The elements within each of these parts of an organization's environment are described in more detail below and illustrated schematically in Fig. 2.1.

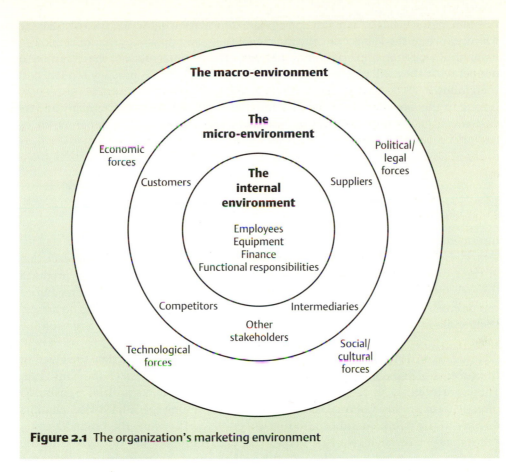

Figure 2.1 The organization's marketing environment

The micro-environment

THE micro-environment of an organization can best be understood as comprising all those other organizations and individuals who directly or indirectly affect the activities of the organization.

The following key groups can be identified.

Customers

These are a crucial part of an organization's micro-environment. In a commercial environment, no customers means no business. An organization should be concerned about the changing requirements of its customers and should keep in touch with these changing needs by using an appropriate information gathering system. Chapter 6 will return to the subject of collecting, analysing, and disseminating information. In an ideal world, an organization should know its customers so well that it is able to predict what they will require next, rather than wait until it is possibly too late and then follow.

Most of this book is devoted to studying the interface between a company and its customers, for example in terms of customers' responses to promotional messages and price levels charged.

Intermediaries

Intermediaries often provide a valuable link between an organization and its customers. Large-scale manufacturing firms usually find it difficult to deal with each one of their final customers individually, so they choose instead to sell their products through intermediaries. In some business sectors, access to effective intermediaries can be crucial for marketing success. For example, food manufactures who do not get shelf space in the major supermarkets may find it difficult to achieve large volume sales.

Channels of distribution comprise all those people and organizations involved in the process of transferring title to a product from the producer to the consumer. These are referred to as intermediaries. Sometimes, products will be transferred directly from producer to final consumer—a factory selling specialized kitchen units directly to the public would fit into this category. Alternatively, the producer could sell its output through retailers, or, if these are considered too numerous for the manufacturer to handle, it could deal with a wholesaler who in turn would sell to the retailer. Sometimes more than one wholesaler is involved in the process.

Because of the importance of intermediaries in making a firm's goods and services accessible to its buyers, a chapter of this book (Chapter 14) is devoted to understanding how they are selected, motivated, rewarded, and controlled. In addition, Chapter 15 reviews physical distribution management and the decisions which firms make in physically moving goods from where they are produced to where customers wish to buy them.

Suppliers

These provide an organization with goods and services which are transformed by the organization into value added products for customers. Very often, suppliers are crucial to an organization's marketing success. This is particularly true where factors of production are in short supply and the main constraint on an organization selling more of its product is the shortage of production resources (e.g. computer manufacturers during the early 1990s when semi-conductors were in short supply). For companies operating in highly competitive markets where differentiation between products is minimal, obtaining supplies at the best possible price may be vital in order to be able to pass on cost savings in the form of lower prices charged to customers. Where reliability of delivery to customers is crucial, unreliable suppliers may thwart a manufacturer's marketing efforts.

In business-to-business marketing, one company's supplier is likely to be another company's customer and it is important to understand how suppliers, manufacturers, and intermediaries work together to create value. The idea of a value chain is introduced later in this chapter. Buyers and sellers are increasingly co-operating in their dealings with each other, rather than bargaining each transaction in a confrontational manner (buyer-seller relationships are discussed further in Chapter 8).

Other stakeholders

In addition to customers, suppliers, and intermediaries, there is a wide range of other organizations and individuals in a firm's micro-environment who can directly affect its marketing activities. Consider the following groups who may affect a company's marketing:

- Local community groups may object to a new production factory, or service outlet, making it difficult to satisfy identified customer demand
- Government regulatory agencies may impose price limits or product specifications which are contrary to those envisaged in a company's marketing plan.
- Members of pressure groups may have never been customers of a company and never likely to be. Yet a pressure group can detract seriously from the image of a company which its marketing department has worked hard to develop.
- Employees are critical to the success of many companies, especially service providers where front-line employees can make or break customers' perceptions of service quality.

These are all examples of 'stakeholders' in organizations. There has been debate about the extent to which organizations have responsibilities towards these groups, in addition to their responsibilities towards customers, intermediaries, and suppliers. The idea of social responsibility will be explored in Chapter 5. For now, it is important to note that companies cannot afford to ignore the needs of this wider group of stakeholders. Although they may not bring in any revenue as customers, failure to recognize and to meet their needs can destroy a company's customer-focused marketing strategy.

Value chains

The concept of a value chain is explored more fully in Chapters 14 and 15 in the context of channels of distribution. Here it is introduced to help understand the complex relationships which can exist between a company and its customers, suppliers, and intermediaries.

Most products bought by private consumers represent the culmination of a long process of value creation. The company selling the finished product probably bought many of its components from an outside supplier, who in turn bought raw materials from another outside supplier. This is the basis of a value chain in which basic raw materials progressively have value added to them by members of a value chain. Value adding can come in the form of adding further components, changing the form of a product, or adding ancillary services to the product offer.

Consider the following example of a value chain for instant coffee:

Value chain member	functions performed
Grower:	produces a basic commodity product—coffee beans
Merchant:	adds value to the coffee beans by checking, grading, and making available to coffee manufacturers
Coffee manufacturer:	by processing the coffee beans, adding other ingredients, and packaging, turns out jars of instant coffee; through promotion, creates a brand image
Wholesaler:	buys bulk stocks of coffee and stores in warehouses close to customers
Retailer:	provides a facility for customers to buy coffee at a place and a time that is convenient to them, rather than the manufacturer
Coffee shop:	adds further value by providing a ready-made cup of coffee in pleasant surroundings

The value of the raw beans contained in a jar of instant coffee may be no more than a few pennies, but the final product may be sold for over £2. Customers are happy to pay this amount because a basic product which they place little value on has been transformed into something which they perceive as valuable. Some consumers would be happy to pay a higher price to buy their coffee ready prepared for consumption in a coffee shop rather than make it themselves at home. Value can only be defined in terms of customers' perceptions, so much of the transformation process described above may be considered by some people to have no value. Some coffee drinkers may consider that processing the coffee to make it into instant granules destroys much of the taste which can be obtained from raw beans. For such people, the most important point in the value creating process probably derives from the growing and selection of the coffee beans.

Who should be in the value chain? The coffee manufacturer might decide that it can add value at the preceding and subsequent stages better than other people are capable of doing. It may, for example, decide to operate its own farms to produce beans under its own control, or sell its coffee direct to customers. The crucial question to be asked is whether the company can add value better than other suppliers and intermediaries could. In a value chain, it is only value in the eyes of customers which matters. If high value is attached to having coffee easily available, distributing it through a limited number of company-owned shops will not add much value to the product.

Relationships between members of an organization's micro-environment

The preceding discussion of value chains emphasizes the point that marketing effectiveness for a firm can be highly dependent upon its relationships with other members of its micro-environment. The individuals and organizations that make up a firm's micro-environment are often described as its *environmental set*. An example of an environmental set for a furniture manufacturer is shown in Fig. 2.2.

Marketers need to be constantly alert to changes in the relationships between members of its environmental set. Consider the following recent changes in firms' environmental sets:

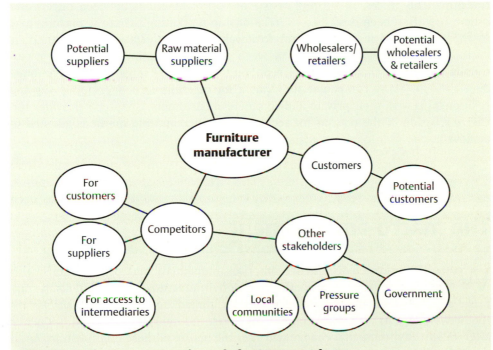

Figure 2.2 The 'environmental set' of a furniture manufacturer

- There have been changes in the balance of power between set members (for example between retailers, wholesalers, and manufacturers).

- New groups of potential customers may emerge (for example elderly people have emerged as new groups of customers for fast food restaurants), while other groups decline.

- New pressure groups are formed in response to emerging issues of widespread social concern.

- Fringe pressure groups have a tendency to become mainstream in response to changes in social attitudes.

In the UK in recent years there has been some significant redistribution in the power of manufacturers relative to retailers. The growing strength of retailers has given them significantly increased bargaining power in their dealings with manu-facturers whose goods they sell. By building up their own strong brands, large retailers are increasingly able to exert pressure on manufacturers in terms of product specification, price, and the level of promotional support to be given to the retailer. It has been estimated that in Britain, the four largest grocery retailers may account for over half of the sales of a typical manufacturer of fast moving consumer goods. The dependency is not reciprocated, with very few retailers relying on one single supplier for more than 1 per cent of their supplies.

Increasingly, firms are changing the way they do business, away from one-off transactions which are individually negotiated, towards ongoing co-operative rela-tionships. The process of turning casual, one-off transactions between buyers and sellers has often been described as 'relationship marketing'. There is nothing new in the way that firms have sought to develop ongoing relationships with their customers, as close relationships between small-scale businesses and their cus-tomers have been characteristic of economies in an early stage of their economic development. Many companies now put a lot of effort into developing ongoing relationships with their private and commercial customers. Chapter 8 provides fur-ther discussion of the reasons for seeking to do this, and the methods adopted to achieve it.

The macro-environment

W^{HILE} the micro-environment comprises individuals and organizations with whom a company interacts, the macro-environment is more nebulous. It com-prises general trends and forces which may not immediately affect the relationships that a company has with its customers, suppliers, and intermediaries, but, sooner or later, macro-environmental change will alter the nature of these relationships. As an example, change in the population structure of a country does not immediately affect the way in which a company does business with its customers, but, over time, it may affect the numbers of young or elderly people with whom it is able to do business.

Most analyses of the macro-environment divide the environment into a number of areas. The principal headings are described below. It must, however, be remembered that the division of the macro-environment into subject areas does not result in watertight compartments. The macro-environment is complex and interdependent. These are the headings for macro-environmental analysis most commonly used.

The macro-economic environment

An analysis of many companies' financial results will often indicate that business people attribute their current financial success or failure to the state of the economy. For example, a retail store that has just reported record profit levels may put this down to a very high level of spending by consumers, while a factory that has just laid off workers may blame a continuing economic recession for its low level of activity.

Few business people can afford to ignore the state of the economy because it affects the willingness and ability of customers to buy their products. Marketers therefore keep their eyes on numerous aggregate indicators of the economy, such as Gross Domestic Product, inflation rates, and savings ratios. However, while aggregate changes in spending power may indicate a likely increase for goods and services in general, the actual distribution of spending power among the population will influence the pattern of demand for specific products. In addition to measurable economic prosperity, the level of perceived wealth and confidence in the future can be an important determinant of demand for some high value services.

The effects of government policy objectives on the distribution of income can have profound implications for marketers. During most of the post-war years, the tendency was for mid-market segments to grow significantly. In the car sector, this was associated with the success of mid-range cars such as the Ford Escort and Sierra. During periods of Labour administration, the sale of luxury cars tended to suffer. However, the boom of the late 1980s and the rapid rise in income of the top groups in society resulted in a significant growth in the luxury car sector. Manufacturers such as BMW, Mercedes Benz, and Jaguar benefited from this trend. At the same time, the worsening of the fortunes of many lower income groups partly explains the growth in very low priced basic cars such as those manufactured by Lada, Skoda, and FSO.

Through models of national economies, firms try to understand how sudden increases in expenditure (whether by government, households, or firms) will affect their sector. The multiplier effect of increases in government spending (or cuts in taxation) can be compared to the effects of throwing a stone into a pond of water. The initial spending boost will have an initial impact on households and businesses directly affected by the injection, but through a ripple effect will also be indirectly felt by households and firms throughout the economy.

A small increase in consumer demand can lead, through an accelerator effect, to a sudden large increase in demand for plant and machinery as manufacturers seek to increase their capacity with which to meet this demand. Demand for industrial capital goods therefore tends to be more cyclical than for consumer goods, so when consumer demand falls by a small amount, demand for plant and machinery falls by a correspondingly larger amount and vice versa.

Companies are particularly interested in understanding business cycles and in predicting the cycle as it affects their sector. If the economy is at the bottom of an economic recession, this may be the ideal time for firms to begin investing in new productive capacity, ahead of the eventual upturn in demand. In the past, firms have often only invested in new capacity once overseas competitors have built up market share, and possibly created some long-term customer loyalty too. Adding new productive capacity during a period of recession is also likely to be much cheaper than waiting until an upturn in the economy puts new pressure on its input prices. During periods of economic boom, firms should look forward to the inevitable downturn which follows. A problem of excess capacity and stocks can result when a firm fails to spot the downturn at the top of the business cycle. Analysing turning-points in the business cycle has therefore become crucial to marketers. To miss an upturn at the bottom of the recession can result in missing out on opportunities when the recovery comes to fruition. On the other hand, reacting to a false signal can leave a firm with expensive excess stocks and capacity on its hands.

It is extremely difficult to identify a turning-point at the time when it is happening. Following the UK economic recession of the early 1990s, there were many false predictions of an upturn. When the predicted revival in domestic consumer expenditure failed to transpire, marketers in product fields as diverse as cars, fashion clothing, and electrical goods were forced to sell off surplus stocks at low prices.

Marketers try to react to turning-points as closely as possible. Many subscribe to the services of firms who use complex models of the economy to make predictions about the future performance of their sector. Companies can be guided by key lead indicators which have historically been a precursor of a change in activity levels for their business sector. For a company manufacturing process plant equipment, the level of attendance at major trade exhibitions could indicate the number of buyers who are at the initial stages in the buying process for new equipment. An alternative to trying to predict the economic performance of their sector a long way ahead is to manage operations so that a firm can respond almost immediately to changes in its macro-economic environment. The use of short-term contracts of employment and out-sourcing of component manufacture can help a company to downsize rapidly at minimum cost when it enters a recession and to expand production when a recovery occurs.

An analysis of the macro-economic environment will also indicate the current and expected future level of competitor activity. An oversupply of products in a market sector (whether actual or predicted) normally results in a downward pressure on prices and profitability. Markets are dynamic and what may appear an attractive market today may soon deteriorate as the market matures. Market dynamics are discussed further in Chapter 11.

The political environment

The political environment can be one of the less predictable elements in an organization's marketing environment. Marketers need to monitor the changing political environment because political change can profoundly affect a firm's marketing. Consider the following effects of politicians on marketing:

- At the most general level, the stability of the political system affects the attractiveness of a particular national market. While western Europe is generally politically stable, the instability of many eastern European governments has led many companies to question the wisdom of investing in those countries.

- Governments pass legislation which directly and indirectly affects firms' marketing opportunities. There are many examples of the direct effects on marketers, for example laws giving consumers rights against the seller of faulty goods. At other times, the effect is less direct, as where legislation requiring local authorities to put out to tender some of their duties, thereby creating more competitive relationships between firms in a market.

- Governments are responsible for protecting the public interest at large, imposing further constraints on the activities of firms (for example controls on pollution which may make a firm uncompetitive in international markets on account of its increased costs).

- The macro-economic environment is very much influenced by the actions of politicians. Government is responsible for formulating policies which can influence the rate of growth in the economy and hence the total amount of spending power. It is also a political decision as to how this spending power should be distributed between different groups of consumers and between the public and private sectors.

- Government policies can influence the dominant social and cultural values of a country, although there can be argument about which is the cause and which is the effect (for example, did the UK government's drive for economic expansion and individual responsibility during the mid-1980s change public attitudes towards the community?).

- Increasingly, the political environment affecting marketers includes supranational organizations which can directly or indirectly affect companies. These include trading blocs (e.g. the EU, ASEAN, and NAFTA) and the influence of worldwide intergovernmental organizations whose members seek to implement agreed policy (e.g. the World Trade Organization and the United Nations).

If there is one topic of political conversation that divides people it is the quest for ever closer European integration. The EU was founded by the Treaty of Rome, signed in 1957 by the original six members of the European Coal and Steel Community—France, West Germany, Italy, Belgium, The Netherlands, and Luxembourg. Britain joined in 1972, together with Ireland and Denmark, to be joined by Greece in 1981, Spain and Portugal in 1986, and Austria, Finland, and Sweden in 1995. The combined population of EU countries in 2000 was estimated at 729 million (Social Trends, Office for National Statistics, London, 1999).

Economic and political integration of the EU are difficult to separate, and, whether they like it or not, marketers throughout Europe are increasingly having to look not just to their own domestic political environment, but also the EU government, comprising the Commission, Council of Ministers, Parliament, and Court of Justice. The Single European Act which came into effect in 1993 removed a lot of the decision-making which affects marketers away from domestic governments to the EU. Directives made by the EU affecting issues such as product design and advertising required member states to implement through their domestic legislation. If new legislation looked threatening, it became futile to lobby the domestic government—it was the EU which inspired the legislation. As an example, it seemed in 1998 that the EU would effectively ban tobacco advertising throughout the EU. The tobacco industry realized that the directive must be stopped at Brussels before it was incorporated into member states' legislation. Through its industry group, the Tobacco Manufacturers Association, it had failed through its previous lobbying to stop the directive, so moved to challenge the directive in the European Court of Justice, arguing that the EU has no authority to make a public health directive under its powers to harmonize the internal market.

The EU is accounting for an increasing proportion of the legislation that affects marketers, and, with the advent of the single European currency, its influence on the macro-economic environment has increased. But are marketers simply opportunistic in their support for greater integration of member states? As an example, brewers have in the past condemned the European Commission's plans for tighter control over the labelling of beer, claiming their national beer is unique, but this has not prevented them also campaigning for a harmonization of taxes where the tax paid in their country is higher than the EU average.

The social and cultural environment

It is crucial for marketers to appreciate fully the cultural values of a society, especially where an organization is seeking to do business in a country which is quite different from its own. Attitudes to specific products change through time and at any one time between different groups.

Even in home markets, business organizations should understand the processes of gradual cultural change and be prepared to satisfy the changing needs of consumers.

Consider the following examples of contemporary cultural change in western Europe and the possible responses of marketers:

- Leisure is becoming a bigger part of many people's lives and marketers have responded with a wide range of leisure related goods and services.
- The role of women in society is changing as men and women increasingly share expectations in terms of employment and household responsibilities. This is reflected in the observation that women made up 47 per cent of the UK paid work-force in 1997, compared with 37 per cent in 1971. Examples of marketing responses include cars designed to meet the aspirational needs of career women and ready prepared meals which relieve working women of their traditional role in preparing household meals.
- Greater life expectancy is leading to an ageing of the population and a shift to an increasingly 'elderly' culture. This is reflected in product design which emphasizes durability rather than fashionability.
- The growing concern among many groups in society with the environment is reflected in a variety of 'green' consumer products.

There has been much recent discussion about the concept of 'cultural convergence', referring to an apparent decline in differences between cultures. It has been argued that basic human needs are universal in nature and, in principle, capable of satisfaction with universally similar solutions. Many companies have sought to develop one product for a global market, and there is some evidence of firms achieving this (for example Coca-Cola and McDonalds). The desire of a subculture in one country to imitate the values of those in another culture has also contributed to cultural convergence. This is nothing new. During the Second World War, many individuals in western Europe sought to follow the American lifestyle, and nylon stockings from the USA became highly sought after cultural icons by some groups. The same process is at work today in many developing countries where some groups seek to identify with western cultural values through the purchases they make.

New challenges for marketing are posed by the diverse cultural traditions of ethnic minorities, as seen by the growth of travel agencies catering for families wishing to visit relatives or to go on religious pilgrimages.

The demographic environment

Demography is the study of populations in terms of their size and characteristics. Among the topics of interest to demographers are the age structure of a country, the geographic distribution of its population, the balance between male and females, and the likely future size of the population and its characteristics. Changes in the size and age structure of the population are critical to many firms' marketing. Although the total population of most western countries is stable, their composition is changing. Most countries are experiencing an increase in the proportion of elderly people and companies who have monitored this trend responded with the development of residential homes, cruise holidays, and financial portfolio management services aimed at meeting this group's needs. At the other end of the age spectrum, the birth rate of most countries is cyclical resulting in a cyclical pattern of demand for age-related products such as baby products, fashion clothing, and family cars. Consider the following changes in the structure of the UK population and the effects on marketers:

■ There has been a trend for women to have fewer children (the average number of children for each woman born in 1930 was 2.35, 2.2 for those born in 1945, and it is projected to be 1.97 for those born in 1965). There has also been a tendency for women to have children later in life (the average age at which women in the UK have their first child has moved from 24 years in 1945 to 28 in 1994). There has also been an increase in the number of women having no children (according to the Office of Population Census and Surveys, more than one-fifth of women born in 1967 are expected to be childless when they reach the age of 40, compared with 13 per cent of those born in 1947). Fewer children has resulted in parents spending more per child (more designer clothes for children rather than budget clothes) and

Figure 2.3 Ageing of the population is a major opportunity for many organizations. This manufacturer of stairlifts has targeted a segment of the population which is expected to grow rapidly in most western countries. (Reproduced with permission of Stannah Stairlifts)

has allowed women to stay at work longer (increasing household incomes and encouraging the purchase of labour-saving products).

■ Alongside a declining number of children has been a decline in the average household size (from an average of 3.1 people in 1961 to 2.3 in 1997). There has been a particular fall in the number of very large households with 5 or more people (down from 9 per cent of all households in 1961 to 5 per cent in 1997) and a significant increase in the number of one-person households (up from 11 per cent to 27 per cent over the same period). The growth in small or one-person households has had numerous marketing implications, ranging from an increased demand for smaller units of housing to the types and size of groceries purchased. A single-person household buying for him- or herself is likely to use different types of retail outlets compared to the household buying as a unit.

■ Marketers also need to monitor the changing geographical distribution of the population (between different regions of the country and between urban and rural areas). The current drift towards rural and suburban areas has resulted in higher car ownership levels and a preference for using out-of-town shopping centres.

Statistics have continued to chart the decline of the typical nuclear family of two parents and 2.4 children. However, advertisers have continued to portray this ideal type family in their advertising, despite the fact that fewer people can relate directly to it. The fast food restaurant McDonald's recognized this trend with an advertising campaign launched in 1995 which portrayed a boy arranging for a meeting between his separated parents in a branch of McDonald's. Behind the departure from the happy-families norm in fast food marketing is the realization that the number of families in the UK with single parents has risen from 8 per cent in 1971 to 21 per cent in 1992. McDonald's claimed that it could not credibly position itself as a family restaurant and show only pictures of mum and dad and two kids without the risk of alienating parents and children from different households. But could McDonald's incur the wrath of critics who might accuse McDonald's of actually contributing to family breakdown? With an eye on such worries, McDonald's advertisements left the impression that the couple were going to get together again.

The technological environment

The pace of technological change is becoming increasingly rapid and marketers need to understand how technological developments might affect them in four related business areas:

■ New technologies can allow new goods and services to be offered to consumers—telephone banking, mobile telecommunications, and new drugs, for example.

■ New technology can allow existing products to be made more cheaply, thereby widening their market through being able to charge lower prices. In this way, more efficient aircraft have allowed new markets for air travel to develop.

■ Technological developments have allowed new methods of distributing goods and services (for example, bank ATM machines allow many banking services to be made available at times and places which were previously not economically possible).

■ New opportunities for companies to communicate with their target customers have emerged, with many financial services companies using computer data-bases to target potential customers and to maintain a dialogue with established customers. The Internet opens up new distribution opportunities for many companies.

Monitoring and responding to environmental change

IT was stated earlier that the relationship between a firm and its business environment is crucial to marketing success. There are many examples of firms who have neglected this relationship and eventually withered and died. To avoid this fate, a firm must:

■ understand what is going on in its business environment, and
■ respond and adapt to environmental change.

As organizations become larger and national economies more complex, the task of understanding the marketing environment becomes more formidable. Information about a firm's environment becomes crucial to environmental analysis and response.

Information collection, processing, transmission, and storage technologies are continually improving, as witnessed by the development of Electronic Point of Sale (EPOS) systems. These have enabled organizations to enhance greatly the quality of the information they have about their operating environment. However, information is becoming more accessible not just to one particular organization, but also to its competitors. Attention is therefore moving away from how information is collected, to who is best able to make use of the information.

Information about the current state of the environment is used as a starting-point for planning future marketing strategy, based on assumptions about how the environment will change. Information is also vital to monitor the implementation of an organization's marketing plans and to note the cause of any deviation from plan. Information therefore has both a planning function and a control function.

Organizations learn about their environment using a number of sources of information:

■ Marketing intelligence comprises unstructured sources of information used by marketers to paint a general picture of their changing environment. Intelligence can be gathered from a number of sources, such as newspapers, specialized cutting services, employees who are in regular contact with market developments, inter-mediaries and suppliers to the company, as well as specialized consultants.

- Marketing research complements marketing intelligence, for whereas the latter concentrates on picking up relatively intangible ideas and trends, marketing research focuses on structured and largely quantifiable data collection procedures. This can provide both routine information about marketing effectiveness—such as brand awareness levels or distribution effectiveness—and one-off studies, such as a survey of changing attitudes towards diet.

- In addition to collecting these external sources of data, companies can learn a lot about their environment by carefully examining data which they routinely collect. An analysis of sales patterns may reveal changes in the types of products bought by particular market segments, which in turn may be indicative of a change of atti-tudes in some groups of society.

Collecting information about the environment is one thing, but analysing it and using it can be quite another. Large organizations operating in complex and turbu-lent environments therefore often build models of their environment, or at least sub-components of it. Some of these can be quite general, as in the case of the models of the national economy which many large companies have developed. From a general model of the economy, a firm can predict how a specific item of government policy (for example, increasing the rate of Value Added Tax on luxury goods) will impact directly and indirectly on sales of its own products.

The crucial role of information in effective marketing management is returned to in Chapters 6 and 21.

SWOT analysis

SWOT analysis (an acronym for Strengths, Weaknesses, Opportunities, and Threats) is a useful framework for assessing an organization and its marketing environment. SWOT analysis summarizes the main environmental issues in the form of opportuni-ties and threats facing an organization. These external factors are listed alongside the organization's internal strengths and weaknesses. An opportunity in an organiza-tion's external environment can only be exploited if it has the internal strengths to do so. If, on the other hand, the organization is not capable of exploiting these because of internal weaknesses then they should perhaps be left alone. For this reason, the terms opportunities and threats should not be viewed as 'absolutes', but assessed in the context of an organization's resources and the feasibility of exploiting them.

The principles of a SWOT analysis are illustrated in Fig. 2.4 by examining how an established manufacturer of ready prepared chicken products might view its strengths and weaknesses in terms of the opportunities and threats which it faces in its environment.

Marketing opportunities can come in many forms and each should be assessed for its attractiveness and success probability. Attractiveness can be assessed in terms of

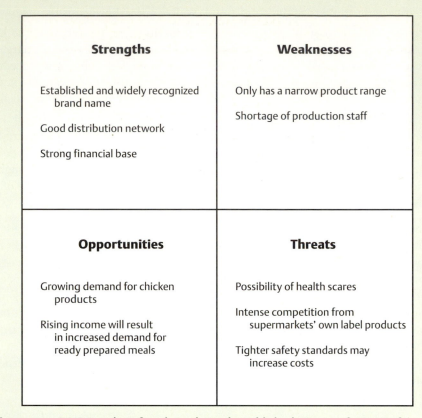

Strengths	**Weaknesses**
Established and widely recognized brand name Good distribution network Strong financial base	Only has a narrow product range Shortage of production staff
Opportunities	**Threats**
Growing demand for chicken products Rising income will result in increased demand for ready prepared meals	Possibility of health scares Intense competition from supermarkets' own label products Tighter safety standards may increase costs

Figure 2.4 SWOT analysis for a hypothetical established UK manufacturer of ready–prepared chicken meat

potential market size, growth rates, profit margins, competitiveness, and distribution channels. Other factors may be technological requirements, the extent of government restrictions, availability of government grants, ecological concerns, and energy requirements. Measures of attractiveness must be qualified by the probability of success which depends on the company's strengths and competitive advantage. Probability of success is likely to be influenced by, among other things, its access to cash, lines of credit or capital to finance new developments, technological and productive expertise, marketing skills, distribution channels, and managerial competence. A simple matrix (Fig. 2.5) can be constructed to show the relationship between attractiveness and success probability.

An environmental threat is 'a challenge posed by an unfavourable trend or development in the environment that would lead, in the absence of purposeful marketing action, to the erosion of the company's or industry's position' (Kotler 1997). In this case the threats should be assessed according to their seriousness and the probability of occurrence. A threat matrix can then be constructed.

In order for an environmental analysis to have a useful input to the marketing

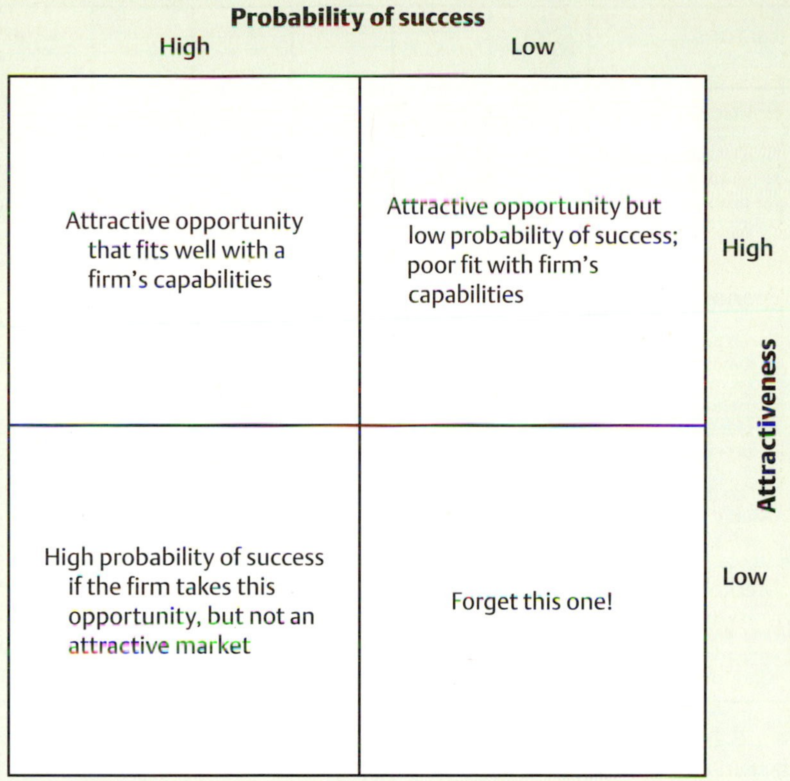

Probability of success

	High	Low	
	Attractive opportunity that fits well with a firm's capabilities	Attractive opportunity but low probability of success; poor fit with firm's capabilities	High
Attractiveness	High probability of success if the firm takes this opportunity, but not an attractive market	Forget this one!	Low

Figure 2.5 Opportunity matrix

planning process, a wide range of information and opinions needs to be summarized in a meaningful way. The information collated from the detailed analysis can be simplified in the form of an Environmental Threat and Opportunity Profile (ETOP). This provides a summary of the environmental factors that are most critical to the organization (Fig. 2.6) and can be useful in stimulating debate amongst senior management about the future of the business. Some analysts suggest trying to weight these factors according to their importance and then rating them for their impact on the organization.

The internal environment

FINALLY, we must remember that marketers do not operate in a vacuum within their organizations. Internally, the structure and politics of an organization affect the manner in which it responds to environmental change. We are all familiar with

Factor	Major opportunity	Minor opportunity	Neutral	Minor threat	Major threat	Probability of occurrence
Political						
New transport policy sees introduction of tax on use of cars in town centres					✓	0.1
Economic						
Tax on petrol increases by 5p				✓		0.4
Household spending falls for two quarters in succession					✓	0.2
VAT on new cars reduced	✓					0.1
Market						
Overseas competitors enter market more aggressively				✓		0.3

Figure 2.6 Environmental Threat and Opportunity Profile, applied to a car manufacturer

lumbering giants of companies who, like a super-tanker, have ploughed ahead on a seemingly predetermined course and have had difficulty in changing direction. During the late 1990s such well-respected companies as Sainsbury's and Marks & Spencer were accused of having internal structures and processes which were too rigid to cope with a changing external environment. Simply having a strong marketing department is not necessarily the best way of ensuring adaptation to change. Such companies may in fact create internal tensions which make them less effective at responding to changing consumer needs than where marketing responsibilities in their widest sense are disseminated throughout the organization.

Two aspects to a marketing manager's internal environment are of importance here—firstly, the internal structure and processes of the marketing department itself (where one actually exists), and secondly, the relationship of the marketing functions to other business functions.

Marketing departments allocate responsibilities to individual managers on a number of bases, the most common being functions performed, products managed, customer segments, and geographical areas, although, in practice, most marketing departments show more than one approach to structure. Chapter 21 will review some of the advantages and disadvantages of each of these approaches.

In a genuinely marketing-oriented organization, marketing activities cannot be confined to something called a marketing department. As Drucker (1973) noted, marketing is so basic that it cannot be considered to be a separate function—it has to be the whole business seen from the customer's point of view. In marketing-oriented organizations, customers should not simply be the concern of the marketing department, but also of all those operational and administrative personnel whose actions may directly or indirectly affect customers' perceptions of quality and value. Some of the most successful companies are those that have successfully integrated marketing into all functional areas of the organization.

An important element of an organization's internal environment is its dominant 'culture'. Culture in this sense refers to a set of values that are shared by all members of the organization. Some organizations, for example, have a culture that stresses that the customer is always right while others have a bureaucratic culture which stresses the need to conduct business in an administratively 'correct' way. Numerous comparative studies into the performance of European, American, and Japanese managed organizations have identified the concept of culture as a possible explanation for differences in competitive effectiveness. It can be very difficult to change cultural attitudes within an organization, and the process of change can be painful for many. Some organizations have appeared to have successfully managed the transition from a production-oriented culture to one which is focused on customers (for example, the Rover car company). In many cases, however, this change has been a slow process, leading to competitive disadvantage where culture does not keep up with changes in the external environment. As an example, UK clearing banks have continued to be dominated by a culture based on prudence and caution when in some product areas such as insurance sales, a more aggressive approach to marketing management is called for.

The flexible organization

The management of change is becoming increasingly important to organizations, driven by the increasing speed with which the external environment is changing. Flexibility can be called for on a day-to-day basis and long term. Chapters 14 and 15 will return to issues of supply chain management which allow companies to respond very quickly to changing customer demand. Flexibility is also required at a more strategic level.

Flexibility within an organization's workforce can be achieved by segmenting it into core and peripheral components (Fig. 2.8). Many organizations have given their core workers greater job security, with defined career opportunities. In return for this relative job security core workers may have to accept what Atkinson (1984) terms 'functional flexibility' by becoming responsible for a variety of jobs, as and when required. During their career with a company, such employees may undertake a variety of roles. In contrast to this group, peripheral employees have less job security and relatively limited career opportunities. They are 'numerically flexible', and often employed on short-term contracts or treated as self-employed subcontractors. It is not just operational staff whose jobs have been casualized in this way. Increasingly, many management jobs are being 'outsourced', and undertaken by consultants who are taken on as and when required. There is, however, debate about whether excessive use of short-term, flexible labour increases the effectiveness of an organization. Many have pointed to a possible downside in the form of reduced commitment of employees to the firm, which can ultimately damage the company's dealings with its customers.

Organizations differ in the speed with which they are able to exploit new opportunities as they appear in their environment. Being the fastest company in a market to adapt can pay good dividends, so recent years have seen major attempts by firms to increase their flexibility, for example by moving human resources from areas in decline to those where there is a prospect of future growth. For example, in order to retain their profitability, retailers must have the ability to move floor space and personnel away from declining or static products in favour of more promising growth areas.

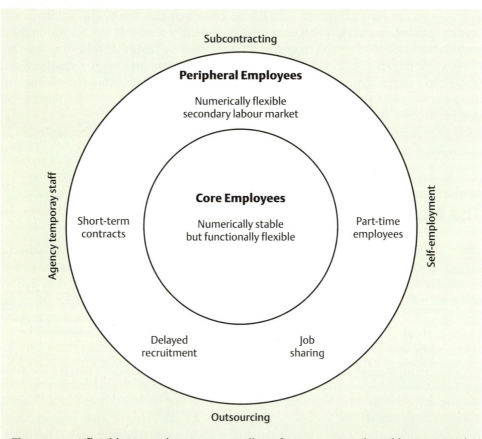

Figure 2.7 A flexible internal environment allows firms to respond quickly to external environmental change

Chapter summary and key linkages to other chapters

Marketing-oriented firms begin their business planning by looking outward to what their customers require, in contrast to production-oriented companies who begin by focusing on what they prefer to produce. Talking to existing customers in order to understand their needs may be good enough for a small business in a stable environment. But as organizations get larger and their environments more turbulent, firms must devote more effort to reading signs in their environment which might indicate what customers will want next, or even the nature of customers' demand in five years time.

This chapter has provided a brief overview of a firm's micro-environment (comprising individuals and organizations with whom it is in regular contact); the macro-environment (comprising pressures and forces which will eventually affect the firm's dealings with people in its micro-environment) and its internal environment (structures and processes internal to the organization which may help or hinder the achievement of marketing objectives).

Marketing management can be seen essentially as an attempt by firms to respond using multiple tools to changes in these multiple dimensions of their marketing environment. In reading the following chapters of this book, the influence of environmental factors must always be born in mind in guiding the marketing management actions which are discussed.

Chapter 1: What is marketing?: You will recall that marketing is essentially about responding to external needs, especially the needs of customers. Remember also that companies need to be aware of competitors in their environment, and the increasing need to be seen as a 'good citizen'.

Chapter 3: Segmentation: Macro-environmental change results in different rates of growth in demand between segments (for example, political and economic forces in the 1990s led to a widening of the gap between the richest and poorest groups, resulting in growth in segments for high value and budget goods, at the expense of mid-market segments).

Chapter 4: Branding: The strength of brands in any market reflects, among other things, the state of economic and social development of that market. Cultures differ in the value they place on brands.

Chapter 5: Marketing and ethics: What does it take for a company to be a 'good citizen'? Does marketing further contribute to the growing sense of division within society where groups feel disenfranchised from society because they cannot share the benefits of economic growth which marketing makes painfully aware to them?

Chapter 6: Marketing research: What methods of research are most appropriate for understanding a firm's micro- and macro-environments?

Chapter 7: Buyer behaviour: What effect does social, economic, and cultural change have on the way people make purchases?

Chapter 8: Buyer–seller relationship development: What pressures within an organization's 'environmental set' are likely to encourage co-operation rather than confrontation between set members?

Chapters 9/10: Developing a product portfolio: How is new product development guided by underlying changes in a firm's marketing environment?

Chapter 11: Developing a sustainable competitive advantage: How does an effective system for collecting information about environmental change, analysing it, and acting upon it give a firm a sustainable competitive advantage?

Chapters 12/13: Pricing theory and applications: Changes in the macro-economic environment can create new competitive pressures on firms, leading to pressure on prices. How does legislation affect a firm's pricing decisions?

Chapter 14: Intermediaries: Most producers need to use intermediaries to get their goods and services to their final consumers, but the relationships between producers, intermediaries, and consumers are going through a period of change.

Chapter 15: Physical distribution management: How can economic, technological, and political change in a firm's marketing environment affect the costs and opportunities for distributing its products?

Chapters 16–20: Principles of promotion/advertising/public relations/personal selling/direct marketing: What opportunities are opened up by new technologies to allow firms to communicate with target customers? How does regulation constrain their promotional activities?

Chapter 21: Organizing for marketing: How should an organization organize its internal environment to ensure that its marketing is effective?

Chapter 22: Services marketing: The services sector is growing in importance, with the majority of employees now working in services sectors. Customers expectations of service are rising.

Chapter 23: Global marketing: What factors are leading to the globalization of firms' marketing environments? How are global brands developed? What problems and opportunities are there in trying to extend marketing operations from the domestic market to one overseas?

Case study

Consumers confound marketers

Household spending by all UK households amounted to over £500 billion in 1997, or 63 per cent of gross domestic product. This level of expenditure is very closely related to conditions in the country's macro-economic environment. For marketers, it is crucial to be able to read the macro-economic environment and to predict the effects of change in demand for their goods and services. Identifying turning-points in the economic cycle has become a work of art as well as science, as consumers frequently confound experts by changing their expenditure levels in a way which could not have been predicted on the basis of past experience.

During the autumn of 1998, mortgage rates in the UK were falling; unemployment was close to its lowest level for two decades; pay rises were keeping ahead of inflation;

and share prices were recovering from their recent falls. Yet expenditure by British households was falling sharply. For three consecutive months retail sales fell in value, with retailers such as Marks & Spencer and Storehouse reporting below expected levels of sales. Retailers have traditionally found excuses to justify poor sales to their shareholders, including weather which is too cold/too hot. Even the death of Diana Princess of Wales was widely blamed for keeping people out of the shops.

Throughout 1998, prices of consumer goods had fallen significantly, with consumer durables down in price by an average of 2 per cent in a year and clothing by 5 per cent. Economic theory would have suggested that lower prices would have resulted in higher sales, especially considering the other favourable elements of the macro-environment. However, this did not appear to be happening.

What else could have been happening in the marketing environment to explain falling household expenditure? At the time, the media was full of reports of an impending global economic crisis, triggered by difficulties in the Asian economies. Consumer confidence is crucial to many high value household purchases such as houses and cars, with consumers reluctant to commit themselves to regular monthly repayments when their source of income is insecure. Even this may be only a partial solution, as a survey of consumer confidence carried out in October 1998 by GFK on behalf of the European Commission showed that although consumers were pessimistic about the state of the national economy, they were quite upbeat about their personal financial situation.

One possibility was that consumers had become more canny. If prices are falling, why not wait longer until prices have fallen further? Consumers had also witnessed the effects of previous over-borrowing and had been more cautious during the recent period of economic growth, resulting in a historically low level of personal sector indebtedness. In 1997, 9 per cent of disposable household income was saved, compared with just 3 per cent at the height of the economic boom of 1988.

For companies who need to commit resources a long while in advance in order to meet consumers' needs, an accurate understanding of the market environment is crucial if stock surpluses and shortages are to be avoided. But this case shows that getting it right can still be very difficult.

Case study review questions

1 Identify all of the environmental factors that can effect the demand for consumer durables and assess the magnitude and direction of their impact.

2 In what ways can a manufacturer of consumer durables seek to gain a better understanding of its marketing environment?

3 How can a manufacturer of consumer durables seek to respond to environmental change as rapidly as possible?

Chapter review questions

1 (*a*) Explain briefly what you understand by the 'marketing environment' of a business.

(*b*) Prepare a list of recommendations which would aid a business to address change in its technical environment (CIM Marketing Environment examination, December 1994, Q.3)

2 'Suppliers and intermediaries are important stakeholders in the micro-environment of the business'.

(*a*) Explain the evolving role and functions of these stakeholders in the marketing orientated business of the 1990s.

(*b*) With examples, comment on the growing importance of relationship marketing in this regard (CIM Marketing Environment examination, June 1995, Q. 3)

3 Using a company of your choice, produce and justify an environmental set. You should include and rank at least five factors in your set. (CIM Marketing Environment examination, June 1995, Q.10, part ii.)

4 Clearly distinguish between an organization's micro- and macro-environments. What is the relationship between the two?

5 With reference to specific examples, examine the ways in which organizations can increase their flexibility in order to respond more rapidly to environmental change.

6 Identify the likely consequences of demographic change for a financial services company. Discuss both the micro- and macro-environmental effects.

References

Atkinson, J. (1984), 'Manpower Strategies for Flexible Organizations', *Personnel Management*, Aug.

Drucker, P. F. (1973), *Management: Tasks, Responsibilities and Practices* (New York , Harper & Row).

Kotler, P. (1997), *Marketing Management: Analysis, Planning, Implementation and Control*, 9th edn. (Englewood Cliffs, NJ: Prentice Hall).

Suggested further reading

Marketing's changing role within commercial organizations is discussed in the following articles:

■ Achrol, R. (1991), 'Evolution of the Marketing Organization: New Forms for Turbulent Environments', *Journal of Marketing*, Oct., pp. 77–93.

- Gummesson E., (1991), 'Marketing-Orientation Revisited: The Crucial Role of the Part-Time Marketer', *European Journal of Marketing*, **25**, 2, pp. 60–75.

- Piercy, N. (1991), *Market-Led Strategic Change: Making Marketing Happen in Your Organization* (London: Thorsons).

- Webster, F. E. (1992), 'The Changing Role of Marketing in the Corporation', *Journal of Marketing*, **56**, Oct., pp. 1–17.

The following references provide further discussion of relationship marketing and supply chain management:

- Buttle, F. (ed.) (1996), *Relationship Marketing: Theory and Practice* (London : Paul Chapman).

- Cravens, D. W., and Piercy, N. F. (1994), 'Relationship Marketing and Collaborative Networks in Service Organizations', *International Journal of Services Management*, **5**, 5, pp. 39–53.

- Gordon, I. (1998), *Relationship Marketing: New Strategies, Techniques and Technologies to Win* (Chichester: Wiley).

- Gummesson, E. (1994), 'Making Relationship Marketing Operational', *International Journal of Services Management*, **5**, 5, pp. 5–20.

- —— (1999), *Total Relationship Marketing* (London: Butterworth-Heinemann).

- Payne, A., Christopher, M., Peck, H., and Clark, M. (1999), *Relationship Marketing, Strategy and Implementation*, (London: Butterworth-Heinemann).

The difficulties of understanding and assessing the impacts of change in the economic environment on a firm's marketing activities are discussed in the following:

- Artis, M. J. (ed.) (1996), *Prest and Coppock's The U.K. Economy: A Manual of Applied Economics*, 14th edn. (Oxford: Oxford University Press).

- Curwen, P. (1997), *Understanding the UK Economy*, 4th edn. (Basingstoke: Macmillan).

- Dunnett, A. (1997), *Macroeconomic Environment* (Harlow: Longman).

- Griffiths, A., and Wall, S. (eds.) (1997), *Applied Economics: An Introductory Course*, 7th edn. (Harlow: Longman).

- Hildebrand, G. (1992), *Business Cycle Indicators: A Complete Guide to Interpreting the Key Economic Indicators* (Chicago: Probus Publishing).

- Kay, J. (1996), *The Business of Economics* (Oxford: Oxford University Press).

The nature of the political environment and its impacts on marketing decisions is discussed in the following:

- Graham, P. (1995), 'Are Public Sector Organizations Becoming More Customer Centred?', *Marketing Intelligence and Planning*, **13**, 1, pp. 35–47.

- Latham, V. (1991), 'The Public Face of Marketing', *Marketing*, 2 Nov., pp. 22–3.

- McKenzie, S., and Rosewell, T. (1997), 'Party Time', *Marketing Business*, Sept., pp. 18–22.

The relationship between pressure groups and and commercial organizations is discussed in the following:

- O'Sullivan, T. (1994), 'The Price of Persuasion', *Management Today*, Oct., pp. 81–5.

- Richardson, J. J. (ed.) (1993), *Pressure Groups* (Oxford: Oxford University Press).
- Wilson, K. G. (1990), *Interest Groups* (Oxford: Blackwell).

  Some of the principles of internal marketing are discussed in the following:
- Diener, B. J. (1998), 'Internal Marketing, Your Company's Next Stage for Growth', *Journal of Consumer Marketing*, **14**, 2–3, pp. 250–1.
- Piercy, N., and Morgan, N. (1990), 'Internal Marketing: The Missing Half of the Marketing Programme', *Long Range Planning*, **8**, 1, pp. 4–6.

  Organizational culture has been referred to in this chapter as having a major impact on an organization's marketing effectiveness and the following references explore internal and external dimensions of culture:
- Cray, D., and Mallory, G. (1998), *Making Sense of Managing Culture* (London: International Thomson Publishing).
- Goffee, R., and Jones, G. (1998), *The Character of a Corporation: How your Company's Culture Can Make or Break your Business* (London: HarperCollins).
- Hofstede, G. (1991), *Culture and Organizations* (London: McGraw-Hill).
- Smith, M. (1998), 'Culture and Organisational Change', *Management Accounting*, **27**, 7, pp. 60–2.
- Stapley, L. F. (1996), *The Personality of the Organization: A Psycho-dynamnic Explanation of Culture and Change* (London: Free Association Books Ltd.).

Useful web links

UK Open Government home page: http://www.open.gov.uk/
EU home page: http://europa.eu.int/
European Union in the US: http://www.eurunion.org/
UK Office of National Statistics: http://www.ons.gov.uk/
DTI Technology Foresight programme: http://www.dti.gov.uk/ost/challeng.htm OR
 http:///www.dti.gov.uk/public/search (for specific report searching)
UK Central Office of Information:http://www.coi.gov.uk
Euroseek: http://www.euroseek.com
EnuNet:http://www.euro-emu.co.uk
The library of official EU and UK documentation: http://wwww.euro-emu.co.uk/offdocs/
 indexmain.shtml
International Business Resources on the Internet: http://www.ciber.bus.msu.edu/
 busres/europe.htm
On-line European Information Resources: http://www.euro-info.org.uk/Resources.html
Statsbase: http://www.statsbase.gov.uk/

Chapter 3

Segmentation and Targeting

Chapter objectives

Customers are becoming increasingly diverse in their needs and aspirations, and less inclined to accept an 'average' product. Some of the bases for identifying different types of customer are familiar and readily observable, such as age, gender, and geographical location. Others, such as attitudes and lifestyle may be more difficult to identify, but can be crucial for understanding consumers' buying processes. The purpose of segmentation is to identify groups of buyers who respond in a similar way to any given marketing stimuli. This chapter explores the bases for market segmentation and how this is subsequently translated by companies into marketing plans which target specific segments.

Why segment markets?

From Chapter 1 it will be recalled that a focus on meeting customers' needs is a defining characteristic of marketing. Organizations which make presumptions about customers' needs or produce goods and services which are chosen for their convenience in production, are probably not practising the marketing concept. A true marketing orientation requires that companies focus on meeting the needs of individual customers. In a simple world where consumers all have broadly similar needs and expectations, a company could probably justify developing a marketing programme which meets the needs of the 'average' customer. In the early days of motoring, Henry Ford successfully sold as many standard, black Model T Fords as he was able to produce. In the modern world of marketing, few companies can have the luxury of producing just one product to satisfy a very large market. Some still can—for example, water supply utility companies generally produce a single standard of water for all of their customers. But this is the exception rather than the rule. Most companies face markets which are becoming increasingly fragmented in terms of the needs which customers seek to satisfy. So while the customers of Henry Ford may have been quite happy to have a plain black car, today's car buyers seek to satisfy a much wider range of needs when they buy a car. The 'average' customer to whom Henry Ford appealed is becoming increasingly a myth.

Segmentation then, is essentially about identifying groups of buyers within a market-place who have needs which are distinctive in the way that they deviate from the 'average' consumer. Some consumers may treat satisfaction of one particular need as a high priority, whereas to others this need may be regarded as being quite trivial. We will return to the subject of needs as buying motivators in Chapter 7 when we look at buying behaviour. For now, consider the case of the new car market. Buyers no longer select a car solely on the basis of a car's ability to satisfy a need to get them from A to B. Additionally, a buyer may seek to satisfy any of the following needs from a new car purchase:

■ to give them status in the eyes of their peer group;
■ to provide safety and security for themselves and their family;
■ to project a particular image of themselves;
■ to provide a cost-effective means of transport;
■ to be seen making a gesture towards the environment by buying a 'green' car.

There are many more possible factors which might influence an individual's choice of car. The important point here is that the market is composed of buyers who approach the decision to buy a car in very different ways. Therefore the features which they each look for in a product offer may differ quite markedly from the market average. It follows that with a wide dispersion of market needs, a marketing plan which is based on satisfying the needs of the average buyer will be unlikely to succeed in a competitive market-place. If another company can satisfy the needs of small specialist groups better, then the company which seeks to serve them with just an 'average' product offer will loose business from this group.

The process of identifying groups of buyers who differ in the needs which they seek to satisfy from a purchase is often referred to as market segmentation. We will define the process of market segmentation as:

the identification of sub-sets of buyers within a market who share similar needs and who have similar buying processes

In an ideal world, each individual buyer would be considered to have a unique set of needs which they seek to satisfy, and firms would tailor their product offering to each of their customers. In the case of some expensive items of capital equipment bought by firms, this indeed does happen (for example, there are very few buyers of large power stations in the UK, so firms can justifiably treat each customer as a segment of one). In the case of products which are relatively low in value and high in sales volumes, it would be impossible for firms to cater to each individual's needs, although there is evidence that new developments in technology are allowing for a much greater degree of customization than has previously

Figure 3.1 From mass market to market segmentation

been the case (we will return to this in Chapter 20 when we discuss Direct Marketing).

Segmentation should not be regarded as a technique which is unique to marketing. In fact, wise marketers are simply following a critical approach to decision-making which is shared by many other professions and disciplines. The critical approach revolves around breaking a large problem down into a number of smaller problems and resolving those smaller problems in the most appropriate way. In this case, the 'problem' for the marketer is how to get the market to buy its products. The problem can be broken down into the sub-problems of how to get particular segments within those markets to buy its products. The solution to each of these problems might be quite different. Analogies can be drawn with many other problems of decision-making. An engineer designing a bridge breaks the bridge down into component parts when specifying materials to be used. The needs of the different parts of the structure would probably call for quite different strengths of material. Just as the marketer would not use one product to satisfy the needs of the entire market, the engineer would not use just one gauge of metal to build the entire bridge structure. Both the marketer and the engineer have used critical thinking to break a large problem down into smaller problems (Fig. 3.2).

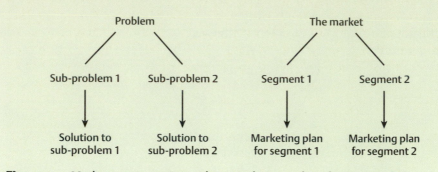

Figure 3.2 Market segmentation and a critical approach to decision-making

Criteria for effective segmentation

MARKET segmentation should be regarded as the product of critical thinking rather than some predetermined set of procedures. There is no underlying theory to the process of market segmentation. It follows that what is an appropriate basis for segmenting one market may not be appropriate to other markets.

Before we begin to look at the bases on which marketers can segment any given market, we need to be aware of the criteria by which the effectiveness of any segmentation basis can be assessed. We will consider here four important criteria: usefulness to a company's marketing planning; size of the resulting segments; their measurability; and accessibility.

Is the basis of market segmentation useful to the company?

It is easy to develop bases for market segmentation and lose sight of the purpose of the exercise. Essentially, the exercise is only worth while if it allows a company to penetrate a greater proportion of its market profitably than would have been the case without undertaking the exercise. Groups identified as homogeneous market segments must be just that—similar in terms of the needs and buying behaviour of the individuals that they contain. Many companies still fail because their assumptions about homogeneity within a segment overlook some critical differences within a segment which produce a varied response to a product offer which has been specific-ally targeted at the segment. For example, a segment defined as 'affluent, married, working women' for overseas package holidays may overlook the fact that women within this segment have very divergent views on the features they seek from a holiday, depending on the age and structure of their family. The buying behaviour of those affluent, married, working women who seek to take their children away with them is quite likely to be significantly different from those who seek to travel by themselves or just with their partner. To be more effective, market segmentation must recognize the diversity of needs within this group.

Are the segments of an economic size?

Any basis for segmentation should yield segments which are of a size that a company can profitably exploit. Companies face a dilemma here, because as segments get smaller, they get closer to achieving the marketing philosophy of satisfying each customer's needs as though they were the centre of all the company's attention. The problem for the company is that smaller segments may be uneconomic to provide for. What is a reasonable size segment varies from one market to another, and is constantly changing over time. In the financial services industry it is possible to develop quite specific products to target very small segments of a market. For example, it would involve relatively little effort by an insurance company to develop motor insurance policies which specifically meet the needs of people driving 'classic' vintage cars, further subdivided into those who live in the north of England, and further subdivided into those aged over 50 years. In principle, there are few production reasons why an insurance company should not focus on a segment so small. At the other extreme, a company manufacturing paint for the private household market may find it difficult to offer a range which is as customer focused as this. For example, a paint manufacturer might wish to produce a variant for a segment of users who are averse to painting (perhaps developing a product which is non-spill and delicately perfumed); the 'professional' home decorator segment who seeks perfection through multi-coat application; the time constrained perfectionist segment who seeks a one coat paint with durable finish; and the adventurous who seek special effect patterns from their paint (e.g. mottled effect paint). For each new variant of its paint, it would probably have to stop its production lines in preparation to make another specialized product. Worse still, it would have to persuade its wholesalers and retailers to stock each variant of paint. When each colour variant is multiplied by the number of segment specific formulations, the stockholding problems for retailers and wholesalers can be imagined.

Over time, manufacturers are becoming increasingly able to offer specialized goods to meet the needs of small market segments. Service industries have had this flexibility for some time, and are now exploiting this to the full with the use of information technology. Within the manufacturing sector, flexible manufacturing systems are allowing smaller production runs to be achieved economically. For Henry Ford, producing even a slight variant of his original car would have meant stopping the production line and re-tooling for a new model. Today, car assembly lines can employ numerical process control equipment, which, combined with interchangeability of components, allows many different models to come off the same line.

Can the market segments be measured?

Ideally, companies should be able to know the precise size of all market segments that it has identified. This is important in order that segments can be compared and their profit potentials assessed. Unfortunately, data are often not available to quantify market segments. Marketers therefore face a further dilemma in defining market segments. Should they go for segments which they feel exist but cannot measure, or should they define segments which can accurately be measured, but which may have little bearing on the homogeneity of consumers' needs and buying processes? As an example, the UK Population Census gives a lot of valuable information which is frequently used as a basis for identifying market segments (for example, the age profile of an area, number of people per household, etc.). However, marketers are often interested in a more subjective assessment of individuals, such as their attitudes and lifestyles. Unfortunately, there is very little published information on these more subjective aspects of market segments. While we know quite accurately the size of the segment of people aged over 60 and living alone in a particular area, there is very little readily accessible information about how many people living in that area can be described as 'environmentally aware' or 'liberal in attitudes' or any other measure of attitudes or lifestyles. Inevitably, marketing managers must make a trade-off between the need for information which is objective and reliable on the one hand and subjective and creative on the other. Fortunately for marketers, the sources of information available which can be used to segment markets are constantly increasing. In addition to traditional government statistical sources, many private sector organizations (for example Mintel, the Economist Intelligence Unit, and the Henley Centre) frequently commission and publish research based on surveys of samples of the population.

Are the segments accessible to the company?

There is little point in going to a lot of effort in defining segments of a market when those segments are not accessible to the company, nor ever likely to be. Inaccessibility can come about for a number of reasons:

- The company may be prohibited by law from entering certain markets (for example, many overseas governments restrict the rights of foreign companies to serve their domestic market).
- Some buyers in a market may be tied to suppliers by long-term supply contracts. In the case of subsidiaries of large corporations, the holding company may require its subsidiaries to obtain its purchases from within the group.

■ Although it may be possible, the cost of gaining access to a market segment may be prohibitive. A supplier of building materials in the UK may in theory be able to supply a segment of small building contractors in southern Italy, but the cost of transporting its bulky goods over the distances involved may effectively make the segment inaccessible.

Although a segment may be inaccessible to a company now, this may not always continue to be the case. Changes in legislation may make possible something which was previously illegal for a company. Policies of large companies towards the contracting out of supplies may present new opportunities. Even segments which seemed inaccessible because of high transport costs may become accessible through the development of a joint venture company.

Bases for market segmentation

A basis for segmenting a market should satisfy the criteria described above. It was noted at the time that companies often need to make trade-offs in arriving at a basis for market segmentation which meet these criteria. It follows therefore that firms seldom use one basis for market segmentation alone. In Fig. 3.3 a number of

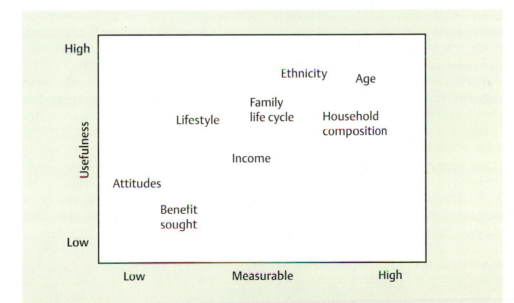

Figure 3.3 An evaluation of segmentation basis for a manufacturer of ready-prepared meals, based on their usefulness and measurability

segmentation bases are plotted in terms of their measurability and usefulness to a typical manufacturer of ready-prepared meals (segmentation here is defined in terms of final consumers, although, as Chapter 14 will discuss, segmentation can also be applied to different types of intermediaries who will handle the product).

The following specific methods of segmenting markets will be considered here: demographic approaches; socio-economic approaches; and psychographic approaches. These are not water-tight definitions and you will recognize that the segmentation methods discussed below show considerable areas of overlap.

Demographic bases for segmentation

Demography can be defined as the study of population characteristics and demographers have used a number of key indicators in their studies of populations. In this section we consider a number of demographic related bases for segmenting markets: age, the stage in the family life cycle, gender, and household composition.

Age

Age is probably one of the most widely used bases for market segmentation. It satisfies many of the criteria for effective segmentation discussed above. It is useful to companies because demand for many products appears to be age related. There are many obvious examples: for example, music buying peaks among the 18–25 year age group and the purchase of cruise holidays increases after the age of 50. There are also more subtle age-related patterns of demand within particular categories of product. Within the UK retail sector, for example, many chains are associated with particular age groups. So while the Arcadia clothing chain's Top Man brand attracts a mainly young 18–30 age segment, its Principles for Men brand is more attractive to the 21–40 segment, and its Burton brand has traditionally appealed to the 25+ segment. The usefulness of age can be partly explained by the observation that people's tastes change as they grow older. Some of this may be related to their stage in the family life cycle which is age related as well as changes in disposable income (see below).

Age segmentation meets another important criterion in that it is generally easy to measure the size of segments. Population censuses record respondents' age, while many privately collected sources of information (such as company-sponsored questionnaires) frequently ask for such information. A company can therefore, for example, be reasonably confident about how many people belong to a particular age segment within a specific area. This information might be vital to a retail chain seeking the best areas to locate new branches, given that demand for its format of stores is very age specific.

Of course age alone is not usually a good basis for market segmentation. Within any age segment, individuals can be observed who exhibit quite different buying behaviour. However, differences often relate to the preference for specific brands rather than the consumption of a particular product. Thus while consumption of whisky is related to age, considerable diversity exists within age segments in brand preferences.

A further reservation on the use of age as a segmentation variable is that there may be little correlation between an individual's actual biological age and their perceived age. This can be seen at one extreme in 'Wannabe' teenagers who seek to act out the lifestyle of their older peers and at the other extreme by the 'Young at Heart' who think themselves into believing that they are ten or twenty years younger than they actually are. There has been interesting research into the increasing desire of older people to perpetuate their youth and the effects on marketing of differences between actual age and self-ascribed age (e.g. Mayo and Jarvis 1981). It could be argued that the most important determinant of a person's buying behaviour is the age that they think they are, rather than their actual age. However, while information on the latter is readily available, the former is much more difficult to come by.

Family life cycle

Individuals typically go through a number of family roles, beginning with that of a dependent child; a young single adult; a married adult with dependent children; a married adult with independent children; and finally a sole survivor. At each stage of development, an individual's buying preferences are likely to change, and, just as importantly, their ability to pay for those purchases will change too. There are many obvious marketing opportunities associated with specific stages in the life cycle. For example, a young adult with no financial responsibilities is a prime target for many leisure-related items such as music, while an individual with a young dependent family is an important target for firms selling childcare products. Fig. 3.4 illustrates some of the changes in food buying habits which may arise as an individual progresses through the family life cycle.

Of course, the family life cycle shown in Fig. 3.4 is an ideal type and most western countries are seeing increasing deviation from it. Later marriage, a rising divorce rate, and the number of single-parent families have created family units which do not fit into this ideal. Marketers have responded to such change by, for example, offering domestic support services aimed at busy, affluent single-parent families.

Gender

It is quite evident that gender differences account for many variations in consumer buying behaviour. At first sight it may seem obvious that companies providing a wide range of goods and services have developed product offers which are particularly targeted at males or females. Thus there are men's clothes and women's clothes; magazines aimed at women and those aimed at men; and cosmetics which emphasize their appeal to one gender rather than the other. Gender is a very commonly used basis for segmenting markets. Not only does it often correspond to crucial differences in buying behaviour, it is also an easy one to measure. Firms can have a reasonably good idea of the gender specific market in any given area.

We do, however, need to be careful how we use gender as a basis for market segmentation. Firstly, it has to be remembered that one of the criteria for effective

Stage in family life cycle	Possible main emphasis of buying food
Dependent child	Main food purchased is for snacks. Attracted by the novelty and packaging of food.
Young independent adult	Eating out, possibly at fast food outlets. Minimum effort put into preparing food at home—home consumed food is often simple ready made meals.
Adult, married, no children	Quite likely to eat out at restaurants. Willing to experiment in home cooking, although may still buy ready made meals for home comsumption.
Adult, married, dependent children	Eating out is reduced and cooking at home concentrates on meeting the needs of the whole family. Budgeting becomes tighter and economy replaces variety as a driving force behind food purchases.
Adult, married, independent children	Greater time and money now available for eating out and being adventurous with home prepared food. Can afford ready-made meals, but prefers to prepare own food.
Sole survivor	Average size of food purchse declines. Emphasis on food items which are easy to prepare.

Figure 3.4 Effects of stage in family life cycle on an individual's food buying behaviour

segmentation is that it should identify homogeneity in *buying* behaviour. There is a lot of evidence that, for many products, a person of one gender may buy a product which is intended for use by another gender. It has been estimated in the UK, for example that over half of all men's underwear is purchased by women, with men having a relatively minor part in the buying process. The segment of men's underwear buyers which should be of interest to manufacturers should therefore be women. The way that women buy underwear, the retailers that they buy from, and the features that they look for are likely to be quite different from the processes of men and the features that they look for. It follows therefore that the female buyer segment represents an important segment for manufacturers of men's underwear.

A further reservation to the use of gender as a segmentation basis is its frequent confusion with a classification based on sex. The latter is essentially a biological description, whereas gender is a social construct. Western societies have seen a convergence in many male and female values, although there remains argument about just how far this has gone. Many marketers have therefore moved on from segmentation based on a dichotomous male/female classification to a segmentation basis which recognizes a wide range of gender orientations. For example, the lifestyle and buying behaviour of career women is likely to be quite different from that of housewives. Many companies have developed marketing programmes which are aimed at segments of gay or lesbian people, whose buying behaviour may not fit neatly within dichotomous measures of gender.

Ethnic

The United Kingdom, like many other western countries, has become much more diverse in the ethnic backgrounds of its population. Despite years of integration, there is evidence that many ethnic groups retain distinctive preferences in their purchases which distinguish them from the native community. For example, many Chinese migrants who have settled in the UK continue to buy authentic eastern-style food, providing a marketing opportunity for many small retailers which has not been fully exploited by the larger supermarkets. Ethnic groups remain important segments for travel-related services, for visiting friends and relatives, and for pilgrimages. As in the case of gender, segmentation purely on the basis of biological origins may not be as useful as an individual's self-ascribed ethnic background. While some members of an ethnic group may be proud of their background and make purchases which reinforce their ethnicity, other sub-segments may wish to associate themselves primarily with the values and lifestyle of their host community.

Household composition

A wide range of goods and services are bought by households as an economic unit. The weekly household shopping, the annual holiday, and the family car are typically purchased to meet the needs of the economic unit as a whole rather than just that of the individuals within it. Households differ in their size and composition and these differences are often associated with diverse buying behaviour. Segmenting markets on the basis of the size of the household buying unit therefore makes a lot of sense for many products. Furthermore, there is a lot of readily available information about household structure from the national census and other sources.

One indicator of household structure is the number of people that comprise the household. In the UK, as in most western countries, the average size of household units has declined as extended families have given way to nuclear families. More recently, there has been growth in the number of single-person households, which now account for over 10 per cent of all households. You should be familiar with the distinctive buying needs of single-person households, for example, smaller pack sizes and products that single-mindedly satisfy the needs of the buyer rather than the whole household. As with all bases of segmentation, it is important to avoid over-generalization, as the single-person household comprising a retired state pensioner is likely to behave very differently from a young, professional single person.

A second indicator of household structure is the composition of individuals' roles within it. This is much more difficult to measure than size alone, but can be very useful because it is associated with quite distinctive buying patterns. In recent years, most western countries have seen a growth in the numbers of households which are composed of something other than the ideal type family of husband, wife, and two children. A rising divorce rate has meant a growing segment of consumers who live in single-parent households, who are often (but not always) poorer than a two-person family in terms of money and time. Some travel companies have specifically targeted this segment to fill capacity at quiet times of the year. Other types of household which may present opportunities to particular companies include those comprising groups of friends sharing; an elderly parent living with their grown up children; and those living in institutionalized homes.

Socio-economic bases for segmentation

It has been traditional to talk about class differences in the way that goods and services are purchased. While an individual's perception of their class may be an important influence on their buying behaviour (discussed further in Chapter 7), marketers find the concept of social class too value laden and imprecise to be of much practical use. Instead, more objective indicators of social class are used, in particular occupation and income.

Occupation

Since 1921, government statisticians in the UK have divided the population into six classes, based simply on their occupation. This has resulted in the following familiar classification system:

Class Category	Occupation
A	Higher managerial, administrative, or professional
B	Intermediate managerial, administrative, or professional
C1	Supervisory or clerical, and junior managerial, administrative, or professional
C2	Skilled manual workers
D	Semi and unskilled manual workers
E	State pensioners or widows (no other earners), casual or lower grade workers, or long-term unemployed.

These segment labels have been widely used; for example, most newspapers have traditionally stressed the number of A/B readers that they have. However, it became increasingly clear that six classifications could not fully explain the impact of class on buying behaviour. In 1998 the UK government published a report which proposed to redefine Britain's class structure for the first time in eighty years, because so many people had joined the ranks of the middle classes. The effect was to increase the number of classes from six to seventeen. The new seventeen classifications would be determined by a range of factors, including how highly an individual is valued by their employer, how many perks they receive, and how stable their job is. The uncertainty of work and the demise of a job for life had undermined the old classification system, so the new system would take account of such things as the size of an individual's organization and their pension rights, effectively reflecting an individual's status in the purchasing market-place. Teachers and librarians were among the winners in the new system, rising to class 3. Nurses and police officers also rose, to class 4. Among the losers were lorry drivers and traffic wardens, down to 12, and hairdressers and plumbers, down to 10. New levels were added to cover the under-class of people who have never worked and the long-term unemployed. Despite the improvements noted above, segmentation based on occupation remains fairly crude when compared with the advances achieved using geodemographic methods (discussed below).

Income

Many studies have shown that, as an individual's income increases, their expenditure on a category of product increases. For example, Mintel in a study of the leisure industry found a strong correlation between income and expenditure on a range of leisure activities.

There are three commonly used approaches to measuring income:

- Total income before taxation: gross income, which is widely quoted and under-stood by most people.

- Disposable income: this refers to the income that individuals have available to spend after taxation. It follows that, as taxes rise, disposable income falls.

- Discretionary income: this is a measure of disposable income less expenditure on the necessities of life, such as mortgage payments. Discretionary income can be significantly affected by sudden changes in the cost of mortgages and other items of expenditure, such as travel costs, which form a large component of household budgets.

All of these can be measured at the unit of the individual, or the whole household.

Marketers are most often interested in consumers' discretionary income. A casual analysis of advertisements on television will show that most are aiming to gain an increased share of that discretionary income—on an overseas holiday, a new car, or a value added meal ingredient, for example.

Despite its apparent correlation with buying behaviour, the use of income as a segmentation variable has some limitations. Obtaining data on individuals' income can be much more difficult than for occupation and people are often reluctant to give this information when asked. Surveys which attempt to gather this information can be subject to misreporting by individuals. Even within any segments of similar dis-cretionary income, differences in actual spending levels arise between segments, accounted for by differences in spending/saving ratios.

Psychographic bases for segmentation

So far, most of the bases for segmentation have been reasonably measurable. How-ever, they are often criticized for missing the unique personality factors that dis-tinguish one person from another. Under the heading of psychographic factors, we will consider the effects of lifestyle, attitudes, benefits sought, and loyalty.

Lifestyle

People of a similar age and socio-economic status can nevertheless lead quite different lifestyles, and firms have been quick to adapt products to meet the needs of these lifestyles. It is very difficult to describe a lifestyle accurately and even more difficult to have any realistic measure of the size of segments of different lifestyle groups. Nevertheless, as societies fragment into ever smaller groups of shared interests and activities, companies have recognized the need to develop ideal types of lifestyle segments. The level of research which underlies these approaches to segmentation is very variable, with many segments being held up as ideal type segments with no empirically derived basis. Thus segments described by terms such as 'Yuppies' and 'Dinkies' have come to acquire a meaning among marketers, if only as an unquantified ideal type of the segment which is being targeted. Many lifestyle segmentation methods have been developed for specific sectors. Thus in one study of grocery retailing in the UK, the Henley Centre for Forecasting identified four segments of shoppers using a multi-variable approach which took account of demographic factors such as age, sex, and income as well as lifestyle, personality, and finally, attitude to the shopping experience. As with so many of these studies the resultant new breeds of shopper were given glib titles:

- The Harried Hurrier was typically burdened with squabbling children and crippled by a severe lack of time. Hurriers were averse to anything that eats into their precious minutes such as having too much choice, which makes them impatient.

- Young-at-Hearts spend less money than Harried Hurriers, tend to be middle-aged, but in contrast to the first group have time on their hands and like to try new products.

- An important and growing species of grocery shopper was identified as the Young, Affluent, and Busy (or 'YABs') for whom money is not a major constraint in their quest for convenience and more interesting products, but they do have a low boredom threshold.

- The Fastidious were attracted by instore hygiene and tidiness and are expected to grow in importance

- Begrudgers were mainly male and tended only to shop out of obligation to others.

- The Perfect Wife and Mother was concerned with the balanced diet, but appeared to be on her way out.

- To compensate for the decline in the Perfect Wife and Mother, the numbers of Obsessive Fad-Followers has been increasing. This group's choice of food tended to be dominated by brand image and current trends.

There have been many similar approaches to lifestyle segmentation. While they may be very useful for defining a target market, they are difficult to operationalize because of the absence of data beyond sample surveys.

What does an individual's choice of sandwich say about them? In 1998, the retailer Tesco undertook research that showed how complex the market for ready-made sandwiches had become, with clear segments emerging who sought quite different types of sandwiches. In an attempt to define and target its lunch customers more precisely, the company found that well-paid executives invariably insisted on 'designer' sandwiches made from ciabatta and focaccia with sun dried tomatoes and costing about £2.50. Sales people and middle ranking executives were more inclined to opt for meaty triple-deckers. Upwardly mobile women aged 25–40 chose low-calorie sandwiches costing around £1.49. Busy manual workers tended to grab a sandwich that looked affordable, simple and quick to eat, such as the ploughman's sandwich that Tesco sold for £1.15. Tesco's research claimed that sandwiches have become an important statement made by individuals and need to be targeted appropriately. What do your snack meals say about you?

Attitudes

Lifestyles are observable, even if it is difficult to estimate how many of each lifestyle group exist in a particular population. Attitudes are much more difficult to identify and may only be revealed in subtle ways. More importantly for marketers, what is a hidden attitude for an individual today, may tomorrow become behaviour which is manifested in purchase decisions to support a chosen lifestyle. Many people may possess an attitude towards an item but are afraid of being an early adopter of behaviour associated with that attitude. Among males, there may be a significant segment of the population that possesses an attitude that it should be acceptable for men to use cosmetics traditionally associated with women. They may, however, be reluctant to buy and use male cosmetics until they consider that it has become socially acceptable to do so. For this segment, the marketing programme should emphasize the need to gain gradual acceptability of the product among this group, for example by appealing to wives/girlfriends as key influencers on their decision to purchase.

Benefits sought

The same product may provide a variety of benefits to different people. A watch, for example, can be purchased by one segment primarily as an accurate timepiece, by another as a fashion item above all else, while others may select brands of watches as items of ostentatious consumption. There will also be segments who buy a watch as a gift to give to somebody else. Each segment is likely to respond in different ways to variations in product design, packaging, pricing, and promotion. Inevitably, overlap between benefit categories exists and it is only really possible to determine the size of each segment on the basis of sample surveys.

Loyalty

In many markets, a segment can be found which shows considerable loyalty to one brand, while other groups are prepared to switch between brands in response to products which offer more benefits and/or lower prices. For some people, loyalty may occur through inertia and a reluctance to take the perceived risk of changing supplier.

Geodemographic bases for segmentation

Marketers have traditionally used geographical areas as a basis for market segmentation. Very often, there have been very good geographical reasons why product preferences should vary between regions. The long, dark, and cold winter nights of northern England and Scotland have led the inhabitants of these regions to take proportionately more winter sun holidays than their counterparts in the south of England, despite the latter having higher average levels of disposable income. Many companies have managed to adapt their product offer to meet the needs of different regional segments. National newspapers, for example, produce regional editions to satisfy readers' needs for local news coverage and advertisers' needs for a regional advertising facility.

More recently, geographical segmentation has been undertaken at a much more localized level, and linked to other differences in social, economic, and demographic characteristics. The resulting basis for segmentation is often referred to as geodemographic. The premiss of geodemographic analysis is that where a person lives is closely associated with a number of indicators of their socio-economic status and lifestyle. This association has been derived from detailed investigations of multiple sources of information about people living in a particular neighbourhood. A very widely used system of geodemographic analysis is MOSAIC, provided by Experian Ltd. (Fig. 3.5).

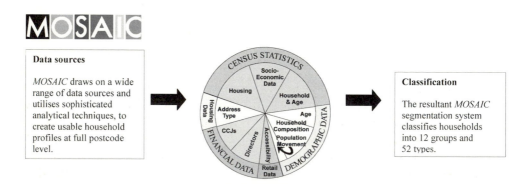

Figure 3.5 MOSAIC is a widely used method of market segmentation, drawing on multiple sources of data to classify households in the UK into 12 groups and 52 types. (Reproduced with permission of Experian Ltd.)

Situational bases for segmentation

A further group of segmentational variables can be described as situational because an individual may find themselves grouped differently from one occasion to the next.

Stage in buying process

For some high value goods, it may take a considerable time for an individual to arrive at a purchase decision. It has been estimated that the average time private buyers take in deciding on a replacement for their current car is about one year. At each stage of the process, their needs will be quite different. A price incentive during the early stages of their search process may achieve no success for the seller, but may do for a buyer who has gone through the search and evaluation processes and is now ready to commit themselves to a particular product.

Use occasion

We often buy a product at different times for quite different reasons. A meal in a restaurant taken during the lunch hour will probably be seen quite differently compared to the same meal taken as part of a social occasion at the weekend.

Frequency of purchase

Infrequent buyers of a product may approach their purchase decision with caution and seek reassurance throughout the process. Their knowledge of prices and competing facilities available in the market may be low. At the other end of this segmentation spectrum, frequent buyers may have become much more price sensitive, or more demanding in the features which they expect from a category of product. A promotional programme which guides buyers through the stages of purchase will be less appropriate for this group.

Comprehensive approaches to segmentation

The preceding discussion has presented a seemingly bewildering array of segmentation variables, each of which has its strengths and weaknesses. In practice, companies would use a number of key variables which are most relevant to their product/market. Geodemographic segmentation has become particularly popular because of the close correlation between where an individual lives and other indicators of income, occupation, and lifestyle. Companies are also likely to combine subjective approaches to segmentation with more traditional quantifiable techniques (Fig. 3.6).

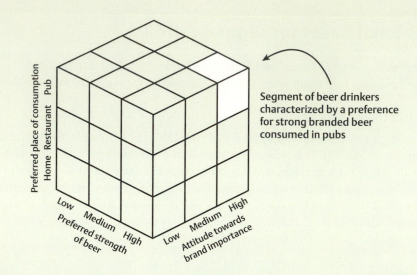

Segment of beer drinkers characterized by a preference for strong branded beer consumed in pubs

Figure 3.6 A multidimension segmentation of the beer market based on buyers' attitude toward brand importance, strength, and place of consumption

The days when all pubs in a town seemed to look alike are long gone, as pub operators segment their markets with increasingly refined detail. But how does a company handle the masses of information about customers' preferences and match these with specific pub locations? The brewery and leisure group Bass uses 'fuzzy logic' to match the sites of new pubs with its preferred segments of customer who have been given labels such as 'blue-collar hunters', 'premium wanderers', and 'pint and pensioners'. Blue-collar hunters, for example, are characterized by unskilled manual workers who spend most of their income in pubs with juke boxes and arcade games and prefer draft cider and ordinary lager. Bass operates a number of pub formats, such as Vintage Inns, Harvester, and O'Neills, targeted at these different groups. Now the company has developed a computerized mapping programme that can help identify the best location for any given format of pub. The programme uses a computer code called fuzzy logic to come up with locations that fit the bill, as well as those that nearly match what the company wants.

Bases for segmenting business markets

T**HE** process of defining market segments for business buyers is similar in principle to that applied to consumer markets. Many of the bases described above, such as frequency of purchase and benefits sought apply equally to private consumer purchases and business purchases. However, others, such as demographic bases, have little role to play, especially in segmenting very large corporate buyers. The following are additional bases for segmentation which are commonly used in business markets.

Size of firm

Within any industry sector, variations in corporate size are likely to be reflected in individual order sizes and the manner in which those orders are placed. In the printing industry, for example, very large printers obtain their inks direct from manufacturers, while smaller printers tend to rely on wholesale merchants. For a small intermediary, the latter may represent an important and accessible segment, whereas the former may be considered inaccessible.

Formality of buying processes

As organizations grow, they have a tendency to formalize their buying processes. Nevertheless, within any size category of firm, variation can be observed in the formality of the buying process, in terms of the number of people involved in making a decision and the level of the management hierarchy at which approval is required. Large state-owned organizations have been noted for having slow and complicated ordering procedures. While many large private companies are similar, some have managed to delegate buying to a very local level, thereby speeding up and simplifying the process. In general, the more complex a firm's buying process, the greater the complexity of a seller's marketing which is called for. Instead of having to appeal to one individual with one set of needs, it must appeal to multiple influences, who may each seek different benefits from a purchase. The complexity of organizational buying processes is returned to in Chapter 7.

Industry sector

An industry sector may be a natural user of certain types of products, but have little use for others. Within particular product categories, niche segments may appear in industries with quite specific needs. Many suppliers of industrial goods and services therefore target particular industry sectors. In the case of Information Technology equipment, Fujitsu ICL has successfully targeted the special computing needs of the retail segment, while NCR has targeted the special needs of the banking segment.

Evaluating market segments

DEFINING market segments is a relatively passive task of analysis. While sound analysis is always important, the vital next stages involve evaluating each of the identified market segments and selecting one or more for targeting. In this section, we consider the questions that a company should ask in deciding whether a segment is worth going after. In fact, a company may avoid a dichotomous classification of 'develop/ignore' and prefer instead a ranking of segments ranging from 'very attractive opportunity' to 'let's ignore this one'.

Size of segment

In our criteria for effective segmentation, it was stated that, to be useful, a segment must be of a sufficient size that the company can serve economically. What is an economic size varies between companies. A package holiday company selling low cost holidays to popular destinations may only be able to operate economically with segments of several tens of thousands of customers. On the other hand, a small company with lower overhead costs may be able to justify serving much smaller segments who have distinctive needs. It was noted earlier that the size of market segments which can be economically served has tended to come down with the development of flexible production systems.

Growth prospects

Our definition of marketing (Chapter 1) spoke not only about identifying current customer demands, but also of *anticipating* what these will be in the future. Markets are seldom static in nature and what is an attractive segment today may not be so in the future. Many UK companies who targeted the 'yuppie' segment in the late 1980s realized this when the lifestyle and spending patterns of this group retreated sharply during the recession of the early 1990s. On the other hand, some segments which were once small have gone on to be very large before fragmenting into smaller sub-segments. In the UK, the segment of adult ice-cream consumers who sought sensual pleasures from consuming ice-cream was small in the early 1980s, but grew significantly during the following decade. Suppliers of 'luxury' ice-cream who had targeted this group saw their sales grow significantly faster than the ice-cream industry average.

Profitability

Just because a market segment is large does not necessarily imply that segment can be profitably served. Many markets are characterized by a large segment which seeks low prices and in which companies can only make good profits by stringent control of their costs, while a smaller segment is prepared to pay a premium for a product for which the cost of differentiation is less than the price premium charged.

Competition for the segment

Of course, the profitability of a segment is significantly affected by the level of competition for it. When a company is identifying potentially profitable segments to develop, the chances are that its competitors are doing exactly the same thing. The result is that an attractive segment soon becomes unattractive when large numbers of new entrants, all following the same logic, create intense competitive pressure. In evaluating a market segment, a company should consider not only how well it can develop the segment, but also how well its competitors could develop it. If its competitors in fact have more strengths in respect of this segment, the segment is likely to become less attractive to it. Too many marketing plans fail because they make assumptions about a static market, when in fact they are dynamic with a changing composition of segments and of firms who supply to those segments.

Fit with company objectives

Many segments may appear large and profitable, but are rejected because they would not sit easily within a company's broader marketing objectives and strategies. These are some examples of market segments which might not 'fit' a company well:

■ A manufacturer of high value cars might be reluctant to serve a market segment which seeks more basic, low value vehicles. What would happen to the image of BMW if it decided to develop the market segment for low priced family hatchbacks?

- Will the image of a company be harmed by appearing to be too closely associated with a segment which is perceived by the public as being 'bad'? Many companies treat as a priority the preservation of their reputation, and being seen supplying products to a repressive government, for example, may cause unquantifiable damage to its long-term reputation.

- Has the company a core competence in serving this segment? Would its funds and management effort be better applied to a project which would fit better with its competencies, and therefore leave this segment to a competitor who may have a stronger base for developing it?

Selection of target markets

THE time has now come for a company to select one or more market segments for further development. At this point, marketing becomes a blend of scientific analysis and creative thinking. The foregoing segmental analysis cannot produce answers—it can only guide decision-making, which is influenced by a range of company and environment-specific factors, many of which cannot be easily quantified.

A fundamental issue for a company is how many segments to exploit and the manner in which it seeks to enter those segments. A number of targeting strategies can be identified: undifferentiated mass marketing; single-segment specialization; and multiple-segment specialization (Fig. 3.7). These three ideal type targeting strategies are presented, but companies frequently combine elements of these approaches. The characteristics of each approach are described below.

Undifferentiated mass marketing

This does not really involve segmentation and targeting at all, as a company seeks to satisfy the entire market with a single formulation of its product. It worked well for Henry Ford, and cases can still be seen where companies serve the entire market with one product (for example, electricity supply companies who have traditionally offered one standard of service delivery to all of their customers). Over time, consumers' needs tend to fragment into segments of different needs. Where markets are competitive, a company may no longer be able to ignore the special needs of small groups of its customers, because, if it does, its competitors my exploit the opportunities available. Very often, these groups with special needs represent the most profitable segments to serve. In the UK, even the market for electricity has fragmented,

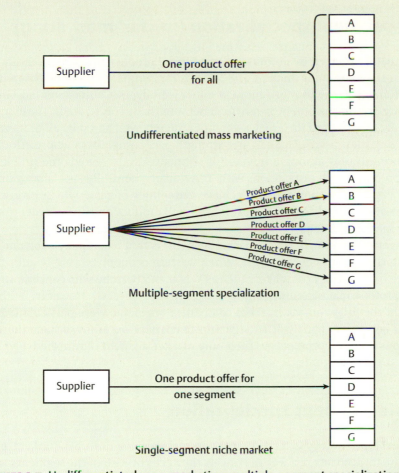

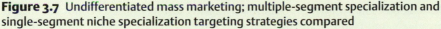

Figure 3.7 Undifferentiated mass marketing; multiple-segment specialization and single-segment niche specialization targeting strategies compared

spurred on by increasing competition which raises the expectations of consumers that their distinctive needs are capable of being met. Thus customers now often have the choice of regular uninterrupted electricity at the regular price, or a service which can be interrupted at peak times, in return for which they pay a reduced price.

Attempting to serve the entire market with one standard product offer is an extreme case of undifferentiated mass marketing. In its lesser form, companies seek to exploit as much of the market as possible without attempting to meet the needs of particular subgroups within it.

Single-segment specialization ('niche' marketing)

Many companies succeed by producing a specialized product aimed at a very focused segment of the market (or 'niche'). The Morgan car company has done this with its sports cars aimed at the connoisseur segment of car buyers. Coutts Bank has done so in appealing only to customers of very high net wealth. By this strategy, the company gets to know the needs of its target segment extremely well and puts all of its efforts into satisfying their needs. This can give strength over competitors whose efforts are spread more diffusely among a number of segments. It also avoids the problem of tarnishing a brand with associations with 'inferior' segments. By specializing on one particular segment, a company can achieve economies of scale which give it cost advantages over competitors who must make small production runs in order to serve its chosen market segment.

The danger of targeting a single-market segment is that a company's fortunes rise or fall with those of its chosen target. When western economies were booming during the late 1980s, luxury car makers such as Jaguar and Porsche who concentrated on affluent, professional segments enjoyed exceptional success. However, with the recession of the following years, these companies' segments were particularly badly hit and the companies had no other segments to fall back on. Many of them therefore faced serious financial problems as their only market segment diminished.

Multiple-segment specialization

A third ideal type strategy is for a company to seek to serve multiple markets, but to differentiate its products in a way that meets the needs of each of the segments which it seeks to serve. The aim here is to develop slightly differentiated products which add to customer value faster than they add to production costs. Car manufacturers have become quite skilful at adapting a basic car to meet the needs of different groups (see below). Many retailers have developed different brand formats to target different groups (for example the Arcadia group with its Top Shop, Principles, and Dorothy Perkins chains, among others).

Segment development plans

Most companies entering a new market realize that it would be unrealistic to use their limited financial and management resources to satisfy all possible segments from the outset. They therefore develop a strategy to roll out their marketing plan throughout further segments. The roll out plan can be defined geographically (McDonald's restaurants did this in the UK, working out from the London-based

Henry Ford would have been amazed at the lengths which the car company he founded now goes to in order to satisfy the needs of specific market segments. Car manufacturers have for some time recognized the differing needs of differing groups of buyers, for example:

- 'Boy racers': these typically seek plenty of features and external manifestations of the power and status of their car (e.g. 'go-faster stripes' and spoilers).
- Affluent elderly males: emphasis on refinement of interior; seeks comfort and reliability, but no vulgar manifestation of status.
- The family buying a 'runabout' car: seeks low initial cost and subsequent running costs; not too worried about comforts; needs to be hard wearing to stand up to rough treatment by dogs, children, etc.
- The professional career woman: a difficult market to typify, but often seeks a light and airy colour, light paintwork, reliability, and easy to maintain.
- Company car buyers: an economical and reliable car which will have a high residual value after three years and which will satisfy the status needs of employees

A look through the brochure for a Ford model such as the 'Fiesta' indicates how far the company has been able to adapt its cars to meet the needs of each of these segments: the 'Sport' has been aimed at the 'boy racers'; the 'Ghia' is aimed at the affluent elderly males; the 'Popular' is a low cost version produced as the family runabout. In the past, the company has produced versions of the car specifically targeted at women, such as the Fiesta Cosmopolitan. Company car buyers find that the L and GL models serve them well.

The logistical problems of satisfying so many segments have been significant, with one basic car available in three basic body forms, with five different engines, twelve colour options and the choice of automatic or manual transmission. Allowing for permutations that are not available, Ford promotes seventy-two versions of its basic car. Making these available on demand at each of its dealers has called for flexible manufacturing systems and a centralized stock management system.

market to provincial markets). Very often, companies initially target high value segments. Such segments may be prepared to pay a premium for the benefits of novelty, but soon the premium attached to this novelty wears off. The company meanwhile has established an upmarket image for itself from which to appeal to aspiring segments of potential buyers. In the UK, mobile telephone companies have moved from segments of business users who are prepared to pay a premium for a mobile phone which will give them a competitive advantage, to more price sensitive segments for whom a mobile telephone is a useful but not essential accessory.

Developing a position within the target market

HAVING chosen a segment to target, a company must decide how to position itself in relation to the competitors for that segment. Positioning could be on the basis of the product's unique selling proposition, its price, design characteristics, method of distribution, or any other combination of factors that allow for differentiation. Within any market, position maps can be drawn to show the relative positions adopted by the principal competing products in respect of key customer evaluation criteria. In Fig. 3.8, a position map has been drawn relating two important criteria which are used by customers in selecting a restaurant; speed of service and the range of services provided by staff (e.g. whether the restaurant is self-service or waiter service). A number of UK restaurants have been plotted on this map in terms of the two criteria.

The fact that a position on a map is unoccupied does not necessarily mean that it is an unexploited opportunity waiting to be exploited. There is always the possibility that a product offering in that position will not satisfy the needs of a sufficiently large market segment. However, many gaps on product position maps have been identified and exploited successfully. In the UK there has for long been a gap between low value fast food restaurants and higher priced gourmet restaurants. Restaurant chains such as Brewers Fayre and Harvester have since successfully exploited this position.

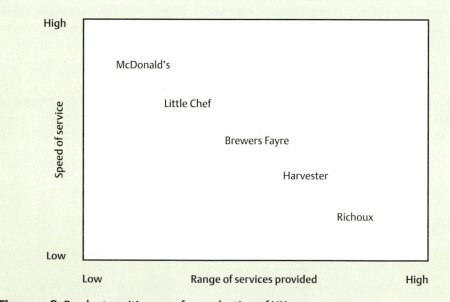

Figure 3.8 Product position map for a selection of UK restaurants

It must be emphasized that a product position map is essentially product focused rather than customer focused. By itself, it does not address the underlying needs of customers that a company seeks to satisfy. The process of adopting a product position is essentially about selecting specific target markets. In a market-oriented company, product features are only developed in response to the needs of clearly identifiable segments of consumers. The subject of competitive positioning is discussed in more depth in Chapter 11.

Chapter summary and key linkages to other chapters

This chapter has emphasized the need for market-oriented companies to break markets down into segments which comprise groups of people with similar needs and buying processes. Numerous bases for segmenting markets have been identified, but there is no unique 'right' way of segmenting a market. The best way is the one that allows a company to exploit the greatest possible share of a market profitably. Segmentation alone does not produce a marketing plan. For this to come about, a company must evaluate the segment opportunities open to it and asses how well it is able to exploit them. There are a number of approaches for entering a market and companies often seek to exploit one segment at a time with products that are uniquely adapted to that segment.

   The crucial importance of segmentation to the philosophy of marketing is reflected in the extensive linkages between this chapter and other chapters:

Chapter 1: What is marketing?: Marketing as a philosophy is customer focused and market segmentation is a method of trying to put each individual company at the centre of all its activities.

Chapter 2: The marketing environment: Market segments grow and decline in importance over time. Much of this change can be understood and predicted by a careful analysis of the marketing environment (e.g. demographic change results in the changing size of age-related segments).

Chapter 4: Branding: Market segments differ in the importance they attach to brands and the reassurance they seek from them.

Chapter 5: Marketing and ethics: Should a company discriminate in favour of, or against, particular groups (e.g. targeting young adults with incentives for cigarettes)?

Chapter 6: Marketing research: How do you quantify the size of market segments?

Chapter 7: Buyer behaviour: What are the distinctive processes of buying that can define market segments?

Chapter 8: Buyer–seller relationship development: Are some segments more amenable to the development of long-term buyer–seller relationships?

Chapters 9/10: Developing a product portfolio: How does an understanding of different segments' needs influence the development of new products and adaptations of existing products?

Chapter 11: Developing a sustainable competitive advantage: Does a company have the strengths to remain competitive in a market segment, relative to the strengths of its competitors in that segment?

Chapters 12/13: Pricing theory and applications: To what extent do market segments differ in their responses to price changes?

Chapters 14/15: Intermediaries/physical distribution management: What channels of distribution does a segment prefer to use? How can intermediaries themselves be categorized into segments of buyers?

Chapters 16–19: Principles of promotion planning/advertising/sales promotion/ personal selling: Which segments make up the target markets for a firm's promotional efforts? How do different segments respond to promotional stimuli?

Chapter 20: Direct marketing: Are there some market segments who are more amenable than others to buying goods and services direct from their producer? Direct marketing essentially appeals to segments of one.

Chapter 21: Organizing for marketing: Should marketing management responsibilities be allocated by market segment or by product category?

Chapter 22: Services marketing: Because of the inseparable nature of services, segmentation methods can be more effective than for goods.

Chapter 23: Global marketing: How do you define market segments at an international level of analysis?

Case study

Polaroid focuses its cameras on new market segments

The American-based Polaroid company has become synonymous with instant photography, but this alone was insufficient to prevent a sharp decline in its fortunes. By the end of 1998, the company's stock market value had fallen to just one-third of what it was a year earlier. During 1998 alone, sales revenue had dropped by 13 per cent and profits by 18 per cent. At the end of the 1990s the company was desperately trying to re-target its products at segments of the market that previously did not buy Polaroid products.

Polaroid was established in the 1940s by Edwin Land and from the start the company laid great stress on its research and development projects. But the company tended to be product led rather than market led and carried out very little market research. Its emphasis on technical excellence caused it to lose out on opportunities which by Polaroid's standards might have been regarded as frivolous. It saw its traditional target market as private individuals and businesses that needed high quality instant photographs for serious purposes, for example, many professional photographers would take an instant picture with a Polaroid camera in order to judge the composition of a picture that they would later take with a standard camera.

Unfortunately, Polaroid's traditional target market had ceased to grow and was increasingly challenged by new forms of electronic imaging which were just beginning to be affordable for business users, although still prohibitive for most private buyers.

A new Chief Executive, Gary DiCamillo, took over in 1995 and set out to remake the company. A key part of this task involved moving the company's positioning away from one of technical excellence to one of fun. The company reasoned that if serious users of instant photography were becoming harder target markets, segments of more casual users may be more promising.

The company's most promising new market segments were the under 17s, a far cry from its previous targeting strategy. For this segment, the company created a Barbie instant camera which retailed for under $20 and in 1997 became one of the hottest Christmas toys, according to *USA Today*. In addition, the company created instant film that children could draw on and planned a camera that would turn photographic images into stickers. Children represented an ideal target market for Polaroid. Their impatience and need for instant gratification gave big advantages over conventional photography which required a typical wait of a week until a parent had been pestered into taking the film to be developed. Developing this theme further, the company has been working on a fun camera for adults which can be used as a toy and retails for $18. Users would be able to experiment with a range of abstract images when they take a picture.

While the 'fun' segment of the photography market has been seen to have a lot of potential, there remain some opportunities for more professional market segments. One area of growth has been instant imaging for official identification documents. The increasing security consciousness of firms and their desire to issue staff with identity cards has helped to fuel this growth. The UK government's intention to include a photograph on driving licences resulted in a new source of demand which Polaroid successfully won.

Further questions remains about the company's targeting strategy. The costs of developing its own electronic cameras are high and the competition likely to be fierce from the major electronics companies. To gain a profitable market share among more serious users, the company may have to spend considerable amounts of money, something that would not go down well with its shareholders, given the company's recent financial performance. The emerging markets of eastern Europe represent hoped-for market segments, but, with their economies floundering, penetration of these markets has been difficult.

Case study review questions

1 How can Polaroid overcome an image problem that may result from serving both the 'professional' and 'fun' market segments?

2 Given the development of electronic imaging and Polaroid's limited resources to develop electronic cameras, suggest a targeting strategy that would be appropriate for Polaroid.

3 Suggest a framework by which Polaroid can assess the attractiveness of the under 17s market segment. Is this segment likely to be sustainable over the longer term? If not, what should the company do to develop this segment?

Chapter review questions

1 'Too much segmentation can be costly and results in a paralysis by analysis'. Discuss the view that for many markets, Henry Ford's approach of producing a limited range of products for the 'average' customer may be the most profitable option for a company.

2 It is common to talk about individuals belonging to social class A/B or C1, and newspapers often quote their readership figures in these terms. In reality, how useful is this as a basis for market segmentation?

3 Critically evaluate the likely future trend in segmentation techniques. Illustrate your answer with reference to a specific market sector.

4 Given the increasing fragmentation of society, and an apparent desire for greater individuality among consumers, are current scientific methods of analysis and segmentation a short-sighted oversimplification?

5 Discuss the criteria that might be used by a recently established small confectionery manufacturer in deciding which market segments to target.

6 For a market sector of your choice, analyse the positions adopted by companies in the market.

References

Mayo, E. J., and Jarvis, L. P. (1981), *The Psychology of Leisure Travel* (Boston: CBI Publishing Co.).

Suggested further reading

For further discussion of market segmentation methods, the following references build on the previous discussion:

■ Bucklin, R., Gupta, S., and Siddarth, S. (1998), 'Determining Segmentation in Sales Response Across Consumer Purchase Behaviours', *Journal of Marketing Research*, **35**, 2, pp. 189–97.

■ Dibb, S., and Simpkin, L. (1997), 'A Program for Implementing Market Segmentation', *Journal of Business and Industrial Marketing*, **12**, 1, pp. 51–64.

■ Green, P., and Kreiger, A. (1995), 'Alternative Approaches to Cluster Based Market Segmentation', *Journal of the Marketing Research Society*, July, **37**, 3, pp. 221–340.

■ Kara, A., and Kaynak, E. (1997), 'Markets of a Single Customer: Exploiting Conceptual Developments on Market Segmentation', *European Journal of Marketing*, **14**, 6, pp. 463–77.

- McDonald, M., and Dunbar, I. (1998*), Market Segmentation: How to do it—How to Profit from it*, 2nd edn. (Basingstoke: Macmillan).

- Mitchell, A. (1997), 'Segmentation: Finding a Niche', *Marketing Business*, Nov., pp. 16–21.

- Rangan, V. K., Moriarty, R. T., and Swartz, G. S. (1992), 'Segmenting Customers in Mature Industrial markets', *Journal of Marketing*, Oct., pp. 72–82.

- Riquier, C., Luxton, S., and Sharp, B. (1997), 'Probabilistic Segmentation Modelling', *Journal of the Market Research Society*, **39**, 4 , pp. 571–87.

- Schaffer, C. M. and Green P. E. (1998), 'Cluster Based Market Segmentation: Some Further Comparisons of Alternative Approaches', *Journal of the Market Research Society*, **35**, 2, pp. 155–63.

- Weinstein, A. (1994), *Market Segmentation, Using Demographics, Psychographics and Other Niche Marketing Techniques to Predict Model Customer Behaviour* (Chicago: Probus Publishing).

Social classification has been discussed widely and the following references are useful in a marketing context:

- Bottomore, J. (1991*), Classes in Modern Society*, 2nd edn. (London: Routledge).

- Crompton, R. (1993), *Class and Stratification: An Introduction to Current Debates* (Cambridge: Polity).

- Sivados, E., Matthews, G., and Curry, D. (1997), 'A Preliminary Examination of the Continuing Significance of Social Class for Marketing: A Geodemographic Replication', *Journal of Consumer Marketing*, **14**, 6, Nov.–Dec., pp. 463–77.

Targeting is discussed in the following references:

- Dibb, S., and Simkin, L. (1996), *The Market Segmentation Workbook: Target Marketing for Marketing Managers* (London: Routledge).

- Herweg, A., and Herweg, F. (1997), *Radio's Niche Marketing Revolution FutureSell* (London: Butterworth-Heinemann).

- Tevfik, D., and Leeuw, M. (1994), 'Niche Marketing Revisited: Concept, Applications and some European Cases', *European Journal of Marketing*, **28**, 4, pp. 39–55.

Chapter 4
Developing a Brand

Chapter objectives

Branding lies at the heart of marketing strategy and seeks to remove a company from the harsh competition of commodity-type markets. By differentiating its product and giving it unique values, a company simplifies consumers' choices in markets which are crowded with otherwise similar products. Branding requires considerable investment by a company in product quality and promotion if a brand is to be trusted by customers. Out of such investment have emerged powerful global brands which are very valuable assets to their owners. This chapter reviews the underlying philosophy of branding and the strategies used by companies to develop strong brands.

The purpose of branding

TRADITIONAL economic theory has been based on assumptions of perfectly competitive markets in which a large number of sellers offer for sale an identical product. All suppliers' products are assumed to be perfectly substitutable with each other and therefore, through a process of competition, prices are minimized to the level which is just sufficient to make it worth while for suppliers to continue operating in the market (price determination in competitive markets is discussed further in Chapter 12).

Perfect competition may at first sight appear very attractive for the welfare of society as a whole, but it can pose problems for suppliers. In a perfect market, an individual firm is subject to considerable direct competition from other firms and must take its selling price from the market. An implication of perfect competition is that firms are unable to make a level of profits which is above the norm for their market. If they did achieve higher than normal profits, this would act as an invitation to new market entrants, whose presence would eventually increase the level of competition in the market and drive down profits to the minimum level which makes it attractive for firms to continue in the market.

To try to avoid head-on competition with large numbers of other suppliers in a market, companies seek to differentiate their product in some way. By doing so, they create an element of monopoly power for themselves, in that no other company in the market is selling an identical product to theirs. To some people, the point of difference may be of great importance in influencing their purchase decision and they would be prepared to pay a price premium for the differentiated product. Nevertheless, such buyers remain aware of close substitutes which are available and may be prepared to switch to these substitutes if the price premium is considered to be too high in relation to the additional benefits received. The coexistence of a limited monopoly power with the presence of many near substitutes is often referred to as imperfect competition (see Chapter 12).

For a marketing manager, product differentiation becomes a key to gaining a degree of monopoly power in a market. It must be remembered, however, that product differentiation alone will not prove to be commercially successful unless the differentiation is based on satisfying clearly identified consumer needs. A differentiated product may have significant monopoly power in that it is unique, but if it fails to satisfy consumers' needs, its uniqueness has no commercial value.

Out of the need for product differentiation comes the concept of branding. A company must ensure that customers can immediately recognize its distinctive products in the market-place. Instead of asking for a generic version of the product, customers should be able to ask for the distinctive product which they have come to prefer. A brand is essentially a way of giving a product a unique identity which differentiates it from its near competitors. The means by which this unique identity are created are discussed in more detail in this chapter.

Summarizing previous research, Doyle (1989) described brand building as the only way to build a stable, long-term demand at profitable margins. Through adding values that will attract customers, firms are able to provide a firm base for expansion and product development and to protect themselves against the strength of intermediaries and competitors. There has been much evidence linking high levels of advertising

Figure 4.1 Perfect competition, imperfect competition, and the role of brands

expenditure to support strong brands with high returns on capital and high market share (e.g. Buzzell and Gale 1987).

Branding through product differentiation may not be possible in all markets. Where products involve consumers in low levels of risk and there are few opportunities for developing a distinctive product, competitive advantage may be based on cost leadership rather than brand development (Porter 1980). Examples of commodity strategies are evident in many low value consumer and industrial markets where a significant segment of customers seek a product with a basic and substitutable set of characteristics. The supply of sulphuric acid to commercial buyers is a good example of a market in which branding has failed to make much progress.

The history of branding

THE term 'branding' pre-dates modern marketing and is generally believed to have originated in agricultural practices of the middle ages. Farmers who allowed their cattle to graze on open common land needed some means of distinguishing their cattle from those which were owned by other farmers sharing common grazing rights. They therefore 'branded' their animals with a branding iron, leaving an indelible mark which would clearly identify to whom a particular animal belonged. The role of a brand to identify products with a particular source is shared by the medieval farmer and the modern corporation.

Economies in an early stage of development are characterized by small-scale production processes and relatively local markets. In such systems, relationship development between producer and consumer is relatively easy to achieve (see Chapter 8). Where there were few opportunities for economies of scale in production, brands had little role to play. With poor transport facilities and few opportunities to expand business profitably beyond the immediate area of production, consumers could readily identify the source of goods. Thus in early nineteenth-century Britain, most communities had their own baker, brewer, and carpenter. None had developed the ability to achieve competitive advantage through economies of scale and poor road and rail transport would have prevented their goods being exported to neighbouring communities. People in local communities knew where their goods had come from and were not confused by competing products from distant towns. In a very simple economy, a community would have had '*the* baker, *the* butcher and *the* candlestick maker'. Buyers were able to learn through personal experience of the abilities, consistency, and reliability of a supplier, while suppliers were able to adapt simple production methods to the needs of individual customers who were known personally. Through personal knowledge and trust, a supplier was likely to be able to judge the creditworthiness of each customer.

In the UK, the industrialization of the nineteenth century meant that many goods could now be produced efficiently in centralized factories rather than in small cottage industries. An efficient centralized factory could produce more output than could be consumed by the local community. Furthermore, improvements in transport infrastructure allowed the surplus production to be shipped to markets around the country. What one company could do efficiently in one factory, another company could probably do equally as well in another factory elsewhere. Therefore, firms became involved in competition in distant markets. This, however, led to a problem for buyers whose buying process was now made more complicated. Instead of having just *the* brewer's products available, they now had a range of brewers' beers available. Buyers probably had little knowledge of the distant firms who were now supplying their market, or of the quality and consistency of their products. Branding essentially emerged to simplify the purchase processes of buyers who faced competing sources of supply.

In impersonal mass markets, consumers who cannot judge a product on the basis of a trusted relationship with a supplier instead seek reassurance through other means. The brand emerged as a means of providing reassurance of consistent quality to spatially dispersed customers who, because of the use of intermediaries, had no direct relationship with the consumers of their products. In a market characterized by choice, a brand was used by buyers to select a product which they had come to trust and which satisfied their needs through the particular benefits of the product.

It can be argued that brands emerged where buyers were unable through personal contact to trust the suppliers of goods, something which was normal in a simple small-scale economy. Where competitive advantage for firms is gained by operating on a large scale, branding has been the traditional route by which firms have sought to reassure distant customers of consistent product quality. However, technological developments in the areas of database and production management now give large-scale producers an ability to keep in touch with customers and thereby recapture some of the relationships for which brand development has provided a surrogate. The question remains, however, whether direct marketing organizations can profitably build sales without the development of a strong brand.

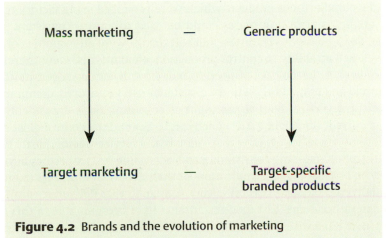

Figure 4.2 Brands and the evolution of marketing

Key characteristics of a brand

A brand is essentially a way of distinguishing the products of one company from those of its competitors. To have value, a brand must have consistency; reduce buyers' level of perceived risk; and offer a range of functional and emotional attributes which are of value to buyers.

Consistency

Consistency is at the heart of branding strategy. To have value in simplifying buyers' purchasing processes, consumers must come to learn that a brand stands for the same set of attributes on one purchase occasion as on all subsequent and previous occasions. Consider a brewery offering draft bitter to the market. The distinctive characteristics of the beer which contribute towards its brand values may be described as:

taste: light hop flavour
strength: above average gravity
appearance: clear light colour

Consumers come to prefer a particular taste/strength/appearance of beer which is described in shorthand by a brand name. If the taste of a brand varies between one pint and the next, the ability of the brand name to act as a shorthand description of a whole bundle of attributes is significantly weakened. Next time, the buyer may not bother sticking with the brand which it does not trust, if it has just as much chance of achieving the desired bundle of attributes from another product.

The ability of a company to secure consistency of product delivery is therefore crucial to the development of branding. This helps to explain why branding was fastest to develop for those products which were produced using factory techniques in which quality control procedures could be used to ensure consistent standards every time. Soap powders, cigarettes, and soft drinks were all examples of products which developed an ability to control production standards and were therefore early adopters of brands. In the case of beer, brands have been developed most strongly among canned and bottled beer where consistency can be ensured, compared to 'real ale' where the quality of beer at the point of consumption is dependent on many factors (e.g. correct storage in a bar) which can be beyond the control of a brewery.

Brands have been relatively slow to develop in the services sector, partly because of the difficulty of maintaining consistent standards. Some service sectors have successfully taken on board the 'industrialization' of their production process to ensure that a service delivered on one occasion is very similar to that delivered on all previous and subsequent occasions. Fast food restaurants have been notable in this field, and have been associated with the development of many strong international brands. On the other hand, many one-to-one services such as those provided by hairdressers,

Figure 4.3 Many of our most familiar fast-moving consumer goods brands have a long history. Typhoo-tea, which can trace its origins back to 1820, is typical of a brand which has been associated with consistency in its appeal. Despite numerous changes in ownership of the brand, many consumers remain loyal to the Typhoo brand, and this loyalty is often passed down through generations of families.

solicitors, and dentists have difficulty in 'industrializing' their service offer and consequently brands have had much more limited impact.

The term 'consistency' was noted above as an important attribute of a brand. As well as referring to specific product attributes (as in the case of the beer above), consistency can refer to more general values about a producer or its range of products. As an example, McDonald's core brand values stand for consistency in quality, service, and value.

Risk reduction

In simple economies where buyers personally knew the producers of the goods and services that they bought, the personal relationship helped to manage the buyers' exposure to risk. In the absence of that relationship, a brand acts as a substitute in managing buyers' exposure to risk. Branding has been found to simplify the decision-making process by providing a sense of security and consistency for buyers (Barwise and Roberston 1992) which may be absent outside of a relationship with a supplier.

A brand addresses a number of dimensions of purchase risk, which have been identified as:

- physical (will the product cause me harm?);
- psychological (will this product satisfy my need for peace of mind?);
- performance (does the product work in accordance with my requirements?); and
- financial (will this product provide adequate performance within my budget?)

Risk levels are perceived as being higher for products that fulfil important needs and values and for which there is a high level of involvement by the consumer.

What makes a 'superbrand'? The magazine *Marketing* reported on the 1998 biannual Superbrand awards, selected by a panel of industry experts for brands which 'offer consumers significant emotional and/or physical advantages over their competitors which (consciously or sub-consciously) consumers want, recognize and are willing to pay for'. Although there were few surprises in the list, with Coca-Cola the overall winner, the list provided an interesting mix of established brands along with others which have made their mark in recent years through aggressive branding and marketing campaigns. Included in the list were companies such as Microsoft, Nike, and American Express, which had resolutely supported marketing in order to achieve high levels of recognition with consumers. The power of logos was emphasized in research carried out among a sample of shoppers with nine out of ten recognizing the golden arches of McDonald's, even with all reference to the company's name removed. Eighty-three per cent recognized the National Lottery's crossed fingers and 82 per cent correctly identified BT's piper.

The idea of a Superbrand extends beyond mere consumer recognition, and according to research can have a major impact on consumer purchasing patterns. Over 50 per cent of consumers who buy so-called Superbrand products said they would not buy an own-label version even if the price were substantially lower, according to findings by Infratest Burke, a consumer research company. The company polled 270 people across thirty UK towns to find out about the strength of a consumer's relationship to a brand, asking questions about six grocery categories: mineral water, chocolate wafers, ice-cream, baked beans, and digestive biscuits. In four of the six categories, the Superbrands of Walkers Crisps, Kit Kat, Heinz Baked Beans, and McVities Digestives dominated buying patterns. Between 40 per cent and 60 per cent of buyers of these brands said that they would not switch to own label, no matter how cheap the own-label alternative was. Depending on the brand, between 15 per cent and 30 per cent of consumers said they would be 'irritated or angry' if the brand was not available in a shop, with Heinz Baked Beans and Walkers Crisps generating the most concern.

There have been many claims that the days of gullible consumers buying overpriced brands are coming to an end as they switch to supermarkets' 'own label'. But there is a lot of evidence that superbrands are as strong as ever. Why should this continue to be? And for what types of products, and for which types of consumers are superbrands most likely to be enduring?

Functional and emotional attributes

There have been many conceptualizations of the unique positioning attributes of a brand. These usually distinguish between tangible dimensions which can be objectively measured (such as taste, shape, reliability) and the subjective values that can only be defined in the minds of consumers (such as the perceived personality of a brand). In an early study, Gardner and Levy (1955) distinguished between the 'functional' dimensions of a brand and its 'personality'. Similar attempts to distinguish the dimensions of brands have been made by others—for example, utilitarianism versus value expressive (Munson and Spivey 1981), need satisfaction versus impression management (Solomon 1983), and functional versus representational (de Chernatony and McWilliam 1990). With increasing affluence, the non-functional expectations of brands have assumed increasing importance.

A number of dimensions of a brand's emotional appeal have been identified, including trust, liking, and sophistication and it has been shown that products with a high level of subjective emotional appeal are associated with a greater level of customer involvement than where a product provides essentially objective benefits (Laurent and Kapferer 1985). This has been demonstrated in the preference shown for branded beer as opposed to a functionally identical generic beer (Allison and Uhl 1964) and in the way that the emotional appeal of brands of analgesics contributed significantly in relieving headaches (Branthwaite and Cooper 1981). As consumers buy

Envy the girl.

Envy the car.

Envy the lifestyle.

NV. The system.

KENWOOD
The new wave in music
NV-series from Kenwood

Figure 4.4 Manufacturers of luxury goods frequently position their products as aspirational. In this advertisement for Kenwood audio equipment, there is very little mention of product features. Instead, creative use of language postions Kenwood as a brand whose ownership gives some measure of status. (Reproduced with permission of Kenwood Electronics)

products, they learn to appreciate their added value and begin to form a relationship with them. For example, as Pitcher (1985) observed, there are many companies selling petrol and credit cards, but individual companies such as Shell and American Express have created brands with which customers develop a relationship and guide their choice in a market dominated by otherwise generic products.

There is an extensive literature on the emotional relationship consumers develop between a brand and their own perceived or sought personality. Brands are chosen when the image that they create matches the needs, values, and lifestyles of customers. Through socialization processes, individuals form perceptions of their self, which they attempt to reinforce or alter by relating with specific groups, products, and brands (Solomon and Buchanan 1991). There is evidence that branding plays a particularly important role in purchase decisions where the product is conspicuous in its use and purchase and in situations where group social acceptance is a strong motivator (Miniard and Cohen 1983).

Are universities unique places of learning, or brands to be marketed just like any other product? The language of brand management has been entering the lexicon of university vice-chancellors throughout the UK. 'Good' universities have known for some time that they have their reputation to preserve, but more recently, many universities have begun talking about managing brand values. Research among applicants to UK universities has consistently shown that prospective students have very poor knowledge about the actual facilities on offer, such as the standards of teaching, accommodation, and library facilities. However, certain universities have come to be rated more highly than others, often on the basis of non-academic information such as the triumphs of the university's sports teams or the night life in town. Many new universities have made a priority out of developing a strong brand image with which to challenge the established universities. Even students feel it is important to have a degree from a university which has a 'good' name, just like people have always wanted to belong to 'good' clubs. The view has spread that a university's good name needs to be nurtured and maintained in just the same way as any fast moving consumer good. Simply having technical excellence is not good enough.

De Montfort University has been one of the pioneers in university brand building, supporting its efforts with television advertising. It undertook research among current students which showed, perhaps surprisingly, that many preferred limited university funds to be spent on a brand building advertising campaign, rather than improvements in academic facilities, such as additional books for the library. Graduating from a known rather than an unknown university was seen as being important to many students. Cynics have been quick to criticize efforts to market universities as brands. How can any brand be sustained over the long term if the infrastructure and facilities of a university are under pressure from ever diminishing resources?

Creating a distinctive brand

THE brand is the focal point for many organizations' marketing activity. Branding creates a product with unique physical, functional, and psychological values and can help to transform commodities into unique products. To be successful, a brand must have a competitive advantage in at least one aspect of marketing, such that it meets the complex needs of consumers better than competitors. This section discusses the strategic issues involved in creating a strong and distinctive brand.

Choice of name

A brand is more than a name. Nevertheless, a name is usually vital to the identity of a brand and can be the most difficult to change. Many products have been redesigned and relaunched as they have gone through their life cycle, yet their brand name has remained unchanged. In the car market, Volkswagen introduced its first Golf model in 1974. Since then, the car has gone through four completely new body designs, three new series of engines, and countless minor modifications to styling, features, engine ranges, and colours. The Golf of 2000 is larger and much better equipped than its predecessor of twenty years ago. Yet the brand name remains the same. Instead of symbolizing a set of narrowly defined product characteristics, the name Golf has come to stand for reliable, mid-size, safe, value for money motoring. These values have been essentially unchanged over twenty-five years. The public has come to learn what is associated with the name Golf and therefore new model launches do not have to start from scratch in explaining what the car stands for.

Companies frequently engage specialist firms to develop brand names for their new products. This is often a wise investment, in view of the possible downside costs of getting a name wrong, and the difficulties of subsequently changing it. A brand-naming team may be made up of linguists, psychologists, sociologists, and media analysts, among others. These are some of the factors which previous experience shows should lead to a brand name being successful.

- The name should have positive associations with the benefits and features of the product (e.g. Bostik suggests adhesive qualities; Flash sounds like it will clean thoroughly and quickly).
- There should be no negative associations with words which sound similar (e.g. Volkswagen had to think long and hard about the wisdom of using the name Sharan in the UK for its passenger van range. Although the name worked well in other countries, it sounded too similar to Sharon, a girl's name which at the time had been much maligned in the media).

Getting a brand name wrong can cost a company dearly. For a major brand, re-tooling to change product formulations can be a relatively minor matter compared to the costs of changing a brand name. Sometimes, brands fail because the underlying product has failed to meet customers' expectations. At other times, a brand name fails because it was chosen with insufficient care. Occasionally, the world around a brand name changes in a way that destroys the appeal of a once well-liked name, for example, the slimmers' biscuits called Aids had to be renamed in the light of HIV scares.

With increasing globalization of markets, firms have to be careful that a brand name is capable of translation into overseas languages without causing offence or ridicule. Here are some examples of brand names that may have been well thought out in their own home market, but failed to take account of local interpretations in potential overseas markets:

■ General Motors may have wondered why its Nova car wasn't selling well in Spain, then realized that in Spanish the brand name suggested that the car 'doesn't work'

■ British visitors to Spain are often amused to find Bum crisps on sale—they probably wouldn't go down too well in an English-speaking market.

■ Similarly, the French drink Sic wouldn't be easy to export to Britain.

■ The name should be easy to pronounce and memorable (there is research to show that names which include the letter 'x' are particularly memorable, such as Andrex, Durex, Radox, etc.).

■ The name must be in a tone of language which is understood and appreciated by the product's target market.

■ The name must be checked by legal experts to ensure that it does not infringe on another company's brand name.

Nevertheless, brand names exist which appear to break all the rules and would almost certainly not have been chosen today. In a world which is sceptical of offal from animals, who would have named a range of meat products 'Brains'?

Distinctive product features

Sometimes the distinctive features of a product do not really require a brand name to prompt immediate recognition. Distinctiveness can be based on the physical design of a product (e.g. the distinctive shape of Toblerone chocolate); distinctive packaging (e.g. the lemon shaped container used to package Jif lemon juice); or distinctive service processes (e.g. the manner in which waiting staff in a TGI Fridays restaurant serve customers). Companies make great efforts through the use of patents to protect the distinctive characteristics of their products from competition, although this can be much more difficult in the case of intangible service processes.

Creation of a distinctive brand personality

It will be recalled that a brand possesses functional and emotional attributes. The emotional attributes are of particular importance in contributing to a brand's personality. This can best be described as the psychological disposition which buyers have towards a particular brand. Brands have been variously described as having personalities which are 'fun', 'reliable', 'traditional', and 'adventurous'. The Virgin group has evolved a personality for its brand which can be described as reliable, slightly offbeat, and value for money. This personality has been developed consistently across the group's product ranges, from air travel to banking and investment services.

There has been debate about whether the emotional aspects of a brand are becoming more or less important in consumers' overall evaluation of a product. One argument is that consumers are becoming more 'marketing literate' and increasingly sceptical of firms' attempts to create abstract images which are not underpinned by reality. On the other hand, there is no doubt that as consumers become more affluent they buy products to satisfy a much wider and more complex range of needs, which they seek to satisfy with distinctive brands (Maslow 1943; see Chapter 7). A brand personality can help an individual to reinforce their own self-identity, for example in the way that clothes are worn bearing brand names that have a personality of their own. An individual who wears a Benetton sweat shirt is probably identifying themselves with the personality that Benetton has created for its brand.

Figure 4.5 Packaging can be an important source of differentiation for an otherwise fairly generic product. *Toblerone*, with its unique triangular design, has managed to provide a highly visible point of differentiation for its product which distinguishes it from competing chocolates.

Distinctive visual identity

Companies often go to great lengths to invest their brands with a distinctive visual identity. Sometimes, this can be achieved simply on the basis of a colour. Within the cigarette market, Silk Cut has come to 'own' the colour purple, with the result that an advertisement need not mention any brand by name, but the presence of the colour will achieve recognition for the brand. The importance of colour was demonstrated in 1996 when Pepsi Cola sought to adopt the colour blue in the UK cola market to distinguish itself from its predominantly red competitors. The fact that the change appeared to result in no increase in sales provides a reminder that buyers are becoming increasingly marketing literate and may not be taken in simply by a colour change. One of Pepsi's arch rivals, Virgin, exploited the opportunity by stating in advertisements that it pays more attention to the *contents* of the can rather than its colour.

The extent to which a company can legitimately 'own' an identifying colour is questionable. Many suppliers of generic products have copied the colours used by their branded competitors, for example many supermarkets' own brands of coffee share a very similar colour scheme to the threat of the market leader, Nescafé. This has frequently led to allegations that they are 'passing off' their goods as if they were the branded product, especially where the packaging and typography are also used to imitate the brand leader. During 1997 Sainsbury was forced to climb down in a dispute with Coca-Cola over the visual similarity of its own brand cola with that of Coke.

Colours have often come to be associated with certain product features. Bright reds and yellows are often used to signify speed (e.g. fast food, one-hour film developing), and white is often associated with purity (low fat, additive-free foods). However, the meaning of colours has to be seen in their cultural context, so although white may be associated with purity in most western countries, in other countries it is associated with bereavement.

To achieve maximum effect, corporate visual identity should be applied consistently. For a typical service-based company, this would mean applying a design and colour scheme to the company's advertising, buildings, staff uniforms, vehicles and the tangible elements of the service offer.

Logos are an important part of corporate visual identity. The aim of a logo is to encapsulate the values of a brand and to provide an immediate reminder of the brand each time that it is seen by customers and potential customers. A good logo should:

■ give some indication of the business which a company is in, or the product category to which its output belongs (e.g. the logos for many water utility companies include stylized waves of water);

Many companies have rule books stating quite precisely how their logo should be applied. But could this consistency be counter-productive and result in the organization being seen by its customers as boring, stuffy, and lacking in creativity? Research by British Airways showed that its brand image was seen as stuffy and British. In an increasingly global market for airline services, it needed to shed this image, yet at the same time still stand for something in the eyes of customers throughout the world. The solution adopted by British Airways was to develop multiple identities based on art from around the world. The designs were applied in a highly visible manner to such items as aircraft tail wings, baggage labels, and furnishings in airport lounges. Traditionalists were horrified at the changes, but they undoubtedly helped to overcome the previous stuffy image. BA was not alone. The BBC, similarly regarded as stuffy, has developed a playful series of images for its BBC2 television channel. The theme is the figure 2, with interpretations including rubber ducks, a fly killer, and a toy car. How many more companies would benefit from a loosening of logo designs? Against this, how does a company maintain some degree of consistency in its brand values?

- stress particular advantages of a product or organization (e.g. the most advanced, the fastest, most caring, longest established);

- not be over-complicated. The simplest logos tend to stand the test of time best (for example, one of the earliest logos to be used was the plain triangle adopted by the brewer Bass. The company still uses essentially the same logo);

- be updated to keep it in tune with styles and fashions of the time (for example, the Shell oil company's logo has gone through numerous minor styling changes during its seventy-year history, which have retained the central theme of a shell, but adapted the shape and the emphasis on particular details.

Logos are sometimes used by public and not-for profit sector organizations, and here the public often expects to have its views about what is an acceptable logo taken into account. How far should an organization go in meeting the needs of its wider public stakeholders rather than those of its target customers?

Like many areas seeking to promote inward tourism, Leicester sought a logo for the city. The local tourism promotion company decided that a logo which featured a fashion clad, ethnic dancer was ideal for promoting some of the key tourism benefits of Leicester: a lively city with a lot of night life, the centre of the fashion industry, and a multi-ethnic choice of artistic events and restaurants. Faced with this new logo, the immediate reaction of many long-standing Leicester residents was 'Where's the Clock Tower?', a well-known landmark in the centre of the city. The marketers rejected the use of this symbol in the city's tourism logo because it conveyed nothing of the special attributes of the city. The Clock Tower may be an important reference point for local residents, but could tourists from outside really identify with it and be induced to visit the city?

Figure 4.6 These logos are so powerful that most people could readily identify with the 'true' owner, despite the use of a false name

Branding strategy

ONCE a firm has decided on a distinctive brand identity for a product, the next issue is to have a strategy for developing the brand. In this section, a number of alternative strategic routes are explored which each lead to a company differentiating its products from those of its competitors. One strategy is to develop a single strong brand. As an alternative, differentiated brands or brand families may be developed. Finally, once a strong brand has been developed, companies are often keen to extend its use.

Development of a single strong brand

One approach to branding is to apply the same brand name to everything that a company produces. The big advantage of this approach is the economies of scale in promotion which this can bring about. Instead of promoting many minor brands through small campaigns, a company can concentrate all of its resources on one campaign for one brand. This approach has been used successfully by many large multinational companies, such as IBM, Kodak, and Cadbury's, who, with a few exceptions, put their single brand name on everything they sell.

The main disadvantage of this approach is that it can pose significant risks of confusing the values of a brand. If a company positioned its product range as premium priced, top quality, confusion may arise in consumers' minds if it applied the

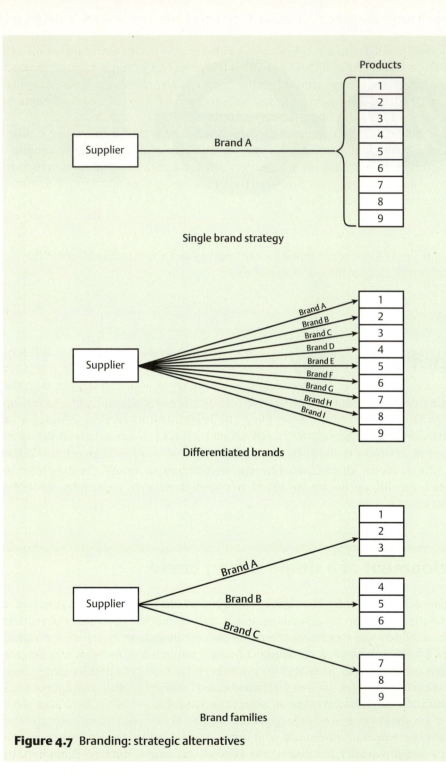

Figure 4.7 Branding: strategic alternatives

same brand name to a budget version of its product. Does the brand still stand for top quality?

Worse still for a company, a poorly performing product carrying its brand can tarnish all products carrying that name. This is a particular problem for new product launches which are of unproven reliability (for example, the Virgin group's reputation for dependable, no-nonsense service suffered when it applied its brand name to train services with a very poor reliability record).

A final problem of the strong single corporate brand is that it can make it more difficult for a company to dispose of the manufacture and marketing of products which no longer fit in its corporate plan. Very often, the main value of the products to a corporate buyer is their brand name, so the company may be forced into a monitoring agreement to protect its brand name from abuse by a company that has acquired the right to use it. Because of changes in corporate strategy, many of the products carrying the Cadbury's and Virgin brand names are not in fact produced by these companies, yet they still need to preserve the values which the names stand for.

Differentiated brands

To overcome the problem of confused brand values, firms often develop different brand names to serve different market segments. In this way, the clothing retailer Arcadia uses a number of different brand names to target different segments of the clothes buying market in terms of their age, disposable income, and lifestyle. So Top Man serves a relatively downmarket young male segment, while Principles serves a relatively affluent and slightly older female market. The Principles brand has been further differentiated with the development of Principles for Men. Because only the gender of the final user distinguishes the segments served by the two stores, the company can justify using the Principles brand name—it has the same fundamental values for men and women.

Brand family

The example of the Principles clothes store brand illustrates the emergence of a brand family. This occurs where a company uses a number of brand names, but identifies each product range or market segment served with a different brand name. The range is then developed to include a line of products. In this way, the Colgate Palmolive company has developed a number of product ranges, including soap, shampoos, and toothpaste, each with their own brand name. Within each range are a number of variants, for example Colgate toothpaste comes in original, baking soda, and total protection formats, among others.

Very often, companies promote brand names at a number of levels. As well as the corporate brand name, the name of the product category might be promoted. In addition, a special package offer within the basic product category may develop its own brand name. Thus British Airways has developed a corporate brand (British Airways), brands for individual routes (e.g. Shuttle), brands for Club Class and Economy Class, and finally brands for special offer tickets (e.g. World Savers). The danger of brand proliferation is confusion in the minds of consumers about what each brand stands for.

Brand extension

Where a company has invested heavily in a brand so that it has many positive attributes in the minds of buyers, it may feel tempted to get as much as possible out of its valuable asset. Given the increasing costs of developing strong brands, many companies have attempted to extend their brand to new product ranges. The attraction is quite clear. Rather than having to start from scratch with a new product and a new name, the company can at least start with a name with whose values buyers are familiar. So if a manufacturer of chocolate has developed a brand which stands for good taste and consistency, those values will be immediately transferred to a new range of ice-cream products that the company may consider adding to its range.

Of course, extending a brand to new products poses dangers as well as opportunities. If the extension goes too far into unrelated product areas, the core values of the brand may be undermined. Consider the case of BP oil which introduced a line of dish-washing detergent to the private consumer market. How could consumers avoid the feeling that the detergent was oily?

Protecting a brand

ONCE they have been created, brands can become very valuable assets to the companies that own them. CDR International, a brand protection consultant, carried out research in 1998 to assess just how desirable some of our favourite brand names are. When shown a white T-shirt, consumers said they would, on average, pay a premium of 33 per cent if it carried a designer label. This premium was even higher (at 37 per cent) for those in the 16–35 age group, or in the C1 socio-economic group (who would be prepared to pay 42 per cent more). Protecting a brand name against illegal counterfeiting is always a challenge, and over half of respondents in CRD's survey claimed that they would be happy to buy good counterfeits. Which brands were considered the most desirable by carrying the highest price premium? The top brand was Nike, followed by Calvin Klein, Rolex, Adidas, and Levi Strauss.

Attempts to value brands usually try to estimate the price premium which they command in their market, multiplied by estimated sales. A discounted cash flow calculation takes into account the value of earnings in future years. The enormous value of brands such as Coca-Cola is a reflection of the significant price premium that they can command and their enormous annual sales worldwide.

Like any object of value, criminals will be tempted to appropriate the asset for themselves. If somebody else has developed a strong brand name, why not 'borrow' it to promote your own goods? The result is counterfeit goods which carry all the superficial manifestations of brand identity, but may fail to deliver the performance which has come to be expected with the brand. Counterfeiting of goods with false brand names has been found in products as diverse as beverages, perfumes, watches, computer chips, and aircraft engine components. Sometimes consumers may be quite happy buying a low priced branded product knowing that it is a counterfeit copy. This is especially true of goods bought for conspicuous consumption, such as the fake Rolex watches which many tourists bring back from the Far East for just a few pounds. At other times, buyers may be defrauded into thinking that they have bought the genuine brand, often with dangerous consequences where the integrity of the product has safety implications.

For the owner of a brand, counterfeit copies hit it in two ways. Firstly, it looses sales to counterfeiters which it would have made itself. Secondly, and more importantly, buyers may come to mistrust the brand. How can they be sure that they are buying the genuine article? Firms often go to great lengths to stay one step ahead of counterfeiters, for example by introducing regular new designs which are hard to copy.

Brand owners resort to the law to protect their assets. The common law provides a general remedy against companies seeking to 'pass off' counterfeit products as though they were the real thing. Passing off can include attempts to copy any of the distinctive brand characteristics which were discussed above. As an example, a bus operator was accused of passing off by painting its buses a similar colour to those of its main competitor and running on a similar route. It had been relying on public confusion to pass off its service as the one which people had been expecting. Further protection is provided by legislation. The Trade Marks Act 1994 (which implements the EU Trade Marks Harmonisation Directive No. 89/104/EEC) provides protection for trade marks, which are defined as any sign capable of being represented graphically which is capable of distinguishing goods or services of one undertaking from those of other undertakings (Trade Marks Act 1994, s.1(1)). Where a company has a patent for a product, the Patents Act 1977 provides protection against unauthorized copying of the product specification during the currency of the patent.

The changing role of branding

THE philosophy and practices of branding have seen a number of developments in recent years. Many have argued that brands no longer have a role in an age of greater public awareness of product characteristics, associated with increased scepticism about brands. At the same time, many intermediaries have taken on board the practices of branding, frequently challenging manufacturers at their own game.

The end of branding?

There have been many suggestions that the processes of branding are in retreat. When the manufacturer of Marlboro cigarettes cut the price of the brand to beat off competition from the rapidly advancing generic competitors, many began to write the obituaries for brands as we have come to know them. Both the functional and emotional dimensions of brands have come under increasing pressure. Research has suggested that consumers are becoming increasingly critical of the messages of brand building advertising, especially those aimed at creating abstract brand personalities (Biel 1990). It is also claimed that consumers are becoming increasingly confident, ready to experiment and to trust their own judgement and less tolerant of products that do not contribute to their own values.

The traditional functional qualities of a brand have also come under pressure from increasing levels of consumer legislation. Characteristics such as purity, reliability, and durability may have traditionally added value to a brand, but these are increasingly enshrined in legislation and therefore less capable of being used to differentiate one product from another. An example of the effects of legislation on brand loyalty can be observed in the taxi market by contrasting buyer behaviour in areas with strict licensing (e.g. London) with areas where a relatively unregulated market exists. In the former case, legislation has reduced the product to a commodity meeting strictly specified standards, whereas in the latter, customers are more likely to seek the reassurance of a branded operator.

Defenders of brands argue that much of the success of generic products during the early 1990s can be attributed to the economic recession rather than any fundamental change in attitude by consumers. As household disposable incomes declined during the recession, many households were forced to cut back on items of optional expenditure, which could have meant substituting a premium priced brand with a cheaper generic product. By this analysis, expenditure on branded products would be expected to rise as household incomes recover. More significantly, it has been argued that many of the cheaper substitutes were in fact branded by the retailer supplying them. The concept of branding was alive and well, but now more in the hands of retailers.

The emergence of retailers' own brands

The suggestion that the growth of generic products is challenging traditional product branding strategy can be partly explained by a shift in buyers' brand allegiance, away from a narrow focus on manufacturers' product image to a broader concern with the image of intermediaries. Through continued investment in product improvement, retailers have been able to develop products which have comparable functional qualities to manufacturers' branded products. The important role played by own brands in building up a store's corporate identity and hence customer loyalty has been noted by Simmons and Meredith (1984) based on a study of the UK, where own label brands are relatively well developed. A comparable study in the USA (Uncles and Ellis 1989) challenged this analysis, although it can be argued that there are differences in positioning between US and UK grocery multiples.

A number of studies have associated high levels of retail market concentration with a desire by retailers to develop customer loyalty (de Chernatony 1989, Duke 1991). Such loyalty can be generated both by own-label brand development strategies and by relationship marketing strategies. With improved product ranges and corporate image strategies, intermediaries have sought to extend the functional aspects of their branding (e.g. quality of products, range of products) with the emotional appeal of the corporate brand. The use of distinctive colour schemes and alignment with good causes can help to develop an emotional relationship between the store and its customers.

The organization as a brand

The traditional role of a brand has been to differentiate a product from competing products and to create liking of it by target customers. The process of branding has been increasingly applied to organizational image too. This has been particularly important for services where the intangibility of the product causes the credentials of the provider to be an important component of consumers' choice. The notion of an emotional relationship to a product has been extended to develop an emotional relationship between an organization and its customers.

Many service organizations have found the development of brands to be attractive where their service offer is highly complex and consumers find the offer mentally as well as physically intangible. In the UK, the pensions industry has found it difficult to explain its products to an audience which is not receptive to the technical details of a product, which is nevertheless considered by most people to be a vital provision for old age. Furthermore, the Financial Services Act 1986 limits the ability of companies to promote their pensions in creative ways (for example, companies may only quote standard industry-wide expected rates of return). This has led many companies to embark on comprehensive brand building programmes which say very little about the details of the products on offer, but a lot about the nature of the company offering them. Thus the Prudential Assurance Company has built its brand image on the superior lifestyle which can result from dealing with the company, while Legal and General has the brand image of an umbrella as the symbol of a protective company.

It is not only in the service sector that brand building has been refocused from the product to the organization. During the 1990s, many companies have moved expenditure from 'above the line' brand building activities to 'below the line' product

Brand building is at the very heart of marketing for fast moving consumer goods. But could a strong focus on branding work for an intangible service such as a pension?

In the spring of 1998, Axa Sun Life embarked on an £8 million UK marketing campaign to make the Axa brand the Coke of pensions. Research had constantly shown that customers want two things from financial services: security and simplicity. Existing advertising by financial service companies had failed to deliver either in spite of the annual £14 million spending by the sector. Few companies had created real brand strength where their values were understood and trusted. With the emergence of new entrants such as supermarkets to the sector, buyers' decision processes were becoming even more confused. Axa set itself a major task if it was to emulate the brand strength of Coca-Cola. How would it be able to establish a distinctive identity when most competing financial services are basically similar and constrained by legislation? What opportunities would there be for creating an aspirational brand? And would the public be able to forget the pensions mis-selling scandal of the 1980s which harmed the image of the sector as a whole?

support by means of direct marketing activities. In one notable case, the Heinz company decided to cut the money it spent on supporting individual product brands and instead promote the Heinz brand for core values of tradition and wholesomeness. Individual products were supported by direct marketing, which included the incentives of offers and suggestions for how its products could be used creatively (see Chapter 20). The company, rather than individual products, becomes the dominant brand and brand equity is based on customers' willingness to pay premium prices for the company's products.

The development of global brands

With the volume of international trade currently growing at around four times the rate of world Gross Domestic Product, companies are increasingly having to include exports as part of their marketing plan. It follows therefore that the process of branding should be considered in global terms. Economies of scale can be achieved by developing a global brand, for example visitors from overseas can automatically recognize a McDonald's restaurant, giving it an advantage over a local branded restaurant which starts with no overseas name recognition.

There are many pitfalls in the development of brands which work in overseas markets as well as the domestic one. This chapter has highlighted some of the problems which occur with an inappropriate choice of name. The subject of global brands is returned to in Chapter 23.

Chapter summary and key linkages to other chapters

The process of branding allows a company to develop a distinctive identity for itself and its products, so as to differentiate its products from those of competitors. By doing this, a company can avoid the worse excesses of price competition. If branding is to be implemented effectively, a strategy needs to be carefully thought through and implemented sensitively. Despite doubts among some cynics about the value of brands, their development continues to play a central role in firms' marketing management.

Because of the pivotal role of brands within marketing planning, the subject impinges on many other aspects of marketing which are covered in other chapters of this book:

Chapter 1: What is marketing?: For many companies, the creation and sustenance of strong brands is a central part of the value creation process which delivers packages of benefits which meet the needs of clearly identified groups of consumers. Marketers must understand the nature of the benefits that consumers seek from a brand.

Chapter 2: The marketing environment: The strength of brands in any market reflects, among other things, the state of economic and social development of that market. A competitive marketing environment is likely to create pressure for brand development as companies seek to distinguish their product offers from those of their competitors.

Chapter 3: Segmentation: Market segments differ in the importance they attach to particular aspects of brands, for example more affluent segments may seek primarily emotional benefits of a brand while those satisfying more basic levels of need will seek the reassurance of the functional aspects of a brand.

Chapter 5: Marketing and ethics: Does the creation of aspirational brands create divisions within society where groups feel disenfranchised from society because they cannot enjoy the benefits of brands which have been promoted as being highly desirable? What harm will be done to a brand if a company is revealed to have acted as a 'bad citizen'?

Chapter 6: Marketing research: What methods of research are most appropriate for understanding how consumers perceive a brand?

Chapter 7: Buyer behaviour: Brands help to simplify the buying process. Do different groups evaluate brands differently in the buying process?

Chapter 8: Buyer–seller relationship development: Is a relationship marketing approach a substitute for, or complementary to, a brand development approach?

Chapters 9/10: Developing a product portfolio: How important are the physical design and process characteristics of an organization's product offers, in comparison to the brand values which they carry?

Chapter 11: Developing a sustainable competitive advantage: How does the development of a strong brand contribute to a company's sustainable advantage? Can a company be successful without having strong brands?

Chapters 12/13: Pricing theory and applications: To what extent can a company sustain a price premium in respect of its brands?

Chapters 14/15: Intermediaries/physical, distribution management: Brands are used to 'pre-sell' products direct to purchasers. How important is the role of an intermediary in influencing the purchase decision, relative to the role of the brand? How have intermediaries themselves created their own strong brands?

Chapter 16: Principles of promotion planning: How successful is a promotional campaign in developing distinctive brand values? What message is most appropriate in achieving this?

Chapter 17: Advertising: What message and media are most effective in developing brand values?

Chapter 18: Personal selling: To what extent is a strong brand essential to support the efforts of sales personnel?

Chapter 19: Public relations and sales promotion: Does sales promotion activity undermine the values of brand advertising?

Chapter 20: Direct marketing: Are consumers willing to buy products directly which are not supported by strong brand building efforts? Can strong brands be built by direct marketing methods alone?

Chapter 21: Organizing for marketing: Should marketing management responsibilities be allocated by brand, by product category, or by market segment?

Chapter 22: Marketing of services: For many intangible services, buyers seek the reassurance of strong brands. However, many services are highly variable and brand development becomes very difficult.

Chapter 23: Global marketing: How are global brands developed? What problems and opportunities are there in trying to extend a successful domestic brand into overseas markets?

Case study

Fairy's brand bubble never seems to burst

The detergent market is often regarded as one of the early pioneers of modern marketing. Differentiating one product from another in the minds of consumers can be extremely difficult, with one packet of detergent looking very much like another, and in many cases also performing similarly. It is often said that aspiring marketers who can succeed in the detergent market can go on to market any product successfully.

In 1960 Proctor & Gamble launched Fairy Liquid in the UK market. At that time, the washing up market was still in its infancy with only 17 per cent of households using a liquid and the rest using soap powder or soap. The first task of Procter & Gamble was therefore to educate the public in the benefits of using washing up liquid. As market leader, P&G stood to gain most from a change in consumers' habits. The launch of Fairy involved distributing 15 million trial bottles to about 85 per cent of households in the UK.

Creating early awareness and trial of the product led to Fairy gaining a market share of 27 per cent by 1960. Strong promotional support has been a key to the brand's success. Since its launch, promotional messages have focused consistently on the mildness of the product, its long-lasting suds, and a proud positioning as a slightly more expensive product which is better value and worth paying the extra for. Mother and child images have been used extensively in advertising. This helps to create brand values of a soft, caring, homely image. Messages have been adapted around this core theme in response to changing attitudes, for example a commercial in 1994 used a father instead of a mother at the kitchen sink. Various celebrities have been used to endorse the brand's values, including a lengthy spell of endorsement by the actress Nanette Newman. The consistency of the brand's message has been reinforced with a promotional jingle that has been modified only slightly since it was first introduced in 1960.

During the first twenty years of the brand's life, product innovation had been relatively modest. However, since then an increasingly competitive market and more discerning customers have forced the company to innovate in order to maintain and strengthen its market share. With the emergence of many 'me-too' competitors from supermarkets, Fairy needed to offer additional unique advantages to supplement its long-lasting suds.

In 1984/5 the company introduced a lemon variant of Fairy and its total market share increased to 32 per cent. By 1987 market share had increased to 34 per cent with the recently introduced lemon variant accounting for one-third of sales. In 1988 a new formulation was launched offering '15 per cent extra mileage', as well as being more effective in dissolving grease.

In 1992 the original Fairy Liquid was replaced with Fairy Excel which claimed to be '50 per cent better at dealing with grease'. This helped to increase market share to 50 per cent. In the following year, a concentrated version of Fairy Excel Plus was launched with the slogan 'the power of four for the price of one'. The company launched this low bulk, high concentration product with one eye to retailers who were tiring of filling their valuable shelf space with more and more variants of basically low value products. Excel Plus offered supermarkets more cost-effective and profitable use of their shelf space.

During the lifetime of Fairy Liquid, the market for detergents in different European countries had gradually converged. As a result, Excel Plus was launched simultaneously in the UK, Belgium, Denmark, Finland, Germany, Holland, Ireland, and Sweden.

Case study review questions

1 How would you explain the success of the Fairy brand?

2 How do you think Procter & Gamble has been able to increase its market share at a time when competition from supermarkets' own-label brands has intensified?

3 To what extent can the principles and practices of brand management used for Fairy Liquid be applied to other goods and services, such as televisions and package holidays?

Chapter review questions

1 Critically assess the suggestion that as the education level of consumers increases, buyers will increasingly see through the claims of brands and will buy cheaper generic alternatives.

2 Critically evaluate the factors in the marketing environment which are crucial to the development of strong brands within a market sector.

3 With increasing levels of consumer protection legislation designed to protect buyers from faulty products and misleading advertising claims, do we still need brands? How can brands adapt to increasing levels of legislation?

4 Are brands a unique invention of marketers? Discuss the role that sociology and psychology can contribute to the understanding of how brands function.

5 To what extent should companies seek to put a financial value on their brands? Critically assess the rationale for brand valuation.

6 What can a brand owner do to protect the investment that it has made in its brand? Critically assess the options available with reference to specific branded products.

References

Allison, R., and Uhl, K. (1964), 'Influence of Beer Brand Identification on Taste Perception', *Journal of Marketing Research*, **1**, 3, pp. 36–9.

Barwise, P., and Roberston, T. (1992), 'Brand Portfolios', *Europe Management Journal*, **10**, 3, Sept.

Biel, A. L. (1990), 'Love the Ad, Buy the Product?', *Admap*, Sept., p. 12.

Branthwaite, A., and Cooper, P. (1981), 'Analgesic Effects of Branding in Treatment of Headaches', *British Medical Journal*, **282**, 16 May, pp. 1576–8.

Buzzell, R. D., and Gale, B. M. (1987), *The PIMS Principle* (New York: The Free Press).

De Chernatony, L. (1989), 'The Impact of the Changed Balance of Power from Manufacturer to Retailer in the UK Packaged Grocery Market', in Pelligrini, L. and Reddy, S. (eds.), *Retail and Marketing Channels* (London: Routledge), pp. 258–73.

—— and McWilliam, G. (1990), 'Appreciating Brands as Assets Through Using a Two-Dimensional Model', *International Journal of Advertising*, **9**, 2, pp. 111–19.

Doyle, P. (1989), 'Building Successful Brands: The Strategic Options', *Journal of Marketing Management*, **5**, 1, pp. 77–95.

Duke, R. (1991), 'Post-Saturation Competition in UK Grocery Retailing', *Journal of Marketing Management*, **7**, 1, pp. 63–76.

Gardner, B., and Levy, S. (1955), 'The Product and the Brand', *Harvard Business Review*, **33** Mar./Apr., pp. 33–9.

Laurent, G., and Kapferer, J. (1985), 'Measuring Consumer Involvement Profiles', *Journal of Marketing Research*, 22 Feb., pp. 41–53.

Maslow, A. (1943), 'A Theory of Human Motivation', *Psychological Review*, **50**, 4.

Miniard, P. W., and Cohen, J. B. (1983), 'Modelling Personal and Normative Influences on Behaviour', *Journal of Consumer Research*, **10** Sept., pp. 169–80.

Munson, J. M., and Spivey, W. (1981), 'Product and Brand User Stereotypes among Social Classes', *Journal of Advertising Research*, **21**, 4, Aug., pp. 37–46.

Pitcher, A. (1985), 'The Role of Branding in International Advertising', *International Journal of Advertising*, **4**, 3, pp. 241–6.

Porter, M. E. (1980), *Competitive Strategy: Techniques for Analysing Industries and Competitors* (New York: The Free Press).

Simmons, M., and Meredith, B. (1984), 'Own Label Profile and Purpose', *Journal of the Marketing Research Society*, **26**, 1, pp. 3–27.

Solomon, M. (1983), 'The Role of Products in Social Stimuli: A Symbolic Interactionism Perspective', *Journal of Consumer Research*, **10**, Dec., pp. 319–29.

—— and Buchanan, B. (1991), 'A Role Theoretic Approach to Product Symbolism: Mapping of Consumption Constellation', *Journal of Business Research*, **22**, 2, pp. 95–109.

Uncles, M. D., and Ellis, K. (1989), 'The Buying of Own Labels', *European Journal of Marketing*, **23**, 3, pp. 57–73.

Suggested further reading

For a general introduction to the roles of brands in marketing planning, the following are useful:

■ Doyle, P. (1989), 'Building Successful Brands: The Strategic Options', *Journal of Marketing Management*, **5**, 1, pp. 77–95.

■ Hart, S., and Murphy, J. (eds.) (1997), *Brands: The New Wealth Creators*, (Basingstoke: Macmillan).

■ Kapferer, J.-N. (1997), *Strategic Brand Management* (London: Kogan Page).

■ King, S. (1991), 'Brand Building in the 1990s', *Journal of Marketing Management*, **7**, 1, pp. 3–13.

■ Kochan, N. (ed.) (1996), *The World's Greatest Brands* (Basingstoke: Macmillan).

■ Randall, G. (1997), *Branding* (London: Kogan Page).

For evidence and examples of how great brands are developed, refer to the following:

■ Aaker, D. (1996), *Building Strong Brands* (New York: The Free Press).

■ De Chernatony, L., and McDonald, M. (1998), *Creating Powerful Brands in Consumer, Service and Industrial Markets*, 2nd edn. (Oxford: Butterworth-Heinemann).

■ Gardiner, P., and Quintin, S. (1998), 'Building Brands Using Direct Marketing—a Case Study', *Marketing Intelligence and Planning*, **16**, 1, pp. 6–12.

■ Kapferer, J.-N. (1997), Strategic Brand Management (London: Kogan Page).

The following discuss the use of corporate identity as a component of brand building:

■ Balmer, J. M. T. (1998), 'Corporate Identity and the Advent of Corporate Marketing', *Journal of Marketing Management*, **14**, 8, pp. 963–96.

■ Howard, S. (1998), *Corporate Image Management: A Marketing Discipline for the 21st Century* (Oxford: Butterworth-Heinemann).

■ Markwick, N., and Fill, C. (1997), ' Towards a Framework for Managing Corporate Identity', *European Journal of Marketing*, **31**, 5-6, pp. 396–410.

■ Van Riel, C. B. M., and Balmer, J. M. T. (1997), 'Corporate ID: The Concept , its Measurement and Management', *European Journal of Marketing*, **31**, 5-6, pp. 340–55.

The following discuss challenges from generic 'own-label' products:

■ Buck, S. (1997), 'Has Own Label Now Passed its Peak', *Marketing*, 17 Feb., pp. 16–17.

■ De Chernatony, L. (1989), 'The Impact of the Changed Balance of Power from Manufacturer to Retailer in the UK Packaged Grocery Market' in L. Pelligrini and S. Reddy (eds.), *Retail and Marketing Channels* (London: Routledge), pp. 258–73.

■ Marquis, S. (1997), 'Lookalikes can go Further on a Little Difference', *Marketing*, p. 20.

■ Simmons, M., and Meredith, B. (1984), 'Own Label Profile and Purpose', *Journal of the Marketing Research Society,* **26**, 1, pp. 3–27.

■ Uncles, M. D., and Ellis, K. (1989), 'The Buying of Own Labels', *European Journal of Marketing*, **23**, 3, pp. 57–73.

Trade marks and patent laws are discussed in the following references:

■ Firth, A. (1995), *Trade Marks*: *The New Law* (Bristol: Jordan Publishing).

■ Johnston, D. (1995), *Design Protection*: *A Practical Guide to the Law on Plagiarism for Manufacturers and Designers*, 4th edn. (Aldershot: Gower).

■ Phillips, J., and Firth, A. (1995), *Introduction to Intellectual Property*, 3rd edn. (London: Butterworth).

Useful web links

The following sites provided by advertising agencies give an insight into the services they offer clients to create strong brands:

Altus Group Communications: http://www.altus-group.com.
Cogbox: http://www.cogbox.com.
Lyon Advertising: http://www.lyonadvertising.com/

The following site includes details of UK advertising agencies with their own web site:

http://www.lime.co.uk/agencies.html
http//www.mailbase.ac.uk/lists/corporate-id-all/: A 'superlist' for a group of discussion lists on the subject of corporate identity.

Chapter 5
Marketing Ethics

Chapter objectives

The adoption of marketing can undoubtedly bring benefits to society. Nevertheless, some aspects of marketing may be questionable on ethical grounds. This chapter discusses the social responsibility of organizations and the nature of their responsibilities to society. Ethics is a complex concept to define, and an attempt is made to understand ethical behaviour in a marketing context.

Introduction

'THE customer is king' is a traditional marketing maxim and, according to this, everything that a company does should be geared towards satisfying the needs of its customers. But should commercial organizations also have responsibilities to the public at large? The question is becoming increasingly important, as marketers have never before been subjected to such a critical gaze from those who are quick to identify the harmful side effects of market-led growth.

There are philosophical and pragmatic reasons why marketers should act in a socially responsible manner. Models of a responsible society would have marketers doing their bit to contribute towards a just and fair society, alongside the contributions of other institutions such as the family and the Church. More pragmatically, marketers need to take account of society's values because if they do not, they may end up isolated from the values of the customers they seek to attract. In increasingly discriminating markets, buyers may opt for the more socially responsible company. Acting in an unsocial way may have a long-term cost for a company and ultimately not serve the needs of those customers who prefer to deal with a socially acceptable company.

This chapter explores the complex moral and practical issues behind the concept of social responsibility by business.

The societal marketing concept

SOME marketers have argued that marketing itself cannot claim to be a discipline if it is unwilling to investigate systematically issues of social welfare and the impacts of market-based distribution systems (e.g. Anderson 1982). The existence of external costs and benefits and the presence of multiple 'stakeholders' in an organization serve to emphasize this point. Stakeholders can be defined as any individual or company who is affected by the activities of an organization. External costs occur where a company causes another person or company to incur costs for which the latter cannot claim reimbursement from the former. An example is a manufacturing plant that causes pollution costs to local residents, who cannot reclaim the costs of additional cleaning or of medical problems that result from the pollution. Many stakeholders may be involved in such external costs and benefits and these are discussed later in this chapter.

Supporters of the societal marketing concept point to a change of heart by companies who attach importance not just to satisfying their customers' needs, but the needs of society as a whole. A distinction should, however, be made between social philanthropy and the societal marketing concept. There have always been companies which have given to good causes quite independently of their marketing strategy.

Rising consumer incomes have resulted in the growing importance of the augmented elements of a purchase. The external benefits provided by consumer purchases are becoming a larger element of the total product offering, which consumers use to judge competing products in increasingly competitive markets. Fragmentation of consumer markets has resulted from growing diversity in the needs which consumers seek to satisfy. To most people, goods and services no longer have to provide for the most basic level of physiological or social needs.

According to Maslow, when individuals' basic physiological and social needs are satisfied, higher order needs become motivators which influence their buying behaviour. In these circumstances, consumers seek to satisfy a relatively intangible inner need for peace of mind, which may come about through knowledge that their purchase is helping to change the world in a way which they consider desirable. Fifty years ago, a packet of washing powder would have largely satisfied a need to produce tangible cleanliness. With most of the population being able to afford cleaning powders which could produce this effect, emphasis moved to promoting washing powder on the basis of satisfying social needs. So one brand was differentiated from another by signifying greater care for the family or was seen to produce results which were visibly valued by peer groups. Today, manufacturers of washing powder recognize that a significant segment seeks to buy more than the packet of washing powder—they seek also to buy a chance to change the world by reducing ecological damage caused by washing powders containing high levels of harmful phosphates (Fig. 5.1).

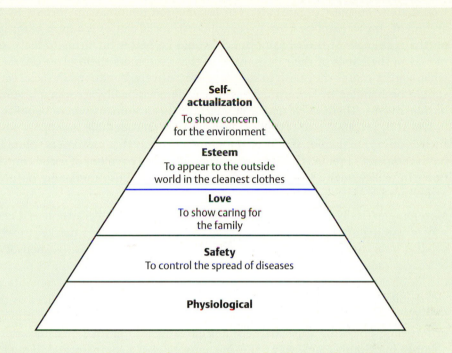

Figure 5.1 Maslow's hierarchy of needs can be used to illustrate how changing levels of needs have influenced the dominant factors influencing the purchase of washing powder

Possible examples of societal marketing approaches adopted by firms include:

- designing products which minimize ecological damage (e.g. using recycled paper for burger containers, rather than styrene);
- supporting charitable causes (e.g. newspapers and supermarkets giving tokens with which schools can buy books);
- promoting the fact that a company recruits heavily among disadvantaged groups in society such as the disabled.

Critics of the societal marketing concept see it as short-term and cynical manipulation by a company of its principal stakeholders. Others have pointed out that there is not necessarily any incompatibility between traditional marketing objectives and societal objectives. For example, Arbratt and Sacks (1988) give the reminder that the societal marketing concept does not involve a company in forgoing its long-term profitability and survival objectives.

Criticisms of the societal marketing concept can take two forms: philosophical and pragmatic:

- At a philosophical level, it has been argued by the followers of Milton Friedman that firms should concentrate on doing what they are best at—making profits for their owners. The idea of social responsibility by firms has been criticized as it would allow business organizations to become too dominant in society. By this argument, any attempt by firms to contribute to social causes is a form of taxation on the customers of their businesses. It would be better for firms to leave such money in the hands of their customers, so that customers themselves can decide what worthy causes they wish to support. Alternatively, donations to social causes should be handled by government which is democratically accountable, unlike business firms. There is particular strength in this argument where benefits are provided by private sector organizations who have considerable monopoly power, such as utility companies. It may be too simplistic to say that customers voluntarily buy a company's products and therefore consent to the payment of social contributions. In reality, many markets are uncompetitive and customers may have very little choice.

■ More pragmatically, companies often support social causes because it is a cheap way of gaining attention and a unique selling proposition. In a market in which product offers are all broadly similar and with saturation advertising, sponsorship of a social cause may allow a company to develop a unique identity for its products. Critics of the societal marketing concept argue that most external benefits provided under the guise of societal marketing are in fact rapidly internalized by their provider. As examples, litter bins sponsored by a fast food restaurant, the provision of recycling points by supermarkets, and donations to animal charities are not altruism but simply a new way of buying awareness of a company and liking of it, using values which are currently fashionable.

Large retailers have been fighting to make moral as well as financial capital from their marketing. Sainsbury's decision to extend its school equipment promotion (whereby customers could collect vouchers for their local school on every used carrier bag or £10 spent in store), showed that 'social' promotions can be highly beneficial to a retailer. Sainsburys saw a dual benefit from the scheme: a perception that the company cares about the community, and a build-up in sales as parents are encouraged to shop at Sainsbury's to benefit their local school. Numerous companies have gone along the route of social promotions. All argue that their initiatives are not altruism, but good business practice. But questions remain to be asked. Why do customers prefer to pay a few extra pennies for their groceries to a 'social' retailer, rather than giving their money directly to a good cause? Does social marketing give too much power to business?

Governments have recently sought to pass on responsibility for many aspects of social provision (e.g. sponsorship of the arts). Is there a danger in expecting the commercial sector to undertake such a role? Commercial organizations tend to be very selective in which sections of society they support. Firms have a habit of supporting causes which have popular appeal (e.g. animal charities and equipment for schools), but may fail to protect minorities in society who command very little public prestige. For example, very few commercial organizations support activities in the fields of mental illness or freedom for political prisoners. It can be argued that responsibilities for such causes cannot be given up by the public sector and handed to private sector organizations.

Collectively, consumers represent roughly the same group as the electorate. Electors have always expected government to act in the best public interest, otherwise—in the extreme—the government will not be elected. Consumers are developing similar expectations towards the suppliers of private sector goods. If they do not feel the company is acting in the public interest, their goods will not be purchased. In taking on this role, some have suggested that private sector companies are becoming more important than governments in setting the agenda for ecological reform. There are examples of where this has happened, such as the development of organically grown vegetables and the replacement of CFCs in aerosols. These initiatives originated primarily with the private sector rather than the government.

Business ethics

Eᴛʜɪᴄs is essentially about the definition of what is right and wrong. However, a difficulty occurs in trying to agree just what is right and wrong. No two people have precisely the same opinions, so critics would argue that ethical considerations are of little interest to business. It can also be difficult to distinguish between ethics and legality, for example it may not be strictly illegal to exploit the gullibility of children in advertisements, but it may nevertheless be unethical.

Culture has a great effect in defining ethics and what is considered unethical in one society may be considered perfectly acceptable in another. In western societies, ethical considerations confront marketers on many occasions. For example:

■ A drug company may advertise a product and provide information which is technically correct, but omit to provide vital information about side effects associated with using the product. Should a marketing manager be required to spell out the possible problems of using its products, as well as the benefits?

■ A dentist is short of money and diagnoses spurious problems which call for unnecessary medical treatment. How does he reconcile his need to maximize his earning potential with the need to provide what is best for his patient?

■ In order to secure a major new construction contract, a sales person must entertain the client's buying manager with a weekend all-expenses paid holiday. Should this be considered ethical business practice in Britain? Or in south America?

It is suggested that society is becoming increasingly concerned about the ethical values adopted by its commercial organizations. With expanding media availability and an increasingly intelligent audience, it is getting easier to expose examples of unethical business practice. Moreover, many television audiences appear to enjoy watching programmes which reveal alleged unethical practices of household name companies. To give one example, the media has on a number of occasions focused attention on alleged exploitative employment practices of suppliers used by some of the biggest brand names in sportswear.

Firms are responding to increasing levels of ethical awareness by trying to put their own house in order. These are some examples of how firms have gone about the task:

- Many companies have identified segments of their market who are prepared to pay a premium price in order to buy a product which has been produced in an ethical manner, or from a company that has adopted ethical practices. Many personal investors are concerned not just about the return that they will get, but the way in which that return will be achieved. This explains the increasing popularity of ethical investment funds that avoid investing in companies which are considered to be of a socially dubious nature. In the food sector, many consumers would consider the treatment of cattle grown for meat to be inhuman and unethical and would be happy to buy from a supplier who they knew acted ethically in the manner in which the cattle were raised and slaughtered. Many with particularly strong convictions may refuse to buy meat at all.

- Greater attention to training can make clear to staff just what is expected of them, for example that it is unethical (and in the long run commercially damaging) for a pension company's sales personnel to try to sell a policy to a person when it really does not suit their needs. Training may emphasize the need to spend a lot of time finding out just what the true needs of the customer are.

- More effective control and reward systems can help to reduce unethical practices within an organization. For example, sales personnel employed by a financial services company on a commission only basis are more likely to try to sell a policy to a customer regardless of the customer's needs compared to a salaried employee who can take a longer-term view of the relationship between the company and its clients.

There are many documented cases to show that acting ethically need not conflict with a company's profit objectives, and indeed can add to profitability. For example, good safety standards and employment policies can improve productivity. In the UK, the DIY retailer B&Q has reduced discrimination against older workers by employing predominantly older people in some of its stores. It is claimed that these stores have become the firm's most profitable.

The 1980s and 1990s saw a great growth in investment funds which claimed to invest only in businesses which are run ethically. Many investors preferred to know that their investment was not just benefiting themselves, but society as a whole. It was also claimed that a good ethical investment fund need perform no worse than one run without explicit ethical considerations. By 1998 there were over thirty ethical investment funds in the UK. However, a report by the Social Affairs Unit was scornful of ethical investment, because ethics is about judgements on what people do with products. It cited the example of funds' refusal to invest in the nuclear industry, which implied that the industry was totally bad, despite the valuable role which nuclear radiation plays in medicine. Similarly, it is very much an individual judgement whether nuclear electricity generation is good or bad. So what is the role of ethical investment trusts? Ethics is very much about statements of what is right and wrong, and these vary between individuals, between cultures, and they change through time. Can an investment trust ever be said to represent the views of a society as a whole?

The stakeholders of organizations

THE traditional mantra of marketing-oriented organizations is that the 'Customer is King'. Companies whose marketing managers focus only on satisfying the short-term needs of customers may end up paying a high price if the interests of a wider group of stakeholders are not satisfied. Customers are crucial to the success of commercial organizations. However, without the support of other key groups in its environment, a company's marketing aims may not be achieved.

It is common to describe stakeholders as those organizations and individuals who may not necessarily have any direct dealings with a company, but are nevertheless affected by its actions. In turn, a company can be significantly affected by the actions of its stakeholders.

It has been argued that business organizations have a moral responsibility to take account of the interests of these stakeholders. More pragmatically, it can also be argued that a company that does not take the needs of this broader group of stakeholders into account will find it increasingly difficult to achieve its narrower commercial goals.

The following principal stakeholders in business organizations can be identified (Fig. 5.2):

Customers

There is an argument that the customer is *not* always right in the goods and services they choose to buy from a company. Customers may sometimes not be aware of their true needs or may have these needs manipulated by exploitative companies. Taking a long-term and broad perspective, companies should have a duty to provide goods and services which satisfy these longer-term and broader needs rather than immediately felt needs. There have been many examples where the long-term interests of

Figure 5.2 A stakeholder approach to business organizations

customers have been ignored by companies. Increasingly, legislation is saying that the customer is *not* always right and companies have a duty to consider the long-term interests of customers as stakeholders. This has been very clearly seen in the mis-selling of pensions in the UK during the 1980s. Private pension companies knew that many members of occupational pension schemes would have undoubtedly been better off remaining in their scheme, rather than making alternative pension arrangements. Nevertheless, many employees were tempted by short-term incentives to leave their employers' scheme and to take out a private pension, leaving them financially worse off over the longer term. Regulatory authorities have recognized the wider interests of customers by requiring the pensions companies to provide compensation to customers who were sold a pension which was inappropriate to their long-term needs.

There are many more examples of situations where customers are probably not right and their long-term interests have been neglected by companies, including:

- tobacco companies who fail to impress upon customers the long-term harmful effects of buying and consuming their cigarettes;

- manufacturers of milk for babies who should make mothers aware of the significant long-term health benefits to children of using breast milk rather than manufactured milk products;

- car manufacturers who add expensive stereo equipment to cars as standard equipment, but relegate vital safety equipment to the status of optional extras.

In each of these cases, most people might agree that, objectively, buyers are being persuaded to make a choice against their own long-term self-interest. But on what moral grounds can society say that consumers' choices in these situations are wrong? According to some individuals' sense of priorities, an expensive hi-fi system may indeed be considered to offer a higher level of personal benefit than an airbag.

Customers as individual consumers usually fail to evaluate the external costs that they cause other consumers collectively to incur. External costs can take many forms, such as:

- congestion which one car driver causes to other drivers;
- the pollution suffered by residents living near waste tips caused by disposing of fast food packaging;
- noise nuisance suffered by people living near a noisy nightclub.

In each case, market mechanisms have failed to make buyers of a good or service pay for the external social costs that they have forced on others. Strategic marketers would recognize that socially unacceptable levels of external costs may bring pressure for legislation which results in higher costs or prohibition of an activity completely. For the marketer, this will have the effect of raising selling prices to customers or making impossible the provision of goods and services demanded by customers.

Employees

It used to be thought that customers were not concerned about how their goods were made, just so long as the final product lived up to their expectations. This may just have been true for some manufactured goods, but probably never was for services where production processes are highly visible. Today, increasingly large segments of the population take into account the ethics of a firm's employment practices when evaluating alternative products. If all other things are equal, a firm that has a reputation for ruthlessly exploiting its employees, or not recognizing the legitimate rights of trade unions may be denigrated in the minds of many buyers. For this reason, some companies, such as Marks & Spencer, have gone to great lengths to challenge allegations made about the employment practices of their overseas suppliers.

Firms often go way beyond satisfying the basic legal requirements of employees. For some businesses, getting an adequate supply of competent workers is the main constraint on growth and it would be in their interest to promote good employment practices. This is true of many high-tech industries. In order to encourage staff retention, in particular of women returning after having children, companies have offered attractive packages of benefits, such as working hours which fit around school holidays and sponsoring events which promote a caring image.

Can going beyond legal requirement for employees ever be considered altruistic rather than just good business? Quaker companies such as Cadbury's have a historic tradition of paternalism towards their staff. But could such altruism result in a payback in terms of better motivated staff?

Local communities

Market-led companies often try to be seen as a 'good neighbour' in their local community. Such companies can enhance their image through the use of charitable contributions, sponsorship of local events, and being seen to support the local environment. Again, this may be interpreted either as part of a firm's genuine concern for its local community, or as a more cynical and pragmatic attempt to buy favour where its own interests are at stake. If a metal manufacturer installs improved noise installation, is it doing it genuinely to improve the lives of local residents, or merely attempting to forestall prohibition action taken by the local authority?

Government

The demands of government agencies often take precedence over the needs of a company's customers. Government has a number of roles to play as stakeholder in commercial organizations:

- Commercial organizations provide governments with taxation revenue, so a healthy business sector is in the interests of government.
- Government is increasingly expecting business organizations to take over many responsibilities from the public sector, for example with regard to the payment of sickness and maternity benefits to employees.
- It is through business organizations that governments achieve many of their economic and social objectives, for example with respect to regional economic development and skills training.

As a regulator which impacts on many aspects of business activity, companies often go to great lengths in seeking favourable responses from such agencies. In the case of many UK private sector utility providers, promotional effort is often aimed more at regulatory bodies than final consumers. In the case of the water industry, promoting greater use of water to final consumers is unlikely to have any significant impact on a water utility company, but influencing the disposition of the Office of Water Regulation, which sets price limits and service standards, can have a major impact.

Intermediaries

Companies must not ignore the wholesalers, retailers, and agents who may be crucial interfaces between themselves and their final consumers. These intermediaries may share many of the same concerns as customers and need reassurance about the company's capabilities as a supplier who is capable of working with intermediaries to supply goods and services in an ethical manner. Many companies have suffered because they failed to take adequate account of the needs of their intermediaries (for example, Body Shop and McDonald's have faced occasional protests from their franchisees where they felt threatened by a marketing strategy which was perceived as being against their own interests).

Suppliers

Suppliers can sometimes be critical to marketing success. This often occurs where vital inputs are in scarce supply or it is critical that supplies are delivered to a company on time and in good condition. The way in which an organization places orders for its inputs can have a significant effect on suppliers. Does a company favour domestic companies rather than possibly lower priced overseas producers? (Marks & Spencer has traditionally prided itself on buying the vast majority of its merchandise from UK producers, so a few eyes were turned when it announced in 1998 that it was to source a greater proportion from lower cost overseas producers.) Does it divide its orders between a large number of small suppliers, or place the bulk of its custom with a small handful of preferred suppliers? Does it favour new businesses, or businesses representing minority interests when it places its orders?

Taking into account the needs of suppliers is again a combination of shrewd business sense and good ethical practice.

The financial community

This includes financial institutions that have supported, are currently supporting, or who may support the organization in the future. Shareholders—both private and institutional—form an important element of this community and must be reassured that the organization is going to achieve its stated objectives. Many company expansion schemes have failed because the company did not adequately consider the needs and expectations of potential investors.

Corporate governance

THE media is taking a great interest in major companies whose internal style of governance appears to be inconsistent with their role as a trusted market-led organization. Recent examples of poor corporate governance have included numerous cases of so-called 'fat cat' directors paying themselves large salary increases while worsening the employment conditions of their lower paid employees.

In the UK, a number of attempts to develop blueprints for corporate governance have been developed (e.g. those by the Cadbury and Greenbury committees). 'Good practice' in corporate governance is increasingly being defined in terms of:

■ having in place internal control systems which prevent the type of abuse of directors' power which occurred in the former Maxwell group of companies;

'Handcuffs courtesy of Yale' could be the future as British police forces recruit marketing officers and embrace the practices of sponsorship. From 1994, British police forces have been able to raise up to 1 per cent of their overall budget through sponsorship. Proposals so far have included police vehicles being sponsored by car manufacturers and insurance companies being called in as sponsors for anti-burglary and crime prevention crack downs. But the head of public relations for West Yorkshire Police conceded that this would not mean police officers walking around with McDonald's logos on their uniforms. Nevertheless, the sponsoring of vital public services does raise ethical issues. What would happen if a sponsor was itself being investigated of a suspected criminal act? Are there some essential public services which should be driven solely by social policy needs and not by market forces?

- having an appropriate structure for the board of directors which combines full-time executive directors with non-executive directors brought in from outside;
- striking a balance when remunerating senior directors and employees between the reassurance of a long-term salary and performance for results;
- recognizing employees as increasingly important stakeholders in organizations. There have been many initiatives, such as Investors in People to promote the training and development of an organization's workforce.

Good corporate governance is culturally conditioned and what may constitute bad governance in one culture may be accepted as normal in others, reflecting economic, political, social, and legal traditions in each country. Despite convergence, differences still predominate, for example in attitudes towards the disclosure of directors' salaries.

Green marketing?

ISSUES affecting our natural ecology have captured the public imagination in recent years. The destruction of tropical rain forests, and the depletion of the ozone layer leading to global warming have serious implications for our quality of life, not necessarily today, but for future generations. Marketing is often seen as being in conflict with the need to protect the natural ecology. It is very easy for critics of the marketing function to point to cases where greed and mismanagement have created long-lasting or permanent ecological damage. Have the rain forests been destroyed partly by our greed for more hardwood furniture? More locally, is our impatience for getting to our destination quickly the reason why many natural habitats have been lost to new road developments?

There is argument about whether ecological problems are *actually* getting worse, or whether our perceptions and expectations are changing. Charles Dickens's description of Victorian London painted a grim picture of heavy manufacturing industry causing widespread pollution and using up natural resources in a manner which today would be considered quite profligate. Objectively, any comparison with industry today will probably leave the impression that environmental issues are lessening in their technical importance. Supporters of this view will point to the relatively clean air which we enjoy today, compared to the smogs which previously descended upon industrial areas, often for very lengthy periods. When salmon were caught in the River Thames in the 1990s for the first recorded time in over fifty years, it would be easy to gain the impression that the ecological environment was improving. Set against this is the worry that the actions that we are taking today could be storing up major ecological problems for the future. A lot of ecological change—such as the depletion of the ozone layer over Antarctica—is happening at a much faster rate than previously and there is no certainty about the magnitude of the consequence.

A market-led company cannot ignore threats to the natural ecology. Commercial organizations' concern with the ecological environment has resulted from two principal factors:

- there has been growing pressure on natural resources, including those that directly or indirectly are used in firms' production processes. This is evidenced by the extinction of species of animals and depletion of hardwood timber resources. As a result of overuse of physical resources, many industry sectors, such as North Sea fishing have faced severe constraints on their production possibilities;
- the general public has become increasingly aware of ecological issues, and, more importantly, has shown a greater willingness and ability to spend money to alleviate the problems associated with ecologically harmful practices.

At a macro-environmental level, support for the ecological environment has sometimes been seen as a 'luxury' which societies cannot afford as they struggle to satisfy the essentials of life. As these necessities are satisfied, individuals, and society collectively, can move on to satisfy higher order needs to protect what are seen as aesthetic benefits such as fresh air and a rich flora and fauna. The idea of environmentalism being a luxury is supported by the observation that countries with the strongest environmental movements, such as the USA and western Germany, tend also to be the richest economically. Many poorer countries tolerate poor environmental conditions in order to gain a competitive cost advantage over their more regulated western competitors.

Assessing ecological impacts

It can be difficult for an organization to know just what is meant by the idea of being friendly to the ecological environment. Consumers may be confounded by alternative arguments about the consequences of their purchase decisions, with goods which were once considered to be environmentally 'friendly' suddenly becoming seen as enemies of the environment as knowledge and prejudice change. The following are

recent examples which show how it can be difficult to evaluate the ecological credentials of a product:

- Recycling of old newspapers has traditionally been thought of as a 'good' thing, but
  recent thinking has suggested that the energy used to transport and recover used
  paper is less than burning it and planting new trees to grow fresh materials.

- In the 1980s, diesel was seen as a relatively clean fuel because it produced less
  greenhouse gases and diesel engines were more efficient than petrol engines. By
  the 1990s, particulates released into the environment by diesel engines had become
  linked with increasing levels of asthma and the environmental credentials of diesel
  were downgraded.

- Similarly, some of the shine was taken off unleaded petrol when studies began
  showing that an additive of unleaded petrol—benzine—was carceogenic.

- Both the supporters and opponents of proposals to build bypasses around towns
  use environmental arguments to support their arguments. Opponents argue that a
  new road in itself will create more road traffic which is environmentally harmful,
  while supporters argue that environmental impacts will be lessened by moving
  traffic out of town where it causes less harm

Most members of the public are not experts on the technical aspects of the ecological
impact of business activities. They may therefore be easily persuaded by the most
compellingly promoted argument, regardless of the technical merit of the case. Very
often, a firm may have a technically sound case, but fail to win the hearts and minds
of consumers who seem intent on believing the opposite argument that is in accordance with their own prejudices. This was seen clearly in the debate about how to
decommission Shell's Brent Spar oil platform. Government and the scientific community appeared to agree that environmental risks would be minimized by dumping the platform in deep water. Considerable risks would result from breaking it up
on land, removing toxic materials, and dumping the remains in landfill sites. Despite the backing that Shell received from the UK government and members of the
scientific community, the public sympathy was with Greenpeace, which mounted a
campaign against Shell. The public appeared to trust Greenpeace rather than a
multinational oil company. Damage to the marine environment was easier for the
public to conceptualize and become emotional about, compared to unrecognized
risks on land which would occur 'somewhere else'. A highly effective campaign
promoted Shell as the villain of the piece, causing great harm to Shell's reputation.
Because of this, Shell was forced to back down and settle for dismantling its platform on land.

Is marketing's pursuit of more consumption fundamentally opposed to ecological
interests? Taken to its logical extreme, consumption of the vast majority of goods and
services can result in some form of ecological harm. For example, the most environmentally friendly means of transport is to avoid the need for transport in the first
place. The most environmentally friendly holiday is for an individual to stay at
home. Individuals with a true concern for preserving their ecological environment
would choose to reduce their consumption of goods and services in total. At the
moment, such attitudes are held by only a small minority in western societies, but

One of Britain's leading tour operators—British Airways Holidays—has drawn up a 'green list' of environmentally friendly hotels in the Caribbean. In a survey among its customers, more than half said they would choose an airline or tour operator which took into account environmental issues. British Airways decided to follow a number of German tour operators by using a survey of 100 hotels carried out by the International Hotels Environment Initiative (IHEI) and the Caribbean Hotel Association. Thirteen hotels which were identified as having the best environmental practices, achieving at least a 75 per cent 'pass rate' in key areas, were given an eco-logo in the British Airways brochure. British Airways may be following public sentiment, but will its eco-friendly labels significantly influence buyers' choices? How large is the segment that would actually be prepared to pay a higher price for an environmentally friendly hotel, rather than simply saying it would? Might this approach work for upmarket holiday destinations such as the Caribbean, but be largely irrelevant to the more price-sensitive market for holidays in Spain?

the development of a widespread anti-consumption mentality would have major implications for marketers.

How business can capitalize on green consumerism

The green consumer movement can present marketers with opportunities as well as problems. Proactive companies have capitalized on ecological issues by reducing their costs and/or improving their organizational image. These are some examples of how firms have adapted to the green movement:

- Many markets are characterized by segments which are prepared to pay a premium price for a product that has been produced in an ecologically sound manner. Some retailers, such as Body Shop, have developed valuable niches on this basis. What starts off as a 'deep green' niche soon expands into a larger 'pale green' segment of customers who prefer ecologically sound products, but are unwilling to pay such a high price premium.

- Being 'green' may actually save a company money. Often, changing existing environmentally harmful practices primarily involves overcoming traditional mind sets about how things should be done (e.g. using recyclable shipping materials may involve overcoming traditional one-way supply chain logistics operations).

- In western developed economies, legislation to enforce environmentally sensitive methods of production is increasing. A company which adopts environmentally sensitive production methods ahead of compulsion can gain experience to competitive advantage ahead of other companies.

Tourism is often seen as a clean industry, but marketers in the travel and tourism sector are having to address increasing concern about the environmental damage caused by tourism. Every year, 120 million glossy brochures are produced, of which an estimated 38 million are thrown away without being used. In resorts, the development of tourism frequently produces problems of waste and sewerage disposal, while local residents find themselves competing for scarce water supplies. British travellers may worry about the damage that tourism causes to the environment, but recent surveys have shown that one in ten of them prefers to holiday in unspoilt or environmentally sensitive areas. Green Flag International, a non-profit-making organization was set up to promote conservation and to persuade tour operators that being 'green' can actually save them money. Among other things, it advocates using small, privately run guest houses and hotels, shops and public transport, and employing local people as guides. Hotels are advised on saving water and electricity, for example by not changing room towels every day. The organization also seeks to educate tourists to evaluate the environmental impact of their visit before booking a holiday and urges tour operators to include in their brochures a statement of their environmental policies. Why do so few people who claim to be green still seek out the cheapest package holiday, regardless of its ecological impacts? And if being green doesn't always cause additional cost, why do so many tour operators seem set in their ways?

Chapter summary and key linkages to other chapters

In a mature business environment, marketing managers must think beyond their own customers to society as a whole. There are good philosophical and pragmatic reasons why firms should act in a socially responsible manner. At a time of increasing competition in many markets, good social credentials can act as a differentiator in the eyes of increasingly sophisticated buyers. Although social responsibility by firms can achieve long-term paybacks, there can still be doubt about what is the most responsible course of action. Discussion about ecological issues and ethics is often muddied by lack of agreement on what is right and wrong.

The following key linkages to other chapters should be noted:

Chapter 1: What is marketing?: Marketing is about satisfying customers' needs profitably. Can this be achieved if a company portrays itself as socially irresponsible?

Chapter 2: The marketing environment: A firm's marketing environment sets the expectations for social responsibility that it is expected to follow.

Chapter 3: Market segmentation: Consumers' attitudes towards social responsibility is increasingly being used as a basis for market segmentation.

Chapter 4: Branding: Brands stand for a whole bundle of attributes and, increasingly, social responsibility is becoming a brand attribute. Firms go to great lengths to protect the integrity of their brands against accusations of anti-social activity.

Chapter 6: Marketing research: How do you assess the reaction of the general public to a firm's social marketing credentials? How do you further assess the effects on sales?

Chapter 7: Buyer behaviour: How important is a firm's perceived social responsibility within the whole process of buying a product?

Chapter 8: Buyer–seller relationship development: How can successful buyer–seller relationships be developed in an environment where customers do not trust the social credentials of a seller?

Chapters 9/10: Developing a product portfolio: What ethical and ecological issues are raised by a firm's new product development proposals? Are there any products that should be dropped from the product portfolio on ethical grounds?

Chapter 11: Developing a sustainable competitive advantage: In the long term, is a socially unacceptable position sustainable? If a company's activities are rapidly depleting natural resources, how can production be sustained over the long term?

Chapters 12/13: Pricing theory and practice: Are any ethical issues raised about the way in which a company sets its prices and discriminates between different groups?

Chapters 14/15: Intermediaries/physical distribution management: What constitutes ethical practice in relation to intermediaries? Is it 'green' to develop a physical distribution system which results in excessive transport of goods between large, efficient distribution centres?

Chapters 16–20: Principles of promotion planning/advertising/sales promotion/personal selling/direct marketing: Promotion often relates to specific products as well as the ethical image of a company. In what ways might advertising be considered to be unethical?

Chapter 21: Organizing for marketing: What constitutes good corporate governance? How can appropriate structures and processes avoid unethical acts of behaviour?

Chapter 22: Services marketing: Concerns about the ecological environment have been greatest for manufactured goods, but the intangibility of services, which are provided on trust, raises many ethical issues.

Chapter 23: Global marketing: In what ways do ethical considerations differ in each of a company's overseas markets?

Case study

Smoking may be bad, but tobacco companies' profits have never looked so good

After the arms industry, the tobacco industry must be one of the most politically incorrect business sectors. Yet during the late 1990s tobacco companies in the UK appeared to be very popular with the Stock Market, outperforming the FTSE all-share index by 36 per cent during 1998.

Tobacco companies now place less emphasis on fighting the health lobby, and no longer pretend that tobacco is anything other than harmful. But fortunately for the tobacco firms, nicotine is an addictive drug. Although cigarette consumption has declined in most developed countries, one person in four still smokes. Moreover, among some groups, especially young women, the rate of smoking has shown some increase in recent years. Tobacco companies also benefit from periods of economic recession. While job cuts may be bad news for most consumer goods and services companies, it has historically also been linked to an increase in smoking.

The tobacco companies have survived many years of attempts to control tobacco sales throughout Europe, but the planned EU directive banning all tobacco advertising would make it increasingly difficult for tobacco companies to get new brands established. As a result, the big three UK companies, BAT, Gallagher, and Imperial Tobacco looked at strengthening their brands with promotional campaigns and joint ventures. BAT linked up with the Ministry of Sound nightclub to push its Lucky Strike brand, while Gallagher tried to promote the Benson and Hedges name through a branded coffee. One industry expert expected to see an army of cigarette girls pushing cigarettes in pubs and corner shops, thereby getting round controls on advertising.

While the costs of promoting cigarettes in Europe have been increasing, tobacco companies have been keen to exploit overseas markets where there are fewer measures to protect the public. In the countries of eastern Europe, the companies have pushed their products, hoping to capitalize on the hunger for western brands. Gallagher has a plant in Kazakhstan and has heavily promoted its Sovereign brand in the former Soviet Union. The biggest opportunities for western tobacco companies, however, are in China which is the world's biggest market in terms of volume. The Chinese smoke 1.7 trillion cigarettes a year, making the British market of just 77 billion look quite small. State owned brands such as Pagoda dominate the market with an estimated 98 per cent market share. With import duties of 240 per cent, most foreign cigarettes enter the Chinese market through unauthorized channels, including those smuggled by the Chinese army. Greater trade liberalization will inevitably give freer access to the Chinese market for western tobacco companies. These will undoubtedly pay significant levels of taxes to the authorities, so a financially strained government may be unwilling to reduce tobacco consumption too much, especially when smoking is so pervasive through the population.

Case study review questions

1 How effective are controls on tobacco advertising? What measures could governments take to bring about a significant reduction in smoking?

2 What factors could explain a booming share price at the same time as Europeans' attitudes towards smoking are becoming more hostile?

3 How would you defend a western tobacco company in its attempts to develop the Chinese market for cigarettes?

Chapter review questions

1 Giving examples, explain what is meant by the term 'environmental lobbies'. Provide a resume of the tactics you would advise a high profile company to use in managing relations with special interest groups.

(CIM Marketing Environment examination, December 1994)

2 (*a*) Identify *two* stakeholder groups and briefly assess the nature and terms of their stake in the organization.

(*b*) Prepare a brief for your marketing director outlining the concept of social responsibility and indicating how this might be applied to your customers and how it might be of overall benefit.

(CIM Marketing Environment examination, December 1994)

3 For what reasons might a fast food restaurant company choose to adopt the societal marketing concept? By adopting the concept, is it really changing the way it does business?

4 Is it possible to define an ethical code of conduct which is applicable in all countries? How should a multinational company attempt to define a global ethical code of conduct?

5 What is meant by good corporate governance, and why has the topic become an important issue in many countries?

6 What should be the response of businesses to pressure groups' claims that their activities are causing ecological damage?

References

Anderson, P. (1982), 'Marketing, Strategic Planning and Theory', *Journal of Marketing*, Spring, pp. 15–26.

Arbratt, R., and Sacks, D. (1988), 'Perceptions of the Societal Marketing Concept', *European Journal of Marketing*, **22**, pp. 25–33.

Suggested further reading

For a general review of 'environmentalism', the following references provide a useful overview of the issues involved:

■ Bromley, D. (ed.) (1995), *The Handbook of Environmental Economics* (Oxford: Blackwell).

■ Cairncross, F. (1991), *Costing the Earth* (Boston: Harvard Business School Press).

■ Morris, J. (1997), *Green Goods?: Consumers, Product Labels and the Environment* (London: Institute of Economic Affairs, Environment Unit).

The general discussion on environmental issues can be followed up with a discussion on the impact of such issues on business organizations:

■ Howard, E., and Bansal, P. (1997), *Business and the Natural Environment* (Oxford: Butterworth-Heinemann).

■ Roberts, J. A., and Bacon, D. R. (1997), 'Exploring the Subtle Relationship Between

Environmental Concern and Ecologically Conscious Behaviour', *Journal of Business Research*, **40**, 1, pp. 79–89.

■ Welford, R. (1995), *Environmental Strategy and Sustainable Development: The Corporate Challenge for the Twenty-First Century* (London: Routledge).

Responses by business to environmental issues are covered in the following:

■ Arason-Correa, J. A. (1998), 'Strategic Proactivity and Firm Approach to the Natural Environment', *Academy of Management Journal*, **41**, 5, pp. 556–67.

■ Dutton, G. (1996), 'Green Partnerships', *Management Review*, **85**, 1, pp. 24–8.

■ Fineman, S., and Clarke, K. (1996), 'Green Stakeholders: Industry Interpretations and Response', *Journal of Management Studies*, **33**, 6, pp. 80–105.

■ Garrett, A. (1996), 'Do the Right Thing', *Marketing Business*, July, pp. 12–15 (about ethical standards).

■ Menon, A., and Menon, A. (1997), 'Environmental Marketing Strategy: The Emergence of Corporate Environmentalism as a Marketing Strategy', *Journal of Marketing*, **61**, 1, January, pp. 51–67.

■ Peattie, K. (1995), *Environmental Marketing Management: Meeting the Green Challenge* (London: Pitman).

For a discussion of business ethics and good corporate governance, the following references are useful:

■ Davies, P. (ed.) (1997), *Current Issues in Business Ethics* (London: Routledge).

■ Donaldson, J. (ed.) (1992), *Business Ethics: A European Casebook*, 7th edn. (London: Academic Press).

■ Epstein, E. M. (1998), 'Business Ethics and Corporate Social Policy: Reflections on an Intellectual Journey, 1964–1996, and Beyond', *Business and Society*, **37**, 1, pp. 7–40.

■ Harvey, B. (1994), *Business Ethics: A European Approach* (Englewood Cliffs, NJ: Prentice Hall).

■ Hoffman, M., and Frederick, R. E. (eds.) (1995*), Business Ethics: Readings and Cases in Corporate Morality*, 3rd edn. (New York: McGraw-Hill).

■ Robin, D. P., and Reidenbach, E. E. (1987), 'Social Responsibility, Ethics and Marketing Strategy: Closing the Gap between Concept and Application', *Journal of Marketing*, **51**, pp. 44–58.

■ Schlegelmilch, B. B. (1998*), Marketing Ethics: An International Perspective* (London: International Thomson Business Press).

■ Solomon, R. C. (1992), *Ethics and Excellence* (Oxford: Oxford University Press).

■ Weiss, J. W. (1998), *Business Ethics : A Stakeholder and Issues Management Approach*, 2nd edn. (Fort Worth: Dryden).

Useful web links

Greenpeace International: http://www.greenpeace.org/

Greenpeace UK Homepage: http://www.greenpeace.org.uk/

Friends of the Earth: United Kingdom: http://www.foe.co.uk/

Friends of the Earth International: http://www.xs4all.nl/~foeint/

Institute of Directors page on corporate governance (gives a list of services and resources): http://www.corpfinet.com/EP_Corp_Gov.html

Corporate Governance Institute: Blueprint for Good Governance in the 1990s: http://www.pli.edu/chb/Corporate_Gover.html

Articles on investment responsibility: http://www.corpgov.net/

Corporate Governance (an OECD outline of structure and topics): http://www.oecd.org/daf/fin/netcorp.htm

Directorship Online (a research and consulting firm that specializes in corporate governance): http://www.directorship.com/

Top Five Consulting services dealing with corporate governance issues: http://www.top5.com/

Corporate Governance News (scans publications and Internet resources to report some of the more important developments in the field of corporate governance): http://www.corpgov.net/news/news.html

PIRC archive of press releases and publications, including information on the Cadbury Report (1992), The Greenbury Committee Report on Code of Best Practice (1995), and Hampel (1997–8) Report: http://www.pirc.co.uk/

A disussion group on current issues in business ethics: http://www.mailbase.ac.uk/lists/business ethics

Part II

Understanding Customers

Chapter 6
Marketing Research

Chapter objectives

Information is a valuable asset which can help a company improve its knowledge of customers and its ability to meet their needs profitably. Later chapters will address the vital role of information within the marketing management process. This chapter focuses on researching customers' needs. Marketing research is essentially about keeping in touch with a company's customers and competitors and this chapter reviews the main methodological approaches. Sources of data are discussed in terms of their timeliness and relevance. It is important that a company knows not just about its markets as they are now, but as they are likely to be in the future, therefore demand forecasting becomes a crucial exercise.

Introduction

DEFINITIONS of marketing focus on a firm satisfying its customers' needs. But how does a firm know just what those needs are? And how can it try to predict what those needs will be in a year's time, or five years time? A small business owner in a stable business environment may be able to manage by just listening to his or her customers and forming an intuitive opinion about customers' needs and how they are likely to change slowly in the future. But how can such an informal approach work in today's turbulent business environments, where the owners of very large businesses probably have very little contact with their customers?

Marketing research is essentially about the managers of a business *keeping in touch* with their markets. The small business owner may have been able to do marketing research quite intuitively and to have adapted their product offer accordingly. Larger organizations operating in competitive and changing environments need more formal methods of collecting, analysing, and disseminating information about their markets. It is frequently said that information is a source of a firm's competitive advantage and there are many examples of firms who have used a detailed knowledge of their customers' needs to develop better product offers which give them a competitive advantage.

The range of techniques used by firms to collect information is increasing constantly. Indeed, companies often find themselves with more information than they can sensibly use. The great advances in EPOS (Electronic Point of Sale) technology has, for example, given retailers a wealth of new data of which not all firms have managed to make full use. As new techniques for data collection appear, it is important to maintain a balance between techniques so that a good overall picture is obtained. Reliance on just one technique may save costs in the short term, but only at the long-term cost of not having a good holistic view of market characteristics.

The terms 'market research' and 'marketing research' are often used interchangeably. This is incorrect and the distinctive characteristics of each should be noted.

- Market research is about determining the characteristics of a market, for example in terms of its size, growth rates, market segments, and competitor positioning.
- Marketing research is about researching the whole of a company's marketing processes. In most organizations, such research would probably include monitoring the effectiveness of its advertising, intermediaries, and pricing position.

This chapter focuses on how a company goes about assessing its customers' needs. Of course, research into areas such as customers' perceptions of advertising messages is closely related to an understanding of their needs and expectations, so it is unwise to see the two aspects of research as completely separate.

Market research should be seen as just one component of a firm's information gathering procedures. It is usual to talk about integrating market research within a company-wide marketing information system, which itself is part of a wider management information system. The topic of marketing information systems is covered further in Chapter 21 in the context of management decision-making. For now, it would be useful to put market research in the context of the broader marketing information system. In Fig. 6.1, an attempt has been made to show the focus of the marketing research aspect of a typical firm's marketing research function.

The marketing research process

THE small business owner may have been able to get by with a fairly intuitive system of market research. Larger organizations operating in complex environments need to adopt a more structured approach to their market research activities. To be useful, keeping in touch with customers' needs should be carried out objectively and accurately. Casual, unstructured research is at best wasteful, and at worst misleading. Data collected should be as up to date and relevant to a problem as time and cost constraints allow.

The stages of the marketing research process can be described in a simple, linear

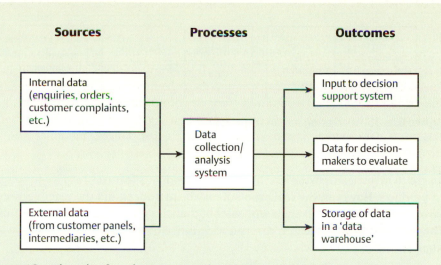

Figure 6.1 The role of marketing research within a marketing information system

Is marketing an art or a science? This age old debate has been given new impetus in recent times by developments in information technology which allow marketing managers to make supposedly scientific decisions, rather than relying on gut instinct. But when all marketing managers have access to the same data analysis packages, might this not result in a series of 'me-too' decisions being made? A survey carried out in 1997 by Taylor Nelson AGB found that 59 per cent of 105 marketers who were interviewed believed that marketing is more of an art than a science. Many marketing managers shelter behind their pile of numbers and use research as a crutch, thereby avoiding having to make their own judgements. Many of the great marketing developments of recent times have come about from individuals taking inspired decisions which might have seemed irrational when assessed by scientific processes. Science may reduce the risk of failure, but does it inhibit originality?

format. A model of this process, which begins with the definition of the research problem and ends with the presentation of the findings is shown in Fig. 6.2. It can be seen that this process follows the basic pattern of enquiry that is adopted for other forms of scientific or academic research.

The trigger for research can usually be related to a gap in the market information which is currently available to a firm. For example, a company may have comprehensive information on the current market for its products, but lack information on new market opportunities for which its product range could be adapted.

Very often, marketing research activity fails because the 'problem' to be researched has been inadequately thought through and expressed as a research brief. For example, a company may be facing declining sales of a product and commission

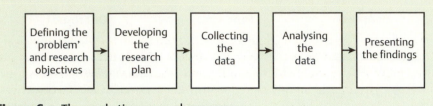

Figure 6.2 The marketing research process

research to investigate customers' liking of the product's features relative to competitors' products. However, the real problem may be to understand the macro-economic environment which may explain why sales of that category of product are declining.

The term marketing research covers a wide range of activities, varying in the level of analysis that is called for.

- At the simplest level, a researcher may be required to provide a normative description of market characteristics (e.g. defining the attributes that buyers evaluate when choosing between competing personal computer brands, or describing the buying behaviour of families buying a personal computer for the first time).

- The research task may call for the measurement of market characteristics (e.g. by measuring the size of the UK personal computer market and the market shares of the main suppliers).

- A more thorough investigation would require an analysis of data, both quantitative and qualitative (e.g. an analysis of personal computer buying behaviour according to the age, income, or lifestyle of different segments of the population).

Once the objectives of a research exercise have been defined, plans can be developed to collect relevant data. Data collection methods are considered below. A time plan is essential to ensure that decision-makers can have the most up-to-date information on market characteristics as they currently are, rather than as they were some time ago. In rapidly changing markets, timeliness can be crucial. The outcome of market research should be actionable by those who receive it.

The task of undertaking marketing research is often subcontracted to outside organizations. A large industry of market research firms (such as BMRB, MORI, and Taylor Nelson AGB) exists to provide specialist support. Market researchers fall into two groups:

- Those employed by manufacturers and services companies (often referred to as 'client' companies) collect internal data and may have responsibility for commissioning research from outside organizations.

- Researchers employed by marketing research companies work on behalf of clients for a fee. Staff employed by these companies can achieve a high level of expertise in particular research techniques or particular product areas (for example, Verdict Research has achieved particular skills in the field of retailing). Some of these

companies undertake 'omnibus' surveys on behalf of a number of clients simultaneously, thereby saving costs.

The research process shown in Fig. 6.2 allows for the expertise of both groups to be
used at different stages. Client company researchers initially define a research problem, after internal discussion with marketing and other management. This is usually
communicated to potential suppliers in the form of a research brief. The objectives of
the study are determined by matching management information needs with what
can realistically be obtained from the market-place, particularly in the light of time
and budgetary constraints, and may well be defined after initial discussions with
possible suppliers.

Specialist market research suppliers tend to dominate at the stage of data collection,
for two main reasons. The first is that very few client companies, however large or
diverse their product range, can generate sufficient research to warrant employing full-
time specialist interviewers throughout the country. Much research is seasonal or one-
off and it would be more expensive for a company to retain research capacity which is
only required intermittently, rather than buying it in as and when required. The second
reason is that respondents are more likely to give honest answers to third parties
than when replying directly to representatives of the organization being discussed.

Relationships between client companies and their suppliers can involve high levels
of trust and co-operation and many relationships between the two are very long
standing. The involvement of the client company in the research process is largely
dependent upon the size and expertise of its research department. Before deciding on
the final plan, however, most client companies approach several possible suppliers
and ask for their suggestions in the form of a research proposal.

How extensive should a firm's marketing research processes be? The amount of
time and effort must balance the benefits of the information that can be gained by
undertaking research with the cost of making a badly informed decision. Where the
capital costs involved in developing a new product are low, and the market is changing rapidly, it may make sense to do very little research and go straight to the
market with a new product. This is true of many fashion designers who can run up
sample items and see how well they sell. If they go well, follow-up production can be
put in hand. If they fail to sell, they can be consigned to a bargain clearance store.
Little would have been lost, but, had the designer taken time to carry out lengthy
market research, it could have got its designs to the market just as the current fashion
was changing again, rendering its research historic and obsolete. Contrast this to the
marketing research needed for a much more risky major infrastructure investment
such as an airport which will have a high capital cost and a long lifespan (Fig. 6.3).

A larger sample
and longer survey
improves confidence
level of the results

But a short, quick
survey may contribute
to a firm's cost
advantage and allow it
to get to market early

Figure 6.3 Balancing the costs and benefits of undertaking marketing research

We may be living in the information age in which marketing managers are linked by computer networks to seemingly endless sources of data. But do marketing managers use such information to help them make better decisions? Research commissioned by the decision support software specialist Business Objectives in 1997 painted a worrying picture of the way managers use information to make decisions. Of 100 senior managers from Times Top 1000 companies, more than three-quarters claimed to rely mainly on gut instinct rather than hard facts when making decisions. Sixty per cent of managers claimed not to receive the right quality or quantity of information to make a decision, even though almost all of them had access to a personal computer. More worryingly, a majority of sales and marketing managers surveyed claimed that they relied on other people for information which they are dubious about, or which is out of date. The picture emerges of an information underclass who rely on instinctive decision-making processes.

It must be remembered that information cannot in itself give answers. Indeed too much information can lead to a 'paralysis by analysis'. In a turbulent marketing environment, it is the quality of interpretation of data which gives a firm a competitive advantage. Should the managers reported in the survey be criticized for their failure to use hard information, or applauded for being bold and creative in their decision-making?

Major uses of marketing research

As markets become more competitive, marketing research is being called upon to perform an ever increasing range of tasks. Some of the more important specific marketing research activities are listed below.

- **Research into Customer Needs and Expectations:** research is undertaken to learn what underlying needs individuals seek to satisfy when they buy goods and services. Identifying needs which are currently unmet by existing products spurs new product development. Needs should be distinguished from expectations and a variety of qualitative techniques are used to study the often complex sets of expectations that customers have with respect to a purchase. For example, when buying a personal computer, what are customers' expectations with respect to reliability, after-sales support, and design, etc.?

- **Customer Surveys:** these are a means of keeping in touch with customers, either on an *ad hoc* basis or as part of a regular programme of survey research. A variety of survey methods are available (see below). Surveys can have the dual functions of providing a company with valuable information as well as providing a public relations tool by allowing customers to feel that they have made their feelings known to the company.

- **Customer Panels:** these are often used to assess the effectiveness of a company's marketing strategy, for example whether its advertising has been remembered by the target audience, or whether a price reduction was large enough to bring about the trial of a new product. Customer panels are also used to provide valuable information about proposed new product launches.

- **Similar Industry Studies:** by researching other companies, including competitors and companies in completely unrelated business sectors, marketing managers can learn a lot about how to improve their own marketing effectiveness. Through a process sometimes referred to as 'benchmarking', an organization can set itself targets based on best practice in its own, or a related, industry.

- **Key Client Studies:** where a company derives the majority of its income from just a small number of customers, it may make special efforts to ensure that these customers are totally satisfied with its standards of service and prices. The loss of their business as a result of shortcomings of which it is unaware could otherwise be catastrophic. In some cases, the relationship with key customers may be of such mutual importance that each partner may spend considerable time jointly researching shared problems (for example, airport operators sharing with airlines the task of researching customers' perceptions of the airport's handling procedures).

- **Research into Intermediaries:** agents, dealers, and other intermediaries are close to consumers and therefore form a valuable means for gathering information about consumers' needs and expectations. In addition, intermediaries are themselves customers of manufacturers and service principals. It follows that the latter should be very interested in how they are perceived by their intermediaries, for example in relation to reliability, delivery times, and after-sales service.

- **Employee Research:** for many services organizations, front-line employees are close to customers and are valuable sources of information about customers' needs. Research can also focus on employees as 'customers' of an organization, for example by measuring their attitudes towards the company. Employee suggestion schemes can form an important part of research into employees.

Qualitative v. quantitative research

I**T** was noted above that research techniques need to be varied and appropriate to the problem being studied. One important decision that needs to be made when developing a survey-based research plan is whether to conduct a qualitative or quantitative survey, or a combination of the two. Although quantitative and qualitative research are often seen as opposite ends of a research techniques spectrum, their methods overlap.

Qualitative research

Qualitative marketing research involves the exploration and interpretation of the perceptions and behaviour of small samples of individuals, and the study of the motivators behind observed actions. It is highly focused, exploring in depth, for example, the attitudes that buyers have towards particular brand names. The techniques used to encourage respondents to speak and behave honestly and unselfconsciously are derived from the social sciences, in particular psychology.

During the early stages of the research process, definitions and descriptions may be needed and it is here that qualitative research is at its most useful. It can define the parameters for future studies, and identify key criteria among consumers that can subsequently be measured using quantitative research. For example, if a supermarket observed that its older customers were unwilling to register for its loyalty card programme, it might conduct some focus groups drawn from its older customers in order to develop hypotheses about why this particular group was reluctant to subscribe. It is important, however, that selected customers are asked in as objective and sympathetic a form as possible. Qualitative research plans generally incorporate a discussion outline for those collecting the information, but are essentially unstructured and respondent led.

Quantitative research

This is used to measure consumers' attitudes and behaviour where the nature of the research has been defined and described. Quantitative research is designed to gather information from statistically representative samples of the target population. The sample size is related to the size of the total population being studied and the degree of statistical reliability required, balanced against time and cost constraints. In order to achieve margins of error small enough to make the final measurements useful, however, quantitative research, as its name implies, is usually conducted amongst several hundred, sometimes thousands, of respondents. For this reason, information is generally obtained using standardized structured questionnaires. Qualitative surveys may give the appearance of a rigorous, scientific approach, but their credibility can be questioned where the sample is inappropriately selected or the questions are ambiguous and do not relate to the information needs of the researcher.

Primary v. secondary research

A **FURTHER** question is whether to use primary data collection techniques, secondary research, or a combination of the two. Data sources are traditionally divided into two categories according to the methods by which they were collected. Secondary research is often referred to as desk research, while primary research is often called field research.

Most organizations would approach a research exercise by examining the available sources of secondary data. Secondary data refers to information which in some sense is secondhand to the current research project. Data could be second hand because the information has already been collected internally by the organization, although for a different primary purpose. Alternatively, the information could be acquired second hand from external sources.

Internal information, on products, costs, sales, etc., may be accessed through an organization's marketing information system. Where such a system does not exist formally, the information may still be available in relevant departmental records, though it would probably need to be reworked into a format that market researchers can use. It was mentioned earlier that many firms amass data which they have no immediate means of analysing, so the task of digging deep into piles of old data, whether in manual or electronic format, is not unusual.

Secondary, or desk research can be a useful starting-point for a research exercise. If somebody else has collected data or published a report in a closely related area, it is often much cheaper to buy that report rather than starting to collect data afresh. Reports by organizations such as the Economist Intelligence Unit (EIU) may at first sight seem to be very expensive, but set against the cost of undertaking the research from scratch, their cost begins to look relatively good value. Secondary research can be carried out internally by a company's own employees, although some specialist knowledge is required in knowing which sources of information are likely to be useful. Undertaking unnecessary primary research when similar information is available through secondary sources is an expensive and time-consuming exercise.

Primary, or 'field' research, is concerned with generating new information direct from the target population. The phrase *keeping in touch* was highlighted earlier, and marketing researchers spend most of their time designing and implementing such studies, either on a one-off or a continuous monitoring basis. Primary research tends to be much more expensive to conduct than secondary research, but the results are invariably more up to date and specific to a company's research objectives. Many marketing research agencies and consultancies commission their own primary research and sell the results to clients. Of course, by the time that they are published they have all the limitations of secondary research.

The range of primary research techniques is constantly increasing and some of the important ones are discussed later in this chapter.

Companies such as Direct Line continually set new standards for the use of IT in marketing management. But it seems that such companies are in a minority. According to a report in *Marketing*, 26 February 1998, probably only 30 per cent of marketing departments in UK companies are using IT effectively and a mere 2 or 3 per cent operate strategic customer management systems. It may be that many marketing directors in their forties and fifties were not brought up on IT and simply do not understand it.

Where companies do invest in IT, there is evidence that much of this investment is wasted. Unless a company installs the right systems to be used in the right way, it could be money down the drain. Another factor that emerges is the sometimes confused communications between marketing and IT departments within a company, with systems often failing to meet expectations because needs have not been defined accurately. As in other aspects of marketing, getting the inter-functional dynamics of a company right can be crucial in the quest for competitive advantage, and may explain the lead gained by Direct Line Insurance.

Sources of information for secondary research

A GOOD starting-point for secondary research is to examine what a company already has available in-house. Typically, a lot of information is generated internally within organizations, for example sales invoices may form the basis of a market segmentation exercise. To make the task of desk research as easy as possible, routinely collected information should be analysed and stored in a way that facilitates future use. Of course, a balance needs to be struck between having data readily available, and the cost of collecting and storing data which may be subsequently used.

The range of external sources of secondary data is constantly increasing, both in document and, increasingly, in electronic format. These sources include government statistics, trade associations, and specialist research reports. A good starting-point for a review of these is still the business section of a good library. Some examples of secondary data sources are shown below:

■ Government departments and official publications—e.g. General Household Survey, Social Trends, Transport Statistics;

- National media—e.g. *Financial Times* country surveys;
- Professional and trade associations—e.g. Association of British Travel Agents, British Roads Federation;
- Trade, technical, and professional media—e.g. *Travel Trade Gazette*, *Marketing Week*;
- Local chambers of trade and commerce;
- Year-books and directories, e.g. *Dataquest*;
- Companies' annual reports and accounts;
- Subscription services, providing periodic sector reports on market intelligence and financial analyses, such as Keynote, MEAL, Mintel, etc.;
- Subscription electronic databases, e.g. Mintel OnLine.

In many cases, other organizations, possibly even competitors, would have conducted similar studies to the one which is proposed. These may be available to purchase (or may be publicly available, as in the case of companies' annual reports which often contain useful market information). There is also a dark world of espionage where companies seek to gather information from competitors. Numerous catalogues exist which list sources of external secondary market research data (e.g. Arlington Management Services, in conjunction with the UK Department of Trade, produce a regularly updated publication called *MarketSearch*, an international directory of published market research).

Field research methods

THE subject of primary, or field research is becoming increasingly sophisticated and the following can only give a brief overview of the range of techniques available. There are now many texts which go into market research methods in great detail.

Sampling procedures

Once research objectives have been established, the next step is to identify the population from which a sample is to be drawn. There are a number of widely used techniques for sampling:

- A random sample implies that everyone within the target population has an equal chance of being selected for inclusion in the sample. For a completely random sample of all adult members of the population, the Electoral Register is frequently used for this purpose and a proportion of names selected at random. A variant on this approach is stratified random sampling in which the population is divided into a number of subgroups and a random sample obtained from each subgroup. The proportion sampled from each subgroup can be varied according to the researcher's interest.

■ Rather than picking specific individuals to be included in the sample, the researcher can specify the characteristics of each subgroup and the number required from each group. The interviewer is then free to include in their *quota* sample individuals who meet the specification. This method of sampling is only as good as the specification of the quota's characteristics. If data collectors are given too much freedom to choose their sample, it can best be described as a *convenience* sample and is likely to be biased in terms of respondents' characteristics. These may bias the results and limit their generalizability to the population as a whole.

■ Some survey techniques are effectively *self-selecting* in their sampling procedure. Where questionnaires are made widely available to the public, the researcher has little control over who will actually return a questionnaire. There is evidence that responses tend to be dominated by vociferous minorities of very satisfied or very dissatisfied customers, which may not be typical of the views of the large group of 'average' customers.

Data collection methods

The range of field research techniques is constantly increasing. Two main approaches to collecting primary data can be identified: by observation of the individuals in whom the researcher is interested, or by interaction with them through a survey.

Observation techniques

Observational techniques are limited to descriptions of behaviour, and cannot explore reasons which might explain such behaviour. However, they do claim to be highly objective and free of bias from respondents.

These are some examples of observation techniques:

■ When a retailer is assessing the attractiveness of a proposed new store location, it may undertake observational research into pedestrian or vehicle flows past a proposed site.

■ Many firms routinely monitor their competitors' marketing programmes, for example by collecting their brochures or by observing prices and products on offer in retail outlets.

■ The use of 'mystery shoppers' is becoming increasingly common among services companies who use them to check on standards of service delivery. Typical uses have been the efficiency and friendliness of restaurant waiting staff, the attention received from staff in a car showroom, and observing whether a travel agent recommended a sponsoring tour operator's products.

■ Experimental laboratory research may observe how consumers interact with a product, for example in observing how and in what order an individual reads an advertisement.

Would you want a 'mystery shopper' trying to measure your performance while you are working? They're not spies, but assessors, insists the market research industry. In fact, mystery shoppers are now highly trained, professional assessors. In the early days of mystery shopping, subjective questions were the norm. Today, 80–90 per cent of mystery shopping questionnaires are objective, for example questions for a mystery shopper survey of a pub include: 'How long was it before I was served?; Was I served in turn?; Was I offered a clean glass when reordering?' Rather than being seen as sneaky spying, companies should place a lot of importance in involving staff in the whole measurement process. Not only do staff provide useful insights to the programme, they can feel a sense of ownership of the programme.

Survey-based research methods

A survey questionnaire involves some form of interaction with the subject being studied and would normally request some attitudinal, personal, or historical information about the respondent. Questions in a survey can be asked face to face, by telephone, or distributed for self-completion.

Face-to-face interviewing is a traditional method of carrying out surveys. It can achieve high rates of response and is free of the self-selection bias commonly associated with self-completion surveys. Bias can, however, occur where respondents give an answer which they believe the interviewer expects them to give, rather than one which they truly believe. Face-to-face interviewing, whether carried out house to house (which is the best approach for sampling purposes), in the street or in hired locations is labour intensive. The cost and difficulty of obtaining good quality trained staff to undertake survey research, often at unsocial times of the day, has led researchers to search for lower cost alternatives. There have been innovations with electronic questionnaires, especially on the Internet, although sampling and the reliability of answers remains a problem.

Another alternative to face-to-face interviewing is the telephone survey. While considerably cheaper than face-to-face interviews, the refusal rate for telephone surveys can be up to three times higher than for personal interviews. The increased use of computer-assisted information collection for telephone (CATI) and personal interviews (CAPI) has speeded up the whole survey process dramatically, with responses being processed as they are received. Immediately prior to the 1997 UK General Election these systems were used in the next-day publication of survey results from total sample sizes extending into thousands.

In the case of self-completion surveys, respondents obviously self-select, so no matter how carefully the original sample to be contacted is chosen, the possibility of bias is highest. Furthermore, the response rate may be lower than 10 per cent, particularly where a postal survey is used.

In qualitative research, the open-ended nature of the questions, and the need to establish the confidence of respondents, precludes the use of telephone and self-completion interviews. Face-to-face depth interviews are used particularly in business-to-business research, where confidentiality is especially important, and it is usually most convenient for respondents to be interviewed at their place of work.

In consumer markets, focus group discussions are frequently used. Groups normally consist of about eight people, plus a trained moderator—quite often a psychologist—who leads the discussion. Respondents are recruited by interviewers, who use recruitment questionnaires to ensure that those invited to attend reflect the demography of the target market, and to filter out unsuitable respondents. In national markets, groups are arranged at central points throughout the country, the number of groups in each region once more reflecting the regional breakdown of the target population. Focus group research also has a role to play in business-to-business markets, although the scheduling difficulties and cost of getting a group of busy buyers together in one place can be a major problem.

In recent years there has been an evident explosion in the amount of time and effort spent by firms collecting information about their customers. The result is that we can hardly visit a restaurant, buy a new item of electrical equipment, or take an airplane journey without being invited to give our comments. Sometimes we are approached unsolicited for our views, whether in the street or by telephone. Information is a key element of a firm's competitive advantage, so they are putting more and more effort into collecting information about customers. The result is a torrent of surveys asking customers and potential customers about their expectations and perceptions.

But with so much information gathering going on, is there a danger of 'survey fatigue' setting in? Just how many times can a company ask customers questions about what they think of the company, before the whole process of carrying out a survey becomes an irritation in itself? Do customers think that their comments will ever be taken notice of by management? Careful organization of surveys can improve response rates. Stopping people when they are in a hurry to catch a train will not make an interviewer popular, but approaching them when they are captive with nothing else to do (e.g. waiting for baggage at an airport following a flight) may be more successful. Many companies offer prize incentives in return for participating in a survey, but does this encourage people to skip through the questions without much thought, simply in order to qualify for the incentive? If companies leave questionnaires for self-completion with no prize incentive and no intervention by an interviewer, how can they be sure that they get a representative sample of respondents? It has often been noted that customers who are very happy or very dissatisfied are the most likely to volunteer to take part in a survey. But what about the mass of people who hold average views about a service? These are likely to be under-represented and a challenge for marketers to learn about.

Marketing intelligence

MARKET research has so far been described in terms of establishing customers' characteristics and preferences in a structured manner. Another approach is to gather relatively unstructured information about their environment in a format that is often referred to as 'marketing intelligence'. Business owners have for a long time developed the art of 'keeping their ear close to the ground' through informal networks of contacts. With the growing sophistication of the business environment, these informal methods of gathering intelligence need to be supplemented. In contrast to market research, intelligence gathering concentrates on picking up relatively unstructured ideas and trends, especially about competitors' developments. Marketing managers can gather this intelligence from a number of sources, including the following:

- By regularly scanning newspapers, especially trade newspapers, a company can learn about competitors' planned new product launches.

- There are now many specialized media cutting services which will regularly review published material and alert a company to items which fall within predetermined criteria.

- Employees are a valuable source of marketing intelligence, especially in services organizations where they are in regular contact with customers. Staff suggestion schemes and Quality Circles are often used to gain market intelligence, in addition to informal methods of listening to front-line employees.

- Similarly, intermediaries are close to customers and their observations are often encouraged through seminars, consultation meetings, and informal communication methods.

- When a firm considers that it does not have the resources to undertake any of the above, it may retain consultants to provide regular briefings.

Demand forecasting

AN important function of market research is to try to predict the likely level of demand for a new product, or to judge the effects on total demand resulting from a change in its price or some other characteristic. There have been many examples of spectacular failures to forecast demand accurately, such as:

- When the Prudential Assurance company launched its new Egg bank account, it experienced an unexpectedly high level of take-up, resulting in delays and frustration for potential customers.

- The promoters of 'Teletubby' dolls were caught by surprise in Christmas 1997 when shops were overwhelmed by buyers trying to get hold of one of the models which had been made unexpectedly famous by the success of the television series.
- Forecasts of the number of people likely to use the Channel Tunnel have proved to be far too optimistic, with competing ferry operators retaining a much higher share of custom than had been expected.

The amount of effort that a firm puts into refining its demand forecasting techniques calls for a balancing of the cost of undertaking a detailed study, against the cost of making an inaccurate forecast. Where capital costs are low, it may make sense to go straight to the market with a product to see what happens. At other times, a more analytic approach to demand forecasting is required (refer back to Fig. 6.3).

A number of approaches to demand forecasting are available. Qualitative and quantitative techniques may be used as appropriate. In looking at the future, facts are hard to come by. What matters is that senior management is in a position to make better informed judgements about the future in order to aid strategic marketing planning.

A starting-point for demand forecasting is to examine historical trends. At its simplest, a firm identifies a historic and consistent long-term change in demand for a product over time and seeks to explain this in terms of change in some underlying variables, such as household income levels or price levels. Correlation and regression techniques can be used to assess the significance of historical relationships between variables. However, a simple extrapolation of past trends has a number of weaknesses. One variable, or even a small number of variables is seldom adequate to predict future demand for a product, yet it can be difficult to identify the full set of variables which have an influence. New variables may emerge over time. There can be no certainty that the trends identified from historic data are likely to continue in the future and the data are of diminishing value as the length of time for which they are used to forecast increases.

Models have become increasingly sophisticated in their ability to forecast consumer demand. This can be partly explained by a growing amount of readily available data which can be used to build and validate a model. Reliability is improved by increasing the volume of data on which a model is based and the number of variables which are used for prediction.

Inevitably, models, no matter how sophisticated, need interpretation. This is where the creative side of marketing management is called for, especially in combining market intelligence with harder economic approaches. In interpreting quantitative demand forecasts, management must use its judgement based on a holistic overview of the market situation.

'Marketing information can be misused by marketers, just like a drunk misuses a lamppost. Both statistics and lampposts can give support, but may provide very little illumination.'

Chapter summary and key linkages to other chapters

Understanding customers is critical to business success and this chapter has discussed some of the approaches to market research. Marketing management is a combination of a science and an art and this is reflected in approaches to gathering and analysing marketing information. An ideal programme of research usually combines qualitative and quantitative techniques, using secondary data where it is available, but supplemented by primary research.

The following key linkages to other chapters should be noted:

Chapter 1: What is marketing?: Marketing is about satisfying customers' needs profitably. Market research is crucial to identifying what those needs are and how they can be met profitably for a company.

Chapter 2: The marketing environment: Market research is essentially about a company keeping in touch with its environment, especially its customers, but also its intermediaries, employees, and government agencies.

Chapter 3: Market segmentation: The ability to segment markets requires information about the characteristics of past, present, and potential customers.

Chapter 4: Branding: Market research should be able to establish the perception of a brand in consumers' minds and the price premium that they are prepared to pay for it.

Chapter 5: Marketing and ethics: How is the ethical position of a company perceived by its customers? How large is the group of buyers which takes an ethical standpoint? How large is it likely to grow in the future?

Chapter 7: Buyer behaviour: Market research is crucial to an understanding of the processes by which buyers evaluate and choose between competing products.

Chapter 8: Buyer–seller relationship development: Gathering information for a customer database often yields valuable market research data.

Chapters 9/10: Developing a product portfolio: Market-led companies are informed by the results of their market research when developing a product policy.

Chapter 11: Developing a sustainable competitive advantage: Does market research suggest that a company's product offer and price position are sustainable over the long term? What does competitive intelligence suggest might be the response of competitors to new initiatives?

Chapters 12/13: Pricing theory and application: How much are buyers prepared to pay for a product? Are there segments who differ in their willingness to pay premium prices?

Chapter 14: Intermediaries: How can intermediaries' first hand knowledge of customers be passed up the distribution chain? How can intermediaries' expectations of a supplier be assessed?

Chapters 16–20: Principles of promotion planning/advertising/sales promotion/ personal selling/direct marketing: How effective is a firm's promotional effort in the eyes of consumers? Which elements were most effective in leading to sales?

Chapter 21: Organizing for marketing: Market research information is of little value if management does not act on it. Appropriate structures and processes are therefore crucial to ensure that the right information gets to the right people at the right time.

Chapter 22: Researching services can be much more difficult for services than for goods, given the lack of tangible evidence and the fact that services can often only exist in the minds of potential customers. Because of the inseparability of services, it is difficult to research the service offer in isolation from the service provider.

Chapter 23: Global marketing: When a firm enters an overseas market, it faces new and unfamiliar risks. Market research is a means of limiting exposure to risk and this chapter discusses the use of various methods to gather information about an overseas market.

Case study

Market research companies run out of information

A ready supply of information about customers, actual and potential, is vital to marketing managers. Consumers have become increasingly fragmented and sophisticated in their buying habits, while the growth in size of business units calls for information which can be easily analysed and acted upon. Gone are the days when most market research could be done simply by the owner/manager of a business listening to their customers.

Specialist data collection companies have come to play an important role in the task of collecting information about buyers. Organizations such as Experian, CACI, and Claritas have developed a role in providing socio-economic and lifestyle data which are sold on to client companies to make their targeting more effective. With the growth in direct marketing, it is important to many clients to have specific information about each individual customer, rather than a general aggregate for the whole market. This applies to information about new prospects, as well as new and additional information from people already on their databases, which are important because people's circumstances change. In contrast to client firms' need for this information, consumers by the end of the 1990s were showing increasing resistance to providing information for commercial purposes.

The market research industry has been concerned for a number of years about falling response rates to quantitative surveys. A Market Research Society report of 1997 pointed out that the public rarely distinguishes between anonymous research, database building, or telephone calls that start off asking for information but end up with a hard sell. A report prepared in 1998 by the Future Foundation found that only 50 per cent of consumers were happy to provide personal information to firms with which they deal, down from over 60 per cent in 1995. A core of people appear to be not interested in taking part in data collection exercises at all, and won't fill in questionnaires. For the marketing industry, this is a worrying development. All marketing, and not just direct marketing, is based on what is known about customers—their needs, wants, attitudes, and behaviour. If the public does not offer this information, it makes the life of the marketer more difficult.

There are a number of factors that may explain this trend. The first is that many more companies are now seeking to obtain information from buyers. The Market Research Society estimated that, in 1998, more than £300 million was spent on quantitative studies and £150 million on continuous tracking studies and omnibus surveys. In addition, direct marketing companies have been building marketing databases of their own customers. Saturation appeared to be setting in.

Secondly, consumers are becoming increasingly aware that information which only they can reveal about themselves has commercial value. Research from the Future Foundation suggested that the majority of people were happy to provide personal details if the result was better products or services. However, the public's experience of how well these data are used often falls short of their expectations in terms of how it benefits them personally.

How can response rates to questionnaires be improved? Developing some form of meaningful relationship with a recipient prior to receiving a questionnaire seems to be important. At its simplest level, an individual would receive a very simple first form. If they complete and return this, it is followed a couple of months later with a reward pack of money-off vouchers and samples, plus a second, more detailed questionnaire. As an example, research by Air Miles concluded that the company gets much better, more robust data if it saves detailed questions until members have had some experience of its services, rather than asking detailed questions of new recruits. And drinks retailer Bottoms Up was able to persuade 10,000 members of its loyalty programme, the Imbibers Club, to agree to telephone interviews on their drinking habits, something that would be very difficult to do out of the blue.

A more sophisticated approach is used by Consodata, which has a contract to collect, manage, and analyse household data for the 'Jigsaw' Consumer Needs Consortium (Kimberly-Clark, Unilever, and Cadbury Schweppes). The chosen vehicle is a magazine with special offers, which over time is tailored to the individual needs of respondents as more is learned about them. As an incentive, everybody gets a reward, instead of being offered a minuscule chance of winning a jackpot. Industry sources suggested that the response rate to the first issue of the Jigsaw consortium's magazine was 30 per cent, in line with the results sometimes claimed for similar, data collecting surveys undertaken via customer magazines. Again, the point is clear that consumers are freer with their information when dealing with organizations they already know and trust.

Bigger bribes to encourage people to provide data are part of the researcher's armoury. This ploy has reached new heights in the USA with reports of home shopping companies offering free computers and Internet access in return for household data and the acceptance of advertising on their screen. But large bribes can lead to another problem of samples being biased towards a new breed of professional market research respondents. There have been reports that focus groups are increasingly being dominated by a small circle of individuals who can make a reasonable living off the fee paid to participants. For the research companies, such people may be readily available and need less training and instruction than a novice. But is the information that they yield of any great value?

Adapted from 'Data Firms React to Survey Fatigue', *Marketing*, 29 April 1999, pp. 29–30.

Case study review questions

1 Suggest additional methods which companies can use to improve the effectiveness of their consumer data collection. What examples have you encountered?

2 Discuss the limitations of statistically based consumer databases of the type discussed here. Do qualitative approaches based on small groups offer any advantages?

3 What effects do you expect the development of interactive electronic media will have on the collection of marketing research information from consumers?

Chapter review questions

1 In what ways does information contribute to a firm's competitive advantage? Can a company ever have too much information?

2 What factors should influence the amount of time and money that a firm commits to the collection, analysis, and dissemination of marketing information?

3 Why is it important to have a structured approach to marketing research?

4 Identify the most likely marketing research objectives for a hotel chain.

5 The view is often expressed that quantitative survey techniques fail to tell the whole truth about customers' perceptions of a company's products. To what extent is this true and how can companies address this issue?

6 Compare and contrast the roles of marketing research and marketing intelligence. Is there a clear distinction in aims and methodologies, or are they part of a continuum?

Suggested further reading

For a general discussion of the principles of marketing research, the following texts are recommended:

■ Birn, R. J. (1999), *Effective Use of Marketing Research* (London: Kogan Page).

■ Chisnall, P. (1996), *Marketing Research*, 5th edn. (Maidenhead: McGraw-Hill).

■ Crimp, M. (1995), *Marketing Research*, 2nd edn. (Hemel Hempstead: Prentice Hall).

■ Gofton, L. and Mitchell, N. (1997), *Business Market Research* (London: Kogan Page).

■ Greenbaum, T. L. (1998), *The Handbook for Focus Group Research*, 2nd edn. (Thousand Oaks, CA., and London: Sage Publications).

■ Proctor, T. (1997), *Essentials of Marketing Research* (London: Pitman).

■ Quee, W. T. (1998), *Marketing Research*, 3rd edn. (Oxford: Butterworth–Heinemann).

■ West, C. (1999), *Marketing Research* (Basingstoke: Macmillan).

The important role played by information in marketing planning is discussed in the following articles:

■ Collis, D. J., and Montgomery, C. A. (1998), 'Creating Corporate Advantage', *Harvard Business Review*, **76**, 3, pp. 71–83.

■ Curran, P. J. (1998), 'Turning Information into Knowledge for Competitive Advantage', *Management Accounting* (*British*), Apr., **76**, 4, pp. 26–7.

■ Czerniawska, F., and Potter, G. (1998), *Business in a Virtual World: Exploiting Information for Competitive Advantage* (Basingstoke: Macmillan).

■ O'Brien, J. A. (1997), *Introduction to Information Systems: An Inter-networked Enterprise Perspective*, 2nd edn. (Boston: Irwin/McGraw-Hill).

■ Porter, M., and Millar, V. (1985), 'How Information Gives You Competitive Advantage', *Harvard Business Review*, **85**, July–Aug., pp. 149–60.

The following reference develops the above point by analysing the interpersonal dimension of information exchange within organizations:

■ Moorman, C., Zaltman, G., and Deshpande, R. (1992), 'Relationships Between Providers and Users of Market Research: The Dynamics of Trust Within and Between Organizations', *Journal of Marketing Research*, **29**, Aug., pp. 314–28.

For a review of information sources relating to the UK economy, the following statistical data are published regularly by the Office for National Statistics:

■ UK National Accounts (The Blue Book): the principal annual publication for national account statistics, covering value added by industry, the personal sector, companies, public corporations, central and local government. Published annually.

■ Economic Trends: a monthly compendium of economic data which give convenient access from one source to a range of economic indicators.

For statistics on the changing structure of UK society and its habits, the following regularly updated publications of the Office for National Statistics provide good coverage:

■ Family Expenditure Survey: a sample survey of consumer spending habits, providing a snapshot of household spending. Published annually.

■ Social Trends: statistics combined with text, tables, and charts which present a narrative of life and lifestyles in the UK. Published annually.

■ Regional Trends: a comprehensive source of statistics about the regions of the UK allowing regional comparisons.

■ Population Trends: statistics on population, including population change, births and deaths, life expectancy, and migration.

The following official publications of the EU are also useful for monitoring current developments:

■ Basic Statistics of the Community

■ Bulletin of the European Commission of the European Communities

Useful web links

Office for National Statistics: http://www.ons.gov.uk

The library of on-line official EU and UK documentation: http://www.euro-emu.co.uk/atoz/indexmain.shtml

The Market Research Society: http://www.thebiz.co.uk/markres.htm

Market Research Directory (A Market Research Directory, Market Research Guide, and Index of Links related to Business Size): http://www.ahandyguide.com/cat1/m/m25.htm

A forum for teachers and researchers working in the ara of Business Information Management, Business Information Systems, and Business Information Technology: http://www.mailbase.ac.uk/lists/business-information-all

Mintel Marketing Intelligence home page (gives a brief overview of recent Mintel reports): http://ww.mintel.co.uk

Home page of MORI (Market & Opinion Research International, the largest independently owned market research company in Great Britain: http://www.mori.com

A. C. Nielsen is a major supplier of market research, information, and analysis: http://acnielsen.com

The European Society for Opinion and Marketing Research (ESOMAR) unites 4,000 members in 100 countries, both users and providers of opinion and marketing research: http://www.esomar.nl

Chapter 7
Buyer Behaviour

Chapter objectives

Faced with competing products, it is important for companies to understand how buyers go about choosing between the alternatives. A thorough understanding of buyer behaviour should be reflected in changes to product design, pricing, promotion, and distribution which should pay attention to the needs of individuals' buying processes. This chapter explores basic theories of buyer behaviour. Distinctions between personal and organizational buyer behaviour are noted, especially in the composition of the decision-making unit.

Introduction

A COMPANY may think that it has developed the perfect product that customers will be queuing up to buy. But despite putting possibly years into new product development, it could find its efforts wasted as buyers reject their product in the few minutes, or sometimes even seconds, that it may take them to choose between competing products. The company may have failed to understand the complex processes by which buyers make purchasing decisions. They may, for example, have underestimated the role played by key influencers in the decision process and gone ahead and aimed their marketing effort at those individuals who really do not count for a lot in the final decision. The company may have spent the bulk of its promotional effort at a time when buyers were not at a receptive stage in the buying process.

Companies undertake marketing activities in order to elicit some kind of response from buyers. The ultimate aim of that activity is to get customers to buy their product, and to come back again. Most of this book breaks marketing activities down into distinct areas of decisions which have to be made by management, for example pricing decisions and promotion decisions. However, while companies may break their planning down into small manageable chunks, customers make an assessment based on a view of the total product offer. How customers perceive the whole offer and react to it may be quite different from what the company had expected when it was developing its marketing plan. In the case of sales to commercial buyers, the task of understanding who is involved in the buying process and what procedures are adopted becomes even greater. Faced with a sometimes bewildering array of choices, buyers seek to simplify their choice process, for example by sticking with brand names with which they are familiar.

In short, buying processes can be complex, involving many people over a sometimes lengthy period of time. Making false assumptions about these processes can result in an otherwise good product not being bought.

This chapter will explore a number of dimensions of the complexity of buying behaviour:

■ What factors motivate an individual to seek out a purchase?
■ What sources of information are used in evaluating competing products?
■ What is the relative importance attached by decision-makers to each of the elements of the product offer?
■ What is the set of competing products from which consumers make their final choice?
■ Who is involved in making the purchase decision?
■ How long does the process of making a decision take?

Of course, buying processes vary between products and between individuals. For the purpose of studying buying behaviour, a number of categories of buying situations can be identified:

■ **Routine rebuy:** the buyer makes a purchase decision in these situations almost instinctively without giving the process any thought. It is like routinely buying the same daily newspaper.

■ **Modified rebuy:** you may be familiar with a class of product, but this time want something a little different. For example, you may be familiar with buying paint, but on this occasion you need a tin of paint specifically for a job in hand which may be novel to you (such as covering external masonry), so you are likely to engage in search processes for identifying and evaluating alternatives.

■ **Completely novel:** where the buyer has no previous experience of buying a type of product, the search process is likely to be longer, with a greater range of information sources being consulted.

In addition, the sophistication of the buying process is influenced by the level of *involvement* that a buyer has in the product being purchased.

■ For high involvement products, buyers have a close relationship with the product. The manner in which the product is used has the capacity deeply to affect our happiness and we cannot easily ignore the product. Items of clothing and many personal medical services fall into this category.

■ Low involvement products have less consequence for an individual's psychological well-being. If a mistake is made in choosing an unsuitable product, we would not worry about it unduly. We can live with the consequences of making a mistake in our washing powder purchase, but a mistake in our choice of outer clothing may affect our self-image.

Figure 7.1 Simplified stages in the buyer decision process

Involvement is closely associated with risk. High involvement purchase decisions are seen as being more risky in terms of their outcomes, so we are likely to spend more time and effort in trying to avoid a bad purchase for such products.

Further variety in the buying process is evident from the major differences which can occur between private individuals and organizations in the way that they make purchase decisions. These differences are considered later in this chapter.

The buying process

THE basic processes involved in purchase decisions are illustrated in Fig. 7.1. Simple models of buyer behaviour usually see an underlying need triggering a search for need satisfying solutions. When possible solutions have been identified, these are evaluated according to some criteria. The final purchase decision is seen as a product of the interaction between the final decision-maker and a range of influencers. Finally, after purchase and consumption, the consumer develops feelings about their purchase which influence future purchase decisions. In reality, purchase decision processes can be complex iterative processes involving large numbers of influencers and a variety of decision criteria. It is often unrealistic to see the stages of the buying process as being completely separate; for example, evaluation often takes place while the search for information is still continuing.

Needs as buying process initiators

A need for something triggers the buying process. Needs provide a motive for an individual's action and can be very complex. Because they are a deep-seated initiator of buying behaviour, marketers are very keen to understand how needs are formed and manifested.

A need can be defined as a perceived state of deprivation, which motivates an individual to take actions to eliminate that sense of deprivation. A *need* refers to something which is deep rooted in an individual's personality. How the individual seeks to satisfy a need will be conditioned by the society of which they are a member. As an example, the need for status may be fairly universal, but its expression differs between cultures. In many less developed economies the need for status may be acquired by owning large numbers of cattle. In western countries the need is more likely to be satisfied by ownership of particular brands of car. These are sometimes referred to as *wants*. Wants are the culturally influenced manifestation of a deep-seated need. Of course, we can all want many products but do not or cannot buy the product. Marketers are ultimately interested in *demand*, which can be defined as a willingness and ability to buy a product that satisfies a need.

An individual's needs are influenced by a wide range of psychological and sociological factors. We can begin our understanding of needs by focusing on those psychological factors that are inherent to an individual.

Physiological and psychological bases of needs

Genetic make-up clearly has some effect on buying behaviour; for example, physiological factors can influence an individual's appetite for food. Some people are said to be more 'impulsive' shoppers than others, and researchers have attributed part of the explanation for this behaviour to genetics. Differences have also been noted in the needs of male and female buyers and the way they approach purchasing decisions. Of course, there is continuing debate about the extent to which such behaviours are inherent in our nature, or whether they are the result of nurture through a socialization process. Either way, it is important for marketers to recognize differences between individuals in what motivates them to buy.

It is wrong to equate needs solely with physiological driver. We no longer live in a society in which the main motivation of individuals is to satisfy the basic needs for food and drink. Maslow (1943) recognized that once individuals have satisfied these basic physiological needs, they may seek to satisfy social needs—for example, the need to have meaningful interaction with peers (see Fig. 7.2). More complex still, western cultures see increasing numbers of people seeking to satisfy essentially internal needs for self-satisfaction. Products therefore satisfy increasingly complex needs. Food is no longer seen as a basic necessity to be purchased and cooked for self-consumption. With growing prosperity, people have sought to satisfy social needs by eating out with friends or family. When such social needs are satisfied, it may be supplemented with a higher order need to experience different types of meals. The great growth in eating out which occurred during the 1970s and 1980s has been followed by a growing diversity of restaurants which cater for people's need for

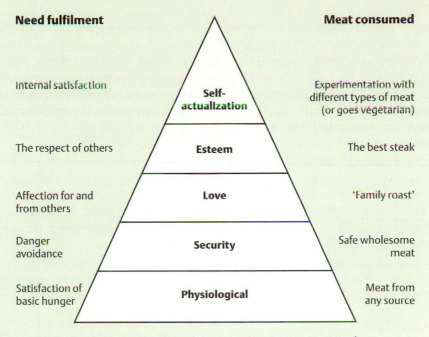

Figure 7.2 Maslow's hierarchy of needs—an application to meat products

variety and curiosity, hence the emergence in many larger European towns of Balti, Creole, and Far Eastern restaurants.

Maslow's hierarchy of needs is no more than a conceptual model and it is difficult actually to measure the level of an individual's needs. Furthermore, it is essentially based on western values of motivation. How, for example, would you explain religious sacrifice and penance which are an important motivator for many non-western consumers?

Maslow has presented one model of motivation which marketers have adopted widely as a conceptual framework. There are other frameworks for understanding the psychological bases for human motivation.

Freudian analysis sees human behaviour being directed by repression of feelings from early childhood. What comes naturally to a young child is often considered socially unacceptable, so such behaviour is socialized out before the child reaches adulthood. Behaviour is the outcome of the interaction between the id (the primitive unconscious basis of the psyche dominated by primary urges) and the ego (conscious perceptions that act as an inhibiting agency).

Stimulus-response models of motivation have been widely used by marketers to understand needs. Analogies have been drawn between Pavlov's dog (who came to associate a bell with food) and everyday marketing situations. The existence of cues in the environment, such as advertising, can help to trigger the buying process, even though the initial cue has no direct connection with the need which an individual is

Freudian analyses of human motivation based on repression have sometimes achieved notoriety for their explanations of human behaviour. Is smoking really a substitute for the repressed desire of a child to suck their thumb? Think about the two following cases of supposedly repressed feelings, their explanation and possible opportunities for marketers:

1. Children inherently dislike order and prefer creative chaos: it is only adults that teach children to be tidy and to structure their lives. Possible marketing opportunity: adult toys and novelties which recreate a sense of chaos, such as 'silly string' and party poppers.

2. Children like to be cared for by a mother figure: as adults we take on board our responsibilities, but we would be happy to go back to a simple dependent child–mother relationship. Possible marketing opportunity: a wide range of personal services aim to pamper adults as though they were children again, including hairdressing, beauty salons, and health farms. Who else can exploit this desire to be a pampered, dependent child? Restaurants? Airlines?

Is an analysis of repression of any use to marketers in trying to understand human motivation? Or is it a highly speculative approach which may be intuitively appealing, but one of only a number of possible explanations of the observed behaviour?

seeking to satisfy. In this way, the sight of a well-known celebrity endorser can trigger the process of seeking out a brand of food which they endorse.

Situational factors influencing needs

In addition to our inherent physiological and psychological make-up, our needs are influenced by the situation in which we currently find ourselves. The subjects of age and socio-economic status can have profound effects on buying behaviour, as you will recall from the discussion in Chapter 3 in the context of market segmentation. In addition, the stage that an individual has reached in the 'family life cycle' also has a significant influence on needs. Wells and Gubar (1966) identified a number of stages in an adult's life, each associated with distinctive sets of needs:

1. Bachelor stage: young, single people not living at home.
2. Newly married couples: young, no children.
3. Full nest 1: youngest child under 6.
4. Full nest 2: youngest child over 6.
5. Full nest 3: older married couples with dependent children.
6. Empty nest 1: older married couples, no children living with them.
7. Empty nest 2: older married couples, retired, no children living at home.
8. Solitary survivor 1: still working.
9. Solitary survivor 2: retired.

There are other definitions of family life-cycle stages which are themselves becoming increasingly complex with the breakdown of the traditional nuclear family and the emergence of deviations from the norm such as single-parent families. However, all make the same important point: an individual's needs are likely to change as they go through life. An individual moving from a bachelor stage to one with dependent children will face a reordering of priorities, reflected in a different set of needs. This will also most likely be matched by a reduction in discretionary expenditure.

Sociological influences on needs

You will recall that needs were defined earlier as being inherent in an individual. The manifestation of these needs is influenced by the society in which an individual lives. A number of levels of influence can be identified:

- The family influences a child's perception of the world and this influence lasts into adulthood. Examples of this effect on buying processes can be found in adults' selection of a particular brand of breakfast cereal, because it is the one that they were brought up with.
- Individuals are surrounded by peer groups which act as a guide for behaviour. Peer groups can be primary and direct in their influence (e.g. colleagues at work and school) or they can be secondary and indirect (e.g. the guidance to behaviour which is provided by pop stars or media figures).
- Individuals can identify with a social class and the values of this class can influence behaviour. As an example, individuals who identify with the 'working class' may feel alienated by an upmarket retail outlet such as The Gap compared to the traditional values epitomized in Woolworth's.
- Culture in its widest sense influences our buying behaviour. Concepts such as self-centredness, the desire for immediate results, and deference to suppliers all differ significantly between cultures (see Hofstede 1991).

Information search

Once a need has triggered the search for need-satisfying solutions, a search for information will begin. But where do buyers look for information when making purchases? In the case of the routine repurchase of a familiar product, probably very little information is sought about the product. But where there is a greater element of uncertainty, buyers will seek out information about the alternative ways in which they can satisfy their needs, especially where a high level of risk is involved. The following information sources are likely to be used:

- Personal experience will be a starting-point, so if a buyer has already used a company's products, the suitability of the proposed purchase may be assessed in the light of the previous purchases.

- Word-of-mouth recommendation from friends is important for many categories of goods and services where an individual may have no previous need to make a purchase. When looking for a plumber or a solicitor, for example, many people will seek the advice of friends.

- Rather than referring to individuals on a face-to-face basis, we may use various other reference groups to guide us. What type of sports shoes are sports heros wearing at the moment? What drink is considered to be fashionable with their age group?

- Newspaper editorial content and directories such as those published by the Consumers' Association may be consulted as a relatively objective source of information.

- Advertising and promotion in all of its forms is studied, sometimes being specifically sought and at other times being casually seen without any search activity involved.

The greater the perceived risk of a purchase, the longer and more widespread the search for information. Of course, individuals differ in the extent to which they are prepared to collect information methodically—some may make a purchase more impulsively than more calculating individuals.

Evaluation

In the process of gathering information, the total range of products available in the market-place is gradually filtered down to a manageable number for evaluation. Choice is made from a select set of possibilities and these consumer choice sets can be classified according to their selectivity:

- The total set comprises all products that are capable of satisfying a given need.
- The awareness set comprises all those products of which the consumer is aware (the unaware set is the opposite of the awareness set).
- The consideration set includes those items within the awareness set which the consumer considers buying.
- The choice set is the group of products from which a final decision is ultimately made.
- Along the way to defining the choice set, some products would have been rejected as they are perceived to be unavailable, unaffordable, unsuitable, etc. These comprise the infeasible set.

Research should seek to establish the choice set against which a company's product is being compared, and on this basis the marketing programme can be adapted in order to achieve competitive advantage against other members of the choice set.

A private buyer seeking to buy a low value, low involvement product such as an

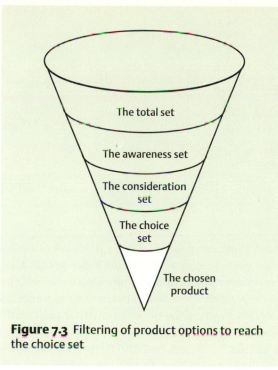

The total set

The awareness set

The consideration set

The choice set

The chosen product

Figure 7.3 Filtering of product options to reach the choice set

electric kettle may have narrowed down the choice set to four kettles. Analysts of buyer behaviour have developed a number of frameworks for trying to understand how a consumer chooses between these competing alternatives. One approach is for the consumer to use a sense of intuition as to what seems best. Such non-systematic methods of evaluation may be quite appropriate where the product in question involves low levels of cost, risk, and involvement.

Even apparently intuitive bases of evaluation can be reduced to a series of rules, implying some systematic basis. One framework is a multiple attribute choice matrix which holds that consumers refer to a number of component attributes of a product to evaluate its overall suitability. Fig. 7.4 shows a typical matrix where four competing electric kettles are compared in terms of five important attributes. In this matrix, the four short-listed kettles in the choice set are shown by the column headings A, B, C, and D. The left-hand column shows five attributes on which buyers are deemed to base their purchase decision (e.g. price, reputation of the brand name, colour, styling, capacity). The second column shows the importance which the consumer attaches to each attribute of the service (with maximum importance being given a score of 10 and a completely unimportant attribute a score of zero). The following four columns show how each kettle scores against each of the five evaluation attributes.

If it is assumed that a consumer evaluates each product without weighting each attribute, kettle B will be preferred, as it has the highest overall rating. It is more realistic to expect that some factors will be weighted as being more important than others, therefore the alternative *linear compensatory* approach is based on consumers

	Importance weights	A	B	C	D
Price	10	10	7	8	10
Brand name	9	10	9	8	8
Colour	8	10	10	9	9
Styling	7	10	10	10	5
Capacity	6	4	10	10	4
Overall rating		44	46	45	36
Weighted rating		7.3	7.2	7.0	6.1

Figure 7.4 A hypothetical choice set for motor insurance: a multiple attribute matrix

creating weighted scores for each product. The importance of each attribute is multiplied by the score for each attribute, so in this case, kettle A is preferred as the attributes which consumers rank most highly are also those which are considered to be the most important. A third approach to evaluation is sometimes described as a *lexicographic approach*. This involves the buyer in starting their evaluation by looking at the most important attribute and ruling out those products that do not meet a minimum standard. Evaluation is then based on the second most important attribute, with products being eliminated which do not meet their standard. This continues until only one option is left. In Fig. 7.4, price is given as the most important attribute, so the initial evaluation may have reduced the choice set to A and D (these score highest on price). In the second round, brand name becomes the most important decision criterion. Only A and D remain in the choice set, and as A has the highest score for brand name, it will be chosen in preference to D.

Decision

It is important to understand who is actually responsible for making a purchase decision. Both private and organizational purchases usually involve large numbers of people (e.g. household purchases may involve joint decision-making between a husband and wife with other family members acting as influencers). The subject of purchase decision-making units is considered later in this chapter.

   The outcome of the evaluation process may be a decision to buy now; not to buy at all; to defer the process; or to start the process again. Even when a positive decision to buy a product is made (e.g. the electric kettle used in the example above), further decisions have to be made to put the main decision into effect, for example:

■ when will the product be bought? from which retailer?
■ how many will be bought?
■ will any optional accessories be bought?
■ how will the purchase be paid for (e.g. cash or credit card?).

Post-purchase evaluation

Wise marketers realize that the purchasing activity does not end when a sale has been made. The buyer takes the product away and continues to develop feelings about the product that will influence their decision next time they need to make a purchase in that product category. The buyer will also be likely to tell their friends about their purchase, and these can be either favourable or unfavourable comments. Many companies regard satisfied customers as their best form of advertising.

Buyers approach a purchase with a set of expectations about the performance of the product they are purchasing. A company's advertising and sales messages often serve to heighten expectations about the product's performance. Of course, these expectations are often not met. Maybe the product did not perform adequately, or the buyer's expectations were simply unrealistically high. In either case, the result is to create what is often referred to as cognitive dissonance, in which our expectations are out of line with the reality around us. We can handle dissonance in a number of ways.

- We can often simply return the goods and make a fresh purchase decision. The failed decision becomes part of a learning experience.
- Sometimes it is not possible to return the product. In the case of services which have already been consumed, this option is generally impossible. We may alternatively go about complaining and telling our friends about the bad product. Estimates vary, but it is reckoned that on average, a dissatisfied customer tells between five and ten people of their bad purchase.
- We can try to reduce dissonance by internal psychological processes. We may

Figure 7.5 Through a message on the back of its till receipt, this company encourages word-of-mouth recommendation, but also tries to reduce the effects of negative word-of-mouth publicity

convince ourselves that we did not really make a bad decision, but our expectations were simply too high. We may clutch at minor features of the product that we like, to offset the major features that we dislike. We do not like to think that we made a mistake, so we try to convince ourselves that we were right in our choice.

Companies often devote part of their promotional budget to reminding customers that they made the right choice in their purchase. Many companies write a short letter to recent customers, providing further reassurance to waverers that they made the best choice. A convinced happy customer will be more likely to recommend a product to their friends and to return to the same supplier next time.

It is important for companies to understand the feelings of customers once they have purchased and consumed their products. But how far should companies go in actively encouraging customers to complain? There have been suggestions that Britain—well known for its traditional reserve—has developed a breed of professional complainers who abuse systems set up by companies to invite complaints and feedback about their products. Food manufacturers, rail operators, and hotels have handed out thousands of pounds in vouchers and compensation to bogus complainants who are exploiting firms' fear of losing their loyal customers. Companies seem to be the victim of importing the American philosophy that once a customer has had a complaint successfully dealt with, they will stay loyal for life. It is commonly accepted that the cost of recruiting a new customer can be around five times the cost of keeping an existing one. But how do companies reconcile the need to satisfy complaining customers with the need to stem the tide of bogus complaints? One company, Sainsbury's now logs all of its complaints centrally in order to try to identify frequent complainers.

The decision-making unit (dmu)

IN practice, few purchase decisions are made by an individual without reference to others. Usually other people are involved in some sort of role and have a bearing on the final purchase decision. It is important to recognize who the key players in this process are, in order that a product can be configured to meet their needs, and that promotional messages can be adapted and directed at the key individuals involved in the purchase decision. A number of roles can be identified among people involved in the decision process (Fig. 7.6):

- **Influencers**: These are people or groups of people to whom the decision-maker refers in the process of making a decision. You will recall from above that reference groups can be primary in the form of friends, acquaintances, and work colleagues, or secondary in the form of remote personalities with whom there is no two-way interaction. Where research indicates that the primary reference group exerts

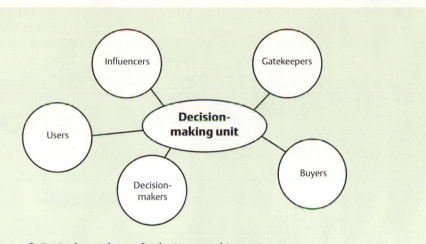

Figure 7.6 Typical members of a decision-making unit

major influence on purchase decisions, this could indicate the need to take measures which will facilitate word-of-mouth communication—for example, giving established customers rewards in return for the introduction of new customers. An analysis of secondary reference groups used by consumers in the decision process can be used in a number of ways. It will indicate possible personalities to be approached who may be used to endorse a product in the company's advertising. It will also indicate which opinion leaders an organization should target as part of its communication programme in order to achieve the maximum 'trickle down' effect. The media can be included within this secondary reference group—what a newspaper writes in its columns can have an important influence on purchase decisions.

- **Gatekeepers**: These are most commonly found among commercial buyers. Their main effect is to act as a filter on the range of products that enter the decision choice set. Gatekeepers can take a number of forms—a buying manager's personal assistant barring calls from sales representatives has the effect of screening out a number of possible choices. In many organizations, it can be difficult to establish just who is acting as a gatekeeper—identifying a marketing strategy which gains acceptance by the gatekeeper, or bypasses them completely is therefore made difficult. In larger organizations and the public sector in particular, a select list of suppliers who are invited to submit tenders for work may exist—without being on this list, a supplier is unable to enter the decision set.

Although gatekeepers are most commonly associated with purchases made by organizations, they can also have application to consumer purchases. In the case of many household goods and services, such as buying wallpaper or booking an overseas holiday, an early part of the decision process may be the collection of samples or brochures. While the final decision may be the subject of joint discussion and action, the initial stage of collecting the items for the decision set is more likely to

We'd try anything once. But now we're back with BT.

Why are so many people who left, coming straight back to BT? Unfulfilled promises? Complicated bills? Savings not quite what they thought? Only those who've come back know for sure. But here's one thing you can be sure of. If you're considering moving to another company because you think it will save you money, call BT first. We have the facts you need to help you make the right choice.

Free*fone 0800* **444 123**
for accurate call cost comparisons

BT *Stay in touch*

Figure 7.7 The buying process does not end with a purchase. In this advertisement, BT encourages its UK phone customers who have recently switched to a rival company to reflect on their feelings towards their new supplier. As well as encouraging former customers to return, this advertisement makes current BT customers feel more comfortable with their current supplier, by reducing the temptation to search for alternatives. (Reproduced with the permission of British Telecommunications plc)

be left to one person. In this way, one member of a family may pick up holiday brochures or samples of wallpaper, thereby acting as a gatekeeper, and restricting subsequent choice to the products of those companies whose brochures or samples were originally collected.

- **Buyers**: In some cases, ordering a product may be reduced to a routine task and delegated to an individual. In the case of industrial goods and services, low budget items which are not novel may be left to the discretion of a buyer. In this way, office stationery may be contracted by a buying clerk within the organization without immediate reference to anybody else. In the case of modified rebuys, or novel purchases, the decision-making unit is likely to be larger.

- **Users**: The users of a product may not be the people responsible for making the actual purchase decision for a category of product. This is typical of many items of clothing bought within household units. For example, it has been estimated that over half of all men's socks are bought by women. Parents buy products for their children, with varying levels of influence (or 'pester power') from the children who will be the actual users of the product. In the case of organizational purchases, there is often a separation between users and buyers and research should be undertaken to reveal the extent to which users are important elements in the decision process. In the case of the business air travel market, it is important to understand the pressure which the actual traveller can exert on their choice of airline, as opposed to the influence of a company buyer (who might have arranged a long-term contract with one particular airline); a gatekeeper (who may discard promotional material relating to new airlines); or other influencers within the organization (e.g. cost centre managers who might be more concerned with the cost of using a product, in contrast to the user's overriding concern with its quality).

- **Decision-maker**: This is the person (or groups of individuals) who makes the final decision to purchase, whether they execute the purchase themselves or instruct others to do so. With many family-based consumer products, it can be difficult to identify just who within the family carries most weight in making the

What role do children play in the purchase of goods which they ultimately consume? There has been considerable debate about the extent of 'pester power' where parents give in to the demands of children. Increasingly, advertisers are aiming their promotional messages over the heads of adults and straight at children. The ethics of doing this have been questioned by many, and some countries have imposed restrictions on television advertising of children's products. However, even with advertising restrictions, companies have managed to get through to children in more subtle ways, for example by sponsoring educational materials used in schools and paying celebrities to endorse their products. When it comes to such items as confectionery and toys, just what influence do children exert on the purchase decision? And when football clubs deliberately change their strip every season, is it unethical for the clubs to expect fanatical children to pester their parents to buy a new one so that they can keep up with their peer group?

final decision. Research into family purchases has suggested that in the case of package holidays and furniture, wives dominate in making the final decision, whereas in the case of financial services, it is the husband who dominates. An analysis of how a decision is made can only realistically be achieved by means of qualitative in-depth research. In the case of decisions made by organizational buyers, the task of identifying the individuals responsible for making a final decision—and their level within the organizational hierarchy—becomes even more difficult.

Models of buyer decision-making

THE buying process has now been portrayed as highly complex and one in which a variety of personal and environmental factors influence the decisions we make. We can process a lot of information with outcomes that can sometimes be seen as quite irrational. So how do we arrive at a decision to purchase one product rather than another?

A simple starting-point is to take a 'black box' model of consumer response (Fig. 7.8). The inputs to the decision process are the range of psychological, sociological, economic, and situational factors. The outcome is the decision (e.g. whether or not to purchase; whether to purchase now or to defer; where to buy from; how many, etc.). In between is the 'black box' comprising our decision-making processes. The black box determines how we translate complex information into decisions. As individuals, we differ in the way that our processing occurs.

Of course, a black box is a simple representation of the input–decision–outcome process. In itself, it does not explain how a decision is actually made. For this, a number of models of buyer behaviour have been developed. If a model is to have value to marketing managers, it should be capable of use as a predictive tool, given a set of conditions on which the model is based. For this reason, a number of researchers have sought to develop models which explain how buying decisions are made in specified situations, and from this to predict the likely consequences of

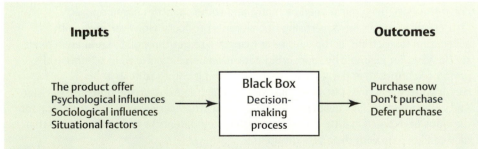

Figure 7.8 A simple black box model of consumer responses

changes to marketing strategy. Modelling buyer decision processes poses many problems. At one extreme, simple models may help in very general terms in developing marketing strategies, but are too general to be of use in any specific situation. At the other extreme, models of buyer behaviour based on narrowly defined sectors may loose much of their explanatory and predictive power if applied to another sector where assumptions on which the original model were calibrated no longer apply. In any event, most models of buyer behaviour provide normative rather than strictly quantitative explanations of buyer behaviour and there can be no guarantee that the assumptions on which the model was originally based continue to be valid.

One widely used model which has been widely applied and subsequently developed is that developed by Howard and Sheth (1969). The principles of their model are shown in Fig. 7.9.

The Howard–Sheth framework incorporates a number of elements:

- **Inputs:** This element comprises information about the range of competing products which may satisfy a consumer's need. Information may be obtained from personal or published sources.

- **Behavioural determinants, psychological and social influences:** Individuals bring to the purchase decision a predisposition to act in a particular way, which is influenced by the culture that they live in, family, and personality factors, among others.

- **Perceptual reaction:** Inputs are likely to be interpreted in different ways by different individuals, based on their unique personality make-up and conditioning which results from previous purchase experiences. While one person might readily accept the advertising messages of a bank, another might have been disappointed by that bank in the past, or by banks' advertising in general. They are therefore less likely to perceive such inputs as credible.

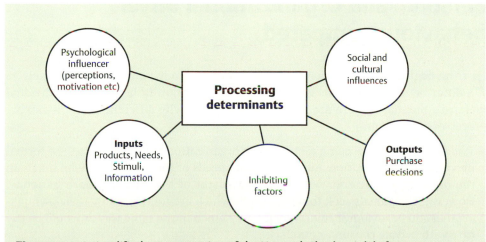

Figure 7.9 A simplified representation of the Howard–Sheth model of consumer behaviour

- **Processing determinants:** This part of the model focuses attention on the way in which a decision is made. Important determinants include the motivation of the individual to satisfy a particular need, the individual's past experience of a particular product or organization, and the weight attached to each of the factors which are used in the evaluation. For some consumers of some products, critical product requirements may exist which must be present if a product is to be included in the decision set. At other times, consumers attach weight to each of its attributes and select the product with the highest weighted score (see Fig. 7.4).

- **Inhibitors:** A number of factors might prevent an individual moving towards making a decision to purchase a particular product, such as ease of access to the product, its price, and the terms and conditions for delivery.

- **Outputs:** The outcome of the decision process may either be to go ahead and purchase, or, alternatively, not to buy or to defer a decision to a later date.

More specific models of buyer behaviour have been developed as a result of research into specific sectors. Many of these have sought to rank in order of importance the factors which contribute towards the purchase decision and to identify critical factors, the absence of which will exclude a possibility from a decision set. As an example, research into restaurant choice decisions by Auty (1992) identified five key factors, ranking food quality as the most important, followed by image and atmosphere. However, it was also noted that the importance attached to each of these factors differed according to the purpose of the visit to the restaurant—the factors influencing a choice of restaurant for a celebration were quite different from those used for a general social occasion.

Personal and organizational buyer behaviour compared

At the beginning of this chapter it was noted that buying processes are likely to differ between situations where it is an organization rather than an individual making a purchase. There are a number of reasons why different decision-making processes often occur.

- Two sets of needs are being met when an organization buys a product—the formal needs of the organization and the personal needs of the individuals who make up the organization. The former might be thought of as being the more 'rational'. However, individuals seek to satisfy needs which are influenced by their own perceptual and behavioural environment, very much in the same way as would be the case with private consumer purchases.

- More people are typically involved in organizational purchases. High value purchases may require evaluation and approval at a number of levels of an organization's management hierarchy. Research might indicate for particular organizations or types of organizations the level at which a final decision is made. The analysis of the decision-making unit (see above) might also reveal a wider range of influencers present in the decision-making process.

■ Organizational purchases are more likely to be made according to formalized routines. At its simplest, this may involve delegating to a junior buyer the task of making repeat orders for services which have previously been evaluated. At the other extreme, many high value purchases may only be made after a formal process of bidding and evaluation has been undertaken.

■ The elements of the product offer that are considered critical in the evaluation process are likely to differ. For many products, the emphasis placed on price by many personal buyers is replaced by reliability and performance characteristics by the organizational buyer. In many cases, poor performance of a product can have direct financial consequences for an organization—a low price but unreliable computer might merely cause annoyance and frustration to a private buyer, but might lead to lost production output or lost sales for an organizational buyer.

■ The greater number of people involved in organizational buying also often results in the whole process taking longer. A desire to minimize risk is inherent in many formal organizational motives and informally present in the motives of individuals within organizations. This often results in lengthy feasibility studies being undertaken. In some new markets, especially overseas markets, trust in suppliers might be an important factor used by purchasers when evaluating competing suppliers and it may take time to build up a trusting relationship before any purchase commitment is secured.

Buyer behaviour and relationship marketing

A^{NY} casual glance through academic or practitioner marketing journals may leave you with the impression that relationship marketing is a very new development. In reality, companies have always taken measures—some more so than others—to ensure that a sale is not so much as the end of one transaction, but the beginning of the next one.

The need for organizational buyers' risks to be reduced and their desire to seek the active cooperation of suppliers in tackling shared problems has resulted in greater attention being paid to the development of organizational buyer–seller relationships over time, rather than seeing individual purchases in isolation. It has been pointed out by Ford *et al.* (1998) and Gronroos (1990) that as the complexity of product offerings increase, the organizational buying unit perceives a greater need for confidence and trust in its suppliers. The following chapter examines the ways in which companies have sought to develop ongoing buyer–seller relationships.

Chapter summary and key linkages to other chapters

A sound understanding of buying processes is essential for the development of an appropriate marketing mix. A purchase decision is influenced by a wide range of personal, social, economic, and situational factors, and varies between different types of product and different individuals. The outcome of a decision-making process may be to buy now, not to buy, or to defer a decision. Few buying decisions are made without reference to others, so it is important to identify the members of the decision-making unit. This is particularly true in the case of organizational purchases where it is important to know what product features and promotional messages motivate different individuals.

The following key linkages to other chapters should be noted:

Chapter 1: What is marketing?: Marketing is above all else about making an organization customer focused rather than internally focused. A true marketing orientation must take account of customers' buying processes, however irrational these may at first sight appear.

Chapter 2: The marketing environment: The way we make decisions is very much influenced by the culture in which we live. Culture and reference groups influence how we behave. The state of the economy affects our evaluation criteria.

Chapter 3: Market segmentation: An important basis for segmenting markets is buying processes, for example a segment of impulsive shoppers is likely to act very differently from those seeking value by shopping around. Buyer behaviour segments are usually correlated with other socio-economic and lifestyle segmentation variables such as age, gender, occupation, etc.

Chapter 4: Branding: Brands are very important in simplifying the decision-making process. When making a routine rebuy, or a modified rebuy, we are likely to be guided by a brand that we have come to trust. Even in the case of the purchase of a novel type of product, we may trust a particular brand even if we know very little about the product itself.

Chapter 5: Marketing and ethics: Companies are often tempted to act unethically in the way they procure sales, for example by giving misleading information or bribing individual members of a Decision-Making Unit. Are bad ethics also in the long term bad business practice?

Chapter 6: Marketing research: It is crucial to understand in detail the processes by which buyers make purchase decisions and for this reason qualitative and quantitative research is routinely undertaken.

Chapter 8: Buyer–seller relationship development: The development of ongoing relationships is one means by which buyers seek to simplify their purchases and to minimize their exposure to risk. Many see relationship marketing theory as a natural development of buyer behaviour theory.

Chapters 9/10: Developing a product portfolio: With changes in customers' preferences and buying processes, a company's portfolio of products could rapidly become unsuited to customers' needs.

Chapter 11: Developing a sustainable competitive advantage: A company may think it has the best marketing mix among its competitors, but it must think holistically about its customers' perceptions of its offer and take account of the way that buyers evaluate competing products.

Chapters 12/13: Pricing theory and application: It is important to understand how important price is in evaluating competing products. Price sensitivity is likely to differ between market segments.

Chapter 14: Intermediaries: Most goods and services are bought through intermediaries, so it is important to understand how buyers evaluate intermediaries. If a product is not readily available, will it fail to enter the choice set?

Chapters 16–20: Principles of promotion planning/advertising/sales promotion/ personal selling/direct marketing: It is vital to know who within a buying Decision-Making Unit to target with messages, what messages they will be receptive to, and when they will be most receptive.

Chapter 21: Managing the marketing effort: It is the task of marketing management to co-ordinate the activities of a firm so that the product offer is in accordance with buyers' decision processes.

Chapter 22: Services marketing: Services are usually more risky purchases than goods, so additional measures may be taken to reduce levels of perceived risk. The simultaneous consumption and production of services makes prior evaluation of a service difficult.

Chapter 23: Global marketing: A company may understand its customers' buying processes in the domestic market, but they can be very different overseas. For example, promotional messages that worked at home may fail overseas. Packaging and colour schemes may need to be adapted.

Case study

Research company tries to show that you can only understand consumer behaviour by living with their behaviour

How can any marketer get inside your mind to understand how you actually make purchase decisions? Structured questionnaire surveys may have a role for collecting large-scale factual data, but they have major weaknesses when it comes to understanding individuals' attitudes. Qualitative approaches, such as focus groups can get closer to the truth, but participants often still find themselves inhibited from telling the full story. Many marketing managers, especially those without large research budgets, inevitably end up relying on their own personal experiences to understand how consumers behave. This may be easy for target markets which are in the 20–40 age range (the age of typical marketers), but how do you get inside the mind of teenagers, or elderly people?

A means of getting close to the truth has been devised by the advertising agency BMP DDB, and involves a company researcher living with a family for several days to record their every move. BMP hopes that Project Keyhole will be used by clients who are looking for more than the data gathered using traditional quantitative and qualitative research techniques. Participants record their views and actions on a digital video camera, in the presence of a researcher who stays with them from 8 a.m. until 10 p.m. for a few days. A normal project would last four or five days and the client may be invited along for part of the time. Participants are paid £100 for their trouble. What did they do with the direct mail when it came through the letter box? Did they use the coupon offer which it contained? Who drinks the fresh orange juice in the house? How long do they spend cooking dinner? How do they actually cook the ready prepared meals they bought earlier? Does the family eat together? These are examples of the vital information that sponsoring companies hope to get hold of in order to position their products more effectively.

According to the company, the advantage of this method over conventional research is that it picks up inconsistencies between what people say they do and what they actually do. Following them throughout the day allows the researcher to see why a person's habits might change according to random factors like their mood, the time of day, or the weather. Crucially it reveals the quirks in our behaviour that marketers are desperate to gain an insight into. For example, a person's store card data might tell you that they buy butter and margarine, but it does not tell whether they eat the bread fresh, or toast it first before putting margarine on it.

In 1998, the magazine *Marketing* put this novel research method to the test with a guinea pig family called the Joneses. It then compared the results of this approach with more traditional methods of profiling customers. In short, established systems such as CACI, Claritas, and Experian might say one thing about the buying behaviour of a family, using lifestyle and electoral roll data, but did they bear any relation to reality?

The information that the researcher gathered in a short space of time told a lot about the Joneses. By contrast, the database information about the Joneses, although detailed and often accurate, could not capture the quirks and details that make up the personality of the family. For example, it transpired that the Joneses had a keener than average eye on value for money. Although information on them from the four database companies correctly suggested that they enjoy luxuries like good food and foreign holidays, it did not say anything about the real-life factors that influence their purchasing decisions. The most noticeable of these was that although they like good food, Mrs Jones mixed her shopping between the supermarket and a local discount store which sells cut-price brands. This means that she only bought at Tesco or Sainsbury's what she could not get cheaper elsewhere. She showed the researcher a can of branded plum tomatoes which she got for 10p at the discount store as an example, explaining that it would have cost 26p in the supermarket. Mrs Jones prided herself on being able to hunt down bargains like this and occasionally rewarded herself by buying 'something luxurious', such as smoked salmon from Marks & Spencer. The freezer had an important role to play as it allows Mrs Jones to buy things she sees on special offer even if she does not need them immediately.

Mrs Jones's eye for an offer made her a keen scrutineer of direct mail. She checked mailings for 'catches' in the small print and for any special offers. She collected mailers worth chasing up on a clip on the fridge door, along with vouchers collected from magazines. Mrs Jones's financial nous means that she managed the family's money.

Not surprisingly, these details did not come out in database information. Of the commercial databases, CACI's People UK and Lifecycle UK databases seemed to be most at variance with the reality of the Joneses' life. They got their ages wrong, incorrectly surmised that they took business flights, and incorrectly attributed Mr Jones with being computer literate. Nobody in the household read the *FT* or the *Independent* as predicted—they read the *Daily Mail* instead. Some of the other points made by CACI were right, but were felt to be very generalized and could apply to anybody.

Claritas seemed to be much closer to reality. The Joneses predicted jobs were about right and the database was correct in stating that they had credit and store cards. They managed to say that the Joneses liked antiques, perhaps learnt as a result of them occasionally buying *Homes and Antiques* magazine. They similarly were correct in stating that they like gardening, DIY, foreign travel, and eating out. The database had predicted that the family would be most likely to own a Ford or Renault car. In fact, Mrs Jones owned a Ford, while Mr Jones had a company Renault.

Based on 'Keeping up with the Joneses', *Marketing*, 19 November 1998, pp. 28–9

Case study review questions

1 Why is it important to study the composition of the decision-making unit? To what extent do you think this research approach will give a complete understanding of how family units make purchases?

2 What new possibilities, if any, for market segmentation are opened up by this approach to the study of buyer behaviour?

3 Critically assess the scope for expanding this type of research as a means of learning more about buyer behaviour.

Chapter review questions

1 Is it realistic to represent the buying process as a simple linear process? What factors might complicate such apparently smooth progress?

2 What is the link between the size of a buying unit and the buying processes that it adopts?

3 Critically evaluate methods by which firms can learn more about how customers go about buying their products.

4 In what ways does a buyer's level of involvement with a product influence their buying process?

5 How can firms encourage positive post-purchase feelings? With reference to an example, assess whether a company is doing enough in this respect. What improvements could it make?

6 Is there really a major difference between how private individuals and organizations make purchases? Discuss the effects of a growing small business sector and the complexity of household units on possible convergence in buying processes.

References

Auty, S. (1992), 'Consumer Choice and Segmentation in the Restaurant Industry', *The Services Industries Journal*, **12**, 3, pp. 324–39.

Ford, W. S. *et al.* (1998), *Communicating with Customers: Service Approaches, Ethics, and Impact*, (Cresskill, NJ: Hampton Press).

Gronroos, C. (1990), 'Relationship Approach to Marketing in Service Contexts: The Marketing and Organizational Behavior Interface', *Journal of Business Research*, **20**, pp. 3–11.

Hofstede G. (1991), *Culture and Organizations*, (London: McGraw-Hill).

Howard, J. A., and Sheth, J. N. (1969), *The Theory of Buyer Behaviour* (New York: John Wiley and Sons).

Maslow, A. (1943), 'A Theory of Human Motivation', *Psychological Review*, **50**, 4, pp. 370–96.

Wells, W. D., and Gubar, G. (1966), 'Life Cycle Concepts in Marketing Research', *Journal of Marketing Research*, **3**, Nov., pp. 355–63.

Suggested further reading

There are numerous textbooks which cover the topic of buyer behaviour in greater detail, including the following:

- Bettman, J. R., Luce, M. F., and Payne, J. W. (1998), 'Constructive Consumer Choice Processes', *Journal of Consumer Research*, **25**, 3, p. 187.

- Engel, J. F., Blackwell, R. D., and Miniard, P. W. (1997), *Consumer Behaviour*, 8th edn. The Dryden Press Series in Marketing (Fort Worth: Dryden Press).

- Foxall, G. R., and Goldsmith, R. E. (1994), *Consumer Psychology for Marketing* (London: Routledge).

- Rice, C. (1997), *Understanding Customers*, 2nd edn. (London: Butterworth-Heinemann).

- Smith, I. (1997), *Meeting Customer Needs*, 2nd edn. (London: Butterworth-Heinemann).

Chapter 8

Buyer–Seller Relationship Development

Chapter objectives

This chapter presents a natural development from the previous chapter on buyer behaviour. It explores how companies seek to turn one-off casual transactions into ongoing relationships with customers, to the point that customers simplify their choice process and remain loyal to one company. Relationship marketing has become increasingly important in marketing planning in recent years. This chapter reviews its underlying theories and critically assesses the usefulness of relationship marketing paradigms.

Why develop ongoing relationships with customers?

'RELATIONSHIP marketing' has become an important part of marketing planning during the 1990s, attracting considerable recent interest from marketing academics and practitioners. Practitioners have seen the potential advantages of reducing levels of customer 'churn' by improving the retention rates of profitable customers (Reichheld and Sasser 1990; Webster 1992). Within the academic community, although some have viewed relationship marketing merely as an applied topic of marketing with an insubstantial theory base, others have argued that relational exchange represents a paradigm shift in marketing thought (Gronroos 1994; Morgan and Hunt 1994). During the 1990s, numerous academic articles have appeared on the subject of relationship marketing, supplemented by a growing range of practitioner publications. The general thrust of such articles has been to extend relational exchange as a paradigm beyond its traditional domain of high value industrial goods. Today, relationship marketing has been applied to the relatively low value, high volume goods and services sold to private consumers (Sheth and Parvatiyar 1995; Christopher, Payne, and Ballantyne 1991).

Relationship marketing is essentially about extending and deepening the business which a company does with each of its customers. So rather than letting customers drift away to competitors, the emphasis of relationship marketing is on retaining those profitable customers that a company has previously acquired, probably at quite a high acquisition cost in terms of the advertising and inducements needed to get their first purchase.

There have been many attempts to demonstrate the benefits to a company of retaining its existing customers rather than continually seeking new customers to replace lapsed ones (e.g. Reichheld and Sasser 1990). The benefits can be demonstrated in the following simple example of a bank's customers.

Before the development of relationship marketing

- Assume that the bank has 500,000 customers and looses 10 per cent of these each year, for one reason or another.
- This implies that the average length of relationship between the company and its customers is 10 years.
- It costs £100 to recruit a new customer (in advertising, incentives, and processing costs). In order to replace its lapsed customers, it spends £5,000,000 (50,000 lapsed customers to replace × £100) on advertising and customer recruitment.
- The company makes an average profit of £50 per year from each of its customers.

After the introduction of a relationship marketing programme

- A customer care programme is introduced which costs £25 per customer (this may include the cost of sending a magazine to all customers; setting up an improved customer service centre, or offering rewards for loyalty).
- The customer defection rate falls from 10 per cent p.a. to 5 per cent.
- The average relationship duration is therefore extended from ten to twenty years.

Financial effects on the company

- Each new customer now represents a gross profit potential of twenty years × £50 p.a. = £1,000, rather than ten years × £50 = £500, a gain of £500.

- The net effect, after taking into account the additional expenditure of £25 per customer p.a. for a customer care programme, is to increase the lifetime profitability of each new customer by £250.
- If the company was content to maintain a stable volume of business, it could cut by half the number of new customers it needs to recruit each year, from 50,000 to 25,000. At a recruitment cost of £100 per new customer, this saves the company £2,500,000 pa.

Of course, this simple example is based on many assumptions, for example that all customers are of equal profit potential. Nevertheless, it powerfully illustrates the potential financial benefits to a company resulting from successfully developing a relationship marketing strategy.

What is the lifetime value of a restaurant customer? A first-time customer may only be spending £20 on this occasion, but if they like what they get, how much are they likely to spend in the future? A typical diner eating out just once a month could be worth £1,200 in just five years. If they are happy, they are likely to tell their friends. If they're not, they are likely to tell even more of their friends. It follows that customers should be seen as investments, to be carefully nurtured over time. When things go wrong (e.g. through overbooking) it would probably be to the restaurant's advantage to spend heavily on putting things right for the customer (e.g. by offering money off a future meal). Judged on the basis of the current transaction, the restaurant may make a loss, but it has protected its investment in a future income stream. Like all investments, some are worth more than others. How should a company decide which customers are priority relationships to invest in? And what level of investment can be justified in terms of the future from the relationship?

Is relationship marketing a new phenomenon?

R**ELATIONAL** exchange is not a new concept, having been observed, for example, in the pattern of exchanges between textile manufacturers and intermediaries in Victorian England (Clegg 1956). Also, while relationships may have been rediscovered in the west, they have remained a fundamental part of exchange in many eastern cultures (Ohame 1989).

In modern times, organizations' interest in developing closer relationships with their private and corporate customers has come about for two principal reasons:

1. The increasingly competitive nature of markets has resulted in good product quality alone being inadequate for a company to gain competitive advantage. Superior ongoing relationships with customers supplement a firm's competitive advantage

(Christopher, Payne, and Ballantyne 1991). This is evident in the car market, where the focal point of marketing has shifted from a preoccupation with better design, to better service, to better relationships. Today, many buyers of cars choose a car which comes with the best support package which keeps the car financed, maintained, insured, and replaced at the end of a specified period (Fig. 8.1). For many, the three-yearly purchase of a car has been turned into an ongoing relationship with a car company to supply all the services which make a car available to the consumer.

2. The emergence of powerful, user-friendly databases has enabled large companies to know more about their customers, recreating in a computer what the small business owner knew in his or her head (Treacy and Wiersema 1993). Many of the current developments in relationship marketing would have been unthinkable without modern information technology capabilities.

Relationship marketing strategies are not appropriate to all buyer–seller relationships. Sellers of generic commodity products may find relationships difficult to achieve in a market where customers have no reason to remain loyal to one supplier and routinely seek out the supplier which is the lowest cost and/or most accessible.

The extent to which the development of ongoing relationships represents a desirable marketing strategy is dependent upon (1) the characteristics of the product; (2) the characteristics of customers; and (3) the characteristics of suppliers.

1. **Characteristics of the product**. Where services are complex and involve a high degree of uncertainty on the part of buyers, the likelihood of customers seeking a relationship is increased. Risk is a component of trust—as risk increases, so the need to be able to trust a supplier increases. Relationships are often a necessity where the stream of product benefits is produced and consumed over a period of time—a programme of medical treatment, for example. For some products, a relationship may allow preferential treatment or semi-automatic responses to requests for service, thereby reducing transaction costs associated with multiple service ordering (Williamson 1975). It has also been suggested that both suppliers and customers seek the security of relationships where the market environment is turbulent.

2. **Characteristics of customers**. A stream of research has sought to segment buyers according to the importance they attach to the economic as against the social aspects of an exchange (e.g. Jackson 1985, Fern and Brown 1984). Customers

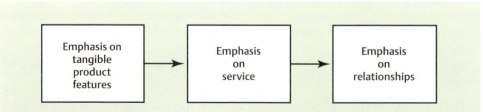

Figure 8.1 The changing focus of marketing: an application to the car market

differ in their receptiveness to relationship development and in the level of suspicion they show towards attempts to create relationships. Customers who are transaction oriented may have greater concern with the economic outcomes of their purchase, whereas relationship-oriented individuals are more concerned with the social exchange aspects of the purchase transaction process (Blau 1989). Research has also suggested that the importance attributed to components of a relationship differ between groups, for example in the way that women place more emphasis on trust and commitment in their relationships compared to men (Shemwell, Cronin, and Bullard 1994).

3. **Characteristics of suppliers**. By developing relationships with their customers, suppliers add to the differentiation of their products and give customers a reason to remain loyal. The extent to which organizations are relationship rather than product oriented can be related to their structure, processes, and core values (Achrol 1991; Quinn 1992). Organizations differ in the extent to which they are able, or willing, to calculate the lifetime value of a customer (Rust and Zahorik 1993).

Defining relationship marketing

DISCUSSION of relationship marketing has suffered from a general failure to position the concept. To some, relationship marketing has been associated primarily with attempts by sellers to buy loyalty, rather than bringing about a deep-seated commitment to a seller on the part of buyers. Viewed as a short-term tactic, relationship marketing may give no long-term strategic advantage to a firm. However, relational exchange which profitably adds to customer perceived value corresponds closely to definitions of the philosophy of marketing (e.g. Narver and Slater 1990).

The term 'relationship marketing' has become widely used and covers a disparate range of activities. Conceptually, it has been positioned anywhere between being a set of marketing tactics, in which any interaction between buyers and sellers is described as a relationship, regardless of the parties' commitment to each other, and a fundamental marketing philosophy which goes to the core of the marketing concept through its customer lifetime focus. To some, relationship marketing is seen as little more than database marketing.

Building on Berry's conceptualization of three levels of relationship marketing (Berry 1995), the published literature on relationship marketing can be classified into three broad approaches.

1. At a *tactical* level, relationship marketing is used as a sales promotion tool. Developments in information technology have spawned many short-term loyalty schemes (Treacy and Wiersema 1993). However, the implementation of such schemes has often been opportunistic, leading to expensive loyalty schemes which create loyalty to the incentive rather than to the supplier (Barnes 1994).

Figure 8.2 WH Smith is one of many retailers offering benefits to customers who sign up for their loyalty programmes. In this example, WH Smith stresses the exclusive benefits that members of its programme can obtain at a special event. (Reproduced with permission of WH Smith Ltd)

2. At a more *strategic* level, relationship marketing has been seen as a process by which suppliers seek to 'tie-in' customers through legal, economic, technological, geographical, and time bonds (Liljander and Strandvik 1995). Again, it has been pointed out that such bonds may lead to customer *detention* rather than *retention* (Dick and Basu 1994) and that a company which has not achieved a more deep-seated affective relationship with its customers may be unable to sustain those relationships if the legal or technological environment changes. What often passes as a relationship, therefore, is an asymmetric association based on inequalities of knowledge, power, and resources, rather than mutual trust and empathy. Where tying-in is achieved through mutually rewarding co-operation, mutual dependence, and shared risk, the relationship is likely to show greater stability and endurance.

3. At a more *philosophical* level, relationship marketing goes to the heart of the marketing philosophy. Traditional definitions of marketing focus on the primacy of customer needs and relationship marketing as a philosophy refocuses marketing strategy away from products and their life cycles towards customer relationship life cycles. Recent conceptualizations of marketing as being the integration of a customer orientation, competitor orientation and inter-functional co-ordination (Narver and Slater 1990) stress the key features of a relationship marketing philosophy; using all employees of an organization to meet profitably the lifetime needs of targeted customers better than competitors.

Considerable double-speak is often present in attempts by firms to develop customer relationships. In the service sector, many organizations are simplifying and 'industrializing' their processes, usually in an attempt to improve their operational efficiency and consistency of performance. Such companies may talk about relationship development with customers, based on dialogue which is driven by information technology. But such relationships can be qualitatively quite different from those based on social bonds founded on affective commitment and trust. While UK clearing banks have become vigorous in their development of customer databases and named personal banking advisers, many customers would feel that the relationship with their bank is qualitatively worse than when a branch manager was able to enter into a more holistic dialogue with customers.

Managers of firms seeking to develop relationships with their customers should avoid the arrogant belief that customers seek such relationships. Surveys have indicated that many categories of buyers are becoming increasingly confident in venturing outside a business relationship and reluctant to enter into an ongoing relationship. Relationship marketing strategies may fail where buyers' perception is of reduced choice and freedom to act opportunistically rather than added value which comes from a relationship. Added value must be defined by sellers in terms of buyers' needs, rather than focusing on customers as captives who can be cross-sold other products from a firm's portfolio.

Customers represent just one category of relationship in firms' value creation activity. The effectiveness of internal relationships and relationships with suppliers can have a significant impact on the quality of customer relationships. A company that

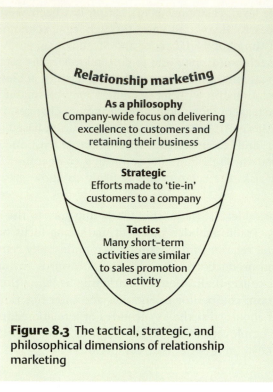

Figure 8.3 The tactical, strategic, and philosophical dimensions of relationship marketing

resorts to opportunistic behaviour in relation to its employees and suppliers may find it difficult to sustain quality and commitment in its relationships with customers. Christopher, Payne, and Ballantyne extend discussion of relationship marketing to encompass six relationship markets of customers, internal markets, employee (recruitment) markets, supplier markets, influence markets, and referral markets (Fig. 8.4).

Components of buyer–seller relationships

A NUMBER of attempts have been made to identify the principal elements of buyer–seller relationships, drawing on frameworks developed in social psychology and organizational behaviour. In the case of one-off transactional exchanges, the elements are relatively easy to identify, as the presumption is made that the parties involved bring no previous history of exchanges to the current exchange, nor do they expect the outcome of the current exchange to influence future exchanges. In the case of ongoing relational exchange, the last condition is not met, and any analysis of exchange elements must consider a wide range of social and economic factors that form part of an exchange.

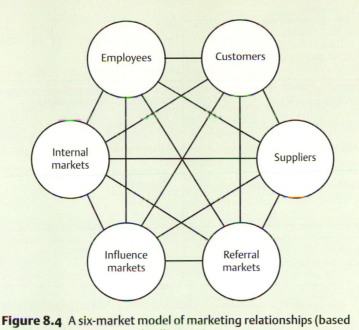

Figure 8.4 A six-market model of marketing relationships (based on Christopher, Payne, and Ballantyne)

Within the context of industrial buyer–seller relationships, Hakansson (1982) identified four elements which are exchanged between a buyer and seller: a product; money; information; and sociality. While the first two are common to most commercial exchanges, information and sociality assume greater importance where the relationship has a time dimension.

The meaning of the social element of exchange can differ between cultures. Although social ties have received considerable attention in the context of industrial buyer–seller relationships, they can also be important in private buyer–seller. relationships. In cultures where social aspects of exchange form a relatively important part of the total exchange benefits received by a buyer, attempts by other suppliers to attract buyers on the basis of more tangible economic benefits may fail. Most analyses of relational exchange identify a number of crucial components which must be present for a buyer–seller relationship to develop.

Quality in perceived delivery

Without satisfactory delivery of promised goods and services, it is difficult for a sustainable ongoing relationship to be developed between a company and its customers. Delivery may be the responsibility of a wide range of front-line and back-up staff, resulting in quality being dependent on extensive customer–producer encounters. In

Traditional transaction oriented marketing	Relationship marketing
Focus on a single sale	Focus on customer retention
Short-term orientation	Long-term orientation
Sales to anonymous buyers	Tracking of named buyers
Salesperson is the main interface between buyer and seller	Multiple levels of relationships between buyer and seller
Limited customer commitment	High customer commitment
Quality is the responsibility of production department	Quality is the responsibility of all

Figure 8.5 The components of transactional and relational exchange compared

the case of high contact services with multifaceted interaction between an organization and its customers, quality is assessed both by processes of service production and final outcomes. However, in the case of products which involve very little contact between an organization and its customers, the sales personnel may be crucial in the development of ongoing relationships.

Trust

Much attention has been given to the role of trust, which can be defined as 'a belief that a party is reliable and will fulfil its obligations in an exchange relationship' (Schurr and Ozanne 1985). Many analyses of trust in a marketing context build upon models used in social psychology to explain its role in interpersonal dyads (e.g. Pruitt 1981, Rotter 1967). In their analysis of the development of trust, Swan and Nolan (1985) conceptualize three stages. In the first stage, there has been no opportunity for exploration of each party's credentials, therefore the level of trust between buyer and seller is at a minimum until a minor exchange occurs. Once exchanges have occurred, trust development moves into the second stage in which the buyer has the opportunity to check actual delivery of a service against the promises that the seller has made. Trust is established where the perceived performance matches the promised performance. Finally, trust established through interaction is combined with other external factors (e.g. word-of-mouth opinions and media reports about the seller) to form an overall perception of trust in the seller. Trust may in fact occur without any prior interaction between buyer and seller, being based on the recommendation of trusted friends.

Organization's customer orientation/empathy

A number of studies have sought to measure the extent to which a company's personnel are customer oriented and are able to empathize with their customers' needs (e.g. Saxe and Weitz 1982, Michaels and Day 1985). In the case of front-line sales personnel, customer-oriented selling has been defined by Saxe and Weitz as 'the practice of the marketing concept at the level of the individual salesperson and customer'.

Saxe and Weitz analysed customer orientation in terms of two factors: 'relations' and 'ability to help'. The former refers to the abilities of sales personnel to develop long-term relationships with customers on the basis of trust, co-operation, and conflict resolution, while ability to help refers to sales personnel's ability to help customers satisfy their needs.

Employees' abilities to empathize with customers have been identified by a number of researchers as a prerequisite to successful selling (Saxe and Weitz 1982). Even where a fault has occurred, the ability of a company's staff to empathize with the customer can help build a stronger relationship. This can be particularly important for highly variable services where the ability of an employee to empathize with customers can make the difference between a complete failure and the development of a closer relationship.

Sellers' ethics

Complex goods and services often provide future benefits that are difficult to prove at the time of sale. The inability of many consumers properly to evaluate such products can put them at the mercy of sales personnel. A preoccupation by sales personnel with short-term goals may result in unethical behaviour which could subsequently endanger the possibility of developing long-term relationships with customers.

Relationship life cycles

BUYERS and sellers proceed through a relationship if they believe that staying in it will enable them to achieve their objectives better than would be possible outside it. The decision whether to invest or divest in a relationship can be seen as dependent on the quality of the relationship so far. There has now been much research into the factors that hold buyers and sellers together in a relationship. Emerging from general models of buyer behaviour, a number of theoretical and empirically based models have been developed to explain the processes of interaction between buyers and sellers, both in the industrial sector (e.g. Ford 1981, Hakansson 1982), and for consumer markets (Dwyer, Schurr, and Oh 1987, Crosby, Evans, and Cowles 1990). Many models of buyer–seller relationship development use frameworks developed in social psychology for the study of interpersonal relationships (for example, an analogy with marriage has been drawn by Tynan (1997).

A life cycle theoretical approach was used by Dwyer, Schurr, and Oh (1987) to develop a model of buyer–seller relationship. Their model identified five stages of relationship development—awareness, exploration, expansion, commitment, and dissolution. They proposed that a relationship begins to develop significance in the exploration stage when the emerging relationship is characterized by attempts by the seller to attract the attention of the other party, to bargain and to understand the nature of the power, norms, and expectations held by the other. They see the expansion phase of the relationship resulting from the successful conclusion of the initial exploratory interaction between the parties. Exchange outcomes in this stage provide clues about the suitability of long-term relationships. The commitment phase of a relationship implies some degree of exclusivity between the parties and results in a minimal information search for alternatives—if it occurs at all. However, the possibility of a relationship being terminated is always present and can occur during any of the previous stages. However, the consequences of termination are greatest where a party has made significant investments in the relationship (e.g. through dedicated equipment which has no alternative use).

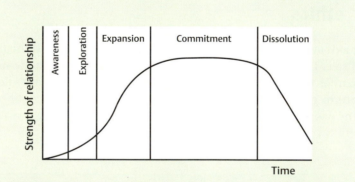

Figure 8.6 A buyer–seller relationship life cycle (based on Dwyer, Schurr, and Oh 1987)

Methods used to develop customer relationships

RELATIONSHIP marketing may sound like a good idea to many companies, but actually implementing a programme that develops true customer loyalty can pose many problems if the end result is not to be mere rhetoric. It was noted earlier that a buyer–seller relationship can be defined at a number of levels, and it is the task of a company to move an individual from being a mere prospect to a strong advocate. It is quite common to talk about this transition in terms of a 'ladder of loyalty' (Fig. 8.7).

Here are some methods used by companies to develop successful ongoing customer relationships.

Total customer satisfaction

In a competitive market-place, customer satisfaction is the surest way to ensure that buyers return repeatedly. To achieve high levels of satisfaction requires the effort of all functions within an organization. Relationship development cannot be simply left to a relationship manager. There are many notable cases of companies that have not

Figure 8.7 The 'ladder of loyalty'

developed any explicit relationship marketing programme, but nevertheless achieve very high levels of customer advocacy. Consider, for example, the chocolate retailer Thorntons which has developed strong loyalty from customers who return to its shops for indulgence and gift purchases of chocolate, despite having no formally stated relationship marketing programme.

Of course, many companies enjoy a high level of repeat business without providing high levels of customer satisfaction. Many customers of train companies may complain about the price and reliability of their train service, but return to it because they have no realistic alternative.

Even companies which have an apparently poor standard of service can achieve high levels of repeat business by charging low prices. Retail chains such as Aldi and Lidl have developed strong loyalty from price sensitive customers who consider that the total service offer (access to the store, range of products, cleanliness, and friendliness, etc.) are acceptable in return for the price that they have paid. The danger here is that competitors may enter the market with similarly low prices, but offering higher levels of service. Would customers still remain loyal?

Adding value to a relationship

Companies must ask 'Why should a customer want a relationship with us?'. The answer is that a relationship, to be sustainable, must add value in the eyes of customers. This value can come about in a number of ways, including:

- Making reordering of goods and services easier (for example many hotels record guests' details and preferences so that they do not have to be re-entered each time that a guest checks in).

- Offering privileges to customers who wish to enter into some type of formal relationship (for example, many retailers hold special preview events for card holders, and send a free copy of the store's magazine).

- Developing an ability to solve problems jointly. For example, a car repair garage may take on board identifying exactly what the problem is that a customer seeks fixing, rather than leaving it to the customer to have to specify the work that they require to be carried out. Such joint problem solving requires a considerable level of trust to have been developed between the parties.

Loyalty programmes

Loyalty programmes became something of a 'flavour of the month' during the 1990s. Loyalty programmes work on the basis of providing rewards to customers in return for their continuing patronage. For the customer, a loyalty programme can add to the value of a relationships in the ways described above. For the seller, the main attractions are based on the ability to gather large amounts of information about identifiable individuals, rather than aggregate level data about the 'average' customer. A loyalty programme can also have the effect of 'tying-in' a customer, at least in the short term while the customer collects sufficient points in order to obtain a reward.

There is of course nothing new in the idea of a loyalty programme—Co-operative Society shops have given a 'dividend' to members in proportion to their expenditure since the early days of the Co-operative movement. The recent proliferation of loyalty programmes has been encouraged by developments in Information Technology which allow previously unimaginable amounts of customer information to be collected and analysed. They are particularly useful in sectors where knowledge of individual buyers' behaviour has been very limited. For example, the typical grocery retailer would have little idea about the specific product combinations bought by shoppers, on the basis of which merchandising could be refined.

Modern loyalty programmes have spread rapidly between sectors, learning a lot from the early experiences of the airline sector. However, there is evidence that, while the innovator in any sector may generate additional profitable business with their loyalty programme, it is very easy to copy and soon ceases to act as a competitive differentiator.

Creating barriers to exit

Companies can try to keep their customers by making it difficult for them to defect to a competitor. Customers can unwittingly walk into traps where they become dependent upon a supplier for continuing support. Suppliers of industrial machinery create ongoing relationships where they are the sole supplier of spare parts or consumable items which the purchaser must buy if they are to continue using their equipment. Many companies negotiate exclusive supply agreements with a supplier in return for a promise of preferential treatment. In both cases, the customer is dependent in the short term. However, such ties can usually be broken eventually (for example when the machinery is replaced or when an exclusive supply contract comes up for renewal), and it is at that point that the true loyalty of a customer is put to the test.

> The mobile phone company One-2-One had large numbers of customers using their phones only during the low price evening period and who left them switched off during the day. How could it encourage its customers to switch on all day, thereby increasing potential use of its service and extending its relationship with them? The company developed a promotional campaign that involved ringing a different customer every minute throughout the day. Those who answered were eligible for a range of prizes. One-2-One claimed that the promotion was a success, as 60 per cent of phones were switched on during the promotion period, compared with just 50 per cent immediately before. But were customers being loyal to this promotion or had the promotion itself brought about a profitable long-term change in their behaviour?

Limitations to the development of customer relationships

SHOULD relationship marketing be viewed as a universal blueprint suitable for all businesses, or a special case that suits just a few types of organization? The arguments in favour of pursuing strategies designed to obtain a greater share of customers' total expenditure have now been well rehearsed. However, as relationship marketing has been extended from high value capital goods to relatively low value consumer goods, limitations have become apparent. Relational exchange may be an unrealistic pursuit in any of the following circumstances: where there is no reason why a buyer would ever wish to return to a seller; where buyers seek to avoid an asymmetric relationship in which they become dependent upon a seller; where buying processes become formalized in a way that prevents a seller developing relationships based on social bonds; where buyers' confidence lowers the need for risk reduction which is an outcome of relationship development; and where the costs associated with relationship development put a firm at a cost disadvantage in a price sensitive market. From a social welfare perspective, relationships have been associated with anti-competitive practices which limit buyers' choice. Finally, a relationship marketing strategy which has worked in the domestic market may fail when exported overseas.

These limitations to the concept of relational exchange are considered below.

Buyers or sellers may have no expectation of ongoing relationships

One of the defining characteristics of relational exchange identified by Macneil is a time orientation within which exchange takes place (Macneil 1980). However, it may be naïve to assume that a longer time orientation implies a greater relational orientation. In the short to medium term, relational exchange may be seen by one or both parties as a means of gaining competencies which they can subsequently use to encroach on their relational partners' value adding activity. In this way, UK manufacturing firms may have seen strategic alliances with Japanese companies as a short to medium-term strategy to acquire skills from their Japanese partners, whereupon they have broken off their partnership to operate independently (Hamel 1991).

Secondly, many businesses serve market segments where customers have no underlying need to make further purchases of a category of product that a company is able to supply. In the extreme case, a small-scale company may appeal to the curiosity of buyers for whom a second time purchase will have little of its original value—curiosity. This phenomenon is present in many tourism related businesses in destinations of symbolic rather than aesthetic quality (for example, many people make a religious pilgrimage once in their lifetime with little incentive to return again).

Power imbalances between a buyer and seller may create a desire by one party to reduce their dependence

Sellers often have a lot of power over buyers while the buyer has little or no power over the seller. A food manufacturer selling 80 per cent of its food to one retailer may perceive that the latter exerts considerable power over it, whereas for the retailer the manufacturer may represent just a small proportion of its total purchases. The manufacturer may seek to lessen its dependence on the relationship with one powerful buyer.

In the absence of symmetrical power and dependence, one party will have little incentive to show flexibility, because no guarantee exists that such actions will be reciprocated. In fact, short-term disturbances might represent opportunities for individual parties to pursue opportunistically short-term advantages. Balanced, or symmetrical dependency represents a mutual safeguard and a collective incentive to maintain the relationship.

Formalized buying processes may prevent the development of ongoing relationships based on social bonds

Much of the literature on buyer–seller relationship development, especially in the business to business sector, has highlighted the importance of developing social bonds between buyers and sellers (e.g. Liljander and Strandvik 1995). Social bonds have been observed to reduce buyers' perceived levels of risk and to simplify the reordering process.

An alternative view is that social bonds can become too pervasive to the point where they allow economic inefficiencies to develop. In the extreme case, corrupt networks of buyers and sellers may acquire sufficient market power to cause an overall loss of economic welfare. Counterbalances are needed to offset such possible relationship-based inefficiencies.

Measures to suppress buyer–seller relationships based on social bonds have been most evident in the formalized ordering procedures for government contracts. Tightly specified supplier–buyer relationships, and a requirement for contracts to be resubmitted for tender after a specified period, reduces the scope for ongoing socially based relationships to be developed within a system of Compulsory Competitive Tendering. It has been argued that the emphasis on obtaining value for money has emphasized cost reduction at the expense of more qualitative measures of efficiency and effectiveness (Walsh 1991).

Buyers' increasing level of confidence reduces their need for an ongoing relationship

In many consumer markets, buyers' need for ongoing trusting relationships has been reduced by legislation which has had the effect of reducing the risk associated with buying goods and services from previously unknown sources. In the UK, for example, statutory provision for investors' compensation funds has lessened the need for investors to rely on an intermediary who they have come to trust. Legislation has reduced the chances of a poor relationship being developed and provided means for compensating investors who suffer loss as a result of failure by an intermediary, thereby encouraging greater transactional orientation.

Recent developments in Information Technology have emphasized the benefits to producers in being able to gain an asymmetrical position of power in private buyer–seller relationships. With further development, IT may strengthen the willingness and ability of private consumers to engage in multiple sourcing of purchases at the expense of ongoing relationships. For example, Internet searches can enable a buyer to identify the lowest cost/highest value source of supply, which they may be prepared to buy, regardless of any previous transactions they have entered into for that category of product.

Relationship marketing can add to costs, as well as to revenues

For sellers, the most rewarding relationships with customers result from continued investment to create deep-seated attitudinal loyalty, rather than financially based incentives. Excessive use of financial incentives to create loyalty may put a firm at cost disadvantage in a market where cost leadership is important. While pioneers in a sector may introduce incentive schemes and gain additional profitable business from competitors, incentives for loyalty can rapidly become a sector norm which customers expect. In the case of airlines' frequent flyer programmes, a cycle of development has been described which began in the 1980s where the first companies to launch such programmes achieved revenue benefits. By the 1990s, the use of frequent flyer programmes had become more widespread and their revenue benefits marginal. Most major airlines had developed programmes, yielding little advantage from this tool. Meanwhile, budget airlines have prospered and the absence of a loyalty programme has helped them to increase their market share.

Networks of relationships can have anti-competitive implications

It has been observed that the pattern of doing business in many countries may be based on a tightly knit network of relationships between buyers, sellers, suppliers, and distributors, typified by Japan's manufacturing and distribution keiretsus. The high cost of goods and services in Japan has been attributed to these keiretsus which have the effect of stifling competition.

Also, modern computer-based systems for developing ongoing relationships between buyers and sellers have been accused of creating anti-competitive behaviour among companies who share information, to the detriment of companies who do not have access to this information. It has been observed that airlines' co-operation through Computerized Reservation Systems (CRS) have been used to create significant disadvantages for new market entrants, again possibly detrimental to overall welfare.

Relationship marketing strategies which have worked in the domestic market may fail in a different overseas marketing environment

Finally, relationship marketing based on western ideas of databases and incentive schemes may fail in cultures where buyer–seller relationships have to be understood in the broader context of the structure of social relationships. As western societies become increasingly litigious, questions must be asked about the compatibility of socially based business relationships within a broader context of contractual agreements. Socially based business relationships can be associated with corruption and economic inefficiency and can lead to a dilemma between the need for ongoing business relationships and financial accountability.

Chapter summary and key linkages to other chapters

Relationship marketing is becoming an important part of many companies' marketing plans as they realize that it can be much more profitable carefully to retain the customers they currently have, rather than expensively searching for new customers to replace lapsed ones.

A number of factors account for the growing interest in relationship marketing, including the increasingly competitive nature of many markets and the expanding capabilities of information technology. Companies use various methods to develop ongoing relationships with their customers, but some of these are short term and tactical, rather than deep rooted and long term. Relationship marketing is not a universal panacea applicable to all companies' marketing plans.

The principles of relationship marketing described in this chapter can be related to the following chapters in this book:

Chapter 1: What is marketing?: Marketing as a philosophy is customer focused and relationship marketing puts customers and their life cycles at the centre of a firm's attention, rather than products

Chapter 2: The marketing environment: Changes in customer expectations and developments in information technology have led to the modern development of relationship marketing.

Chapter 4: Branding: Is a branding strategy a substitute for, or complementary to, a relationship marketing strategy?

Chapter 5: Marketing and ethics: Are there limits beyond which a company should not seek to extend a relationship with its customers (e.g. should a credit card company use information about its customers' card use to target them with offers which reflect their spending patterns?).

Chapter 6: Marketing research: How do companies understand the relationship expectations of their customers? Or their perceptions of relationship quality?

Chapter 7: Buyer behaviour: Relationship marketing can be seen as an extension of many models of buyer behaviour.

Chapters 9/10: Developing a product portfolio: How does a company develop a product portfolio with which it can broaden and deepen the relationship it has with its existing customers?

Chapter 11: Developing a sustainable competitive advantage: If implemented strategically, relationship marketing can give a company a sustainable advantage among key groups of customers with whom it seeks to develop relationships.

Chapters 12/13: Pricing theory and applications: Should pricing be related to the point a customer is in their relationship life cycle (e.g. low introductory prices followed by rising real prices which reflect a greater sense of commitment by customers)?

Chapter 14: Intermediaries: It must not be forgotten that manufacturers seek to develop close relationships not only with their final customers, but also with their intermediaries.

Chapters 16–19: Principles of promotion planning/advertising/sales promotion/ personal selling: A company's promotional efforts should be aimed at reassuring existing customers, as well as appealing to potential new customers.

Chapter 20: Direct marketing: To many people, direct marketing and relationship marketing are seen as very closely related.

Chapter 21: Organizing for marketing: Should customer relationship managers be included in the organizational structure? How can the company assess the true potential lifetime value of different categories of customers?

Chapter 22: Services marketing: For many manufacturers, providing an ongoing relationship is the essential element of the service that they provide. It was noted in this chapter that for many companies, the quality of relationships has replaced service quality as a differentiator.

Chapter 23: Global marketing: Will relationship marketing strategies work in overseas markets where customers' expectations may be quite different?

Case study

Relationships do not always help Marks & Spencer to sparkle

The retailer Marks & Spencer has often been held out as an example of how to manage effective relationships—with suppliers, employees, and customers. For many years the company was a favourite of the Stock Market, with regular and increasing levels of profitability. It seemed that loyalty from dedicated manufacturers and its employees was feeding through into high levels of customer loyalty, with customers prepared to pay a price premium for the company's products. An analysis of relationships with the company's suppliers gives some indication of how value can be created by close working relationships.

An important reason for the high standing of Marks & Spencer's products and perceived value for money is that the company hasn't bought its products 'off the shelf' from suppliers. Instead, technologists, designers, buyers, and merchandisers from both sides—along with the raw material producers—have worked together to identify new products and designs. For many manufacturers, the 'customer' is regarded as the retail company's buyer. Many manufacturers have very little direct involvement with the final consumers of their products, which limits the opportunities for feedback. This problem has been tackled at M&S, whose suppliers are made aware of who the ultimate customer is and share with the retailer and other raw material producers a focus on the end consumer.

M&S doesn't have a specific research and development budget, but encourages its suppliers to invest to the mutual benefit of both companies. Competitive advantage is gained for the supply chain as a whole, through sharing Marks & Spencer's knowledge of its customers with its suppliers' knowledge in production, distribution, logistics, and information technology. The result can be that the sum of all companies' distinctive competence is more powerful than all companies acting alone. It also allows greater flexibility to changing retail trends. Joint input into manufacturing techniques means equipment can be reconfigured relatively easily, so neither side needs to commit to large amounts of merchandise before market testing.

With food, M&S has innovated to improve availability. As an example, the company decided in 1989 to explore ways of extending the strawberry growing season. M&S technologists, working with suppliers, applied the best scientific methods, and now UK growers can supply the company for seven months a year rather than two. This allowed M&S to become the largest strawberry retailer in Europe. There are many more examples of how M&S has worked closely with its producers to improve its profitability. Since ready prepared Indian takeaway meals were pioneered with supplier Northern Foods, the company claims to have become the world's biggest Indian takeaway.

Northern Foods is M&S's largest food supplier. It has been supplying M&S for over thirty years and has eight factories committed to M&S production. Despite the duration and breadth of their working relationship, there is no formal partnership between the two. Like relationships with all of its suppliers, mutual trust is important to continued success. Some relationships with M&S have failed where suppliers have felt that the retailer pays too little to justify its continued investment, which is especially dangerous where a very high proportion of the supplier's business is with M&S. A small wallpaper manufacturer, for example, may put 80 per cent of its business with M&S, but this would represent only a fraction of 1 per cent of M&S's total business. Power imbalances have to be recognized and sensitively handled.

The idea of one integrated supply chain competing with another became crucial to gaining competitive advantage during the 1990s. Rivals such as Sainsbury's and Debenham's had been equally busy improving their supply chain, even if it did not always mean entering into such close relationships as M&S. By the end of the 1990s, however, observers were beginning to ask whether M&S's supply relationships would be sufficient to guide it through an economic downturn. During 1998, the company issued a profits warning and its share price fell sharply. The company had been accused of arrogance in the way it assumed the loyalty of its customers. Its selling prices had slowly crept up to significantly greater than its competitors, while competitors' services levels had matched M&S's. Faced with a downturn in its business, the company sought to lower its costs and one obvious source of saving was to buy more of its goods overseas. Its competitors had been taking advantage of the high value of sterling to pass price savings on to customers, but M&S's trusted network of domestic suppliers seemed to be a millstone round its neck. Could these relationships survive M&S's cost saving attempts? Or does it prove the case of cynics who argue that relationships—contractual or informal—tie a company down and prevent it being opportunistic and exploiting new opportunities as they arise?

Case study review questions

1 Critically assess whether close relationships with its suppliers have helped or hindered Marks & Spencer's task of gaining competitive advantage.

2 What factors are crucial to the development and maintenance of long-term supplier–retailer relationships?

3 To what extent is it important for there to be consistency in the standards of relationships between a company and its employee, customer, and supplier markets?

Chapter review questions

1 What factors explain recent interest in relationship marketing? Is it really a new topic or old ideas dressed up in new language?

2 Critically assess the factors that are crucial to the success of a relationship marketing programme.

3 It is often suggested that relationships are imposed on unwilling buyers. What evidence do you have of this? How can companies seek to make relationships more consensual?

4 What criteria might a company use to assess whether a prospective customer is likely to be worth developing a relationship with?

5 Critically discuss what is meant by customer loyalty. Do contemporary customer loyalty programmes justify their title?

6 In what ways can marketers improve the effectiveness of relationship marketing activities through a thorough understanding and application of psychological and sociological theory?

References

Achrol, R. (1991), 'Evolution of the Marketing Organization: New Forms for Turbulent Environments', *Journal of Marketing*, Oct., pp. 77–93.

Barnes, J. G. (1994), 'Close to the Customer: But is it Really a Relationship?', *Journal of Marketing Management*, **10**, 7, pp. 561–70.

Berry, L. L. (1995), 'Relationship Marketing of Services—Growing Interest, Emerging Perspectives', *Journal of the Academy of Marketing Science*, **23**, Fall, pp. 236–45.

Blau, G. (1989), 'Testing the Generalizability of a Career Commitment Measure and its Impact on Turnover', *Journal of Vocational Behavior*, **33**, pp. 88–103.

Blau, J. R. (1989), *The Shape of Culture* (Cambridge: Cambridge University Press).

Christopher, M., Payne, A., and Ballantyne, D. (1991), *Relationship Marketing* (Oxford: Butterworth-Heinemann).

Clegg, P. (1956), *A Social and Economic History of Britain 1760–1955* (London: Harrap).

Crosby, L. A., Evans, K. R., and Cowles, D. (1990), 'Relationship Quality in Services Selling: An Interpersonal Influence Perspective', *Journal of Marketing*, **54**, July, pp. 68–81.

Dick, A. S., and Basu, K. (1994), 'Customer Loyalty : Toward an Integrated Conceptual Framework', JAMS, **22**, 2, pp. 99–113.

Dwyer, F. R., Schurr, P. H., and Oh, S. (1987), 'Developing Buyer–Seller Relationships', *Journal of Marketing*, **51**, Apr., pp. 11–27.

Fern, E. R., and Brown, J. R. (1984), 'The Industrial Consumer Marketing Dichotomy: A Case of Insufficient Justification', *Journal of Marketing*, **48**, Spring, pp. 68–76.

Ford, D. (1981), 'The Development of Buyer–Seller Relationships in Industrial Markets', *European Journal of Marketing*, **14**, pp. 339–53.

Gronroos, C. (1994), 'From Marketing Mix to Relationship Marketing', *Management Decision*, **32**, 1, pp. 4–20.

Hakansson, H. (ed.) (1982), *International Marketing and Purchasing of Industrial Goods* (New York: IMP Group, John Wiley and Sons).

Hamel, G. (1991), 'Competition for Competence and Inter-Partner Learning Within Strategic Alliances', *Strategic Management Journal*, **12**, Jan.–Feb., pp. 83–103.

Jackson, B. B. (1985), 'Build Customer Relationships That Last', *Harvard Business Review*, Nov.–Dec., pp. 120–8.

Liljander, V., and Strandvik, T. (1995), 'The Nature of Customer Relationships in Services', in T. A. Swartz, D. E. Bowen, and S. W. Brown (eds.), *Advances in Services Marketing and Management* (London: JAI Press).

Macneil, I. R. (1980), *The New Social Contract: An Inquiry into Modern Contractual Relations* (New Haven: Yale University Press).

Michaels, R. E., and Day, R. L. (1985), 'Measuring Customer Orientation of Salespeople: A Replication with Industrial Buyers', *Journal of Marketing Research*, **22**, Nov., pp. 443–6.

Morgan, R. M., and Hunt, S. D. (1994), 'The Commitment-Trust Theory of Relationship Marketing', *Journal of Marketing*, **58**, July, pp. 20–38.

Narver, J., and Slater, S. (1990), 'The Effect of Market Orientation on Business Profitability', *Journal of Marketing*, **54**, 4, Oct., pp. 20–35.

—— and —— (1994), 'Marketing Orientation, Customer Value and Superior Performance', *Business Horizons*, **37**, 2, pp. 22–9.

Ohame, K. (1989), 'The Global Logic of Strategic Alliances', *Harvard Business Review*, **67**, 2, pp. 143–54.

Pruitt, D. G. (1981), *Negotiation Behavior* (New York: Academic Press).

Quinn, J. B. (1992), *Intelligent Enterprise* (New York: The Free Press).

Reichheld, F. F. (1993), 'Loyalty Based Management', *Harvard Business Review*, **71**, 2, pp. 64–73.

—— and Sasser, W. E. (1990), 'Zero Defections', *Harvard Business Review*, **68**, 5, pp. 105–11.

Rotter, J. B. (1967), 'A New Scale for Measurement of Interpersonal Trust', *Journal of Personality*, **35**, 4, pp. 651–65.

Rust, R. T., and Zahorik, A. J. (1993), 'Customer Satisfaction, Customer Retention and Market Share', *Journal of Retailing,* **69**, pp. 193–215.

Saxe, R., and Weitz, B. A. (1982), 'The SOCO Scale: A Measure of the Customer Orientation of Salespeople', *Journal of Marketing Research*, **19**, Aug., pp. 343–51.

Schurr, P. H., and Ozanne, J. L. (1985), 'Influence on Exchange Processes: Buyer's Perceptions of a Seller's Trustworthiness and Bargaining Toughness', *Journal of Consumer Research*, **11**, pp. 939–53.

Shemwell, D., Cronin, J., and Bullard, W. (1994), 'Relationship Exchanges in Services: An Empirical Investigation of Ongoing Customer Service-Provider Relationships', *International Journal of Service Industry Management*, **5**, 3, pp. 57–68.

Sheth, J. N., and Parvatiyar, A. (1995), 'Relationship Marketing in Consumer Markets: Antecedents and Consequences', *Journal of the Academy of Marketing Science*, **23,** 4, pp. 255–71.

Swan, J. E., and Nolan, J. J. (1985), 'Gaining Customer Trust: A Conceptual Guide for the Salesperson,' *Journal of Personal Selling & Sales Management*, **5**, 2, pp. 39–48.

Treacy, M., and Wiersema, F. (1993), 'Customer Intimacy and Other Value Disciplines', *Harvard Business Review*, **71**, 1, pp. 84–93.

Tynan, C. (1997), 'A Review of the Marriage Analogy in Relationship Marketing', *Journal of Marketing Management*, **13**, 7, pp. 695–704.

Walsh, K. (1991), *Competitive Tendering for Local Authority Services—Initial Experiences*, Department of the Environment (London: HMSO).

Webster, F. E. (1992), The Changing Role of Marketing in the Corporation', *Journal of Marketing*, **56**, Oct., pp. 1–17.

Williamson, O. (1975*), Markets and Hierarchies: Analysis and Antitrust Implications* (New York: The Free Press).

Suggested further reading

For an introduction to the general principles of relationship marketing and its current status within marketing planning, the following are useful:

- Arias, J. T. G. (1998), 'A Relationship Marketing Approach to Guanxi', *European Journal of Marketing*, **32**, 1–2, pp. 145–55.

- Bagozzi, R. P. (1995), 'Reflections on Relationship Marketing in Consumer Markets', *Journal of the Academy of Marketing Science*, **23**, 4, pp. 272–7.

- Buttle, F. (ed.) (1996), *Relationship Marketing: Theory and Practice* (London: Paul Chapman).

- Copulsky, J. R., and Wolf, M. J. (1990), 'Relationship Marketing: Positioning for the Future', *Journal of Business Strategy*, July–Aug., pp. 16–20.

- Dick, A. S., and Basu, K. (1994), 'Customer Loyalty: Toward an Integrated Conceptual Framework', *Journal of the Academy of Marketing Science*, **22**, 2, pp. 99–113.

- Ford, D. (1981), 'The Development of Buyer–Seller Relationships in Industrial Markets', *European Journal of Marketing*, **14**, pp. 339–53.

- —— Gadde, L.-E., Hakansson, H., and Lundgren, A. (1998), *Managing Business Relationships* (New York: John Wiley and Sons).

- Gummesson, E. (1993), 'Relationship Marketing—A New Way of Doing Business', *European Business Report*, **3Q**, Autumn, pp. 52–6.

- —— (1999), *Total Relationship Marketing* (London: Butterworth-Heinemann).

- Payne, A., Christopher, M., Peck, H., and Clark, M. (1999), *Relationship Marketing, Strategy and Implementation* (Oxford: Butterworth-Heinemann).

- Peppers, D., and Rogers, M. (1993), *The One to One Future: Building Relationships One Customer at a Time* (New York: Doubleday).

- Reichheld, F. F. (1993), 'Loyalty Based Management', *Harvard Business Review*, **71**, 2, pp. 64–73.

For a more thorough understanding of the theoretical underpinnings of buyer–seller relationships, the following are frequently cited:

- Duncan, T., and Moriarty, S. E. (1998), 'A Communication-based Marketing Model for Managing Relationships', *Journal of Marketing*, **62**, 2, pp. 1–14.

- Heide, J. B. (1994), 'Interorganizational Governance in Marketing Channels', *Journal of Marketing*, **58**, pp. 71–85.

- John, G. (1984), 'An Empirical Investigation of Some Antecedents of Opportunism in a Marketing Channel', *Journal of Marketing Research*, **21**, Aug., pp. 278–89.

- Liljander, V., and Strandvik, T. (1995), 'The Nature of Customer Relationships in Services' in T. A. Swartz, D. E. Bowen, and S. W. Brown, (eds.), *Advances in Services Marketing and Management*, **4** (London: JAI Press).

- Morgan, R. M., and Hunt, S. D. (1994), 'The Commitment-Trust Theory of Relationship Marketing', *Journal of Marketing*, **58**, July, pp. 20–38.

- Sheth, J. N., and Parvatiyar, A. (1995), 'Relationship Marketing in Consumer Markets: Antecedents and Consequences', *Journal of the Academy of Marketing Science*, **23**, 4, pp. 255–71.

For a more sceptical view of relationship marketing and its limitations, the following are useful:

- Barnes, J. G. (1994), 'Close to the Customer: But is it Really a Relationship?', *Journal of Marketing Management*, **10**, 7, pp. 561–70.

- O'Brien, L., and Jones, C. (1995), 'Do Rewards Really Create Loyalty?', *Harvard Business Review*, May–June, pp. 75–82.

Useful web link

Association for the Advancement of Relationship Marketing (a US non-profit organization): fttp://www.aarm.org

Part III

Developing the Marketing Mix

Chapter 9
The Product

Chapter objectives

The product is at the heart of a company's marketing activity. Customers buy a firm's products in order to satisfy their needs as cost-effectively as possible. This chapter begins by discussing the nature of the product offer. Products comprise complex bundles of attributes which must be translated into benefits for customers. Companies typically offer a range of products, each of which can be expected to go through some form of life cycle. Product mix planning is discussed in the context of the product life cycle.

What do we mean by a product?

PRODUCTS are the focal point by which companies seek to satisfy customers' needs. The term 'product' can mean many things to many people. Most people, when they consider marketing and the marketing of products, tend to think of fast-moving consumer goods (FMCGs) such as soap powder or chocolate bars. In fact, the term 'product' can mean many things. In this chapter, a 'product' is any tangible or intangible item that satisfies a need. In other words a product can be:

- a material good;
- an intangible service;
- a combination of the above;
- a location;
- a person;
- an idea.

It must be remembered that people do not buy products as an end in themselves. Products are only bought for the benefits which they provide. In other words a product is only of value to someone as long as it is perceived as satisfying some need.

It is useful to begin this chapter by identifying the wide range of products that exist. Although a truly marketing-oriented company will focus on customers, it is important to understand how product characteristics affect marketing the company's efforts. Within the different categories of products that are described below, some broad similarities in marketing requirements can be identified. Fig. 9.1 attempts to classify products according to two important dimensions:

1. the level of involvement required on the part of the purchaser (e.g. the purchase of sugar calls for only very low levels of emotional involvement by the buyer, whereas this may be very high in the case of fashion clothing);
2. the level of availability that is typically required by purchasers (e.g. a buyer will expect a can of soft drink to be available immediately and without having to travel to it, whereas the buyer would be prepared to travel further, and possibly wait, to buy garden furniture).

These are just two dimensions that contribute towards the design of an appropriate marketing mix. Others could include buyers' price sensitivity, brand loyalty, frequency of purchase, etc. The idea of placing products somewhere on a position map is introduced at this stage to emphasize the reason for categorizing products in the first place—that is, to explore whether marketers of one product can learn from the marketing of another product which may at first appear to be quite different, but is really quite similar in terms of marketing needs.

Material goods

Material goods can be classified under two major headings: consumer goods and industrial goods (the latter are often referred to as business-to-business goods).

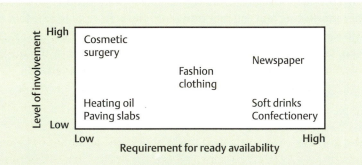

Figure 9.1 A hypothetical classification of product categories based on buyers' level of involvement and desired level of access to the product

Consumer goods

Consumer goods are those that are purchased to satisfy individual or household needs and can be classified into the following: convenience, shopping, speciality, and unsought.

- **Convenience goods**: Convenience goods are those items that tend to be relatively cheap and are purchased on a regular basis such as tea, coffee, toothpaste etc. They are often referred to as fast-moving consumer goods (FMCGs). The purchase of this type of product is likely to involve very little decision-making effort on the part of the buyer and in many cases an individual will tend to purchase a particular brand of item on a regular basis.

    Within the broad category of convenience goods, products as diverse as ice-cream and toothpaste may at first appear to have very little in common, but in fact the marketing of them can be quite similar. Convenience goods are generally sold through many retail outlets so that buyers have easy access to the product. There is therefore a tendency to spend large amounts on advertising and on sales promotions aimed at the buyer rather than at the retailer. The packaging aspect of the marketing mix is also likely to be important with the package acting as a promotional tool in its own right. These items tend to be cheaply priced with the aim of selling high volumes at low margins.

- **Shopping goods**: Consumers generally put a lot more effort into choosing 'shopping' goods. Such goods involve making decisions about price, credit facilities, guarantees, after-sales service, etc. Examples of these would be fridges and freezers (these are examples of what is known as 'white goods') stereos, cameras, etc.

    Such products are distributed through fewer retail outlets and therefore there is likely to be a higher margin for the retailer. Customers are usually more willing to travel to an outlet to find a good, rather than expecting it to be available on their doorstep. Large amounts of money may be spent on advertising these goods and developing strong brands, and the amount of effort put into personal selling tends to be greater than for fast moving consumer goods.

- **Speciality goods**: For these products, consumers may spend a great deal of effort in the decision-making process. Speciality goods have one or more unique characteristics and are sold in relatively few outlets. A quality image is usually communicated as a result. Designer clothing would be an example of a speciality good. These goods are bought infrequently, and tend to be expensive. Buyers may go to considerable effort in finding the product of their choice.

- **Unsought goods**: Some goods may initially be considered not to be needed by an individual but are nevertheless sold aggressively on the market. For many people, double glazing may be viewed as an unsought good which they will only buy if it is sold to them aggressively.

Industrial goods

Industrial, more commonly referred to today as 'business-to-business', goods are those which are purchased for use in a firm's production processes or to make other goods. Industrial goods are often bought by a large decision-making unit, in which organizational as well as individuals' objectives needs have to be satisfied (see Chapter 7).

Industrial goods can be divided into the following types: raw materials, major equipment, accessory equipment, component parts, and consumable supplies.

- **Raw materials**: Raw materials are those basic materials that are needed to produce the physical item, e.g. iron ore, chemicals, etc. They are often purchased in bulk and sold as a commodity with little attempt at product differentiation which justifies a price premium.

- **Major equipment**: This category includes large machines and tools used in production processes. They tend to be expensive and are expected to last a number of years. The decision to purchase this type of equipment tends to be made at a very high level in an organization and the purchase process can take a good deal of time and involve a number of people. There is a need for the building of important relationships between buyers and sellers in this process as it is likely to involve not only the agreement to purchase the equipment but also agreement on financing, maintenance contracts, guarantees, future purchases, etc.

- **Accessory equipment**: Accessory equipment involves those goods which are used in the production process or allied activities but are separate from the final 'product' itself. Examples of accessory equipment include computer software, tools, etc. These goods are generally cheaper than major equipment and the purchase process is less involved. They are generally considered as standardized items that can be purchased on a regular basis from a larger number of outlets.

- **Component parts**: Component parts are those items that, when put together, produce a finished good. Buyers purchase such items according to their own requirements for quality and delivery time so that they can ensure that their own end product can be produced effectively and efficiently. Just-in-time delivery of component parts is becoming an important element of the total product offer.

- **Consumable supplies**: Consumable supplies are those goods that help in the production process and do not become part of the product, for example lubricating oil is vital to many production processes but does not become incorporated into the product. These items are typically purchased routinely by organizations with very little search effort.

Intangible services

Services can be described as 'products', although some people still find it amusing that bank accounts, package holidays, and even pop stars can be described as products. Although the term product is traditionally associated with tangible goods, it can more correctly be defined as anything of value that a company offers to its customers. This value can take tangible or intangible forms.

There has been a big increase in recent years in service industries which do not offer physical goods for sale but offer intangible benefits to buyers. A car mechanic offers his/her expertise in maintaining vehicles, decorators or plumbers sell their service. It is essentially their skills in performing a service process that are being offered for sale, rather than a physical good. In most western economies, services now account for over three-quarters of Gross Domestic Product.

The marketing of services can be quite different from the marketing of goods, although in practice many products are a combination of a good and a service (e.g. a meal in a restaurant combines the tangible elements of the food with the intangible service which is provided). The distinguishing features of services, and their implications for marketing, are considered in more detail in Chapter 22. For now, it is worth noting a number of distinguishing features of products that are essentially service based.

- **Intangibility**: Services cannot be seen, tasted, or touched. This means that it is very difficult for a customer to know what is about to be purchased in advance. Although the feature of intangibility is important, the distinction between material goods and intangible services is not as clear cut as it would at first seem. There are in fact few material goods which have no intangible service aspects to them and there are likewise very few services which have no physical elements. Indeed it is likely to be a question of degree of intangibility which will help in the identification of whether a product is a service.

   An interesting distinction that can be made between material goods and services is that material goods tend to use intangible features such as pre-sales and after-sales service to help differentiate the product from the competing products. In contrast, service providers tend to use physical aspects such as decor, livery, etc., to differentiate themselves from competing services.

- **Inseparability**: The provision of a service normally requires the involvement of both customer and service provider simultaneously. Production and consumption cannot be separated in the way that manufacturing companies are able to mass produce their goods in a central factory and transport them to customers for consumption.

- **Variability**: As a result of inseparability, each service is unique and the standard of service delivery can vary from one occasion to the next. A consequence of this is that service quality is difficult to standardize and to guarantee. The best that can be achieved are minimum standards (e.g. answering the telephone after a stated number of rings) or standards that relate to the physical aspects of the service (such as the temperature of a fast food meal).

- **Perishability**: Services cannot be inventoried like material goods. If a service product is not sold at the time that it is produced (e.g. an empty airline seat after a plane has departed), then the service offer disappears for ever. This has important implications for service providers as they cannot store up services when demand is low in order to satisfy demand when it increases.

In much the same way as for goods, services can be further broken down into categories, such as consumer services, business-to-business services, and personal services. These are explored further in Chapter 22.

Locations and people

The term 'product' can also be used to denote places (e.g. holiday resorts) and people (e.g. footballers, rock stars). These involve both tangible and intangible elements and therefore the marketing mix should be configured accordingly.

The principles of product management have been extended to areas that would have been thought completely off limits only a few years earlier. A sign of the times occurred during the late 1990s when the Royal Family took on board many of the principles of product management, although nobody went as far as to describe its activities by that name.

In more general terms, the marketing of such people would seem to necessitate a consideration of what the 'product' actually is (the Queen, the Royal Family, or both) and to identify those aspects of the monarchy's role which the public find appealing. When the population sees the Queen on television, whether at Balmoral or on state occasions, it may not perceive the Royal Family as having great benefits to the population.

A major innovation was the establishment of the Way Ahead Group which is chaired by the Queen, and attended by senior Family members and advisers. The group's primary function has been to look at the official work of the Royal Family and to make sure it is properly targeted and in tune with the needs of the country.

Many of the initiatives of the Way Ahead Group would seem to be taken straight from a textbook on product management. The research organization MORI was commissioned to ascertain the Royal Family's public image. In response to the group's research findings, a number of innovations in the 'product' were developed. Negative feelings of aloofness came through in the group's research and were overcome by developing greater informality among the Royal Family, such as a visit in 1998 to a branch of McDonald's in Chester which was given the appearance of Her Majesty just dropping in for a bite to eat. In came a communication secretary in an attempt to develop a more coherent image in the eyes of the media. Dialogue with the Royal Family was facilitated by the establishment of the Royal web site which by 1998 was receiving about 2 million hits a week.

Commercial viability has entered the lexicon of the Royal Family, with initiatives such as the opening of Buckingham Palace to visitors and the creation of the Royal Collection Trust, to make the Queen's world famous art and antiques collection commercially available.

Can product management be taken to these limits? And is it right to treat the Royal Family as a product to be marketed? If the approach is accepted, how do you set appropriate goals and measure the success or otherwise of such product management?

Ideas

Ideas can also be considered as 'products'. Political parties have developed marketing strategies to promote their own particular policies to the electorate as have groups who are attempting to market particular issues such as the environment, equal opportunities, etc.

The key feature of these types of product is that they are intangible and have many similar characteristics to services.

To sum up, the term 'product' can mean more than merely a physical item that is purchased to satisfy an individual's particular want at a given time. Many items can be classified as a 'product' in its broader sense and this chapter will use the word as a generic term for any overall offering that is made available to the customer.

Analysis of the product offer

PRODUCTS can be complex entities and it is useful to identify a number of levels of the product offer. Three levels will be identified here (see Fig. 9.2):

- the core level;
- the secondary level;
- the augmented level.

The core level

Every product exists to satisfy a need and therefore an individual is searching for a product that at the very least will have satisfaction of this basic need as its core benefit. The best way to think of this is to consider an item and identify the key benefit from its ownership. For example, the core benefit of owning a car to most people is transport and the core benefit of undertaking a marketing course is personal development.

Every product has a core element and it is the secondary and augmented elements that put 'flesh on the bones' and give a product an individual identity.

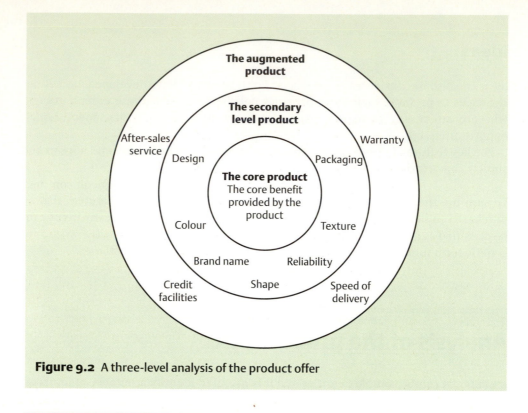

Figure 9.2 A three-level analysis of the product offer

The secondary level

The secondary level of a product includes those physical features that the product actually possesses. Such secondary elements include colour, design, shape, packaging, size, etc. A television, for example, may have entertainment as a core benefit but the secondary elements would include such features as the shape of the box, the type of screen, the size of screen, the quality of sound, the colour of the unit, whether there is a stand, etc.

The augmented level

It is this that differentiates a particular product from its competitors. The augmented level of a product tends to include intangible features such as pre-sales and after-sales service, guarantees, credit facilities, brand name, etc.

The three-level analysis may be appropriate to tangible goods, but has less value in the analysis of intangible services. For services, the augmented level may be the key distinguishing feature of the service. It is more appropriate therefore to talk about two levels of the product offer, with a core level representing the core benefit and a secondary level representing the distinguishing characteristics of the service.

Quality

QUALITY is an important feature of a product and buyers make choices between competing products on the basis of the ratio of quality to price. Most people would accept that a Sony CD player is of higher quality than one made by Amstrad and would be prepared to pay a higher price for it. Many people will nevertheless be quite happy with the quality of the Amstrad machine, preferring its lower price.

But what do we mean by product quality? Quality is an extremely difficult concept to define in a few words. At its most basic, quality has been defined as 'conforming to requirements' (Crosby 1984). This implies that organizations must establish requirements and specifications; once established, the quality goal of the various functions of an organization is to comply strictly with these specifications. However, the questions remain: whose requirements and whose specifications? A second series of definitions therefore state that quality is all about fitness for use (Juran 1982), a definition based primarily on satisfying customers' needs. These two definitions can be brought together in the concept of customer perceived quality—quality can only be defined by customers and occurs where an organization supplies goods or services to a specification that satisfies their needs.

The problem remains of identifying precisely what consumers' needs are. A company may think that it has the best quality product based on its own criteria, but customers may have completely different criteria for judging quality. Sometimes there are benchmarks for measuring quality which can be readily agreed upon, for example a 22 carat gold ring is better quality than one which is only 15 carats. In the case of intangible services, it can be much more difficult to agree the criteria for assessing quality, because few tangible manifestations exist. This has led to many people drawing a distinction between technical and functional dimensions of quality.

Technical quality refers to the relatively quantifiable aspects of a product which can easily be measured by both customer and supplier. Examples of technical quality include the waiting time at a supermarket checkout and the reliability of a new car. However, consumers are also influenced by *how* the technical quality is delivered to them. This is what Gronroos (1984) has described as functional quality and cannot be measured as objectively as the elements of technical quality. In the case of the queue at a supermarket checkout, functional quality is influenced by such factors as the environment in which queuing takes place and consumers' perceptions of the manner in which queues are handled by the supermarket's staff.

A lot of research has gone into trying to understand the processes by which buyers form expectations about the quality of a product (e.g. Zeithamal, Berry, and Parasuraman 1993). It is widely accepted that a product could be deemed to be of poor quality simply because it did not meet the buyer's expectations. A company's promotional material may have built up unsustainable expectations, resulting in perceptions of poor quality, even though an objective outside observer may have considered technical quality to be high.

To try to provide reassurance to buyers, many companies incorporate some sort of guarantee of quality into their product offer. These can take a number of forms, including:

■ Specifying the standards in the product descriptions (e.g. bread made without pre-servatives; light bulbs tested for a life of 10,000 hours; clothing manufactured to be water-resistant).

■ Often, product quality statements are backed up by specific guarantees of perform-ance (e.g. the paintwork on a new car may be guaranteed to remain intact for six years).

■ Customer charters are becoming increasingly important as a means of stating the standards of service that a customer can expect (train operating companies have customer charters which, among other things, can provide compensation for late-running trains).

■ A company can state that its product standards are in accordance with a widely recognized general standard. Many firms proudly claim that they have been accredited with British Standard 5750 (or its international equivalent ISO 9002). Contrary to popular belief, a company operating to ISO 9002 does not guarantee a high level of quality output. Instead, the ISO accreditation is granted to organiza-tions who can show that they have in place management systems for ensuring a consistent standard of quality—whether this itself is high or low is largely a sub-jective judgement.

Packaging

IT was noted earlier in this chapter that packaging is an important tangible element of any product. At its basic level, the packaging of a physical product performs three major functions: handling, transport, and storage.

Packaging is needed to ensure that a product is delivered to customers in a sound condition. The packaging should enable both distributors and the end user to handle and transport the product from one place to another. In addition, packaging should also allow the product to be stored and therefore the shape should be conducive to stocking on shelves and, where appropriate, in the home, office, or business. In addition to these functions, packaging should allow for the protection of the product from deteriorating (in the case of perishable foods) and from breakage.

Where goods are sold to customers using self-service methods, packaging can per-form an important information and promotional role. The package can inform the customer of what is inside and indeed can communicate a large amount of infor-mation directly. In addition, the package can communicate the brand name, both directly through name association, and indirectly by associating the brand with a

The British have a long tradition of buying fresh bottles of milk delivered daily to the front door. Powdered milk had been around for a long time and, despite being nutritious, was looked down upon by most people. Yet a market existed for dried milk as a 'reserve supply' of milk for those times when fresh milk was temporarily not available. But the product still had an image problem, not helped by many people's wartime memories of rations of dried milk being provided in tins and boxes. One solution identified by St Ivel was to put its dried milk in familiar shaped milk bottles. It could then sit in the fridge next to the fresh milk. The image of the product improved and sales soared.

distinctive type of packaging (for example, most people would recognize a bar of Toblerone chocolate by the shape of its packaging alone).

The results of redesigning packaging without changing the contents can sometimes be quite dramatic. For example, since its relaunch in 1989, Felix tripled its share of the cat food market and established itself as the number two brand. This dramatic increase in fortune was initiated by a redesign of the packaging.

The product life cycle

THERE is a general acceptance that most products go through a number of stages in their existence, just as humans and most living organisms go through a number of life cycle stages. When a new product comes on to the market, there is likely to be a good deal of promotional effort on the part of the firm making the product to secure sales. It is likely that the firm has incurred high costs in the development of such a product which in the early stages may not be covered by revenue. Potential customers for a new product may very well be few and far between and therefore sales in the early stages may be quite slow. This stage is known as the *introduction stage*.

If the new product becomes a success, more people may start to show an interest and start purchasing it. As more people buy, the firm will discover a number of cost savings in producing larger quantities. Raw materials can be purchased in bulk and therefore at a cheaper cost per unit. Machinery can start to be used to a greater capacity and individual employees will become far more efficient at producing larger quantities. Any initial teething problems with the product start to be ironed out and more people will purchase the product on the basis of word of mouth rather than merely the firm's formal promotion campaign. All of these savings on the part of the firm are known as economies of scale. Falling costs and rising revenues improve profitability in what is usually referred to as the *growth stage*.

As sales of the product increase, other competitors are likely to be attracted to the

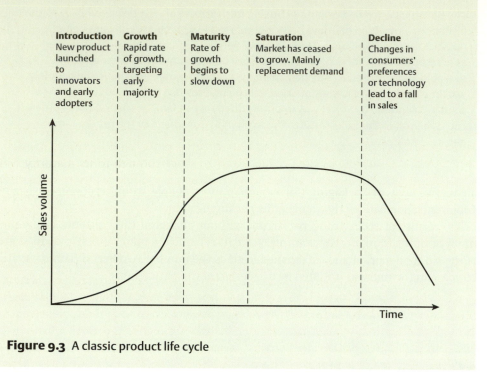

Introduction	Growth	Maturity	Saturation	Decline
New product launched to innovators and early adopters	Rapid rate of growth, targeting early majority	Rate of growth begins to slow down	Market has ceased to grow. Mainly replacement demand	Changes in consumers' preferences or technology lead to a fall in sales

Figure 9.3 A classic product life cycle

market and as a result may start to compete on price. Promotion on the part of all competitors tends to increase and yet the number of customers for the product has ceased to grow. Over a period of time, the increase in sales starts to slow down and this is known as the *maturity stage*.

As time goes on, sales start to stabilize—*the saturation stage*—and eventually, sales of the product start to fall. This is the *decline stage*. Fig. 9.3 displays this classical product life cycle. There is a certain degree of logic and common sense to this view of a product life cycle. Indeed, this fits well with the explanation put forward of how new products are adopted (Rogers 1962). Different types of customer are identified according to the speed at which a new product is adopted.

When a new product is introduced on to the market, only a small number of people will be interested in purchasing it as it is an untested item and usually quite expensive. Such people are categorized as *innovators* and tend to buy new products because they like to be seen as owning something new and generally untried. People in this category are likely to have been among the first to buy mobile phones, digital cameras, and wide-screen television when they were launched. Despite the existence of innovators, new product launches may nevertheless be unsuccessful, as witnessed by the launch of the BSB 'squarial' or the Sinclair C5 vehicle.

As the successful product starts to move to the growth stage, more people show an interest in it. The price of the product by this time has started to fall, and as innovators inform other people of benefits, more people purchase it. The next wave of people to buy the product are known as *early adopters*. A key characteristic of early adopters is that they can be very influential in the groups with whom they interact, so they can be considered as opinion leaders. These individuals are generally looked on as experts in a particular field among the group and therefore if they feel generally happy with the purchase of this relatively new product, they are likely to influence others to purchase it as well. This next group of customers are known as the *early majority* and the product is now firmly in the growth stage of its life cycle.

As the competition starts entering the market and prices fall even more quickly, the next group of people start to consider purchase and these people are known as the *late majority*. It is at this point that the number of potential new customers for a product starts to decline as the product starts to move through to its maturity and saturation stages. Products are sold at very low prices as companies try to sell excess stock and start to try to place a new model or new product on to the market. There is a relatively small group of people who tend to purchase products at the end of their life cycles and such people are known as *laggards* This pattern of product adoption is illustrated in Fig. 9.4.

The concept of the life cycle is useful in that any marketing activity applied to a product can be closely related to the stage in the life cycle that the product has reached. Promotional planning, for example, can be closely related to the life cycle. Emphasis will typically be placed in the introductory phase on creating awareness through public relations activity, building on this through the growth phase with advertising. The use of sales promotion activity will typically be used as the market reaches maturity and becomes more competitive, and, finally, all promotional activity may be dropped in the decline stage as the product is allowed to die naturally. Similarly, other aspects of the marketing mix can be altered to fit the various life cycle stages. For example, a high price may be achievable in the introductory stage, eventually falling as the competition gets stronger and costs fall. Similarly, different distribution policies can be applied to the different stages.

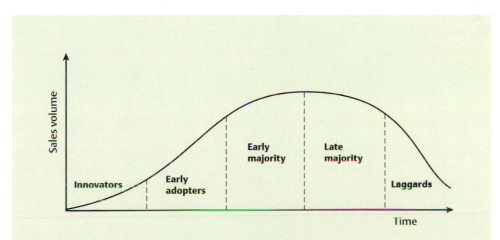

Figure 9.4 Patterns of adoption for a new product (based on Rogers 1962)

Is there one particular pattern of product life cycle that is applicable to all products? In fact, different products move through the stages at different speeds and not all products follow the 'classic' shaped cycle. Some products have an introduction stage and fail to go any further. Some products reach the growth stage and then for some reason sales fall very rapidly after this point. Other products go through the introduction, growth, and maturity stages but stay at this stage seemingly for an indefinite period. In reality, a number of different types of life cycle can exist and some of these can be seen in Fig. 9.5.

In the first example, the product has a high level of sales at an early stage but, from then on, there seems to be no change in sales either positively or negatively. In the second example, there is a constant increase in sales volume in each subsequent time period. The third example displays the complete opposite. In this example, each subsequent period of time brings with it a fall in sales volume after sales initially being strong. This could be a result of the entry of strong and powerful competition. The fourth life cycle displays the situation where a firm actually influences the degree to which a product follows the life cycle. In this situation, the product has been saved from decline either through intense sales promotion activity or possibly through some form of product modification. Alternatively, external factors such as a change in customer tastes, etc., may have led to the improvement in sales. Whatever the cause, the product here displays further growth before moving once again through to a decline phase although sales are still higher now than they were at the original

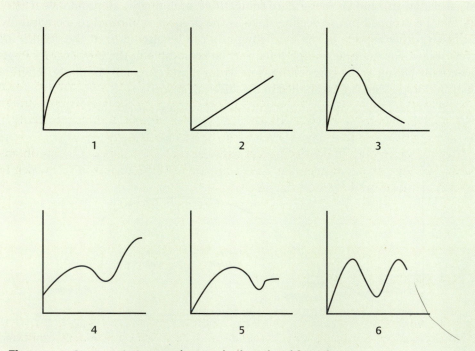

Figure 9.5 Some variations to the standard product life cycle

decline phase. The fifth example once again shows that the product has been saved from decline but, in this case, the new cycle is at a lower stage than existed at first. The final example displays a typical life cycle pattern for a fashion item where there is a steep drop in sales once the product is considered unfashionable, but it may subsequently become popular again.

The product life cycle concept can play a useful role in a firm's management of its overall portfolio of products. However, it is important to be aware that there have been some criticisms of the concept and its application.

In reality, life cycles may be difficult to apply for short-term forecasting purposes or developing short-term marketing operational decisions and they are therefore more useful in strategic planning and control decisions. Even so, as can be seen in Fig. 9.5, there are so many life cycle shapes that it is extremely difficult to make accurate predictions on how the product is performing at any given time. Another problem in applying the concept is that it is difficult for marketers to identify where a product currently lies on a life cycle. For example, if sales are stabilizing, it is difficult to ascertain whether the product has reached its peak in terms of growth and is about to decline or whether there is just a temporary stabilization due to external influences and that, if left alone, sales may very well start to increase once again in the near future. Indeed, the shape of the life cycle can very well be influenced by the actions of the marketer and as a result there could be a self-fulfilling prophesy. For example, if there is a belief that the product is about to reach the decline phase, marketers may consciously reduce the marketing effort in response to this belief. As a result of this action, sales may fall and the product indeed moves into the decline phase!

Another observation is that the shape and duration of a life cycle is dependent upon whether it is the product class, product form, or a specific brand that is being considered. For example, the life cycle of men's trousers is quite flat, taken over a long period of time, compared to specific types of trousers (e.g. jeans, chinos) which come and go out of fashion. Within each type of trouser, brand names will go through a life cycle of popularity (e.g. Levis rose in the 1980s but suffered a loss of popularity in the late 1990s). These differing life cycles are illustrated in Fig. 9.6.

Finally, the product life cycle concept assumes that all products that are in any particular stage experience similar risks and enjoy similar opportunities which in practical terms is unlikely to be the case.

The product mix

THE product mix comprises the complete range of products that a company offers to the market. Product life cycle theory reminds us that a product's profit and sales performance are likely to change over a period of time, and therefore there is a need for a proactive approach to product mix management by the firm. Knowing that

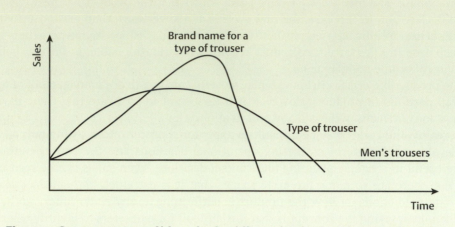

Figure 9.6 A comparison of life cycles for different levels of product specification

a product will at some time be expected to go into decline should be a spur to the development of new products to replace those going into decline. It would therefore seem sensible for companies to keep a variety of products within their portfolio which are at different stages of their life cycle.

A number of elements of a typical product portfolio can be identified and the following terms are commonly used (see Fig. 9.7):

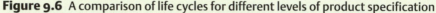

Product item

This is the individual product, with its core, secondary, and augmented elements (e.g. a 1 litre bottle of non-biological washing powder).

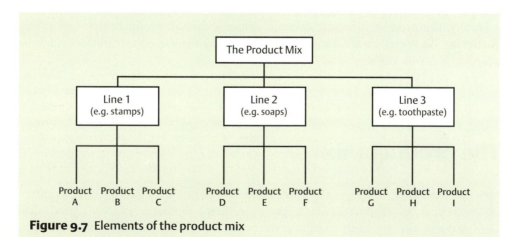

Figure 9.7 Elements of the product mix

Product line

This is a collection of product items which are related by way of type of raw materials used, similar technology used, or merely as a common-sense grouping (e.g. soap powder).

A truly effective product line should be customer focused and therefore should link to the range of needs of the particular segment/s targeted by the firm (e.g. the need for skin maintenance).

Product mix

This is the total range of products that the company has on offer to customers and within this product mix there is what is known as the *depth* of the product mix and the *width* of the product mix.

The depth of the product mix refers to the number of products offered within a product line. The more products within a line, the greater the depth of the product mix. For example, the electrical retailer Dixon's could have many different types of computer within its line of computers.

The width of the product mix refers to the number of product lines a company has and, the more lines, the greater the product mix width. Dixon's, for example, would have other lines as well as computers, including televisions, audio equipment, cameras, etc.

Chapter summary and key linkages to other chapters

Products are the means by which a company satisfies its customers' needs. However, it must be remembered that customers seek the benefits of the product rather than the product itself. Despite this, products can be grouped according to the similarity of their marketing requirements and a number of bases for classifying products have been suggested. Services can be described as products, but the characteristics of 'pure' services can be quite distinct from those of 'pure' goods. For all products, quality is an important defining characteristic. Most products go through some form of life cycle which affects the way they are marketed. Because most products eventually go into decline, it is important that a portfolio of established and new products is maintained. The theme of new product development is taken up in the following chapter.

The following key linkages to other chapters should be noted:

Chapter 1: What is marketing?: Marketing is about satisfying customers' needs profitably and products are the means by which those needs are satisfied.

Chapter 2: The marketing environment: A sound analysis of the marketing environment should identify changes in consumers' preferences which trigger the development of new products. The marketing environment may also indicate developments in technology which allow new products to be created.

Chapter 3: Market segmentation: Products are increasingly being adapted to satisfy the specific needs of small market segments.

Chapter 4: Branding: A brand is often an essential attribute of a product. Often, buyers may have difficulty understanding or evaluating competing products, and make their judgement primarily on the basis of the brand.

Chapter 5: Marketing and ethics: What does a company do when the competitive nature of its environment calls for it to make a product in an unethical way, or to offer for sale a product which is considered socially unacceptable?

Chapter 6: Marketing research: Many would consider market research to be crucial to determining the product mix, although products often emerge as a result of laboratory discoveries.

Chapter 7: Buyer behaviour: What are the principal features of a product on which buyers base their evaluation? How can a product be designed to allow more favourable evaluation by potential buyers?

Chapter 8: Buyer–seller relationship development: Where a class of product purchase is regarded as risky, a strong relationship with a seller may help to reduce the perceptions of risk.

Chapter 10: New product development: The next chapter carries on where this chapter left off by discussing ways in which new products are brought into a company's portfolio.

Chapter 11: Developing a sustainable competitive advantage: No amount of promotion can sell poor products. A company must continually ensure that the products it offers are in accordance with buyers' changing preferences. A company cannot sustain its profitability on the basis of one short-life fashionable product, so it must invest in new product development.

Chapters 12/13: Pricing theory and application: Price should reflect the value that customers put on a product. Most markets can be segmented into premium price/ quality segments and other segments where low price is expected, even at the sacrifice of product quality.

Chapter 14: Intermediaries: Intermediaries can be a crucial link in allowing buyers easy access to a company's products. How can intermediaries be motivated to handle a company's products? Can intermediaries be valuable sources of ideas for new product development?

Chapters 16–20: Principles of promotion planning/advertising/sales promotion/ personal selling/direct marketing: Promotional messages must be consistent with a product's capabilities. Advertising that over-promises product performance may simply result in perceptions of failed quality.

Chapter 21: Managing the marketing effort: Managing a product portfolio is a crucial management task that demands a timely source of information about product performance, market trends, etc.

Chapter 22: Services marketing: Many have argued that goods marketing is quite different from the marketing of services. The nature of these differences is discussed in further detail.

Chapter 23: Global marketing: How should products be adapted when a company seeks to enter overseas markets?

Case study

Ford tries to focus on more exciting cars

Ford has survived the pressures of the increasingly competitive car market and expanded its market share in a number of key markets. At times the company has been accused of selling boring cars with a tired image. On other occasions (as with the launch of the Sierra), it has been accused of replacing tried and tested products with designs that alienate the car buying public. By 1998, Ford found the European car market to be extremely competitive and its product range wasn't helping its profitability.

Despite the fact that the 1998 Ford range of cars were the best-sellers in the UK and major performers in mainland Europe, results showed that Ford lost $273 million (£165 million) in Europe in the third quarter of 1998, almost double the $147 million (£90 million) lost in the third quarter of 1996. Europe could not be carried along on the profits of the company's profitable North American operations. In the year to September 1998, Ford held an 18.2 per cent share of the UK car market, with sales of 335,327 cars (according to the Society of Motor Manufacturers and Traders). That was down slightly from 18.31 per cent for the same period the previous year. More worryingly, profit margins had been falling and critics were accusing the company of lowering prices to tempt people to buy cars which didn't really sparkle. The launch of the Ford Focus was seen as a response to the apparent problems of the company's dull product range.

The Focus in its various formats was the successor to the Ford Escort which was the UK's biggest seller and a strong performer across Europe. The aim was to reinforce Ford's presence in the medium-light car sector which is the largest, most important, and the most competitive part of the European car market. Although the Escort was still to be on sale until the year 2000, the Focus was to become the core of the future Ford range.

The Focus was the first product resulting from the company's four-year reorganization plan, code-named 'Ford 2000'. Announced in 1995, the plan aimed to change Ford from a company organized geographically to one with a more efficient, global structure. It aimed to cut costs on new cars by developing models that used common parts and which could be sold in many of Ford's markets around the world. By taking this approach, the company claimed to have been able to cut $1,000 (£625) from the production costs of each car, increasing its profit margins.

There was a view that Ford's models in the recent past had not had the positive image that they once had and the Focus was an attempt to improve this. It was believed that one reason for Ford's difficulties in Europe was the amount of money it had spent on modifying recent variants of the Escort. Although it was first launched in 1968, by 1990, a fourth generation version was introduced and was criticized heavily for a variety of problems which included sloppy handling and noisy engines. As a result, Ford had to invest so much money improving the situation, marketing the model, and cutting prices to sell it, that it had become unprofitable. This time, Ford wanted to make sure that it got the Focus right and spent about $100 million (£60.6 million) on marketing and development costs.

The Focus aimed to stretch the boundaries of the medium-light car sector and attract a new group of buyers who would be different from Escort buyers. However, it was likely to be difficult to expand this sector too much without cannibalizing sales of the company's larger Mondeo model.

On its initial launch, the Focus received a positive response from motoring correspondents although there were a few difficulties. For example, it had a radical and unique design which could have deterred some car buyers in the medium car sector. Secondly, it entered the dealers' showrooms seven months after a new Vauxhall Astra and five months after a new Volkswagen Golf. This could have been a disadvantage although the Focus could have benefited from being the most recent entrant to the market.

The expectation within the industry was that the Focus would succeed in repairing previous damage. By cutting development and production costs, Ford had increased the likelihood of the car's profitability.

Adapted from *Marketing Week*, 22 October 1998.

Case study review questions

1 What do you consider to be the core, secondary, and augmented levels of the Ford Focus product offer?

2 Using the product life cycle approach, why do you think the development of the Focus was necessary?

3 In the light of subsequent performance, to what extent has Ford's strategy been successful?

Chapter review questions

1 Why is the term 'offering' sometimes used instead of the term 'product'?

2 Is there a case for considering different product strategies based on each of the following types of product: material goods, services, locations, people, and ideas?

3 To what extent is the product life cycle concept a useful tool for the product manager?

4 Why is it considered prudent for a firm to have a 'basket' of products?

5. To what extent is the application of portfolio analysis helpful to the marketing manager?

6. What role/s can packaging perform in the product strategy process?

References

Crosby, P. B. (1984), *Quality Without Tears* (New York: New American Library).

Gronroos, C. (1984), 'A Service Quality Model and its Marketing Implications', *European Journal of Marketing*, **18**, 4, pp. 36–43.

Juran, J. M. (1982), *Upper Management and Quality* (New York: Juran Institute).

Rogers, E. M. (1962), *Diffusion of Innovation* (New York: The Free Press).

Zeithamal, V., Berry, L. L., and Parasuraman, A. (1993), 'The Nature and Determinants of Customer Expectations of Sevice', *Journal of the Academy of Marketing Science*, **21**, 1, pp. 1–12.

Suggested further reading

Some practical applications of product life cycle theory are discussed in the following:

- Birou, L. M., Fawcett, S. E., and Magnan, G. M. (1998), 'The Product Life Cycle: A Tool for Functional Strategic Alignment', *International Journal of Purchasing and Materials Management*, **34**, 2, pp. 37–51.

- Grantham, L. M. (1997), 'The Validity of the Product Life Cycle in the High-tech Industry', *Marketing Intelligence & Planning*, **15**, 1, pp. 4–10.

- Niss, H. (1996), 'Country of Origin Marketing Over the Product Life Cycle: A Danish Case Study', *European Journal of Marketing*, **30**, 3, pp. 6–22.

- Prasad, B. (1997), 'Re-engineering Life-cycle Management of Products to Achieve Global Success in the Changing Marketplace', *Industrial Management & Data Systems*, **97**, 3–4, pp. 90–8.

The development of product portfolios is discussed in the following:

- John, D. R., Loken, B., and Joiner, C. (1998), 'The Negative Impact of Extensions: Can Flagship Products be Diluted?', *Journal of Marketing*, **62**, 1, pp. 19–33.

- Product Portfolio Development Workbook—1st Class Customer Service. The Learning Business (1996), Pergamon Open Learning (Oxford: Butterworth-Heinemann).

There is now an extensive literature on the topic of quality and the following references provide an introduction to key issues involved in the definition and management of product quality:

- Bolton, R., and Drew, J. (1991), 'A Multistage Model of Customers' Assessments of Service Quality and Value', *Journal of Consumer Research*, **17**, Mar., pp. 375–84.

- Buttle, F. (1996), 'SERVQUAL: Review, Critique, Research Agenda', *European Journal of Marketing*, **30**, 1, pp. 8–32.

- Dobb, F. (1999), *ISO 9000 Quality Registration Step by Step* (Oxford: Butterworth-Heinemann).

- Oakland, J. S. (1997), *TQM: A Pictorial Guide for Managers* (Oxford: Butterworth-Heinemann).

- Parasuraman, A., Zeithamal, V., and Berry, L. (1988), 'Servqual: A Multiple-Item Scale for Measuring Consumer Perceptions of Service Quality', *Journal of Retailing*, **64**, 1, pp. 12–40.

- Szmigin, I. T. D. (1993), 'Managing Quality in Business-to-Business Services', *European Journal of Marketing*, **27**, 1, pp. 5–21.

Useful web links

Department of Trade and Industry: Marketing—The Way Forward: Define your total product by what it does for the customer: http://www.dti.gov.uk/mbp/bpgt/m9ka00001/m9ka000014.html

A 'superlist' for a group of Total-Quality discussion sites: http://www.mailbase.ac.uk/lists/total-quality-all

A forum for the exchange of ideas and information by researchers and practitioners involved in the field of quality management and continuous improvement practices: http://www.mailbase.ac.uk/lists/quality-management

Chapter 10
Innovation and New Product Development

Chapter objectives

The previous chapter showed how products often go through a life cycle. This chapter explores the methods used by companies to keep their product ranges up to date. Innovation is an important differentiating factor for many firms and this chapter discusses methods by which innovative products can be developed, tested, and brought to market. When products approach the end of their life cycle, it is important that they are deleted in a rational and cost-effective manner.

What is innovation?

THE previous chapter discussed the concept of a product life cycle and noted that most products eventually go into decline. It is therefore important for a company to develop new products to replace those that have reached the end of their life. Marketing managers must recognize the need to develop new products in response to shortening life cycles, which in turn result from rapidly changing technology and competitive pressures.

The *Oxford English Dictionary* defines innovation as 'making changes'. For many managers, innovation means new or better products. Innovation has often been identified as a source of a company's long-term competitive advantage. Indeed, some nations as a whole can be described as more innovative than others, and there appears to be a link between a country's spending on research and development and its economic performance.

It should be remembered that innovation is not confined to a company's product offer, but applies to all marketing functions, such as distribution and promotion.

Innovation must be linked to a firm's objectives and of course must relate to what customers need.

Many new products are merely modifications of old ones which do not tend to take the market-place by storm. However, there is also a need to consider the possibilities of producing major new products in response to changing customer demands, external environmental forces, and internal strengths and weaknesses.

Gap analysis

GAP analysis looks at the difference between a firm's forecast profits over a given time and the profits it would like to make. This difference is known as the *planning gap* and it consists of a number of elements: usage gap, distribution gap, product gap, and competitive gap. New product development can help to overcome the planning gap.

Usage gap

This is the gap that exists between the total future market potential and the current actual usage in the market. The measurement of the total market potential really has to be a judgement based on market research and from other statistical and demographic data. Current usage information is the basis for the calculation of market shares. The difference therefore between the total potential market and the total current market is the usage gap.

Distribution gap

This gap is the difference between a firm's present distribution system and the potential for it to be increased. Increasing distribution outside the present network is not automatically a good thing, however. A possible key feature of a speciality product (expensive perfume, for example), is the limited number of sales outlets, and increasing the number of these could lower the perfume's prestige image. Ensuring maximum distribution within existing outlets would be the preferable option in this instance.

Product gap

This gap (sometimes known as the segment or positioning gap) represents those aspects of the market in which the firm has difficulty in trading due to the nature of its products. For example, a firm that produces specialist hi-fi equipment would have difficulty in selling such goods to a mass market due to the highly specialized specifications of the product and the high price at which it is sold.

Competitive gap

This is the difference between the effectiveness of an individual firm's marketing strategy and the effectiveness of its competitors' strategies in the same market. This difference is influenced by such factors as promotional strategy, pricing policy, distribution systems, etc.

The constituent elements of the planning gap are illustrated in Fig. 10.1.

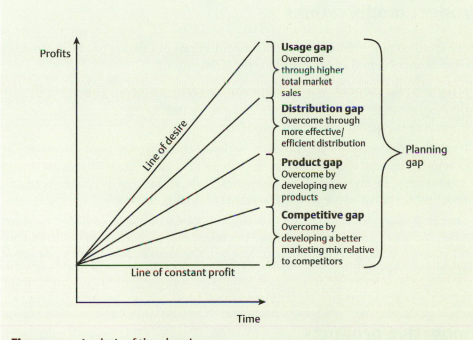

Figure 10.1 Analysis of the planning gap

What are new products?

ANALYSING gaps, whatever types they may be, has a tendency to lead to incremental changes to existing products in existing markets. Indeed, it may not be that easy actually to define what is meant by a 'new product'.

The degree of newness of products is worth considering. New products could comprise any of the following:

- improvements/revisions to existing products;
- additions to existing lines;
- new to the world products;
- new product lines;
- repositioning (existing products in new segments/markets);
- cost reductions.

We will consider below the distinction between product modifications and innovative products.

Product modifications

Many so-called new products are in fact modifications of existing products. Changes tend to be incremental and may include the following:

- Making minor changes to how the product actually performs. This could involve the addition of new features and/ or changing the packaging.
- Improving the quality of the basic product.
- Modifying the style of the product, without changing its basic function (for example, cars tend to undergo styling changes to keep in line with current design preferences). In style-conscious industries such as fashion clothing, regularly updating a product's style can be crucial to continuing success.
- Changing non-product attributes to produce a change of image. A change in advertising message can be used to change the image of a product. This occurred with the change in image of Guinness from a working-man's stout to a trendy social drink, for example.

Innovative products

Truly new products are comparatively rare compared to product modifications, but can be very important under certain circumstances:

- If consumers' tastes are changing radically, existing products may no longer satisfy their needs (this is often the case in many parts of the fashion clothing industry).

- Technological change may make present products obsolete (e.g. dot matrix printers have been made obsolete by the development of ink jet and laser printers).

- New products may be required as a result of changes in internal processes such as accounting, office management, or labour relations. If a product becomes dangerous or illegal to produce (as has happened in the UK with many derivatives of beef products), a motivation is provided for a new replacement product to be developed.

- New products may be required to meet the need of intermediaries (e.g. the existing range of products may be too complex to be handled by many distributors).

- The environment may have changed, creating new needs in the market. For example, the communications revolution resulting from cable technology has spawned many new products such as modems, digital television receivers, etc.

- If competitors are actively developing new products, a company must do likewise if it is not to lose market share.

- New products may be developed to fill under-utilized capacity (for example, many business hotels have filled their empty rooms at the weekend by offering innovatory weekend leisure activity breaks).

The above analysis still does not explain the development of those major innovations, such as computers and mobile phones, which occur now and again and which totally transform the market-place. Indeed, it is highly unlikely that the use of the standard marketing approaches would have been that helpful in developing such products. If

Putting the spoken word into print has seen a quickening pace in the technologies available to do the job as quickly and accurately as possible. The typewriter eventually gave way to the word processor and keyboard. But what about the likely fortunes of a new speech recognition service launched in 1998? A UK company called Speech Machines used computers to receive dictation over the telephone or as voice messages sent through the Internet by e-mail. The dictation is transcribed automatically by computer with a claimed 95 per cent accuracy. Specially written software manages the incoming dictation and automatically sends the transcribed document to one of an army of contract typists the company uses for checking and correction of the final manuscript. It is then sent back to the customer through the Internet. The service has found a useful niche in the USA with the legal and medical professions, offering a speedy and efficient alternative to employing a secretary in-house. But how long a life can this service expect before it is overtaken by increasingly sophisticated and user-friendly voice recognition software that allows users to complete the task in-house? If it is to maintain its business, how can the company offering this new service continue to develop its service offer so that it meets customers' changing needs better than any of the alternatives currently available?

potential customers (if these could have been identified!) had been asked about their likely interest in purchasing such products, there would probably have been difficulties in using the responses given, because the major innovations had not been heard of or understood by these people. The firm would have to educate customers about the new product as part of its research strategy.

Critical to the development of many new products has been a 'product champion' within an organization. A champion can continually press the case for a new product to be developed and provide the impetus for development which may be lost if responsibility is dispersed too widely. Without such people, it is likely that many innovations which we take for granted today would not have been seen through to development and launch.

Although standard marketing procedures may very well have limited use in the development of 'earth-shattering' new products, they are generally useful in reducing the risk of failure of new products.

The new product development process

Having a formal new product development process in place is still more likely to be effective than a haphazard approach. Indeed, where costs and risks are high (as they are in many major infrastructure developments), a system needs to be in place to keep these risks to a minimum. It is usual to talk about a new product development process comprising a number of stages (Fig. 10.2).

Idea generation

New products come from a variety of sources rather than merely being initiated by the firm through the use of market research and the identification of untapped needs.

An important source of new product ideas is the customer. In the industrial context, new uses for an existing product or ideas for new ones tend to be communicated to the sales force. For services, the important characteristic of inseparability means that there are plenty of opportunities for customers to inform service providers of new ideas or improvements to service processes.

Another source of new product ideas is a firm's competitors. Creative imitation does not have the same risks as developing something totally new. A consideration of the flaws that exist in a competitor's product can also produce useful ideas for new products.

Some organizations see the importance of developing new products as part of their long-term competitive strategy and try to instill an internal organizational culture

Figure 10.2 The new product development process

which positively thrives on new ideas. For example, Sony, the electronics company, encourages employees to move around and get involved in other departments. New perspectives and new ideas therefore come from every level of the organization resulting in hundreds of new products every year. Similarly, 3M expects to receive new product ideas regularly from *all* members of staff rather than just the Research and Development Department. Its corporate ethos includes two rules: 'the 15 per cent rule' and 'the 25 per cent rule'. The '15 per cent rule' states that every member of the organization must commit 15 per cent of his/her time to thinking of new ideas and the 25 per cent rule states that every manager must ensure that at least 25 per cent of his/her portfolio of products are less than five years old. As a result, a number of products which are now accepted in the market-place have originated from this approach (e.g. Post-It notes).

Despite the need to be market led, many new product ideas arise quite by accident in laboratory tests. As an example, the anti-impotence drug Viagra became a major commercial success when it was launched in 1998, but researchers were originally developing an anti-angina drug. Unexpected side effects of the drug led to further development and a market opportunity.

What would consumers think of exploding volcanic soufflés, whistling steamed pudding, or *Jurassic* rock buns with 'fossilized' currants? These are examples of some new product ideas developed out of a brainstorming session.

Marketing Business reported on the techniques being used by design and development company Cambridge Consultants Ltd. (CCL), to help develop new products for a wide variety of market sectors. A structured brainstorming session (as compared to the usual *ad hoc* approach) is one part of this process. Team members are briefed in advance, and therefore there is a clear understanding of the required focus participants are expected to have in the development of solutions to a predefined problem.

The above examples were proposed in a simulation session where a team was given the task of proposing new product ideas for the Frazzle Company, a fictitious manufacturer of microwavable convenience foods. Any ideas were deemed possible as long as they were not bread based (this would create conflict with a sister company), and that they should be microwavable and have some sort of synergy with existing product lines. During the fifteen-minute simulation, more than 100 ideas were generated. Apparently, 300–400 ideas is not uncommon in a three-hour session.

The brainstorming team includes a facilitator whom the team can trust and with whom participants can confide. This person's role also involves cajoling and encouragement when necessary. There is also likely to be an individual from another area who can bring a fresh, independent view on the project.

At first, the process aims to produce as many ideas as possible without any judgement on their feasibility, all being accepted equally without criticism. Indeed, silly ideas may spark off a new line of thought in other team members. At this stage, the quantity of ideas is the key.

Later, a screening process does take place. Team members are required to prioritize their ideas with the strongest being picked for further development. The whole process can have up to seven stages and be spread over several weeks, although it has been carried out in nine days for one client. Throughout the whole process, nothing is thrown away as ideas can be combined and may be used later.

Idea screening

Whether a firm responds positively to ideas for new products depends a good deal on its internal resources. As well as considering whether there are the financial resources to develop a new product (particularly, the availability of cash flow in the short term), a firm needs to consider other internal issues. For example, is there enough production capacity to cope with likely demand? Are there enough suitably trained personnel? Will new staff have to be recruited or present staff retrained? In addition, the firm needs to consider the availability of the raw materials or components required to produce the new product.

Another consideration is time. New product development can take a long time from inception to final production and launch. The relevance of time depends a great deal on the type of product being developed and the market for which it is being developed. Some developments can take as little as a few weeks whereas others can take years to come to fruition, especially where safety testing is protracted, as in the case of new drugs. The pressures of competition now mean that speed is increasingly becoming more important.

An important aspect that needs to be considered is the possibility that the new product could take sales from another product that is already in the firm's portfolio through a process of 'cannibalization'. If this is likely to be the case, the firm needs to prepare a response to minimize its impact. Alternatively, adding a new product may help to improve the sales of existing products as the product line now becomes more comprehensive.

Whether a proposed new product fits with the firm's marketing strategy must be considered. To what extent does the new product complement existing product lines? Can existing distribution patterns be used? Can present consumer awareness and attitudes be built upon? The new product should be consistent with the organization's existing products in terms of consumer perceptions of price and quality. Producing a higher priced and higher quality product than those that already exist may be counter-productive as would producing a lower priced, poorer quality product.

Screening should ensure that the new product fits within the firm's overall corporate and marketing strategies. At this stage, many new product ideas will be dropped because they do not fit with overall marketing strategy. If the proposal passes this filter, the company proceeds to the next stage.

Concept development and testing

It is often estimated that more than 80 per cent of new products fail and therefore it is important that the number of potential failures are kept to a minimum. In other words, unsuccessful ideas should be eliminated as quickly as possible.

The new product concept can be tested using a number of methods and such testing should take place before any significant amount of further investment in product development takes place. Initial market research should aim to discover potential customer attitudes to the concept and more particularly whether they would be interested in purchasing the product if it came on to the market. This may be quite a difficult task if the new product is a major innovation and customers have no experience of such an idea. A case in point is the experience of Barclaycard. In 1995, two cards were proposed: Barclaycard Sense which was associated with the caring nineties and Barclaycard Gold which was associated with high status. Qualitative research indicated that the Sense card would be successful and that the Gold card would fail. In this instance, the company were not convinced of the results and went ahead with both cards. Gold turned out to be hugely successful and the Sense card underperformed.

Business analysis

A financial analysis needs to take place in order to assess whether the product concept can be made into a profitable proposition. An income statement together with the associated balance sheet and cash flow analysis therefore needs to be prepared. The key to this financial analysis is that the product should at least break even over a period of time. However, any financial forecasts may be based on very crude assumptions about the likely volume of sales, the selling price, distribution costs, and the cost of producing the item. Cost and revenue estimates can be closely linked with each other, so that high volume sales result in lower unit production costs, which in turn improves profitability. Because there are many unknowns in the financial analysis, a sensitivity analysis is often carried out to assess the impact on overall profitability of changes in the underlying assumptions. Would the concept still be profitable if selling prices were only half those which had been predicted?

Product development and testing

This is the translation of the idea into an actual product that is capable of delivery to customers. It is at this point that the decision is made actually physically to develop the product and large amounts of money can be poured in at this stage. The various elements of the product have to be designed and tested. However, this testing should be more rigorous than at the concept testing stage. Customers can now see the product as it might actually look and identify possible problems that need to be resolved.

There is a need to consider the requirements for repeat purchase in addition to the single one-off purchase decision and therefore the factors that influence trial, first purchase, adoption, and purchase frequency need to be identified. In addition, customer response to promotional material also needs to be measured.

Even given the increased rigour in this testing process, there are still difficulties. Testing customer response to intangible elements of a new product is difficult. This is a particular issue when developing new services.

Test marketing

The test market aims to replicate everything that is likely to exist in the real market but on a smaller scale. Test marketing can therefore take place in a television viewing area, a test city, particular geographical regions, or, in the business-to-business context, a sample of key customers.

Designing a test marketing exercise involves asking a number of questions: Where should the test market be? What is to be tested? How long should the test last? What criteria should be used to determine success or otherwise?

Although test marketing should reduce the potential risks before launch, it is important to realize that there are still potential problems. Test marketing is not cheap and in some cases can be nearly as expensive as full-scale launch. Even a large test market is not going to be totally representative of the market; in reality small test markets are likely to lead to distortions. Test marketing is also likely to warn competitors of what is to come and, as a result, the competition may act more quickly in response or they may interfere with the test itself.

Product launch

How a product is launched is an important issue. Replacing one product with the new one tends to be a popular approach. There is likely to be an existing customer base for the new product and therefore the risks are lower. For a period of time, however, there may be two products being offered simultaneously.

Time is a key issue. The longer a new product goes through the various developmental stages, the greater the chance that competitors will enter the market beforehand. Timing of entry is also important. The firm can be a pioneer and enter the market first or be a follower and reduce the risks considerably.

In 1997, the Virgin group launched a new 'Virgin One' account which allows customers to control their mortgage, banking, credit cards, loans, and savings from a single account, with twenty-four hour telephone access. The service targeted busy people with neither the time, nor inclination, to shop around for financial services. But how many customers should the company have geared itself up to handle when it launched its new product? Launching a new product often involves a lot of guesswork. If the number is underestimated and the company doesn't have the capacity to cope with large numbers, frustration and harm to the brand reputation can soon build up. Many new product launches have been victim of their own success as potential customers queue seemingly endlessly for a telephone to be answered and are then answered by an overstretched operator. Tesco and Standard Life both seriously underestimated the number of people who might respond to their newly launched banking services, leading to frustrated customers and overstretched staff as call centres were swamped with calls.

Virgin undertook testing of its new banking service among a small group of customers before launching it to all its existing customers in November 1997. This allowed it to understand more about demand when it eventually went for a full public launch in January 1998. The company appeared to have managed an orderly launch of its new service and maintained the integrity of its brand, something that has been harmed by other companies in their rush to get to the market.

Integrating the new product development process

So far, the stages of new product development have been presented as if they are steps which necessarily have to be tackled in a sequential order. In fact, the time taken to go through this process can be considerable, allowing competitors to gain a lead. There have therefore been many attempts to carry out some of the steps simultaneously. Virtual reality systems, for example, are allowing customers to get a feel of the final product at a very early stage, allowing it to take place at the same time as concept testing and avoiding the need to wait while all steps of the process are progressed. Even simple administrative matters such as rapid communication following the results of one stage can help to speed up the new product development process.

As can be seen, the new product development process can be time consuming and complex. However, given the degree of risks involved, it would seem prudent to utilize a logical system rather than attempting to act 'off the hoof'. Indeed, a US-developed computer system designed to prevent the potential waste of resources is now being marketed in the UK. This system has been used by Procter & Gamble, AT&T, and Pepsi Cola to name but a few and combines both qualitative and quantitative methods of customer research. Although this is not an outright replacement for all the usual research techniques, the system attempts to ensure that only the most viable of a company's ideas will be subjected to the usual expensive and time-consuming processes.

Planning the new product portfolio

THE previous chapter introduced the idea of a product mix which comprises the range of products offered by a company. The product life cycle reminds us that a product mix cannot remain static, as some products will eventually cease to be profitable elements of that mix. But which direction should the new product mix take?

Product management involves ensuring that there is a succession of products available that are at different stages of their life cycle. It is widely accepted that the planning process should involve the firm's business being managed in the same way as an investment portfolio, with attention paid to developing, maintaining, phasing out, and deleting specific elements. This process can lead management to identify where there may be future potential and therefore where investment can be most profitably made.

Portfolio analysis attempts to produce specific marketing strategies aimed at achieving a balanced mix of products that will bring maximum profits in the long run. Two important influences on profitability are likely to be market share and stage in the product life cycle. The product portfolio approach allows for an evaluation of each of the firm's products by considering these two measures simultaneously.

A widely used type of portfolio analysis was developed by the Boston Consulting Group (BCG) in the 1960s, which developed a matrix linking market growth and market share. A company's strategic business units (SBUs) are plotted on the matrix according to the rate of market growth and the company's market share (see Fig. 10.3). This forces management to consider both the future potential of the market and the SBUs' competitive position, which offers the opportunity to balance cash flows within the organization. The aim is for some products to generate cash (and provide profit) which is used to support the development and growth of tomorrow's high performers.

The BCG model identifies four categories within the matrix, each indicating a different type of business with a different cash usage and generation rate. Each category has a set of strategy alternatives that are applicable to the products in that category (Fig. 10.4). The four categories are often referred to as Stars, Question Marks, Cash Cows, and Dogs.

This particular model, however, can be criticized and there may be shortcomings associated with the reliance on a growth-share analysis. Other factors may influence cash flow and indeed cash flow may not be of as much importance as return on investment as a means of comparing attractiveness. There are numerous other portfolio matrices which share the common aim of trying to create a rational approach to investment in new products. Other approaches use competitive capabilities and profitability prospects as ratings (Shell's Directional Policy Matrix and Abell and Hammond's 3 × 3 chart) and others have used competitive position and stage of industry maturity (Little's Strategic Condition Model).

Portfolio analysis will be returned to in the following chapter in the context of developing a sustainable competitive advantage. For now, however, it should be noted that although portfolio approaches are useful for guiding new product development, they do have a number of weaknesses.

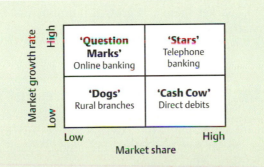

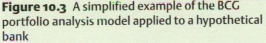

Figure 10.3 A simplified example of the BCG portfolio analysis model applied to a hypothetical bank

Product type	Likely marketing strategy
Question Marks	Promotion mainly through Public Relations Selective distribution channels Premium price aimed at innovators
Stars	Public relations/advertising Distribution and pricing adjusted to appeal to early majority
Cash Cows	Heavy advertising with increasing use of sales promotion activity Extensive distribution with severe pressure on prices
Dogs	May withdraw promotional support completely and 'harvest' the product with the highest price that existing customers will bear

Figure 10.4 Marketing strategies associated with different positions in the BCG matrix

Too simplistic an approach

Although it may be accepted that a portfolio approach enables managers to think strategically in a proactive way, it can lead to too great an emphasis on market share growth and entry into high growth businesses to the neglect of managing the current business. Indeed, market share and growth rate may not be particularly good measures of industry attractiveness and competitive position.

Other important strategic factors are not considered

Other factors which are a function of the external competitive environment such as technological change, social, legal, political, and environmental pressures may be being ignored in a simple portfolio model.

Difficult to use in practice

Many of the definitions of the terms used are matters of judgement rather than fact, therefore there may be difficulties in actually measuring many of the variables.

Problems with the product life cycle concept

A major problem with the portfolio planning approach is its reliance on the product life cycle concept itself and these limitations have already been noted in the previous chapter.

Even taking the above criticisms into account, there would seem to be some value in using the product life cycle concept and portfolio planning as broad planning and forecasting tools. They highlight the need for marketing strategy to change over time and aid investment decisions. They can also improve the allocation of resources and levels of control.

Deleting products

Good portfolio management demands not only that new products are developed, but that failing ones are deleted. Deciding when a product has reached the decline stage of its life cycle can be quite difficult, because a downturn could simply be a temporary blip. If a downturn seems to have set in, it can sometimes be difficult to decide whether it is worth trying to revive the product, or to just let it die. Even the manner of a product's deletion requires careful thought—should it be allowed to die gradually, or suddenly killed off?

In general, there is a tendency to 'add on' rather than subtract and therefore many products do not die but merely fade away, consuming resources of an organization which could be better used elsewhere. 'Old' products may not even cover overheads. In addition there are a number of hidden costs in supporting dying products that need to be taken into consideration:

- A disproportionate amount of management time can be spent on them. This can delay the search for new products.
- Short and relatively uneconomic production runs may be required where the demand for a product is small and irregular.
- They often require frequent price and stock adjustments.

Firms should have a logical planning system for deciding which products to delete.

It would be naïve, however, to assume that deletion is a simple process. In reality, there are a number of reasons why logical deletion procedures are not readily followed:

■ Often firms do not have the information which they need to identify whether a product needs to be considered for elimination. Even if an organization is aware of a potential deletion candidate, the reasons for its failure may not be known and therefore management may just leave things as they are and hope that the problem will go away by itself.

■ Managers often become sentimental about products, hoping that sales will pick up when the market improves. Sometimes, marketing strategy will be blamed for the lack of success and there may be a belief that a change in advertising or pricing, for example, will improve the situation.

■ Political issues within organizations may create barriers to deletion. Some individuals will have vested interests in a product and may fight elimination efforts. In fact, some individuals may hide the true facts of a product's performance to ensure that deletion is not considered at all.

■ Finally, a company may fear that the sale of other products in the product range will fall if a product is deleted. With the growing importance of relationship marketing, many firms are keen to ensure that they are able to satisfy all of their target customers' needs for a particular category of product. If a product is deleted, the whole relationship may be lost.

Where weak products are identified, a number of possibilities may be open for trying to revive a product, including:

■ Modifying the product so that it meets changed market requirements.
■ Decreasing promotional expenditure, in order to minimize costs. This may be a sensible idea if there is a small loyal market.
■ Increasing promotional expenditure, assuming that sales are sufficiently responsive to this increased promotion.
■ Decreasing the price, if demand is elastic and an increase in sales revenue is likely to result.
■ Increasing the price, if there remains a core market which is strongly loyal to the product.
■ Changing the distribution system, in order to cut costs, and/or open up new sales opportunities segments.

If none of these options is considered feasible, the company must decide how best to delete the product. This is not always a simple task and a number of options can be identified:

■ Ruthlessly eliminate 'overnight'. This may seem the simplest solution, but will customers take their business to other competitors? Will they take their business for other products in the company's mix with them? There may also be the problem of what to do with existing stocks of finished goods and work in progress. A sudden withdrawal of a product without notice may create bad publicity for a company, especially if customers have come to depend upon it.

- Increase the price and let demand fade away. This may sound to many loyal customers like exploitation, but it could mean that the firm makes good profits on the product while demand lasts.
- Reduce promotion or even stop it altogether. Again this could increase profitability while demand lasts.

Chapter summary and key linkages to other chapters

In most markets, customers' needs are constantly changing. Rising expectations mean that a product that was considered adequate a few years ago may now be considered lacking. Technological development has played a major role in allowing for new production possibilities and this in turn has further fuelled consumers' expectations.

This chapter has emphasized new product development as a process. The length of this process will depend upon product and market characteristics. Short new product development times can give a firm a competitive advantage, but shortening the process can also increase the risk of a failed launch. The result of new product development should be to strengthen the product range of a company in order that it can sustain a long-term profitable portfolio of products. The opposite of new product development is deletion and a rational approach to deletion can prevent a firm becoming weighed down with a large number of minor products which consume a lot of management time but return very little, if any, profit.

The aim of new product development and deletion strategies is to give a company a desired portfolio of products. A number of conceptual frameworks for studying product portfolios have been discussed.

The following key linkages to other chapters should be noted:

Chapter 1: What is marketing?: Marketing is about satisfying customers' needs profitably and products are the means by which those needs are satisfied. Where needs change, new products must be developed.

Chapter 2: The marketing environment: A sound analysis of the marketing environment should identify changes in consumers' preferences which trigger the development of new products. The marketing environment may also indicate developments in technology which allow new products to be created.

Chapter 3: Market segmentation: New products and adaptations of existing products have proliferated as a result of the fragmentation of society into smaller market segments.

Chapter 4: Branding: Many new products have been successfully launched on the strength of a strong brand. However, if a new product does not perform to customers' expectations, the brand itself may be harmed.

Chapter 5: Marketing and ethics: What does a company do when the competitive nature of its environment calls for it to develop new products that are socially unacceptable?

Chapter 6: Marketing research: Do new products necessarily have to involve lengthy market research? It may help to cut the chances of failure, but if the research takes too long, a company can be beaten to market. Also, there are many examples of new products that have emerged from laboratories without research into customers' needs.

Chapter 7: Buyer behaviour: How can a new product be designed to allow more favourable evaluation by potential buyers?

Chapter 8: Buyer–seller relationship development: New products are often developed to allow a company to broaden its relationships with customers.

Chapter 9: The product: New product development should develop a company's product mix in a way that takes account of the product life cycle.

Chapter 11: Developing a sustainable competitive advantage: A company cannot sustain its profitability on the basis of one short-life fashionable product, so it must invest in new product development. Chapter 11 follows up the discussion in this chapter on product portfolio analysis.

Chapters 12/13: Pricing theory and application: Genuinely innovative new products may command an initial price premium before lookalike competitors catch up.

Chapters 14/15: Intermediaries and distribution: Intermediaries can be useful sources of ideas for new product development. Before a new product is launched it is often important to research intermediaries' attitudes towards handling it.

Chapters 16–20: Principles of promotion planning/advertising/sales promotion/ personal selling/direct marketing: The promotion mix for an innovative new product may emphasize public relations. For lookalike copies, advertising and sales promotion may be more appropriate.

Chapter 21: Managing the marketing effort: New product development is greatly facilitated by a management structure in which an individual champions a proposal and has adequate information and interdepartmental co-operation.

Chapter 22: Services marketing: The intangible nature of services results in many incremental variations in services, with relatively few major innovations.

Chapter 23: Global marketing: An overseas market may have such different characteristics that the only way a company can succeed is to develop new products specifically for it.

Case study

Tensator the innovator

Tensator is a small company which until a few years ago was not known for its innovation. The company's Sales and Marketing Director Terry Green stated that 'I'm a very firm believer that innovation doesn't need to be revolutionary. There's nothing my company has done that couldn't be done by anyone else'.

Tensator is a light engineering business which manufactured the Constant Force Spring, a device used in the manufacture of car seat belts throughout Europe. Although the company continues to produce this product for this market, it is now far more successful in the production of more recently introduced new product lines.

When Green joined the company in 1989, he realized that there was much more potential for the company. In 1978 it had put forward plans for the use of the Constant Force Spring in the production of queuing barriers for supermarkets and banks, etc. 'We hadn't done much with it', recalled Green, 'even though there was a feeling it could be developed further'. He persuaded the company to focus on this new product idea.

Research was undertaken where customers, current and potential, were asked to give opinions on the viability of such a product and how it could improve on the products that were currently available. The market research proved to be invaluable. 'It was hardly rocket science, but it made us realize that what matters is what the customer wants to buy', noted Green.

As a result of the company's research and development, Tensabarrier was launched. By 1996, the product was being exported to thirty-six countries and accounted for £3 million turnover. This was a dramatic improvement on the sales generated by the original product which was developed in 1978 and which had now become just a small part of the company's turnover.

There are now a variety of Tensabarriers in a variety of shapes and forms. There is a bolt-down barrier and a special checkout version which incorporates an electronic movement sensor to prevent theft. These and other innovations were developed very proactively. 'It's so easy once you realize that the key is to talk to your customers about how you can find solutions to their problems.'

Tensator launched thirteen new products in the years 1995 and 1996. Total turnover had risen more than threefold since 1988 to £10 million, with employee numbers only rising over the same period from 120 to 200. Green makes the point, 'Innovation is about the successful implementation of new ideas, it's as simple as that. It's not necessarily about coming up with new inventions. It boils down to pretty basic stuff. It's about tweaking the way you do things rather than jettisoning one big idea for another'.

Adapted from *Marketing Business*, January 1996.

Case study review questions

1 Why do you think the new application of the Constant Force Spring is more successful than its predecessor?

2 To what extent is the above a good example of product portfolio planning?

3 Where do you think the new product is in its life cycle? Give reasons for your answer.

Chapter review questions

1 Is innovation always a good thing for a company?

2 How can Gap Analysis aid in the planning process?

3 To what extent can the various stages in the NPD process be distinguished? To what extent should they be integrated more fully?

4 What possible problems could be encountered by a service firm trying to develop new services?

5 What is the relationship between innovation and profitability? Can a firm succeed without being an innovator?

6 With reference to specific examples, examine the practical problems of deleting products from a company's product range.

Suggested further reading

For a discussion on the general nature of innovation and the impact of new technologies, the following provide a useful introduction:

- Cervantes, M. (1997), 'Diffusing Technology to Industry', *OECD Observer*, **207**, pp. 20–3.

- Coombs, R. (1998), 'A Reflection on the Major Themes of the 1997 R & D Management Conference', *R & D Management*, **28**, 3, pp. 213–14.

- Doyle, P., and Bridgewater, S. (1998), *Innovation in Marketing* (Oxford: Butterworth-Heinemann).

- McCartney, L. (1998), 'Getting Smart About Knowledge Management: Managing Intellectual Resources Can Maximize Innovation and Competitiveness', *Industry Week*, **247**, 9, pp. 30–3.

Further discussion on the processes of new product development is provided in the following:

- Caffyn, S. (1997), 'Extending Continuous Improvement to the New Product Development Process', *R & D Management*, **27**, 3, pp. 253–67.

- Cunningham, F. (1998), 'Cultures that Bring New Products to Life', *Management Today*, June, pp. 100–1.

- Gordon, G. L., Schoenbachler, D. D., Kaminski, P. F., and Brouchous, K. A. (1997), 'New Product Development: Using the Salesforce to Identify Opportunities', *Journal of Business & Industrial Marketing*, **12**, 1, pp. 33–50.

- Jones, T. (1996), *NPD: An Introduction to a Multi-Functional Process* (Oxford: Butterworth-Heinemann).

- Madhavan, R., and Grover, R. (1998), 'From Embedded Knowledge to Embodied Knowledge: New Product Development as Knowledge Management', *Journal of Marketing*, **62**, 4, pp. 1–29.

- Maylor, H. (1997), 'Concurrent New Product Development: An Empirical Assessment', *International Journal of Operations and Production Management*, **17**, 11–12, pp. 1196–1214.

- Moorman, C., and Miner, A. S. (1997), 'The Impact of Organizational Memory on New Product Performance and Creativity', *Journal of Marketing Research*, **34**, 1, pp. 91–116.

■ Schilling, M. A., and Hill, C. W. L. (1998), 'Managing the New Product Development Process: Strategic Imperatives', *The Academy of Management Executive*, **12**, 3, pp. 67–81.

■ Scott, G. M. (1998), 'The New Age of New Product Development: Are We There Yet?', *R & D Management*, **28**, 4, pp. 225–36.

■ Song, X. M., and Parry, M. E. (1997), 'A Cross-National Comparative Study of New Product Development Processes: Japan and the United States', *Journal of Marketing*, **61**, 2, pp. 1–18.

Approaches to launching new products are discussed in the following:

■ Dwek, R. (1998), 'The Ghastliest Product Launches' (causes of failed product launches), *Fortune*, **136**, 5, p. 44.

■ Mahajan, V., and Muller, E. (1998), 'When is it Worthwhile Targeting the Majority Instead of the Innovators in a New Product Launch?', *Journal of Marketing Research*, **35**, 4, pp. 488–95.

■ Raymond, D. (1997), 'Famous Flops', *Forbes*, **159**, 11, pp. S101–3.

The literature on product deletion is less extensive than that on new product launches, but the following elaborate on some of the points raised in this chapter:

■ Barrett, P. (1996), 'The Good (and bad) Die Young', *Marketing*, 11 July, p. 16.

■ Boulding, W., Morgan, R., and Staelin, R. (1997), 'Pulling the Plug to Stop the New Product Drain', *Journal of Marketing Research*, **34**, 1, pp. 164–76.

Useful web link

UK government's technology Foresight programme: http://www.foresight.gov.uk

Chapter 11

Developing a Sustainable Competitive Advantage

Chapter objectives

In a competitive marketing environment, a company must use all elements of the marketing mix to make its products the preferred choice of buyers. Subsequent chapters will focus on the management of individual marketing mix elements. The purpose of this chapter is to provide an overview of what is involved in creating a competitive advantage. A sustainable competitive advantage occurs where a company delivers superior value not only today, but understands how it can continue to deliver superior value in the future. Strategies for growth will be discussed in this context. The chapter begins with an analysis of who the competitors to a company are.

Introduction

MARKETING is a dynamic process of ensuring a close fit between the capabilities of an organization and the demands placed upon it by its external environment. It follows that the marketing mix will need to evolve continually over time in order to meet changes in a company's internal objectives and in its business environment. It is not good enough for a company to develop a marketing mix strategy that works for a short period, but then fails to make good long-term profits for the company.

History is full of marketing plans that looked too good to be true. A company may have found a very high level of sales in the short term, but failed to earn sufficient profits over the longer term. It may be that such a company has underpriced its products, leaving it insufficient margin to cover its fixed costs. Or it may have invested heavily in product design and promotion but failed to generate a sufficient level of sales to pay for such investment. It is not difficult to develop short-term marketing strategies which at first appear highly successful when judged by sales levels. It is much more difficult to develop a marketing strategy that is sustainable over the longer term by producing adequate levels of continuing profits.

Many companies that have been hailed as successful market-led businesses have not managed to achieve a sustainable long-term success. In the UK, companies such as Next, Amstrad, Laura Ashley, and British and Commonwealth have all risen rapidly and gained many 'Business of the Year'-type awards on the way. But each of these examples ended up in serious financial difficulties just a short while later, and in some cases even went into receivership. It has been noted that very few of the so-called 'excellent' companies identified by Peters and Waterman in their book *In Search of Excellence* were considered to be excellent fifteen years later. The marketing strategy that had led to short-term success was clearly not sustainable.

Who are the competitors?

THE importance of seeing marketing management as a process of analysis, planning, implementation, and control was noted in Chapter 1. Any plan to develop a competitive advantage must be based on a sound analysis of just who a company's competitors are. At first, it may seem obvious who the competitors are, but, as Theodore Levitt pointed out, a myopic view may focus on the immediate and direct competitors while overlooking the more serious threat posed by indirect and less obvious sources of competition. When railway companies in the 1930s saw their main competitors as other railway companies, they overlooked the fact that the most serious competition would derive from road-based transport operators. More recently, banks have been made to realize that their competitors are not just other banks, or even other financial services organizations, but any organization which has a strong brand reputation and customer base. Through these, supermarkets, airlines, and car companies have all developed various forms of banking services which now compete with mainstream banks.

Even without considering the possibility of new market entrants appearing, it is possible to identify direct and indirect competitors. Direct competitors are generally similar in form and satisfy customers' needs in a similar way. Indirect competitors may appear different in form, but satisfy a fundamentally similar need. Consider the examples of products, an underlying need which they satisfy, and their direct and indirect competitors shown in Table 11.1.

A sound analysis of the direct and indirect competitors for a firm is crucial in defining the business mission of an organization (discussed further in Chapter 21). In the example presented in Table 11.1, the Parker pen company may see itself as being not so much in the pen business, or even the writing implement business, but rather the gift business. On this basis, its competitors may include the producers of such products as diverse as clocks, books, and glassware.

A useful framework for analysing the competition facing a company has been provided by Michael Porter. His model illustrates the relationship between existing

Table 11.1

Product	Underlying need	Direct competitors	Indirect competitors
Overseas holiday	Relaxation	Rival tour operators	Garden furniture
Restaurant-prepared meal	Social gathering	Other restaurants	Ready-prepared gourmet meal for home consumption
Television programme	Entertainment	Other television programmes	Internet service provider
Parker pen	Gift giving	Other pens	Any gift products

competitors and potential competitors in a market and identifies five forces requiring evaluation:

- the threat of new entrants;
- the threat of substitute products;
- the intensity of rivalry between competing firms;
- the power of suppliers;
- the power of buyers.

Understanding the structure of competition within a market is a crucial prerequisite for developing a strategy to develop a sustainable competitive advantage. The model is shown in Fig. 11.1 and the nature of these five forces is discussed below.

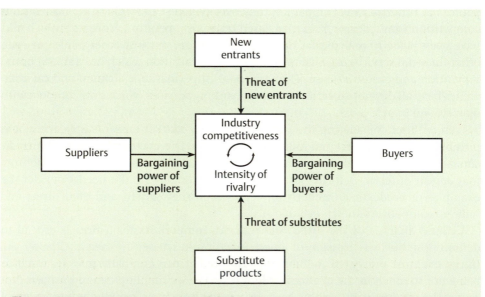

Figure 11.1 Porter's Five-Forces model of industry competition, based on M. E. Porter (1980), *Competitive Strategy: Techniques for Analyzing Industries and Competitors* (New York: Free Press)

The threat of new entrants

The threat of new entrants is greatest where there are low barriers to entry. New entrants may already be active in a similar market sector, but in another geographic market. The threat becomes reality when a company which is strong in one geographical market decides to exploit other geographical markets. As an example, a number of South Korean car manufacturers, including Hyundai and Daewoo, moved into the UK and other European markets during the 1980s and 1990s from their strong base in Far Eastern markets. The Hungarian bus manufacturer Ikarus posed a threat to western bus manufacturers in the post-Soviet era when it turned its attention to western markets.

Alternatively, new entrants may arrive from outside the industry. BIC, whose technology base was plastic moulding, was well established in the disposable ball-point pen market. They were able successfully to diversify into the wet shave razor market with plastic disposable razors, thereby challenging established market leaders such as Gillette and Wilkinson in their core business.

The threat of substitute products

Substitute products are likely to emerge from alternative technologies, particularly as the economics of production change. Initially the new technology may have high costs associated with it and serve only small niche markets. As the technology and experience develops, the level of investment rises and production volumes increase, resulting in economies of scale which are associated with falling production costs. Many products have been consigned to obscurity by the development of new technologies, for example the market for typewriters has been considerably reduced by the development of personal computers and the market for sugar has been reduced by the development of artificial sweeteners. These substitutes may change the whole economics of an industry and threaten the survival of manufacturers of the traditional product.

Intensity of rivalry between competing firms

The intensity of rivalry may be high if two or more firms are fighting for dominance in a fast growing market. For example, this occurred among Internet Service Providers (ISP) such as AOL, Freeserve, and Line One who have fought hard in the early stages of growth of this market to become consumers' preferred entry port (or 'portal') to the Internet. A company needs to become established as the dominant technology or brand before the industry matures, as entering the market later may require considerably greater investment (although the costs of early mistakes may be avoided). In a mature industry, particularly if it is characterized by high fixed costs and excess capacity, the intensity of competitive rivalry may be very high. This is because manufacturers (e.g. of cars) or service providers (e.g. airlines) need to operate at near maximum capacity to cover overhead costs. As the industry matures, or at times of cyclical downturn, firms fight to maintain their maximum level of sales. Price cuts and discounting may become commonplace and profits eroded. Low-cost producers with high brand loyalty have the best chance of survival.

The power of suppliers

The power of suppliers is likely to be high if the number of suppliers are few and/or the materials, components, and services they offer are in short supply. The suppliers of microprocessor silicone chips and compact discs have in the past held a powerful market position due to their dominance of technology and high demand for their products.

The power of buyers

Buyer power is likely to be high if there are relatively few buyers, if there are many alternative sources of supply, and if the buyer incurs only low costs in switching between suppliers. During the 1980s and 1990s Britain's grocery retailing has become increasingly dominated by seven very large organizations. According to the Nielsen Grocery Service (Nielsen 1998) Asda, Co-operative, Iceland, Safeway, Sainsbury, Somerfield, and Tesco held 77.8 per cent market share by turnover in 1997. Thus the power in the market-place has shifted away from the manufacturers of grocery products to the retailers, seven of whom buy around three-quarters of many manufacturers' output.

Developing a sustainable competitive advantage

WHAT makes some companies, such as BP and Lloyds Bank, enjoy long periods of steady success, while others may rise fast, but fall equally quickly? A snapshot of businesses may produce quite a misleading impression, as success can only really be judged over a period of many years. Comprehensive, longitudinal studies of the factors contributing to marketing success are relatively few and far between. However, a major study undertaken by the Chartered Institute of Marketing and Cranfield School of Management is a useful starting-point for discussing long-term competitive advantage (McDonald 1994). Their research focused on some of the world's most successful companies, such as Shell, Tesco, and Zeneca, who were monitored on a continuous basis over several years. The study identified ten guidelines for 'world-class marketing'. These are reviewed briefly below and some are returned to later in this chapter.

1. **Develop a true marketing orientation**: Successful companies put a genuine concern for their customers above all else. A true customer orientation must be developed in all functions and not confined to something called the marketing department. Leadership of senior management is crucial to developing a marketing orientation—if they are not customer focused, then the chances of customer orientation permeating the whole organization are reduced. Firms that preoccupy themselves with looking inwardly are not likely to succeed. Bureaucratized approaches to Total Quality Management, ratio management, and cost reduction are pointless if they lose sight of customers' needs. Only customers can judge quality and value.

2. **Develop a differentiated product offer**: Successful companies differentiate their products so that they avoid competition between identical products which is based on price alone. Differentiation can arise from offering superior product quality, innovative product features, a unique product, a strong brand name, superior service levels, and wide distribution coverage. Of course, differentiation along these lines will only serve a company well if they are based on a thorough understanding of customers' needs. Differentiation that is based on production considerations alone may not create value in the eyes of customers. World class companies continuously strive to meet customers' needs more cost-effectively than their competitors, giving them a sustainable differential advantage. Michael Porter's prescription for competitive advantage based on differentiation is discussed later in this chapter.

3. **Monitor changes in the marketing environment**: Firms' operating environment is changing faster than ever before, with the result that a strategy that worked a few years ago may be completely irrelevant today. The example is given of IBM which in the 1980s seemed to be unquestioningly stable and profitable. But the company failed to respond quickly enough to changes in the structure of the computer market, leading to its recent problems. It is vital that firms monitor changes in their marketing environment. At the macro-environmental level, analysis can be classified under the headings of political, economic, technological, and societal environments. Within a firm's own industry sector environment, key trends to watch include market size and potential; customers' behaviour; changes in market segment structure and composition; suppliers; intermediaries; industry practices; and the level of profitability within this and related sectors.

4. **Understand your competitors**: It is not good enough for a company just to

focus on its customers. Its competitors are probably focusing equally on those same customers, so it is important for any company to understand the actions of its competitors. Competitors can appear at a number of levels. The most obvious which most firms monitor are direct competitors (e.g. one bank monitoring other banks). It is less common, but still very important, to monitor potential competitors (e.g. supermarket chains who are potential competitors for many banks' services). Many industry sectors have been transformed by new entrants who were previously not seen as competitors. Competitors could also emerge in the form of suppliers and intermediaries diversifying their roles within the supply chain. Many manufacturers of branded groceries have faced strong competition from retailers who have developed their own strong brands which have clearly satisfied customers' needs in respect of quality, price, and availability. Sometimes competition can arise when customers change their preferences to a substitute product (for example, sales of beef in the UK fell in the late 1990s as many consumers shifted their preference to white meat).

Figure 11.2 The DIY retailer, Homebase, keeps an eye on its competitors by checking thousands of prices every week and guaranteeing its customers unbeatable value for money at all times by offering to match prices of thousands of products. Such a guarantee provides a valuable reassurance to potential customers that further "shopping around" is unnecessary.

5. **Market segmentation is crucial**: The days of being able to make a generic product and offer it to a mass market are over for most products. In order to succeed in modern markets, it is important to recognize that not all customers have the same needs. The ability to recognize groups of customers who share similar needs and then develop appropriate product offers has always been a crucial factor underlying success. This understanding should include a detailed knowledge of market structure; the spending habits of different segments; and the motivators which drive each group to buy. However, it is just as important to monitor continuously the needs of targeted segments as they change over time and to adapt the product offer to meet these changing needs. Over time, there has been a tendency for market segments to fragment, so it may be necessary to develop new variants of a product to meet the needs of new sub-segments.

6. **Understand your strengths and weaknesses**: As a result of their environmental scanning, successful companies have a good idea of the opportunities and threats facing them. A key management task is to match these with the organization's internal strengths and weaknesses, in respect of each identified market segment. Successful companies have processes for conducting regular audits of their business which can help to understand their strengths and weaknesses in different market segments. Too many companies have failed by trying to serve market segments for which they have no competitive advantage.

7. **Understand the dynamics of product/market evolution**: It was noted earlier that companies must continuously monitor their marketing environment. Most markets are in a state of transition as a result of technical change, changes in social attitudes, competitive pressures, etc. It is important that companies understand not only how a market has evolved to date, but how it is likely to continue to evolve in the future. Although it is often criticized for its simplicity, the product life cycle concept is a reminder that an apparently successful product may enjoy only transient success as markets pass from a growth phase to maturity and decline. Successful managers are proactive in seeing a product through these life cycle stages, and in extending the stages before decline sets in.

8. **Pay attention to portfolio management**: Companies have finite resources and must allocate these resources to create a sustainable portfolio of products and markets. A balanced portfolio will include a number of 'cash cows', and 'rising stars', which will help to support new product development. The number of 'dogs' which are at the end of their life cycle must be kept to a minimum. The management of a balanced portfolio would not allow for the inclusion of only stars or cash cows—sooner or later these will go into decline, so it is important that there are new products emerging in the portfolio to supersede these.

9. **Identify strategic priorities**: Those organizations that define their key target markets, their sources of differential advantage, and their intended sources of revenue tend to be the most successful over the long term. It is comparatively

easy for anyone to develop a marketing plan showing forecasts and budgets. Too often, this is the outcome of a very bureaucratic process. It is more difficult to spell out clearly how the stated budgets are to be achieved, and by whom. Resources available to a company should be focused on the best opportunities for achieving continuous growth in sales and profits.

10. **Develop professional management skills**: There are many examples of small entrepreneurs who have succeeded with few, if any, professional qualifications. However, for continued and sustainable growth, it is essential to have professional marketing skills, which implies formal training in the underlying concepts, tools, and techniques of marketing. At the very least, marketing managers should understand the importance of market research, market segmentation, portfolio management, and the marketing mix.

Creating a strategy for differential advantage

THERE have now been many prescriptions for marketing strategies that give a firm a long-term competitive advantage. A framework that has received much attention is based on the work of Michael Porter (Porter 1980). The basis of his analysis is that firms identify those activities for which they have a competitive advantage over their competitors. Competitive advantage-based strategies can be divided into three generic types: cost leadership; differentiation; and focus.

Overall cost leadership

In many markets, selling price is crucial to gain business and may be by far the most important basis on which buyers evaluate competing products. This is typical of many commodity-type markets such as petrol. To achieve competitive advantage in such markets, a company needs to put a lot of effort into lowering its production and distribution costs so that it can charge lower prices than its competitors. The important point here is to achieve sustainably low prices. Companies that gain market share without cutting their operating costs will eventually deplete their financial resources and run the risk of becoming insolvent. For companies operating in very price sensitive markets, ruthless control of costs is crucial and firms have met this challenge by such means as replacement of staff with machines, flexible working practices, and improvements to production processes.

Cost leadership can result from being able to achieve economies of scale. In industry sectors that use high technology, or which require highly trained labour skills, a learning curve effect may be apparent (also called a cost experience curve). By operating at a larger scale than its competitors, a firm can benefit more from the learning curve and thereby achieve lower unit costs. While this may be true of some industries, others face only a very low critical output at which significant economies of scale occur—many craft industries and hairdressing, for example. For organizations in these sectors, cost leadership would be a difficult strategy as many rival firms would also be able to achieve maximum cost efficiency. A cost leadership strategy is more likely to be effective where a high level of output relative to market size is necessary in order to achieve economies of scale, as is the case with car manufacturing.

Differentiation

Companies do not like operating in commodity-type markets, as selling price is essentially dictated by the market. Competitive market pressures generally mean that the going price is only just enough to keep an efficient organization profitable. In order to try to reduce their dependence on market forces, many firms have sought to differentiate their products. They seek to achieve superior performance by adding value to the product which is reflected in the higher price that customers are prepared to pay. Added value as perceived by customers could come about in a number of ways, including:

- offering greater quality relative to price than competitors;
- offering completely new products which are not yet available from competitors;
- improving existing products;
- making products more easily available.

As an example, a bank could seek superior performance in areas such as the greatest number of branches, the highest rates of interest, the greatest number of cash machines, or the most convenient home banking service. An organization can realistically aim to be leader in one of these areas, but not in all at the same time. It therefore develops those strengths which will give it a differential performance advantage in one of these benefit areas. A bank which has the most comprehensive branch network may build upon this by ensuring that they are open at times when customers wish to visit them; that there is no excessive waiting time and that they present a bright and inviting image to customers.

Of course, a differentiation strategy only works for as long as it takes competitors to catch up. Sometimes, a company can protect its differentiation strategy by patenting its products. This is especially important in the pharmaceutical industry where years of research can be rewarded with an exclusive right to sell a unique product for a number of years. At other times, firms must rely on differentiation through simple style changes or the addition of features that cannot be protected by patent. For a differentiation strategy to be sustainable, a company must continually invest in new product development and try to anticipate future trends.

Focus

An organization may focus on one or more small market segments rather than aiming for the whole market. A focus strategy involves an organization becoming familiar with the needs of specific market segments and gaining competitive advantage by cost leadership or differentiation within its chosen segments, or both.

A focus strategy requires an organization to segment its market and to specialize in products for that market. By concentrating on a narrow geographical segment, or producing specialized services for a very small segment, the organization can gain economies of scale in production. In this way a retailer of specialist musical equipment could focus on the needs of professional musicians living in the south-east of England. By building up volume of sales, it may achieve operating economies, by spreading overhead costs over a large number of customers. By focusing on the south-east market, it can reduce the costs which may result from attempting to arrange distribution to more remote areas.

Despite the advantages of a focus strategy described above, there are also dangers. The segments which form the focus may be too small to be economical in themselves. Moreover, an over-reliance on narrow segments could leave an organization dangerously exposed if these segments go into decline.

For firms pursuing a similar strategy aimed at similar market segments, Porter contends that the one which pursues its strategy most effectively will meet its objectives most effectively. Of all the car manufacturers pursuing a cost leadership strategy, the one which actually achieves the lowest level of costs will be the most successful. Firms which do not pursue a clear strategy are the least effective. Although they try to succeed in all three strategic alternatives, they end up showing no cost leadership, no differential advantage, and no clear focus on one customer group. Like many models, Porter's model has been challenged. Critics have pointed to successful firms who have managed to pursue multiple strategies simultaneously.

Positioning strategy

POSITIONING strategy is used by a company to distinguish its products from those of its competitors in order to give it a competitive advantage within a market. Positioning puts a firm in a sub-segment of its chosen market, thus a firm which adopts a product positioning based on 'high reliability/high cost' will appeal to a sub-segment which has a desire for reliability and a willingness to pay for it. For some marketers (e.g. Trout and Rivkin 1996) positioning has been seen as essentially a communications issue where the nature of the product is given and the objective is to manipulate consumer perceptions of it. However, others have pointed out that positioning is more than merely advertising and promotion but involves the management of the whole marketing mix. Essentially, the mix must be managed in a way that is internally coherent and sustainable over the long term. A marketing mix positioning of high quality and low prices may attract business from competitors in the short term, but the low prices may be insufficient to cover costs of delivering high quality, and therefore profits may be unsustainable over the long term.

A company must examine its opportunities and take a position within a marketplace. A position can be defined by reference to a number of scales—level of comfort and price are two dimensions of positioning which are relevant to cars. It is possible to draw a position map in which the positions of key players in a market are plotted in relation to these criteria. A position map plotting the positions of selected cars in respect of their price and level of comfort is shown in Fig. 11.2. Both scales run from high to low, with price being a general indication of price levels charged relative to competitors and level of comfort a subjective evaluation of features provided with the car. The position map shows that most cars lie on a diagonal line between the high comfort/high price position adopted by Mercedes Benz and Lexus and the low price/ low comfort position adopted by Proton and Lada. Points along this diagonal represent feasible positioning strategies for car manufacturers. A strategy in the upper left quadrant (high price/low quality) can be described as a 'cowboy' strategy and generally is not sustainable. A position in the lower right area of the map (high quality/low price) may indicate that an organization is failing to achieve a fair exchange of value. Of course, this two-dimensional analysis of the car market is very simplistic and buyers make judgements based on a variety of criteria. Low levels of comfort may be tolerated at a high price, for example, if a car carries a strong, aspirational brand name.

The example of cars used two very simplistic positioning criteria. Wind (1982, pp. 79–81) has suggested six generic scales along which all products can be positioned. These are examined below by reference to the positioning opportunities of a leisure centre:

- **by benefits or needs satisfied**: the leisure centre could position itself somewhere between meeting pure physical recreation needs and pure social needs. In practice,

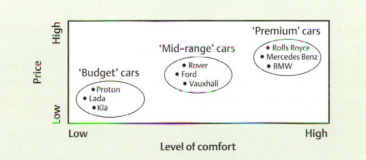

Figure 11.3 A simplified product positioning map for selected cars

positioning may combine the two sets of needs, for example by giving up gym space to allow the construction of a bar.

■ **by specific product features**: for example, a leisure centre can promote the fact that it has the largest swimming pool in the area, or the most advanced solarium.

■ **by usage occasions**: the centre could be positioned primarily for the occasional visitor, or the service offer could be adapted to aim at the more serious user who wishes to enter a long-term programme of leisure activities.

■ **by user categories**: a choice could be made between a position aimed at satisfying the needs of individual users and one aimed at meeting the needs of institutional users such as sports clubs and schools.

■ **by positioning against another product**: the leisure centre could promote the fact that it has more facilities than its neighbouring competition.

■ **by positioning by product class**: management could position the centre as an educational facility rather than a centre of leisure, thereby positioning it in a different product class.

Of all the position possibilities open to a company, which position should it adopt? Selecting a product position involves a number of basic steps (illustrated in Fig. 11.4).

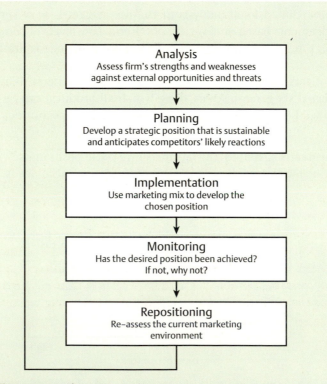

Figure 11.4 The process of positioning a product offer

1. **Undertake a marketing audit to analyse the position opportunities relative to the company's strengths**: A SWOT analysis should be undertaken to assess the opportunities and threats in a market-place and the strengths and weaknesses of the company in meeting opportunities as they arise. An important consideration is often the position that customers currently perceive a company as occupying. If a company is perceived as being downmarket, this may pose a major weakness in exploiting opportunities arising for more upmarket products. An organization which is already established in a particular product position will normally have the advantage of customer familiarity to support any new product launch. A car manufacturer such as Mercedes Benz which has positioned itself as a high quality/high price can use this as a strength to persuade customers to pay relatively high prices for a new product range, in this case a small compact car. Sometimes a weakness can be turned into a strength for positioning purposes, for example, the Avis car rental chain has stressed that by being the number two operator, it has to try harder.

   It often happens that opportunities are greatest in budget range, low quality, low price positions. If a company has established a position as a premium position supplier, should it seek to exploit a lower market position when the opportunity arises? It must avoid tarnishing its established brand values by association with a lower quality product. One solution is to adopt a separate identity for a new product which assumes a different position. In this way, the Volkswagen car group offers three different price/quality positions with its Volkswagen, Audi, and Skoda brands.

2. **Evaluate the position possibilities and select the most appropriate**: In undertaking a SWOT analysis, a number of potential positions may have been identified, but many may have to be discarded if they result in uneconomically small market segments, or are too costly to develop. Other positions may be rejected as being inconsistent with an organization's image. Selection from the remaining possibilities should be on the basis of the organization's greatest differential advantage in areas which are most valued by target customers. When it entered the Indonesian market, the UK retailer Marks & Spencer realized that its UK positioning would be unsustainable against low cost local competition. It therefore adopted a much more exclusive position with smaller shops, limited product ranges, and relatively high prices.

3. **Use the marketing mix to develop and communicate a position**: Organizations must develop programmes to implement and promote the position that they have adopted. If a car manufacturer seeks to adopt a position as a supplier of premium quality cars at premium prices, it must have in hand production facilities for ensuring consistently high quality. It must also effectively communicate this quality to potential customers in order to justify customers paying premium prices.

Repositioning

Markets are dynamic and what was once an appropriate position for a company may eventually cease to be so. A company's environmental monitoring should identify any factors that may call for a repositioning. Repositioning could become necessary for a number of reasons:

■ The original positioning may have been based on an overestimation of a company's competitive advantage or of the size of the sub-segment to whom the positioning was intended to appeal. Positioning strategy could have become untenable.

■ The nature of customer demand may have changed, for example in respect of preferences for high quality rather than low price. It has, for example been argued that UK customers' attitudes towards package holidays have changed during the 1990s away from an emphasis on low price towards greater emphasis on high quality standards. Many tour operators accordingly repositioned their offering to provide higher standards at higher prices.

■ Companies often try to build upon their growing strengths to reposition towards meeting the needs of more profitable high value sub-segments. In many sectors, companies start life as simple, no frills, low price operations, subsequently gaining a favourable image which they use to 'trade up' to relatively high quality/high price positions. This phenomenon is well established in the field of retailing and has become known as the 'Wheel of Retailing'. This contends that retail businesses start life as cut-price, low cost, narrow margin operations which subsequently 'trade up' with improvements in display, more prestigious premises, increased advertising, delivery, and the provision of many other customer services which serve to drive up expenses, prices, and margins. Eventually, retailers mature as high cost, conservative, and 'top-heavy' institutions with a sales policy based on quality goods and services rather than price appeal. This in turn opens the way for the next generation of low cost innovatory retailers to find a position which maturing firms have vacated.

Developing a portfolio of products/markets

MANAGING a portfolio of products was noted above as a key factor in creating a sustainable competitive advantage. The previous chapter noted that portfolio analysis can be useful in guiding new product development. Portfolio planning can be applied to the types of products/markets served and the stage of products in their life cycles.

Risk spreading is an important element of portfolio planning which goes beyond marketing planning. Giving strategic direction to an organization is not simply a case of analysing the needs of consumers and gearing its resources to earn good short-term profits from meeting these needs. Maintaining a balanced portfolio of activities can be just as important as earning adequate short-term profits. In this respect, a bank may be meeting a proven need by lending money to fund property purchase and earning acceptable returns from it. However, a strategic approach to portfolio management may lead it to diversify into some other activity with a counterbalancing

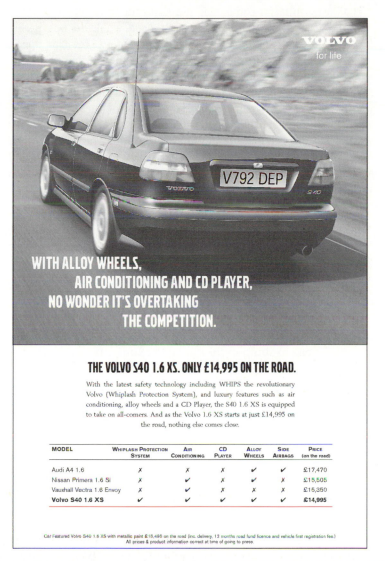

Figure 11.5 In this advertisement the unique product benefits of a Volvo car are contrasted with those offered by competing products. Compare this approach to identifying benefits with the approach of other car manufacturers who make emotional appeals about their products. (Reproduced with permission of Volvo Cars UK)

Should a company 'stick to its knitting' and do what it is good at, or search continually for new products and new markets? Countless companies have reported disastrous results after going into areas they knew very little about. The rapid growth of Next from its core of fashion retailing to newsagents and home furnishings contributed to its near collapse in the late 1980s. TSB Bank diversified into car leasing but regretted it later. WH Smith went through bad years in the mid-1990s when the newsagent's diversification into DIY retailing and television failed to work.

But isn't change essential for companies, especially those facing static or declining markets? One of the UK's leading grocery retailers, Asda, would not be where it is today had not the Associated Dairy company taken a risk and set up a retailing operation. The security services company Securicor company knew that it was taking a risk when it invested in a joint venture with British Telecom to create the successful Cellnet mobile phone network. And a small company called WPP (standing for Wire Plastic Products) took huge risks on its way to becoming the owner of one of the world's leading advertising agencies, J. Walter Thompson.

It is fine with hindsight to criticize a firm's decisions about which direction its product portfolio should take. But in an uncertain world, risks have to be taken. A sound analysis of a company's strengths and weaknesses and of its external environment certainly helps, but success also depends upon an element of luck.

level of cash flow and risk, turning away business which may seem attractive in the short term.

Some companies deliberately provide a range of products which—quite apart from their potential for cross selling—act in contrasting manners during the business cycle. There is a long tradition to this practice, for example the ice-cream manufacturer Walls became more sustainable as a business unit by adding sausages to its product portfolio. Sausages tended to have their highest demand in winter, counterbalancing the sharp peak in summer for ice-cream. Similarly, accountancy firms have become potentially more stable units as they have amalgamated, by allowing procyclical activities such as management buy-out expertise and venture capital investment to be counterbalanced by contra-cyclical activities such as insolvency work.

Sometimes, statutory requirements may require a balanced portfolio of output. The Bank of England's regulation of the UK banking system, for example, imposes constraints on banks' freedom to be market led in the pattern of their lending decisions.

For a company to put all of its efforts into supplying a very limited range of products to a narrow market segment is potentially dangerous. Over-reliance on this one segment can make the survival of the organization dependent upon the fortunes of this one segment and its liking for its product. In any event, the fact that most markets change to some extent over time would imply that its products will eventually move out of line with customers' requirements. Also, with the development of relationship marketing strategies, firms are increasingly keen to develop opportunities for offering customers a broad range of products which attract a higher share of their total expenditure. For all of these reasons, organizations seek to manage their growth in a manner that maintains a desired portfolio of products.

Portfolio position analysis

Organizations seek to match their own internal strengths with the opportunities available in their environment. A number of attempts have been made to show in the form of a portfolio position map the mix of products within a company's portfolio. Such position maps can facilitate management thinking in the development of balanced portfolios and the allocation of strategic priorities. In Fig. 11.6 a typical portfolio position map is shown. The grid comprises two dimensions—market attractiveness and competitive position. Market attractiveness includes such factors as the size of a market, its projected growth rate, and earnings performance. Competitive position refers to brand strength, experience in a market, and the availability of financial, technical, and human resources to serve that market. In developing an index, weights must be attached to each of these components and a sometimes subjective assessment made of each component. Ownership of a strong brand may be an essential element of competitive advantage for a soft drinks firm and would therefore be given a relatively high weighting, although the task of assessing how strong a brand is remains very subjective.

For the purpose of analysis, each of these scales is divided into two classifications, resulting in a matrix of four cells.

Box 1: A market may appear attractive, but if a company has only a weak competitive position, it should think carefully before investing large amounts of cash. The market will appear attractive to other companies who have a stronger competitive position.

Box 2: A highly attractive market for which a company has a strong competitive position is the best position in the matrix and the company should invest and build for future growth.

Box 3: Unattractive markets for which a company does not have a strong competitive position should be avoided. However, a company may find that it has products in this box which were previous high performers, but market characteristics have changed.

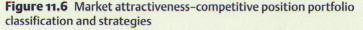

Figure 11.6 Market attractiveness–competitive position portfolio classification and strategies

The best that a company can do with the remaining products in this box is to refrain from new investment and to manage the products for the cash they generate.

Box 4: Market attractiveness is low, but the company's competitive position is strong. The company should exploit its strengths by selectively investing and building for future market growth.

As a portfolio model the grid can be used to analyse the current offering of a business. As a basis for strategy formulation, the grid focuses attention on finding strategies which match an organization's internal strengths and weaknesses with the opportunities and threats presented by its operating environment. The key to making this model useful in formulating marketing strategy is to measure the two dimensions of the grid, not only as they are at the present, but as they are likely to be in the future.

It must not be forgotten that market attractiveness is a dynamic measure and, for planning purposes, the prime consideration is how attractive a market will appear at the time when a proposed strategy is implemented. If a market appears attractive to one company, then it probably appears equally attractive to others as well, who may possess equal competitive advantage in addressing the market. If all such firms decide to enter the market, oversupply results, profit margins become squeezed, and the market becomes relatively unattractive. This is especially true of easy to copy goods and services.

Planning for growth

MOST private-sector organizations pursue growth in one form or another, whether this is an explicit aim or merely an implicit aim of its managers. Growth is often associated with increasing returns to shareholders and greater career opportunities for managers. Growth may be vital in order to reach a critical size at which economies of scale in production, distribution, and promotion can be achieved, thereby contributing to a company's sustainable competitive advantage.

Of course, the growth pursued by many companies has proved to be unsustainable. There have been many spectacular failures where too rapid a rate of growth has left a company close to bankruptcy, including Next, Coloroll, and the Fascia Group. It is therefore important to consider the options open for growth and the levels of risk and sustainability inherent in each of these.

Market/product expansion choices

A frequently used approach to understanding growth is to analyse two key dimensions: market development and product development. These dimensions form the basis of the product/market expansion grid proposed by Ansoff (1957). Products and markets are each analysed in terms of their degree of novelty to an organization and growth strategies identified in terms of these two dimensions. In this way, four possible growth strategies can be identified. An illustration of the framework, with reference to the specific options open to a grocery retailer, is shown in Fig. 11.7. The four growth options are associated with differing sets of problems and opportunities for a company. These relate to the resources required to implement a particular strategy, and the level of risk associated with each. It follows, therefore, that what might be a feasible growth strategy for one organization may not be for another. The characteristics of the four strategies are described below.

1. **Market penetration strategies**: This type of strategy focuses growth on the existing product range by encouraging higher levels of take-up of a service among the existing target markets. In this way a food manufacturer serving the growing market for organic produce could—all other things being equal—grow naturally, simply by maintaining its current marketing strategy. If it wanted to accelerate this growth, it could do this firstly by seeking to sell more products to its existing customers and secondly by attracting customers from its direct competitors. If the market was in fact in decline, the company could only grow by attracting customers from its competitors through more aggressive marketing policies and/or cost reduction programmes. This strategy offers the least level of risk to an organization—it is familiar with both its products and its customers.

2. **Market development strategies**: This type of strategy builds upon the existing product range which an organization has established, but seeks to find new groups of customers for them. In this way the organic foods manufacturer which had saturated its current market might seek to expand its sales to new geographical regions or overseas markets. It could also aim its marketing effort at attracting custom from groups beyond its current age/income groups, for example by targeting children with organically produced snacks. While the company may be familiar with the production side of its growth plans, it faces risks because it may have poor knowledge of different buyer behaviour patterns in the markets which it is attempting to enter. For an organic food company that has built its business in south-east England, it may have little knowledge about consumer buying

		Products	
		Existing	New
Markets Existing		**Market penetration strategy** Achieve higher market share among population within catchment area of its existing shops	**Product development strategy** Develop new restaurant facilities at its stores
New		**Market development strategy** Open new shops in different areas of the country	**Diversification** Develop a food processing operation

Figure 11.7 An application of Ansoff's product/market growth matrix to a grocery retailer

behaviour in northern England, or in continental European countries, for example. It may face even greater risk in developing a marketing strategy aimed at children, whose needs it has little previous experience of satisfying.

3. **Product development strategy**: As an alternative to selling existing products into new markets, a company may choose to develop new products for its existing markets. The organic food company may add new ranges of ready meals, or drinks, for example. While the company minimizes the risk associated with the uncertainty of new markets, it faces risk resulting from lack of knowledge about its new product area. Often a feature of this growth strategy is collaboration with a product specialist who helps the organization produce the new products, leaving it free to market it effectively to its customers. Rather than setting up its own facility to produce ready prepared meals, the organic foods company may leave the specialized task of doing this and undertaking quality controls to a more experienced food manufacturer.

4. **Diversification strategy**: Here, a company expands by developing new products for new markets. Diversification can take a number of forms. The company could stay within the same general product/market area, but diversify into a new point of the distribution chain—for example, the organic food producer may move into retailing of its products, rather than just selling its products exclusively to wholesalers and retailers. Alternatively, it might diversify into completely unrelated areas aimed at quite different market segments, for example by offering residential cookery courses. Because the company is moving into both unknown markets and unknown product areas, this form of growth carries the greatest level of risk from a marketing management perspective. Diversification may, however, help to manage the long-term risk of the organization by reducing dependency on a narrow product/market area.

The personal style of Richard Branson may seem slightly offbeat compared to the typical Chief Executive, but he has been much admired for his charismatic leadership of the Virgin group. But just how far can the Virgin group spread itself and risk getting into businesses for which it has few competencies? Growth has taken the business from its roots in the music industry through airlines, beverages, and condoms. The key behind the group's success has been a customer focus and a clear positioning as a slightly unconventional, respected, and reliable supplier of goods and services. However, many observers were sceptical about Virgin's move into the financial services sector. In early 1995, a Personal Equity Plan (PEP) was launched by Virgin in association with Norwich Union, focusing on the Virgin brand's association with reliability, value for money, and a sometimes slightly offbeat approach to marketing. Critics within the established financial service sector were quick to point out that while it was good to have the charismatic figure of Richard Branson raising the profile of their industry, he was really stretching the Virgin brand too far. It is argued that Branson's passion is airlines and, given that he has pulled out of other business areas, will he have enough enthusiasm for financial services, which have to be seen as essentially long term?

In practice, most growth that occurs is a combination of product development and market development. In very competitive markets, a company would most likely have to adapt its product slightly if it was to become attractive to a new market segment.

Organic growth v. growth by acquisition

The manner in which an organization grows can affect the sustainability of that growth. There are two basic means by which an organization can grow—through organic growth and by acquisition, although many organizations grow by a combination of the two processes. The manner of growth has important marketing implications, for instance in the speed with which an organization is allowed to expand into new market opportunities and the level of risk to which it exposes itself.

Organic growth is considered to be the more 'natural' pattern of growth for a company. The initial investment by the company results in profits, an established customer base, and a well founded technical, personnel, and financial structure. This provides a sound basis for future growth. In this sense, success breeds success for the rate of the organization's growth is influenced by the extent to which it has succeeded in building up internally the means for future expansion.

An organization may grow organically by tackling one market segment at a time, using the resources, knowledge, and market awareness it has gained in order to tackle further segments. Organic growth into new segments may occur in a number of ways. Many grocery retailers have grown organically by developing one region before moving on to another. In the UK, Sainsbury's grew organically from its southern base towards the northern regions, while Asda grew organically during the 1970s and early 1980s from its northern base towards the south. Other organizations have grown organically by aiming a basically similar product at new segments of the market. Mobile phone companies started by aiming their services at business users and have since widened their market to open up segments of personal and purely leisure users.

There are limits to a firm's rate of organic growth. If the markets for its products are only growing slowly, organic growth alone will be slow. Companies with relatively high capital requirements will find organic growth relatively slow. Organic growth limits a company's exposure to major risk, as development is essentially incremental and the company can learn from its previous trading experience. However, where markets are fast moving and new opportunities arise, organic growth alone may be insufficient to give a firm a competitive advantage.

Growth by acquisition may be attractive to organizations where opportunities for organic growth are low. It is sometimes almost essential in order to achieve a critical mass which is necessary in order to gain a competitive cost advantage. The DIY retail sector in the UK is one where chains have needed to achieve a critical mass in order to pass on lower prices resulting from economies in buying, distribution, and promotion. Small chains have not been able to grow organically at a sufficient rate to achieve this size, resulting in their take-over or merger to form larger chains. The market leader—B&Q has seen mainly organic growth, while the Homebase chain grew significantly with the acquisition of the rival Texas chain.

Many firms have used growth by acquisition to diversify into new product or market areas. The time and risk associated with starting a new venture in an unknown market sector may be considered too great, so acquiring an established business is seen as less risky. A take-over can be mutually beneficial where one company has a sound customer base but lacks the financial resources to achieve a critical mass while the other has the finance but needs a larger customer base.

Although growth by acquisition may allow a company to gain a competitive advantage, it can also present considerable risks. An acquisition often involves a company raising new loans which must be repaid, regardless of the financial performance of the business being acquired. A high level of 'gearing' (that is, a high proportion of loans to equity capital) can leave a company dangerously exposed where the economy goes into recession. A company that has grown organically may be able to defer paying a dividend to shareholders, but holders of loans will expect payments on those loans to be made on time, regardless of the company's profitability or cash flow. There have been many cases of companies that have expanded through acquisition in order to gain a competitive advantage, but collapsed under the weight of their debt (for example, the hotel chain Queens Moat House became unable to pay the interest charges on its newly acquired hotels when the sector faced a downturn in the early 1990s).

A further problem for firms growing by acquisition is that they may be unable to prevent key personnel at the acquired company leaving, taking critical skills and knowledge with them. Worse still, these employees could defect to the acquiring company's competitors. During the late 1980s, many financial institutions acquired estate agencies, but found the value of their investments reduced when key staff left—with their list of contacts—to work for competitors.

Chapter summary and key linkages to other chapters

Developing a sustainable competitive advantage involves a sound understanding of a firm's strengths and weaknesses relative to the opportunities and threats in its market environment. A marketing mix is developed, based on a combination of scientific analysis and personal judgement. The only effective marketing mix strategy is one that is sustainable over the long term. A position in the market-place must be adopted which is internally coherent and sustainable against competitors' reactions. Most organizations have an inherent tendency to grow, but some types of growth are more sustainable than others.

The following key linkages to other chapters should be noted:

Chapter 1: What is marketing?: Chapter 1 discussed the basic theories and tools of marketing, which form the basis of developing a sustainable competitive advantage discussed in this chapter.

Chapter 2: The marketing environment: Continual monitoring of the changing marketing environment is critical to retaining a profitable position in the market-place.

Chapter 3: Market segmentation: An important task of marketing management is to prioritize market segments and identify those segments where it can sustain a competitive advantage.

Chapter 4: Branding: For many companies, brands are among their most valuable assets which give them a competitive advantage. However, to be sustainable, brands need maintenance if they are to retain their value in the eyes of customers.

Chapter 5: Marketing and ethics: Buyers are increasingly judging the ethical standpoint of a company, and some companies have developed a strong position based upon their ethical behaviour.

Chapter 6: Marketing research: Successful companies have effective systems for collecting, analysing, disseminating, and acting on information which allow them to maintain a competitive position.

Chapters 7/8: Buyer behaviour and buyer–seller relationship development: Processes by which customers buy should be carefully understood in order that ways of doing business are convenient for customers and not just the company.

Chapters 9/10: Developing a product portfolio: The product is at the heart of what a company offers its customers. With changes in customers' preferences and the development of new technologies, a company's portfolio of products could rapidly become unsuited to customers' needs, diminishing any competitive advantage.

Chapters 12/13: Pricing theory and application: Pricing is the one element of the marketing mix that brings in revenue—the others are cost items. Prices must be sufficiently high to cover costs and generate an adequate level of profits.

Chapter 14: Intermediaries: Wholesale and retail outlets are often a source of a firm's competitive advantage. A company may have the best product on offer, but will not benefit from it if the product is not readily available through intermediaries.

Chapters 16–20: Principles of promotion planning/advertising/sales promotion/ personal selling/direct marketing: Promotion is closely related to positioning. A company must communicate its unique positioning to potential customers.

Chapter 21: Managing the marketing effort: The current chapter has discussed the general principles of creating a sustainable competitive advantage. Chapter 21 discusses how this can be made to happen in practice.

Chapter 22: Services marketing: For many manufacturing companies, superiority in service aspects of the product offer competitive advantage. Services are easy to copy and cannot be protected by patent, so a firm must ensure that its service quality is continually ahead of its competitors.

Chapter 23: Global marketing: The tasks of creating a sustainable competitive advantage in overseas markets are in principle similar to those in the domestic market, but risks are likely to be greater in view of the uncertainty of the overseas business environment.

Case study

Complacency can be the biggest enemy of retailers

'There's no need to ask the price—it's a penny' was the proud claim of Marks & Spencer a hundred years ago. From the start, it had developed a unique position in its market— an emphasis on low price, wide range, and good quality. Over time, the Marks & Spencer position has been steadily developed, along with its profitability. By the 1990s it looked unstoppable as a retailer, as it progressively expanded its product range from clothing to food, furnishings, and financial services. The world seemed to be waiting for M&S to exploit, and despite disappointing starts in the USA and Canada, it developed steadily throughout Europe and the Far East. Then, just like any star who has been put on a pedestal, the media began to savage the company. After a sudden drop in profits and sales during 1998, critics claimed that the company had lost its position in the market-place. It appeared to be like a supertanker, ploughing straight ahead with a management that had become much less adaptable to change than its nimbler competitors.

Many observers had commented on the fact that the company did not have a marketing department until 1998. Marketing, at least in terms of advertising the brand, had become so important to its competitors, but had never been high on Marks & Spencer's agenda. According to Media Monitoring Services, M&S's total media spending between December 1997 and November 1998 was just £4.7 million, almost a drop in the ocean compared to the spending of Sainsbury's (£42.1 million); Tesco (£27.5 million); and Woolworth's (£21.5 million). While other retailers had worked hard on building a brand image, M&S has relied on the quality of its stock to do the talking. The argument was that everyone knew what they were getting with M&S underwear or shirts—good quality at fair, but not cheap, prices. Similarly with food, M&S's offering was about quality rather than price. M&S believed its customers knew what the brand stood for and advertising was much less important than ensuring that it could obtain the right products at the right price.

In 1998, M&S looked to marketing to help turn around its performance, describing its new marketing division for UK retail as 'a significant development in our retailing philosophy'. Many suspected that M&S's conversion to marketing had been encouraged by the example set by the star of modern retailing, Tesco. There are many similarities between the problems facing M&S and those which Tesco faced a decade previously. In the early 1990s Tesco was a brand which looked like it had seen better days. The retailer's format was tired, its stores poorly laid out, and the positioning of the company was still based on its founder's principle of 'pile it high and sell it cheap'. Its arch-rival, Sainsbury's, was regarded as the more upmarket store for the middle classes, who shopped for quality food in a more pleasant environment. Since then, Tesco had transformed its brand and its profitability. It realized that the trend in shopping was towards a more concerted focus on customer service and that store design, product quality, and, crucially, its relationship with customers would be vital to success. Gaining a competitive edge was becoming even more important as saturation in the sector gave most people a choice of supermarkets which were within easy reach for their shopping. Tesco responded to the competitive challenge with more store assistants, new store designs, petrol stations, coffee shops, a new fascia, the

Tesco Clubcard, and twenty-four-hour store opening. The list of Tesco's marketing initiatives seemed to be unstoppable, in an attempt to keep one step ahead of its competitors.

In contrast, M&S had failed to keep pace with customer service. In many issues of retail development, such as out-of-town shopping centres, Sunday opening, and loyalty cards, it had lagged behind its main competitors. While it has stood still, the likes of Tesco and Sainsbury's marched ahead until there was no longer much that felt exceptional about the M&S shopping experience. Analysts argued that M&S had failed to make its store layouts help shoppers bring clothing together to make outfits. In a typical M&S store, all jackets would be located in one area and all cardigans in another, for example. Its competitors had made much greater progress in bringing together co-ordinated sets of clothing which would encourage shoppers to spend more. M&S has also been criticized for making things difficult for customers by not accepting payment by major credit cards.

In response to its current troubles, the newly created marketing department of M&S launched its first national campaign towards the end of 1998. The ads followed an initial attempt at regional TV advertising earlier in the year, with which the company was said to be very pleased. The newly appointed Chief Executive claimed 'It's not that people don't like what we're selling, but that we haven't got the message across. There are an awful lot of people who love us for our knickers, but they don't love our home furnishings because they don't even know they are there.' Many critics thought the problems were much more deep seated and blamed the store's problems on the fact that its autumn fashions were seen as dull and uninspiring, and out of touch with consumers' preferences. Greater authority was pledged to the marketing department when it came to new product design.

In response to its pledge to listen to what its customers wanted, new designers were brought in to try to give the company's ranges more sparkle. The company even thought the previously unthinkable by proposing to stock manufacturers' own branded products, instead of relying entirely on M&S's own-label products. If customers wanted to obtain variety at M&S, the new thinking was that the company must adapt and offer it. Another area identified for development was direct marketing of fashion products— an area where the company had begun to lag behind its rivals who had developed interactive web sites.

Serious questions remained about the company. How quickly could it change in response to its changed environment? The company had not been known for speedy decision-making, so probably a major structural overhaul was essential before it could get down to the serious business of adapting to customers' changing needs. Also, there was a great danger of changing the company's position too far and too fast, thereby alienating its traditional customers without gaining sufficient new ones. As a warning of how not to change, M&S's rival Laura Ashley had repositioned itself so radically from its original format that it now failed to gain the support of any major group. M&S had itself tried to become more fashion conscious during the mid-1980s with similar effect, and had to make a hasty retreat to its traditional, more staid image.

Based on 'Time for M&S to follow Tesco', *Marketing*, 28 January 1999.

Case study review questions

1 What do you understand by positioning, and what tools are available to Marks & Spencer to give it a positioning advantage?

2 There has been a lot of debate about whether the existence of a marketing department can actually be harmful to services companies because it absolves everybody else of marketing responsibilities. What, then, do you make of M&S's decision to introduce a marketing department?

3 What are the dangers to M&S of moving its market position too far and too fast? How can it try to alleviate these problems?

Chapter review questions

1 What factors might explain why so many of the firms in Peters and Waterman's study of excellent US firms had been eclipsed a few years later?

2 In the context of a sustainable competitive advantage, what is meant by customer value? How can a company ensure that it continues to deliver value?

3 Why is it important for a company to undertake a SWOT analysis not only of itself, but also of its competitors?

4 Using examples, discuss the problems that are likely to result from a firm seeking to reposition its product offer.

5 From a marketing perspective, critically assess the advantages and disadvantages of a strategy of growth by diversification.

6 What are the benefits of growth for organizations' marketing activities? Using relevant examples, can excessive growth have a detrimental effect on marketing?

References

Ansoff, I. H. (1957), 'Strategies for Diversification', *Harvard Business Review*, **25**, 5, pp. 113–24.

McDonald, M. (1994), *Marketing—the Challenge of Change* (London: Chartered Institute of Marketing).

Nielsen Grocery Service (1998), The Retail Pocket Book (NTC Publications).

Porter, M. E. (1980), *Competitive Strategy: Techniques for Analysing Industries and Competitors* (New York: The Free Press).

Trout, J., and Rivkin, S. (1996), *The New Positioning* (London: McGraw-Hill).

Wind, Y. J. (1982), *Product Policy: Concepts, Methods and Strategy* (Reading, Mass: Addison-Wesley).

Suggested further reading

The ways in which marketing strategy can give a firm a competitive advantage are discussed in the following:

■ Bharadwaj, S. G., Rajan, P., and Fahy, J. (1993), 'Sustainable Competitive Advantage in Service Industries: A Conceptual Model and Research Propositions', *Journal of Marketing*, **57**, pp. 83–99.

■ Egan, C. (1998), *CIM Handbook of Strategic Marketing* (London: Butterworth-Heinemann).

■ Fifield, P. (1998), *Marketing Strategy—How to Prepare it: How to Implement It* (London: Butterworth-Heinemann).

■ McDonald, M. (1992), 'Strategic Marketing Planning, A State of the Art Review', *Marketing Intelligence and Planning*, **10**, 4, pp. 4–22.

■ Narver, J., and Slater, S. (1994), 'Marketing Orientation, Customer Value and Superior Performance', *Business Horizons*, **37**, 2, pp. 22–9.

■ Peters, T. J., and Waterman, R. H. (1982), *In Search of Excellence: Lessons from America's Best Run Companies* (New York: Harper & Row).

■ Piercy, N. (1997), *Market Led Strategic Change* (London: Butterworth-Heinemann).

■ Taylor, B. (1997), 'The Return of Strategic Planning, Once More with Feeling', *Long Range Planning*, **30**, 3, pp. 334–44.

■ White, D. S., and Griffith, D. A. (1997), 'Combining Corporate and Marketing Strategy for Global Competitiveness', *Marketing Intelligence & Planning*, **15**, 4–5, pp. 173–9.

Positioning strategy is discussed in the following:

■ Kalra, A., and Goodstein, R. C. (1998), 'The Impact of Advertising Positioning Strategies on Consumer Price Sensitivity', *Journal of Marketing Research*, **35**, 2, pp. 210–25.

■ Trout, J., and Rivkin, S. (1996), *The New Positioning* (London: McGraw-Hill).

Chapter 12
Pricing: Underlying Principles

Chapter objectives

This is the first of two chapters dealing with the price element of the marketing mix. In this chapter, the economic theory underlying price decisions is explored. Perfectly competitive markets are presented as one extreme in which the marketer must take prices as given from the market. Various other market structures are discussed and their impact on pricing decisions assessed. This chapter develops underlying theories of pricing—the following chapter will apply this to the development of pricing strategy.

Introduction

Most of the decisions made by marketing managers involve spending their company's money—advertising, paying sales personnel, setting up distributor networks, new product development, and so on. Price is the one element of the marketing mix which directly affects the income that a company receives. In businesses with high turnover and low profit margins, a miscalculation of selling prices can have a big effect on a firm's annual profits. If the company charges too little for its products, it may find that, although it has achieved a very respectable level of sales, the low price charged is insufficient to give it any profit. Too high a price and it may be unable to sell sufficient output to cover its fixed overhead costs. It may also end up with unsold stocks of obsolete products.

For most firms, setting prices is a difficult task which involves both scientific analysis and intuitive trial and error. This is especially true of new product launches where a company has no historical precedent on which to base its expectations of how much customers will be prepared to pay.

Two chapters are devoted to issues of pricing. In this chapter, we will look at some of the basic principles and theory which underly firms' pricing decisions. Taking a broad perspective, firms cannot ignore market forces, so it is important to understand the relationship between market structure and the way in which prices are determined. The approach to pricing of a firm operating in a fiercely competitive market will differ quite markedly from the approach of a firm in an oligopolistic market. Consumers do not act with complete rationality, so it is important to understand something of the psychological processes that influence their evaluation of prices. Finally in this chapter, the effects of regulation on firms' pricing decisions will be considered. We are living in a world where governments increasingly seek to control prices of key goods and services, so it is important to understand how firms can reconcile the sometimes conflicting approaches of market forces and regulation.

The following chapter will consider more applied issues of pricing. Firms develop strategies in order to respond to the competitive nature of their environment, for example they may aim to be a price leader across their range of products. For individual new product launches a company may pursue a strategy of starting with a high price, and gradually lowering it over time. In terms of setting prices for individual products, firms pursue a variety of approaches, including basing their selling price on their production costs, the prices which competitors are currently charging, and customers' ability and willingness to pay.

Of course, pricing should never be seen as an isolated element of a firm's marketing decision-making. What the company is able to charge is closely related to, among other things, the quality of its products, the advertising images that it has created, and its distribution strategy.

Effects of market structure on pricing

THE market conditions facing suppliers of goods and services vary considerably. Customers of gas and water supply companies may feel they are being exploited with high prices and poor service levels provided by companies who know that their customers have little choice of supplier. On the other hand, customers are constantly being wooed by seemingly countless travel and motor insurance companies, all trying to offer deals which buyers will consider to be better than those offered by competitors. The differences in the pricing behaviour of these two groups of organizations can be related to the structure of the markets in which they operate. The term 'market structure' is used to describe:

- the number of buyers and sellers operating in a market;
- the barriers which exist to prevent new firms from entering the market (or prevent existing companies from leaving it);
- the extent to which the supply of goods and services is concentrated in the hands of

a small number of buyers (or, less frequently, the extent to which purchases are concentrated in the hands of a few buyers);

■ the degree of collusion which occurs between buyers and/or sellers in the market.

An understanding of market structure underpins all pricing decisions made by marketers. Market structure influences not only the pricing decisions made by marketers within a firm, but also the nature of the response from other firms operating in the market.

Economists have developed a number of labels to describe different types of market structure. At one theoretical extreme is the model of perfect competition and at the other is pure monopoly. In practice, examples of the extremes are very rare, and most markets are referred to as being in a state of imperfect competition (Fig. 12.1).

We are going to spend some time looking at perfectly competitive markets. These are characterized by the following conditions:

■ There are many producers supplying to the market, each with similar cost structures and each producing an identical product. No single supplier can on its own influence the market price.

■ There are also many buyers in the market, none of whom can, on their own, influence the market price.

■ Both buyers and sellers are free to enter or leave the market, that is, there are no barriers to entry or exit.

■ There is a ready supply of information for buyers and sellers, for example about competing alternatives.

These may seem quite unrealistic conditions for many markets, although a few markets do come close to meeting them (e.g. the 'spot' market for oil products and

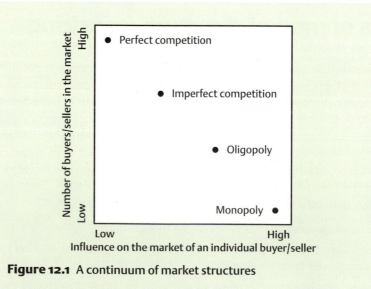

Figure 12.1 A continuum of market structures

```
212½   79   UK Land          191   ...  2.6  11.6
256½  186½  Warner           254½  ...  5.5  15.7
375   230   Warnford         360   ...  2.2  19.1
99     65¼  Wates             96½  ...  0.4  46.3
825   450   Workspace Grpt   817½ − 2½  2.4  26.2
```

RETAILERS, FOOD

```
188    53   Alldays           55  −  2½ 10.9  ...
78½    58   Budgens          73½  + 1   2.7  11.4
92     53¼  Dairy Farm Intl  55¾  − ¼  6.5  29.5
172½  102   Fyffes†          170   ...  2.0  ...
2687½ 1912½ Greggs          2020   ...  2.1  16.4
317½  224½  Iceland Group    256  − 7   2.3  11.4
175   113   Morrison (W)     131  + 4   1.0  18.4
304   160¾  Safeway†         209¾ − 4¼  6.0   9.8
480   286   Sainsbury J      351  − 1   4.1  25.2
```

WATER

```
845   480   Anglian Water    484  − 45   8.9  7.2
285   187   East Surrey      187   ...   7.1  7.4
836   220   Hyder†           225½ − 14½ 17.9  4..
124¼   86¼  Hyder Cm Prf†     86¼ − ¼    9.1  ..
552½  270   Kelda            295   ...   8.0  5.3
665   322½  Mid Kent Hdgs    327½  ...  11.1  3.5
1162½ 490   Pennon           500  + 5    7.2  6.6
1023  571¼  Severn Trent†    646½ − 16½  7.4  7.5
437½  302½  South Staffs     325  + 6½   3.8 10.
1179  670   Thames†          765  − 16   5.7  7.7
894½  471   Utd Utilities†   623½ − 36    7.2  7.3
```

Figure 12.2 Stock markets come close to meeting the requirements of perfect competition, with large numbers of buyers and sellers resulting in daily fluctuations in a company's share price

stock markets where shares are bought and sold). However, the real value of studying competitive markets is that it teaches us the basic rules of supply, demand, and price determination.

The theory of supply and demand

THE term 'market forces' is inextricably linked to the concept of supply and demand. In perfectly competitive markets, firms are price *takers* and their ability to set prices is limited by the level of demand and supply within the market which they serve. If total demand goes up, all other things being equal, the going rate of prices in the market for their product will rise. Likewise if there is a drop in total supply for whatever reason (e.g. due to bad weather), there will be further pressure for prices in the market to rise. The final price paid in the market will reflect the balance between supply side and demand side factors.

A market as defined here need not be a physical location where buyers and sellers meet (as happens in retail and wholesale grocery markets). A market in the economist's sense refers to all individuals and firms who wish either to buy or sell a specified product, regardless of where they are located. Very often a market is defined in terms of product and geographic descriptions, so the UK soft drinks market refers to all individuals in the UK who seek to buy soft drinks and the suppliers to that market.

Demand

Demand refers to how many people in a market are actually able and willing to buy a product at a given price and given a set of assumptions about the product and the environment in which it is being offered. Demand is also expressed in terms of a specified time period, for example thousands of litres of soft drink per week. It is important to add the caveat that demand is about the quantity of a product that consumers are *willing* and *able* to buy at a specific price over a given period of time. It is important to distinguish these conditions from what people would merely *like* to buy, after all, most people would probably like to buy expensive holidays and cars.

For most products, as their price falls, so the demand for them (as defined above) can be expected to rise. Likewise, as the price falls, demand could be expected to rise. This relationship can be plotted on a simple graph. In Fig. 12.3, a *demand curve* for dessert strawberries is shown by the line D1. This relates—for any given price shown on the vertical axis—the volume of demand, which is shown on the horizontal axis. So at a price of £8 per kg, demand is 20,000 units per period within a given area, while at a price of £4, the demand has risen to 40,000 units.

The demand curve shown in Fig. 12.3 refers to *total* market demand from all consumers and is not simply measuring demand for one strawberry grower's output. The importance of this distinction will become clear later, because, in imperfect markets, each producer seeks to develop a unique demand function for its own differentiated product.

In drawing the price-volume relationship D1, a number of assumptions were made. These include, for example, assumptions that the price of substitutes for strawberries will not change, or that consumers will not suddenly take a disliking to strawberries. Demand curve D1 measures the relationship between price and market demand for *one given set of assumptions*. When these assumptions change, a new demand curve is needed to explain the new relationship between price and quantity demanded.

In Fig. 12.4, two sets of fresh assumptions have been made and new price–volume relationship curves D2 and D3 drawn, based on these new sets of assumptions. For new demand curve D2, more strawberries are demanded for any given price level (or alternatively, this can be restated in terms of any given number of consumers

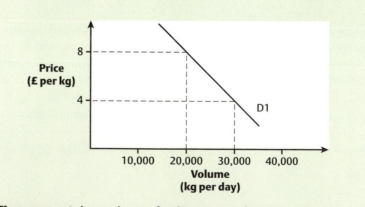

Figure 12.3 A demand curve for dessert strawberries

demanding strawberries being prepared to pay a higher price). A shift from D1 to D2 could come about for a number of reasons, including:

- Increased spending power available to consumers could lead to more of all goods, including strawberries being bought.
- The demand for strawberries may be dependent upon demand for some complementary goods. For example, if demand for cream increases (perhaps because of some newly discovered health benefit), it is just possible that demand for strawberries will also rise.
- There could have been an increase in the price of substitutes for strawberries (such as peaches or raspberries), thereby increasing demand for strawberries.
- Heavy advertising of strawberries may increase demand for strawberries.
- Consumer preferences may change. This may occur, for example, if strawberries are found to have positive effects on health

In the case of the fall in the price–volume relationship from D1 to D3, corresponding but opposite explanations can be put forward, including: reduced spending power of consumers; a fall in demand for a complementary product; a fall in the price of substitutes; reduced advertising; and new evidence linking strawberries with harmful effects on health.

Most price–volume relationships slope downwards, as in Figs. 12.3 and 12.4, indicating that as price rises, demand falls and vice versa. While this is usually the case, there are exceptions. Sometimes, as the price of a product goes up, buyers are able and willing to buy more of the product. This can occur where a product becomes increasingly desirable as more people consume it. The Internet was of little value when only small numbers of people were connected to it, so opportunities for buyers to communicate with others was limited. But as more customers are connected to the World Wide Web, the value of an Internet connection increases, so individuals are correspondingly willing to pay a higher price to advertise on it.

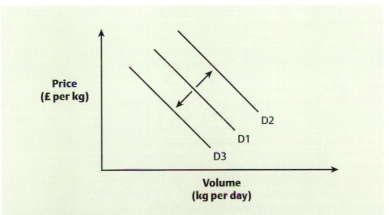

Figure 12.4 Alternative demand curves for strawberries, based on differing assumptions

Upward sloping demand curves can also be observed for some products sold for their 'snob' value. Examples include some designer label clothes where high price alone can add to a product's social status. Upward sloping demand curves can be observed over short time periods where a 'bandwagon' effect can be created by rapidly rising or falling prices. For example, in stock markets, the very fact that share prices are rising may lead many people to invest in shares.

Although the price–volume relationships shown in Figs. 12.3 and 12.4 are straight, this is a simplification of reality. Demand curves would usually be curved, indicating that the relationship between price and volume is not constant for all price points. There may additionally be discontinuities at certain price points where buyers in a market have psychological price barriers. For example, many buyers would not consider an item of clothing if it cost £100 or more, but may be happier to consider the purchase if it was priced at £99.99, just below their psychological price barrier (see Fig. 12.5).

Drawing a conceptual diagram relating price to volume of demand is relatively easy compared to the problems of collecting data and validating the relationship. The problems are both theoretical and practical. Data can be obtained by one of two principal methods:

1. Data could be collected at one point in time by comparing sales volumes in one area at a given price, with sales volumes in another area where a different price is charged. Retailers often experiment by charging different prices at different stores to build up some kind of picture about the relationship between price and volume. This is referred to as *cross-sectional data*. To be sure that this is accurately measuring the price–volume relationship, there must be no extraneous differences between the points of observation (such as differences in household incomes) which could partly explain differences in price/volume relationships.
2. Alternatively, a firm can change the price of a product over time and see what

Figure 12.5 £9.99 represents an important price point in many people's minds. Through a process of rationalisation, customers of this shop may be able to justify spending £9.99 on a luxury, whereas £10 may have been considered unacceptable

happens to sales volumes. This is referred to as *longitudinal data*. Again, it can be difficult to keep assumptions constant throughout the duration of the data collection, so that rising incomes or changing consumer preferences could explain sales variations, just as much as changes in a product's selling price.

Supply

Firms' willingness to supply products to a market will be influenced by the prevailing price in the market. If the price which they receive for selling their goods is low, they will be less willing to supply to the market than if the selling price is high. As in the case of demand, a price–volume line can be drawn, relating the market price of strawberries to volumes supplied by all farmers to the market (Fig. 12.6).

The supply curve in Fig. 12.6 slopes upwards from left to right, indicating that as the market price rises, more suppliers will be attracted to supply strawberries to the market. Conversely, as prices fall, marginal producers (such as those who operate relatively inefficiently) will drop out of the market, reducing the daily supply available.

Supply curve S1 is based on various assumptions about the relationship between price and volume supplied. If these no longer hold true, a new supply price–volume relationship needs to be drawn, based on the new set of assumptions. In Fig. 12.7, two new supply price–volume relationships, S2 and S3 are shown. S2 indicates a situation where, for any given price level, total supply to the market is increased. This could come about for a number of reasons, including:

- In the short term, extraneous factors (such as favourable weather conditions) could result in a glut of perishable strawberries which must be sold and the market is therefore flooded with additional supply.

- Improvements in production methods, resulting in suppliers being prepared to

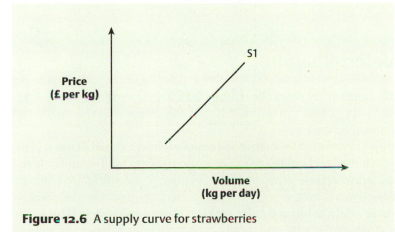

Figure 12.6 A supply curve for strawberries

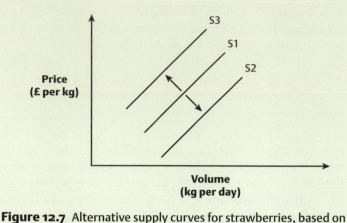

Figure 12.7 Alternative supply curves for strawberries, based on differing assumptions

supply more strawberries at any given price (or, looked at another way, for any given volume supplied, suppliers are prepared to accept a lower price).

- Governments may give subsidies to strawberry growers, thereby increasing their willingness to supply to the market at any given price level.

New supply curve S3 indicates a situation where, for any given price level, total supply to the market is reduced. This could come about for a number of reasons, including: adverse extraneous factors (e.g. bad weather for growers); increased production costs (e.g. rising wage costs); and reduction of government subsidies and/or imposition of taxes.

It should be noted that some changes in the actual volume of supply may take time to occur. So if strawberry prices went up today, it may not be until the next growing season that this results in increased planting of strawberry plants and hence a larger supply of strawberries to the market.

Price determination

In perfectly competitive markets, selling prices are determined by the interaction of demand and supply. This can be illustrated by superimposing the supply curve on the demand curve (Fig. 12.8).

The supply curve indicates that, at lower prices, fewer strawberries will be supplied to the market. But, at these lower prices, customers are willing and able to buy large volumes of strawberries—more than the suppliers collectively are willing or able to supply. The demand and supply curves intersect at precisely the point where the price–volume relationship is similar for both buyers and sellers. This is the point of equilibrium where demand and supply are precisely in balance. At any lower price,

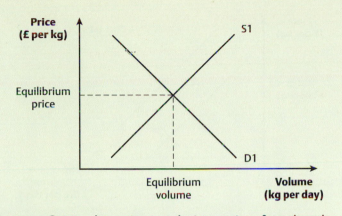

Figure 12.8 Price determination: the interaction of supply and demand for strawberries

there will be more demand than suppliers are willing to cater for. At any higher price, excessive supply could result in the build up of unsold stocks.

Changes in the equilibrium market price can come about for two principal reasons:

1. assumptions about buyers' ability or willingness to buy change, resulting in a shift to a new demand price–volume relationship;
2. assumptions about suppliers' ability or willingness to supply change, resulting in a shift to a new supply price–volume relationship.

The effects of shifts in supply are illustrated in Fig. 12.9. From an equilibrium price of £7 and volume of 15,000 kgs, the supply curve has shifted to S2 (perhaps in response to higher wage costs). Assuming that demand conditions remain unchanged, the new point of intersection between the demand and supply lines occurs at a volume of 12,000 kgs and a price of £6. This is the new equilibrium price. A similar analysis could be undertaken with a shift in the demand curve and noting the new point of intersection between the demand and supply lines.

Markets vary in the speed with which new equilibrium prices are established in response to changes in demand and/or supply. In pure commodity markets where products are instantly perishable, rapid adjustments in price are possible. Where speculators are able to store goods, or large buyers and sellers are able to influence a market unduly, adjustment may be slower. The extent of changes in price and volume traded is also dependent on the elasticity of demand and supply, which are considered in a later section.

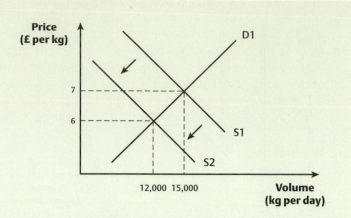

Figure 12.9 New equilibrium market price for strawberries, based on a shift in the supply price–volume relationship

Imperfections to competition

The model of perfect competition presented above is rarely seen in practice. The forces of competition may be ideal for consumers because of the tendency of market forces to minimize prices and/or maximize outputs. But in such markets, suppliers are forced to be price *takers* rather than price *makers*. In a perfectly competitive market, firms are unable to use marketing policies to affect the price at which they sell. At a higher price, buyers will immediately substitute identical products from other suppliers. Lower prices would be unsustainable in an industry where all firms had similar cost structures.

It is not surprising therefore that firms try to overcome the full effects of perfectly competitive markets. There are two principal methods by which a firm can seek to deviate from the workings of perfectly competitive markets to its own advantage: operating at lower costs than other firms in the market; and differentiating its products.

Operate at a lower cost

If a company operates at a lower cost than other firms, and is able to remain at a lower cost than other firms, it will be able to sustain lower prices than its competitors. In many industries, economies of scale are available to firms, so that as they grow bigger, their unit costs fall. This allows them to charge lower prices and still make an adequate profit. Lower prices result in more demand for a firm's products which can in turn allow it to achieve even more economies of scale. This virtuous circle of lower costs leading to competitive advantage can result in a small number of firms gaining a dominant position in the market-place. This can lead to a situation of oligopoly or monopoly (see below), in which the dominant firms have significant power to dictate prices.

Of course, gaining a competitive advantage through economies of scale is not an option open to firms in all industries. Where production and distribution methods are simple, there may be no economies of scale available to exploit. As an example, many firms in service industries such as plumbing and decorating would find it difficult to gain a cost advantage over competitors by operating at a larger scale. Indeed, there may be diseconomies of scale associated with being too large.

Differentiate the product

Perfect competition is based on the premiss that products offered in a particular market are identical. An entrepreneur can seek to avoid head-on competition by trying to sell a product which is somehow differentiated from the products offered by its competitors. So in the market for strawberries, a strawberry grower may try to get away from the fiercely competitive conditions which occur in wholesale fruit and vegetable markets. In such a market, the price at which it sells is determined by the market. Instead, it could try a number of differentiating strategies, including:

- concentrating on selling specially selected strawberries, for example ones which are of a particular size or ripeness;
- offering strawberries in distinctive protective packaging;
- offering a delivery service to local customers;
- offering a money-back guarantee of quality;
- offering strawberries in combination with other complementary elements of a fruit salad;
- the supplier might process the strawberries by tinning or freezing them;
- as a result of any of the above actions, the supplier could develop a distinct brand identity for its strawberries, so that buyers don't ask just for strawberries, but for Brand X strawberries by name.

In this example, the supplier has taken steps to turn a basic commodity product into something which is quite distinctive, so it has immediately cut down the number of direct competitors which it faces. In fact, if its product really was unique, it would have no direct competition (in other words, it would be a monopoly supplier of a unique product). For some differentiated products, this may seem very true in many customers' minds, for example some people would see a Rolex watch as being quite different from any other watch. Part of the differentiation may only be in buyers' minds, resulting from brand images and lifestyle associations which have been built up over time.

It must not, however, be forgotten that although the way a supplier has presented its product may be unique, it is still broadly similar to many competing products in terms of the ability to meet buyers' basic needs. The strawberry trader therefore still faces indirect competition, just as Rolex still faces competition from other suppliers of watches.

If a supplier has successfully differentiated its product, it is no longer strictly a price taker from the market. So the strawberry supplier which has specially selected or packaged its strawberries may be able to charge a few pennies per kilogram more than the going rate for basic commodity strawberries. However, it will only achieve this higher price if customers consider that the higher price is good value for a better product. It will be able to experiment to see just how much more buyers are prepared to pay for its differentiated product.

Elasticity of demand

In imperfectly competitive markets, firms will most likely find that, if they lower their prices, demand would rise by a certain amount. Price elasticity of demand refers to the extent to which demand changes in relation to a change in price. Price elasticity of demand is a useful indicator for business organizations because it allows them to predict what will happen to volume sales in response to a change in price.

Price elasticity of demand can be expressed as a simple formula:

$$\frac{\text{Price elasticity}}{\text{of demand}} = \frac{\text{(\%) change in demand}}{\text{(\%) change in price}}$$

Where demand is relatively unresponsive to price changes, demand is said to be *inelastic* with respect to price. Where demand is highly responsive to even a small price charge, demand is described as being *elastic* with respect to price.

Two demand curves are shown in Fig. 12.10. D1 is more elastic than D2, as indicated by the greater effect on volume of a change in price, compared with the effects of a similar price change with D2.

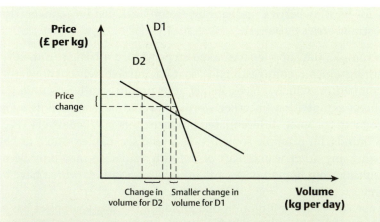

Figure 12.10 Price elasticity of demand: a comparison of a relatively inelastic elastic demand function (D1) with a relatively elastic one (D2)

Firms face a downward sloping demand curve for their products, indicating that, as prices fall, demand increases and vice versa. By lowering its price, a firm may be able to increase its sales, but what is important to firms is that they increase their total revenue (and profits). Whether this happens depends upon the elasticity of demand for the product in question.

- If it is possible to substitute a product with one which is very similar, price elasticity will be increased. What constitutes a similar and substitutable product can only be defined in the minds of customers. Two cars may seem technically similar, but their images may be so different that for many buyers they are not at all substitutable.

- The absolute value of a product and its importance to a buyer can influence its elasticity. As an example, most people would not bother shopping around for the best price on infrequently purchased boxes of matches. However, the same percentage difference in price between competing brands of television sets may be sufficiently large to encourage buyers to shop around.

In fact, a number of demand curves describing a firm's market can be described, ranging from the general to the specific brand. For example, in the market for beverages, the demand curve for beverages in general may be fairly inelastic, on the basis that people will always want to buy drinks of some description (Fig. 12.11). Demand for one particular type of beverage, such as Cola, will be slightly more elastic as people may be attracted to Cola from other drinks such as fruit juices and milk on the basis of their relative price. Price becomes more elastic still when a particular brand of Cola is considered. To many people, Coca-Cola can be easily substituted with other brands of Cola, so if a price differential between brands developed, switching may occur.

In general, firms will find that their products are much more inelastic to changes in

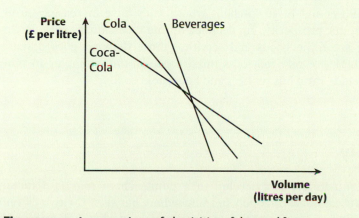

Figure 12.11 A comparison of elasticities of demand for beverages at different levels of product specificity

How easily swayed are consumers of fast food by a price cut? The market for fast food in the USA and western Europe has become increasingly saturated, leading McDonald's, the market leader, to initiate a number of price initiatives. One campaign in 1997 cost $200 million in promotion and involved reducing the cost of a Big Mac from $1.90 to 55 cents. But price alone seemed to have little effect in the continuing war against arch-rival Burger King. The heart of the problem seemed to be that baby-boomers had got older and cared more about taste. Yet armies of fast food critics argued that McDonald's had failed to improve the taste and range of its meals in the 1990s as much as its rivals, to the point where even price-cutting would not prevent customers wandering down the road to the second placed Burger King or the third placed Wendys.

price over the short term, when possibilities for substitution may be few. But over the longer term, new possibilities for substitution may appear. (For example, petrol is very inelastic over the short term but much more so over the long term, when motorists have a chance to adapt to less fuel intensive methods of transport.)

In addition to price elasticity of demand, economists measure a number of other types of elasticity which are of relevance to marketers in determining selling prices. Probably the most important of these is income elasticity of demand, which measures the responsiveness of demand to changes in buyers' incomes and can be expressed in the following way:

$$\text{Income elasticity of demand} = \frac{\text{percentage change in demand}}{\text{percentage change in income}}$$

In general, as an individual's income rises, their demand for most products rises, giving rise to a positive income elasticity of demand. Where there is a particularly strong increase in demand in response to an increase in incomes, a product is said to have a high income elasticity of demand. This is true of luxuries such as long-haul package holidays and fitted kitchens whose sales have increased during times of general economic prosperity, but declined during recessionary periods. On the other hand, there are some goods and services whose demand goes down as income increases. These are referred to as inferior goods and examples in most western countries include rural bus services and household coal.

Oligopoly

Imperfect competition can develop to a point where market structure can be described as *oligopolistic*. Oligopoly lies somewhere between the two extremes of perfect competition and pure monopoly. An oligopoly market is dominated by a small number of sellers who provide a large share of the total market output. The crucial point about oligopoly markets is that all suppliers in the market are interdependent.

One company cannot take price or output decisions without considering the specific possible responses of other companies.

Markets are most likely to be oligopolistic where economies of scale are significant, for example oligopoly is typical of oil refining and distribution, pharmaceuticals, car manufacturing, and detergents. Customers of oligopoly organizations may not immediately appreciate that the products they are buying come from an oligopolist, as such firms frequently use a variety of brand names (the detergent manufactures Unilever and Proctor & Gamble between them have over fifty apparently competing detergent products on sale in the UK).

Oligopolists pay particular attention to the activities of their fellow oligopolists and there is often a reluctance to upset the established order. One firm is often acknowledged as the price leader and firms wait for their actions before adjusting their prices. In the UK household mortgage market, for example, Halifax has often been the initiator of price changes which other banks and building societies then follow. It has been suggested that firms may not match upward price movements, in the hope of gaining extra sales, but they would match downward price changes for fear of losing market share. Price wars between oligopolists can be very expensive to participants, so there is a tendency to find alternative ways to compete for customers, such as free gifts, coupons, added value offers, and sponsorship activities.

Oligopolists have often been accused of collusion and creating barriers to entry for newcomers (such as signing exclusive distribution rights with key retailers).

Monopolistic markets

In its purest extreme, monopoly in a market occurs where there is only one supplier to the market, perhaps because of regulatory, technical, or economic barriers to entry which potential competing suppliers would face. A pure monopoly means that one person or organization has complete control over supply to that market. But this rarely occurs in practice. Even in the former centrally planned economies of eastern Europe, there have often been active 'shadow' markets which have existed alongside official monopoly suppliers.

A monopolist can determine the market price for its product and can be described as a 'price maker' rather than a 'price taker'. Where there are few substitutes for a product, and where demand is inelastic, a monopolist may be able to get away with continually increasing prices in order to increase its profits.

Sometimes, monopoly control over supply comes about through a group of suppliers acting in collusion together in a cartel. As with the pure monopoly, companies would join a cartel in order to try to protect themselves from the harmful consequences of competition. Cartels have been suspected in many industry sectors—for example rings of cement suppliers in a region who covertly agree to share markets between themselves and not to undercut each other's prices.

It can, however, be difficult to define just what is meant by monopoly control of 'the market', as most products have some form of substitute which reduces the monopolist's ability to set prices. While in Britain there may be just a few companies who between them have a near monopoly in the supply of bananas, when looked at in the context of the fruit market more generally, monopoly pricing power diminishes. Also, a firm which has significant monopoly pricing power at home may nevertheless face quite severe price competition in its overseas markets.

A company may have monopoly power over some of its users, but it may face competition if it wishes to attract new segments of users. It may therefore resort to differential pricing when targeting the two groups. As an example, many rail operators in the London area have considerable monopoly power over commuters who need to use their train services to arrive at work by 9 a.m. on weekdays. For such commuters, the alternatives of travelling to work by bus or car are very unattractive. However, leisure travellers wishing to go shopping in London during off-peak periods may be much more price sensitive. For them, the car or bus provides a realistic alternative, and so train companies offer a range of price incentives aimed at off-peak leisure markets, while charging full fare for their peak period commuters.

In theory, a company with significant monopoly power could continually raise its prices in order to exploit its monopoly. However, marketing managers who think strategically may be reluctant fully to exploit their monopoly power. By charging high prices in the short term, a monopolist could give signals to companies in related product fields to develop substitutes which would eventually provide effective competition. Blatant abuse of monopoly power could also result in a referral to the regulatory authorities (see below).

Americans are devoted to the idea that air travel is cheap following deregulation in the 1970s. But are low prices in fact a myth? And what are the implications for air fares in Europe as air services throughout Europe are deregulated?. The theory of airline deregulation in the USA was irresistible. Any airline would be allowed to operate on any route, setting its fares as it liked. New airlines soon appeared and initially held down fares through competitive pressures. However, the major carriers have since acquired such a dominant position that US air fares rose on average 20 per cent during 1997. What went wrong? The established airlines have managed to control 'slots' at the principal hub airports, making it difficult for new entrants to obtain slots. Many of the larger airlines have resorted to predatory pricing to keep away newcomers. This involves offering low fares on routes and at times that are competitive with other airlines, but charging higher fares where it has an effective monopoly. The final straw for price competition came with the bad publicity generated by the cut-price airline Valujet whose aircraft crashed in 1996. The lesson from US airline deregulation is that price competition may be expected in theory, but there are many reasons why it doesn't happen in practice.

Regulatory influences on pricing

BECAUSE of the presumed superiority of competitive markets, the law of most developed countries has been used to try to remove market imperfections where these are deemed to be against the public interest. In addition to some publicly provided services where prices are set as a matter of social policy, many private-sector companies must take account of various regulations in setting their prices. These can be classified as:

- direct government controls to regulate monopoly power;
- government controls on price representations.

Direct government controls to regulate monopoly power

Governments have a range of measures which can be used to prevent exploitative pricing by monopolists. At a European level Articles 85 and 86 of the Treaty of Rome limit the ability of firms to collude with their fellow producers or distributors in fixing prices. In the UK, the Resale Prices Act 1976 and Competition Act 1998 limit the extent to which producers of goods and services can control selling prices as their products pass through a distribution channel. Manufacturers of goods often like to be able to control the price of their products as they pass through wholesalers and retailers, but this can have the effect of restricting competition between distributors. A manufacturer of hi-fi equipment that has positioned its products as exclusive, high value items may want to prevent retailers 'piling it high and selling it cheap'. Given a high elasticity of demand, the retailer may increase its own sales and profitability. But for the manufacturer, the discount strategy may devalue the image of its equipment and merely switch sales away from retailers who give good customer support and service to a retailer that concentrates all its efforts on cutting costs.

The Resale Prices Act prevents a manufacturer insisting on a price at which a retailer or wholesaler must sell its products to their customers. It is illegal for manufacturers to do anything which has the effect of limiting retailers' ability to charge whatever prices they think fit—for example it would be illegal for the manufacturer to withhold supplies unless there was another non-price related reason for doing so.

A firm is only allowed to fix selling prices through its distribution channel where to do so can be shown to be in the public interest. Until September 1995, UK publishers were able to insist that bookshops sell books at the publishers' recommended retail price (through the Net Book Agreement). The argument was put forward that if small bookshops could not make profits by selling best sellers at full price, they would not be able to cross-subsidize the specialist titles which it would be in the public interest to make available. The agreement was therefore upheld by the Restrictive Practices Court and its demise was brought about largely as a result of a change in the structure of the market for books in the UK.

In the UK, the Office of Fair Trading has power to order an investigation by the Competition Commission, previously the Monopolies and Mergers Commission, of any anticompetitive practices which may have the effect of restricting choice or causing prices to be higher than they need be. One referral in respect of the credit card industry, for example, criticized the existing pricing structure, stating that it involved cross-subsidization between different groups of consumers and imposed unnecessary restrictions on retailers handling credit card sales. In response to this, most credit card companies revised their pricing structure by lowering interest charges levied on those who use their cards as a means of credit and balancing this by a fixed annual charge on all cards, including those held by customers who use their card solely as a means of payment.

Government controls on price representations

In any market-place, buyers and sellers need rules which govern their conduct and prevent abuses of their respective positions. So as well as controlling or influencing the actual level of prices, government regulation can have the effect of specifying the manner in which price information is communicated to potential customers. At a general level, the Consumer Protection Act 1987 requires that all prices shown should conform to the Code of Practice on pricing—misleading price representations which relegate details of supplementary charges to small print or give attractive low lead-in prices for services which are not in fact available are made illegal by this Act. There are other regulations which affect specific industries. The Consumer Credit Act 1974 requires that the charge made for credit must include a statement of the Annual Percentage Rate (APR) of interest. Also within the financial services sector, the Financial Services Act 1986 has resulted in quite specific requirements in the manner which charges for certain insurance-related services are presented to potential customers.

Governments have taken measures to regulate the prices charged by monopoly suppliers of utility services. Attempts have been made to increase competition, in the hope that this in itself will be instrumental in moderating price increases (for example, numerous companies have been licensed to compete with British Telecom in the UK). However, in many cases, measures to increase competition have had only limited effect, as in the very limited competition faced by the privatized water supply companies. Here, governments have created regulatory bodies which can determine the level and structure of prices which can be charged by these utilities. In this way, British Gas and the regional water companies are controlled by Ofgen and Ofwat respectively.

Chapter summary and key linkages to other chapters

This chapter has discussed the underlying theory of price determination. The forces of supply and demand interact to determine a price which is acceptable for a willing seller to part with their goods in return for money and a willing buyer to part with money in return for goods. Perfect competition is an idealized market structure which rarely occurs in its pure extreme. Most markets show some degree of imperfection which affects the manner of price determination. Because imperfect markets are generally held to be against the public interest, various regulatory measures exist to improve the competitiveness of markets.

The following key linkages to other chapters should be noted:

Chapter 1: What is marketing?: Marketing is about satisfying customers' needs profitably. Pricing is the mediating device between customers receiving value for money and companies achieving an adequate financial return.

Chapter 2: The marketing environment: Pricing of any product must have regard to the marketing environment of the product. Pricing should be flexible enough to respond to changes in the marketing environment (e.g. a weakening economy may put pressure on prices).

Chapter 3: Market segmentation: Segmentation is fundamental to pricing in a competitive market. Different market segments are likely to place different limits on what they would expect to pay for a product.

Chapter 4: Branding: Brands add to the perceived value for many products for many market segments. Products carrying a strong brand usually attract a price premium compared to similar but unbranded products.

Chapter 5: Marketing and ethics: Is it ethical to provide misleading price indications, or to discriminate prices in favour of, or against, particular groups?

Chapter 6: Marketing research: How do you predict the price that customers will be prepared to pay for a new product?

Chapter 7: Buyer behaviour: How important is price within the whole process of buying a product? What is the level of price awareness?

Chapter 8: Buyer–seller relationship development: Price is often used to initiate and maintain relationships.

Chapters 9/10: Developing a product portfolio: Are the opportunities for new product development matched by prices which will allow for profitable exploitation of the opportunity?

Chapter 11: Developing a sustainable competitive advantage: Can a price position be maintained in the face of a competitive and changing marketing environment?

Chapter 13: Pricing theory: This chapter has discussed the underlying theory of pricing. The following chapter discusses practical application of the theory discussed here.

Chapters 14/15: Intermediaries/physical distribution: How can price levels be maintained through distribution channels? Can price be used to motivate intermediaries?

Chapters 16–20: Principles of promotion planning/advertising/sales promotion/ personal selling/direct marketing: Does a company's promotional effort provide a basis for charging a sustainable price premium?

Chapter 21: Managing the marketing effort: How are prices determined within the organization? Are the organization's processes fast enough to adjust prices in response to a changing marketing environment?

Chapter 22: Services marketing: Similar principles apply to goods and services, although the prices of services are more likely than goods to be regulated by government agencies.

Chapter 23: Global marketing: What factors influence prices in a company's overseas markets? Should it seek to maintain globally uniform prices, or locally adapted prices?

Case study

A single market—so why no single price?

The laws of supply and demand imply that a price equilibrium will be reached where the quantity of a product that buyers want to buy exactly matches the quantity that sellers want to sell. Why then should this equilibrium price differ, sometimes quite markedly, between different countries?

The price charged for the same goods varies widely between European countries. A study undertaken in 1998 by Lehman Brothers found that, on average, prices differed from the mean by 24 per cent. A Ford Mondeo car cost almost 50 per cent more in Germany than in Spain; a Big Mac priced at Bfr 109 in Belgium cost 20 per cent more than one at Pta 375 in Spain. For drugs, where government intervention plays a big part, the difference between the cheapest and most expensive countries was as big as 300 per cent. Part of the reason for this variation can be found in different tax rates. For example, the rate of VAT levied on some electrical goods varies between zero in Finland and over 30 per cent in France. Transport costs can also make a big difference to bulky goods which have to be moved to areas where local production is not possible. The standard deviation around the average price was relatively low for low volume, high value goods which can enter international trade relatively easily.

Regional tastes can also make a difference to prices. For example, the Dutch on average eat nine times as much yoghurt as the Irish. The higher turnover of yoghurt in Dutch supermarkets results in mass market competition which helps to drive down prices, while it remains a relatively niche market product in Ireland. The result is that yoghurt costs one-third as much in the Netherlands as it does in Ireland. Even for broadly similar products, differences in tastes may lead to reconfiguration of a product, thereby losing economies of scale and putting upward pressure on prices. As an example, the fish fingers sold in Belgium taste different from those sold in the UK. Where such product differences are noticeable, the possibilities for importing goods from a low price market to a high price one are made more difficult.

Travel, education, and international media channels are leading to a homogenization of tastes, but regional differences remain strong and are likely to remain so. For example, Heinz's baked bean pizza is unlikely ever to find much favour outside the UK. Differences in climate and geography will continue to result in differences between markets in the products consumers prefer to buy, so thermal underwear will remain a niche market product in Greece, but a mass market product in Norway.

The development of a single European currency seems set to bring about some harmonization of prices throughout Europe. When all prices are quoted in Euros, consumers will be able to make immediate price comparisons and it may be difficult for sellers to maintain price differentials. This may be bad news for companies who have relied on high prices in some national markets to boost their global profits. The consultant McKinsey made a study of the automotive components business and calculated that a 1 per cent change in price can result in a 10–15 per cent change in profits.

Is a harmonization of prices across Europe inevitably going to result from the introduction of a single European currency? Evidence from the USA suggests that price differentials may still remain. There, despite the existence of a common currency, price variation around the mean is about 12 per cent, or half the level currently found in Europe.

Case study review questions

1 Using an analysis of supply, demand, and equilibrium price, explain why price differences for certain goods exist between different countries in Europe.

2 Using appropriate economic analysis, explain the processes by which price levels are likely to become more harmonized throughout Europe as a result of the development of the Euro.

3 Identify the barriers that may prevent a common price equilibrium occurring for goods and services throughout Europe.

Chapter review questions

1 Using examples, identify the characteristics of commodity-type markets which are highly competitive.

2 Critically assess methods used by companies to reduce the effects on them of intense price competition.

3 'Elasticity of demand is a fine theoretical concept of economists, but difficult for marketers to use in practice'. Critically assess this statement.

4 What are the main challenges facing an oligopolist when determining prices? Is the task of an oligopolistic marketer more or less difficult than that of a marketing manager in a sector dominated by small businesses?

5 It has sometimes been suggested that the deregulation and privatization of many public services in the UK has led to greater control of prices than before. Using examples, to what extent do you think this is true?

6 Taking a broad view, what can marketers gain from a thorough understanding of price theory?

Suggested further reading

This chapter has provided only a very brief overview of the principles of economics as they affect pricing. For a fuller discussion, one of the following texts would be useful:

- Chrystal, K. A., and Lipsey, R. G. (1997), *Economics for Business and Management* (Oxford: Oxford University Press).

- Davies, S., Lyons, B., Geroski, P., and Dixon, H. (1991), *Economics of Industrial Organizations* (Harlow: Longman).

- Lipsey, R. G., and Chrystal K. A. (1999), *Principles of Economics*, 9th edn. (Oxford: Oxford University Press).

- Stanlake, G. F., and Grant, S. J. (1995), *Introductory Economics*, 6th edn. (Harlow: Longman).

Competition policy and law is reviewed in the following references:

- Cini, M., and McGowan, L. (1997), *Competition Policy in the European Union* (Basingstoke: Macmillan).

- Ernst, J. (1994), *Whose Utility? The Social Impact of Public Utility Privatization and Regulation in Britain* (Buckingham: Open University Press).

- Helm, D., and Jenkinson, T., (1997), *Competition in Regulated Industries* (Oxford: Clarendon Press).

- Dosi, G., Teece, D., and Chytry, J. (1997), *Technology, Organization and Competitiveness* (Oxford: Oxford University Press).

- Korah, V. (1994), *An Introductory Guide to EC Competition Law and Practice*, 5th edn. (London: Sweet and Maxwell).

Useful web links

Website of the UK Competition Commission (formerly the Monopolies and Mergers Commission) which provides reports of investigations into alleged anti-competitive pricing: http://www.mmc.gov.uk

MMC News & Current References: http://roof.ccta.gov.uk/mmc/news2.htm

UK Office of Fair Trading: http://www.oft.gov.uk/

Trading Standards Central: http://www.tradingstandards.gov.uk/business/award.htm

EuroCommerce Press Releases: http://www.eurocommerce.be/

Chapter 13
Pricing: Application

Chapter objectives

The previous chapter set the scene for the theory which underlies firms' pricing decisions. This chapter focuses on situations where firms have developed some degree of uniqueness, such as a brand, which sets them aside from perfectly competitive markets. Corporate objectives influence pricing strategy, which can take a number of forms. The strength of demand, the strength of competitors, and a company's costs are important reference points for pricing. Various methods are discussed by which companies implement pricing decisions on a day-to-day basis.

Introduction

THE previous chapter considered some of the factors that underpin firms' pricing decisions. It was noted that firms seek to reduce their dependence on market forces by creating products which are distinctive in the minds of buyers, and for which there is therefore relatively little direct competition. The creation of a distinctive product clearly involves many marketing decisions, for example in relation to the physical design of the product, the promotional message used, and the ease with which buyers are able to get hold of it. The end result of this differentiation should be a product which buyers perceive as preferential to a basic commodity product within that product category, and for which they are prepared to pay a price premium.

This chapter extends the analysis of pricing by examining the marketing management decisions open to firms who are able to act as price makers rather than price takers, in other words, they have established some degree of differentiation from the rest of the market. Marketers must consider pricing not just at one point in time, but over the life of a product. So a price based on differential advantage over competitors may need to change over time as competitors gradually erode a company's differential advantage. Simplistic economic analyses of pricing also tend to overlook the complex interdependencies which can exist between different products within a firm's product range and this chapter will explore the subject of product mix pricing.

Pricing objectives

SIMPLE models of perfect competition assume that firms are motivated primarily by the desire to maximize their short-term profits. In a commodity market where prices are taken from the market, a company cannot be expected to have any other objectives, or it would soon go out of business. However, where a company has differentiated its products to give it a degree of monopoly power, it is able to pursue a more diverse range of possible objectives. In the following section the effects of diverse objectives on an organization's pricing policies are explored.

Profit maximization

Economists' models of perfect competition assume that firms in a market act rationally in order to maximize their profits. In less competitive markets, the notion of profit maximization becomes much more complex to understand. The first complicating issue is the possible divergence between short-term and long-term profit objectives. A company which aims to maximize its profits over the short run may unwittingly reduce its ability to achieve long-term profit objectives. By charging high prices in a new market, it may make that market seem very attractive to new entrants. This could provide a major incentive for new competitors to appear, thereby increasing the level of competition in subsequent years, and therefore reducing long-term profitability. Drugs companies selling medicines which have just come out of their period of patent protection must decide whether to continue charging the high prices to which buyers have been accustomed, or to lower the price to a point where it deters new market entrants who can no longer be sure of making a quick short-term profit.

Organizations differ in the urgency with which they need to make profits from a new product. It is frequently suggested that the open shareholding structure of UK firms makes shareholders restless for short-term profits. Managers are therefore likely to set prices to achieve these short-term objectives, even if this is at the expense of longer-term profitability. By contrast, the relatively closed capital structure of many Japanese companies has allowed them to take a longer-term view on profitability, relatively free of short-term stock market pressures. A longer-term profit objective may allow an organization to tap relatively small but high value segments of its markets in the first year and save the exploitation of lower value segments until subsequent years.

Finally, while it is easy to talk about maximizing profits during the present planning period, many marketing managers in reality have little understanding about the relationship between costs, sales volumes, and profitability. This can be especially true of new and emerging markets where there is little historical data on which to predict the outcome of price changes.

Sales growth

Management often does not directly receive any reward for increasing its organization's profits, so its main concern may be to achieve a *satisfactory* level of profits rather than the *maximum* possible. Managers are often in a position to benefit personally where their company pursues a sales growth strategy. This has been suggested by many behaviourial studies of how managers actually act (e.g. Cyert and March 1963). Many managers may go for maximum sales growth as a means of boosting their ego. In addition, they may recognize numerous tangible benefits which such a strategy may bring them, especially better promotion prospects and personal job security. In reality, managers may have been able to secure a better return for shareholders by being more cautious and cutting back on unprofitable activities.

There are also some very good reasons why a company may benefit over the longer term by seeking to boost its short-term sales growth, even if this does mean charging very low prices in order to do so. In many industries it is essential to achieve a critical size in order to achieve economies of scale in buying, production, promotion, and distribution. On the basis of these economies of scale, a firm may be able to achieve a competitive advantage. Companies in sectors as diverse as grocery retailing, civil aviation, and publishing have used low prices to achieve short-term sales growth in the hope that this will lead to long-term profit growth.

Finally, sales growth may be an important objective influencing pricing because managers have practical difficulties in establishing relationships between marketing strategy decisions and the resulting change in profitability. Going for growth may be perceived by managers as their safest option.

Survival

For many struggling companies, the objective of maximizing profits or sales volume is quite unrealistic when they are fighting desperately to avoid bankruptcy. In these circumstances, prices may be set at a very low level, simply to get enough cash into the organization to tide it over. Many retailers have found themselves in this situation when there has been a sudden downturn in consumer demand and they are left with too much stock and expensive overheads to pay. Cash was tied up unnecessarily in stock. In a bid to stay afloat, many desperate retailers have held stock liquidation sales in which stocks were sold at almost any price, just to keep cash flowing in. Even if the prices charged did not cover the original cost of goods, pricing could satisfy managers' short-term objective of survival.

Figure 13.1 This company probably has very little pricing discretion if it is forced to liquidate its stock in a hurry

Social considerations

Talk about maximizing sales or profits may have little meaning within the public and not-for-profit sectors, where the emphasis is on maximizing social benefits (e.g. the number of operations performed by a hospital). The price of many public services represents a tax levied by government based not on market forces, but on an individual's ability to pay, with many services being provided at no charge. In the UK, many basic health services are provided without charge to patients, and where charges are made, these often reflect the ability of individuals to pay, rather than the need for the health authority to maximize their revenue (e.g. lower dental and prescription charges for disadvantaged groups).

Even where public services are provided in a more competitive market environment, pricing decisions may still be influenced by wider social objectives. As an example, many Business Link organizations have been set up in the UK to offer a range of subsidized training courses to local businesses, but with the expectation that such courses should be able to charge commercial prices for their services once they have been established.

Although social objectives are normally associated with public-sector services, they are sometimes adopted by private-sector organizations. Many companies provide goods and services for their staff (such as canteens and sports facilities) at below their market price, with the aim of adding to staff's motivation and sense of loyalty to their organization.

Pricing strategy

S TRATEGY is the means by which an organization seeks to achieve its objectives. Strategic decisions about pricing cannot be made in isolation from other strategic marketing decisions, so, for example, a strategy that seeks a premium price position must be matched by product development strategy that creates a superior product and a promotional strategy that establishes in buyers' minds the value that the product offers.

The concept of positioning was discussed in Chapter 11 where it was noted that combinations anywhere along a line from high price/high quality to low price/low quality are sustainable strategic positions to adopt. A strategy that combined high price with low quality may be regarded by customers as poor value and they are likely to desert such companies where they have a choice of suppliers. For most companies, such a strategy is not sustainable. A high quality/low price strategic position may appear very attractive to buyers, but it too may not be sustainable. Many companies in their public pronouncements claim this to be their strategic position, but it can pose problems for them:

■ Are they selling themselves short and failing to recover their full costs in their bid to please customers? Unless they are operating more efficiently than other companies in their sector, there is the possibility that they are failing to make sufficient profits. In the mass market restaurant sector, for example, portion control can be quite critical to financial success. Customers may love the value offered by bigger servings, but many restaurants have gone out of business because they offered their customers too much value.

■ If a company genuinely is able to offer lower prices for any given level of quality on the basis of greater efficiency, it must realize that its competitors may soon learn and copy its own levels of efficiency. Its prices will therefore no longer be the only sustainable low prices in the sector. In the European scheduled airline industry, many low cost operators have appeared to undercut the established airlines. However, their competitive advantage has often been eroded where the established operators have implemented many of the cost-cutting measures pioneered by their new competitors.

Pricing and the product life cycle

In Chapter 9, the concept of the product life cycle was introduced and it was noted that many aspects of a product's marketing strategy are closely related to the position that it has reached in its life cycle. Pricing strategy is no exception. An effective marketing strategy must identify how the role of price is to function as a product goes through different stages in its life from the launch stage through growth to maturity.

Where a company is supplying to a market where product differentiation is possible, it is able to take a long-term view on its price position. However, pressure on the product's price, and hence on its profitability will vary during the life of the product. Fig. 13.2 illustrates the typical pressures on a product's price as it progresses through its life cycle.

Lifetime pricing

You will recall from Chapter 8 that the development of ongoing buyer–seller relationships is becoming a much more important part of business strategy. Rather than bargaining each transaction, companies are trying to view each transaction with a customer in the context of those that have gone before, and those that they hope will occur in the future. Pricing levels with a prospective client may start off relatively low and build up progressively as both buyer and seller come to recognize the value of their relationship. In practical terms, imagine a new customer going into a restaurant. Should the profit of that diner walking in be measured just in terms of that one meal, or the lifetime of meals that they may subsequently be expected to buy? Viewed in the latter context, there may be scope for offering price or non-price incentives to encourage trial of the restaurant.

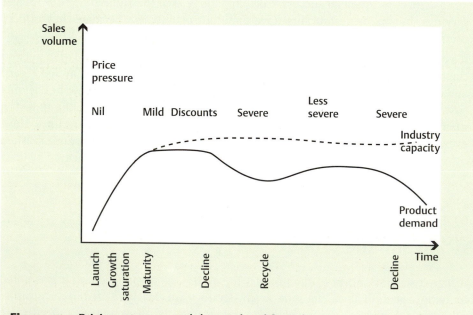

Figure 13.2 Pricing pressure and the product life cycle

Price skimming strategy

O**NE** approach to life cycle pricing is for a firm to start by charging a high price for a newly launched product, on the basis of its uniqueness. However, as its uniqueness is copied by other firms, its price will have to be reduced to match the competitors.

This strategy is suitable for products which are genuinely innovative: the first microwave cookers in the 1970s; the first portable phones in the 1980s, and the first digital cameras in the 1990s, for example. Such products are aimed initially at the segment of users who can be described as 'innovators' (discussed in Chapter 10). These are typically consumers who have the resources and inclination to be the trend setters in purchasing new goods and services. Following these will be a group of early adopters, followed by a larger group often described as the 'early majority'. The subsequent 'late majority' group may only take up the new service once the product market itself has reached maturity. 'Laggards' are the last group to adopt a new product and would only do so when it has become commonplace and/or its price has fallen sufficiently.

The basic principle of a price skimming strategy is to gain the highest possible price from each market segment, beginning with the highest value segments and moving on to lower value ones when the purchasing ability of the first segment appears to be approaching saturation level. At this point, the price level is lowered in order to appeal to the early adopter segment which has a lower price threshold at which it is prepared to purchase the product. This process is repeated for the following adoption segments.

As with so much of product life cycle theory, identifying the points during the life cycle at which action is needed can be very difficult. It can be very difficult to map out a price strategy with any degree of confidence. Consider the following problems which make a price skimming strategy difficult to formulate:

- What is the saturation level of individual market segments? At what point should the company decide to lower its prices to appeal to lower value segments?

- How long will the firm's product remain genuinely innovative in the eyes of consumers? Will the appearance of competitors diminish its uniqueness and therefore the firm's ability to charge premium prices?

- Should the firm avoid charging very high initial prices, as this may be a signal to competitors to enter the market?

Price skimming strategies work for consumer markets as well as business-to-business markets. It can be argued that diffusion patterns for products sold mainly to business buyers differ from those for consumer products. Business buyers generally have less of a desire to be a trend setter for its own sake and a different kind of rationality in purchase decisions. This limits the opportunities for price skimming to

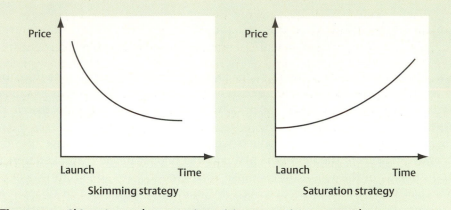

Figure 13.3 Skimming and penetration pricing strategies compared

situations where commercial buyers can use innovative products to give them a productivity advantage which in turn gives buyers a competitive advantage in selling their own products to their customers at a lower price and/or to a higher standard.

For many innovative products, falling prices may be further stimulated by falling production costs. Lower costs can occur due to economies of scale in production, promotion, and distribution (e.g. the cost of microwave cookers and mobile phones came down partly as a result of improved production efficiency which itself was partly a reflection of economies of scale). Costs may also fall as a result of the experience effect. This refers to the process by which costs fall as experience in production is gained. By pursuing a strategy to gain experience faster than its competitors, an organization lowers its cost base and has a greater scope for adopting an aggressive pricing strategy.

Penetration pricing strategy

GENUINELY innovative new product launches are few and far between. The vast majority of product launches are simply copies of products which consumers can already buy in substantially the same form. Consider the following new product launches:

- a new television listings magazine;
- a new type of chocolate biscuit;
- a new long-distance telephone service.

The principle of initially appealing to high value segments and then dropping the price will be unlikely to work with these new product launches, as buyers in all segments have access to competitors' products which are essentially similar. Buyers must have a good reason for choosing to try the new product instead of sticking with the product which they currently purchase. There are many ways that a company can encourage trial of its product, including a product design which offers real benefits to buyers, heavy promotion, sales promotion, and sponsorship activity. One way used by many companies to encourage trial is by offering prices which are sufficiently low that a large number of buyers will switch from their existing supplier. Sometimes the product will even be given away at no price in order to get potential buyers to try the new product (for example, samples of new shampoos are often given away with women's magazines).

Naturally, companies will not want to go on charging low prices for very long. Their hope is that once buyers have tried and enjoyed their product, they will come back again. By this stage, the price can be raised to something that approaches competitors' price levels. The buyer no longer has to be tempted with a low price. Over time, they may even come to prefer the product over competitors' products, so the company may be able to charge a price premium.

Of course, penetration pricing strategies have their dangers. Companies often find it difficult to develop loyalty from customers that will allow them to raise prices. Customers who were attracted by low penetration prices may be just as easily lost when a competitor or another new market entrant tries offering low prices. This pricing strategy also presupposes that buyers have a high awareness of prices. Research has shown that in many markets, buyers have a very poor knowledge of prices, so competing for market share on the basis of low price alone may not work.

Companies use many pricing tricks to gain a trial and then exploit a consumer's preference. Knowing that a customer who was attracted by a low price may just as easily be lost to a competitor who tries to tempt them back with low prices, companies try to lock customers in once they have tried a new product. Many new magazines launch with low prices and include series or articles to which readers get attached to and will probably carry on buying, even after the publisher has put the price up midway through the series. Many fast-moving consumer goods manufacturers include competitions or gift offers with their launch sales, for which tokens need to be collected. However, the price of the product may increase while customers are part-way through collecting the required number of tokens. In some cases, a company can exploit the fact that customers have become hooked on their product. So with the biscuit Hob Nobs, a suspicion arose that individuals could become addicted to the biscuit, regardless of its price.

Traditional price theory makes assumptions that there is a high level of knowledge in markets about prices charged by different competitors. In reality, this is simply not true. Many companies realize this and do not compete on price for most of their products, other than a few 'loss-leaders' for which buyers are able to make price comparisons.

The telephone company BT regularly monitors buyers' perceptions of prices of a variety of goods and services, doubtless aware that people still think of telephone charges as being very expensive. Its 1997 Business Price Perception Survey showed how knowledge of many prices was wide of the mark. Respondents gave the average price of a five minute peak national call as £2.15, whereas in fact it was only 44p. Another sector with confusing price structures is railways. Here, respondents estimated the price of a second-class return ticket from London to Edinburgh at £54, compared to the actual price of £64. In contrast to the wide variations in many service price estimates, respondents were quite accurate in their assessment of the price of a pint of beer. The average estimate of £1.73 for a pint of lager was just 2p off the true average.

Pricing methods

STRATEGIES need to be translated into methodologies for actually setting prices. Faced with a new product, the task of determining a selling price can sometimes appear to be quite daunting. If it is a completely new product, there may be very little guidance in setting prices. Many entrepreneurial companies may resort to a hunch or guesswork. However, even guesswork can be reduced to a series of rule-based decisions. Essentially there are three questions that need to be asked when setting the price for any product:

1. How much does it cost us to make the product?
2. How much are competitors charging for a similar product?
3. What price are customers prepared to pay?

We can identify an additional factor that affects marketing managers in many public utility sectors:

4. How much will a government regulator allow us to charge customers?

The relationship between these bases for pricing is shown in Fig. 13.4. Let us consider each of these in turn.

Costs and prices

The cost of producing a product sets the minimum price that a company would be prepared to charge its customers. If a commercial company is not covering its costs

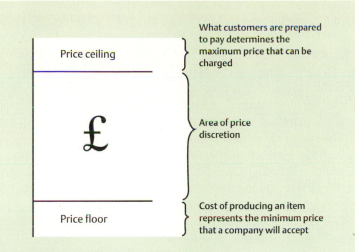

Figure 13.4 Bases for determining prices

with its prices, it cannot continue in business indefinitely (unless, perhaps, the business has a wealthy owner and the business is kept going for reasons of prestige, as in the case of many national newspapers). The principle of a direct linkage between costs and prices may be central to basic price theory, but marketing managers rarely find conditions to be so simple. Consider some of the problems in relating costs to prices:

- The cost of a particular product is often very difficult to calculate. This is especially true where production costs involve high levels of overhead costs which cannot easily be allocated to specific products.

- While it may be relatively easy to calculate historic costs, it is future costs that may be crucial in determining profitability. An office furniture manufacturer, for example, may find it difficult to set fixed prices for customers today for furniture which will be built and delivered at some time in the future. It may be difficult to predict inflation rates for labour and materials used.

- Cost-based pricing in itself does not take account of the competition which a particular product faces at any particular time, nor of the fact that some customers may value the same service more highly than others.

Despite these shortcomings, cost-based pricing is widely used in many sectors. In its most straightforward form, 'cost-plus' pricing works where a company calculates its total costs, and divides these by the total volume of resources used to determine the average cost of each unit of resource used. It then calculates a selling price by estimating the number of units of resources to be used, multiplying this by the unit cost and adding a profit margin. It is widely used by solicitors, plumbers, and other labour-intensive service industries where the cost of labour is a major component of total costs. So a plumber may price a job on the basis of the total number of hours estimated to complete a job (calculated on the basis of historical costs including overheads), plus materials used, plus a profit margin. The principles are illustrated in Fig. 13.5.

Another form of cost-based pricing that is widely used is referred to as 'marginal' cost pricing. Here, a company calculates what would be the marginal cost of producing one additional unit of a product (that is, what would be the addition to the company's total costs of selling one extra item?). In some industries with high levels of fixed costs, the marginal cost of producing one extra unit of output can be surprisingly small. The cost of carrying one extra passenger on an airplane which is about to depart can be little more than the cost of the airport departure tax, a meal, and marginally additional fuel. This explains why many airlines are keen to offer last-minute standby airfares, as some revenue is better than having an unsold seat, just so long as the price charged more than covers the marginal costs.

Pricing based on marginal costs may work up to a point, but companies must realize that sufficient customers must be willing to pay full costs in order for others to be charged a much lower price reflecting only marginal costs. Many airlines and holiday companies have gone bankrupt because too high a proportion of their customers have been sold tickets at the marginal cost, leaving the fixed overhead costs uncovered.

Calculating marginal costs can sometimes be quite difficult. In the long term, all of a company's costs are marginal in that the option is open to close down whole business units or even the whole company. While the marginal cost of one seat on an airplane may be low, if the unit of analysis is the whole journey or even the whole route, the level of marginal costs becomes much higher (see Fig. 13.6).

Cost information for most recent trading year:

Total employees' wage costs	£700,000
Total hours worked	70,000
Cost per employee's hour	£10.00
Total other overhead costs	£200,000
Overhead cost per employee hour worked	£2.86
Total chargeable amount per hour	£12.86
Required profit markup	20%

Price calculations for a job requiring 100 hours of labour and £500 materials:

100 hours @ £12.86 per hour	£1,286
Materials	£ 500
Sub-total	£1,786
Add 20% markup	£ 357
Price	£2,143

Figure 13.5 Cost-based approach to pricing for a building contractor

Product	Fixed costs	Marginal costs
Building maintenance	Transport equipment Tools	Materials used Labour Fuel
Meal in a restaurant	Building maintenance Rent and rates Waiters and cooks	Food
Bank mortgage	Staff time Building maintenance Corporate advertising	Sales commission Paper and postage
Hairdresser	Building maintenance Rent and rates	Shampoos used

Figure 13.6 Fixed and marginal costs compared

Competitors and pricing

Very often, a marketing manager may go about setting prices by examining what competitors are charging. But who is the competition against which prices are to be compared? Competitors can be defined at different levels:

■ similar in terms of product characteristics;
■ or more broadly, just similar in terms of the needs which a product satisfies.

As an example, a video rental shop can see its competition purely in terms of other video shops, or it could widen it to include cinemas and satellite television services, or wider still to include any form of entertainment.

Once it has established what market it is in and who its competitors are, a company can go about setting comparative prices. It must first establish what price position it seeks to adopt relative to its competitors. This position will reflect the wider marketing mix of the product, so if the product is perceived by buyers as being of superior quality than competitors' products, it may justify a relatively high price. Similarly, heavy investment in promotion or distribution channels may give it a competitive advantage which is reflected in buyers' willingness to pay relatively high prices.

In commodity-type markets which are characterized by a fairly homogeneous product offering, demand can be so sensitive to price that a firm would risk loosing most of its business if it charged just a small amount more than its competitors. On the other hand, charging any lower would result in immediate retaliation from competitors, resulting in nobody being any better off. This situation is found in many street markets with rival traders selling items such as plain T-shirts and fresh vegetables at very similar prices to each other. Petrol retailers within an area often keep a watch on rivals' prices, resulting in a fairly standard price for petrol within a locality.

Solicitors in the UK have traditionally enjoyed a high professional status in which high charges and slow service almost became an expectation. But a series of measures at deregulation (e.g. the authorization of licensed conveyancers to share the solicitors' previous monopoly on house conveyancing) has led to much greater price awareness among buyers. This has been particularly true in the case of legal services provided to businesses, where many companies now routinely shop around for the lowest priced solicitors. The old loyalty of client to lawyer has almost died as clients are seduced by the lure of low fees elsewhere. But are legal services a commodity which buyers can shop around for as and when they are required? Lawyers argue that the practice of 'lowballing' (offering ludicrously low fees) can create problems for client as well as lawyer. Clients believe that by holding down fees on professionals who are guaranteed to provide a competent service, they have nothing to lose by going for the cheapest possible deal. But are those practices willing to provide services at rock bottom prices likely to try to achieve a profit by cutting corners? Rather than offering low fees, is there a significant segment of business clients who would prefer value to be added to a business relationship, for example by organizing seminars on subjects of topical interest?

This approach to pricing can resemble the economists' ideal type of perfect competition.

Many markets have a small number of dominant suppliers and a large number of smaller suppliers. Perfect competition and pure monopoly are two extremes which rarely occur in practice. In markets which show some signs of interdependency amongst suppliers, firms can often be described as price makers, or price followers. Price makers tend to be those who as a result of their size and power within a market are able to determine the levels and patterns of prices which other suppliers then follow. Within the UK insurance industry, the largest firms in the market often lead changes in rate structures. Price takers, on the other hand tend to have a relatively low size and market share and may lack product differentiation, resources, or management drive to adopt a proactive pricing strategy. Smaller estate agents in a local area may find it convenient simply to respond to pricing policies adopted by the dominant firms—to take a proactive role themselves may bring about a reaction from the dominant firms which they would be unable to defend on account of their size and standing in the market.

Where it is difficult for a company to calculate its production costs (perhaps because of the high level of fixed costs), charging a 'going rate' can simplify the pricing process. As an example, it may be very difficult to calculate the cost of renting out a video film, as the figure will be very dependent upon assumptions made about the number of uses which the initial purchase cost can be spread over. It is much easier to take price decisions on the basis of the going rate charged by nearby competitors.

Many industrial goods and services are provided by means of a sealed bid tendering process where interested parties are invited to submit a bid for supplying goods or services in accordance with specifications. In the case of many government contracts, the organization inviting tenders is often legally obliged to accept the lowest priced

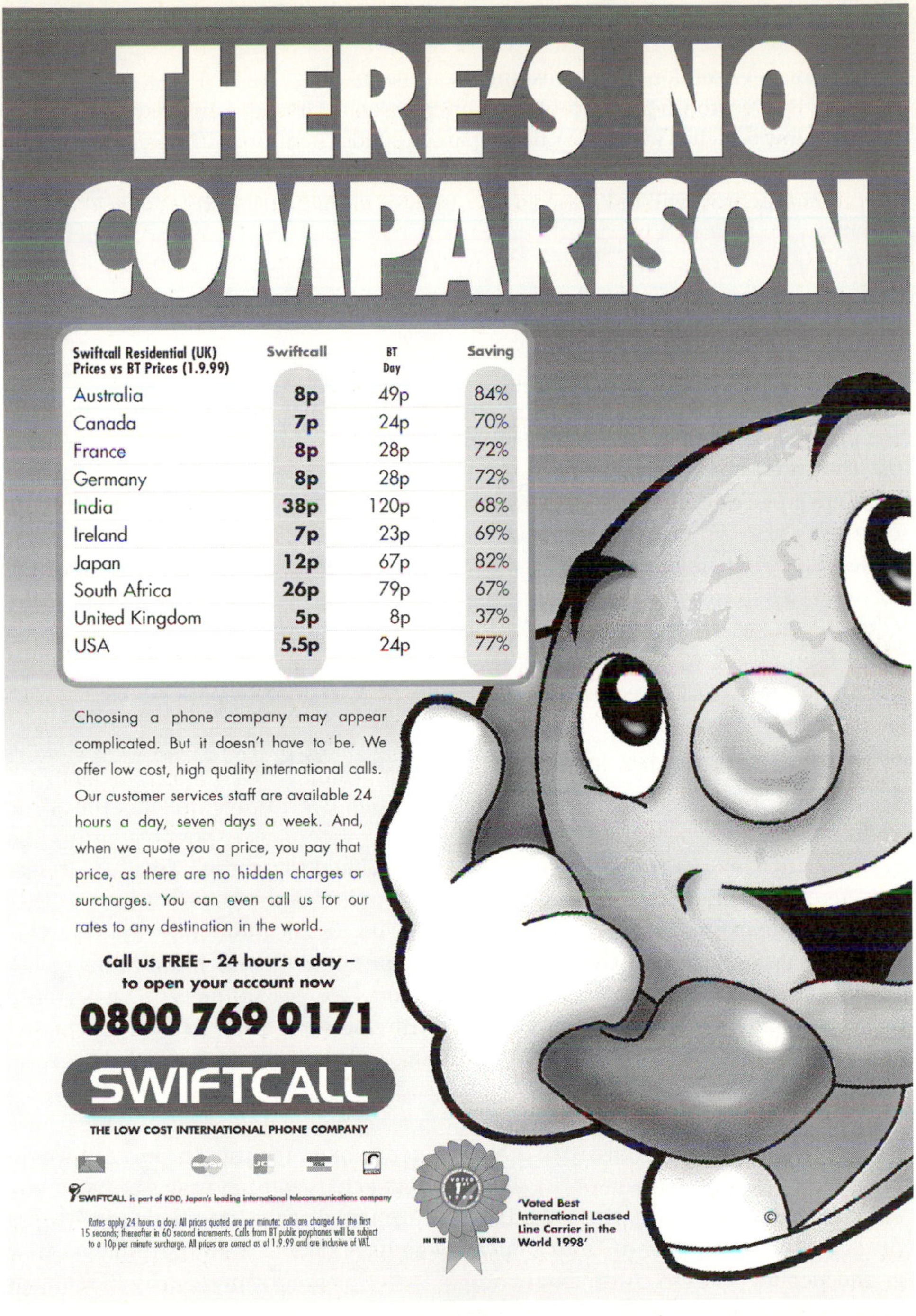

Figure 13.7 The telephone company Swiftcall uses price as an important part of its positioning strategy. For many consumers, telephone services are a generic product for which the only basis of comparison is price. Swiftcall has chosen to focus on a few key prices, for which comparisons can be readily made. In reality, many telephone companies' price schedules are much more complex, with a few low headline prices while other services are offered at higher margins. (Reproduced with permission of Swiftcall Ltd.)

tender, unless exceptional circumstances can be proved. The first task of a bidding company is to establish a minimum bid price based on its costs and required rate of return, below which it would not be prepared to bid. The more difficult task is to try to put a maximum figure on what it can bid. This will be based on expectations of what its competitors will bid, based on an analysis of their strengths and weaknesses.

Demand-based pricing

What customers are prepared to pay represents the upper limit to a company's pricing possibilities. In fact, different customers often put differing ceilings on the price that they are prepared to pay for a product. Successful demand-oriented pricing is therefore based on effective segmentation of markets and price discrimination which achieves the maximum price from each segment.

The bases for segmenting markets were discussed in Chapter 3 and are of direct relevance in determining discriminatory prices. It was noted that in addition to socio-economic factors, the geographical location of buyers, their reason for purchase, and time of purchase are important bases for segmentation. Their impact on price determination is considered below:

Price discrimination between different groups of buyers

Sometimes, price discrimination can be achieved by simply offering the same product to each segment, but charging a different price. This is possible with some services which are not transferable from one individual to another. So a hairdresser can offer senior citizens a haircut which is identical to the service offered to all other customer groups in all respects except price. The justification could be that this segment is more price sensitive than other segments, and therefore additional profitable business can only be gained by sacrificing some element of margin. By performing more haircuts, even at a lower price, a hairdresser may end up having increased total revenue from this segment, while still preserving the higher prices charged to other segments.

On other occasions, however, price discrimination would not be sustainable where one segment was paying more than other segments for an identical product. It would always be open for members of the segment being charged high prices to try to buy their goods in low price markets. Sometimes they will do this directly themselves, as witnessed by the number of British buyers who have taken advantage of lower new car and alcohol prices in continental Europe. Sometimes, entrepreneurs will seek out goods in low priced market segments and offer them for resale in the high price market (a practice which retailers such as Superdrug and Tesco have carried out in respect of branded perfumes which are sold at lower prices in many overseas markets, compared to the UK).

To be sustainable, price discrimination is often associated with slight changes to the product offer. This can be seen in the market for trans-Atlantic air services.

Many service sector companies have offered reduced prices for segments of senior citizens, calculating that these segments are more price sensitive than others and could usefully fill spare capacity at a profit, even at the lower prices charged. But can this apply to the sale of goods? With services, a supplier can insist that only the senior citizen receives the benefit of the service they have paid for (for example by insisting on seeing proof of age during a train journey). But goods can be bought by a low price segment and sold on to a relatively high price one. The pitfalls of this approach to market segmentation were learnt by a German grocery retailer which offered 20 per cent off the price of all purchases made by senior citizens. Entrepreneurial senior citizens were then seen lining up outside the supermarket offering to do other customers' shopping for them. The 20 per cent price saving was split between the senior citizen and the person needing the goods, saving effort for the latter, providing additional income for the former, but making a mockery of the retailer's attempts at price discrimination.

Airlines offer a variety of fare and service combinations to suit the needs of a number of segments. One segment requires to travel at short notice and is typically travelling on business. For the employer, the cost of not being able to travel at short notice may be high, so this group is prepared to pay a relatively high price in return for ready availability. A subsegment of this market may seek extra comfort and space and is prepared to pay more for the differentiated first-class accommodation. For nonbusiness travellers, another segment may be happy to accept a lower price in return for committing themselves to a particular flight two weeks before departure. Another segment with less income to spend on travel may be prepared to take the risk of obtaining a last minute standby flight in return for a lower priced ticket still.

Price discrimination by point of sale

Some companies charge different prices in different places. Hotels frequently charge much higher prices in some prime locations, compared to the average for the chain as a whole, despite there being little difference in facilities offered between locations. The reason for this discrimination can be a combination of cost factors (e.g. land and staff costs for a hotel are higher in central London compared to northern England) as well as demand factors (to large segments of potential buyers, a hotel room in central London will be considered more valuable than one located in northern England).

Within Britain, price discrimination by area is frequently used by train operating companies for journeys to and from London. Fares from provincial towns to London are frequently priced at a lower rate than equivalent fares from London, reflecting—among other things—the nature of demand at each end of a route and the differing competitive pressures in each market.

Price discrimination by area is much more effective for services than goods. Services cannot generally be transferred from the point where they are produced to another area where a buyer most wants to consume them (for example, a Sheffield hotel room can only be consumed in Sheffield and cannot be brought to London where it would be more valuable). By contrast, differences between areas in the price

Will the development of the single European currency eventually lead to uniform prices for a product throughout Europe? Advocates of the Euro claim that this will be one of the currency's benefits, as price discrepancies become blatantly obvious and consumers shop around in the cheapest market. But what about price discrepancies that exist between different regions of the UK? The going rate for petrol in one town can be between 5 and 10 per cent different from that in a town just twenty or thirty miles away. This may seem remarkable considering the mobility of buyers and the ease of shopping around for petrol. Similarly, there is no immediately obvious reason why the price of used cars should vary between different regions of the UK. Similar price variations are present in the USA which has much longer experience of a single currency. There, prices of most consumer goods tend to reach a high in the affluent north-east and are lowest in the relatively poor areas of the deep south. Why should this be? And what hope is there of the single European market harmonizing prices when there are such discrepancies of commodity-type products within a single country?

of goods will soon be exploited by entrepreneurs who are able to buy in the lower price market and sell on in the higher price one (as has happened with cosmetics sourced from low price Far Eastern markets and resold in the UK).

Price discrimination by type of use

A similar product can be bought by different people to satisfy quite different needs. A train journey may be perceived as an optional leisure purchase by one person, but to another person a means of getting work done on the way to an important business meeting. Train operating companies have therefore developed different fares aimed at groups with different journey purposes (e.g. off-peak fares for price sensitive leisure travellers and first-class facilities for business executives).

Even the same person may repeatedly buy a product but seek to satisfy different needs on each occasion. There are many examples of this. Most people when eating out are more likely to be price sensitive for a regular midday meal during their lunch hour, compared with a social meal with friends in the evening. Many restaurants have responded to this by offering special lunch menus which are very similar to meals offered in the evening, except that the price is lower.

Price discrimination by time of purchase

It is quite common for suppliers of services to charge different prices at different times of supply. Services often face uneven demand which follows a daily, weekly, annual, seasonal, cyclical, or random pattern. At the height of each peak, pricing is usually a reflection of:

- the greater willingness of customers to pay higher prices when demand is strong, and
- the greater cost which often results from service operators trying to cater for short peaks in demand.

The greater strength of demand which occurs at some points in a daily cycle can occur for a number of reasons. In the case of rail services into the major conurbations, workers must generally arrive at work at a specified time and may have few realistic alternative means of getting to work. A railway operator can therefore sustain a higher level of fares during the daily commuter peak period. Similarly, the higher rate charged for telephone calls during the daytime is a reflection of the greater strength of demand from the business sector during the day. As well as price discrimination between different periods of the day, it can also occur between different periods of the week (e.g. higher fares for using many train services on a Friday evening), or between different seasons of the year (e.g. holiday charter flights over bank holiday periods).

Price discrimination by time can be effective in inducing new business at what would otherwise be a quiet period. Hotels in holiday resorts frequently lower their prices in the off-peak season to try to tempt additional custom. Many of the public utilities lower their charges during off-peak periods in a bid to stimulate demand—for example, lower telephone charges at weekends.

Pricing a product range

MOST organizations sell a range of products and the price of each individual item should recognize the pricing strategy adopted for other products in the range. Some companies may have many thousands of individual items, for each of which a price must be set.

For any given product, a company can allocate the other items in its product range to one of three categories for the purposes of pricing:

- optional additional items;
- captive items;
- competing items.

Optional additional items are those which a buyer chooses whether or not to add to the main product purchased, often at the time that the main product is purchased. As a matter of strategy, an organization could seek to charge a low lead-in price for its core products, but to recoup a higher margin from the additional optional items. Simply breaking a product into core and optional components may allow for the presentation of lower price indicators, which through a process of rationalization may be more acceptable to many customers. Research may show that the price of the core product is in fact the only factor that potential customers take into account when choosing between alternatives. In this way, many travel agents and tour operators cut their margins on the core holiday which they sell, but make up some of their margin by charging relatively high prices for optional extras such as travel insurance policies and car hire.

tel : 375336

PRICE LIST

cut -	Ladies -	£25
	Gentlemen -	£17
cut & blow dry -	Ladies -	£32
	Gentlemen -	£25
permanent waving -	*from*	£42
colouring	- by quotation	
highlights	- by quotation	

SPECIAL RATES

senior citizens - 10% off all prices
Monday-Thursday only
students - 20% off on Wednesday afternoon
children - 25% off all prices

Figure 13.8 This price schedule for a hairdresser's salon illustrates how even the smallest business can practise discriminatory pricing between different types of customers and different times of purchase

Captive items occur where the core product has been purchased and the provision of additional services can only be provided by the original provider of the core product. Where these are not specified at the outset of purchasing the core product, or are left up to the discretion of the service provider, the latter is in a strong position to charge a high price. Against this, the company must consider the effect which the perception of high exploitative prices charged for these captive items will have on customer loyalty when buyers are next considering the purchase of the core product. An example of captive product pricing is provided by many car manufacturers who charge high prices for specialist replacement parts for which they hold a design patent. Against the wish to maximize profits from charging high prices, car manufacturers must consider the effects of such pricing on repeat purchase of its cars.

Competing items within the product range occur where a new product targets a segment of the population which overlaps the segments served by other products within the organization's mix. By a process of 'cannibalization', a company could find that it is competing with itself. In this way, a confectionary company with a large market share which launches a new chocolate bar may find that its new launch is taking sales away from its existing range of chocolate bars.

Price bundling is the practice of marketing two or more products in a single package for a single price. Bundling is particularly important for goods and services which have a high ratio of fixed to variable costs. Furthermore, where there is a high level of interdependency between different types of output from an organization, it may be difficult and meaningless to price each individual item. In this way, the provision of a cashpoint card and cheque guarantee card becomes an interdependent part of the current bank account offering which most UK banks do not charge for separately.

Price bundling of diverse services from an organization's product mix is frequently used as a means of building relationships with customers. In this way, a mortgage could be bundled with a household contents insurance policy or a legal protection policy. Where the bundle of service represents ease of administration to the consumer, the service organization may be able to achieve a price for the bundle which is greater than the combined price of the bundle's components.

Different groups of consumers have differing expectations about what they would expect to see in a price bundle. Car buyers in the UK, for example, expect a high level of equipment (such as radio, wheel trims, etc.) to be bundled in with the main price of a car, while many buyers in continental Europe would expect to pay for each item separately.

The pricing of public services

MANY of the pricing principles discussed above, such as price discrimination and competitor-based pricing may be quite alien to some public services. It may be difficult or undesirable to implement a straightforward price–value relationship with individual users of public services for a number of reasons:

- External benefits may be generated by a public service for which it is difficult or impossible for the service provider to charge individual users. For example, road users within the UK are not generally charged directly for the benefits which they receive from the road system, largely because of the impracticality of road pricing. Instead, road services are provided by direct and indirect taxation.

■ Pricing can be actively used as a means of social policy. Subsidized prices are often used to favour particular groups, for example prescription charges favour the very ill and unemployed, among others. Sometimes, the interests of marketing orientation and social policy can overlap. Charging lower prices for unemployed people to enter museums may provide social benefits for this group, while gaining additional revenue from a segment that might not otherwise have been able to afford a visit to the museum.

■ Benefits to society at large may be as significant as the benefits received by the individual, so there may be a case for government subsidizing low prices. Education and training courses may be provided at an uneconomic charge in order to add to the level of skills available within an economy generally.

Problems can occur in public services which have been given a largely financial, market-oriented brief, but in which social policy objectives are superimposed, possibly in conflict. Museums, leisure centres, and car park charges have frequently been at the centre of debate about the relative importance to be attached to economic and social objectives. Museums have sometimes overcome this dilemma by retaining free or nominally priced admission charges for the serious, scholarly elements of their exhibits, while offering special exhibitions which match the private sector in the standard of production and the prices charged.

Chapter summary and key linkages to other chapters

This chapter has discussed some of the bases on which practising managers go about setting prices. While the fundamental principles of price determination which were discussed in the previous chapter should never be forgotten, this chapter has suggested that markets are rarely perfectly competitive and setting prices is not a straightforward task. Determining pricing objectives and strategy is important for a company which is not merely a price taker. Prices can be set in relation to production costs, the strength of demand, competitors prices, or a combination of all three.

The following key linkages to other chapters should be noted:

Chapter 1: What is marketing?: Marketing is about satisfying customers' needs profitably. Pricing is the mediating device between customers receiving value for money and companies achieving an adequate financial return.

Chapter 2: The marketing environment: Pricing of any product must have regard to the marketing environment of the product. Pricing should be flexible enough to respond to changes in the marketing environment (e.g. a weakening economy may put pressure on prices).

Chapter 3: Market segmentation: Segmentation is fundamental to pricing in a competitive market. Different market segments are likely to place different limits on what they would expect to pay for a product.

Chapter 4: Branding: Brands add to the perceived value for many products for many market segments. Products carrying a strong brand usually attract a price premium compared to similar but unbranded products.

Chapter 5: Marketing and ethics: Is it ethical to provide misleading price indications, or to discriminate prices in favour of, or against, particular groups?

Chapter 6: Marketing research: How do you predict the price that customers will be prepared to pay for a new product?

Chapter 7: Buyer behaviour: How important is price within the whole process of buying a product? What is the level of price awareness?

Chapter 8: Buyer–seller relationship development: Price is often used to initiate and maintain relationships.

Chapters 9/10: Developing a product portfolio: Are the opportunities for new product development matched by prices which will allow for profitable exploitation of the opportunity?

Chapter 11: Developing a sustainable competitive advantage: Can a price position be maintained in the face of a competitive and changing marketing environment?

Chapter 12: Pricing theory: This chapter has discussed applied issues of pricing. The underlying theory of pricing should never be forgotten.

Chapter 14: Intermediaries/physical distribution: How can price levels be maintained through distribution channels? Can price be used to motivate intermediaries?

Chapters 16–20: Principles of promotion planning/advertising/sales promotion/ personal selling/direct marketing: Does a company's promotional effort provide a basis for charging a sustainable price premium?

Chapter 21: Managing the marketing effort: How are prices determined within the organization? Is it fast enough to adjust prices in response to a changing marketing environment?

Chapter 22: Services marketing: Services are often difficult to evaluate and price may be the main method by which buyers judge a service offer in relation to other offers.

Chapter 23: Global marketing: What factors influence prices in a company's overseas markets? Should it seek to maintain globally uniform prices, or locally adapted prices?

Case study

Adding value to petrol

Of all the textbook definitions of a pure commodity, petrol must represent one of the best practical examples. Differentiating petrol is very difficult—all the main players have standard offerings, which must conform to government set standards. In the past, attempts to differentiate the core product have met with only moderate success, as witnessed by the only very limited uptake of low sulphur diesel. In the case of Shell's attempts to differentiate its petrol with Formula Shell, the result was disastrous with complaints from customers of damage to engines.

In a market that has competed chiefly on price, the two principal options for firms to achieve profitability are to keep squeezing costs and investing in added value services. Most companies have tried developing brands, but the generic nature of petrol has resulted in highly fickle customers showing very little brand loyalty. In the UK, the market for petrol has been made more complex by the impact of supermarkets. Between 1996 and 1997, supermarket forecourts increased their share of the market from 18.8 per cent to 23.3 per cent, according to Datamonitor. The productivity of the supermarkets is very high, given that all of the major supermarket chains had only 1,000 sites between them in 1998, compared with Esso's 1,874 and Shell's 1,841.

Towards the end of the 1990s the drive towards lower costs was translated into a series of mergers between the big oil companies. During 1998, Esso's announcement that parent company Exxon had put together the world's biggest merger, with rival Mobil, followed on from BP's merger with Amoco and Total's proposed take-over of its Belgian competitor PetroFina. The hope was that economies of scale could be achieved through the rationalization of outlets and distribution, allowing lower costs to be passed on in sustainably lower prices, and thereby maintaining market share and profitability.

To complement the strategy of lowering costs, petrol retailers sought to diversify their retail sites in order to gain a higher share of consumers' spending. The quality of retail facilities has been crucial to this strategy. Shell has been among the leading petrol companies to diversify into retail, thereby reducing its dependence on price sensitive petrol sales. In effect, it was counter-attacking the supermarkets that had diversified in the reverse direction. Shell even recruited a former Tesco marketing director to develop its retail business. The new kinds of petrol station retail outlets stock all the kinds of products that would normally be found in a Tesco Metro—including snack foods, newspapers, and chilled ready meals. These products offer much higher profit potential than petrol. It also means that Shell is competing directly against the supermarkets which have had the most impact on the petrol market. Esso and BP have taken a slightly different route by making agreements with supermarkets to lure motorists on to their forecourts. Esso signed a deal with arch-rival Tesco to open Tesco Express shops on Esso forecourts. BP struck a similar deal with Safeway, while Elf announced a plan to develop convenience stores with the retailer Somerfield at some of its sites.

With regard to the pricing of the petrol itself, recent years have seen a shift in pricing strategy. Many companies have traditionally offered some form of incentive for buyers to return repeatedly. The offer of collecting a matching set of glasses or kitchenware has in the past lured many drivers, especially those less price sensitive company car drivers who are filling up their car at their employer's expense. More recently, loyalty card schemes have taken over where free glasses and green shield stamps left off. Towards the end of the 1990s there was evidence that these incentives were not working to fend off the advances of the supermarkets. Market leader Esso had relied on its Tiger Tokens loyalty scheme since 1986, but in 1996 abandoned this in favour of Price Watch, a scheme designed to position the Esso brand as the cheapest on the high street. The company claimed to study all competitors within five miles of its outlets and matched any lower prices that it found. This was a direct challenge to the supermarkets who had been pricing petrol low as an alleged loss leader to draw consumers into their stores. Esso had spent the bulk of its £5.5 million advertising budget on supporting its Price Watch campaign during 1997. Despite this, Esso's market share still fell from 20.3 per cent in 1996 to 18.7 per cent in 1997. Meanwhile, Shell stuck with the loyalty programme route and significantly upgraded its Smart loyalty scheme to make it one of the most extensive multi-partner loyalty schemes operating in the UK.

Despite the attempts of the oil companies to increase the non-petrol element of their business, the sector seemed set for further costly competition. With further consolidation among the petrol companies, the prospect emerged of efficient companies with deep pockets determined to take on the supermarkets in a battle for market share. But the supermarkets, financially secure and among the most profitable retailers in Europe, were not going to let their petrol sales slip away. Losing the motorist from the petrol forecourt could result in the loss of the shopper in the main store.

Case study review questions

1 Summarize the main elements of pricing strategy that are open to petrol retailers.

2 How sustainable is a company's guarantee to match competitors' prices, such as that offered by Esso's Price Watch guarantee?

3 What would you expect the effects of rapidly falling or rising market prices for oil products to be on oil companies' retail pricing strategy?

Chapter review questions

1 To what extent is the concept of a product life cycle useful in determining the pricing of a product?

2 How should a company go about assessing the price that buyers would be prepared to pay for an innovative home maintenance service?

3 Analyse the product mix of a multi-product company and identify the pricing strategies used to increase total revenue.

4 Using examples, compare the advantages and disadvantages of cost plus and marginal cost pricing.

5 Using a company of your choice, critically assess how price discrimination is practised between different groups of customers.

6 What is the role of pricing for local authority services? Illustrate your answer with reference to the police or fire services.

Reference

Cyert, R. M., and March, J. G. (1963), *A Behavioural Theory of the Firm* (Englewood Cliffs, NJ: Prentice Hall).

Suggested further reading

For an overview of pricing strategy, the following provide a useful introduction:

■ Creyer, E. H., and Ross, W. T., Jnr. (1997,) 'Tradeoffs Between Price and Quality: How a Value Index Affects Preference Formation', *Journal of Consumer Affairs*, **31**, 2, pp. 280–93.

■ Docters, R. G. (1997), 'Price Strategy: Time to Choose your Weapons', *Journal of Business Strategy*, **18**, 5, pp. 11–15.

■ Hanna, N., and Dodge, H. R. (1995), *Pricing: Policies and Procedures* (Basingstoke: Macmillan).

■ Trout, J., and Rivkin, S. (1998), 'Prices: Simple Guidelines to Get them Right', *Journal of Business Strategy*, **19**, 6 , pp. 13–17.

The following discuss applied cases in price discrimination:

■ Calderwood, J. A. (1998), 'Rate Discrimination', *Transportation & Distribution*, **39**, 8, pp. 128–9.

■ Layson, S. K. (1998), 'Third-Degree Price Discrimination with Interdependent Demands', *Journal of Industrial Economics*, **46**, 4, pp. 511–12.

■ Morwitz, V. G., Greenleaf, E. A., and Johnson, E. (1998), 'Divide and Prosper: Consumers' Reactions to Partitioned Prices', *Journal of Marketing Research*, **35**, 4, pp. 453–4.

■ Woolley, S. (1998), 'I Got it Cheaper than You', *Forbes*, 2 Nov., pp. 82–3.

■ Yelkur, R., and Herbig, P. (1997), 'Differential Pricing for Services', *Marketing Intelligence & Planning*, **15**, 4–5, pp. 190–5.

Chapter 14
Channel Intermediaries

Chapter objectives

Most companies would encounter administrative and logistical problems in trying to deliver their goods and services to each of their end consumers. Instead, companies more often than not use intermediaries to distribute their products. This chapter aims to develop an understanding of the 'place' element of the marketing mix and the role of intermediaries in marketing channels. Approaches to designing a channel of distribution and issues in the management and control of intermediaries are discussed.

Introduction

THIS chapter, and the one following (Chapter 15) discuss issues concerning what is often called the 'place' P of the traditional marketing mix. Decisions about channel intermediaries (or 'middlemen', to use an outdated, yet user-friendly term) and the management of physical distribution fall under this heading. 'Placing' products involves managing the processes supporting the flow of good or services from producers to consumers. We shall examine the distribution of services later in this chapter, but most of our attention will focus on the availability of goods. Goods must be made available in the right quantity, in the right location, and at the times when customers wish to purchase them, all at an acceptable price (and cost to the producer and/or intermediary). Achieving these concurrent aims is not easy but is often essential for an organization wishing to gain a sustainable competitive advantage.

Sometimes, a manufacturer will decide to dispense with intermediaries altogether. For instance Alan Sugar, the outspoken Chairman of Amstrad, was vociferous in his criticism of computer retailers when he withdrew his products from high street outlets (*The Times* 1995). He said that the store chains 'scour the world to buy machines from whoever is prepared to lose money this week ... they are not making any money and the obvious place to turn is the manufacturer. But we are not inclined to subsidize their advertising and after-sales service'. Instead, Amstrad have begun to sell their computers to customers direct, with no 'middleman' involved. Ask yourself what the market conditions were that prompted Sugar to take such a bold decision. Such choices are not easy for manufacturers. In the following pages we intend to explain the complex set of issues involved in managing distribution channels in today's fast-shifting economic environment.

A *marketing channel* has been defined as 'a system of relationships existing among businesses that participate in the process of buying and selling products and services' (Bowersox and Cooper 1992). Channel *intermediaries* are those organizations which facilitate the distribution of goods to the ultimate customer. The complex roles of intermediaries, which are explored in the following section, may include taking physical ownership of products, collecting payment, and offering after-sales service. Since these activities can involve considerable risk and responsibility, it is clear that, in attempting to ensure the availability of their goods, producers must consider the needs of channel intermediaries as well as those of the end consumers. Marketing channel management refers to the choice and control of these intermediaries, although, as we shall see, the ability of manufacturers to exert influence over inter-mediaries such as retailers varies considerably, especially in channels for FMCGs (fast-moving consumer goods).

As more and more tasks are passed on to intermediaries, the producing company starts to lose control and power over its products and how they are sold. A key part of channel management therefore involves the recognition that networks of intermedi-aries represent social systems as well as economic ones. In other words, the careful nurturing of business and personal relationships can be as important as financial considerations. This has become particularly important in the UK where there have been many changes in the retailing environment over the last thirty years. Fernie (1997) points to the facts that consumers have become more mobile, more experi-mental in their behaviour, and more conscious of time pressures on shopping and cooking activities. Consumers now expect products of reasonable quality, via retailers offering variety, good customer service, and easy access. The response from the retail sector has seen a transformation in food shopping: you should be aware of the recent trend towards building larger supermarkets, mainly operating from out-of-town sites, and the resulting decline in the number of small independent shops. You may also be aware of how some town centre intermediaries are trying to fight back. What initiatives spring to mind? Yet the growth in supermarkets' market share remains inexorable: by the mid-1990s the top five UK multiples (e.g. supermarket chains such as Tesco and Sainsbury) accounted for over 60 per cent of the total gro-cery market between them (Randall 1994). In 1997, the proportion had reached over 80 per cent (*Observer* 1997). These changes have meant that it is vital for brand manu-facturers to maintain good relations with their retail intermediaries in order to gain access to consumers.

Retailing has become one of the most dynamic sectors of the UK economy. This is the case not only in groceries, but in areas such as clothes, DIY, electronic goods, chemists, books, and music retailing. As well as the high profile of British market leaders like B&Q, Boots, and Waterstone's, the reputation and status of figures behind different chains like Anita Roddick (Body Shop), Terence Conran (Habitat), and

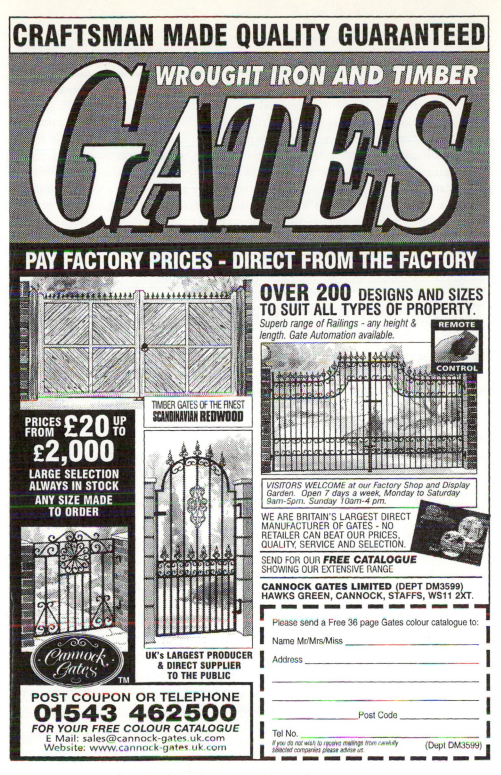

Figure 14.1. Cannock Gates serves a specialist market for gates which it feels is inadequately catered for by intermediaries. In this advertisement, which ran in the UK national press, the company stresses the price and service advantages of dealing directly with it. The fact that gates are generally made to order may make this method of distribution a sensible one, but this strategy is less likely to succeed where the product is relatively standardized and buyers seek variety. (Reproduced with permission of Cannock Gates Ltd.)

Richard Branson (Virgin) are considerable. Such personalities have not, of course, always had a smooth ride in the media: witness the fall from grace of Gerald Ratner when he admitted that his jeweler shops sold 'crap' (*Observer* 1992). In general, though, retailing represents a highly visible sector which gives us plenty of opportunities to analyse the practice of marketing theory. The consumer goods examples already discussed illustrate the significant impact the management of marketing channels can have in the commercial environment, both from the point of view of producers and of the intermediaries themselves. We shall continue our discussion of retailing in the section which follows. However, most of this chapter will examine intermediaries from the perspective of the product manufacturer.

The role of intermediaries in a value chain

THE generic *value chain* of an organization describes the activities involved in the manufacture, marketing, and delivery of a product or service by the firm (see Fig. 14.2).

Michael Porter argues that value can be added during the movement of goods from suppliers (of raw materials or components), through the manufacturing organization, and on to the end customer, at any of the five primary activity stages shown in Fig. 14.2 (Porter 1985). Marketing channels can perform an important role in the three latter stages, i.e. those of Outbound Logistics (e.g. order processing, storage, and transportation), Marketing and Sales (e.g. market research, personal selling, sales promotions), and Service (e.g. repair, training, spare parts). It is rare for a producer

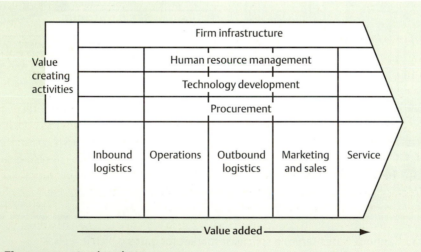

Figure 14.2 A value chain

to control all these activities itself, and therefore the management of channel intermediaries, in terms of both minimizing costs and maximizing competitive advantage, plays a vital part in boosting the value added by any marketing channel.

In order to decide whether a firm should undertake its own distribution direct to consumers or whether it would be more efficient and effective to use intermediaries, it is necessary to understand the functions of these intermediaries.

Functions of intermediaries

Perhaps the most significant role of channel intermediaries is to reconcile the differing needs of manufacturers and consumers. For instance, it is typical for an FMCG manufacturer to gain economies of scale by producing a large quantity of a limited range of goods, whereas consumers often want only a limited quantity of a wide range of goods, goods that are conveniently made available under one roof (i.e. in a retail supermarket). Intermediaries can help overcome this *discrepancy of assortment* (Alderson and Halbert 1968) by reducing dramatically the number of contacts required between suppliers and the end customers. Distribution and selling costs are therefore reduced. This is shown in Fig. 14.3.

Wholesalers can add value by breaking bulk. This might involve purchasing in large quantities from a manufacturer and then selling smaller, more manageable volumes of stock on to retailers. *Discrepancies of quantity* are further reduced by retailers who provide consumers with individual items that suit their needs. Wholesalers can also benefit small producers by combining a large number of smaller purchases from, say, agricultural smallholdings lacking the funds to deliver their goods to consumers, and then combining them into a bulk quantity for transportation.

In many cases, intermediaries can have *superior knowledge* of a target market compared to manufacturers. Retailers can therefore add value to the producer's goods by tailoring their offerings more closely to the specific requirements of consumers, for example by ensuring that goods are stocked which match the economic and lifestyle needs of shoppers. Think of the range of goods Virgin Megastores offer in addition to music software.

Distributors of technical goods might also offer after-sales services in the form of guarantees and customer advice hotlines. If these services can be provided with a high level of expertise, then manufacturers may feel able to relinquish control of these parts of the value chain. For instance, Ahmad and Buttle (1998) describe the relationship between a foreign-based manufacturer of office equipment (fax machines, photocopiers, printers, etc.) and its UK dealers. The manufacturer provides basic service training for the dealers' technical staff and allows them to sell consumables such as toners. More complex repair queries, however, are handled by a head office telephone helpline for both dealers and end users.

Probably the most obvious gaps between consumers and producers in channel

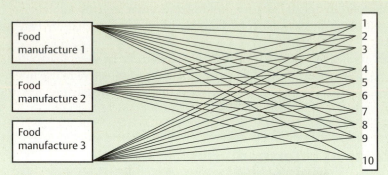

With no intermediaries: 3 producers × 10 customers = 30 contracts

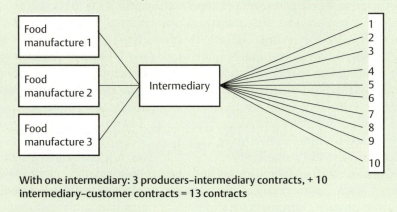

With one intermediary: 3 producers–intermediary contracts, + 10 intermediary–customer contracts = 13 contracts

Figure 14.3 Direct v. indirect channels

management are those of location and time. A *location gap* occurs simply due to the geographic separation of producers and the consumers of their goods. This is rarely the case for services of course (see Chapter 22), nevertheless for the vast majority of FMCGs this location gap exists, especially for companies dealing globally. A *time gap* takes place between when consumers want actually to purchase products and when manufactures produce them. At the most basic level, we can see that most production facilities are at their busiest during standard working hours on Monday to Friday, while most retailers expect their daily takings to be greatest at the weekend, and, increasingly, in the evenings on weekdays. As a student, you probably find sufficient time between (or instead of!) lectures to go shopping—most people, however, are 'time poor' and have to squeeze the weekly shop in after work!

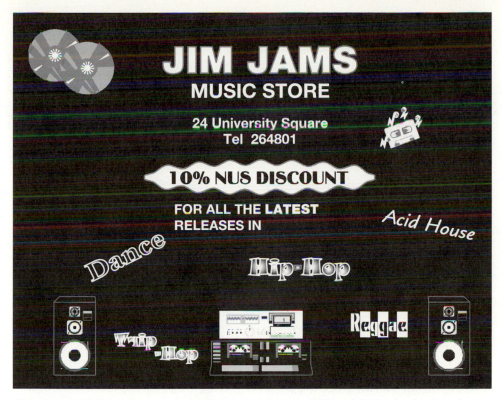

Figure 14.4 This music store provides an assortment of CDs which is clearly aimed at the needs of young, slightly offbeat buyers of music

Types of intermediary

A **VARIETY** of types of intermediary can participate in the value chain, or, perhaps more accurately, the supply chain (see Chapter 15). For most FMCG manufacturers the two most commonly used intermediaries are wholesalers and retailers. These organizations are normally described as *distributors* (or 'merchants') since they take title to products, typically building up stocks and thereby assuming risk, and resell them; wholesalers to other wholesalers and retailers; retailers to the ultimate consumers. Other intermediaries such as agents and brokers do not take title to goods. Instead they arrange exchanges between buyers and sellers and in return receive commissions or fees. The use of agents often involves less of a financial and contractual commitment by the manufacturer and is therefore less of a risk, yet the lack of commitment to the manufacturer's goods from the agent may prove problematic.

As we mentioned earlier, retailing is an extremely high profile area of marketing, and worthy of further discussion. We should not, however, forget the role of *whole-salers* in marketing channels. Wholesalers are typically less obvious to us as individual consumers, but they play an important role in servicing retailers (in consumer markets) and organizational clients (in industrial or business-to-business markets). For example, it can prove prohibitively expensive for a manufacturer of industrial goods, such as a simple bolt fastening, to maintain a large sales force. In this case, access to a wide range of industrial customers may be more efficiently facilitated via a specialist wholesaler. Retailers are often serviced by wholesalers specializing in sourcing and selecting inventory (i.e. stock) for a particular product line, such as greetings cards. These wholesalers can offer detailed product knowledge and in-store merchandising services to retailers, which involves maintaining their own designated selling space within a store. What benefits do you think each party gains from this arrangement?

Classification of retailers

Returning to retailing, we should remind ourselves that a *retailer* is simply an organization that buys products for the purpose of reselling them to consumers. Having said this, a number of different types of retailer may be identified. As the broad classifications below suggest, these stores types have certain characteristics:

- **department stores**, e.g. Debenham's. Here, we find product lines laid out into separate departments such as ladies' and men's clothing, home furnishings, cosmetics, etc. Companies may operate as 'shops-within-shops' and pay rent as a percentage of takings to the host store.

- **supermarkets**, e.g. Sainsbury's. These are large, self-service stores carrying a broad and deep range of FMCGs. They are typically located in out-of-town retail parks, although Tesco have recently embarked upon opening smaller, city centre sites known as Metro stores (Fernie 1997). The supermarket chains are often the first with new customer initiatives such as loyalty cards, although the actual long-term impact of these schemes is still to be proven (East and Hogg 1998). The resulting discounts gained by shoppers, however, are hard for smaller independent stores to match.

- **discount sheds or 'category killers'**, e.g. Toys 'R' Us. These stores often stock bulky items such as furniture and electrical goods. The category killer terminology results from the tendency of some very large specialist stores to put competing independent retailers out of business.

- **speciality shops**, e.g. clothing (Next), music (HMV), newsagents (WH Smith). Typically found in central business districts of towns where prime sites are vitally important. As it is frequently only the large national chains who can afford the high rents of such sites, it might be said that many UK high streets are now remarkably similar in the choice they offer to the shopper. How does your home town compare to its nearest neighbour, for instance?

- **convenience or 'c' stores**, e.g. 7-Eleven. Geographically, and also in terms of the range of products on offer, these stores fill the gap between edge-of-town super-markets and the 'traditional' corner shop situated close to housing estates.

- **markets and cash and carry warehouses**, e.g. Makro. The former usually offer cheaper fresh produce to consumers or catering trades and small retailers. The latter perform a similar function for goods such as alcohol, tobacco, and confectionery.

- **catalogue showrooms**, e.g. Argos. These stores lower their costs by maintaining only a limited display of goods, with consumers making their selection via a catalogue and collecting their purchase from a stockroom attached to the showroom site.

Within these differing types of store, we can find some interesting trends. McGoldrick (1990) points out that one of the most significant changes in retailing structure has been the increased proportion of trade taken by the multiple retailers (i.e. the retail chains). In the grocery sector, multiples are usually defined as retailers with over ten outlets. This change has taken place largely at the expense of independent retailers, but has also eroded the market share of the co-operatives. It is notable that, collectively, the co-operative societies represent one of the largest retailers in the country. The problem for the Co-op is that it comprises a large number of mostly autonomous societies and does not pool its buying resources into a fully integrated retailing organization (McGoldrick 1990). Independent retail stores are typically run by a sole trader or as a family business. The social trends identified at the start of this chapter clearly conspire against the corner shop, which has constantly to look for ways to differentiate itself, usually through flexible opening hours and specialist inventory (Howe 1992). One response of independent retailers has been to form voluntary or 'symbol' groups where buying and marketing is often provided centrally in return for the retailer buying a proportion of their goods from particular wholesalers. Examples include Spar and Happy Shopper for groceries, and Unichem in the chemist sector.

Retail strategies

As significant channel intermediaries, it should not be forgotten that retailers have their own set of strategic choices. *Location* is usually the most critical issue since it is central to attracting the right kind of customer in sufficient volume to make trade viable (Anderson 1993). Retailers are using increasingly sophisticated methods to determine the optimum locations for their outlets. For instance, large car dealerships now examine geodemographic information from database suppliers such as Experian to determine the likely customer profiles of the region surrounding a possible site (Horner 1998) to see if they match those of their typical drivers.

Retailers must also decide whether to own or lease their properties. Companies such as Marks & Spencer invest in the ownership of most of their sites, thereby saving on rents and bolstering their balance sheet. Other retailers choose to lease, making

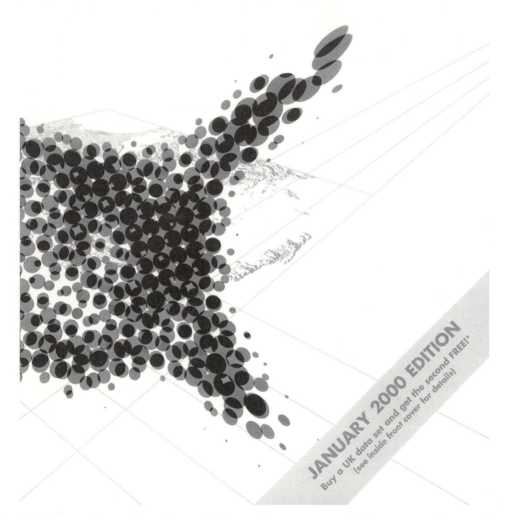

CACI Data Catalogue

A Complete Listing of Demographic, Marketing and Mapping Data
for the UK, Europe and USA

JANUARY 2000 EDITION
Buy a UK data set and get the second FREE!*
(see inside front cover for details)

Figure 14.5. Increasing volumes of information are now available to companies to assist them in store location decisions. The specialist information company CACI lists hundreds of datasets in its catalogue, including local area analyses of household expenditure on home improvements, visits to restaurants, and household income. The company also provides information about overseas markets, for example it can provide local area information throughout the USA about ethnic origin, household net worth, and type of household tenure

operating funds available and providing greater flexibility. Such decisions clearly require the support of the finance department of the organization, emphasizing that the marketing department cannot exist in a vacuum.

In terms of *product/market strategies* it is helpful to examine variations on Ansoff's matrix (1987). See also Chapter 21 which discusses marketing planning and management in greater detail. Kristenson (1983) provides an assortment/market segment matrix which is shown in Fig. 14.6.

Retailers must address the needs of particular market segments, but must also consider which product lines to carry. The matrix has been developed further by Omura (1986) who has added the level of *service* to the horizontal axis, reminding retailers of the need to offer differentiation via service delivery levels as well as through their product assortment. The risk is greatest when retailers attempt to sell new merchandise with unfamiliar service levels, as exemplified by the failure of Asda's move into selling cars (McGoldrick 1990). Retailers must also, of course, position themselves in the minds of consumers. Walters (1988) recommends the use of four strategies to accomplish this; merchandise, trading style/format, customer service, and customer communications. Retailers must ensure that their stores have the appropriate 'atmospherics' (the physical elements of the store's interior and exterior that appeal to consumers and encourage them to buy), and that the store's image is acceptable to the retailer's target market (this can be achieved, for example, via a reputation for integrity, service, product quality, advertising, and retail branding). Refer back to the discussion of clothing retailers in Chapter 4 for some examples, and ask yourself why you patronize your favourite clothes store.

As East (1997) has pointed out, retailers spend large sums of money in attracting customers, and despite factors such as value, choice, friendly service, and quality being important to shoppers, the main reason cited by supermarket users for patronage is close location. Nevertheless, the fact that these other factors are of importance

Assortment Segments	Existing assortment	New assortment
Existing segments	Increased share of market	Expansion, product development
New segments	Expansion, market development	Diversification

Figure 14.6 A product–market segment matrix

to consumers is significant since these are the very determinants of consumer behaviour which are largely out of the control of the manufacturer. In other words, the professionalism with which retailers, particularly those in the UK, have managed their operations, has meant that the design of a channel of distribution which gives access to the desired end consumer has become a difficult decision for goods manufacturers. Just how do they ensure that their products are adequately represented on the shelves of such powerful supermarket businesses?

Designing a channel of distribution

Now that we are more familiar with the roles of channel intermediaries, we need to consider a producer's distribution objectives and how the selection of suitable channels might support these. *Channel objectives* will be (or should be!) set by the organization's positioning strategy. The place element of the marketing mix must be consistent with the remaining marketing tools used by the marketing manager to gain a sustainable competitive advantage (see Chapter 11). This is usually achieved by considering three options:

- **Intensive distribution**. Generally used for FMCGs and other relatively low priced or impulse purchases. Put very simply, the more outlets stocking your product, the greater the likelihood of it being bought. The convenience factor is often very important for these goods. An interesting development here is the increasing range of products available from petrol stations; everything from groceries to snacks and gifts (*Marketing Week* 1995). In terms of the discrepancies of assortment and location discussed earlier, a highly intensive distribution network with wide geographical cover can prove extremely efficient. Although not a conventional 'product', look at the huge number and variety of outlets where National Lottery tickets may be bought.

- **Exclusive distribution**. Here, distribution may be limited to a small number of intermediaries who gain better margins and exclusivity. In return the manufacturer seeks more price controls and dedicated merchandising and sales support from the retailer. Dealers often also agree not to stock competing lines. This is often done for expensive products with an upmarket brand image such as Ray-Bann sunglasses or designer label clothing. Manufacturers can become upset when retailers who they see as not having the appropriate brand image attempt to stock these products or, worse, offer them at discounted prices. Witness the reaction of the perfume industry to Superdrug's stocking of fine fragrances (*Guardian* 1993) or Calvin Klein's protests at Tesco carrying their underwear range.

- **Selective distribution**. This represents a compromise between intensive and selective distribution. The manufacturer is looking for adequate market coverage, but still hopes to select supportive dealers. This usually occurs for 'shopping' products such as audio and video hardware.

Influences on channel selection

There are a number of key influences on channel selection strategies: buyer behaviour, producer's needs, product type, and competition. First, the expectations of the *end customer* must be addressed. This might mean taking into consideration factors such as a geographical preference to buy locally, or to feel more comfortable visiting a particular type of store (say, an independent dance-orientated music store as opposed to Our Price in order to purchase a 'house' 12 inch single), or the need for a retailer capable of offering certain after-sales services, such as washing machine repair warranties. Decisions must be made based on sound marketing research into buyer behaviour patterns (see Chapters 6 and 7). This is also true for industrial markets. For example, suppliers of electronic components need to determine whether business customers prefer to deal with the company's direct sales force (often the case for larger organizational clients with expert purchasing departments) or whether they are happier going to a specialist distributor (typically used by smaller clients without this in-house expertise). In international markets, it may be essential to use an agent with an intimate knowledge of the cultural nuances of doing business in target countries (see Chapter 23).

Producer-related factors include a number of issues in addition to the distribution levels sought. An important constraint is the resources that are available to the manufacturer to bring the product to market. Some companies will lack the finances to recruit and reward a salesforce and so will use a wholesaler instead. This is often the case for companies making a very narrow range of products, unless the product is particularly expensive, such as a mainframe computer system. Also critical is what the manufacturer believes to be its core competence. If, for instance, this is the design and production of innovative goods, then recognizing that the company's employees may lack personal selling skills may indicate that the effective distribution of these goods may well be better left to a specialist channel intermediary. Another area of much contention is the desired level of channel control sought by the manufacturer. This will be discussed later under Monitoring and Controlling Intermediaries.

Product attributes can be important. Clearly, fresh produce that is highly perishable requires fairly short channels. Northern Foods, a manufacturer of chilled meals for Marks & Spencer boasts that it takes just twenty-four hours from the time a fresh egg arrives at the factory to its appearance in a custard tart on the shelves of an M&S store anywhere in the country (*Marketing Business* 1998b). This has implications for the storage and transportation facilities available in the channel (see Chapter 15). Heavy or large goods are frequently not suited to inner-city retail locations where consumers cannot easily drive to pick up their purchases: instead they are often sold at out-of-town sites or not carried by retailers at all and only sold to order via direct distribution. Some products may be so complex that personal contact between supplier and buyer is essential. This can be the case for the installation of highly technical machinery where the later three stages of Porter's value chain (see above) are entirely performed by the producer without the use of any intermediary.

Finally, the activities of the *competition* must be considered. If competitors have exclusive deals with certain intermediaries, then the support of other channel members with similar market-place penetration may be sought. For instance, when Raleigh found Toys 'R' Us to be tied to an arrangement with an American supplier for young children's bicycles, they focused on alternative retailers such as John Lewis and Woolworth's for the successful launch of their new Max 16″ model (Smith 1998). For an FMCG manufacturer, it may be crucial that their product appears on the shelves of the Big Five UK supermarkets, especially if the leading competitor's brand is already there. Sometimes, of course, as we have seen in Chapter 4, a brand's most significant competitor is the 'own label' product of the supermarket itself! When this happens, it can be very difficult to gain retailer support, as shown by the battles of Coca-Cola to gain what it saw as adequate display space in Sainsbury's. A solution may be for the manufacturer to target convenience stores instead, or to set up alternative distribution channels such as company-owned chilled vending machines. Another solution is to set up a vertically integrated channel or a franchised operation, such as those run by many car manufacturers. These approaches will be discussed later in this chapter.

Steps for channel design

A systematic process for *design of a channel* is suggested by Stern *et al.* (1993). From the outset, as we have already mentioned, the demands of the customer must be taken on board. This may be complicated by the fact that there are likely to be differing requirements from different market segments. This end-user analysis will result in the creation of an 'ideal' channel system which offers a multi-channel format catering for the service-level demands of each customer segment. The supplying company should also evaluate its existing channels in terms of efficiency and effectiveness. This should be done in terms of the company's objectives and its positioning relative to the competition. Further, a constraints analysis is needed to identify limits which have to be built into any proposed channel structure. These may include, for example, existing loyalties to certain intermediaries or specific sales targets which distributors must meet.

Once these analyses have been undertaken, the company will be in a position to identify the gaps which exist, i.e. those areas which will need to be addressed in order to move closer to the 'ideal' system. This is not as easy as it sounds since the senior management of many companies can be very reluctant to change the *status quo*, and, surprisingly, a regular strategic review of distribution methods is often neglected when companies search for competitive advantage (Ennis 1995). Why do you think this might be? Finally, the company must consider channel alternatives in the context of the preceding analysis so that it can move towards the 'optimal' channel strategy. This may not be the 'ideal' position identified earlier, yet it should represent the most viable and achievable position for the company.

Channel alternatives

Managers can choose from among three generic marketing channels (Doyle 1998):

- **Direct marketing**. This involves reaching customers via communications media such as telesales, mailshots, catalogues, or advertisements with tear-off reply slips. For more information on direct marketing as part of product promotion, see Chapter 20. Ordered goods are usually sent by mail or a third-party parcel distributor. For example, Reader's Digest uses a company called White Arrow. A key factor for companies operating a telephone-based link to customers is the management of special call centres to handle sales and customer queries. For instance Freeman's, the UK's number three mail order company, recently invested over £10 million in a new purpose-built centre in Sheffield (Isaacs 1998).

  Other media which are growing in importance for direct channels include the Internet and World Wide Web. These new developments will be discussed at the end of this chapter.

- **Salesforce**. Here a company might build its own team of salespeople, or perhaps hire an independent contract salesforce. Issues of sales management are covered in more detail in Chapter 18.

- **Channel intermediary**. This alternative is, of course, what has chiefly concerned us in the present chapter. As Ennis (1995) points out, when products and services which are geared for mass markets are considered, then direct distribution is simply not a practical option for most companies. Several types of channel can be identified: those for consumer markets, for industrial markets, and for services, and we shall now consider them in more detail.

Fig. 14.7 shows some alternative *consumer* channels. Channel A represents producer to consumer. This may involve the techniques of direct marketing or a door-to-door sales force (e.g. Avon Cosmetics) as discussed above. Alternatively, this type of channel includes consumers who pick their own fruit from farmers' fields. Channel B represents producer to retailer to consumer. This is typically used by large retailers such as Sainsbury's, who have the buying power to order large quantities of goods direct from manufacturers with no need of a further middleman. The addition of the wholesaler in Channel C is more commonly used by smaller retailers with limited order quantities and, from the producer's perspective, by manufacturers of convenience goods, such as cigarettes, which need intensive distribution. The even longer structure of Channel D via the inclusion of agents is often used by producers entering foreign markets, where a local agent's expertise may be essential to overcome trade barriers (see Chapter 23).

Fig. 14.8 shows alternative channels used in order to reach *industrial* (organizational) customers. In general, these channels are shorter than those for consumer goods.

The shortest structure, that of Channel E, represents manufacturer to customer. It

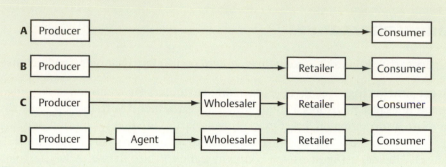

Figure 14.7 Consumer channel alternatives

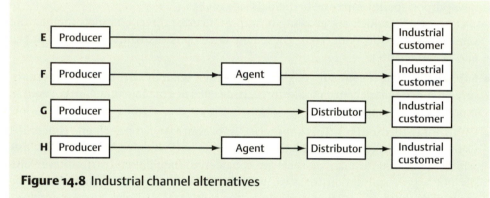

Figure 14.8 Industrial channel alternatives

is a viable alternative for many industrial producers as their customer numbers are fewer and often less geographically widespread than for consumer markets. Channels for large, expensive, and highly technical products such as the railway engines produced by ADtranz in Derby, the development of which may require the solving of considerable mechanical problems, frequently follow this pattern.

Channel F represents manufacturer to industrial distributor to customer. It is used for more frequently purchased, less expensive products that are required by a wider range of industrial customers, for example tools used by garage repair workshops. The use of an agent as in Channel G can occur when a manufacturer chooses not to set up its own dedicated salesforce, and has therefore to 'outsource' the agent's marketing and selling services. This can be a relatively quick option but, as we have noted previously, the support offered by agents may be less than that provided by a title-taking distributor. The lengthier structure of Channel H may arise when it is found that organizational buyers in a particular market prefer to use nearby distributors. This can happen when customers need to be resupplied frequently, for instance with paper for the photocopying machines leased by universities.

Service channels

It is important to remind ourselves that this chapter so far has largely confined itself to discussing channels for tangible goods. What about services? As you will recall from Chapter 9 services have a number of characteristics which can affect their distribution: they are often highly intangible, 'ownership' of services by customers is difficult, their delivery cannot be easily separated from the service provider, and they cannot be stored. These factors, especially the inability to hold an 'inventory' of unsold services, means that the role of a channel intermediary can be very different for services compared to goods. Direct channels for services for which inseparability is a key characteristic include the supply of medical services, hairdressing, cleaning, security personnel, and professional services such as legal or accountancy advice.

Agents have traditionally been used for some markets such as insurance and travel agents, some of which are independent, while others are owned by holiday companies, for example the Lunn Poly chain is owned by Thomson plc. Large-scale changes are afoot in these sectors, however, as exemplified by the massive growth in telephone-based services such as Direct Line insurance. This occurs where there is little competitive advantage enjoyed by existing service suppliers like banks, leaving new entrants the opportunity to use ease of access (availability) as their major competitive weapon. Now that many large supermarkets have begun to offer banking services, note how the high street banks have been forced to widen their opening hours in order to compete. Note also the growth of telephone banking companies, some of which are owned by the traditional banks, such as the HSBC's First Direct. How secure do you think the future is for service providers using traditional channels? Why might some consumers still prefer to use intermediaries?

Multiple channels

You should be aware that some producers in both consumer and business-to-business markets use a variety of channels to distribute their goods. Think of the many different places you can purchase a can of Coca-Cola, for instance.

Also, of course, some manufacturers, such as those in the personal computer sector, sell to both consumers and to organizations. As we also observed in our consideration of service channels, there is rarely one simple solution to the decision over which channel type should be selected by a company's marketing manager. Indeed, bearing in mind the power of some retailers, the problem for producers often comes down to: which channel intermediary will select *us*?! This complexity is explored further in the following section.

Selecting specific intermediaries

Once a decision has been made regarding the type of channel or channels to use, it is necessary to choose individual organizations with which to work. As Ennis (1995) points out, the *selection of intermediaries* can have a major impact on what happens afterwards, for example the success or failure of a product launch. He offers a number of *criteria* which can be used to assess the relative merits of potential channel participants:

- their financial position;
- depth and width of product lines carried;
- are competitive lines carried?;
- evidence of marketing, sales, and promotional ability;
- approach to order processing and order fulfilment;
- evidence of investment in IT;
- reputation within industry;
- willingness to share data.

You should recognize that this list is by no means exhaustive. For instance we might add: market coverage, local market knowledge, and service capability. Also, the relative importance of each criterion should be considered in relation to the customer demands of the particular industry sector. Clearly, the more subjective elements in the list will be harder to evaluate.

The issue of *reverse selection* can also arise. An example would be the design of an exotic pre-prepared meal recipe by a supermarket such as Safeway who then approaches different specialist meal manufacturers for their ability to mass produce the products to the supermarket's specification. The flexibility of such manufacturers as S&A Foods in Derby in providing Asian-style chilled meals to order, as well as in developing their own recipes, has resulted in the company's massive growth and an explosion of choice for the 'time-poor' consumer (*Asian Hotel & Caterer* 1997).

Motivating intermediaries

In order to gain an intermediary's commitment it is frequently necessary to motivate channel members. This is so because of the differing needs of intermediaries and producers: these needs do not necessarily coincide. For instance, a manufacturer may seek exclusive distribution of its products at high prices, whereas a retailer may be pursuing a strategy of market penetration through budget pricing of a wide range of goods. More obviously, of course, simple disagreement over margins can occur when retailers consider the cost price (i.e. the price a product is sold to them by a supplier) to be too high. This is particularly pertinent when the market-place is highly competitive and price wars are common.

The situation is further complicated by the fact that intermediaries and producers often have *different perceptions* about their own roles in the supply chain. The typical intermediary's self-perception is summarized by Hanmer-Lloyd (1993):

- they are fundamentally independent;
- they emphasize their ability to provide a broad range of products and full customer service;
- customers for a product are the *intermediary's* customers, not the manufacturer's;
- they see themselves as large and desirable customers of the manufacturer;
- they are more customer orientated than manufacturer orientated.

In contrast, the manufacturer's view of the intermediary is often that:

- the intermediary is part of the manufacturer's channel structure;
- the intermediary is unwilling to carry sufficient stock to ensure the best customer service;
- the end users (typically consumers) of the product are the *manufacturer's* customers, not the intermediary's;
- the intermediary exists to handle small accounts, and physically distribute the goods;
- the intermediary has a poor level of managerial competence.

Have you ever had a job in a retail store? How true do you think the above points are, especially if you have had to deal with customer queries regarding the availability of stock? Did you blame the manufacturer if a delivery had not arrived?

Such differences can create an antagonistic atmosphere in channel relationships, something which it is important to resolve to ensure sufficiently high levels of co-operation in channels (Ennis 1995). Before turning in more detail to issues of power and conflict, we shall examine ways in which intermediaries can be motivated to devote resources to a producer's lines. Doyle (1998) suggests *two levels of motivator*: promotional and partnership. Promotional channel motivators are usually short-term inducements to support the supplier's goods. These might include trade discounts for large order volumes, providing point-of-sale display materials, or undertaking joint promotional campaigns (e.g. sharing the cost of an advertisement highlighting both the product and a list of dealers). These motivators are often very expensive and do not build particularly high levels of loyalty with intermediaries.

Partnership motivators, on the other hand, seek to build a longer-term relationship between suppliers and channel participants. The types of strategic considerations here may involve the sharing of market research information, providing training to a distributor's sales staff, designing fair incentive schemes for dealer performance, and joint planning over how best to create a competitive advantage in the market which benefits all participants. The Malaysian car manufacturer Proton has invested heavily in dealer development and training in the UK with a view to making dealers stronger, and thus more able to protect the manufacturer's position (*Marketing Business* 1998a).

Evaluation and control of intermediaries

EVALUATION of channel performance is needed to decide which intermediaries to retain and which to motivate, or even, where necessary, to discard. Criteria for evaluation are obviously similar to those used in the initial selection decision (see above). Once the relationship between organizations has been established, criteria can include: the sales volume and value of the producer's goods that are generated through the intermediary's outlets, the profitability of servicing that intermediary, the stock levels the intermediary is prepared to hold, the quality of customer service offered, feedback provided about the market-place, and the intermediary's attitude to inter-channel co-operation. As Jobber (1995) points out, however, the scope for evaluation may be severely limited if power lies with the channel member rather than the producer. In certain retail markets, for instance, some dominant intermediaries simply may not wish to share the information with producers that the producer needs, whereas on the other hand, if manufacturer power is high (say, through having strong brands) or there are many distribution alternatives, evaluation may be more comprehensive, with intermediaries agreeing to have their sales efforts monitored. The latter is often the case for car dealerships who must perform to extremely strict criteria set by the major manufacturers.

Power in marketing channels

IN order to exert effective control, we have seen that it is necessary for the producer to attempt to build channel power. *Power* has been defined by El-Ansary and Stern (1972) as the 'ability to control the decision variables in the marketing or purchasing strategy of another member in the supply chain'. Using power ultimately means getting other channel members to do something they might otherwise not have done. Since members are interdependent, the potential for using power lies with all channel participants. Usually, however, a channel leader emerges. This organization can derive its power from a number of sources, both economic and non-economic (see Fig. 14.9). The former include the size of the firm and the resources it can draw upon, such as available capital or design copyrights. The latter, based on the work of sociologists French and Raven (1959), are commonly classified as follows, with the four later categories often summarized as 'non-coercive':

- **Coercive power**: where a channel member can threaten or persuade another member into performing certain tasks by withdrawing certain benefits. This can only work if one channel member is in a highly dominant position, for example,

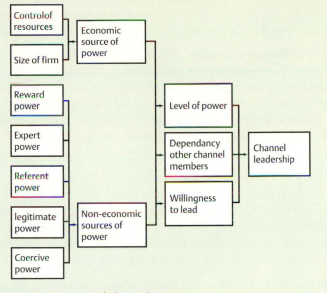

Figure 14.9 Sources of channel power

Source: Adapted from Ronald D. Michman and Stanley D. Sibley, (1980), *Marketing Channel and Strategy*, 2nd edn. (Columbus, OH: Publishing Horizons), p. 143

when a supermarket threatens to delist a particular product line from its shelves unless a manufacturer agrees to offer the retailer cash discounts. A further example might be seen as Tesco's invitation to its UK suppliers to join its 'community' of EDI (Electronic Data Interchange—see Chapter 15) linked companies or find themselves unable to trade with the store chain (Smith and Sparks 1993).

■ **Reward power**: if a channel member does something successfully, then something of value will be given to them. For example, an independent retailer may find itself listed on a co-operative advertisement that is largely paid for by a brand manufacturer as a reward for displaying the particular brand prominently in-store.

■ **Legitimate power**: an understanding that one channel member has a right to exert influence over others. This may be a contractual right derived from a franchise agreement (see ahead) or may be based on a traditional acceptance by members that one member has historically held power. This was once the case in FMCG markets where retailers 'accepted' the power of manufacturers (Davies 1996).

■ **Referent power**: where one channel member is attracted to another and wishes to be associated with the more powerful participant. This is often the case where retailers recognize the prestige value of stocking certain high profile brands and can result in certain manufacturer's products gaining preferential shelf space. The stocking of Rolex watches by jewelers such as Goldsmiths is a good example: even though, frustratingly, some watches can take literally years to order, the kudos of being allowed by Rolex (who control their distribution fiercely) to carry such a highly regarded brand is something the chain would not wish to give up.

- **Expert power**: where one member perceives another to have some special knowledge or expertise. For instance, a small producer might regard a large, experienced wholesaler as having particular skills in managing distribution networks for their particular product line. Also, the possession by supermarkets of detailed sales and customer information through EPOS (Electronic Point of Sale—see Chapter 15) technology can give them considerable influence over producers (Fletcher 1994).

If power is used in a manner believed to be unfair by one or more channel members, then *conflict* may arise. Conflict need not necessarily be destructive, since it can encourage managers to question the *status quo* and find ways of improving their distribution systems. Sometimes, however, strategies employed by firms can create unstable, adversarial relationships between producers and intermediaries. Magrath and Hardy (1987) identified the following such behaviours:

- **bypassing channels**: skipping established intermediaries and selling direct to the customer;
- **over-saturation**: using too many distributors within a given geographical area;
- **too many links** in the supply chain: resulting in small intermediaries having to buy from bigger dealers who can sometimes be viewed as no better than themselves;
- **new channels**: developing innovative means of distribution that pose a threat to established channels;
- **cost-cutters**: using 'discount' intermediaries alongside established dealers, thus damaging the brand image of the goods concerned;
- **inconsistency**: appearing to treat arbitrarily some intermediaries more favourably than others, for example through reward power.

It is worth noting, of course, that some producer strategies which could be classified as contributing to conflict might just as easily be seen as legitimate attempts to fight back against growing retailer power. An example is the formation of the Consumer Needs Consortium (Crawford 1997). This is a marketing alliance between Unilever, Cadbury-Schweppes, Bass, and Kimberly-Clark aimed at building databases of mutual customers who can then be targeted via direct marketing initiatives (see also Chapter 20), thus bypassing intermediaries. In terms of ethical behaviour (see Chapter 5), do you think the above strategies are unfair in what is, after all, a harsh commercial environment?

When conflicts that affect the smooth flow of goods through the channel do arise, various methods can be used to rebuild effective relationships. From the intermediary's perspective, Narus and Anderson (1987) suggest that distributors should:

- **Reach consensus with manufacturers** on the role of intermediaries in the channel: i.e. to achieve the overall channel objective of minimizing the total cost and maximizing the total value to the end customer. This may involve a recognition that, in order to accommodate developments in the market-place (such as changes in consumer shopping habits), compromises in channel practices may be needed to maintain ultimate customer loyalty to both the product and the outlet concerned—see the discussions on Efficient Consumer Response (ECR) ahead.

■ **Appreciate manufacturing requirements**: this can be achieved by intermediaries visiting production plants and observing procedures for ordering and quality control. The sharing of information on likely future sales patterns can also help the manufacturer plan production schedules more accurately (see also Chapter 15).

■ **Fulfil commitments**: manufacturers need reassurance that intermediaries will be proficient in areas such as market penetration ability, prompt payment of bills, and product knowledge. Thus distributors should proactively examine their own performance levels and seek improvements where possible.

Category management and efficient consumer response

Ennis (1995) states that it is in the interests of producers to manage intermediaries on the basis of mutual dependence and trust. As we have seen, the differing perceptions of producers and 'middlemen' as to their respective channel roles can make this difficult. A strong focus should therefore be placed by marketing departments on relationship management (see Chapter 8) with channel participants. A possible way forward for manufacturers is *Category Management*. This is described by Harlow (1995) as 'joint strategic planning with retailers to build total category sales and profit for mutual benefit' and is based on the fact that the retailer wishes to maximize the profits from an overall category rather than from a specific brand. A category is seen as a group of products all satisfying the same consumer need, for example toothpaste as opposed to, say, Crest (Dewsnap 1997).

In terms of promotional strategies, category management is an advance on the 'push' policies of trade marketing (i.e. to the retailer) and provides 'pull' by sharing the ownership of brand strategy with the intermediary. For this to work, the producer should occupy a leading position in the category so that any increase in total category consumption can be exploited. Also, since category management should be built on collaborative research into consumer shopping patterns, it must be used with retailers who are prepared to co-operate fully in the exchange of consumer data. Major brand manufacturers such as Proctor & Gamble and Nabisco have begun to assemble category teams which manage several brands and customize each category's product mix and promotional plans on a chain-by-chain basis (Nielsen 1993). In the case of P&G, the brand managers for individual liquid dishwashing detergents report ultimately to a category manager responsible for all P&G's packaged soaps and detergents. Category teams draw upon specialists from other company departments such as finance, manufacturing, and distribution, resulting in teams acting as small businesses with complete responsibility for the category's performance. Although category management may seem a sensible strategy for brand manufacturers, do you see any disadvantages for producers?

Partnerships between producers and intermediaries are also evident in the *Efficient Consumer Response* (ECR) initiative. ECR involves members of the total supply chain working together to respond to customers' purchasing patterns, thereby ensuring the right products are delivered to store shelves on time. The ECR Scorecard Group (1996) describe the moves made by the manufacturer Johnson & Johnson. These include: agreeing with major retail customers to optimize categories in order to drive mutual business needs; focusing on consumer research in conjunction with retailers; and providing promotional activities that suit target consumers' particular needs. The implications of ECR for IT in enhancing the flow of information between participants are discussed further in Chapter 15. However, it should be noted that the implementation of ECR can require considerable investment from manufacturers to change corporate structures and EDI links (Keh and Park 1997).

Channel competition

As well as the conflict between members at different levels in the channel, we should be aware of other types of competition in marketing channels. In addition to the *vertical* competition which can develop between producer and intermediary, Palamountain (1955) identified three further sorts of rivalry:

■ **Horizontal competition**: this is competition between intermediaries of the same type. The rivalries between different retailers, such as HMV and Our Price or between Body Shop and Bath & Bodyworks, serve as good examples. As we have discussed above, each chain seeks to develop marketing strategies that differentiates itself from its competitors.

■ **Intertype competition**: this refers to competition at the same level in the channel, but between intermediaries of different type. For instance, since legislation in 1994, the availability of magazines from grocery supermarkets as well as from traditional outlets means that the more specialist Confectionists Tobacconists and Newsagents (CTN) are threatened. This is despite the fact that supermarkets only have some 14 per cent of the newspaper market at present (*Marketing Week* 1998).

■ **Channel system competition**: this is where an entire channel is competing with a different, parallel channel. Examples are commonly found where the producer of an item owns the outlets of distribution for that item themselves. This occurs not only for goods, such as petrol where oil companies such as BP control many of their petrol stations, and are in competition with supermarket garage forecourts; it also happens for services such as package holidays where Thomson holidays are bookable through their own Lunn Poly outlets and Airtours holidays from the Airtours-owned Going Places travel agents. As the media gleefully point out (*Observer* 1995), the fact that these holidays are also bookable through independent agents only makes the network of channels more complicated for the confused consumer seeking unbiased advice!

Vertical marketing systems

The ownership or integration by an organization of other participants at different levels in the channel is termed a *vertical marketing system*. These systems are seen as having several advantages over conventional marketing channels (see Fig. 14.10):

- they reduce channel costs by eliminating duplication of functions;
- they minimize conflict amongst channel members;
- they maximize the experience and expertise of members.

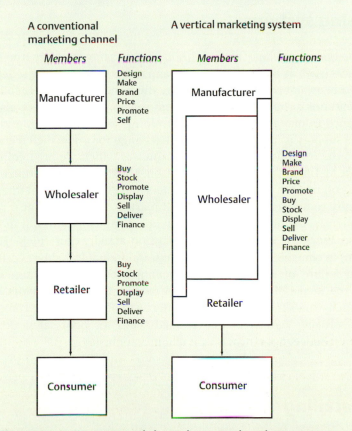

Figure 14.10 Conventional channel v. vertical marketing system

Source: Adapted from David J. Kollat, Royer D. Blackwell, and James F. Robeson, *Stategic Marketing*, New York: Holt, Rinehart & Winston, 1972, p. 321

There are three types of vertical marketing system: corporate, administered, and contractual. The first of these, *corporate*, is actually increasingly rare since many organizations either cannot afford to, or wish to, invest in fixed assets or skills where they do not have a competitive advantage (Doyle 1998). An example that remains is the Dutch-based retailer C&A which owns its own manufacturing plants and whole-sale operations. *Administered* systems arise when participants are financially independent but are effectively controlled by the most powerful channel member. The highly co-ordinated purchasing of a large proportion of its goods from UK manu-facturers by Marks & Spencer illustrates backward integration, whereas the man-agement of car dealers' sale activities by Mercedes represents forward integration. In *contractual* systems channel members' rights and obligations are defined by legal agreements. These can include collaborative agreements such as the voluntary chains discussed earlier in this chapter, where separate firms share resources and agree to joint purchasing initiatives, and franchise arrangements.

Franchising systems

In a franchise system a seller (the franchisor) gives an intermediary (the franchisee) specific services (such as marketing support) and rights to market the seller's product or service within an agreed territory. In return, the franchisee agrees to follow certain procedures and not to buy from unauthorized sellers. The franchisor also typically offers assistance in management and staff training, merchandising, and operating systems. This support is usually provided in exchange for a specified fee or royalties on sales from the franchisee. Examples of businesses which are predominantly fran-chised include McDonald's, Body Shop, Benetton, Tie Rack, and Pronuptia.

Franchising offers both manufacturer/retailers and entrepreneurial intermediaries the opportunity to undertake relatively rapid market development at relatively low risk. Consequently, for many internationally operating companies, franchising has become the cornerstone of their global expansion activity (Burt 1995). Having said this, problems in controlling standards amongst individual franchisees can occur, for example the failure of some of the Body Shop's outlets in France. When this takes place, the image of the franchisor can be seriously dented. From a different perspective, Benetton's franchisees in Germany were outraged at the company's con-troversial advertising campaigns and blamed them for poor sales. Clearly, good communication between partners is essential in franchising.

Global retailing

Chapter 23 explains the importance of global marketing in greater detail, but we shall now briefly discuss the growth of channel intermediaries across national boundaries. Pelligrini (1994) suggests that retail companies have three options for growth: vertical integration, retail diversification, and *internationalization*. Retailing has often been slow to expand globally because of the high level of investment needed to set up in another country, especially when this involves organic growth or risky acquisitions, for example the failure of Marks & Spencer to turn around the fortunes of the Brooks Brothers menswear chain in the USA. Nevertheless, due to the limited possibilities for growth in national markets, many of the more dynamic retailers have increasingly internationalized their operations.

Muniz-Martinez (1998) offers an analysis of the expansion into North and South America of leading European retailers. He points out that the USA and Canada are the favoured targets within these continents, based on the cultural affinity with northern Europe, from where most leading European-based retailers originate. Moreover, the potential for profit in these relatively prosperous countries is greater than in Latin America. Some retailers such as Virgin Megastore and Body Shop use specialization either in product sector or customer segments in order to expand. Other retailers like Carrefour have exported a commercial concept such as the hypermarket, and adapted it to local conditions by altering the extensive ranges of food on offer to suit local consumption. This French company has also collaborated with local firms such as Gigante in Mexico. IKEA, on the other hand, remains centrally controlled, owning virtually all its stores, and deliberately tries to retain its unique 'Swedishness' without changing its product range or retailing approach to local tastes.

Expansion is also taking place by some retailers within Europe. The *Sunday Times* (1998) reported that Marks & Spencer is opening more stores in Germany despite that nation's sluggish economy and reluctance to create a modern service-sector culture. Stores have only been allowed to open until 4.30 p.m. on Saturdays since 1997, and Sunday opening has been out of the question. M&S hopes that its refund policy and the quality of its goods (e.g. the sandwiches aimed at busy office workers) will prove a long-term success in this significant yet moribund market. Have you noticed any other significant differences between retail practices across different countries when you have travelled abroad? Conversely, are markets becoming increasingly similar? How might this be explained?

Retailers as market drivers

Kumar (1997) makes the interesting assertion that there has been nothing less than a revolution in retailing over the last twenty-five years. He states that leading retailers, through consolidation, global expansion, technological sophistication, own-labels, and innovative store formats, have been '*market driving*' rather than 'market driven'. In other words, 'they have shaped consumer behaviour, transformed the market-place, and redefined the rules of engagement with their competitors and suppliers'. Kumar claims that these revolutionary retailers, such as Ahold in the Netherlands, Wal-Mart in the USA, and the Japanese-based Seven-Eleven, are reconfiguring the value chain. They are using their power to demand changes from manufacturers and driving the manufacturers' marketing strategies.

As Randall (1994) observes, manufacturers are now frequently bound into long-term relationships with retailers, and, to succeed, must manage their situation to both parties' mutual advantage. He worries, however, that 'there is room for doubt as to how real talk of partnership is, particularly when the balance of power is so unequal'. Davies (1996) describes the situation as a 'see-saw': the manufacturer uses its branding power and the consumer franchise this produces, while the retailer uses its buying power and the threat of delisting the brand. He calls this the 'power paradigm'. This can be contrasted with the 'partnership paradigm' which should result from the careful management of the relationship between producer and intermediary. If writers like Kumar (1997) above are correct, it is debatable which paradigm will dominate, at least within the retail grocery sector. As we shall see in Chapter 15, however, there is far more scope for the building of successful partnerships when the physical distribution of goods through supply chains is examined.

Channels of the future?

The McCann-Erickson Research Consultancy (1995) believe that manufacturers need to take a holistic view of distribution, and adopt a new 'channel vision' to maximize their opportunities to reach the customer. Fig. 14.11 shows the complex range of channel choices that should be considered by producers of premium branded goods.

Figure 14.11 A new channel vision

Source: Adapted from W. Hamilton (1995), 'Brands Must Change Channels', *Marketing Week*, 16 Feb., p. 28.

As you can see, there are many more options available than merely the traditional retail store.

Direct delivery is being undertaken by specialist companies such as Food Ferry in London, where certain branches of M&S and Sainsbury also offer this service. Moreover, because of the ever-increasing penetration of home computers, it is likely that doorstep deliveries of goods will return on a large scale, particularly now that the Internet provides a network for inexpensively transferring orders. Indeed, Fernie (1997) comments that 'Possibly the most significant likely change to affect the retail environment in the near future will be that associated with the information super-highway'. It remains to be seen whether this distribution option will be exploited primarily by retailers as an 'add-on' service, or by manufacturers as a strategic channel choice.

Some retailers like Tandy have actually closed a number of branches and offered customers instead access to their product range via a web site (*Marketing* 1998). Several UK suppliers of books, music, computer games, and flowers already have the logistical support (see Chapter 15) to develop their business on the Internet (the CD market-place is explored in more detail in the Case Study which closes this chapter). In the longer term, Fernie (1997) suggests that FMCG suppliers may use this channel to regain some of their lost power in channel relationships. In the US, car manufacturers are just beginning to recognize the impact of the Internet on their traditional dealership-based channels of distribution. In 1997, this medium was used for selecting, negotiating, and ordering 11 per cent of all new car sales—a total of 1.5 million cars (*Marketing* 1998). To many car buyers, the dealership has become nothing more than a delivery point. How would you feel about making a major purchase of something like a car over the Internet?

Thanks to their interactive nature, new channels can give manufacturers the opportunity to reassert the notion of dialogue with the consumer. New channels may also present smaller producers or innovative retailers with opportunities to enter the market-place with relative ease, i.e. without the need to find established intermediary partners. Already we have seen the rise of a new type of middleman: the *infomediary*. This intermediary gathers information about customers and uses it on customers' behalf to get a better deal of some sort from a supplier. They might screen commercial messages (like a specialized mailing preference service—see Chapter 20) for customers; represent their interests (say, golfing and gardening) to marketers who want access to information about them; and then find vendors who can deliver the best product at the cheapest price (perhaps in the form of a 10 per cent discount offered by the supplier in return for access to the infomediary's client list). If this happens, then the infomediaries become powerful distribution channels in their own right, effectively 'selling' customers to marketers.

Chapter summary and linkages to other chapters

The management of channel intermediaries plays a key part in a company's attempts to ensure that its goods or services are made available to the desired market segments. If a company can achieve its distribution objectives, it will have made a significant step towards gaining a competitive advantage over rival producers. The design of a marketing channel requires careful analysis and planning. For this to be done effectively, firms must be aware of the roles that intermediaries can perform and of their relative power bases. This is especially important in FMCG markets where the retailer has considerable power. To succeed, a marketing manager must consider both economic and social factors in managing the organizational relationships necessary to facilitate the flow of products to the end customer.

The increasing importance of channel decisions for marketing managers means that issues concerning intermediaries can be related to many other chapters in this book:

Chapter 1: What is marketing?: Customer needs must be properly understood in order to match delivery channels to customers' expectations. The creation of value through making goods available in the right quantity, in the right location, and at the time customers wish to purchase them, is crucial.

Chapter 2: The marketing environment: The impact on channel design of external environmental factors such as changes in consumer shopping habits, the pace of technological innovation, and the typically intense levels of competition that exist among intermediaries, can clearly be considerable.

Chapter 3: Segmentation and targeting: Although the market for groceries is often assumed to be homogeneous, it can be seen that retailers have targeted different segments. Look, for instance, at the positioning of Aldi when compared to Tesco, or of Asda versus Marks & Spencer.

Chapter 4: Branding: The creation of a strong brand can give a manufacturer a significant advantage in negotiations with intermediaries. In the FMCG sector, however, producers are increasingly finding their main rivals to be the retailer's own brands. In order to gain valuable shelf space, many manufacturers are restructuring their organization and making brand managers function as part of a category management team.

Chapter 5: Marketing and ethics: The whole question of power struggles within marketing channels raises questions about ethical behaviour. Also worthy of consideration is the limiting of consumer choice by retailers utilizing ECR techniques, and the debate over the siting of out-of-town retail superstores at the expense of the traditional corner shop, and indeed, of the countryside.

Chapter 6: Marketing research: It is important for marketing managers to discover how, when, and where their potential customers wish to buy. Are there gaps in the market-place which present a company with an opportunity to innovate with a new channel design?

Chapter 7: Buyer behaviour: An understanding of both consumer and organizational buyer behaviour is required in order to make the most appropriate channel management decisions.

Chapter 8: Buyer–seller relationship development: Relationship management is important at two levels. First, between organizational participants in a marketing channel, and, second, between either a retailer or a producer and the end consumer.

Chapters 9/10: Developing a product portfolio and NPD: What are the key characteristics of the company's product or service offering which may impact upon channel design?

Chapter 11: Developing a sustainable competitive advantage: For certain products, such as impulse purchases, intensive distribution is vital in gaining a competitive edge. Whatever a company's product, it is essential to ensure a consistent marketing mix, for example by limiting the stocking of luxury goods to 'high class' intermediaries.

Chapters 12/13: Pricing theory and applications: Before setting prices, marketing managers must consider the impact upon intermediaries' profit margins as well as on the propensity to buy of the end customer.

Chapter 15: Physical distribution management: The need for an effective marketing channel to be underpinned by adequate physical distribution systems. The impact of information technology on distribution management and links in the supply chain.

Chapter 16: Promotion strategy: Trade-offs are often made between promotion strategy and distribution strategy, for example high profile retail locations may reduce the need for promotion. Intermediaries often become involved in joint promotion activities.

Chapter 17: Advertising: The use of co-operative advertising campaigns can highlight both a manufacturer's products and the retail outlets which stock them.

Chapter 18: Personal selling and sales management: The channel option of creating and maintaining a company sales force and the use of agents as intermediaries.

Chapter 19: Sales promotion and sponsorship: Point of sale promotions located within intermediaries' outlets are a valuable means of stimulating impulse purchases. Public relations activity by a manufacturer should address intermediaries as an important 'public'.

Chapter 20: Direct marketing: Traditional direct channels such as door-to-door salespeople, and emerging alternatives to intermediaries like the use of the Internet.

Chapter 21: Managing the marketing effort: Strategic planning issues in managing channel intermediaries. The importance of careful analysis. The problems of motivating and controlling powerful intermediaries.

Chapter 22: The marketing of services: The lack of tangible elements means that services intermediaries play a different role from goods intermediaries. Service intermediaries are essentially involved as co-producer of a service.

Chapter 23: Global marketing: The risks and opportunities faced by retailers when expanding internationally. How different retail organizations may adopt different strategies when entering foreign markets.

Case study

The retailing of compact discs: a bittersweet symphony?

Who'd be the marketing manager for a record label? You might be able to rub shoulders with the stars but ultimately, once the partying is over, it's time to get down to business. And a 'business' is exactly what the music industry is—a very aggressive business. It's all about shifting 'units' (or compact discs to you and me). In 1996, the UK market for pre-recorded music was approximately £1.81 billion, at retailers' selling prices. Since 1991, the market had shown a 43 per cent increase in retail value, and was expected to grow at an annual rate of 7 per cent by the year 2001.

The compact disc (CD) format dominates, accounting for over three-quarters of all albums sold, by volume. Cassettes are losing market share all the time and sales of vinyl, once the traditional format for record albums, have declined rapidly over the last ten years. Innovative formats have been launched, but with no significant consumer impact—do you know anyone who owns a laser-disc or a DAT player? Competition within the CD market-place is largely between major entertainment corporations who record, manufacture, and co-ordinate the distribution of products. The independent recording sector is also important as a source of new talent. The market is extremely subject to sales variation, due to fluctuating reputations and 'hype' surrounding individual artists or related phenomena. Think of the unpredictable ups and downs in the sales of bands like Oasis and of soundtracks like *The Titanic*, for instance. There is also always a huge seasonal variation in volumes because of the Christmas gift-giving market. Looking more broadly, consumer spending on recorded music forms just a part (some 9 per cent in 1997) of the wider leisure and entertainment sector, which typically also includes books, magazines, sports, games, and hobby products. This means that the marketing carried out by record companies has to overcome some pretty big hurdles in order for a particular CD to enter the average consumer's consciousness.

A significant contribution to the marketing of CDs is made by distribution channels. The main intermediaries are the general high street chains like WH Smith and Woolworth's, which sell other goods in addition to music-related products; and the specialist record chains like Our Price (which is also a subsidiary of the WH Smith Group) and HMV. The chief difference between the two types of chain is the range they stock: Woolworth's may sell more units than any other chain, but it keeps a considerably less deep array of titles on display than HMV who are aiming to attract the more 'knowledgeable'—and frequently higher and more regular spending—music fan, in addition to the chart-orientated buyer. More mature consumers tend to shop at outlets like Boots or WH Smith.

Sales in other non-traditional outlets, such as petrol stations and grocery stores, are growing. Supermarkets in particular are now moving strongly into the recorded music sector. Grocery chains like Safeway and Sainsbury's offer a top chart selection, sometimes at discounted prices. Some chains, such as Asda, also offer singles as well as a limited 'back-catalogue' range but these are usually mid-price or budget compilations. The number of Asda stores with record departments had grown from zero in 1991 to 250 by 1996. Over the same period, the number of UK independent record shops had fallen from nearly 2,000 to 1,500. Although record companies welcome the huge volume provided by supermarkets selling music, they fear a repeat of the retail revolution in the

USA which virtually wiped out the small 'indie' record shop. The music industry believes the long-term development of new bands has been harmed because the shops that used to sell debut albums are in decline. Asda's category controller for entertainment says that record companies are in a difficult position because, although publicly they feel that supermarket price promotions are devaluing music, privately they are happy to see any sector performing strongly. However, companies are finding supermarkets, with their high expectations of marketing and merchandising support despite the low margins on CDs compared to groceries, much harder to deal with than specialist chains.

The grocery multiples normally buy their CDs through a wholesaler. It suits them to do so because of the hugely diverse nature of the titles available and the need for frequently changing ranges. The major wholesalers include Entertainment UK, which is part of the Kingfisher Group (who also own Woolworth's) and Total Home Entertainment (THE), which is part of John Menzies. The process for gaining supermarket distribution for a CD title is as follows: the major record companies present their titles to a wholesaler which has an account with a grocery multiple; the wholesaler then recommends a selection to the retailer's buying team; they may also work out the planogram (the actual store shelf layout) and do the merchandising. Cork International Ltd., who are the UK's largest non-food merchandising company, specializing in books and pet accessories (under the Hartz brand) are now also considering moves into CD wholesaling, thus offering retailers an alternative to what some observers feel to be the rather complacent existing suppliers.

The Internet offers new opportunities for major labels and independent record companies to provide access to their products. This could prove to be a significant development in music distribution as domestic modem penetration increases. Already, the sites most commonly visited by 15–24 year olds are music related. Music is well suited to on-line retailing. With no need to see the actual CDs, it is easier to listen to a taster on-line than in a shop. Web sites can also add value by incorporating reviews, concert listings, and discographies. At present, however, record companies seem loath to embrace the Internet due to concerns over the downloading (free of charge) of copyrighted music from pirate 'digital jukeboxes' set up by enthusiastic fans. The boss of one small label believes that 'the retail side and the record companies are trying to stare one another out' over which of them will make the first move into the uncharted waters of selling sounds on-line. An interesting issue here would be that of price—could companies still justify the seemingly high prices for CDs currently levied in stores once music is available in cyberspace?

Case study review questions

1 Identify the key environmental forces that should be considered by CD producers in evaluating strategies for channel design.

2 Contrast the role of a specialist music retailer with that of a grocery supermarket in the channel for CDs.

3 How would you suggest CD producers might control their marketing channels more effectively?

Chapter review questions

1 'Channel intermediaries are nothing but parasites.' Why might some observers think this? Do you agree? If not, why not?

2 Describe some different objectives for channel management. Give examples of the products typically associated with each objective.

3 What channel options are open to a small producer of highly complex measuring equipment for the manufacturing sector?

4 List the criteria you might use in selecting a channel intermediary.

5 Identify an industry where the approach to distribution has changed dramatically over the last few years. What are the marketing implications for suppliers within this industry?

6 Why does conflict so often occur between manufacturers and intermediaries? How might this conflict be resolved?

References

Ahmad, R., and Buttle, F. (1998), 'Bridging the Gaps Between Theory and Practice: A Case of the Retention of Dealers of Office Equipment Products'. in *Proceedings of Academy of Marketing Conference*, Sheffield Hallam University, 8–10 July, pp. 16–21.

Alderson, W., and Halbert, H. N. (1968), *Men, Motives and Markets* (Englewood Cliffs, NJ: Prentice Hall).

Anderson, J. C. (1993), *Retailing* (New York: West).

Ansoff, H. I. (1987), *Corporate Strategy* (Harmondsworth: Penguin).

Asian Hotel & Caterer (1997), 'Indian Ready Meals Giant Goes "Thai"', Oct.

Bowersox, D. J., and Cooper, M. B. (1992), *Strategic Marketing Channel Management* (New York: McGraw-Hill).

Burt, S. (1995), 'Retail Internationalization: Evolution of Theory and Practice'. in P. J. McGoldrick, and G. Davies (eds.), *International Retailing: Trends and Strategies* (London: Pitman).

Crawford, A.-M. (1997), 'Unilever Unveils TV Infomercials to Threaten Ads, *Marketing*, 30 Oct., p. 1.

Davies, G. (1993), *Trade Marketing Strategy* (London: Paul Chapman).

—— (1996), 'Supply-Chain Relationships', in F. Buttle, (ed.), *Relationship Marketing: Theory and Practice* (London: Paul Chapman), pp. 17–28.

Dewsnap, B. (1997), 'Trade Marketing', in D. Jobber (ed.), *The CIM Handbook of Selling and Sales Strategy* (Oxford: Butterworth-Heinemann), pp. 104–25.

Doyle, P. (1998), *Marketing Management and Strategy*, 2nd edn. (London: Prentice Hall).

East, R. (1997), *Consumer Behaviour: Advances and Applications in Marketing* (Hemel Hempstead: Prentice Hall).

—— and Hogg, A. (1998), 'Making a Conquest', *Marketing Business*, Jan., p. 48.

ECR Scorecard Group (1996), *ECR Scorecard: A UK Perspective* (Watford: ECR UK).

El-Ansary, A. I., and Stern, L. W. (1972), 'Power Measurement in Distribution Channels', *Journal of Marketing Research*, **9**, Feb., pp. 47–52.

Ennis, S. (1995), 'Channel Management', in M. Baker (ed.), *Marketing: Theory and Practice*, 3rd edn. (Basingstoke: Macmillan).

Fernie, J. (1997), 'Retail Change & Retail Logistics in the UK: Past Trends & Future Prospects', *Service Industries Journal*, **17**, 3, pp. 383–96.

Fletcher, K. (1994), 'The Evolution and Use of IT in Marketing', in M. Baker (ed.), *The Marketing Book*, 3rd ed. (Oxford: Butterworth-Heinemann), pp. 333–57.

French, R. P., and Raven, B. (1959), 'Bases of Social Power', in D. Cartwright (ed.), *Studies in Social Power* (Ann Arbor: University of Michigan Press).

Guardian (1993), 'MMC in Bad Odour over Superdrug Ruling', 12 Nov., p. 18.

Hanmer-Lloyd, S. (1993), 'Relationship Appraisal: A Route to Improved Reseller Channel Performance', in *Proceedings of 9th IMP Conference*, Bath, Sept.

Harlow, P. (1995), 'Category Management: A New Era in FMCG Buyer–Supplier Relationships', *Journal of Brand Management*, **2**, 5, pp. 289–95.

Horner, C. (1998), 'Geodemographic Systems and Related Targeting Tools', at *Academy of Marketing East Midlands Region Presentation*, Nottingham Trent University, 21 Jan.

Howe, W. S. (1992), *Retailing Management* (London: Macmillan).

Isaacs, M. (1998), 'Freeman's: Marketing Meets the Millennium', *Presentation at CIM East Midlands Regional Branch Meeting*, Nottingham, 8 June.

Jobber, D. (1995), *Principles and Practice of Marketing* (Maidenhead: McGraw-Hill).

Keh, H. T. and Park, S. Y. (1997), 'To Market, to Market: The Changing Face of Grocery Retailing', *Long Range Planning*, **30**, 6, pp. 836–46.

Kristenson, L. (1983), 'Strategic Planning in Retailing', *European Journal of Marketing*, **17**, 2, pp. 43–59.

Kumar, N. (1997), 'The Revolution in Retailing: From Market Driven to Market Driving', *Long Range Planning*, **30**, 6, pp. 830–35.

McCann-Erickson (1995), cited in W. Hamilton (1995), 'Brands Must Change Channels', *Marketing Week*, 16 Feb., p. 28.

McGoldrick, P. J. (1990), *Retail Marketing* (Maidenhead: McGraw-Hill).

Magrath, A. J., and Hardy, K. G. (1987), 'Avoiding the Pitfalls in Managing Distribution Channels', *Business Horizons*, Sep.–Oct., pp. 29–33.

Marketing (1998), 'Our Friends Electric', 29 Jan., pp. 28–31.

Marketing Business (1998*a*), 'Tiger Malaise', Mar., pp. 24–8.

—— (1998*b*), 'Top Marks', July/Aug., pp. 26–30.

Marketing Week (1998), 'Asda Take on the News Trade Giants', 25 June, p. 14.

Muniz-Martinez, N. (1998), 'The Internationalization of European Retailers in America: The US Experience', *International Journal of Retail & Distribution Management*, **26**, 1, pp. 29–37.

Narus, J. A., and Anderson, J. C. (1987), 'Distribution Contributions to Partnerships with Manufacturers', *Business Horizons*, Sept.–Oct., pp. 34–42.

Nielsen, A. C. (1993), *Category Management in Europe: A Quiet Revolution* (Oxford: Nielsen Europe).

Observer (1992), Business Section, 29 Nov., p. 37.

Observer (1995), 'Ticket to Trouble', Business Section, 3 Nov., p. 1.

—— (1997), 'Jam Today', Business Section, 21 Sept., p. 6.

Omura, G. S. (1986), 'Developing Retail Strategy', *International Journal of Retailing*, **1**, 3, pp. 17–32.

Palamountain, J. C. (1955), *The Politics of Distribution* (Cambridge, Mass.: Harvard University Press).

Pelligrini, L. (1994), 'Alternatives for Growth and Internationalization in Retailing', *International Review of Retail, Distribution and Consumer Research*, **4**, 2, pp. 121–48.

Porter, M. E. (1985), *Competitive Advantage* (New York: The Free Press).

Randall, G. (1994), *Trade Marketing Strategies: The Partnership Between Manufacturers, Brands and Retailers*, 2nd edn. (Oxford: Butterworth-Heinemann).

Smith, D. L. G., and Sparks, L. (1993), 'The Transformation of Physical Distribution in Retailing: The Example of Tesco Stores', *International Review of Retail, Distribution and Consumer Research*, **3**, 1, pp. 35–64.

Smith, L. (1998), Presentation at *CIM Midlands Region Excellence in Marketing Awards*, Trent Bridge, Nottingham, 6 July.

Stern, L. W., Sturdivant, F. D., and Getz, G. A. (1993), 'Accomplishing Marketing Channel Change: Paths and Pitfalls', *European Management Journal*, **11**, 1, pp. 1–8.

Sunday Times (1998), 'M&S Branches out in Germany's Heartland', 15 Mar.

The Times (1995), 'Lights go out for Store Chain, 4 Nov., p. 17.

Walters, D. W. (1988), *Strategic Retailing Management: A Case Study Approach* (Hemel Hempstead: Prentice Hall).

Suggested further reading

For a more detailed review of the channels of distribution literature, the following develop many of the issues raised in this chapter:

- Ennis, S. (1995), 'Channel Management', in M. Baker (ed.), *Marketing: Theory and Practice*, 3rd edn. (Basingstoke: Macmillan).

- Hardy, K. G., and Magrath, A. J. (1988), 'Ten Ways for Manufacturers to Improve Distributions Management', *Business Horizons*, Nov.–Dec., pp. 65–9.

- Stern, L. W. and El-Ansary, A. I. (1992), *Marketing Channels*, 4th edn. (Englewood Cliffs, NJ: Prentice Hall).

For more detailed coverage of retailing issues, the following are useful:

- Anderson, J. C. (1993), *Retailing* (New York: West).
- Fernie, J. (1997), 'Retail Change & Retail Logistics in the UK: Past Trends & Future Prospects', *Service Industries Journal*, **17**, 3, pp. 383–96.
- Howe, W. S. (1992), *Retailing Management* (London: Macmillan).
- Keh, H. T., and Park, S. Y. (1997), 'To Market, to Market: The Changing Face of Grocery Retailing', *Long Range Planning*, **30**, 6, pp. 836–46.
- Kristenson, L. (1983), 'Strategic Planning in Retailing', *European Journal of Marketing*, **17**, 2, pp. 43–59.
- Kumar, N. (1997), 'The Revolution in Retailing: From Market Driven to Market Driving', *Long Range Planning*, **30**, 6, pp. 830–5.

The subject of relationship development between members of channel of distribution is explored in the following:

- Anderson, J. C., and Narus, J. A. (1990), 'A Model of Distributor Firm and Manufacturer Firm Working Partnerships', *Journal of Marketing*, **54**, Jan., pp. 42–58.
- Dwyer, F. R., Schurr, P. H., and Oh, S. (1987), 'Developing Buyer-Seller Relationships', *Journal of Marketing*, **51**, Apr., pp. 11–27.
- Ford, D. (ed.) (1990), *Understanding Business Markets: Interaction, Relationships and Networks* (London: Academic Press).
- Harlow, P. (1995), 'Category Management: A New Era in FMCG Buyer–Supplier Relationships', *Journal of Brand Management*, **2**, 5, pp. 289–95.

Useful web links

British Franchise Association: http:// www.british-franchise.org.uk
A discussion group for academics interested in the retail sector: http:// www.mailbase.ac.uk/lists/retail

Chapter 15
Physical distribution and logistics

Chapter objectives

The previous chapter looked at *who* is involved in getting products from a producer to the final consumer. This chapter considers *how* goods are physically moved between the two. It seeks to develop an understanding of the importance of time and service-based competition; the objectives of physical distribution management; strategic approaches to supply chain management; and the key elements of a physical distribution system. The influence of IT on physical distribution and logistics will become apparent throughout this chapter.

Introduction

In addition to our discussion of channel intermediaries in Chapter 14, it is important for marketing managers to understand the *overall* movement, storage, and availability of goods. This chapter looks at the physical distribution processes that allow goods to flow from materials suppliers to manufacturers and on to the end customer. In taking a wider perspective that extends beyond marketing channel considerations, it is common to visualize this entire 'supply chain' (for a definition, see below) as a *pipeline*. As we have seen, the flow of goods *downstream* from manufacturer to consumer frequently relies on channel intermediaries. In the next few pages, as well as examining the movement of goods between producers and these downstream channel participants, we shall also be considering the flow of raw materials and components from suppliers that are *upstream* from the manufacturer. Further, we shall explore the vital role played by the flow of information between supply chain members, as shown in Fig. 15.1.

In Fig. 15.1, second-tier suppliers usually provide the raw materials (e.g. plastic resin) for first-tier suppliers to convert to component parts (e.g. steering wheels),

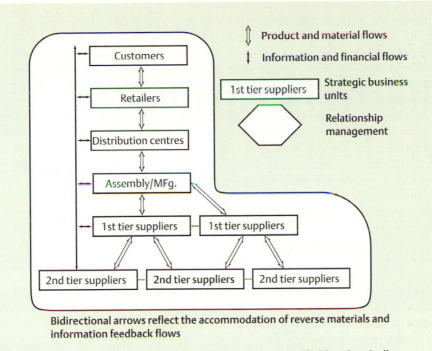

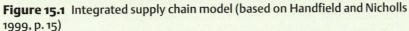

Bidirectional arrows reflect the accommodation of reverse materials and information feedback flows

Figure 15.1 Integrated supply chain model (based on Handfield and Nicholls 1999, p. 15)

which are then manufactured into the end product (e.g. cars) by the producer. Note that not all supply chains will contain both tiers of suppliers: we shall discuss more examples of supply chains later. Note also the position of the producer. As in Chapter 14, it is the producer who forms the major focus of this chapter. In this context, you should try to see yourself as the marketing manager for a manufacturing company where the logistics function is at least closely integrated with your department, if not subsumed within it. How would you describe the orientation of a company where this was the case?

Some definitions

You might be asking yourself why this chapter has reintroduced the term 'logistics'. (You should recall from Chapter 14 that logistics featured in the primary activities of the value chain.) Let us provide some definitions, and attempt to show how the terms physical distribution and logistics differ. Johnson and Wood (1996) state that *physical distribution* refers to the movement of finished goods outward from the end of the manufacturer's assembly line to the customer, frequently via intermediaries. Functions under this heading can include warehousing, transportation

Customer dissatisfaction can all too quickly occur when logistics systems break down. Take, for instance, the seemingly annual shortage of certain toys at Christmas: in 1997 it was the Teletubbies; in 1998 Furbies. As in previous years, retailers appeared to leave it to manufacturers to take the responsibility to ensure supply met demand, without recognizing the need to give suppliers a clear indication of which lines were proving popular during the preceding months. The Teletubbies manufacturer, Golden Bear, claimed that, when retailers were shown the product range back in January, they had shown no interest. A spokesman said, 'If we had received the orders at the beginning of the year we could have coped' (*Derby Evening Telegraph* 1997). No doubt you can recall other similar distribution disasters. Remember Power Rangers and Teenage Mutant Hero Turtles? Clearly something was wrong within these supply chains. Because retailers are closer to customers, shouldn't they be partly to blame for not understanding their customers' changing needs well enough? What about the manufacturers? Should they have developed more flexible production methods which are more responsive to sudden changes in demand? Or do we just have to accept that some fad products are quite unpredictable in their popularity and that their resulting scarcity can be profitably exploited by members of the supply chain? Perhaps even the fact that the product is hard to get hold of adds to the lucky customers' perceptions of value?

(often undertaken by third-party specialists), customer service, and administration. *Logistics* describes the entire process of materials and products moving into, through, and out of a firm. Physical distribution may therefore be seen as 'outbound logistics', while 'inbound logistics' covers the movement of materials from suppliers and is closely linked to the manufacturer's purchasing or procurement function. 'Materials and inventory management' typically describes the movement and stockholding of goods within a firm.

The notion of *supply chain management* is often viewed as somewhat larger than logistics. It links organizations more directly with the manufacturer's total communication network or 'supply pipeline'. The pipeline metaphor, as outlined above, helps us to picture the flows of goods and information up and down the supply chain. The 'supply chain' metaphor itself serves as a reminder that the organizations participating in the delivery of added value to the end customer must work together as 'links' in a chain of interdependent activities (Saunders 1997).

The US Council of Logistics Management (CLM) has defined logistics as:

the process of planning, implementing and controlling the efficient, effective flow and storage of goods, services and related information from the point of origin to the point of consumption for the purposes of conforming to customer requirements.

Building on our discussion of channels in Chapter 14, the management of logistics can be more simply described in terms of delivering the right product to the right place at the right time in the right condition for the right cost. This sense of 'rights' connects *customer responsiveness* to each level of the marketing channel for any product offering. Remember that marketing is essentially about satisfying customer's needs in a way that is profitable to suppliers.

Physical distribution objectives

As with all elements of the marketing mix (see Chapter 11), the ultimate objective of physical distribution management is competitive advantage. The search for a sustainable competitive advantage, however, is becoming increasingly difficult. Christopher (1992) points out that customers are now seeking more than just brand or product value, and are looking for value in a much wider sense. A critical component of such customer value is *service*, and a key part of service value is *availability*. In other words, there is no value in a product until it is in the hands of the customer. Christopher states that customers often only have a *preference* for a particular brand, rather than having strong brand loyalty (see Chapter 4). When that preferred brand is not available, many customers will quite readily choose an acceptable substitute. This is equally true in industrial or consumer markets. For example, the choice of suppliers by a just-in-time (JIT—see below) manufacturer will be hugely influenced by delivery reliability, and not just product quality.

Companies that are responsive to customer needs also need to focus on *time* as a source of competitive advantage (Stalk and Hout 1990). Basically, the shorter it takes for a company, or indeed an entire supply chain, to do things, the more flexible it can be in response to the market-place. Benetton, for instance, is able to respond to the popularity of certain colours in its ranges extremely quickly thanks to its advanced logistics systems. Information flows from points of sale, flexible manufacturing, and global distribution all mean that Benetton's *lead times* (i.e. the time taken from receipt of a customer's order to final delivery) are much shorter than clothing industry averages.

In addition to lead times, manufacturers should consider the impact of shorter life cycles on new product development (see Chapter 10). If innovation is a company's key source of competitive advantage, then the time in getting the product to market will be crucial to prevent obsolescence.

Logistics changes in retailing

A good illustration of industry responsiveness is provided by the UK grocery retailing sector, where the logistics support provided to stores has evolved significantly over the last twenty years (Fernie 1997). Until the 1970s most UK retailers received products direct from the manufacturer. Store inventory levels were controlled by branch managers, who bought direct, often via sales representatives. Because lead times were long, much stock was held in the backroom of the store. In order to improve stock availability, retailers such as Sainsbury's began to *centralize* their distribution through the construction of large warehouses for the receipt of suppliers' goods. Retailers negotiated volume discounts with manufacturers at head office level, and

Figure 15.2 Suppliers of goods and services must consider the location where their goods will have greatest value for end-consumers. Somerfield is one retailer that has identified a market of consumers who are attracted by home delivery of the products sold in its stores. Its logistics task must therefore incorporate this final link in the distribution channel. For increased efficiency, many retailers have set up specialist warehouses which deliver goods to consumers' homes, without passing through their retail premises. (Reproduced with permission of Somerfield Stores Ltd.)

consolidated stock at their warehouses prior to replenishing stores at greatly reduced lead times.

Food retailers also developed the concept of *composite distribution*. Fernie (1997) explains that composites are huge, multi-compartmentalized distribution centres which allow the storage of products at different temperatures under one roof. Delivery trucks are also able to carry mixed product ranges, resulting in a streamlined, efficient system able to support the growth of the grocery superstores. Food manufacturers' own distribution networks have been substantially eroded, and, instead, a new market has been created in the provision of distribution services by specialist logistics companies such as NFC and Christian Salvesen.

The developments outlined above resulted in the movement of stock away from stores' backrooms to distribution centres. Lead times were reduced but inventory was merely pushed further up the channel. This situation is not desirable, for, as we shall see, it is now common to think of inventory not as a safety-buffer against selling out of particular lines, but as a cost. The previous chapter showed us that retailers wield a large amount of power in the grocery supply chain. They are now using their influence to move towards a *JIT system* for the replenishment of stock. Sales-based ordering direct from store level, via head office, and on to manufacturers has increased, thanks to the use of Information Technology (IT—discussed later in this chapter). Products are now delivered more frequently in smaller quantities from factories and *cross-docked* across distribution centres. Cross-docking refers to the rapid breaking down of an in-coming delivery of, say, frozen pizzas, from one supplier and then the allocation of the appropriate proportion of the pizzas to trucks out-bound for individual stores. These trucks will also be carrying other goods from different suppliers which have been cross-docked in the same way.

These efficiency gains do mean, of course, that unless there is an excellent exchange of sales and production information between participants, the cost of holding inventory is passed fully to the manufacturer. Piercy (1997) claims that the Efficient Consumer Response (ECR) initiative (see Chapter 14) represents the application of 'lean supply chain' principles to FMCG channels. He applauds the attempts of ECR to improve organizational efficiency, yet expresses concern over the pressure exerted by powerful US retailers like Krogers on manufacturers such as Procter & Gamble to absorb more and more costs.

From the manufacturer's perspective, the above discussion reminds us that customer service impacts not only on the end user but also on intermediate customers. Christopher (1992) suggests that marketing has traditionally focused on the consumer by seeking to promote brand values and to generate a demand 'pull' within the market for a company's products. We now recognize that this by itself is often not sufficient. Due to the shifts in channel power towards the retailer, it has become vital to develop the strongest possible relations with such intermediaries. In other words, marketers must create a *trade franchise* as well as a *consumer franchise*. (We might best see Christopher's 'franchise' here as being 'worthy' of the right to deal with our customers.) Both these franchises can be enhanced or diminished by the efficiency of the supplier's logistics system. This is shown in Fig. 15.3 below.

Who do you think gains the most from the development of Efficient Consumer Response initiatives? The consumer, the retailer, or the manufacturer? Is the retailer's gain necessarily the manufacturer's loss? And to what extent are efficiency gains passed on to consumers in the form of lower prices and/or better service, rather than added to the profits of retailers and manufacturers? What factors influence the distribution of gains?

It is only when the three components are working optimally together that marketing effectiveness is maximized. Christopher believes that the combined impact depends on the product of all three. (We shall return to the reference to ROI in Fig. 15.3 as the chapter progresses.)

You should note that, apart from the high visibility of transportation companies such as Eddie Stobart, much of the work carried out by the logistics function is 'behind the scenes' as far as the end consumer is concerned. This does not, however, diminish the importance of this work in contemporary marketing practice. In fact, without a high degree of skill being exercised by marketing managers within *industrial* (or business-to-business) markets, it can be argued that most consumer marketing initiatives would be doomed to failure! Thus, many of the examples presented in this chapter will be from an industrial context, with the service that is under discussion typically being a service to *business* or commercial customers.

Customer service in logistics

So, what do we mean by '*customer service*'? In truth, it is a complex concept comprising a number of factors, and an area in which academic researchers have reached different conclusions. For a discussion, see Palmer (1998). In a physical distribution context, a study by LaLonde and Zinszer (1976) showed that customer service could most simply be examined under three headings:

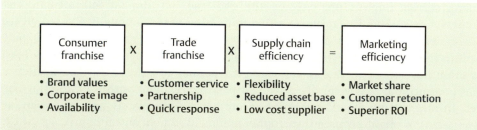

Figure 15.3 The Impact of logistics and customer service on marketing

Source: Adapted from M. Christopher, (1992), *Logistics and Supply Chain Management* (London: Pitman)

- pre-transaction elements;
- transaction elements;
- post-transaction elements.

The evaluation of *pre-transaction* elements of customer service include companies asking themselves such questions as:

- Is our service policy communicated internally and externally?
- Are we easy to contact and to do business with?
- Is there a service management organizational structure in place?
- Can we adapt our service delivery systems to meet particular customer needs?

Transaction element issues include:

- What is the time from order to delivery?
- What is the reliability of this lead time?
- What percentage of demand can be met from stock?
- What proportion of orders are completely filled?
- How long does it take us to provide order status information?

Post-transaction element considerations include:

- What is the availability of spare parts?
- What is the call-out time for our engineers?
- Can we maintain the warranty to customers' expectations?
- How promptly do we deal with customer complaints?

It is fair to say that some of these elements will be more important than others within certain market-places. The key issue for marketers to grasp is that it is essential to understand the differing requirements of different market segments (see Chapter 3), and then to tailor the company's service offering accordingly. For some customers, such as in the retail distribution example above, frequent deliveries of small quantities may be far more desirable than occasional deliveries of large volumes.

The primary objective of any logistics customer service strategy must be to reduce the customer's cost of ownership, that is, it must make the transaction more 'profitable' for the customer (Christopher 1992). For example, a delivery twice a week instead of once reduces the customer's average inventory by half and therefore cuts the cost of carrying that inventory. Similarly, reliable on-time delivery means that a retailer can reduce the need to carry safety stock, again resulting in lower stock holding costs. Research by the National Economic Development Council (1991) carried out among the 'preferred suppliers' (see ahead) to the Nissan car plant in Sunderland proved to be highly revealing. Results implied that the classic competitive dimensions of price and promotion were substantially less important to Nissan than product quality and, crucially, reliability of delivery and responsiveness. Customer service clearly represents a major potential source of competitive advantage.

Cost/service trade-offs

Marketing and logistics managers must also face the fact that there will be significant differences in profitability between customers. Customers will, of course, vary in the volumes of different products they purchase, but the *cost to service* these customers may also vary considerably. The Pareto Law, or '80/20 rule' will often be found to hold, i.e. roughly speaking, some 80 per cent of a company's profits will come from only about 20 per cent of its customers. We need to recognize that there are costs as well as benefits in providing customer service, and therefore the appropriate level of service will need to vary from customer to customer. While we want to attract and retain customers by offering superior service to that provided by our competitors, there comes a point when diminishing returns set in. For instance, a chemicals supplier might continually have to keep huge stocks of a particular product because of the JIT demands of a key customer, say, an oil company. Eventually the cost of holding that inventory (perhaps in terms of storage space, or insurance bills) may force the supplier to reconsider the service levels it offers to the customer. The supplier may attempt to compromise on promises for 'next day' delivery, for example. Fig. 15.4 shows the typical nature of the cost/benefit trade-offs in service-level decisions.

In Fig. 15.4 Christopher (1992) explains that the shape of the revenue curve is dictated by customers' response to the service level offered. The slope is initially fairly flat since in many markets there will be a minimum threshold of acceptable service which most competitors will be providing, for example delivery within seven days. Once the threshold is passed, increasing returns to service improvements (say, getting delivery times down to five, then three days, and so on) should be achieved as customers place more orders with us. At the top, the curve flattens out again when our additional expenditure on service does not pay back. Christopher calls this 'service overkill'. The costs curve is usually a steeply rising curve as shown due to keeping high levels of inventory. By investing in IT to improve the flow of information about customer requirements, we might, however, be able to push this curve to the right, thus boosting overall profitability at all levels of service.

In setting physical distribution objectives, it is important for managers to understand the *total cost* of attempting to meet a specified service level. When testing alternative approaches, the costs of some functions will increase, others will decrease, and still others may remain unchanged: the objective is to find the approach with the lowest overall cost. The concept of cost *trade-offs* recognizes these changing patterns. For example, the 'trading' of information, via IT-based control systems, for inventory; or perhaps, the 'trading' of an extra regional warehouse for a fleet of national delivery trucks.

You will recall that Fig. 15.3 mentioned ROI (return on investment) and a '*reduced asset base*'. As has been mentioned before, the need for marketing managers to work closely with other functional areas, such as finance, is vital. An understanding of accounting should tell you that, since ROI is the product of margin and capital turnover, a company may attempt to improve this ratio by increasing sales revenue and/or

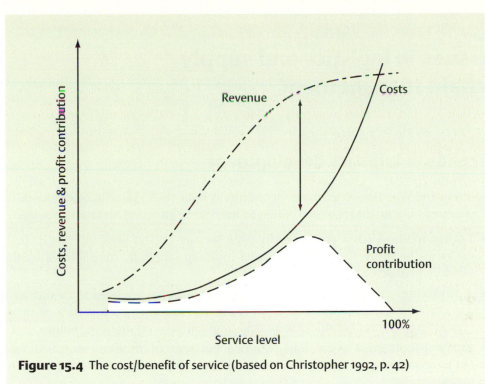

Figure 15.4 The cost/benefit of service (based on Christopher 1992, p. 42)

reducing costs. The company may also use the leverage of improved asset turnover through lowering the value of the assets utilized. This can be achieved by a better management of inventory, thereby *tying up less money in stocks*. The use of JIT techniques to address this issue is discussed later in the chapter.

Marketing logistics

In concluding our discussion of physical distribution objectives, we should quote Doyle (1998), who states that modern managers now use the concept of '*marketing logistics*'. This starts by asking how customers want to receive the product (see Chapter 7 on buyer behaviour) and then works backwards to the design of the materials, final goods, inventory, transportation, warehousing, and customer service in order to meet those wants. The amount of *information* needed by managers to make appropriate marketing logistics decisions is clearly vast. Fortunately, it is becoming increasingly available due to huge advances in technology, and we shall discuss some of these advances in more detail at the end of this chapter.

Issues in logistics and supply chain management

Trends in logistics development

Johnson and Wood (1996) list a number of trends since the 1950s which have made it increasingly important for organizations to focus their attention on logistics issues:

- **Transportation costs rose rapidly**: this became critical with the rise in fuel prices of the 1970s. Transportation costs could no longer be considered a stable factor in planning equations.

- **A fundamental change in inventory philosophy**: as we have seen, retailers used to hold a large proportion of stocks in the marketing channel. Now, it is typical for 90 per cent of stocks to be held by manufacturers and distributors.

- **Product lines grew**: as consumer choice grew, items of inventory such as different package sizes also increased dramatically, making storage and transportation more complex.

- **The advent of computer technology**: without the development of IT and its widespread use by channel participants, logistics theories might well have been impossible to put into practice.

- **The growth of retailer power**: the large chains have demanded and received special treatment from their suppliers (see Chapter 14).

- **Increased public concern over the environment**: this impacts upon logistics in, for example, packaging design and developing return channels for recycled materials.

These developments have resulted in contemporary logistics managers having a huge spending power. In the UK alone, their combined spend has been estimated as well over £750 billion every year (Supply Chain Management Casebook 1996). The Confederation of British Industry (CBI) estimates that, on average, businesses spend just over half their production costs on buying in goods and services. Many organizations also spend 10–20 per cent of production costs on storing, handling, and transporting the goods they have bought, and further amounts on distributing the finished product. For example, purchasing by British Telecom cost £4.5 billion a year, SmithKline Beecham £3.5 billion, and Nat West Bank over £2 billion. Although these are very large British businesses, it is not unusual for a top decision-maker in a medium-sized company to control a purchasing and logistics budget of over £100 million (see Chapter 7 for more on commercial buyer behaviour).

Logistics and supply chain management are areas that cut across every type of industry and service. At the very least, someone has to take responsibility for ensuring an adequate supply of office stationery, and a whole factory could grind to a halt if no one has ordered sufficient packaging for the finished product. The UK professional body, the Chartered Institute of Purchasing and Supply, claims that better logistics management results in substantial savings and increased efficiency, with even a 1 per cent improvement in the management of the supply chain boosting the bottom line of a company by as much as 15 per cent (Supply Chain Management Handbook 1996).

Changes in supply chain management

We have seen that supply chain management is about trying to co-ordinate the entire supply chain, from purchasing the raw material to the point where the end product is consumed. It is common to find complex supply chains in which many participants are dependent on each other to ensure that the right goods are in the right place at the right time. Note the many alternative routes by which food products can find their way to US consumers in the supply chain illustrated in Fig. 15.5.

Problems can arise when the supplies available do not match demand: items may be out of stock, or they cannot be found in the warehouse, or they may have been held up on the production line because parts or commodities were not available. In today's highly competitive markets, it is crucial that such problems are eliminated. This has meant the elevation of supply chain management to a *strategic* level of importance (Bowersox and Closs 1996). Companies have begun to realize that excellence in supply chain management lies in the effective *co-ordination* of a number of overlapping activities:

- Assessing commercial risk, such as the relative benefits of buying components or services from an outside supplier compared to producing/providing them in-house. This is known as 'out-sourcing' and is becoming increasingly common as companies shed their non-core competencies (see Chapter 11).
- Identifying reliable, economic supply sources that meet the company's quality needs.
- Deciding on the nature of business relationships, and which are the most appropriate for the company (see below).
- Ensuring the best contractual arrangements are reached with suppliers and customers (e.g. retailers) to maintain competitive advantage.
- Planning and managing inventories, warehousing and transportation. (We shall discuss these topics in more detail later in this chapter.)

The quality of the relationships between the various members of the supply chain is seen as a vital ingredient in saving costs and improving quality. Christopher *et al.* (1991) cite the work of Reichheld and Sasser (1990) in highlighting the importance of customer retention on profitability. These authors believe that the practice of *relationship marketing* (see Chapter 8) throughout the supply chain can lead to improved customer service, which will lead to closer customer relationships, which in turn

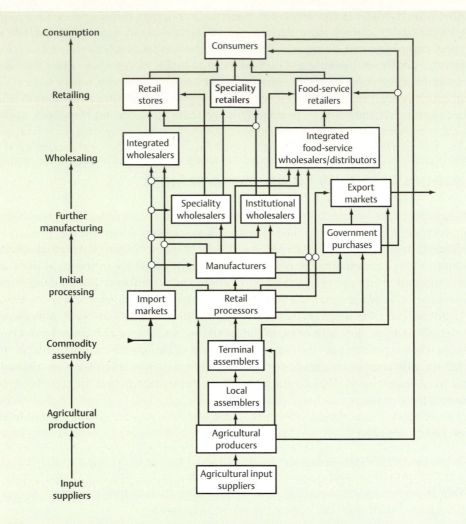

Figure 15.5 Food channel participants in the USA (adapted from Bowersox and Closs 1996)

leads to improved customer retention, and long-term profits for suppliers. The longer a customer stays with a supplier, the more likely they are to see that company as a 'preferred supplier'. This is the case whether the relationship occurs at the downstream or upstream phase (relative to the manufacturer) of the supply pipeline. In Chapter 14 we discussed how producers could manage the *downstream* relations with retailers. The suppliers *upstream* from Nissan, who were discussed at the beginning of the chapter, have earned the status of 'preferred suppliers'. By carefully managing the relationship between themselves and their key customer, their long-term futures are theoretically now more secure. In what other sectors can you see the development of close relationships between organizations? How do Marks & Spencer purchase their textiles, for instance?

One way to deliver competitive advantage is through *partnership sourcing*. Here, the supplier is treated as an associate of the buying organization and price competitiveness is complemented by service, innovation, and shared ambitions (e.g. in NPD, where a supplier might be consulted over the feasibility of developing a new component for a manufacturer's intended product design). Spekman (1988) states that both the buyer and the seller must invest in the relationship. Due to the pressure of increased competition from overseas producers, shorter product cycles, and rapidly changing technologies, manufacturing companies must search for suppliers who can bring their competence and experience to bear on making a contribution to the purchasing company's success, as well as to their own fortunes. Spekman acknowledges that this may be difficult since many purchasers have traditionally held back from forming bonds with a single supplier, and lack the trust and openness necessary to make partnerships work. He claims, however, that 'we are beyond the debate of whether such close ties are feasible. They are now essential'.

A good example of this upstream relationship management is provided by Xerox. Several years ago, the company reduced by over 50 per cent the number of suppliers from whom it bought. From its remaining suppliers, Xerox demanded a commitment to quality, innovation, and cost reduction (*Purchasing* 1985). The company took this difficult decision when it found that its copier manufacturing costs were some 30 per cent higher than those of its Japanese competitors. The resulting closer collaboration with suppliers, over issues like flexible response times and the recycling of parts, formed part of an overall supply chain initiative by Xerox which led to the company achieving record levels of customer satisfaction, yet reducing inventory by over $700 million (*Fortune* 1991).

Bowersox and Closs (1996) believe that the next few years will continue to focus on strategic logistics where managers' considerations will move beyond the 'walls' of existing business structures to encompass suppliers and customers. They predict that logistical competency and channel-wide partnerships will be used to gain competitive advantage. The movement from traditional functional independence towards achieving a fully integrated supply chain is graphically summarized in Fig. 15.6.

Paradigm shifts in logistics

In order to make the necessary changes in the management of the supply chain discussed above, Christopher (1992) claims there is a need for a *paradigm shift* in the way we think about organizations. (You will recall the mention of 'paradigms' in Chapter 14.) He suggests there are five major areas where a paradigm shift is required:

1. *From functions to processes*: this is an important viewpoint worthy of detailed analysis. It challenges the traditional idea that a business is best managed on a functional basis, i.e. a purchasing function, a production function, a sales function and so on (see also Chapter 21). Each of these functions in a conventional organization

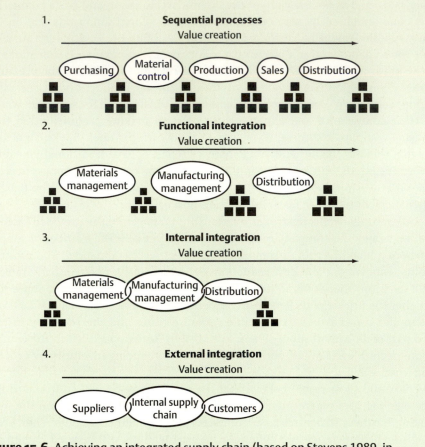

Figure 15.6 Achieving an integrated supply chain (based on Stevens 1989, in Christopher 1992)

is normally run by a senior manager who comes to regard their functional area as their 'territory' and who often jealously guards their own departmental budget. The problems that can occur in this situation include:

■ Inventory building up at functional boundaries when, for example, the production manager wants to minimize costs by running large batch quantities, even though this may mean creating an inventory greater than that which is needed;

■ Functional boundaries impeding process management, i.e. the process of satisfying customer demand by purchasing supplies, manufacturing, and then distributing finished goods to end users, becomes fragmented into water-tight sections where paperwork and constant rechecking takes valuable time;

■ Presenting too many faces to the customer, for example the customer may have to deal with the sales office, credit control, production planning, warehousing, and transport planning, where each function performs its task and then passes the order on as if it was being 'thrown over the wall' to the next functional area.

Christopher feels that the solution to these problems lies in recognizing that the order and its associated information flows should be at the heart of any business. This means moving from an *input focused and budget driven* organization to an *output focused, market driven* one. Stewart (1992) describes three elements in this shift: the development of self-directed work teams to empower employees; managing processes rather than functions; and the rapid sharing of accurate information. As you can see, these are not solutions that will be quick to implement. What problems do you foresee for companies trying to enact them? Think of the crucial role human resource management will have to play.

2. *From profit to profitability*: this means a move from the old notion of profit as being focused around margins. Rather, it recognizes the importance of resource management and asset utilization, meaning that logistics managers will need to control resources and costs (see the discussion of asset turnover above).

3. *From products to customers*: this is clearly not a new concept to you as a reader of a marketing textbook like this one! Because logistics management is ultimately about customer service, it has a central role to play in a company making the transition to a marketing orientation (see also Chapter 1).

4. *From transactions to relationships*: in the past, much of marketing's focus was on winning market share and gaining new customers. There is now a recognition of the need to retain customers as well, through the building of long-term relationships. For the optimum performance of the supply chain, partnerships should be forged with both customers and suppliers.

5. *From inventory to information*: IT is helping managers 'see' from one end of the supply pipeline to the other. By doing so, and thus reducing uncertainty about product availability in relation to market demand, companies can dramatically lower the need for inventory. The impact of IT on logistics is examined later in this chapter.

Ultimately, the message you should take from the preceding section is that, rather than seeing competition merely at the level of company versus company, contemporary thinkers in logistics see it as *supply chain competing with rival supply chain*. How different, if at all, do you think this concept is from the channel system competition mentioned in Chapter 14?

Global logistics

Before we begin to examine the more operational side of physical distribution management, we shall briefly consider the challenges of *global logistics*. At the same time as companies market brands across international boundaries (see also Chapter 23), many will typically also source for global production on a worldwide basis.

Christopher (1992) gives the example of the Singer Sewing Machine Company which buys its machine shells from a subcontractor in the USA, the motors from Brazil, the drive shafts from Italy, and assembles the finished machines in Taiwan.

There are two related developments underpinning the trend towards global logistics management: the focused factory and the centralization of inventory. *Focused factories* enable a company to gain considerable economies of scale by limiting the range and mix of products manufactured in a single location. For instance, despite its enormous capacity, the Toyota factory in Derbyshire makes very few different models of car at a time: in the main, the Corolla model is made there for export to the continent. An obvious trade-off with this approach is the effect on transport costs and delivery lead times. Too great a focus may also reduce the flexibility of a company's production facility to respond to market trends. *Inventory centralization* has taken place as organizations steadily close national warehouses and amalgamate them into regional distribution centres (RDCs) serving a much wider geographical area. For instance, Valeo, a French automotive parts distributor found that it was still able to maintain service levels despite merging its Belgian, German, and French warehouses into a central facility near Paris (Cooper *et al.* 1992). A more recent development has been the recognition that there may be even greater gains made by not physically centralizing inventory, but rather by still locating it near the customer and instead managing and controlling it centrally. What do you think are the advantages of this approach?

Christopher (1992) highlights five key challenges for logistics in a global context:

- **Extended lead times of supply**: the consolidation of global production can lead to difficult decisions in serving the demands of various, geographically widespread markets, possibly requiring local product variations (see Chapter 23).

- **Unreliable transit times**: shipping, cargo consolidation, and customs clearance all contribute to delays and variability (Ploos van Amstel 1990). Local managers tend to compensate by building up buffer stock.

- **Multiple consolidation and break-bulk options**: these include shipping direct from each source to the final market in full containers; or consolidating from each source for each general geographic area, with bulk broken down into intermediate inventory ready for specific markets.

- **Multiple freight mode and cost options**: this follows on from the previous point, with shipping companies offering a complex mix of sea/air services, different container sizes, and scheduled and unscheduled services (see ahead for more on containers and freight handling).

- **Intermediate component shipping with local added value**: some companies, like the US construction plant manufacturer Caterpillar, have examined their value chain (see also Chapter 14) and calculated that there are opportunities for delaying the final configuration of a product until it is as close to the customer as possible. They can then achieve lower costs by shipping generic sub-assemblies to the local operation which typically provides finishing, local language packaging, and direct customer delivery.

A vivid illustration of the problems faced by companies trading internationally is provided by clothing retailer and manufacturer Laura Ashley's financial position in 1990. Due to a huge £89 million debt, banks were demanding that something be done about the company's poor logistics performance. The company had £105 million tied up in stock, yet still could not deliver to its shops on time. Distribution was particularly bad in North America, where that year's autumn/winter collection had arrived some three months late, resulting in the need for immediate mark downs (Peck and Christopher 1994). Shipments of garments for the USA should have been arriving weekly by air, but late processing at the factories meant that they missed the weekly flight. Rather than putting the goods on the next available flight, freight forwarders often held the consignment over to the following week so they could consolidate the loads. These poor deliveries affected the US stores' performance. This resulted in a vicious circle: as the shops' performance deteriorated, they sank lower in priority of delivery, eventually receiving shipments by sea. The company clearly had some major communication problems within its global supply chain!

Whysall (1995) points to another important global consideration in supply chain management, that of 'fair trade'. This reflects an awareness among the advanced manufacturers and retailers in developed countries of their relationships with vulnerable third-world suppliers. Companies such as the Body Shop have made much of their ethical trading practices, claiming that they treat their suppliers with a high degree of principle and integrity (*Guardian* 1995). These claims have been used by Anita Roddick as a form of positioning statement to gain competitive advantage. How credible do you believe such claims to be? Have you read anything that might make you question the Body Shop's stance? (See also Chapter 5.)

An interesting example of the potential problems in the area of environmental supply chain management is the experience of B&Q which set out to audit the environmental integrity of its supply chain, only to discover that the company's environmental policy was inappropriate for industries in developing countries. Suppliers in developing countries found that adapting to the company's environmental policy was financially crippling, and therefore B&Q announced that third-world employees' welfare had to take precedence over wider environmental considerations (Whysall 1995).

Key elements of a physical distribution system

Identification of segments by service requirements

As we discussed under Customer Service above, the marketing logistics manager first needs to determine the dimensions of service that customers most value, for example speed, reliability, or availability. Some form of marketing research is likely to be needed here (see Chapter 6). It is probable that the market will not be homogeneous: some market segments may be willing to pay high prices to obtain premium service, whilst others may attach greatest importance to low prices and be willing to accept minimum service levels. In attempting to meet buyers' requirements, managers must, of course, also consider cost/service trade-offs and the logistics standards set by the competition. Looking at the company's performance in relation to main competitors is known as *benchmarking*, and allows us to identify areas for improvement. For an example, see Fig. 15.7. Which service elements do you think should be addressed by the company concerned?

Once *target service levels* have been identified (e.g. to deliver 95 per cent of orders within two days; to ensure 98 per cent availability of product 'x'), the company must design a physical distribution system which can deliver them at minimum cost. The key issues for marketing logistics managers to consider include:

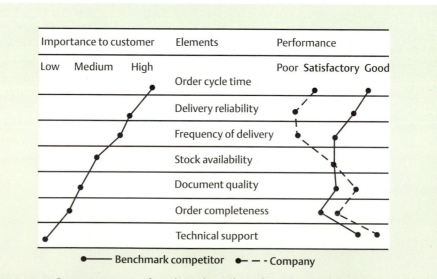

Figure 15.7 Customer service benchmarking (based on Christopher 1992, p. 93)

- how can we speed up communications and order processing?
- where should we produce goods and store them?
- how much stock should be held?
- how can we best handle transportation?

Communications and order processing

Basically, the physical distribution process starts with the company *receiving an order*. This may be direct from the end consumer, as in the case of Dell's sales of its personal computers; it may involve a head office 'order-taker' noting a replenishment order from a major retailer; or it may be generated by an account manager visiting a major client and entering their order for some new technical equipment on to a laptop keyboard. Copies of this order are then usually directed to various company departments. Where relevant, this may include those responsible for inventories, purchasing, credit control, manufacturing, dispatch, warehousing, and invoicing. As we noted in our earlier examination of functionally organized companies, customers may be serviced more efficiently if *communication* between these activities is speeded up. Better still, as far as is possible, the company should ensure that these activities take place *concurrently*, rather than consecutively, i.e. it should try to eliminate the need to 'throw' the order over the company's internal 'walls'.

Significant advances in IT now offer organizations the chance to reduce delays and costs in order processing. Via networked computers, sales people can send order details to the relevant departments as they are given to them by the customer. Using these IT systems, account managers can also provide instant status reports on the progress of their order to customers, examining inventory levels and making recommendations for out-of-stock items as they do so. Once an order is confirmed, integrated computer systems can automatically generate orders to pick goods from warehouse shelves, to ship goods, to bill customers, to update stock records, and to confirm delivery arrangements to the customer.

As we shall see in a later section of this chapter, EDI (Electronic Data Interchange) links and advanced IT programmes can even inform the production department of the potential need to make new stock, and the procurement department of the need to order new supplies, as well as warning suppliers of the producing company's imminent requirements. Cooper *et al.* (1992) report the advantages from EDI enjoyed by L'Oreal (UK): faster transaction times, reductions in administrative costs, and enhanced business relationships with retailers.

Production and warehouse location

As *warehousing* enables finished goods (as well as work in progress) to be stored and subsequently moved according to customer demands, it forms an important link in the supply chain. A key determinant of the availability of goods is the *number and location* of manufacturing facilities and warehouses. We may view decisions here in terms of the familiar trade-offs concept. The greater the number of locations used, the greater the potential for rapid delivery. Conversely, more facilities will increase costs and capital employed, thus reducing ROI. As we have seen, warehouses may not necessarily be owned by manufacturers: many retailers utilize their own warehouse facilities in order to address the challenges of composite distribution and cross-docking (Fernie 1997).

Location decisions are complex due to the enormous number of potential site combinations, especially when the company is operating globally. It is increasingly common for managers to use computer-based mathematical models to aid their decision-making. In doing so, however, companies must not lose sight of the trends we have already discussed, like the move towards focused factories and centralized RDCs, and conflicting views such as locating inventory locally yet controlling it centrally. Also, they should note how alternative transportation arrangements (see below) might circumvent the need to invest heavily in storage facilities in the first place. For instance, the decision by Digital to cut the number of its 'logistics centres' (effectively, RDCs) from twenty-six country locations to between five and seven centres during the 1980s led to a large-scale, yet cost-effective increase in the company's use of carrier services (Cooper *et al.* 1992). This was partly made possible by the removal of trade barriers between countries of the EU.

Inventory management

You should by now be aware of the strategic importance of inventory management. Ultimately, stockholding represents costs such as storage space, obsolescence, deterioration, and interest payments. Yet, ideally, the company should carry enough stock to meet customers' orders immediately. If the desired goods are not available, then a sale may be lost, and worse, a customer may be lost to a competitor. If too much unmoved stock is held, the company may find itself with large quantities of goods which it is forced to mark down. This is often the case in fashion retailing, as we saw with Laura Ashley. Thus, the objective of inventory management is to find a *balance* between customer service and the cost of carrying additional stock.

There are a number of methods used to achieve the desired balance in stockholding. Perhaps the most basic method is that of the *reorder point*. This approach recognizes that waiting to reorder stock until an extremely low level has been reached is risky, due to the fact that it takes time to replenish stock. The reorder point system triggers reordering at a stock level a little higher than 'danger' level, so that by the time new stock is received, the danger level of the old stock has only just been reached. Stock is typically counted manually in small organizations, or via computerized sales systems such as EPOS (see below), which compare daily sales to starting stock levels, in larger organizations. Safety stock levels are usually based on historical sales data. Another approach is to use the *economic order quantity* (EOQ) formula:

$$EOQ = \sqrt{2do/ic}$$

where d = annual demand in units; o = cost of placing an order; i = carrying costs as % of cost of one unit; and c = the cost of each unit. The equation is based on the EOQ model, as shown in Fig. 15.8, which shows an idealized theoretical relationship between order processing costs and inventory carrying costs to give the order quantity size that minimizes total costs.

Unfortunately, as with many economic models, it does not take into sufficient account variations in customer and supplier behaviour. Where demand is unpredictable or when stocks cannot be replenished relatively quickly, the model may be inadequate. Further, as Christopher (1992) points out, the reorder quantity means that a company will be carrying more inventory than is actually required per day over virtually the complete order cycle (the time between placing separate orders with the supplier). For example, if the EOQ were 100 units, and daily usage was 10, then on the first day of the cycle the buyer would be overstocked by 90 units, on the second day by 80, and so on.

This brings us to the *just-in-time (JIT) philosophy*. This is based on the view, commonly attributed to the Japanese, that inventory is waste and that large inventories merely hide problems such as inaccurate forecasts, unreliable suppliers, quality issues, and production bottlenecks. The JIT concept aims to eliminate any need for safety stock, with parts for manufacture (or goods for reselling) arriving just as they are needed. As a result, small shipments must be made more frequently. Order requirements from

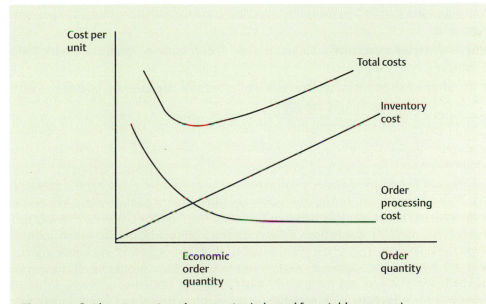

Figure 15.8 The economic order quantity (adapted from Jobber, p. 490)

some companies can specify the exact unloading point and time of day, with suppliers having to respond accordingly. For example, Toyota schedules its production to minimize sharp fluctuations in daily volume, and to turn out a predicted number of each model every day. Suppliers are automatically notified of customer orders and given a stable production schedule so they will not deliver the wrong components on the date of final assembly (Bower and Hout 1988). This level of planning also occurs, for instance, with retailers like Marks & Spencer stipulating delivery 'windows' for its carriers, and with manufacturers such as Rover utilizing the services of third-party distributors like BRS, who consolidate and deliver quantities from several different suppliers resulting in no congestion of delivery vehicles at the production plant (Christopher 1992).

The increasing popularity of JIT delivery among business customers clearly means that, for suppliers, the logistics service elements of availability and reliability plus, of course, uniformly excellent product quality, become paramount. Successful implementation of JIT systems relies on high levels of co-operation between supplying and buying organizations, and the development of long-term partnerships. These closer relations can exist both upstream and downstream from the producer/manufacturer. Isaac (1985) points out the effects of adopting JIT techniques on a company's culture. He contrasts conventional wisdom with 'JIT thinking' in relation to the following issues:

- **Inventories**: large inventories from manufacturing economies of scale and safety stock provision, contrasted with low inventories from reliable, 'continuous flow' delivery;

- **Flexibility**: minimal flexibility with long lead times, contrasted with short lead times and customer service driven flexibility (although you might argue that this throws open to question the stable planning environment often thought necessary for JIT);

- **Seller/carrier relations**: tough, adversarial negotiations, contrasted with joint venture partnerships;

- **Number of suppliers/carriers**: many to avoid sole dependency, contrasted with few in long-term open relationships;

- **Communications**: minimal and with many secrets, contrasted with open communication and sharing of information to enable joint problem solving.

The JIT concept is not without its problems. The *Financial Times* (1994) reported that suppliers in the Japanese plastics industry have been in 'revolt' against JIT, claiming that it is too expensive. During the 1980s, suppliers tolerated the system because it strengthened the relationship between them and the customer. Once manufacturers had become used to a steady flow of materials from one company, they were unlikely to go elsewhere. The cost to the suppliers of additional freight and stock holding was bearable because the Japanese plastics sector was highly profitable. However, in recent years, the demand for plastics has fallen and the costs of frequent small deliveries have become insupportable: some manufacturers had been demanding three deliveries a day. Eventually, *en masse*, the petrochemicals industry association decided to tell their customers that deliveries would be limited to once a day, with additional calls available, but only if paid for by the customer. Buyers were also encouraged to take larger quantities in each order. All of which is pretty ironic, since, after all, JIT is a technique popularized by the Japanese!

Transportation

The appropriate choice of transportation mode is a key part of physical distribution management. This is especially important in markets where JIT delivery is the norm. A number of criteria should be used to select transport: costs, transit time, reliability, capability (important if goods require special handling, such as chilled temperatures), security, and traceability. Each major mode of transport has its own cost and service outcomes that must be considered by the marketing logistics manager. These are described in turn below:

Road: Road haulage has the key advantage of flexibility due to national road networks providing direct access to production facilities, warehouses, and customers. This allows lorries to transport goods from supplier to end user without unloading *en route*. The last twenty years has seen a growth in the number of dedicated contract distribution (DCD) companies such as BRS. DCD organizations now offer both road freight transportation and warehousing to customers. For example, Exel Logistics, a subsidiary of NFC, operates a DCD arrangement for Marks & Spencer to service stores across Europe from an RDC near Paris (Cooper and Johnstone 1990). An issue for users of road haulage is fleet ownership versus outsourcing, and the subsequent loss of control versus flexibility.

Rail: Railways tend to be used for carrying large, bulky freight over long distances. Goods commonly carried by trains include coal, chemicals, and building aggregates. The longer the journey, the more economically competitive rail transport becomes, as can be seen in North America. A significant problem for railways, however, is its lack of flexibility. For most companies, barring those with premises directly adjacent to rail yards, this means the transport of goods to and from rail depots via lorries. Because of this, the railway's share of the European transportation market has declined steadily. The opening of the Channel Tunnel may yet provide a boost in rail haulage's fortunes, but much will depend on the ease of use of freight terminals by customers.

Air: This is both the fastest and most expensive mode of transport. Its great speed over long distances means that it is often used to carry perishable goods and emergency deliveries. As international trade continues to grow, air freight should likewise grow in importance, especially in global JIT systems. Like rail, though, companies must still transport goods to and from air terminals. Air freight is eminently suited to valuable, relatively light goods such as fresh flowers, jewellery, and electronic components.

Water: This can be divided into sea and inland waterways, both of which are slow but fairly inexpensive. Ocean-going vessels carry a large variety of goods, for example oil from the Far East to be refined in British Petroleum's Fawley coastal terminal, or basic consumer goods to small islands like Gran Canaria. Inland water transportation, like rail, is associated with low-value, bulky commodities such as coal or steel. Its low costs mean that European rivers which are linked to canal networks, including the Rhine and the Danube, are still commonly used. How good is your geography? Which waterways in other continents offer companies the chance to exploit water transport?

Pipeline: Pipelines are a dependable and low maintenance form of transportation for liquids and gas. They normally belong to the shipper and carry the shipper's products. The downside of this transport mode is the major investment involved in the construction of the pipeline. A good example of a logistics trade-off is given by the use of pipelines in the North Sea as opposed to oil tankers.

Materials handling

This is essentially concerned with the movement of goods within the producer's factory, warehouses, and transportation depots. Due to the complexity of handling the proliferation of consumer product lines that now exists, mechanization of procedures is becoming increasingly common. In warehouses, this typically involves automatic picking equipment, mobile platforms, cranes, and conveyor belts. In some depots, such as the Bass brewery in Burton, the fork-lift truck fleet is a combination of fully automized, remote controlled vehicles and driver operated trucks. This enables certain basic picking and loading tasks to be carried on into the night shift with minimal staff running costs. The practice of combining multiple packages of, say, cans of Carling Black Label, on to pallets has facilitated these improvements.

In general, provided a company has sufficient funds for initial investment, cutting the human element in locating inventory and compiling customer orders reduces error and increases speed of operation. This was certainly the case for RS Components, which distributes an extraordinarily broad range (over 100,000 product lines) of electronic, electrical, and mechanical goods to industries worldwide. The company invested £60 million in a state-of-the-art distribution facility at Nuneaton, at the heart of the Midlands motorway network. RS Components boasts that its stock control systems and warehousing facilities are now among the most advanced in Europe. The efficiency of the company's order taking, picking, and dispatch processes means that customers' lead time is cut to an absolute minimum (*Business East Midlands Special Report* 1998).

An important development in materials handling is *containerization*. The combining of large quantities of goods into a single large container avoids the need to handle individual items during transit. Once containers are sealed, they can relatively easily be transferred from one mode of transport to another (see back to our earlier discussion of global logistics). This allows the distributor to handle the product as few times as possible, in as large a quantity as possible, and with as much automation as can be achieved. In this way, stock losses and damage are reduced.

Product *packaging* can also play a part in facilitating materials handling. Goods must be capable of withstanding regular loading and unloading, as well as stacking in manufacturers' and customers' warehouses. You will probably have noticed how some goods are displayed on supermarket shelves: often they are either still in large cardboard boxes, designed to show off their contents, or in conveniently shaped individual containers to ensure maximum use of shelf space. At the same time, as Johnson and Wood (1996) remind us, packaging must be as environmentally friendly as possible in terms of its capacity for recycling.

To conclude this section, we may observe that many of the strategies above have been neatly summarized by Anderson Consulting (Christopher 1992) into the following model for logistics planning. Fig. 15.9 suggests a number of key issues that marketing logistics managers should consider as they work their way down the 'pyramid'.

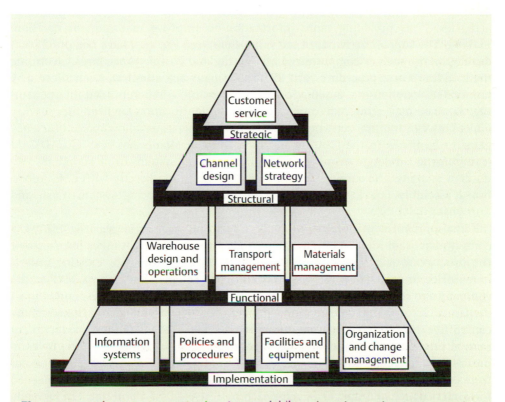

Figure 15.9 A logistics strategic planning model (based on Christopher 1992, p. 215)

Effects of IT on logistics

A CORNERSTONE of the model presented in Fig. 15.9 is the firm's Information Systems. Indeed, throughout this chapter we have seen numerous examples of the impact of Information Technology (IT) on logistics management. IT is facilitating the creation of *integrated logistics systems* that link the operations of the business, such as production and distribution, with suppliers' operations on the one hand and the customer on the other. (See back to our generic supply chain in Fig. 15.1). The use of EDI to enable computer-to-computer ordering and transaction management is becoming increasingly widespread. This section aims to provide an overview, and some further examples, of the effects of IT on marketing logistics. It is important for marketers to be aware of IT as a management tool, but this does mean having to get used to a lot of ugly acronyms!

In discussing the *value chain*, Porter (1985) gives examples of how IT is transforming both the way value activities are performed and the nature of linkages between such activities. IT is providing more information to improve management decision-making. The support activities of the value chain (see Fig. 14.2) have benefited from developments such as computerized accounting and costing procedures, electronic mail, on-line search procedures, and EDI. The primary activities have been affected by automated warehousing, automatic order processing, computer aided manufacturing, database marketing, and computerized fault identification for after-sales service. Links between internal activities and external organizations allow major efficiency gains to be made. In the USA, for instance, General Motors has tied its CAD/CAM (computer aided design/manufacture) and order entry systems to its suppliers' production systems. The suppliers' computers communicate directly with GM's robot-based assembly line in an integrated flexible manufacturing system (Cash and Konsynski 1985).

Remaining in the manufacturing context, *materials requirements planning* (MRP) is a computer-assisted method of managing production inventory. It takes into account the producer's master production schedule (MPS), sales forecasts, existing orders, inventories, and a bill of materials (BOM) listing all the necessary inputs. MRP allows companies to control production inputs carefully, yet still be able to respond to most demand-driven production situations (Johnson and Wood 1996). First, the company establishes its MPS, typically from sales forecasts, for what may be the production of several product lines simultaneously. A complex BOM is then determined by computer in order to keep track of the exact number of parts required during a particular time period. The MRP programme lists (or 'explodes') the production inputs needed for each product, and then aggregates each part needed for all products to be made during each MRP cycle. This cycle takes place several weeks prior to the actual production. At this point, the company places orders with its suppliers and delivery is scheduled just before the parts are needed for the production process.

A more recent development has been *manufacturing resource planning* (MRP II), which adds to MRP information from the firm's marketing, finance, and purchasing functions. In this way, an even more complete picture of the firm's procurement needs can be built up, and internal communications ensure that such activities as the accurate processing of customer orders and invoicing can take place under an integrated system (Hutchinson 1987). More customer focused still is *distribution requirements planning* (DRP) which also adds to MRP information by co-ordinating the warehouse inventory levels of finished goods and plans stock movement via the company's distribution channels (Fig. 15.10). Bowersox and Closs (1996) point out that

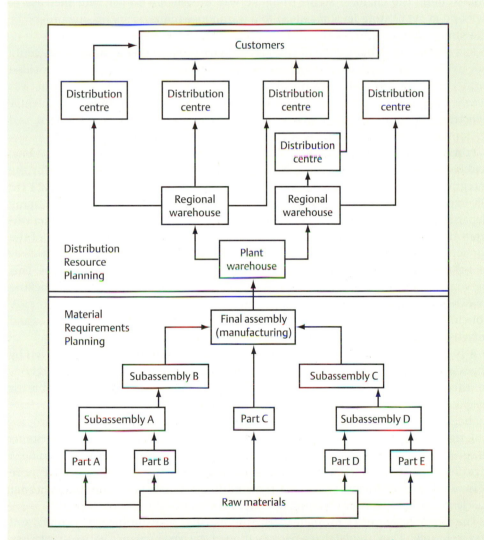

Figure 15.10 Conceptual design of integrated DRP/MRP system (based on Bowersox and Closs 1996, p. 292)

DRP is guided by customer demand whereas MRP is more of an internally driven, production-orientated system.

Sophisticated manufacturers such as Benetton attempt to combine DRP and MRP systems, although they recognize that the marketing environment can be extremely volatile and the potential for sales forecasts to be wrong is always present. Uncertainty can occur in supply chains, despite the best planning. For instance, within complex systems, an 'amplification' effect known as the 'Forrester Effect' can arise where small disturbances in one part of the system quickly become magnified as the effect spreads through the pipeline (Forrester 1961). The vague desire of managers to err on the side of caution can amplify the total demand for a product at individual points along the chain. It stems from the way in which a 10 per cent increase in demand at retail store level may lead to a warehouse manager increasing orders for the same product by 20 per cent, and so on (*Financial Times* 1997).

In a supply chain management context, we have seen that JIT arrangements could not exist without improved information flow between companies. IT has provided both the hardware and software to make this possible. In 1988 agreement was reached over a *common international 'language'* for electronic communication, EDIFACT (electronic data interchange for administration, commerce, and transport), designed to improve data exchange between otherwise incompatible systems.

Previously, a domestic language called TRADACOM (Trading Data Communications) had been promoted by the Article Number Association, a group responsible for the integrated development of barcodes (Fletcher 1994). The importance of EDIFACT for UK exports has been highlighted by Probert (1996). Traditionally, export shipping departments would produce all their instructions on paper and send them to a carrier. All this data would then have to be re-keyed into the in-house systems of the carrier in order to process the booking. These old-style paper-based systems, as well as being slow, were not designed to receive any information from external sources. This prevented the automatic processing of potentially helpful data such as cargo tracking and customs status reports. International standards like EDIFACT are proving invaluable in facilitating improved communication, and thus reductions in lead times and increases in accuracy, throughout the global distribution chain.

A highly focused example of the impact of IT on physical distribution is given by the scheduling and routing of delivery vehicles (Cooper *et al.* 1994). Manual methods for this process are laborious and relatively inefficient. However, it is now possible for *computerized vehicle routing and scheduling* (CVRS) to be used on a daily basis. Here, managers use CVRS to allocate vehicles to sets of delivery locations and build routes linking these destinations. In most cases CVRS is linked to order processing systems to speed up computation and minimize errors. Other benefits to companies include: a significant overall reduction in transport costs, greater vehicle utilization, a more responsive service to customers, and the ability to ask 'what if?' questions without carrying out an expensive operational trial.

The contribution of IT to retail marketing logistics was outlined by Schultz and Dewar in 1984. They argued that a re-evaluation of the *power* balance between retailers and manufacturers was needed. This was due to computer systems and barcodes on products which allowed retailers to track inventory and to have reliable information upon which to base their demands to suppliers. Our discussion of retailer power in Chapter 14 shows this prediction to have been right. IT enables retailers to conduct *direct product profitability* (DPP—see ahead) analysis of individual items, through the use of Electronic Point of Sale (EPOS) scanning data. DPP is an application of logistics cost analysis which recognizes that, for many transactions, the customer (in this case, the retailer) will incur costs other than the immediate purchase price of the product. Through the use of IT, DPP attempts to identify all the costs that are attached to a product or an order as it moves through the distribution channel (Christopher 1992). Thus, after the gross margin has been calculated, costs such as warehousing, transportation, retail space allocation, and stocking labour are subtracted to give the product's net profit contribution to the retailer. It is in the supplier's interest to determine how they might lower the cost element to the retailer by, say, redesigning a product's packaging, and thus influencing the retailer's purchase decision more favourably. Because shelf space is often a limiting factor, the key performance measure becomes DPP per square metre. Some typical examples of average DPP/square metre include: rice = 0.24; ice-cream = 0.99; cigarettes = 6.56. Why do you think there are such large variations between products?

There have been a whole series of major *technological innovations in grocery retailing*. These are summarized chronologically by Keh and Park (1997):

1970s information processing, product handling and display, temperature control;
1980s electronic tills, barcodes, scanner systems (EPOS), database management, EDI;
1990s consumer scanning, data warehousing, computer assisted ordering (CAO), continuous replenishment (CRP), category management, direct store delivery, cross-docking.

In order to illustrate some of these changes, Keh and Park (1997) discuss the ECR initiative (see also Chapter 14) in detail. They state that *EDI* is central to ECR. EDI enables data transfer both internally, typically from terminal to computer (e.g. till to store stock control system), and externally with the integration of two or more independent systems (e.g. retailer's warehouse to supplier's factory). By reducing transaction costs and providing higher levels of service, the implementation of an EDI link reflects a significant commitment to the relationship between distribution channel members. *CRP* works in the following way: the manufacturer supplies the retailer with goods based directly on warehouse shipment and inventory data rather than waiting for the retailer's purchase orders. The manufacturer then determines the order quantity needed, compiles the delivery, and informs the retailer electronically of the impending shipment, which usually takes place the next day. Procter & Gamble, for example, supply over 30 per cent of their US sales volume via CRP. The use of *CAO* can reduce the amount of time a salesperson spends in store taking orders. This is due to item-by-item sales forecasting, mathematically extrapolated from historical sales data, by CAO systems which enable stores to be replenished under JIT conditions using information from the cash tills.

It should be noted, however, that the start-up costs of ECR are high, and not every grocery chain is rushing to implement the system. The careful planning of the introduction of information systems for retailers is also crucial. For instance, Burden and

Proctor (1997) describe how a DIY retailer encountered difficulties in system capacity. After implementation, the entire system was prone to 'crashing', thus making it impossible to place stock orders, receive stock, or enter sales leads for hours at a time! Have you ever been frustrated by a store's systems failures when attempting to make a purchase? What was the ultimate cost to the retailer concerned?

In his examination of IT in marketing, Fletcher (1994) concludes that a sweeping reorganization of work practices is needed for companies to gain full advantage from IT. In an argument that should be familiar, he believes that this means breaking down old functional barriers and redeploying workers in new multidisciplinary ways (see also Chapter 21). This should be possible, Fletcher claims, because of the capacity of IT to provide front-line staff with the knowledge they need to act quickly and effectively via user-friendly software, hand-held terminals, and distributed information systems. This view is echoed by Gummesson (1987) who points out the interfunctional dependency of different parts of the company, including marketing. In effect, he argues that marketing's links with research and development (R&D), manufacturing, and purchasing, as well as with distribution and the sales force, mean that the marketing function is spread throughout the firm. Everyone becomes what he calls a '*part-time marketer*'. What do you think? Does this represent the ultimate in marketing orientation?

Finally, here is some further food for thought. We saw in Chapter 14 that there are many other exciting new avenues for channel intermediaries to explore using the opportunities presented by IT. These included the Internet, database marketing (see also Chapter 20), and even 'infomediaries'. An even more intriguing scenario is that of the '*virtual organization*'. Bowersox and Closs (1996) suggest that formal company structures could one day be replaced with an informal electronic network. In other words, a virtual organization would exist as a provider of integrated performance, but not as an identifiable business unit. In the case of logistics, key teams might be electronically linked to perform critical activities in an integrated fashion. 'Transparent' logistics organizations of the future would be characterized by functional disaggregation in an attempt to concentrate on work flow. Work teams could share common information regarding customer requirements and performance measures while retaining local control to achieve a high level of logistical core competency. This is essentially a form of 'electronic keiretsu' (the keiretsu is a Japanese term for a loosely affiliated group of firms that share common practices and are committed to co-operation). The fact that companies could join forces to achieve common goals and then disband presents significant challenges for the management of partnerships. The jury is still out on whether the virtual firm will become a realistic logistics proposition . . .

Chapter summary and key linkages to other chapters

Marketing managers must be aware of the key issues of supply chain management. They need to recognize the contribution that 'upstream' and 'downstream' channel activities can make to a company's competitive advantage. Logistics is concerned with co-ordinating the flow of goods from suppliers to the manufacturer, through the production process, and on to the customer. In other words, it considers both 'inbound' and 'outbound' logistics (or physical distribution management), as well as the handling of inventory within companies. The overall aim of marketing logistics management is to provide customer value through service which, for many customers (both consumers and commercial) comprises the key elements of availability and timeliness. There have been numerous developments in physical distribution and logistics in the last few decades, most of which have been facilitated by advances in IT.

There are several other chapters in this book which relate to the logistics issues raised in this chapter:

Chapter 1: What is marketing?: Customer needs, in terms of high levels of product availability and shorter lead times, must be met by any organization which claims to be marketing orientated.

Chapter 2: The marketing environment: The massive impact of IT on logistics and physical distribution management. The need for marketing to develop closer relationships with other internal company functions.

Chapter 3: Segmentation and targeting: The segmenting of markets by their service-level requirements and profitability.

Chapter 5: Marketing and ethics: The treatment of so-called third world suppliers should be carefully considered. Also important are societal concerns over recyclable packaging.

Chapter 6: Marketing research: The importance of research to establish customer service requirements.

Chapter 7: Buyer behaviour: It is especially important for marketing logistics managers to understand how commercial customers buy. Business-to-business marketing must address the needs of industrial purchasing managers.

Chapter 8: Buyer–seller relationships development: A fundamental part of supply chain management is the building of close relations with organizational participants, both upstream and downstream from the producer.

Chapter 9: Developing a product portfolio: Product packaging decisions must result in goods being protected and, where relevant, being promoted to the customer, yet should limit harm to the environment.

Chapter 10: Innovation and NPD: The cutting of logistics lead times can be crucial to successful product launches.

Chapter 11: Developing a sustainable competitive advantage: Considerations beyond product and brand value are now necessary for companies to succeed. Product availability is often vital.

Chapters 12/13: Pricing theory and application: The need for logistics managers to balance costs with price/service levels, i.e. trade-offs, as well as the need to control inventory costs. Also, accounting procedures such as DPP calculations.

Chapter 14: Channel intermediaries: The role of intermediaries in the downstream part of the supply chain. The impact of retailer power and the ECR initiative on logistics practices.

Chapters 16–19: Promotion strategy: Promotion may stress the ready availability of a company's products. The company must ensure that it can deliver what its promotion promises. Sales promotion activities may have the effect of creating peaks in demand which a company's distribution system must be able to handle.

Chapter 20: Direct Marketing: This extends the supply chain directly to consumers' front doors. Modern direct marketing relies heavily on the developments in information technology discussed in this chapter.

Chapter 21: Managing the marketing effort: The contemporary debate over functional v. process based organizations. The possible emergence of informal 'virtual organizations'.

Chapter 22: Services Marketing: Providing availability of goods is essentially a service-based activity. Many specialist service companies exist to handle distribution on behalf of manufacturers and retailers.

Chapter 23: Global marketing: How firms operating globally should plan their logistics flows to overcome the many challenges that international markets present.

Case study

The distribution of food products in Zimbabwe: not such a 'dark continent'?

In a landmark article in 1962, the 'management guru' Peter Drucker claimed that physical distribution was the US economy's 'dark continent'. He said, 'We know little more about distribution today than Napoleon's contemporaries knew about the interior of Africa. We know it is there, and we know it is big; and that's about all.' The thirty plus years that have passed since Drucker threw down the gauntlet for companies to embrace logistics management have clearly seen massive advances in efficiency and effectiveness in North American and European markets. What about the actual continent that formed the thrust of Drucker's famous metaphor, however? Are professional logistics practices still a 'dark continent' to physical distribution managers based in Africa itself?

The Southern African state of Zimbabwe presents its businesses with many commercial challenges. The country is moving rapidly towards privatization with formerly state-run 'parastatals' struggling to keep pace in the new private-sector economy. Such a parastatal is the Cold Storage Company (CSC), a registered limited company wholly owned by the government of Zimbabwe. The company was established to procure, process, and market beef and related products. Historically, the CSC enjoyed a monopoly as the main slaughterer and distributor of meat to the domestic and export markets, but plans are now underway to privatize the company. The recent commercialization of the market-place has meant managers having to cope with the change from being production led to market driven. The CSC now competes with private abattoirs in the domestic market, as well as leading beef-producing countries on the international scene such as the USA and Argentina.

The CSC operates abattoirs and cold stores in four major towns and in the nation's second largest city, Bulawayo; plus three additional cold stores and distribution depots in other towns, including the capital, Harare. Four of the company's five abattoirs are widely acclaimed as modern plants using state-of-the-art technology, the exception being the facility in Kadoma. These abattoirs effectively function as factories with a total capacity to slaughter and process 600,000 head of cattle per year. The plants must meet stringent veterinary and export requirements: a significant proportion of the CSC's turnover is derived from sales to the EU. The CSC sells mainly carcass beef and offals, either chilled or frozen. The beef may be sold as a whole side, a quarter, or in specific small cuts. Beef products are graded by quality as Super, Choice, Commercial, Economy, or Manufacturing. The company also sells canned products such as corned beef and stewed beef under the Meadows and Texan brands. More recently, the CSC has introduced some value-added products in the form of pre-packed fresh beef to aid presentation by its retail customers.

The typical supply chain for beef in Zimbabwe begins 'upstream' with stock feed companies supplying foodstuffs to farmers, who raise the herds of cattle. Fully grown animals are dispatched by cattle transporters to meat processing plants like those run by the CSC. From there, the meat must go into cold storage before chilled distribution 'downstream' to the customer. Customers may be private-sector organizations in the hotel and catering trade or in the food manufacturing sector. They may also be retail butchers. Other customers include hospitals, exporters, and some domestic consumers. The number of suppliers of slaughtered beef stock in Zimbabwe has risen dramatically over the last ten years from fifteen to over 200. Competition has focused on issues of price, product quality, regularity of supply, and provision of credit terms. As a result, the CSC has lost market share from 88 per cent in 1986 to 45 per cent in 1996. Conversely, the position of the cattle farmers has remained strong. This is due partly to the erratic supply of cattle in comparison with the high demand from the numerous abattoir operators in Zimbabwe, and partly thanks to the organization of powerful lobby groups amongst farmers like the Cattle Producers Association.

At present, the CSC attempts to source its cattle from company-owned ranches as well as from stock purchased by CSC buyers, typically in 'one-off' transactions, from cattle farmers. There is some debate within the company whether the CSC should concentrate solely on its core business competence of meat processing and shed its ranches. The company is considering entering into long-term contractual agreements with farmers, and aiming to build relationships by offering them consultancy services on 'finishing' cattle to specific slaughter requirements. Payment of suppliers is also being improved by the CSC's investment in a new computerized information system. Unfortunately, the company's chaotic distribution arrangements often mean that its prompt producer payments are being made for unsold beef still in its coldrooms, using borrowed funds. The CSC's transport division had at one stage been a full service centre whose costs were apportioned to the CSC depots and ranches. In recent years an attempt was made to rationalize operations by gradually outsourcing transport services. By 1997, however, these arrangements were perceived as being unworkable. Customers were increasingly demanding close-to-JIT service, and serious complaints were arising about carriers who consistently failed to meet delivery schedules. Market research revealed that customers were happy with CSC's product quality, largely a result of the company's excellent cold storage facilities, but dissatisfied with availability, responsiveness, and reliability.

Comparisons are being drawn by CSC senior management with another parastatal, the Dairiboard Zimbabwe Limited (DZL). This organization was privatized in 1997 but is already fast becoming a commercial success. DZL produces no milk of its own. Instead it buys its supplies from numerous vendors across the country, using competition amongst suppliers to drive prices down. Although this increases profit margins, it can affect product quality. Despite the company's relatively strong growth, managers acknowledge there is still work to be done. A further problem for DZL is the need for the company to carry large buffer stocks of dairy products due to the inconsistency of supply of vital items such as packaging materials. Since interest rates in Zimbabwe are currently extremely high, this inventory represents a large cost to DZL. Internally, there are barriers between functional areas: because there is no co-ordination between marketing and procurement departments, DZL ultimately writes off considerable volumes of obsolescent stock. More positively, managers have made huge cost savings in the area of distribution. The company took the decision to franchise their thirty distribution depots, thus saving on payroll and local delivery costs, and lowering warehouse inventory levels, yet gaining improvements in customer service levels due to the increased commitment of local franchisees. Despite this, managers are conscious that there is no formal customer service policy within DZL itself, and no attempt made to service the differing needs of the company's market segments. These include high density population areas, low density, and rural areas. All areas are targeted with equal resources and thus service overkill often results.

It seems that there is a high level of professional awareness among marketing logistics managers in Zimbabwe, at least within the CSC and DZL. It is clear that the major political and economic changes affecting this formerly tightly controlled market have resulted in considerable problems for each company to overcome. Yet, in recognizing the many shortcomings in the logistics practices evident in the supply chains for both beef and dairy products, managers are gradually coming to grips with the challenges that face them. Physical distribution is certainly no longer a 'dark continent' for Zimbabwe's parastatal food manufacturers. Who knows what improvements we will see as privatization becomes firmly established?

Sources: Drucker 1962, Hakutangwi 1998, Pakai 1998.

Case study review questions

1 Use a flow chart to illustrate the different supply chains that exist for meat products originating in Zimbabwe.

2 What problems does the CSC face in attempting to manage the various participants in its supply chains?

3 What specific physical distribution issues are of the greatest significance in this market-place, for both beef and dairy products? How could the use of IT help to overcome some of the logistics dilemmas you have identified?

Chapter review questions

1 Explain the difference between logistics and physical distribution management.

2 Describe some of the elements of customer service in logistics. Give examples of product sectors where each might be especially relevant.

3 Explain what is meant by trading information for inventory. Outline another typical trade-off in logistics management.

4 Contrast JIT inventory management with conventional reorder methods. Do you think the adoption of JIT techniques is viable for every sector? Where might it not be so relevant?

5 Compare the benefits and disadvantages of using road haulage and air transport to a manufacturer of valuable machine parts.

6 Giving examples from both the manufacturing and retailing sectors, discuss the effects of EDI on logistics and physical distribution management.

References

Bower, J. L., and Hout, T. M. (1988), 'Fast-Cycle Capability for Competitive Power', *Harvard Business Review*, Nov./Dec.

Bowersox, D. J., and Closs, D. J. (1996), *Logistical Management: The Integrated Supply Chain Process* (New York: McGraw-Hill).

Burden, R., and Proctor, T. (1997), 'Information System Development in Retailing', *Marketing Intelligence & Planning*, **15**, 2, pp. 106–11.

Business East Midlands (1998), *Special Report: RS Components*, May.

Cash, J., and Konsynski, B. (1985), 'I.S. Redraws Competitive Boundaries', *Harvard Business Review*, Mar./Apr., pp. 134–42.

Christopher, M. (1992), *Logistics and Supply Chain Management* (London: Pitman).

—— Payne, A., and Ballantyne, D. (1991), *Relationship Marketing* (Oxford: Butterworth-Heinemann).

Cooper, J., and Johnstone, M. (1990), 'Dedicated Contract Distribution: An Assessment of the UK Marketplace', *International Journal of Physical Distribution & Logistics Management*, **20**, 1.

—— O'Laughlin, K., and Kresge, J. (1992), 'The Challenge of Change: Logistics in the New Europe', *International Journal of Logistics Management*, **3**, 2.

—— Browne, M., and Peters, M. (1994), *European Logistics*, 2nd edn. (Oxford: Blackwell).

Derby Evening Telegraph (1997), 'Teletubby Mania', 30 Oct., p. 1.

Doyle, P. (1998), *Marketing Management and Strategy*, 2nd edn. (London: Prentice Hall).

Drucker, P. (1962), *The Economy's Dark Continent, Fortune*, Apr., p. 103.

Fernie, J. (1997), 'Retail Change & Retail Logistics in the UK: Past Trends & Future Prospects', *Service Industries Journal*, **17**, 3, pp. 383–96.

Financial Times (1994), 'Just in Time now Just Too Much', 14 Jan., p. 20.

—— (1997), 'Supply and Over-Demand', 10 Dec., p. 18.

Fletcher, K. (1994), 'The Evolution and Use of IT in Marketing', in M. Baker (ed.), *The Marketing Book*, 3rd edn. (Oxford: Butterworth-Heinemann), pp. 333–57.

Forrester, J. (1961), *Industrial Dynamics* (Cambridge, Mass.: MIT Press).

Fortune (1991), 'The Bureaucracy Busters', 17 June.

Guardian (1995), 'Body Shop adds to Social Audit Team', 20 Jan., p. 16.

Gummesson, E. (1987), 'The New Marketing—Developing Long-Term Interactive Relationships', *Long Range Planning*, **20**, 4, pp. 10–20.

Hakutangwi, V. (1998), *Logistics Management in Dairiboard Zimbabwe Limited*, unpublished MA diss., University of Derby.

Handfield, R. B., and Nichols, E. L. (1999), *Introduction to Supply Chain Management* (Englewood Cliffs, NJ: Prentice Hall).

Hutchinson, N. E. (1987), *An Integrated Approach to Logistics Management* (Englewood Cliffs, NJ: Prentice Hall).

Isaac, G. A. (1985), *Creating a Competitive Advantage Through Implementing Just-in-time Logistics Strategies*, Touche Ross Series (Chicago: Touche Ross).

Johnson J., and Wood, D. (1996), *Contemporary Transportation*, 5th end. (Englewood Cliffs, NJ: Prentice Hall).

Keh, H. T., and Park, S. Y. (1997), 'To Market, to market: The Changing Face of Grocery Retailing', *Long Range Planning*, **30**, 6, pp. 836–46.

LaLonde, B. J., and Zinszer, P. H. (1976), *Customer Service: Meaning and Measurement* (Chicago: National Council of Physical Distribution Management).

National Economic Development Council (1991), *The Experience of Nissan Suppliers* (London: National Economic Development Office).

Pakai, D. (1998), *Logistics Management in The Cold Storage Company*, unpublished MA diss., University of Derby.

Palmer, A. (1998), *Principles of Service Marketing*, 2nd edn. (London: McGraw-Hill).

Peck, H., and Christopher, M. (1994), 'Laura Ashley: The Logistics Challenge', in P. McGoldrick (ed.), *Cases in Retail Management* (London: Pitman).

Piercy, N. (1997), *Market-Led Strategic Change*, 2nd edn. (Oxford: Butterworth-Heinemann).

Ploos van Amstel, M. J. (1990), '*Managing the Pipeline Effectively* ', *Journal of Business Logistics*, **11**, 1.

Porter, M. E. (1985), *Competitive Advantage* (New York: The Free Press).

Probert, S. (1996), 'The Importance of Electronic Commerce and Modern Logistics Systems to the Competitiveness of UK Exports', in *Institute of Export Handbook*, 1996 edn. (London: Institute of Export).

Purchasing (1985), 'Xerox Preaches the Gospel of Just-in-Time to Suppliers', 24 Oct., pp. 21–2.

Reichheld, F., and Sasser, E. (1990), 'Zero Defections: Quality Comes to Services', *Harvard Business Review*, Sept./Oct.

Saunders, M. (1997), *Strategic Purchasing & Supply Chain Management*, 2nd edn. (London: Pitman).

Schultz, D. E., and Dewar, R. D. (1984), 'Technological Challenge to Marketing Management', *Business Marketing USA*, Mar., pp. 30–41.

Spekman, R. E. (1988), 'Strategic Supplier Selection: Understanding Long-Term Buyer Relationships', *Business Horizons*, July–Aug., pp. 75–81.

Stalk, G. and Hout, T. (1990), *Competing Against Time* (New York: The Free Press).

Stevens, G. C. (1989), 'Integrating the Supply Chain', *International Journal of Physical Distribution and Materials Management*, **19**, 8.

Stewart, T. A. (1992), 'The Search for the Organisation of Tomorrow', *Fortune*, May.

Supply Chain Management Casebook (1996), (London: Hobsons Publishing).

Whysall, P. (1995), 'Ethics in Retailing', *Business Ethics: A European Review*, **4**, 3, pp. 150–56.

Suggested further reading

For a discussion of the general principles of logistics and physical distribution management, the following provide an extended coverage of the issues raised in this chapter:

- Bowersox, D. J., and Closs, D. J. (1996), *Logistical Management: The Integrated Supply Chain Process* (New York: McGraw-Hill).

- Christopher, M. (1992), *Logistics and Supply Chain Management* (London: Pitman).

- —— (ed.) (1992), *Logistics: The Strategic Issues* (London: Chapman & Hall).

- Handfield, R. B., and Nichols, E. L. (1999), *Introduction to Supply Chain Management* (Englewood Cliffs, NJ: Prentice Hall).

- Johnson, J., and Wood, D. (1996), *Contemporary Transportation*, 5th edn. (Englewood Cliffs, NJ: Prentice Hall).

- Ploos van Amstel, M. J. (1990), 'Managing the Pipeline Effectively', *Journal of Business Logistics*, **11**, 1.

- Saunders, M. (1997), *Strategic Purchasing & Supply Chain Management*, 2nd edn. (London: Pitman).

- *The Supply Chain Management Casebook* (1996) (London: Hobsons Publishing).

  The subject of just-in-time management of supply chain relationships is covered in more detail in the following:

- Isaac, G. A. (1985), *Creating a Competitive Advantage Through Implementing Just-in-time Logistics Strategies*, Touche Ross Series (Chicago: Touche Ross).

- Oliver, N., and Wilkinson, B. (1988), *The Japanisation of British Industry?*, 2nd edn. (Oxford: Blackwell).

  The more general issue of supply chain relationships is explored in the following:

- Campbell, A. (1997), 'Buyer–Supplier Partnerships: Flip Sides of the Same Coin?' *Journal of Business & Industrial Marketing*, **12**, 6, pp. 417–34.

- Ford, D., Gadde, L., Hakansson, H., Lundgren, A., Snehota, I., Turnbull, P., and Wilson, D. (1998), *Managing Business Relationships* (Chichester: John Wiley).

  The crucial role played by IT in developing supply chains is discussed in the following:

- Cunningham, C., and Tynan, C. (1993), 'Electronic Trading, Inter-organisational Systems and the Nature of Buyer–Seller Relationships: The Need for a Network Perspective', *International Journal of Information Management*, **13**, pp. 3–28.

- Olsen, R. F., and Ellram, L. M. (1997), 'Buyer–Supplier Relationships: Alternative Research Approaches', *European Journal of Purchasing & Supply Management*, **3**, 4, pp. 221–31.

- Probert, S. (1996), 'The Importance of Electronic Commerce and Modern Logistics Systems to the Competitiveness of UK Exports', in *Institute of Export Handbook* 1996 edn. (London: Institute of Export).

  For a review of the internal issues concerning flexible supply chain management, the following are useful:

- Gummesson, E. (1987), 'The New Marketing—Developing Long-Term Interactive Relationships', *Long Range Planning*, **20**, 4, pp. 10–20.

- Storey, J. (ed.) (1994), *New Wave Manufacturing Strategies: Organisational and Human Resource Management Dimensions* (London: Chapman).

Useful Web Links

Institute of Export: http://www.export.org.uk
Institute of Purchasing and Supply: http://www.cips.org
Southern Center for Logistics and Intermodal Transportation
Georgia: http://www2.gasou.edu/coba/centers/lit /
Tibbett & Britten Group (transport, distribution, and logistics services): http://www.tbg.co.uk/intro.htm
Discussion group for all aspects of purchasing and supply chain management: http://www.mailbase.ac.uk/lists/purchasing-supply-chain
A forum for the exchange of research ideas, developments, and findings in the fields of logistics and supply chain management, established by UK academics in conjunction with the Institute of Logistics: http:// www.mailbase.ac.uk/lists/logistics-research-network/

Chapter 16
Principles of Promotion Planning

Chapter objectives

It is sometimes said that a well designed product, appropriately priced and distributed, should require little or no promotion. Instead, customers should be queuing to buy it. Some new products find themselves in the fortunate position of a seller's market and their producers can sell all they can produce without need for promotion. But the reality of most markets is fierce competition between suppliers in which each supplier has to communicate to potential buyers the unique benefits of buying its products rather than the competitor's. This chapter aims to develop an understanding of promotion planning as an integral part of the marketing and business planning process. It then discusses the key stages of the promotion planning process, the range and variety of promotional techniques, basic models of communication, and how promotional activity can be monitored. This chapter concentrates on general principles and subsequent chapters will focus on specific techniques of promotion.

The role of promotion planning as an integral part of the marketing and business planning process

As consumers we are surrounded and constantly bombarded by marketing communications stimuli. These stimuli reach us as a result of organizations implementing a range of promotional activity via advertising, sales promotion, public relations, selling, and direct marketing, delivered through a variety of different channels and media. Alongside such activity, other elements of the marketing mix are also communicating to us. These include aspects of the product, pricing, distribution, and the quality of service we experience.

It is difficult as consumers to identify how such a complexity of activity might form part of a cohesive marketing and business plan. While we commonly become aware of or act upon an advertisement or sales promotion, we may not be aware of how such activity forms part of a more comprehensive and increasingly integrated programme of business and marketing activity.

To understand fully the role of promotion planning, it is necessary to see it within the context of an organization's overall business and marketing plan, and in particular its objectives and strategy. Promotions activity should occur towards the end of the business and marketing planning process and should not be seen as a stand-alone series of activities which bear little relation to the organization's goals, purpose, and markets.

At its most basic, promotions planning can be visualized as a top down process. Fig. 16.1 shows such a process. Promotion should be seen as one element of the business and marketing planning cycle, with the aim of ensuring that:

- the messages being communicated are consistent with an organization's corporate and marketing activity;
- promotions activity supports and adds synergy to the overall business and marketing strategy;
- consumers hear 'one voice' and not a range of disparate messages and behaviour.

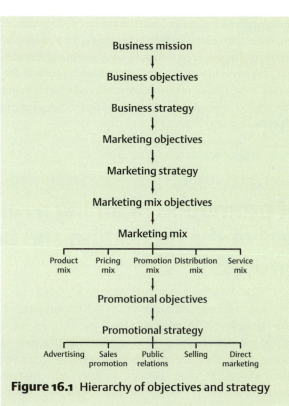

Figure 16.1 Hierarchy of objectives and strategy

Market segmentation, targeting, and positioning

MARKET segmentation, targeting, and positioning has already been discussed in detail in Chapter 3. Brief mention again of this topic here is essential when considering the principles of promotion planning, particularly with regard to the issues surrounding its application. A fundamental principle that underlies most promotional activity is that the communication should be designed and placed to reach a specific type of audience. This audience is defined as a market segment. A market segment is any group of people who exhibit similar needs or demographic, social, psychological, or behavioural characteristics that will enable them to be targeted with a distinct marketing mix. Effective market segmentation presents marketers with a significant challenge. This can be demonstrated by considering the value of the traditional consumer market segmentation variables of demographics and socio-economic grade against more recent variables such as psychographics and behavioural segmentation techniques.

Demographic and socio-economic variables provide the marketer with national data that can be statistically analysed, and can indicate trends or size of segments. Such data can, however, only provide a broad stereotype profile of a market segment when explaining behaviour and does not in itself closely reflect individual consumers' needs. Saga holidays, for example, targets the over-55 age group BC1s with their holiday brochures. Not all over-55 BC1s are, however, targeted by Saga. The company overlays behavioural data against demographic data and specifically targets those over 55s with high disposable income who still wish to lead an active and social lifestyle. Such a holiday would not appeal to all over 55s. The target audience is reached through selected media, in particular magazines which appeal to the audience's lifestyles.

While the overlaying of behavioural data on to demographic and socio-economic data provides the marketer with a richer insight into a target audience's needs, such behavioural data are not provided in the same quantified format. Data collection is based on smaller samples and cannot be analysed with the same statistical rigour. A broader and clearer picture of the market's behaviour is obtained but targeting becomes harder as the market segments become fuzzier. A trade-off has to be made between hard quantifiable data that generally do not represent the diversity of individuals behaviour or needs and qualitative data that more closely represent behaviour but are harder to quantify and target.

Geodemographic data provide a relatively sophisticated method of aggregating quantitative data. Data are initially gathered from the national census and overlaid with other statistics such as financial records and purchase histories. In principle, geodemographics suggest that your buying behaviour is influenced by where you live. The providers of such data classify the country into household types. These

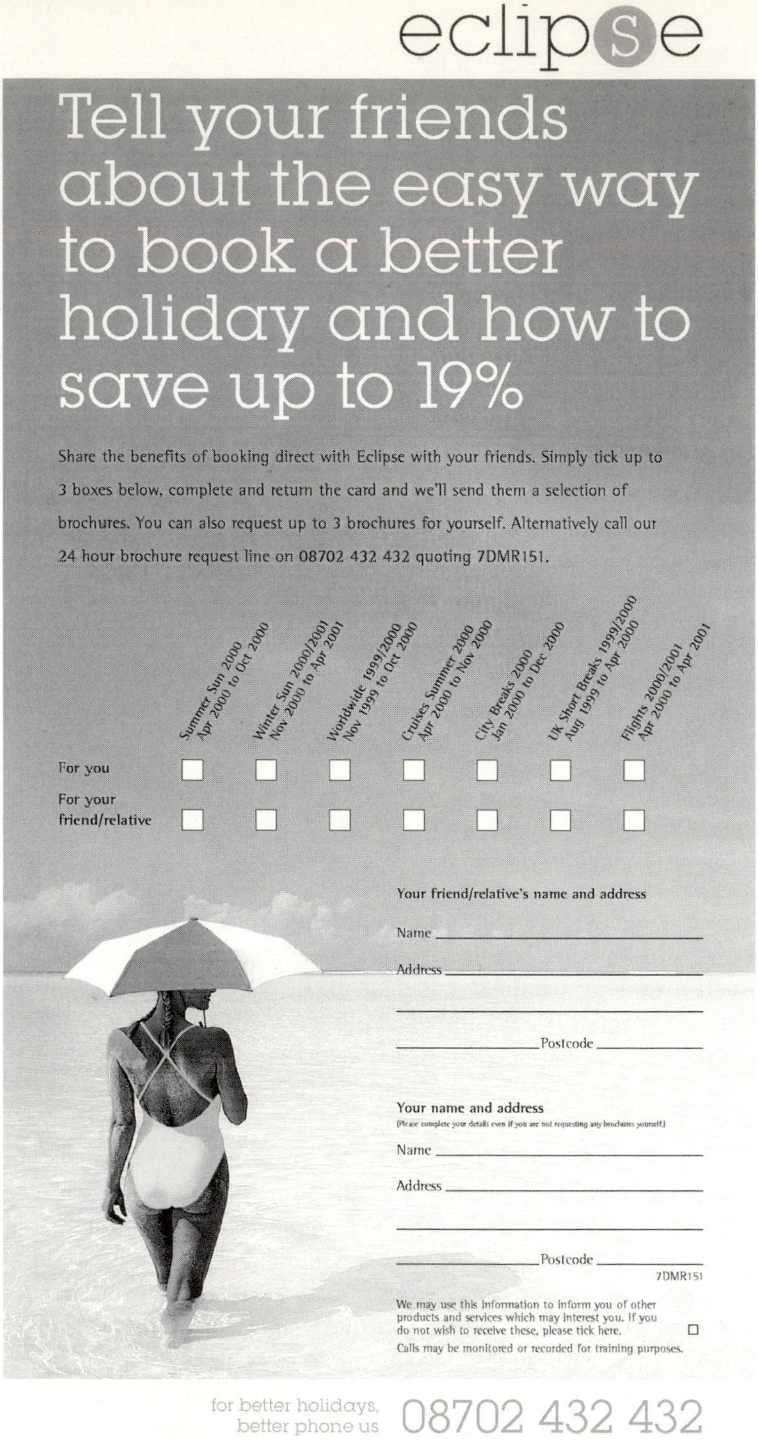

Figure 16.2 It should never be forgotten that the most powerful form of promotion is word-of-mouth recommendation. Companies go to great lengths to encourage their satisfied customers to recommend them to friends. Eclipse Holidays tries to make it easy for customers to recommend them to a friend by providing this reply-paid brochure request form. (Reproduced with permission of Eclipse Holidays Ltd.)

household types are then described in terms of life stage and socio-economic status, alongside specific behavioural and lifestyle information. Although it is increasingly being used by marketers, geodemographics is still flawed. Its primary weakness lies in its lack of individuality and therefore targeting and responses can be varied. Attempts are being made to overlay lifestyle data with geodemographic data to provide richer insights. Such techniques are in their early phase of development and are heavily reliant upon the degree of rigour in the lifestyle information provided. Such issues make the marketer's job of understanding and segmenting markets as much an art as a science. In Chapter 20 you will be introduced to the techniques of direct marketing where some of the more advanced principles, techniques, and applications of market segmentation and targeting will be explored in further detail.

In business-to-business markets, segmentation criteria have traditionally been based upon aggregate data such as regional location, size of organization, or Standard Industrial Classifications (SIC codes). Increasingly however more qualitative data are used to identify organizations' behaviour or situations. These include such variables as the complexity of the decision-making unit, and an understanding of an individual organization's economic situation or benefits being sought. Generally, business-to-business markets are easier to target because of the smaller number of buying units involved, but more complex to understand and reach, particularly where the decision-making unit is complex.

In both consumer and business-to-business markets the challenge for marketers is to classify market segments accurately. This is increasingly being done using state-of-the-art technology to manipulate quantitative and qualitative data. The accuracy of such market information is critical for effective promotions management, specifically with regard to effective use of resources and maximizing responses. The media industry has traditionally been provided with a wealth of market research data such as the Target Group Index which mixes product usage data with demographic, socio-economic, and attitudinal data. The Broadcasters Audience Research Board (BARB) uses a panel of households to monitor television viewing data and National Readership Surveys (NRS) provides data on newspaper and magazine readership. Alongside these data advertising agencies and market research organizations conduct their own detailed research to provide better insights into the identification of appropriate market segmentation variables.

Once the potential market segments have been identified and target segments selected, the marketer will need to determine the positioning of the product or service in the market-place and in the minds of the consumer. It is not feasible to develop promotional plans until a clear understanding of the product positioning has been determined.

Positioning was discussed in Chapter 11, but in view of its importance to promotional planning, a brief overview is provided here. Positioning can be tangible, based upon such criteria as size, taste, quality, and price, or intangible based upon brand image, perceptions, and value. Positioning on tangible factors will require a focus upon product and service design. For the consumer, however, it is often the intangible factors that have a significant influence on their attitudes and purchase decision. Effective management of marketing communications can enable the

Figure 16.3 The language used in an advertisement must be in a form which is easily understood by the target market. Compare these two styles of language. Would the advertisement for a nightclub have much effect on a target market of young people? And would the elderly market segment being targeted in the advert for bifocal glasses be alienated by this use of language?

marketer to position a product or service in the consumer's mind through providing a clear brand proposition that differentiates the offer from competitive products. A principal positioning tool in the marketers toolkit is the utilization of the promotional mix, in particular advertising and public relations.

The Co-operative Bank Case Study (at the end of this chapter) demonstrates the importance of market segmentation, targeting and positioning as a key process within promotion planning. Through a clear understanding of its customer base, the bank was able to deliver a relevant and distinctive message that gained immediate approval from those it targeted. These creative and media strategies were developed to gain maximum effectiveness and impact. Without such a clear understanding of the market segment, campaign effectiveness would have been significantly diminished.

One significant launch in recent years that appears to have broken all the principles of market segmentation is the UK national lottery which has gained wide market appeal with a singular message. For the majority of products and services such a situation is unlikely to occur. The trend is in fact towards increasing fragmentation of markets, while at the same time there is a burgeoning of media availability and choice. Such fragmentation of both markets and media availability confirms the need for increased sophistication of market segmentation and targeting techniques within the promotion planning process.

Other key audiences of promotional planning

It should be remembered that promotion is not always aimed solely at customers or their immediate decision-making unit. Other key audiences alongside the specific target customers should also be clearly identified in terms of their role, influence, and importance in the market-place. These 'interest' groups are commonly referred to as stakeholders. They include the following:

Supply Chain/Market-place
   Suppliers
   Distributors/agents
   Partner organizations
   Competitors

Political/Financial
   Local authorities
   Governments and international bodies
   Financial institutions

Interest Groups
   Pressure Groups
   Employees
   Trade unions

Local community
The media
Opinion leaders

Each group at varying times can have a significant influence upon the organization in terms of its overall effectiveness, efficiency, and image. It is often necessary to strike a balance between the goals of the organization and these key groups. Communication is a vital link between the organization and its key stakeholders. Public relations is the primary tool used for communicating with such stakeholders and is discussed further in Chapter 19.

Introducing the promotional mix

THE promotional mix includes all activities related to advertising, sales promotion, selling, public relations, and direct marketing. Within each of these five categories a further range of options can be identified that can be utilized within the promotional plan. Fig. 16.4 outlines some of the key elements of the promotional mix.

The following section briefly defines the scope of the main elements of the promotion mix. Further discussion will follow in subsequent chapters.

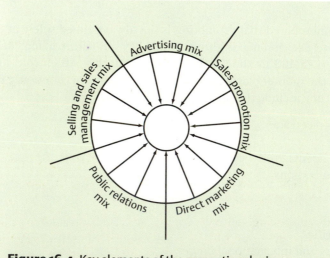

Figure 16.4 Key elements of the promotional mix

Advertising

This is defined as '*any paid form of non-personal communication of ideas goods or services delivered through selected media channels*'.

This definition provides a succinct statement of advertising which encompasses the running of adverts on prime-time television through to placing a postcard in a newsagent's window. The term media simply refers to where the advert is placed. In addition to television and newspapers, a hot air balloon with an advertising message or football hoarding seen at stadiums are all different forms of media. The selection of media is critical. In an ideal world a specific advertisement would be seen and read by all of its intended target audience. In reality such coverage is difficult to achieve. Different media are therefore selected to increase the probability of a member of the target audience seeing the advert at least once. The combination of types of media used for this purpose is often referred to as the media mix.

Advertising is defined as non-personal. Advertisements are targeted at a mass audience and not to a named individual. One of the benefits of advertising is its ability to reach a large number of people at relatively low cost. That is not to say that advertising costs are low. If an advertiser wishes to reach a prime-time television audience or place a full-page advert in a high quality magazine or newspaper then the costs will range from tens of thousands of pounds to hundreds of thousands of pounds just for one spot or insertion. The relatively low cost is when we consider the cost per 1,000. With large audiences or readerships the cost of an advertisement per 1,000 viewers or readers can often fall to less than 10p.

The decision whether to advertise or not to advertise will be determined by an organization's market situation and its objectives. In Chapter 17 we will be looking in more detail at the development of advertising strategy and its implementation.

Sales promotion

The Institute of Sales Promotion defines sales promotions as

a range of tactical marketing techniques designed within a strategic marketing framework, to add value to a product or service in order to achieve a specific sales and marketing objective.

Sales promotions can be targeted at consumers with the aim of pulling sales through a channel of distribution, or at the distributor with the aim of pushing products through the channel or a combination of both. The majority of people are familiar with, and have no doubt responded to or participated in, a sales promotion. The most common consumer sales promotion techniques include special offers, for instance price reductions or 'two for the price of one' offers, competitions or gifts, coupons or incentive schemes such as Air Miles and the retailer loyalty cards. Sales promotions targeted at distributors include seasonal incentives or bulk purchase offers.

Traditionally, sales promotions have been used tactically to encourage brand switching, as a response to competitors' activity, or to create a short-term increase in the level and frequency of sales. Increasingly, sales promotions are now being used more strategically and integrated into an overall communications strategy. While price discounting, coupons and special offers still play an important part in the sales promotion mix, more attention is now being focused on how sales promotions can add value, not detract value from a brand.

The decision of when and how to use sales promotion techniques will be influenced by the competitive situation of a company and its marketing objectives. In cases such as the launch of a new brand of cigarette, sales promotion events are sometimes the only vehicle used to promote the product, primarily due to the limitations placed on advertising the product. Sales promotion will be discussed further in Chapter 19.

Public relations

Public relations is the deliberate, planned and sustained effort to establish and maintain mutual understanding between an organization and its publics. (Institute of Public Relations)

In recent years there has been a significant increase in both interest and expenditure on public relations activity. Despite this interest and the work of the Institute of Public Relations to improve understanding, it still remains a misunderstood subject and fails to achieve the recognition and importance that it deserves.

The key feature of public relations is its focus upon the 'publics', or stakeholder groups that have an interest in, or can influence, an organization's activities and positioning in the market-place. Some of the key groups were identified earlier in this chapter. These groups are often united by a common interest or cause. Each group will have its own set of needs and agendas and will require careful monitoring and communication. As suggested in the definition, a key role of PR is to establish and maintain mutual understanding between the organization and its key stakeholder groups. If the interests and issues raised by these groups are ignored or mishandled then the resulting publicity can do harm to the organization's public image.

Organizations such as the Body Shop and Virgin have in the past made extensive use of public relations activity to establish and reinforce their brands' credentials. Political parties are some of the more recent organizations to recognize the benefits of effective PR.

Public relations encompasses the following areas of activity:

- Media relations/press releases;
- Editorial and broadcast material;
- Publicity and stunts;
- Sponsorship;
- Crisis management;
- Corporate image/corporate identity;
- Employee relations;

How can an advertising manager make their adverts go further? One solution is to get the media to talk about the ads, so that they are given free editorial coverage. This is where advertising must work closely with public relations, and be aware that, as in all PR, control over actual media coverage may be quite limited.

Of course, outrageous adverts have always ended up being talked about in the media, exemplified by Club 18–30 Holidays which have acquired notoriety for saucy adverts on billboards and in newspapers. A turning-point however came in the early 1990s with the deliberate integration of advertising and PR. A pioneer in this was the 'Hello Boys' advertising campaign for Wonderbra which featured posters of the supermodel Eva Herzigova. Advertising agency TBWA worked closely with PR consultancy Jackie Cooper to secure media coverage of the advertising campaign, which it achieved, for example, by arranging media interviews with the supermodel at the centre of the advertising campaign and putting out stories of advertising posters being stolen by collectors. Another example of this close integration was undertaken for an advert for the Renault Clio in 1998 which featured comedians Vic Reeves and Bob Mortimer at Nicole's wedding. Beer Davies Publicity sent 3,000 wedding invitations to national and local press, asking journalists to join Papa at the wedding of his beloved daughter, Nicole, on Friday, 29 May, on ITV at 7.40 p.m. It also invited them to attend a pre-wedding breakfast at the Savoy Hotel the day before, where the advert was unveiled. As a result of this, the story featured in most of the UK national newspapers. Some of the papers also even covered the news that members of Nicole's Internet fan club attended the launch event carrying banners urging Nicole 'Don't do it!'.

But securing PR overage for an advert is not always easy. Journalists may get wise to advertisers' tactics and take no interest in the story. PR must be innovative in giving an editor a story that their audience will want to hear about. There is also a problem where an advert generates negative publicity, something which happened with Help the Aged and its advertising campaign featuring elderly people in a morgue. It may have used shock tactics to gain attention, but did it help advance its cause?

- Lobbying;
- Events management;
- Financial and corporate affairs.

This requires a significant amount of resource if the PR function is to be carried out effectively. Chapter 19 will consider this important and growing field of marketing communication activity.

Selling and sales management

A sales force provides the personal interface between a company and its customers. This contact may be face to face, by telephone or, more recently, by utilizing information technology. It is necessary to explain why selling and sales management appear under a chapter on promotions management. The most significant reason is because the sales function forms an integral part of an organization's integrated communications activity. The salesperson acts as a conduit through which information can be passed between an organization and its customers. Selling offers the opportunity for one-to-one communication and provides an important personal link between an organization and its customers, thereby completing the circle of marketing activity.

To omit selling may be likened to having a football team without a striker, designing a gun without a firing pin, a chemical formula without a catalyst or an organism without the means of reproduction. The item may be absolutely perfect in design, targeted at segments of the consumer population who crave it, promoted with great flair and price structured to meet every possible combination of purchase occasion. However if no professional selling effort is involved the product is likely to remain on the pallets in the warehouse. Selling is about making things happen. (Steward 1993, p. 7)

Sales management is a critical management process which involves five major functions:

- Organization of the sales force;
- Motivation of the sales force;
- Monitoring and control;
- Recruitment and training;
- Interface with other management functions.

The sales manager's primary objective is to ensure that sales and profitability targets are met and that sales personnel are working as a team efficiently and effectively. This can require the application of a significant range of interpersonal, analytical, administrative, and technical skills in an often pressurized environment. At the same time the nature and process of selling is changing from a transactional to a longer-term partnership/relational focus which requires the development of new skills and strategies. Personal selling and sales management are discussed further in Chapter 19.

Direct marketing

In recent years, technological developments have opened up a number of new possibilities for companies to communicate with their customers. Direct mail, telephone response media, and more recently the Internet allow promotional messages to be tailored and targeted to individuals, having regard to their unique needs. The principles and techniques of direct marketing are discussed in Chapter 20.

Promotional messages about a company can come from many different sources within the organization, and not just the traditional promotion channels which originate with marketing departments. Service industries in particular provide opportunities for front-line staff and service outlets to act as live advertisements for a company.

The general appearance of a shop, restaurant, or car dealership can promote the image of a service organization. A brightly coloured and clean exterior can transmit a message that the organization is fast, efficient, and well run. Outlets can be used to display advertising posters which in heavily trafficked locations can result in valuable exposure. Many retailers with town centre locations consider that these opportunities are so great that they do not need to undertake more conventional promotion. Among the large UK retailers, Marks & Spencer until the 1980s paid for very little promotional activity, arguing that over half the population passed one of its stores during any week, thereby exposing them to powerful 'free' messages. Although the company's promotional mix now includes more paid-for advertising, store locations are still considered to be valuable promotional media.

Outlets can also provide valuable opportunities to show service production processes to potential customers, something which is much more difficult to achieve through conventional media. A fast food restaurant displaying modern, state-of-the-art equipment and a solicitor's clean and tidy office all send out promotional messages about the organization.

Marketing communications models

THE development of communication models enables marketers to understand complex relationships, phenomena, and processes within a manageable framework. While many of these models simplify the real world and are primarily designed to highlight specific issues, they do provide a means to explain how interrelationships between variables occur and can provide explanations of causes and outcomes of specific types of behaviour.

A range of models have been developed in the academic literature, each one explaining some part of this complex communication process. In this section some of the key communication models are outlined.

To understand how communication works it is helpful to look at the communication process. The communication process can be seen as an exchange of information between an information sender and an information receiver. Fig. 16.5 outlines how this information is exchanged. The model demonstrates that the communication process is a cycle consisting of six main elements:

1. *The sender* can be an individual or an organization who determines what message will be sent through which medium and how it should be translated (encoded) into

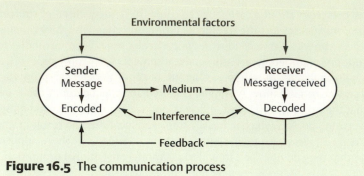

Figure 16.5 The communication process

a meaningful communication to its intended audience. The sender can utilize sound, colour, movement, symbols, words, etc.

2. *The receiver* can be an individual or an organization who hears or sees a message and responds. The range and type of responses will be determined by a range of factors but include such things as relevance and clarity of message, the characteristics of the individual receiver, the environment in which the message is received, etc. The aim of effective communication is to reach and attain a desired response from the target audience.

3. *The medium* is the method through which the message is communicated. This can be via newspapers, leaflets, people, events, etc. The aim of effective communication is to select the most appropriate medium that reaches the target audience in a cost efficient and effective manner.

4. *Interference* highlights those factors that can reduce the impact and effectiveness of the communication. This includes such things as clutter of adverts, non-attentive audience, interruptions whilst message is being relayed etc.

5. *Environmental factors* will influence the process of encoding and decoding the message. These include macro and micro environment factors which can have a significant bearing upon the effectiveness of the communication.

6. *Feedback* identifies the need for monitoring of communications and its effectiveness. Such feedback can be obtained from some form of market research.

The model is useful in identifying the broad dynamics and complexity of the communication process and highlights its key components. The model does not attempt to explain behaviour or communication effect. For those people involved in planning and implementing communications it does provide a general framework for considering how effective communications works.

Hierarchy of effects models

A range of models have been developed that propose a sequence of response that occurs as a result of a message being received by the audience. The two most common of these models are referred to as AIDA and DAGMAR (Fig. 16.6).

The principle that underlies these models is that promotions act as a stimulus which gives rise to a 'conditioned' response. Promotions can therefore be devised to achieve the objective of moving people through the sequence of responses. Advertising may be effective in building awareness or gaining attention or interest. Literature and brochures can provide comprehension and desire, sales promotions and sales activity can provide action. The models suggest that effective communication must carry its audience through the sequence of responses hence its term hierarchy of effects.

Hierarchy of effects models suggest how communications affect the mind and behaviour of the audience. The major value of the models is that they enable the purpose of a particular promotion to be defined and pre- and post-campaign surveys can be carried out to demonstrate the communication effect.

The models have many weaknesses, the most significant being their simplification of a complex psychological and behavioural process. The audience is seen as a passive recipient of messages as opposed to an active seeker and participant in the communication process. Consumer research has shown that many consumers set predetermined parameters within which a purchase decision might be made, such as price range and style of a product. The consumer therefore selects those messages that support them in their purchase decision as opposed to being passively pulled through the sequence. These models also ignore psychological factors such as the influence of attitudes/beliefs, motivation, and perception on behaviour. The model also assumes that the sequence of response is universal. However, instances occur where consumption of a product may occur before any conviction for the product or service is made. Similarly, awareness of, and conviction for, a product can occur at the same time at the point of purchase but with limited understanding, as happens with impulse

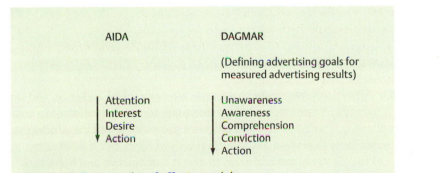

AIDA	DAGMAR
	(Defining advertising goals for measured advertising results)
Attention	Unawareness
Interest	Awareness
Desire	Comprehension
Action	Conviction
	Action

Figure 16.6 Hierarchy of effects models

Figure 16.7 Advertisers must fight to gain the attention of an audience, and simply stating the benefits of a product may be inadequate to gain attention or to create a distinctive identity. This advertisement does not say much about the product on offer and is not likely to achieve any sales in the short term, but it does raise awareness of the Kit Kat brand and helps to give it a distinctive and humorous position in the competitive market for confectionery products.

purchases. These models also ignore the effects of promotional activity that aim to limit brand switching behaviour and prompt repeat purchase.

The assumption that specific promotional effects can be measured in isolation is also a simplification of a complex communication environment. In reality it is difficult to isolate one single cause with a communication effect. We are bombarded daily by a multitude of communication signals, each one playing its part in influencing behaviour.

A model that identifies and integrates psychological and behavioural elements was developed by Timothy Joyce and is shown in Fig. 16.8. This model recognizes that to understand how promotions work we need to understand the nature of the promotion, people's purchase behaviour, their individual psychology, and how the relationship between these factors interrelate. The effect of communication is not seen as a passive relationship but more a continuing relationship with habit and consistency forming an integral part of an individual's behaviour. The inclusion of perception and selective attention to communication stimuli recognizes that the consumer will not take in all of a communication message and that individuals make associations in their own minds as to the nature of the communication they have received. The model also recognizes that attitudes can be influenced by both pre- and post-purchase experience and that, while advertising might succeed in arousing interest or successfully reinforcing attitudes, post-purchase experience and dissonance may have an equal effect.

The model provides a useful framework within which to consider the complexity of the communication process. However, it does not provide a means against which

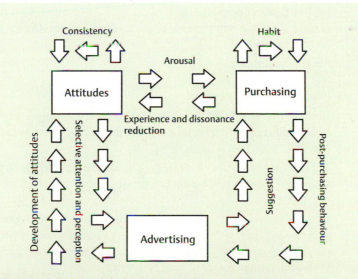

Figure 16.8 A model of communication, incorporating psychological and behavioural elements (adapted from Timothy Joyce, 'What Do We Know About How Advertising Works ?', ESOMAR, 1967)

promotional effects can be measured and does not offer the simple application of the hierarchy of effects models considered earlier.

Alongside these communication models can be considered the buyer behaviour models that you were introduced to in Chapter 7. These overlap with the communications models discussed above by seeking to explain the buying process. With all these models their importance lies in helping us to understand specific elements of a complex process. Despite their inherent weaknesses they provide useful guidelines for planning and implementing effective communication.

Stages of the promotion planning process

PROMOTIONAL activity is unlikely to be effective unless it forms part of a cohesive and integrated promotional plan. A key element of that plan is the decisions on how the elements of the promotional mix should be implemented. However, prior to such decisions, analysis needs to be undertaken and objectives and strategy agreed. A useful framework within which to consider promotional planning is SOST 4Ms proposed by Paul Smith (1995, p. 35).

Situation	(a)	Company—sales and market share trends, summary strengths and weaknesses.
	(b)	Product service range—features, benefits, and Unique Selling Proposition, product positioning.
	(c)	Market structure and growth, opportunities and threats, target markets and competition.
Objectives		Short, medium, and long term
	(a)	Marketing objectives
	(b)	Communication objectives
Strategy		How the objectives will be achieved. This can be a summary of the promotional mix and sometimes includes the marketing mix. (No tactical details here)
Tactics		The detailed activities of strategy. The detailed planning of how, when, and where various promotional activities (communication tools) occur

+4M's

Men	Men and women—who is responsible for what? Are there enough suitably experienced men and women in-house to handle various projects. Have they got spare capacity to take on extra tasks? Are outside agencies needed or should extra permanent staff be recruited?
Money	Budget—what will it cost? Is it affordable? Is it good value for money? Should the money be spent elsewhere? Does the budget include research to measure the effectiveness of various other activities? Is there an allowance for contingencies?

Minutes	Time-scale and deadlines for each stage of each activity—proposals, concept development, concept testing, regional testing, national roll-out, European launch, etc.
Measurement	Monitoring the results of all activities helps the marketing manager to understand what works well and what is not worth repeating in the next campaign. Clearly defined and specific objectives provide yardsticks for measurement. The monitored results also help the manager to make realistic forecasts and ultimately to build better marketing communication plans in the future

The situation analysis should ideally be part of a comprehensive audit of an organization's competitive position. It should highlight market trends, market position, competitor activity, consumer perceptions, etc. From this analysis a clearer understanding of the situation can be obtained and appropriate objectives and strategies agreed. It is also important to conduct an internal audit of the organization to determine resource requirements.

After analysing the situation, objectives can be set. Promotional mix objectives should relate to the organization's marketing and communications objectives. Marketing objectives typically refer to market share, new product development or positioning, etc. Communications objectives refer to how the total communications activity will help achieve marketing objectives. Typically models such as AIDA or DAGMAR can be used but more individualized and specific communications objectives are likely to be identified on completion of the audit. The promotional mix objectives relate directly to what each element of the promotional mix is expected to achieve. Objectives can be set for advertising activity, sales promotions, public relations, selling, and direct marketing activities.

A mnemonic which provides a useful framework by which to formulate objectives is SMARTT. Objectives should be

S	pecific
M	easurable
A	chievable
R	elevant
T	imed
T	argeted

Establishing clear objectives is an important part of the promotional planning process in providing direction and focus to promotional activity. Care should therefore be taken in ensuring that the objectives set are SMARTT.

The choice of promotional strategy will be determined by the objectives. A range of promotional options are likely to be available and the role of the strategist is to determine which is best. Strategy is not about doing things, but about setting the direction, scope, and breadth by which things will be done and allocating resources. The strategy document should provide guidance on the future implementation of promotional activity and its evaluation.

Implementation of the promotional mix will be the most detailed part of the promotional plan. Specific objectives, strategies, and tactics can be set for each element of the mix and timings of activities and budgets allocated. Activities can be time-scaled on a chart as shown in Fig. 16.8.

Setting budgets and monitoring promotional activity

For each promotional mix activity, an organization should allocate a level of expenditure. The level of expenditure should ideally be determined in accordance with the need to achieve the objectives. This is called the objective and task method of budget setting. In reality it is unusual to see this method, primarily due to the complexity involved in calculation and the unstable environment within which most organizations operate. Other methods of budget setting include percentage of sales and matching competitive activity. A combination approach is usually sufficient with a contingency budget set aside for unforeseen circumstances.

Product X				Schedule of Promotional Activity						
	J	F	M	A	M	J	J	A	S	O
TV adverts	X	X				X	X			
Magazine adverts		X	X	X				X	X	X
Press releases	X	X			X	X			X	X
Sales promotions			X	X	X				X	X
Trade promotions	X	X			X	X			X	X
Field sales	X	X			X	X			X	X
Telephone sales	X	X	X			X	X	X		
Sponsorship					X			X		
Exhibition					X					
Community event							X			

Figure 16.9 Setting promotional objectives, strategies, and tactics

Evaluation of promotional activity can be judged using variance analysis of cost against budget. Of more importance to marketers, however, is measuring the effectiveness of the promotional activity. In the subsequent chapters specific examples of measurement techniques will be given for each of the promotional activities. Evaluation of promotional activity performs an important role in the promotional plan, providing feedback to help inform future activity and to enable adjustments to be made to promotional activity if objectives are not being achieved. It is important that enough resource is allocated for evaluation of promotional activity, a point often overlooked by marketers.

Chapter summary and key linkages to other chapters

A company's product offer needs to be communicated with its target market. If the other elements of the mix are not correct, promotion alone is unlikely to make customers buy the product. This chapter has provided an overview of the promotional planning process and application of this process to the main promotion media will be discussed in the following chapters.

Promotion planning can be related to the following chapters in this book:

Chapter 1: What is marketing?: To many people, marketing and promotion are synonymous. It should now be clear that promotion is just a small part of marketing, and that promotion will not be effective if the other elements of marketing orientation are not present.

Chapter 2: The marketing environment: Changes in customer expectations are continually influencing the content and distribution channels for promotional messages. New technology allows new promotional media to emerge.

Chapter 3: Segmentation: Effective promotion depends crucially on an ability to segment audiences and develop a message and medium which is most appropriate to each targeted segment.

Chapter 4: Branding: The development of strong brands usually calls for great investment in promotional activities.

Chapter 5: Marketing and ethics: Unethical promotional practices may be bad for society, but they are also quite likely to be bad in the long term for the promoter.

Chapter 6: Marketing research: Marketing research is essential in order to identify and address target markets and to evaluate the effectiveness of promotion.

Chapter 7: Buyer behaviour: Promotion efforts must recognize the stage in the buying process that a buyer has reached. For commercial buyers, identifying members of the decision-making unit can be crucial for effective targeting of promotion.

Chapter 8: Buyer–seller relationship development: Promotion should be aimed at not just recruiting new customers, but retaining existing ones.

Chapter 9: The product: What are the unique benefits of a product that should be promoted to the target market?

Chapter 10: New product development and innovation: For radically innovative new products, public relations alone may be sufficient to launch a new product. For most products, however, a substantial advertising effort is required to launch a new product, especially where there is relatively little novelty and the market is competitive.

Chapter 11: Developing a sustainable competitive advantage: Promotion alone will not create and sustain a competitive advantage—the other elements of the marketing plan must also be correct.

Chapters 12/13: Pricing theory and applications: Promotion should create awareness of the unique advantages of a product, which justify buyers paying a premium price.

Chapters 14/15: Intermediaries/logistics: Intermediaries are recipients of promotional messages, which may be useful to encourage them to carry a manufacturer's stock. They also frequently work with suppliers in developing joint advertising programmes.

Chapter 17: Advertising: This chapter provides an overview of promotion planning and the communication process, of which advertising is an interrelated component.

Chapter 18: Selling and sales management: This chapter provides an overview of promotion planning and the communication process, of which selling and sales management is an interrelated component.

Chapter 19: Sales promotion and public relations: As an element of the promotion mix, sales promotion is frequently used to encourage a short-term response by buyers. Public relations is essentially a long-term undertaking.

Chapter 20: Direct marketing: New media frequently rely on conventional advertising media for creating awareness and initiating a dialogue.

Chapter 21: Organizing for marketing: Promotional aims must relate to other corporate and marketing aims.

Chapter 22: Services marketing: The intangibility of services often creates a perception of greater riskiness which promotion must seek to overcome.

Chapter 23: Global marketing: How should promotional messages and media be adapted when a company seeks to enter overseas markets?

Case study

Ethical values used to position bank

The Co-operative Bank evolved from its origins in 1872 as a bank for the Co-operative Wholesale and Retail Societies to become by 1992 one of the eight UK clearing banks with a network of over 100 branches. Throughout the 1980s it had enjoyed steady growth as a result of several innovative new products such as free in-credit banking, extended opening hours and interest bearing cheque accounts. However, the bank found its market position being steadily eroded by increased competition from the major clearing banks and particularly from building societies who were able to enter the personal banking sector as a result of the deregulation of the banking sector. The Co-operative Bank is one of the smaller clearing banks. As a result of increased competition it saw its market share fall from 2.7 per cent in 1986 to 2 per cent by 1991. Alongside this trend the bank faced a changing customer profile. Traditionally the bank had attracted a high proportion of its customers from the more affluent ABC1 social groups. By 1992 this position was changing. An increasing number of new accounts were being attracted from the C2DE social groups, while at the same time the bank was losing its core ABC1 accounts. This trend was diluting its position as a more upmarket bank and reducing its potential to cross-sell more profitable financial products.

The bank's research showed that outside of its customer base, it lacked a clear image and that what image there was showed the bank as rather staid, old fashioned, and with left-wing political affinities. Furthermore spontaneous recall of its name had steadily fallen despite extensive advertising of its innovative new products.

The bank realized that immediate action was necessary to rebuild its image and stem the loss of its ABC1 accounts. The size of the bank and its profitability meant that the advertising budget was modest and therefore a focused campaign with maximum effectiveness was crucial.

BDDH was the advertising agency appointed to devise a promotional campaign. The agency 'interrogated' the Co-operative Bank to identify any distinctive competencies that it could build a campaign upon. It discovered that the bank's heritage offered a unique positioning opportunity against other mainstream banks. This derived in particular from its sourcing and distribution of funds which had been governed by an unwritten ethical code, that the bank never lent money to any of the larger environmentally or politically unsound organizations. BDDH set out to transform the results of its interrogation into a relevant and motivating proposition that would appeal beyond the bank's current customer base. A key strategic decision was made to target promotional activity at the growing number of 'ethical consumers' who importantly were found to have a more upmarket ABC1 profile.

The 'ethical bank' formed the foundation upon which BDDH built its campaign. Initially this was tested on its existing customer base where it gained a high level of approval. The bank incorporated its ethical stance into its customer charter. Advertising was initially used to raise awareness of the bank's positioning. The creative work was deliberately provocative and motivating, while at the same time maintaining the bank's credentials as a high street lender. The creative images used were often simple and stark.

The key objectives of the campaign were to :

- build customer loyalty and so stem the outflow of ABC1s;
- expand the customer base, targeting ABC1s;
- expand the corporate customer base.

National press and regional television in the bank's 'northern heartland' were the primary media used in the initial stages of the campaign. Cinema was utilized as the campaign progressed.

The marketing objectives were exceeded as a result of the promotional campaign. The bank established a strong and differentiated brand platform which in 1999 it still continued to build upon. The campaign's success can be put down to a clear understanding of the bank's customer base and its own unique competencies. The campaign was carefully targeted with the aim to achieve maximum impact which enabled the message to be delivered cost effectively. The case clearly demonstrates how effective promotional activity, linked closely to business and marketing objectives and strategy can provide a long-term sustainable competitive position in the market-place.

Adapted from Institute of Practitioners in Advertising 1994, pp. 329–52.

Case study review questions

1 How can the Co-operative Bank assess whether its ethical position has been effective?

2 What dangers does the Co-operative Bank face in promoting an ethical position?

3 Critically assess the promotional positioning of other banks with which you are familiar.

Chapter review questions

1 What is meant by the promotional mix?

2 Evaluate the usefulness of the hierarchy of effect models as an approach to understanding how advertising works. Select two recent advertising campaigns to illustrate your points.

3 To what extent do you think consumers have an active role rather than a passive role in the 'consumption' of promotions?

4 What is the difference between a promotional objective, promotional strategy, and promotional tactics.

5 For an organization of your choice, outline their current promotional strategy. Use the SOST 4Ms framework to support your answer.

6 Show how promotional planning can be integrated into an organization's overall marketing and communications planning framework

References

Institute of Practitioners In Advertising (1994), *Advertising Works 8* (London: NIC Publications Ltd.), pp. 329–52.

Smith, P. (1995), *Marketing Communications—An Integrated Approach* (London: Kogan Page).

Steward, K. (1993), *Market Led, Sales Driven* (Oxford: Butterworth-Heinemann), p. 7.

Suggested further reading

Individual elements of the promotion mix are considered in the following chapters. For a general overview of communication methods and campaign planning, the following are useful;

- Brannan, T. (1998), *A Practical Guide to Integrated Marketing Communications* (London: Kogan Page).

- Canwell, D., and Maitland, L. (1998), *Marketing Campaigns* (London: ITP).

- Fill, C. (1995), *Marketing Communications: Frameworks, Theories and Applications* (Englewood Cliffs, NJ: Prentice Hall).

- Shrimp, T. A. (1996), *Advertising, Promotion and Supplemental Aspects of Integrated Marketing* (Fort Worth: Dryden Press).

- Smith, P. (1998), *Marketing Communications*, 2nd edn. (London: Kogan Page).

- Yeshin, T. (1998), *Integrated Marketing Communications* (Oxford: Butterworth-Heinemann).

Useful web links

Institute of Practitioners in Advertising, Sales & Marketing Resource Directory: http://salesdoctors.com/directory/dircos/3102i02.htm

Institute of Sales Promotion: http://www.thebiz.co.uk/isp.htm

The British codes of advertising and sales promotion: http://www.asa.org.uk/bcasp/bcasp.txt

Institute of Direct Marketing: http://www.thebiz.co.uk/instdirm.htm

Institute of Professional Sales: http://www.iops.co.uk/

Institute of Public Relations: http://www.ipr.org.uk/

Direct Marketing Association: http://www.the-dma.org/

Chapter 17
Advertising

Chapter objectives

The previous chapter introduced general principles of promotional planning. This chapter focuses specifically on the advertising element of the promotion mix. It begins by discussing communication models, introduced in the previous chapter, in the context of advertising. Methods of analysing audiences, developing an advertising strategy, and implementing it are then discussed.

The role of advertising in the promotion mix

ADVERTISING is mass, paid communication which is used to transmit information, develop attitudes, and induce some form of response from the audience. It seeks to bring about a response by providing information to potential customers, by trying to modify their desires, and by supplying reasons why they should prefer that particular company's product. The different elements of the promotion mix were introduced in the previous chapter, but it must be stressed that advertising, like the other mix elements, cannot be seen in isolation. Advertising is frequently used to support sales promotion and direct marketing activity, for example.

The planning process for advertising comprises a number of key stages, which can be related to the fundamental marketing management process of analysis, planning, implementation, and control:

1. 'Where are we now?' In the first stage, an organization seeks to establish how its brand or product offering is perceived in people's minds. This can be ascertained through marketing research.
2. 'Why are we there?' An organization should seek to establish how a particular position was reached by examining and identifying causal relationships.
3. 'Where could we be?' This reflects an organization's objectives in terms of such factors as market share, awareness levels, etc.

4. 'How can we get there?' This refers to the development of an advertising strategy and its tactical implementation.
5. 'Are we getting there?' Having implemented an advertising programme, results must be evaluated and control action taken to address any discrepancy with objectives.

This chapter begins by looking at how advertising communicates with its audiences and then discusses objective setting, strategy formulation, implementation, and monitoring.

How does advertising work?

ADVERTISING involves an ongoing process of communication between an organization and its target markets. The process is defined by the answers to the following questions:

- To whom is the message addressed?
- What response is sought?
- What is the message?

The elements of this process are illustrated in Fig. 17.1 and are described in more detail below.

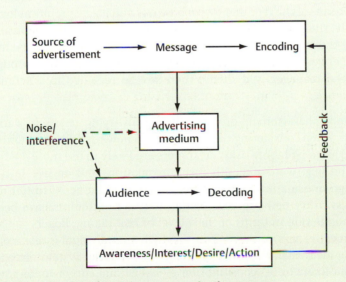

Figure 17.1 The advertising communication process

To whom is the message addressed?

The most important element of the advertising process is the audience at which communication is aimed. The audience of an advertisement determines what is to be said, when it is to be said, where it is to be said, and who is to say it. The target audience of a communication must be clearly defined and this can be done in a number of ways.

- The most traditional method of defining audiences is in terms of social, economic, demographic, and geographical characteristics. In this way, audiences are defined using parameters such as age, sex, social class, area of residence, etc.

- Audiences can be defined in terms of the level of involvement of potential recipients of the communication, for example a distinction can be made between those people who are merely *aware* of the existence of a product, those who are *interested* in possibly purchasing it, and those who *wish to purchase* the product.

- An audience can be defined on the basis of target customers' usage frequency (e.g. regular users of an airline are likely to respond to an advertisement in a different way compared to occasional users).

- Similarly, audiences can differ in the benefits which they seek from a category of product. In this way, airlines aim different messages at leisure travellers who may seek benefits in terms of low cost vacations, compared to business users for whom the benefits of speed, availability, and reliability are of greatest importance.

- In the case of goods and services supplied to corporate buyers, audiences can be defined in terms of the type and size of business and its geographical location. More importantly, the key decision-makers and influencers must be identified and used in defining the audience—e.g. for office stationery, secretaries can be important in choosing between competing products rather than the actual product user or departmental manager, and should therefore be included in a definition of the target audience.

An important characteristic of the audience justifying research is its degree of perceived risk when considering the purchase of a new product. For purchases which are perceived as being highly risky, customers are likely to use more credible sources of information (e.g. word-of-mouth recommendation) and engage in a prolonged search through information sources. Chapter 9 noted that people differ markedly in their readiness to try new products and a number of attempts have been made to classify the population in terms of their level of risk taking. Rogers (1962) defined a person's 'innovativeness' as the 'degree to which an individual is relatively earlier in adopting new ideas than the other members of his social system'. In each product area, there are likely to be 'consumption pioneers' and early adopters, while other individuals only adopt new products much later. This has led to a classification of markets into the following adopter categories:

- innovators;
- early adopters;
- early majority;
- late majority;
- laggards.

The importance of recognizing different adopter categories is reflected in advertising for mobile telephones. In the early stages, advertising stressed the benefits of flexibility and security which appealed to some segments of more affluent private buyers and company buyers. Over time, many segments' resistance to owning a mobile phone has diminished, so by 2000 the message had changed to one of cheapness and lack of contractual formality.

What response is sought?

An advertisement may seek a number of possible responses from its audience, of which securing an immediate purchase is only one. In most cases, customers are seen as going through a series of stages before finally deciding to purchase a product. It is therefore critical to know these buyer-readiness stages and to assess where the target is at any given time. These are the focus of hierarchy of effects models which were discussed in the previous chapter.

An advert will be seeking any one or more of three audience responses:

- cognitive responses—the message should be considered and understood;
- affective responses—the message should lead to some change in attitude;
- behavioural responses—finally, the message should achieve some change in behaviour—a purchase decision.

Communication models portray a simple and steady movement through the various stages, although it should not be seen as ending when a sale is completed. It was noted in Chapter 8 that organizations increasingly seek to build relationships with their customers, so the behavioural change (the sale) should be seen as the starting-point for making customers aware of other offers available from the organization. Advertising is often aimed at customers after they have made a purchase to encourage the belief that they made the correct choice (thereby reducing 'cognitive dissonance') and to foster further purchases from the company.

The UK government's efforts to sell shares in public utilities during the 1990s illustrated the process of pushing the target audience through the buying process. Initial advertising was aimed at creating awareness of an industry which most people took for granted. So the first adverts for the water companies' privatization used images of underground pipework to make people aware of the size and complexity of the organization which was being sold. Following this, the adverts moved towards creating a desire to become a shareholder. The British Gas adverts at this stage created the character of 'Sid' with whom people could identify as a new small shareholder. Telephone numbers given in advertisements allowed potential investors to call to obtain further information. Finally, advertising in the closing stages focused on the need to take immediate action. Newspaper adverts contained application forms and a cut-off date by which forms must be submitted.

Had the advertising been effective in taking people through the buying process? At the outset of the privatization process, cynics had claimed that very few people would want to buy shares in 'boring' public utilities. In the event, shares in the privatizations were nearly all heavily over-subscribed, and much of this could be attributed to the effective advertising.

The message

A^N advertising message must be able to move an individual along a path from awareness through to eventual purchase. In order for a message to be received and understood, it must gain attention, use a common language, arouse needs, and suggest how these needs may be met. All of this should take place within the acceptable standards of the target audience. However, the product itself, the channel, and the source of the communication also convey a message and therefore it is important that these do not conflict.

Three aspects of a communication message can be identified—content, structure, and format. It is the content which is likely to arouse and change attention, attitude, and intention and therefore the theme of the message is important. The formulation of the message must include some kind of benefit, motivator, identification, or reason why the audience should think or do something. Appeals can be rational, emotional, or moral.

Messages can be classified into a number of types, according to the dominant theme of the message. The following are common focal points for messages:

- The nature and characteristics of the organization and the product on offer—for example, British Airway's advertising has emphasized its claim to be the 'world's favourite airline'.

- Advantages over the competition—the mobile phone company Vodaphone has

How do you strike a balance between an advertising campaign being eye-catching and accessible on the one hand, and preserving the core values of the product on the other? Retailers, banks, and insurance companies have all encountered problems when their traditional mature audiences have been alienated by advertising which was aimed at increasing the number of younger customers. Wacky advertising may attract attention, but what does it say about the nature of the product on offer? Liverpool-based John Moores University used an unconventional approach to advertising its courses in 1999. Its prospectus paid relatively little attention to the details of the courses on offer, but gave great emphasis to the pubs and clubs in town. It may well be that this was based on a sound analysis of the factors that influence students' choice of university. Most prospective students have only a limited ability to distinguish between the academic credentials of competing courses, whereas nightlife is an easier point of reference. But the media picked up the story, claiming that this was further evidence of 'dumbing down' in education generally, and at John Moores University in particular. Even existing students claimed that the value of their degrees would be demeaned by advertising which made their institution appear to the outside world like a 'good time university'. But if the university went back to stuffy advertising and prospectuses, would it loose a point of difference with its nearby competitors?

consistently emphasized its greater coverage and better performance compared to competing mobile phone networks.

- Adaptability to buyers' needs—Virgin Bank emphasizes the extent to which its accounts have the flexibility to cater to individuals' specific needs.

- Experience of others—in this way, testimonials of previous satisfied customers are used to demonstrate the benefits of a product and the dependability of the supplier (for example, Aer Lingus has used famous Irish writers to recount their experiences of flying with the airline in its advertisements).

Recipients of a message must see it as applying specifically to themselves and they must see some reason for being interested in it. The message must be structured according to the job it has to do—the points to be included in the message must be ordered (strongest arguments first or last) and consideration given to whether one-sided or two-sided messages should be used. The actual format of the message will be influenced by the medium used, for example, the type of print if published material, type of voice if broadcast media is used, etc.

The credibility of the message source

The source of an advertising message—as distinct from the message itself—can influence the effectiveness of any advertisement.

- If a source is perceived as being credible then the message is more likely to be accepted by the audience. Credibility can be developed by establishing a source as important, high in status, power, and prestige, or by emphasizing reliability and openness. A doctor in a white coat may be seen as a credible endorser of a new headache tablet, and a German engineer may be seen as credible in promoting the reliability of a new car.

■ If a source is perceived as having power, then the audience response is likely to be compliance. If a government advertisement states the benefits of cyclists wearing protective headware, this may be believed more than a message put out by a manufacturer.

■ If a source is liked and perceived as a friend, identification by the audience is a likely response. Many advertisers use well liked personalities, or simply the kind of ordinary person who may live next door, in order to bring about identification with the product and the promotional message.

Closely related to the notion of credibility is the 'halo effect'. Coulston-Thomas (1985) defines this as the 'tendency to impute to individuals and things, the qualities of other individuals and things with which they are associated'. In this way, many advertisers use trusted professionals as message sources, in the belief that they will carry greater credibility. A person purporting to be a doctor may carry more credible messages about a new toothpaste than a television presenter, for example. However, there is also a phenomenon known as the 'sleeper effect' in which the credibility of a source—and hence message retention—is built up over a period of time. The implication of this is that company and product reputation need regular reinforcement, both from advertising and other communication media.

Barriers to effective advertising communication

T**HE** creator of a message needs to encode it into some acceptable form for an audience to decode and comprehend. Unfortunately, there is likely to be interference between the stages of encoding and decoding and although it is difficult totally to eliminate such interference in the communication process, an understanding of the various elements of this 'noise' should help to minimize its effects.

The nature of 'noise' factors can be examined in terms of the simple 'black box' model of buyer behaviour which was discussed in Chapter 7. A communication of some sort (either marketer or non-marketer dominated) is seen as a stimulus to some form of customer response. Response can be expressed in terms of quantity purchased, frequency of purchase, or even non-purchase. The final response, however, is not a straightforward response to the initial stimulus. The initial stimulus is distorted within the 'black box' process, resulting in different individuals responding in different ways to a similar stimulus. The variables at work within the black box are the noise factors and can be divided into two major types:

- those that relate to the individual, i.e. psychological factors;
- those that relate to other groups of people, i.e. sociological factors.

Psychological factors

No two individuals are the same in terms of their psychological make-up. Each person undergoes different experiences influencing their personalities, their perceptions of the world, their motives for action, and their attitudes towards people, situations, and objects. Therefore it is not surprising to find that different people will interpret an advertisement differently.

An individual's past experience of a product or supplier is an important influence on how messages about that company's products are interpreted. Both positive and negative experiences predispose an individual to decode messages in a particular way. For example, an individual may have a negative attitude towards an insurance company as a result of having previously had an insurance claim turned down by that company. This negative attitude is likely to distort the individual's interpretation of any marketing communication from the company. In this context, therefore, the communication should involve an attempt to shift attitude as well as merely to inform.

The personality of specific members of an audience can significantly influence interpretation of a message—for example, an extrovert may interpret a message differently from an introvert. Similarly an individual's motives can influence how a message is decoded.

A number of authors (e.g. Maslow 1954, Bayton 1958) classify motives into those that are biological (such as the need to satisfy hunger, thirst, etc.) and those that are psychological and learned. Maslow talks of safety, social, esteem, and self-actualization needs, while Bayton distinguishes between ego bolstering, ego defensive, and affective needs. Both agree that in different situations, one of these needs becomes dominant over the others and influences perceptions of the outside world (the influences of motivation on buyer behaviour was discussed in more detail in Chapter 7). As an example, an individual who has just come home from work tired and hungry and is about to eat dinner, is unlikely to be amenable to an advertising message promoting banking services. At that moment, they are motivated by lower order needs.

Sociological factors

In addition to the essentially personal characteristics which influence their behaviour, individuals are influenced by the presence of other people around them.

Individuals develop attitudes as a result of a conditioning process which is brought about by the culture they live in and the specific actions of family, friends, and work associates. Attitudes are learnt and are usually formed as a result of past experience. They are extremely enduring and are very influential in determining how a message is perceived.

Attitudes are predispositions to act in a particular situation and involve three elements: cognitive, affective, and conative.

- The cognitive element of an attitude involves the knowledge and understanding of the object, person, or situation to which there is an attitude.
- The affective element refers to the emotional content of an attitude and is usually expressed in terms of either positive or negative feelings.
- The conative element of an attitude refers to the preparedness on the part of the individual holding the attitude to act positively or negatively if a particular situation involving the object or person arose.

People develop attitudes from a number of sources. In addition to the family, there are many other social groupings which influence how consumers see the world and the way in which purchase decisions are made. Great importance is attached to the concept of reference groups. Chisnall (1985) defined reference groups as

groups with which an individual closely identifies so that they become for him/her, standards of evaluation and the sources of personal behavioral norms.

Reference groups can be divided into those of which an individual is a member ('membership groups') and those to which membership is aspired ('aspirational groups'). Both types of reference group influence how an individual perceives his or her environment and their decisions on goods and services purchases. Opinion leaders may exist who have the important task of 'trickling down' a message to other members of an audience. This type of process is most important where the cost of a product is high, the amount of information is low, the product involves significant social and symbolic value, and the purchase involves a high level of perceived risk.

Perception and retention of advertising messages

Past experience, personality, motivation, attitudes, and the influence of reference groups can all produce a 'noise' effect and thereby distort an audience's interpretation of an advertising message. Individuals are constantly being bombarded by numerous stimuli (visual, auditory, tactile, etc.), but are likely to select only the stimuli perceived as being important to them.

- Selective perception occurs where communication is perceived in such a way that it merely reinforces existing attitudes and beliefs.
- Selective reception occurs where individuals make active decisions as to which

stimuli they wish to expose themselves. For example, a committed Conservative Party supporter may consciously avoid advertising by the Labour Party.

- Selective retention occurs when an individual remembers only those aspects of the message perceived as being necessary to the receiver.

Even if an individual decides to give attention to an advert, understands it, and remembers it, comprehension may still be different from that which the advertiser expected. This perceptual distortion could be caused by those noise factors previously noted, poor encoding on the part of the communicator, or poor understanding by the audience itself. It is therefore important to pre-test advertising before a full campaign is launched.

Noise is an extremely difficult variable to eliminate totally from any communication process. However, an understanding of its existence and its potential in hindering effective communication is vital in developing a communication strategy. The best way of minimizing these noise effects is to develop a detailed understanding of the target audience.

Determining advertising objectives

S PECIFYING advertising objectives is important if appropriate messages are to be accurately targeted through the most appropriate media in the most cost-effective manner possible.

A number of factors should guide the formulation of advertising objectives:

- they should reflect the areas of accountability for those who implement the advertising programme;
- the target audience should be defined as accurately as possible;
- there should be a clear statement of the desired response from the target audience (e.g. whether the desired response is a purchase, desire, or merely becoming aware of the product being advertised);
- wherever possible, goals should be expressed in quantitative terms (for example, promotional objectives for a new type of motor insurance policy may begin with an objective to achieve awareness of the brand name by 30 per cent within the 25–55-year-old London-based insurance-buying public within one year of launch);
- a statement of time constraints.

Although it is commonplace to think that advertising can increase sales, it is extremely difficult to prove that advertising alone is responsible for a sales increase. Sales, after all, can be the result of many intervening variables, some of which are internal to the organization (e.g. public relations activity, pricing policy), while others are external (e.g. the state of the national economy). It is therefore too simplistic to set advertising objectives simply in terms of increasing sales by a specified amount. Given the existence of diverse adopter categories and the many stages in the communication process which were described earlier, more appropriate objectives can often be specified in terms of levels of awareness or comprehension.

Determining the advertising budget

ADVERTISING expenditure could become a drain on an organization's resources if no conscious attempt is made to determine an appropriate budget and to ensure that expenditure is kept within the budget. A number of methods are commonly used to determine an advertising budget.

- What can be afforded: this is largely a subjective assessment and pays little attention to the long-term promotional needs of a product. It regards advertising as a luxury which can be afforded in good times, to be cut back during lean times. In reality, this approach is used by many smaller companies to whom advertising spending is seen as the first and easy short-term target for reducing expenditure in bad times.

- Percentage of sales: by this method, advertising expenditure rises or falls to reflect changes in sales. In fact, sales are likely to be influenced by advertising rather than vice versa and this method is likely to accentuate any given situation. If sales are declining during a recession, more advertising may be required to induce sales but this method of determining the budget implies a cut in advertising expenditure.

- Comparative parity: advertising expenditure is determined by the amount spent by competitors. Many market sectors see periodic outbursts of promotional expenditure, often accompanying a change in some other element of firms' marketing mix. As an example, during 1999, increased capacity of ferries operating between Britain and Ireland led to price competition and triggered an increase in advertising by competing ferry operators, with each operator responding to their competitors' increase in advertising expenditure. However, merely increasing advertising expenditure may hide the fact that other elements of the marketing mix need adjusting in order to gain a competitive market position in relation to competitors.

- Residual: this is the least satisfactory approach and merely assigns to the advertising budget what is left after all other costs have been covered. It may bear no relationship to promotional objectives especially as a downturn in the business cycle may call for greater expenditure not less.

- Objective and task: this approach starts by defining promotional objectives. Tasks are then set which relate to specific targets. In this way, advertising is seen as a necessary—even though possibly risky—investment in a brand, ranking in importance with other more obvious costs such as production and salary costs. This is the most rational approach to setting a promotional budget.

Advertising media

EFFECTIVE advertising requires a good understanding of the media habits of the target audience. If a firm's target market is not in the habit of being exposed to a particular medium, much of the value of advertising through that medium will be wasted. As an example, attempts to promote premium credit cards to high income segments by means of television commercials may lose much of their value because research suggests that the higher socio-economic groups tend to spend a greater proportion of their viewing time watching BBC rather than commercial channels. On the other hand, they are heavy readers of Sunday newspaper magazine supplements.

Information about target audiences' media habits is obtained from a number of sources. Newspaper readership information is collated by the National Readership Survey. For each newspaper, this shows reading frequency and average readership per issue (as distinct from circulation) broken down into age, class, sex, ownership of consumer durables, etc. Television viewing information is collected by the Broadcasters Audience Research Board (BARB). This indicates the number of people watching particular channels at particular times by reference to two types of television ratings (TVRs)—one for the number of households watching a programme/advertising slot and one for the number of people watching.

Using such sources of information, the media characteristics of a particular target audience can be ascertained and a media plan produced which achieves maximum penetration of the target audience.

Media characteristics

The choice of media is influenced by the characteristics of each medium and their ability to achieve the specified promotional objectives. The following are some of the most common types of media and their characteristics:

Newspapers. Daily newspapers tend to have a high degree of reader loyalty, reflecting the fact that each national title is targeted to specific segments of the population. This loyalty can lead to the printed message being perceived by readers as having a high level of credibility. Therefore, daily papers may be useful for prestige and reminder advertising. They can be used for creating general awareness of a product or a brand as well as providing detailed product information. In this way, banks use newspapers both for adverts designed to create brand awareness and liking for the organization, as well as adverts for giving specific details of savings accounts. The latter may include an invitation to action in the form of a freepost account opening coupon.

Daily newspapers, however, are normally read hurriedly and therefore lengthy copy is likely to be wasted. Sunday newspapers also appeal to highly segmented audiences and are generally read at a more leisurely pace than daily papers. They are also more likely to be read at home and shared by households, which may be important for appealing to family-based purchase decisions.

Local newspapers offer a much greater degree of geographical segmentation than is possible with national titles. Within their circulation areas, they also achieve much higher levels of readership penetration. In the case of free newspapers, total penetration is achieved, although actual readership levels are more open to question. While national advertising through local newspapers is expensive and inefficient, it is useful for purely local suppliers, as well as national organizations who wish to target specific areas with local messages, or wish to pretest national advertising copy.

Magazines/Journals. Within the UK, and most western countries, there is an extensive selection of magazine and journal titles. While some high circulation magazines appeal to broad groups of people (e.g. *Radio Times*), most titles are specialized in terms of their content and targeting. In this way, *What Car* magazine may be a highly specific medium for car manufacturers, dealers, and loan companies to promote their goods and services to new car buyers. Specialist trade titles allow messages to be aimed at service intermediaries—for example, manufacturers of catering equipment will gain access to an audience of key buyers through *The Caterer* magazine.

Although advertising in magazines may at first seem relatively expensive compared to newspapers, they represent good value to advertisers in terms of the high number of readers per copy and the highly segmented nature of their audiences.

Television. This is an expensive, but very powerful medium. Although it tends to be used mainly for the long-term task of creating brand awareness, it can also be used to create a rapid sales response. The very fact that a message has been seen on television can give credibility to the message source and many companies add the phrase 'as seen on TV' to give additional credibility to their other media communications. The power of the television medium is enhanced by its ability to appeal to both the senses of sight and sound, and to use movement and colour to develop a sales message.

The major limitation of television advertising is its cost. For most small businesses, television advertising rates start at too high a level to be considered. The high starting price for television advertising reflects not only high production costs, but also the difficulty in segmenting television audiences, either socio-economically, or in terms of narrowly defined geographical areas. Also, the question must be asked as to how many people within the target audience are actually receptive to television advertising. Is the target viewer actually in the room when an advertisement is being broadcast? If the viewer is present, is he/she receptive to the message? The use of video recorders and remote controls has important implications for the effectiveness of television advertising.

With the development of digital broadcasting and the proliferation of television channels, the ability of the medium to segment audiences is increasing. There are now numerous channels which have developed distinctive audiences, including The Discovery Channel, MTV, and Sky Sports.

Commercial Radio. Radio advertising in the UK has seen considerable growth in recent years, recovering from its traditional perception as the poor relation of television advertising. The threshold cost of radio advertising is much lower than for tele-

Until a few years ago, the shelves of most newsagents would have been loaded with many general interest women's magazines (e.g. *Woman's Own*, *Women's Weekly*, *Cosmopolitan*), but very few general interest magazines aimed at men. Why? Some cynics might have argued that women were more likely to have spare time at home and could sit around reading, while 'busy' men were out at work, in the pub, or watching sport and did not have time to read magazines. There may just have been a bit of truth in this, but the main reason has been that women's magazines have been popular with advertisers. In the traditional household, it has been women who have made decisions on a wide range of consumer goods purchases. Advertising the benefits of toothpaste, yoghurt, or jam would have been lost on most men who had little interest in what was put in front of them, and played little part in the buying process.

Take a look at the newsstand now and it will carry a wide range of men's general interest magazines, such as *FHM*, *Loaded*, *Maxim*, and *Esquire*. Why have they suddenly mushroomed in number and in readership? Again, the answer lies in their attractiveness to advertisers. Talk of a male identity crisis may have spurred some sales, and it is evident that men are involved in a wider range of purchasing decisions than ever before. While some 'new men' may be taking a more active interest in the household shopping, many more are marrying later and indulging themselves in personal luxuries, an option which is less readily available to their married counterparts. With support from advertisers, the leading men's magazine in the UK, *FHM*, was selling over 750,000 copies per issue in 1999, overtaking the leading women's magazine, *Cosmopolitan*, which sold just under 500,000. Advertising to men had never before looked so attractive.

vision, reflecting much more local segmentation of radio audiences and the lower production costs of radio adverts. A major advantage over other media is that the audience can be involved in other activities—particularly driving—while being exposed to an advertisement. Inevitably, a radio message is less powerful than a television message, relying solely on the sense of sound. Although there are often doubts about the extent to which an audience actually receives and understands a message, it forms a useful reminder medium when used in conjunction with other media.

Cinema. Because of the captive nature of cinema audiences, this medium could potentially have a major impact. It is frequently used to promote local services such as taxi operators and food outlets whose target market broadly corresponds to the audience of most cinemas. However, without repetition, cinema advertisements have little lasting effect, but do tend to be useful for supporting press and television advertising.

Outdoor Advertising. This is useful for reminder copy and can support other media activities. The effect of an advertisement on television or in the national press can be prolonged if recipients are exposed to a reminder poster on their way to work the following day. If strategically placed, the posters can appeal to segmented audiences, for example London Underground sites in the City of London are seen by large numbers of affluent business people. The sides of buses are often used to support new

Figure 17.2 Radio is a useful advertising medium for communicating with audiences when they are captive and/or open to persuasion. This advertisement demonstrates the power of radio in communicating a message about a fast moving consumer good, just at the moment when the audience may be thinking about the product. (Reproduced with permission of the Radio Advertising Bureau)

Figure 17.3 Many outdoor poster sites command captive audiences, which can be powerful where viewers are captive. This advertising message on a bus shelter makes a simple point which has not been lost on advertisers of products targeted at motorists stuck in traffic jams

products available locally (e.g. new store openings) and have the ability to spread their message as the bus travels along local routes. Posters can generally only be used to convey a simple communication rather than complex details.

Electronic media

The Internet has opened up new opportunities for companies to communicate with their target markets. Much of the development in this area has been aimed at allowing companies to enter into one-to-one dialogue with customers, which is not strictly a form of advertising as defined here. The use of the Internet for one-to-one communication and distribution is considered in more detail in Chapter 20. In addition, most medium and large-sized companies now have their own web sites which address mass audiences. Creating an awareness of these sites has become a major challenge for companies, with conventional media often being used to promote the web site address. As a further method of attracting 'hits', companies frequently pay for hot-links out of other companies' web sites.

Other innovative media

Advertising media can become very cluttered by the sheer volume of advertising. Companies who spot new media may avoid some of this clutter by having the field to themselves, at least until it too becomes cluttered. Innovative media which have targeted specific groups in recent years include:

- adverts on milk bottles promoting breakfast cereals;
- adverts on petrol pumps promoting car insurance;
- adverts on the sides of cows promoting ice-cream.

Media selection criteria

FACED with the availability of such a great variety of media, advertising managers need some criteria by which to assess which will be the most effective mix of media to meet their objectives. Increasingly sophisticated computer packages are becoming available which produce a schedule of advertising activities, based on their ability to get through to the target audience cost-effectively. Such programmes are based on a number of important criteria: the *impact* which an advertisement will have on the target audience; the extent to which the effects of a particular advertising message 'wear out' over time; and the cost of advertising through a particular medium. These are considered below.

Advertising exposure

Advertising exposure of a particular communication is determined by two factors: cover/reach and frequency. 'Cover' or 'reach' is the percentage of a particular target audience reached by a medium or a whole campaign, while 'frequency' is the number of times a particular target audience has an 'opportunity to see/hear' (OTS/OTH) an advertising message. The combination of these two factors results in an index of advertising exposure which is usually stated in terms of 'Gross Rating Points' (GRPs). For example, if an objective is to reach 50 per cent of the target audience three times a year, this would be stated as a GRP of 150 (i.e. 50×3).

Within a given budget, there has to be a trade-off between coverage/reach and frequency. A greater emphasis on reach means less emphasis on frequency and vice versa. The actual balance at any given time will depend on advertising objectives. Frequency *may* be a more important objective in situations where a new brand requires increased awareness, to increase loyalty to a non-dominant brand, to match the frequency of competitors' advertising, or to increase the level of understanding of a complex message.

Advertising impact

Impact is usually more closely related to the message than the medium. If, however, the medium is the message, then advertising impact should be an important criterion for media selection. Different media can produce different levels of awareness and comprehension of an identical message. In this way, the image of a high performance car presented via television is very much more powerful compared to that presented via radio.

Wearout

The concept of advertising exposure assumes that all advertising slots have equal value. However, the effect of additional slots may in fact decline, resulting in diminishing returns for each unit of expenditure. There is usually a 'threshold' level of advertising beneath which little audience response occurs. Once over this threshold, audience response tends to increase quite rapidly through a 'generation' phase until eventually a saturation point is reached. Any further advertising leads to a negative or declining response, i.e. 'wearout'. Generally, wearout is more a function of the message but if wearout for the same message does vary between media, this should be taken into account when choosing between media. Wearout may be alleviated by broadening the variety of media being used (although this is likely to increase marginal costs), or alternatively, by incorporating a more 'creative' approach in the message. A typical relationship between advertising repetitions and audience response is illustrated in Fig. 17.4.

The possibilities for overcoming the effects of wearout are dependent upon the pattern of audience responses. Two response functions over time are shown in Fig. 17.5. The 'S' shape response pattern implies that there is a need for a lot of advertising initially in order to ensure that a threshold is reached. This could be achieved by an initial 'burst' campaign, slowly reducing over time. On the other hand, the concave response pattern implies that a more regular 'drip' campaign would be the most appropriate.

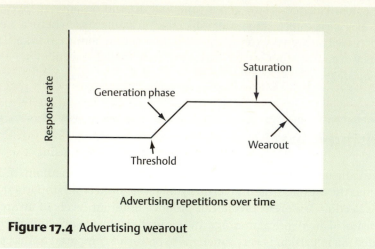

Figure 17.4 Advertising wearout

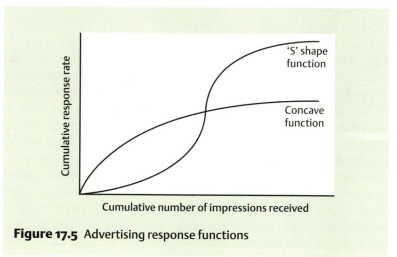

Figure 17.5 Advertising response functions

Cost

The cost of using different media varies markedly. A medium which at first sight appears to be expensive may in fact be good value in terms of achieving promotional objectives, so it follows that a sound basis for measuring cost is needed. There are generally two related cost criteria:

- **Cost per Gross Rating Point**: this is usually used for broadcast media and is the cost of a set of adverts divided by the Gross Rating Points.

- **Cost per Thousand**: this is used for print media to calculate the cost of getting the message seen by one thousand members of the target market.

These measures can be used to make cost comparisons between different media. However, a true comparison needs to take into consideration the different degrees of effectiveness each medium has—in other words, the strength of the media vehicle needs to be considered, as does the location, duration, timing and—where relevant—size of the advertisement plus a variety of more complex factors. These are all combined to form 'media weights' which are used in comparing the effectiveness of different media. Cost effectiveness therefore, is calculated using the following formula:

$$\text{Cost Effectiveness} = \frac{\text{Readers/Viewers in Target} * \text{Media Weight}}{\text{Cost}}$$

The advertising campaign

AN advertising campaign brings together a wide range of media-related activities so that, instead of being a discrete series of activities, they can act in a planned and coordinated way to achieve promotional objectives. The first stage of campaign planning is to have a clear understanding of promotional objectives (see above). Once these have been clarified, a message can be developed that is most likely to achieve these objectives. The next step is the production of the media plan. Having defined the target audience in terms of its size, location, and media characteristics, media must be selected which achieve desired levels of exposure/repetition with the target audience. A media plan must be formulated which specifies:

- the allocation of expenditure between the different media;
- the selection of specific media components—for example, in the case of print media, decisions need to be made regarding the type (tabloid versus broadsheet), size of advertisement, whether use of a Sunday supplement is to be made, and whether there is to be national or local coverage;
- the frequency and timing of insertions;
- the cost of reaching a particular target group for each of the media vehicles specified in the plan.

Finally, the advertising campaign must be coordinated with the overall promotional plan, for example by ensuring that sales promotion activities reinforce advertising messages.

Should a company undertake its own advertising campaign management, or give the task to a specialist advertising agency? There are many benefits in giving the task to an outside agency. The culture of an organization, especially large ones operating in stable or regulated environments, may not be conducive to the creativity which advertising demands and therefore may be better left to an outside organization which has a more creative culture. It may be easier for an outsider to be more customer focused and see opportunities for promotion which are not immediately apparent to insiders who are too close to the product. A further major benefit of using an advertising agency is the ability to use their expertise in developing and executing advertising campaigns. They can usually purchase media on more favourable terms than a single company acting alone.

Against these benefits, advertising agencies are sometimes accused of losing sight of the true nature of a product and its target customers. While an agency may be free to take risky innovations, these can sometimes prove disastrous and have to be disowned by the client company. Relationships between an advertising agency and its client company are critical. There are many examples of very long-lasting relationships which have been mutually beneficial and have given the agency considerable experience in understanding the client's needs. Dissatisfaction with the relationship may result in the client company inviting rival agencies to 'pitch' for its account. Large organizations frequently use a number of advertising agencies, to cover different product and/or geographical areas.

Constraints on advertising

BRITAIN, like most developed countries, recognizes the possibly harmful effects which advertising can have on the values and activities of society. Advertisers therefore face a number of controls on the content and distribution of their adverts. The content of advertisements is influenced just as much by voluntary codes as by legislation, although the effect of EU legislation has been to move more towards legislation. Contrary to popular belief, for example, controls on cigarette advertising in the UK prior to 2000 were based on a voluntary code rather than legislation.

For printed media, the Advertising Standards Authority (ASA) oversees the British Code of Advertising Practice which states that all advertisements appearing in members' publications should be legal, honest, decent, and truthful. It has reprimanded drinks companies who have promoted 'alco-pops' in magazines targeting teenagers, violating the authority's code which prohibits alcohol advertisements in publications or on poster sites where more than 25 per cent of the potential audience is aged under 18. The penalty for breaching the ASA code is the adverse publicity that follows, and ultimately the Authority could ban a business from advertising in all members' publications.

A stronger voluntary code is provided by the Independent Television Commission, which governs all terrestrial television broadcasting. Although the ITC is a statutory body, the Broadcasting Acts have devolved to the Commission the task of developing

Although the primary target audience of an advertisement may be customers, its effects on employees should not be forgotten. This is especially true of labour intensive services industries where an advert can provide encouragement for front-line employees to perform their jobs with pride, as well as encouraging customers to buy. If cabin crew of British Airways see the airline's advertisements casting them in the role of a helpful and friendly problem solver, they should be able to carry out this role effectively and with pride. At times, however, advertisements can only serve to demotivate staff. Advertising claims may be made which front-line staff are incapable of delivering, perhaps due to inadequate training or insufficient resources to keep promises made in the advert. On occasions, adverts can actually annoy staff by casting them in a demeaning role, something which the retailer Sainsbury's learnt to its cost in 1999 following its 'Value to shout about' adverts.

a code for advertisers. Like the ASA code, it too is continually evolving to meet the changing attitudes and expectations of the public. In recent years, restrictions on some products have been tightened up (e.g. cigarette advertising is now completely banned on television in the UK, and loopholes have been closed which allowed tobacco brand names to be used to promote non-tobacco products offered by the manufacturers, such as sportswear and overseas holidays). On the other hand, advertising restrictions for some products have been relaxed in response to changing public attitudes. Adverts for condoms have moved from being completely banned to being allowed, but only in very abstract form, to the present situation where the product itself can be mentioned using actors in life like situations.

Numerous other forms of voluntary controls exist. Many trade associations have codes which impose restrictions on how their members can advertise. Solicitors, for example, were previously not allowed to advertise at all, but now can do so within limits defined by the Law Society.

Assessing the effectiveness of advertising

I**T** can be very difficult to assess the effectiveness of advertising. Lord Rothermere once famously said that half of all advertising was wasted, but the trouble was he couldn't tell which half. While much evaluation relies on instinct and gut feeling, attempts at evaluation are becoming increasingly sophisticated.

It must not be forgotten that evaluation of an advertisement must be made against the objectives set for that advertisement. An advert which had the objective of creating awareness of a brand should not be criticized if it failed to achieve a short-term increase in sales. Instead, evaluation may be based on levels of awareness of the brand among the target market.

ADWATCH

The weekly analysis of advertisement recall

Q: Which of the following TV commercials do you remember seeing recently?

	Last week	Account	Agency/TV buyer	%
1	(1)	**National Lottery**	WCRS/BMP OMD	74
2	(–)	**Orange Mobile Phone Network**	WCRS/BMP OMD	71
3	(5=)	**I Can't Believe It's Not Butter**	McCann-Erickson/Initiative Media	70
4=	(3)	**Andrex**	J Walter Thompson/MindShare	68
4=	(4)	**Pantène Pro V Shampoo and Conditioner**	Grey Advertising/Starcom	68
6=	(5=)	**Homebase**	Abbott Mead Vickers BBDO/New PHD	66
6=	(5=)	**McDonald's**	Leo Burnett/Starcom	66
6=	(12=)	**Sainsbury's**	M&C Saatchi/New PHD	66
9	(9)	**One 2 One**	Bartle Bogle Hegarty/Motive	65
10	(8)	**Bounty Kitchen Towels**	Leo Burnett/Starcom	64
11	(4)	**Halifax Mortgage**	Bates UK/Zenith Media	62
12=	(–)	**BUPA**	WCRS/MediaVest	61
12=	(–)	**British Gas**	BMP DDB/BMP OMD	61
14	(–)	**Intel Pentium III**	Euro RSCG Wnek Gosper/Mediapolis	57
15	(–)	**Kleenex Huggies**	Ogilvy & Mather/Mindshare	56
16	(19=)	**Inland Revenue Better Deal For Working Parents**	St Luke's/MediaVest	55
17	(–)	**Lenor Fabric Enhancer**	Grey Advertising/Starcom	54
18	(–)	**Mr Muscle Foamer Drain Cleaner**	Banks Hoggins O'Shea FCB/Optimedia	53
19	(–)	**Fairy Non-Bio Laundry Detergent**	D'Arcy/Starcom	51
20	(–)	**Asda George**	Publicis/Carat	48

Adwatch research was conducted from October 1 to October 3 by NOP Research Group (0171-890 9445) as part of a weekly telephone omnibus survey among more than 1000 adults. Copies of the Adwatch data and analysis are available from Liz Price at NOP. Advertisements were selected by Xtreme Register (0171-520 6409) and CIA Medianetwork (0171-633 9999).

Figure 17.6 In a weekly telephone omnibus survey, NOP asks a national representative sample of adults aged 15+ about the adverts that they have seen recently. This table, published in *Marketing* magazine, gives some indication of levels of awareness created by individual advertising campaigns. Additional qualitative techniques are useful in order to establish the extent to which the campaigns have changed viewers' attitudes.
(Reproduced with permission of NOP Research group)

Is there any relationship between an advertisement being one which is liked by the public, and one which sells products for the company paying for it? Sadly, some of the most nauseating adverts which we love to hate turn out to be the most successful. The advertising for the soap powder Radion was universally condemned for its brashness and depiction of women as subservient housewives. Yet despite leading in polls as the public's most hated advert, it undoubtedly contributed to the phenomenal sales of Radion. 'Nice' adverts which are applauded by the public for their humour may not be sufficiently forceful to motivate viewers to buy the product. During the late 1990s, many Rover adverts were admired by the public for their humour, but this did not prevent a significant fall in sales.

Used in combination, a number of techniques can be used to try to assess the effectiveness of an individual advert or an advertising campaign:

- Prior to launching an advert, companies use focus groups to test its effectiveness. Researchers are particularly concerned to identify memorable parts of an advert and how far an individual progressed before they skipped to the next subject. Prior evaluation of an advert can help avoid companies running adverts which subsequently turn out to be offensive or misinterpreted.

- It was noted above that routine monitoring of a sample panel's television viewing is undertaken by BARB. Similar monitoring of the press is undertaken by the National Readership Survey. While such monitoring can estimate how many people see an advertisement, they provide little evidence of whether the advert was recalled or acted upon.

- To overcome the above problem, a number of panels are retained by market research agencies and are consulted regularly to ascertain which recent advertisements they can recall, either spontaneously or with prompting. One example is the weekly NOP weekly telephone omnibus survey carried out among 1,000 adults on behalf of sponsoring companies (Fig. 17.6).

Chapter summary and key linkages to other chapters

Advertising is an element of the promotion mix characterized by impersonal, paid-for communication. As with all elements of the promotion mix, effective advertising requires a clear analysis of the market environment of the product being advertised, a clear specification of objectives, an advertising strategy which flows from these objectives, and a detailed programme of implementation. The task of developing an advertising campaign is often left to a specialist agency which can take an independent view and use its experience to the benefit of a client company. It is very difficult to separate the contribution to sales of advertising from other elements of the marketing mix which are discussed in the previous and following chapters.

Advertising can be related to the following chapters in this book:

Chapter 1: What is marketing?: To many people, marketing IS advertising. It should now be clear that advertising is just a small part of marketing, and that advertising will not be effective if the other elements of marketing orientation are not present.

Chapter 2: The marketing environment: Changes in customer expectations are continually influencing the content and distribution of advertisements. New technology allows new advertising media to emerge.

Chapter 3: Segmentation: Effective advertising depends crucially on an ability to segment audiences and develop a message and medium which is most appropriate to each targeted segment.

Chapter 4: Branding: Advertising is usually crucial to the development of strong brands.

Chapter 5: Marketing and ethics: The discussion in this chapter of controls on advertising has indicated that society has an interest in the content of advertisements. Unethical advertising may be bad for society, but it is also quite likely to be bad in the long term for the advertiser.

Chapter 6: Marketing research: Marketing research is essential in order to identify and address target markets and to evaluate the effectiveness of advertising.

Chapter 7: Buyer behaviour: The discussion in this chapter of buyer readiness states relates closely to the chapter on buyer behaviour. For commercial buyers, identifying members of the decision-making unit can be crucial for effective targeting of advertisements.

Chapter 8: Buyer–seller relationship development: Advertising should be aimed not just at recruiting new customers, but at retaining existing ones.

Chapter 9: The product: What are the unique benefits of a product that should be promoted to the target market?

Chapter 10: New product development and innovation: For radically innovative new products, public relations alone may be sufficient to launch a new product. For most products, however, a substantial advertising effort is required to launch a new product, especially where there is relatively little novelty and the market is competitive.

Chapter 11: Developing a sustainable competitive advantage: Advertising alone will not create and sustain a competitive advantage—the other elements of the marketing plan must also be correct.

Chapters 12/13: Pricing theory and applications: Advertising should create awareness of the unique advantages of a product, which justify buyers paying a premium price.

Chapters 14/15: Intermediaries/logistics: Intermediaries are recipients of advertising, which may be necessary to encourage them to carry a manufacturer's stock. They also frequently work with suppliers in developing joint advertising programmes.

Chapter 16: Principles of promotion planning: This chapter provided an overview of promotion planning and the communication process, of which advertising is an interrelated component.

Chapter 18: Selling and sales management: The task of personal selling is facilitated by effective advertising which provides sales leads and facilitates sales negotiations.

Chapter 19: Sales promotion and public relations: Sales promotion frequently undermines efforts to build strong brands through advertising.

Chapter 20: Direct marketing: New media frequently rely on conventional impersonal advertising media for creating awareness and initiating a dialogue.

Chapter 21: Organizing for marketing: Advertising aims must relate to other corporate and marketing aims.

Chapter 22: Services marketing: The intangibility of services often creates a perception of greater riskiness which advertising must seek to overcome.

Chapter 23: Global marketing: How should advertising messages and media be adapted when a company seeks to enter overseas markets?

Case study

Investing in advertising

It is widely accepted that a good proportion of advertising expenditure is wasted and techniques are constantly being developed to ensure that a firm's advertising achieves maximum possible effect. Most effort has been directed at trying to establish the effect of advertising on sales. However, another important dimension is understanding the effects of advertising on a company's share price. With advertising expenditure in the UK reaching over £14 billion by 1998, the search for better evaluation techniques has never been greater.

Recent research carried out in the USA by James Gregory, CEO and founder of brand strategy company Corporate Branding, has suggested that advertising not only helps sales, but has a positive impact on share price too. His analysis indicates that advertising expenditure is the single biggest contributor to brand image. The research built on earlier research, which studied fifty *Fortune* 100 companies over a seven-year period to establish a link between advertising expenditure and corporate reputation. Gregory's work, under way since 1997, widened this to a study of 220 companies. It measured different contributing factors which influenced share price, including a company's size, financial strength, expected cash flow growth and new product developments. Brand image was defined as having two distinct elements: familiarity and favourability. Familiarity is a quantitative measure of the number of buyers familiar with the company. Favourability is the qualitative aspect of its image, based on individuals' perceptions of a company's reputation, management, and investment potential.

Gregory discovered that corporate brand image directly explained 5 per cent of the variation of company share price, which he described as 'hugely significant'. The figure is not large when compared with cash flow, earnings, and dividends (30 per cent), but it is nearly as important as the 6 per cent explained by financial strength (stable earnings and amount of debt). Furthermore, the research indicated that brand image has an indirect influence on 70 per cent of all the other factors which determine the share price. Such indirect influence was manifested through cash flow, earnings and dividends, share price growth and expected cash flow growth. The research also examined the factors that contributed towards brand image, and advertising was shown to contribute 30 per cent of the effect. Company size was also important, contributing some 23 per cent towards brand image, with other factors such as publicity, management changes, and products contributing 22 per cent.

Some validation of Gregory's findings can be seen in separate research undertaken by WCRS and Lehman Bros on behalf of the UK mobile phone operator Orange. The company won the Institute of Practitioners in Advertising's 1998 Advertising Effectiveness Award for its paper, which analysed the contribution of advertising to the success of Orange as a FTSE 100 company. An advertising campaign launched in 1994 through television, radio, and newspapers featured the memorable slogan 'The future is bright, the future is Orange'. Research suggested that the advertising campaign created an earnings payback in excess of six times its expenditure and increased Orange's implied share value by £2.49 billion. At the time of launching the campaign, analysts had accused Orange of not fulfilling its marketing pledge, for example its coverage was perceived as being much inferior to its main competitors, Vodaphone and Cellnet. By the end of 1998, however, the company's market capitalization had increased to around £10 billion, and while much of this further rise could undoubtedly be attributed to the strength of demand for mobile phones, it confounded earlier sceptics who had accused Orange of short-termism and a preoccupation with advertising over network development.

Many factors which affect share price are out of a company's hands, but image is within its control. It is therefore a tool that can be used to manipulate share price performance. It follows that advertising should be seen as an investment which yields measurable results in terms of a company's market value. Debate about how a brand should be valued in a company's balance sheet has continued, but many take-over bids have been focused on the portfolio of brands which a target company owns.

Adapted from 'Waking the City up to the Value of Brand Marketing', *Marketing*, 27 May 1999, p. 19.

Case study review questions

1 What difficulties exist in trying to determine the link between a company's advertising expenditure and its share price performance?

2 What factors other than advertising might have explained the strong share performance of Orange?

3 To what extent should advertising expenditure be capitalized and recognized as an asset in a company's balance sheet?

Chapter review questions

1 To what extent is it possible, or desirable, to identify advertising as a distinct element of the promotion mix?

2 What factors should a company take into account when developing an advertising message for a new product?

3 Why is it so important for advertisers to be rigorous in their analysis and choice of medium?

4 Should advertisers face greater levels of regulatory controls in order to protect society, or do such controls unnecessarily stifle consumers' choice?

5 Is it still true today to say that 'half of all advertising is wasted, but we don't know which half'? To what extent have recent innovations improved marketers' ability to evaluate effectiveness?

6 Is advertising essentially a creative art or a science?

References

Bayton, J. A. (1958), 'Motivation, Cognition, Learning—Basic Factors in Consumer Behavior', *Journal of Marketing*, **22**, 3, pp. 282–89.

Coulston-Thomas, C. T. (1985), *Marketing Communications* (London: Heinemann).

Chisnall, P. (1985), *Strategic Business Marketing* (Englewood Cliffs, NJ: Prentice Hall).

Maslow, A. (1954), *Motivation and Personality* (New York: Harper).

Rogers, E. M. (1962), *Diffusion of Innovation* (New York: The Free Press).

Selected further reading

The following texts provide a more detailed analysis of the principles and practices of advertising:

- Butterfield, L. (1997*), Excellence in Advertising: The IPA Guide to Best Practice* (Oxford: Butterworth-Heinemann).

- Hart, N. A. (1995), *The Practice of Advertising* (Oxford: Butterworth-Heinemann).

- Moriarty, S., and Burnett, J. (1997), *Introduction to Marketing Communications* (Englewood Cliffs, NJ: Prentice Hall).

- Smith, P. R. (1998), *Marketing Communications*, 2nd edn. (London: Kogan Page).

- Wilmshurst, J. (1998), *The Fundamentals of Advertising* (Oxford: Butterworth-Heinemann).

Useful web links

Institute of Practitioners in Advertising: http://www.ipa.co.uk/contents.html

Advertising Standards Authority: http://www.asa.org.uk/

The Advertising Association (UK): http://www.adassoc.org.uk/

Independent Television Commission: http://www.itc.org.uk/

Newspaper Readership Survey: http://www.inma.org/reading.html

American Association of Advertising Agencies home page. AAAA is the national trade organization representing the advertising agency business in the USA: http://www.aaaa.org

European Association of Advertising Agencies home page, with links to national bodies throughout Europe: http://www.eaaa.be

Chapter 18
Selling and Sales Management

Chapter objectives

Selling is a frequently misunderstood aspect of marketing. To some, marketing is synonymous with selling, while many others fail to appreciate the complexity and diversity of selling situations. The aim of this chapter is to examine the scope, characteristics, and importance of personal selling and to understand the changing nature of selling from a transactional to a relational perspective. The chapter will outline the steps involved in making a sale and identify the major steps in sales planning, setting objectives, developing selling strategies, forecasting, setting budgets, and implementation. An overview is given of the main aspects of sales management and the various methods of rewarding sales personnel.

Introduction

A COMMON difficulty when attempting to discuss selling lies not so much in defining what selling and sales management is, but how selling interrelates with marketing. This interrelationship is explored by Steward (1993), who suggests that to omit the importance of selling as an integral component of the marketing activities of an organization is akin to 'omitting a striker from a football team, a gun without a firing pin, a chemical formula without a catalyst and a organism without the means of reproduction'.

There is limited evidence to support the view of Drucker (1973) who stated that if organizations get their marketing activity right they will not need a salesforce as customers will come beating to their door. Such a statement is naïve and does not recognize the complex nature of many purchase decisions and the importance of human relationships and the sales function in business transactions.

A further dimension of the role of selling and sales management relates to the changing nature of how organizations are doing business, particularly with regard to the trend towards strategic partnerships, joint ventures, alliances, and the increasingly integrated nature of supply chain structures. Very few organizations can operate without considering the range of networks that have been established within industry sectors (Ford *et al.* 1998). Being part of a network is often a prerequisite for doing business and once in the network the maintenance and building of relationships becomes a critical aspect of an organization's marketing and sales strategy.

While the above considerations will form an important part of this chapter, this does not negate the need to consider the important role a salesperson plays within most commercial organizations. The salesforce commonly represents the primary link between an organization and its customers. This chapter would therefore not be complete without acknowledging the skill and knowledge required of a salesperson to undertake a role that is at times extremely difficult, frustrating, and soul destroying. The chapter will also consider the important role that sales management therefore plays in managing and motivating the salesforce.

While the focus of this chapter will primarily be on personal selling on a face-to-face basis, consideration will also be given to various types of situations in which the selling function can be found. This includes retail sales assistants, merchandising, and telephone selling.

The scope and importance of selling

PERSONAL selling involves interpersonal dialogue. It requires person-to-person interaction between a prospective customer and a salesperson. Such dialogue may occur face to face or by other personal forms of communication. Personal selling is not simply about persuasion and persistence although undoubtedly such skills and attributes do come in useful. Professional selling is more about gathering market and customer information, listening, interpreting and understanding customer needs, managing the customer–supplier relationship interface, and communicating clearly to the customer the benefits of purchasing a particular product that meets their needs.

Selling as a profession is often devalued and misunderstood. Much of this misunderstanding comes from the activities of sectors of the profession itself, particularly the sleazy end represented by pressurized selling techniques, which traditionally were (and still commonly are) practised in several consumer service and goods industries such as double glazing, financial services, timeshares, and kitchens/bathrooms. In an industrial context professional selling is more highly regarded. However, such regard is often as much a reflection of an organization's orientation towards sales in preference to marketing, rather than its recognition of the role of selling within marketing. In fact, sales orientation is often evident in many industrial organizations where the sales manager/director is given prominence over most marketing functions.

Salesmen are not a highly esteemed group of people in the UK. A survey carried out in 1998 by a leading recruitment consultant put used car salesmen firmly in the bottom place of least desired professions. Doctors and the clergy—two occupations least associated with selling—scored very highly. Similar surveys in the USA have shown quite a different picture, with salesmanship being considered a great virtue. Maybe the British, being typically very reserved, don't like being sold to. Much of the misapprehension about selling may be due to perceived bad practices within a number of sectors. But is bad practice ultimately the salesperson's worse enemy? Is a trusted salesperson more likely to achieve not just a one-off sale, but repeated sales?

McMurry (1961) provides a standard classification of selling situations.

1. The salesperson's job is mainly concerned with delivering the product, e.g. milk, beer, bread, lemonade, etc. He or she possesses little in the way of selling responsibilities. Increases in sales are more likely to stem from a good service and a pleasant manner.
2. The salesperson is predominantly an inside order taker, e.g. the sales assistant in a retail outlet. Opportunities to sell are rather limited, as customers have in many cases already made up their minds.
3. The salesperson is predominantly an order taker but works in the field and is sometimes able to negotiate additional sales. Selling is usually done by senior executives at head office. The field salesperson simply records and processes the customers orders and makes sure that the customer is carrying sufficient stock. Again, good service and a pleasant personality may lead to more orders, but the salesperson has only limited opportunity for creative selling.
4. In missionary selling, the salesperson does not actually take orders but rather builds up goodwill, educates the actual or potential user, and undertakes various promotional activities, e.g. a salesperson for a pharmaceutical company who makes doctors and pharmacists aware of the benefits of prescribing a new drug.
5. In technical selling, many companies in the industrial market use sales engineers or sales people with technical knowledge where product and application knowledge is a central part of the selling function.
6. Creative selling involves both tangible and intangible products and services, e.g. vacuum cleaners, washing machines, encyclopaedias, insurance, banking, and investment advice. Services tend to be more difficult because the product cannot easily be demonstrated.

Many of these roles are still evident within organizations but the list does not do justice to the role of a modern professional field salesperson which involves significantly greater responsibilities and more complex roles than McMurry's list gives credit for. A similar criticism can be made of the following list which highlights one or more of the following tasks as being identifiable within a salesperson's responsibilities (Kotler 1997, p. 686).

Prospecting: searching for prospects or leads.

Targeting: deciding how to allocate time among prospects and customers.

Communicating: skilfully communicating information about the company's products and services.

Selling: knowing the art of sales—approaching, presenting, answering objections, and closing sales.

Servicing: providing various services to customers—consulting on their problems, rendering technical assistance, arranging financing, and expediting delivery.

Information gathering: conducting market research and intelligence work and filling in call reports.

Allocating: deciding which customers will get scarce products during product shortages.

The range of these roles and responsibilities will vary between organizations and sectors particularly in terms of the level of complexity. For a retail salesperson the primary role is to meet customers who enter the shop or store and through dialogue to encourage purchase of a product or service. Such a salesperson may also be responsible for maintaining the appearance of the stock on the shelf and provide support and advice to customers. A telephone salesperson requires a different range of skills, and is often highly trained to handle telephone sales calls either inbound or outbound and to manage customer relationships over the telephone. Importantly they are trained to influence the purchase decision, often following a predetermined and well-tested script.

Such lists provide some value in identifying the traditional role of a salesperson. As suggested above, however, the range of activities which a professional salesperson needs to cover is considerably more diverse than that of order taker, order maker, and sales support.

A particular criticism of the above lists is their transactional orientation which does not recognize the importance of the ongoing relationship between the buyer and the seller. You will recall from Chapter 8 that ongoing relationships between buyers and sellers are becoming increasingly important in many sectors. The modern salesperson is as much if not more interested in the process that maintains a delighted and loyal customer as they are with achieving a transaction (Egan 1997). The relationship between a seller and a customer begins before a sale is made, is consummated at the time of the sale, and is likely to intensify as the relationship evolves and becomes embedded. The salesperson's primary role then becomes one of managing the relationship rather than the transactions that take place within the relationship. This requires a range of new skills from the salesperson, but alongside these personal skills needs to be a range of support mechanisms and processes from the organization. Many organizations believe that because a sales person has established good relationships with a buying team that they are practising relationship marketing. Such a belief is soon shattered when either the salesperson/member of the buying team changes or the marketing environment in which the organizations operate changes (see Levitt 1983).

In recent years the recognition of the importance of selling within marketing-led organizations has increased. This has occurred at the same time as the Institute for Professional Sales has raised its profile and promoted the importance of managing and building a professional sales function. As identified in this chapter the sales function has also become more complex and therefore the need for highly trained and effective sales personnel has never been greater.

Principles of personal selling

THE following section considers the principal factors that lead to effective sales performance. Selling techniques can be placed on a continuum from a high-pressured, sales-orientated approach to a softer solutions-based, customer-orientated approach. As indicated earlier, much of the blame for selling's low professional esteem lies in its reputation for sleazy hard sell. Such a reputation does not do justice to the sales profession and therefore a clearer identification of the factors that lead to effective and professional sales performance need to be considered.

Major areas of knowledge and skill

A professional salesperson will require extensive training in sales and negotiation techniques. Alongside this they also require company, product, service, market, competitor, and customer knowledge. Further important skills are time management, area management, and report writing. Development of these skills and knowledge areas will enable a salesperson to do their job more efficiently and effectively.

Company and product knowledge

A salesperson must have extensive and up-to-date knowledge of both the company they represent and the products it offers. Knowledge of the company should include a clear understanding of its mission and purpose, key personnel, operations and support functions, and its manufacturing and service processes. A salesperson cannot afford to make promises which the organization does not have the competence or capability to meet.

Similarly the salesperson must have knowledge of the products and services they can offer and their applications. The buying organization or individual will commonly expect the salesperson to act as a consultant and adviser on many issues relating to the product or service use. The salesperson will also be expected to have good technical knowledge and both understand and be able to explain the product features and performance attributes. While a salesperson may have sound technical knowledge, it is equally critical that such knowledge can be explained to the customer in terms of benefits and not just features. Every product feature or performance attribute will accrue some benefit to a customer and it is the salesperson's role to sell the benefits (e.g. time saving, efficiency/cost gains, performance improvements etc.).

Market and customer knowledge

The salesperson will be closer to the customer than most other personnel in a selling organization. A key part of their role has to be as the 'eyes and ears' of the organization. The salesperson should act as a communication conduit to the marketing department, providing detailed information on competitor activities, market trends, customer requirements, and changes in key personnel, etc. This is often a neglected part of a salesperson's role and yet the benefits that can accrue from having accurate and timely information justify attention to this aspect of a salesperson's role. The salesperson requires training in both information gathering and analysis plus development in report writing, writing up visit reports, and presentation skills. Reports from the field are an essential element of a salesperson's function but are often neglected, seen by the salesperson as a millstone that consumes time that could be better spent seeing more customers.

Time management and area management

Careful management of time and planning of calls can generate opportunities for the salesperson to make extra sales visits or gather and analyse market and customer information. If a sales person is making three sales calls per day over 300 days this would generate 900 sales visits per annum. If 20 per cent of these visits generated a sale 180 sales would successfully be achieved. One extra sales call per day would generate 300 extra opportunities to sell a product or service. If 20 per cent of these calls were successfully turned into orders this would represent sixty extra sales which represent a 25 per cent increase in sales to that salesperson. The marginal costs of servicing these extra accounts would be minimal and therefore the salesperson's contribution to profit would substantially increase. Spending more time with customers normally generates more business for the organization and therefore a salesperson should be trained in time management so that less time is spent travelling or waiting.

Elements of the selling process

Consider these barriers facing a salesperson, highlighted in an advertisement by the publisher of *Business Week*, McGraw–Hill.

I don't know who you are.

I don't know your company.

I don't know your company's products.

I don't know what your company stands for.

I don't know your company's customers.

I don't know your company's record.

I don't know your company's reputation.

Now—What was it you wanted to sell me?

Prospecting

A key function of a salesperson is to assist in the process of identifying and generating leads in conjunction with marketing. Unsophisticated prospecting involves door knocking, searching through telephone directories, trade directories, and other general listings of companies, etc. The probability is that only a small percentage of the organizations contacted will be interested in what the organization has to offer. Such cold calling is not the most effective method of identifying potential clients. The generation of sales leads from referrals by customers, suppliers, or other business/ social contacts will generally provide better prospects on the basis that prior knowledge of the potential customer is known by the individual making the referral. Similarly leads generated by exhibitions, conferences, seminars, and responses to advertisements will provide 'warmer' leads.

Having established a customer prospect list the salesperson should conduct some form of evaluation of each potential buyer in terms of their business, markets, and products and their probability of purchase. Those prospects that appear to offer the most potential can then be shortlisted for contact.

The following section outlines the classic structure of a sales call. Steward (1993) breaks this down into a number of stages (Fig. 18.1).

Plan Call (Preparation)

Objectives   Anticipate objections
Opening statement   Sales aids

Sales Presentation — Opening

Create impact   State purpose
Summarize

Sales Presentation — Body

Question   Use aids
Listen   Handle objections
Sell benefits

Closing the Sale

Follow up

Figure 18.1 The structure of a sales call

Preparation

Before contacting potential customers a good salesperson will research the customer and find out as much information as possible in relation to the organization's current and previous purchase history. They should obtain as much insight into the organization's history and current business situation and strategy as they can. Much of this information can be gleaned from contacts within the industry or by analysing annual reports and other company publications. The fact that a salesperson has established some knowledge about a prospective customer will make them better equipped to handle the first meeting. Preparation can be as simple as knowing the key contact's name and how long they have been at the organization and in their current role. Clear sales objectives should be set before approaching the customer. Without objectives the call can become just a chat and nothing achieved. It is also important to prepare an appropriate opening statement rather than a general 'how are you today'. This will suggest a greater degree of professionalism and preparation on the part of the salesperson. To avoid being caught unexpectedly in the middle of the sales presentation it is a useful exercise to anticipate potential objections that the buyer might raise and prepare answers to these.

As indicated above, cold calling is not the best way of approaching a potential customer. Appointments should be made and confirmed in writing. It is useful to make clear the nature and purpose of the call early on and to explain how the customer's name was obtained. Any initial contact should be built around general discussion, broadly clarifying the prospect's needs/concerns. Once the appointment is confirmed the salesperson can then plan their sales presentation.

The sales presentation

The sales presentation will vary in style dependent upon the product/service and the nature of the relationship established with the prospective customer. What follows is the general framework and guidelines that a good salesperson will follow when presenting a standard sales pitch to the client.

Create impact

In the opening minutes of a sales call, the sales person should endeavour to create interest and develop rapport with the buyer. This is a critical first stage in the sales presentation. In the first five to ten minutes the prospective customer is determining whether they like you, trust you, and want to give you any time of their day. In this first stage it is important to use the time to put the customer at ease. Some salespersons use a technique called 'matching'. The salesperson will wear appropriate clothes in line with the potential customer's and attempt to adopt similar mannerisms and speech in line with the customer's. Early conversation will revolve around the potential customer's personal interests or issues. This process of matching is best termed the 'dance of rapport'. It is only once good rapport has been established that the salesperson should commence the next stage of the sales presentation.

Asking questions and listening

One of the most important skills of an effective salesperson is their ability to ask questions and listen. The process of asking questions aims to ascertain the exact nature of the customer's needs, concerns, issues, and possible objections to making a purchase. The process of asking questions also has the benefit of keeping control of the sales interview. The general rule at this stage is to keep control by always asking a question. If the salesperson does answer a question they should finish the sentence with another question. Even simple questions suffice such as 'Are the points I have made clear?', 'Are there any further issues you would like to discuss?', 'Can you explain to me in more detail about——?'

The salesperson's ability to listen to what has been said is also a critical skill. Often the buyer will provide clues as to their interest or needs or potential objections which can be missed if the buyer is not listening. Objections are signals of a customer's concern and must be dealt with as they occur. Objections are potential reasons why the customer will not buy your product. Typical objections are comments such as 'That sounds expensive compared to other quotes I have had', or 'You do not appear to offer as extensive a range as your competitor'. Objections are reasons not to buy and therefore must be dealt with to the satisfaction of the buyer otherwise the opportunity to 'close' the sale will be made very difficult. Techniques for handling objections abound but primarily the exact nature and reason for the objection should be made clear and then the objection minimized through asking questions and giving alternatives to the customer's way of thinking. The aim of the salesperson is to provide enough evidence and reassurance to the buyer that the objection is not a relevant or important concern because the benefits of the product or service being offered outweigh the concern.

Selling the benefits

Once the salesperson has clarified the client's needs and interests and answered their concerns, the next stage of the selling process is to sell the benefits of the product to the customer. Customers buy benefits not features and are interested in what the product or service can do for them or their organization. This is a critical phase because the salesperson is looking and listening for 'buy in' from the customer. The presentation may involve a demonstration or use of visual props and may include endorsements from previous clients but always it should be sold in terms of what the particular feature being shown or described means in terms of benefits to the customer.

Buying signals

Signs of interest are called buying signals. A question from the buyer asking for more details is a buying signal. A comment such as 'that's interesting' is a very strong buying signal. All buying signals should be closed by the salesperson. The guidelines to closing are outlined below.

Closing the sale

The term closing the sale refers to the salesperson's technique of asking the buyer for an order. A successful salesperson will take every buying signal that they hear as an opportunity to close. The close might involve simply asking for the order or it might be a question that offers the buyer an alternative. A variety of closing techniques can be found outlined in many textbooks on selling but such techniques are most commonly used in instances where there is a transactional sell. Asking for the order should come naturally when a salesperson knows that they have clarified a customer's needs and key concerns, answered all their questions, and handled potential reasons not to buy to the satisfaction of the customer. Good salespeople do not need to adopt hard sell tactics.

Follow up

The follow up, while being a common courtesy is also an important aspect of the selling process. The buyer may require some form of demonstration of commitment and care or may have a series of minor points that require tying up to ensure the contract runs smoothly. The follow up is also an important relationship builder and can signal the opportunity for potential future repeat business. The follow up may take the form of a letter confirming the issues discussed or a telephone call to ensure the buyer is satisfied.

Industrial/business selling—the complex sale

The industrial market-place comprises businesses that range from small manufacturing units through to multinational/global corporations and includes both goods and service sectors. Although it has been customary to talk about 'industrial marketing', today the term 'business-to-business marketing' is more prevalent. The selling process outlined above needs to be adapted to reflect the nature and demands of the more complex purchase processes that are often evident in business purchase decisions. In a business-to-business context the sales presentations may cover a period of many weeks and months and involve a number of individuals. Such complexities are considered below.

Industrial goods and services are often purchased by professional buyers who are highly trained managers responsible for significant levels of expenditure. These buyers will not be working in isolation but may be part of a project team or committee that is evaluating alternative suppliers. While knowledge of these teams/committees is important, the seller also needs to be aware of the different purchase roles that are evident within industrial/business purchase decisions. The concept of a decision-making unit was introduced in Chapter 7 and is considered further here in the context of commercial buying units. Buying roles have been classified into six distinct categories that create a buying centre or decision-making unit (Webster and Wind 1972).

The Buyer is responsible for identifying, evaluating, and selecting suppliers and negotiating the purchase. They may also be involved in writing specifications. Their choices and decisions are, however, often heavily influenced by other individuals who perform other roles in the purchase decision process.

The User is the person who actually uses the product. These people can be quite influential in initiating a purchase decision and influencing the specification. However, the power of the user is often quite low in the buying centre particularly with regard to decision-making but their role is nevertheless an important one for the seller to identify and respond to.

The Decision-maker: the decision to purchase may be made by an individual or a group and can be dependent upon the value of the purchase and level of authority at which such decisions are made. It is important that the salesperson identifies who the decision-makers are otherwise much valuable time can be wasted selling the benefits of a product or service to an individual who has no authority to make the decision and therefore refers it on to another person or group.

The Approver: once a decision has been made it may have to be forwarded on to get approval. Such authorization is common for high value purchases which have significant financial implications for the organization.

The Influencer is commonly an expert who has specialist knowledge in the area of the purchase being considered. The influencer has a primary role to play in the decision-making unit and therefore has to be identified and reached by the salesperson. Influencers provide advice to the other members of the buying centre and are often employees with technical or professional skills and knowledge. Christopher, Payne, and Ballantyne (1991) suggest that for some purchase decisions the selling organization needs to look outside the confines of the purchase organization and identify key stakeholders who may also have an influence on purchase decisions.

The Gatekeeper is the person who controls the flow of information to people or access by the salesperson to key individuals. Such control can create problems for both the selling organization and within the buying centre as often decisions are being made with incomplete knowledge. It is critical therefore to have knowledge of individuals or departments that are performing this role and overcome the problems directly or bypass the gatekeepers and go direct to the other members of the buying centre.

The business purchase decision is made more complex because of the buying process adopted and time-scales within which decisions are made. A common purchasing technique is to use a tender document requesting specifications and quotes which are sealed and considered by the buying centre but with no salesperson present. Some contracts/projects take several years before decisions are made. The underlying complexity of the industrial or business purchase decision therefore requires the selling organization to move towards a more relational and longer-term selling strategy rather than a short-term transactional strategy.

Every salesperson knows the importance of human relations , interpersonal skills, and positive mental attitude in their daily lives as professional salespeople. But is this enough to make a good salesperson? Unfortunately when combined with the theory of self-motivation and the setting of clearly defined objectives, these interesting and absorbing topics can produce an adverse reaction in some individuals who then spend most of their day conditioning themselves that they feel great, reciting self-motivators like 'success is achieved by those who try and keep trying', or 'when the going gets tough the tough get going' and 'I'm going to be top salesman this year' and forget that their real task is to locate decision-makers and persuade them to buy! Pontificating about success is fine but at the end of the day, salesmen must make it happen!

The impact of relationship marketing on personal selling

I⊤ was noted in Chapter 8 that within the last decade relationship marketing has become a topic of increasing interest to many companies and marketing academics. The origins of relationship marketing can be found within the context of industrial and business purchase decisions. It has been pointed out that while the traditional sales model focused solely on the buyer and the decision-making unit, relationship marketing broadens this perspective to include managing relationships within the buying organization, intermediaries, and, for some organizations such as car and computer manufacturers, the consumer (Peck *et al.* 1999). In many industries the focus of marketing activity has moved from the market-place to managing the supply chain as this is where the competitive battles will now be won. Gronroos (1996) identified three strategic elements of the relationship approach;

1. A service business orientation;
2. A process and not functional perspective;
3. An active seeking of involvement in partnerships and network.

As a result of this reorientation suppliers should broaden their reach to make direct contact with key supply chain members and other key stakeholders. The focus of marketing and sales activity should be on customer retention not acquisition and customer orientation should be embedded within the organization's culture.

The implications of this reorientation for the role of selling within an organization's marketing strategy are significant. Increasingly new organization structures are being developed with new roles such as category managers, customer relations managers, business development managers, key account managers. While the traditional buyer–seller relationship would have been one of contract/price and volume negotiation the new relationship approach involves multifunctional levels of interaction with the key account manager role requiring a greater range of skills to manage these interactions than was necessary under the traditional buyer–seller relationship model (Fig. 18.2).

Shipley (1997) further suggests that a range of generic sales/marketing approaches exist for suppliers to select from. Fig. 18.3 summarizes these different approaches using two axes, the sales and marketing approach on the horizontal axis and the salesperson's primary concern on the vertical axis.

Shipley suggests that the concern of the salesperson is positioned along a continuum running from concern for getting the sales to concern for managing the well-being of the customer. The salesperson's style will be influenced by whether their organization has a transactional or relational orientation, for instance in terms of how performance is evaluated and rewarded, time-scales for achievement of goals, etc.

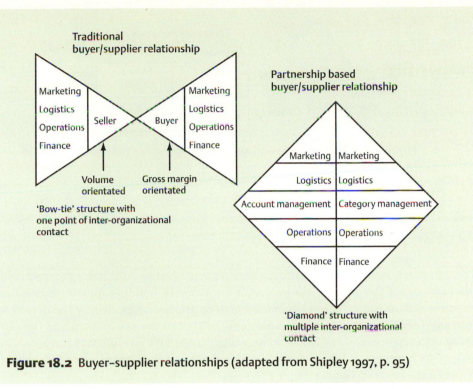

Figure 18.2 Buyer–supplier relationships (adapted from Shipley 1997, p. 95)

Account opener approach

This option represents the classic selling opportunity whereby a sales lead is converted into a sale and the seller and buyer negotiate a one-off transaction. Such an approach is highly transactional in nature and relies on the ability of the organization to generate leads and highly skilled salespeople trained to convert such opportunities into a sale. The salesperson is likely to be rewarded on a commission on sales basis.

Have a nice day approach

Here the company is seeking to build repeat sales via relationships but these relationships are probably only managed as part of a broad customer care programme. The actions and words of the sales people/employees are merely a surface gloss to cover up the organization's transactional orientation. 'Have a nice day' is said as part of a trained ritual but is not meant with any sincerity.

		Company sales orientation	
		Transaction	Relationship
Salesperson's primary concern	The Sale	Account opener	'Have a nice day'
	Customer	Account keeper	Key account manager

Figure 18.3 Supplier sales and marketing approaches (adapted from Shipley 1997, p. 92)

Account keeper approach

This approach reflects the situation where an organization still has a transactional orientation but the salesperson perceives the value in building long-term ongoing business relationships. The salesperson's actions are not supported by the organization and therefore the relationship only exists between the salesperson and the purchase organization and not through inter-organizational cross-functional teams. The lack of such integration negates the likelihood of any relationship being established between the organizations.

Key account manager approach

With this approach, both the salesperson and the organization are committed to building long-term, ongoing relationships with key account customers. The orientation and structure of the organization is such that cross-functional support and adequate resources are committed to enable the 'key account' manager to succeed.

To ensure long-term, mutually beneficial and sustainable relationships, organizations need to move towards a key account management approach. Such an approach imposes new structures and disciplines but the benefits of such a shift in orientation are significant for both the buying and selling organization. The salesperson's role under a key account management approach shifts from a transactional to a relationship orientation, therefore a new set of skills and knowledge are required to succeed in this environment.

Responsibilities of a sales manager

IN the same way that the nature of the salesperson's role is changing so too is the traditional role of the sales manager. The primary role of a sales manager typically covers responsibility for planning, motivating, recruitment, training, and evaluating salesforce performance. These roles are considered below. This section will then consider the changing nature of the sales management role as organizations move towards a relationship marketing orientation.

To understand the firm's goals, strategies, market position, and basic marketing plan, and to convey them to the salesforce

The sales manager has an integral role in both managing the sales force as a conduit of information to pass to the marketing/strategy planners and also to ensure that the marketing plan is implemented effectively by the salesforce. Sales-oriented organizations have traditionally made products which are given to the salesforce to sell. Sales personnel were motivated by being rewarded for hitting sales targets but little thought was given to using the salesforce as a key marketing tool or as a source of market intelligence to develop products and services. The modern salesforce is an integral part of an organization's marketing strategy and therefore the sales manager plays an increasingly important role in ensuring that the organization's objectives and strategies are clearly communicated and understood, and that the salesforce acts in a consistent manner in terms of implementing the marketing strategy. It is essential that the sales manager is therefore involved in the process of developing the marketing plans.

To identify a sales philosophy, salesforce characteristics, selling tasks, a sales organization, and methods of customer contact

The sales manager is responsible for organizing both the structure of the salesforce, its style and approach to selling, and the manner in which sales personnel should operate when contacting customers. Essentially the sales manager is responsible for determining the overall ethos of the salesforce, the allocation of tasks, and the delegation of duties to be carried out. The salesforce can be structured by product or region or a combination of both and can be both field based and office based. These decisions have major implications for both overall selling costs and the nature of customer contacts/relations.

To develop and update sales forecasts

A key aspect of the sales manager's role is to forecast likely future demand based upon knowledge of the market, customer, and competitor trends and other external factors. These forecasts will impact upon decisions made by marketing, financial, personnel, and production/service planners as well as the sales manager's own planning needs. Attention to detail and accuracy are essential to avoid resources being committed to the wrong areas. The sales manager therefore needs to be familiar with forecasting techniques and beware of the pitfalls associated with such techniques when analysing and presenting sales forecasts.

To allocate selling resources based on sales forecasts and customer needs

As indicated above, the sales manager needs to allocate resources based upon the expected future levels of demand. Resource issues that will need to be considered include the number of salespersons employed, their objectives, key tasks, responsibilities, and sales targets. Much of this is encompassed under the sales management function of territory planning. Fig. 18.4 illustrates the range of issues that need to be considered when carrying out this function.

The model illustrates the range of tasks and considerations that need to be undertaken when planning and managing a salesforce. The sales manager's most important task is to allocate roles and responsibilities in a manner that is efficient and effective and seen by the salesforce as fair and equitable. It would be unfair for instance to allocate the same goals and expectations to a garden furniture salesperson covering the region of East Anglia compared with one operating in South London. Many factors will be taken into account by the sales manager, including spread and density of customers, traffic considerations, etc.

To select, motivate, train, compensate, and supervise sales personnel

People management is a crucial role of the sales manager. The selection of sales personnel requires the manager to be involved in specifying job requirements and

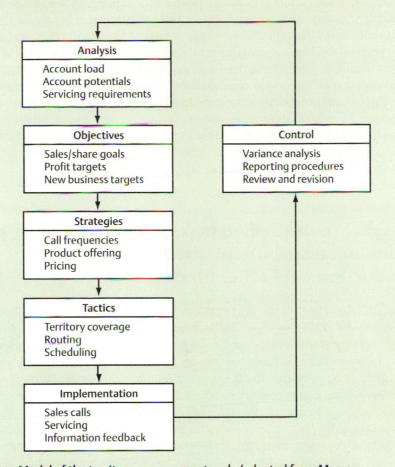

Figure 18.4 Model of the territory management cycle (adapted from Mercer 1993, p. 613)

candidate criteria and to participate in the interview and selection process. It is likely that the sales manager will have responsibility for initial and ongoing training of the salesforce in both selling techniques and product updates, etc. Rewarding staff is also a key part of the sales manager's responsibilities. In principle, methods of paying sales personnel lie on a continuum from straight salary to straight commission. Salaried employees receive no pay related to performance whereas commission-only employees receive pay related to performance, with no salary. It is common to see a combination approach of salary plus commission adopted. The sales manager needs to be aware of the effect different reward techniques can have on a salesperson's behaviour, motivation, and performance. Any reward plan should aim to incorporate at least some of the following characteristics: it should be easily understood, fair and accountable, relate to the sales objectives, and offer the opportunity and incentive to be rewarded for performance.

Motivation and leadership issues represent a significant challenge to the sales manager. The role of a salesperson can be frustrating and lonely and maintaining good motivation through these periods is critical to performance and retention of sales personnel. The sales manager must recognize that there is a range of factors that motivate sales personnel and these will vary from individual to individual depending upon personal attitudes and circumstance. Income, while being a common primary motivator is not necessarily always the most appropriate mechanism to motivate the salesforce. Recognition, career prospects, job satisfaction, and security may be equally salient factors to be considered. The sales manager's leadership capability is also an important factor in motivating the salesforce. Credibility, respect, and good interpersonal skills are essential characteristics for effective leadership.

To synchronize selling tasks with advertising, product planning, distribution, marketing research, production, and other functions

This task relates back to the sales manager's responsibility to liaise and work with the marketing function to ensure that marketing and sales activity work in unison and with maximum effect. This requires good communications and working relationships between the two functions and an understanding of the value each plays in delivering good performance. It is not uncommon to hear of the marketing department launching a new product or offering a sales promotion that the salesforce has heard nothing about until the customer asks them about it. Similarly the salesforce may be focusing their selling activities in the wrong markets or on inappropriate products. A common complaint from marketing departments is that the salesforce withhold important market information. Such inconsistencies should be avoided through proactive attention by both marketing and sales functions.

To assess sales performance by salesperson, product, product line, customer, customer group, and geographic area

Monitoring and evaluation of performance against targets is a critical sales management function. This can be done at individual salesperson, product, customer, and regional level. The most common measurement mechanism is performance against budget or forecast. The sales manager needs to be able to evaluate the performance of individuals using a range of qualitative and quantitative performance measures. Qualitative variables include customer-related measures (e.g. customer retention and customer satisfaction measures) and softer issues of salesforce performance such as salesforce attitudes, motivation, and knowledge of markets. Quantitative measures include sales performance statistics and ratios such as sales volume by value and by unit, sales volume by regions or by customer, profit, cost of calls, number of calls made, number of repeat sales, value of sales, etc. The problem with the link between sales effort and sales success is that a number of variables can impact between the two factors and it is not easy to gain an accurate measure of how much of the success can be attributed to the salesperson and how much to extraneous factors.

In most organizations a key resource is the salesforce. Effective management of this resource is therefore a significant area of responsibility that can have a major impact on the organization's market performance. As can be seen above, the sales manager has a wide-ranging and complex set of responsibilities that require high levels of management skills. A top performing salesperson who wishes to progress their career into sales management may not have the necessary range of skills to cope effectively with this level of responsibility.

As indicated earlier in this chapter, while the traditional sales manager's role is still evident in many organizations there is a trend away from a transaction orientation towards a relationship orientation. The result of this shift is that the traditional sales manager's role has been superseded to some degree by a new breed of manager who is responsible for managing the business relationships with key customers. An increasingly important management role in these organizations is therefore that of the key account manager who requires a different set of skills from those identified above for the sales manager.

Responsibilities of a key account manager

THE key account manager's primary responsibility is to manage the relationship between the organization and its key customers. The key account manager represents the management interface between the multifunctional teams that interact between the organization and the customer and to some extent has responsibility for all the activities, processes, and functions that form part of this relationship. While they may have the responsibility they may not have the power, as functional managers will still have their own line responsibilities and targets to meet. This therefore represents a significant challenge to the key account manager and there is a shortage of qualified individuals who are adequately skilled and knowledgeable to fulfil this complex and demanding role. The key skills required for such a role include the following.

Co-ordination of multifunctional teams

The key account manager is required to co-ordinate cross-functional teams both between the supplier organization and customer and within the separate functions of the supplying organization. In both cases conflicts of interest and differences will occur so high level organization and communication skills are required along with strong leadership and interpersonal skills. The key account manager must ensure that functional specialists in their organization are motivated and able to interact with their counterparts in the customer organization.

Managing personal customer relationships

The key account manager acts as the primary interface between the supplier organization and the customer. The role requires a strongly orientated customer-focused attitude with strong personal relationship skills. The key account manager must be able to demonstrate a strong aptitude towards customer care while at the same time managing the everyday demands of business problems and issues. As well as day-to-day commercial issues a key part of the role is entertainment and regular visits to ensure that a strong bond is built up with the customer at a personal level.

Facilitating the relationship between customer and supplier

Alongside the first two functions the key account manager has to facilitate the relationship between supplier and customer. In particular any problems in the relationship must be dealt with promptly and to the satisfaction of both parties. One of the major problems a key account manager will face is overcoming both customer and supplier organizations' short-term focus. Similarly they will face problems with functional specialists not seeing customer relationship building as part of their responsibility and the key account manager will require a degree of authority and credibility to drive through such barriers. The key account manager should be constantly exploring ways in which the relationship can be strengthened and developed to the mutual long-term gain of both parties. This facilitation role requires careful management as the key account manager has to be seen in a supporting role to the relationship and not a dominant role. A good facilitator will be able to guide the cross-functional teams rather than lead them.

Acting as the customer's 'champion' within the organization

The key account manager will often be required to take the side of the customer when in negotiation with functional teams in their own organization. Often the customer's voice is not heard in internal meetings and therefore the key account manager plays a primary role in ensuring that any strategic or tactical decisions take into account the possible implications to the customer. This can be a difficult role as the customer's requirements may not be in the best short-term interests of the organization or specific function within the organization.

Negotiation and selling skills

While the key account manager's primary role is the management of the customer relationship, they are also responsible for selling the organization's products and services and therefore require the requisite commercial and selling skills. Similarly they will be required to enter into contract negotiations between the two organizations and will therefore require the ability to manage high level negotiations between the supplier and customer and negotiations within their own organization. The key account manager will also need to have the appropriate level of technical knowledge about products to be able to carry out these activities.

Monitoring and evaluation skills

The key account manager will be required to develop appropriate and mutually acceptable short-term and long-term performance measures that accurately monitor the health of the business relationship and the benefits that accrue to both parties for being part of this relationship. This will involve agreement at board level and throughout the functions. Primary measures will cover financial criteria, process measurements, customer measures, and innovation and learning measures.

Talk about the importance of relationship building may be fine, but can it ever be a complete substitute for the hard skills of selling? In all too many companies, it seems that sales and service people see their task as 'account managing' and 'relationship building', and abhor the idea of selling. One of the popular tactics of such people is to show up unannounced at customers and invite themselves in for tea and biscuits. They see tea and biscuits as a good method of building personal relationships. But is such relationship building actually sought by customers? Many claim to hate such intrusion and prefer to be left to get on with their business. Although the salesperson's product may be vital to their business, customers often do not welcome the pressure from 'T&B' reps for personal relationships—they may just want a business relationship.

One further thought about the emergence of relationship managers: how can a company tell whether its relationship managers are performing effectively? How many 'T&B' visits does it take before you would expect evidence of results in the form of sales? Could relationship management be just an invitation for soft management when what is really needed is a hard sell?

Chapter summary and linkages to other chapters

This chapter has introduced the traditional role of the salesperson and sales manager and explored how this role is changing in response to an increasingly competitive market-place and more demanding buyers. The traditional salesperson and sales manager roles, responsibilities, and skills were outlined and discussed in the context of the transactional orientated organization. The need for a shift from a transaction to relationship orientation has been outlined and the changing demands that this placed on both the supplying and buying organization explored. This shift has required both parties to move towards adopting a multifunctional interactive structure which creates implications for organization culture, roles, and responsibilities as well as the nature of the relationships that will be established. The key account manager was identified as having a primary role acting as an interface between customer and supplier and between the functions within the supplying organization itself. The key account manager role requires a new and broader range of skills than that of the traditional sales manager and places immense pressure on the person adopting this role. Without the appropriate organization culture and senior management support such a role would be virtually impossible to fulfil.

This chapter has stressed the close link between selling and other marketing functions, and can be related to the following chapters in this book:

Chapter 1: What is marketing?: To many people, marketing is selling. This chapter has emphasized the need for selling to be closely related to marketing strategy. Very few products do not require selling and sales personnel should be the ears as well as the mouthpiece of an organization.

Chapter 2: The marketing environment: With the move towards relational selling, sales personnel need to address the interests of a wide range of distribution channel members. Developments in technology are providing new opportunities for sales management.

Chapter 3: Segmentation: Effective selling requires a careful analysis of the most promising sales targets and a sales message which is most appropriate to each segment.

Chapter 4: Branding: Having a strong brand to sell can act as a powerful door opener for a salesperson.

Chapter 5: Marketing and ethics: This chapter has discussed some of the high pressure, unethical sales techniques which have given selling, and indeed marketing, a bad reputation in the eyes of many people.

Chapter 6: Marketing research: Marketing research is essential in order to identify and address the most promising sales prospects.

Chapter 7: Buyer behaviour: The discussion in this chapter of selling to industrial buyers relates closely to the chapter on buyer behaviour. For commercial buyers, identifying members of the decision-making unit can be crucial for effective selling.

Chapter 8: Buyer–seller relationship development: This chapter has noted the change in sales personnel's role from one where the focus is on individual transactions to one where creating and maintaining ongoing relationships with customers is crucial.

Chapter 9: The product: Sales personnel must have good knowledge of their organization's products and be able to identify how product features can lead to benefits for buyers.

Chapter 10: New product development and innovation: Sales personnel can be a source of ideas for new products, based on feedback from buyers.

Chapter 11: Developing a sustainable competitive advantage: Selling alone cannot sustain a competitive advantage—the other elements of the marketing mix must also be correct.

Chapters 12/13: Pricing theory and applications: In many selling situations, the salesperson's task is to obtain the highest price possible from a buyer, taking into account the competitive environment and the buyer's willingness to pay.

Chapters 14/15: Intermediaries/logistics: A lot of selling effort is focused on intermediaries. Sales personnel often need to work with intermediaries to ensure stock availability.

Chapter 16: Principles of promotion planning: This chapter provided an overview of promotion planning and the communication process, of which personal selling is an interrelated component.

Chapter 17: Advertising: The task of personal selling is facilitated by effective advertising which provides sales leads and facilitates sales negotiations.

Chapter 19: Sales promotion and public relations: Effective sales promotion and public relations activity can facilitate the task of selling.

Chapter 20: Direct marketing: Direct marketing techniques are sometimes seen as a substitute for face-to-face selling. At other times, direct marketing is used to support sales personnel.

Chapter 21: Organizing for marketing: This chapter has stressed the need for marketing to be closely integrated with other marketing functions.

Chapter 22: Services marketing: The intangibility of services often creates a perception of greater riskiness which sales personnel must seek to overcome. Product demonstrations for services may be more difficult than for goods.

Chapter 23: Global marketing: Should a company have its own salesforce in overseas markets or operate through other organizations, such as agents or joint venture partners?

Case study

Selling the job of key account manager can be a difficult task

Key account managers have become popular in recent years, and seminars abound on how to increase profits through key account management, global account management and European account management. Are key account managers suitable for all organizations? Or is their appointment related closely to an organization's growth pattern?

It has been observed that companies that grow organically will have a tendency to 'grow into' the role of key account managers. If, for example, a small regional enterprise becomes a successful multinational one, it might be expected that the local sales function would become centralized, and may eventually develop into a national, pan-European and eventually even global function.

The effect of growth can be seen in the food retailing sector, when consolidation occurred in the 1960s with the rapid growth of Sainsbury's and Tesco. Both companies' single-figure market shares started to grow rapidly from that time. At that time, Sainsbury's suppliers had to deal with the company's head office. Suppliers to Tesco's, however, were still trying to cover stores on an individual branch level. As Tesco grew, food manufactures' salespeople were still running around at branch level trying to influence managers with a wide range of incentives. As Tesco's share climbed upward, most significantly over a five-year period in the 1970s, it became apparent that supplying/ buying negotiations could be best dealt with at head office rather than branch level.

With the further growth of Asda and Safeway, the grocery retail market was reshaping massively, with the number of independent grocers declining, unable to compete with the popularity of the new generation of supermarkets. Yet food manufacturers were still clinging to salesforces of 300–400 people, despite the fact that buying by retailers was becoming increasingly centralized. It took a long time for suppliers to see that key account management was the most cost-effective way of gaining increased sales with fewer people. It became apparent that the amount of business they were generating among the independents was relatively small and declining and their profitability depended on selling into four or five major customers and the cash and carries.

By the end of the 1990s, Bird's Eye-Walls had a salesforce of just forty or so left from a previous total of several hundreds. Anchor Foods came down to twelve people who dealt with the whole of the grocery trade—several hundreds of millions of pounds of business. Food manufacturers realized that if they did not supply to the majors there were few alternative sources of large-scale, profitable sales. It is easy to see what should have happened in retrospect. Some food manufacturers suffered by delaying the inevitable and should have cut the numbers of their sales professionals earlier.

Why does it often take a long time for a key account management structure to emerge? Many companies do not have the courage to realign their business and discard the regional structure. This may be because jobs are at stake, and also because moving the account from a local to national handler can cause an enormous amount of aggravation, both internally and with customers. Going through the process of dismantling regional sales networks to build a national or key account structure can be soul destroying— especially for sales managers who know the business intimately and have lived within such a structure for a long time. In the early stages, it can be nerve racking for a business to focus on fewer prospects with higher value. The rewards, however, can be great. Suppliers to the likes of Marks & Spencer, once through the hoop, for example, have been adopted to the point of excluding their competitors.

The pharmaceutical industry is another facing a big challenge in the way it sells its products. Typically companies in this sector field hundreds of salespeople, each attempting to make three or four appointments a day—morning appointments with GPs plus, perhaps, a hospital specialist in the afternoon. Their work never generates a direct order. Their role is simply to influence, or hope to influence, the doctor or surgeon so that when the symptoms are relevant, they can prescribe their new drug. In the long term, doctors within the NHS are not going to accept these appointments as a viable, efficient way of accumulating knowledge about what products are available.

When this change occurs, there is likely to be a move towards team selling. The salesperson, traditionally the single point of contact between the buying and selling companies, will become multi-skilled, more highly disciplined, and is likely to orchestrate the activity of a team. Sales professionals in key account management structures typically talk to buyers more about long-term development, and less about closing sales. They talk about the possibilities of building a relationship and might arrange for the companies' respective experts, for example in quality control or packaging, to meet. Gradually the relationship becomes a team sell.

As companies learn the value of getting closer to their customers the role of key account management rises. Team selling is becoming the norm, companies are working closer together than ever before. A new, stronger level of interdependency is driving the act of selling into a new era. To profit now, many companies must change or flounder.

Adapted from John Mayfield, 'Driving Strategic Partnerships', *Winning Business*, 3, 1, Jan.–Mar., 1999.

Case study questions

1 What are the disadvantages of a key account management approach to selling?

2 Suggest methods by which a key account manager for a food manufacturer might be evaluated.

3 How should food manufacturers cater for the needs of small retailers for whom a key account management approach may not be justified?

Chapter review questions

1 What is the relationship between selling and marketing?

2 Outline the key stages in the selling process? Is it appropriate to describe selling as a simple linear process?

3 Outline the primary roles and skills required of a sales manager. Can it be assumed that a good salesperson will also be a good sales manager?

4 Why is the relevance of the traditional transaction approach to selling increasingly being questioned?

5 Explain the implications for an organization moving from a transactional orientation towards a relationship orientation.

6 Outline the primary roles and skills required of a key account manager. What are the primary difficulties associated with such a role?

References

Christopher, M., Payne, A., and Ballantyne D. (1991), *Relationship Marketing* (Oxford: Butterworth-Heinemann).

Drucker, P. (1973), *Management: Tasks, Responsibilities and Practices* (New York: Harper & Row).

Egan, C. (1997), *The CIM Handbook of Selling and Sales Strategy: A Practical Guide to Selling and Implementing Effective Sales Strategies* (London: Chartered Institute of Marketing).

Ford, D., Gadde, L., Hakansson, H., Lundgren, A., Snehota, I., Turnbull, P., and Wilson, D. (1998), *Managing Business Relationships* (Chichester: John Wiley).

Gronroos, C. (1996), 'Relationship Marketing: Strategic and Tactical Implications', *Management Decision*, **34**, 3, pp. 5–14.

Kotler, P. (1997), *Marketing Management: Analysis, Planning, Implementation and Control*, 9th edn. (Englewood Cliffs, NJ: Prentice Hall).

Levitt, T. (1983), 'After the Sale is Over', *Harvard Business Review*, Sept.–Oct., pp. 87–93.

McMurry, R. N. (1961), 'The Mystique of Super Salesmanship', *Harvard Business Review*, **26**, Mar.–Apr., pp. 114–32.

Mercer, D. (1993), *Marketing* (Oxford: Blackwell).

Peck, H., Payne, A., Christopher, M., and Clarke, M. (1999), *Relationship Marketing—Strategy and Implementation* (Oxford: Butterworth–Heinemann).

Shipley, D. (1997), *Selling and Sales Strategy: Selling to and Managing Key Accounts* (Oxford: Butterworth–Heinemann).

Steward, K. (1993), *Marketing Led, Sales Driven: Professional Selling in a Marketing Environment* (Oxford: Butterworth-Heinemann).

Webster, F. E. Jnr., and Wind, Y. (1972), *Organizational Buying Behaviour* (Englewood Cliffs, NJ: Prentice Hall), pp. 78–80.

Suggested further reading

The following sources discuss in more detail the principles and practices of selling and sales management:

■ Brown, R. (1990), *From Selling to Managing: Guidelines for the First-Time-Sales Manager* (New York: Amacom).

■ Donaldson, B. (1998), Sales Management Theory and Practice, 2nd edn. (London: Macmillan).

■ Hartley, B., and Starkey, M. (1996), *The Management of Sales and Customer Relations: Book of Readings* (London: International Thomson Business Press).

■ Newby, C. (1998), Sales Strategies (London: Kogan Page).

■ Petrone, J. (1999), *Building the High Performance Sales Force* (Productivity Management Press).

Useful web links

Institute of Professional Sales: http://iops.co.uk

American Telemarketing Association: http://www.ataconnect.org/

Association for the Advancement of Relationship Marketing: http://www.aarm.org/

National Alliance of Sales & Marketing Executives (US association dedicated to raising the professionalism and public image of the sales and marketing profession): http://www.nasme.com/nasme_inside.html

Winning Business magazine on-line: http://winning-business.com

Chapter 19
Public Relations and Sales Promotion

Chapter objectives

This chapter introduces two of the traditional elements of the promotion mix—public relations and sales promotion. It is emphasized that, to be effective, both must have regard to the other elements of the promotion mix. Public relations is sometimes regarded as 'free advertising', but its use has to be carefully planned and may be difficult to control. Excessive sales promotion activity may undermine the efforts of advertising to develop a strong brand. This chapter concludes by considering sponsorship, which combines a number of elements of the promotion mix.

The characteristics of public relations

PUBLIC relations is an indirect promotional tool whose role is to establish and enhance a positive image of an organization and its products among its various publics. It is defined by the Institute of Public Relations as

the deliberate, planned and sustained effort to establish and maintain mutual understanding between an organization and its publics.

The words 'deliberate', 'planned' and 'sustained' are crucial here, as companies cannot hope to 'do a bit of PR' in isolated bursts and hope for the type of results which come from a more concerted effort. Public relations as a professional activity is treated with suspicion by many people, but this probably reflects a perception of a short-term opportunistic activity, rather than the long-term commitment advocated by public relations professionals. A good long-term public relations strategy will make it much easier for a company to use PR tools when it has a real emergency about which it needs to communicate with its audience. As an example, a food manufacturer which has carefully used PR to develop a good mutual understanding between itself and its principal publics will be better placed to use PR to counter a food safety incident, than a manufacturer who seeks to use PR tools only as and when needed.

Because public relations is involved with more than just customer relationships, it is often handled at a corporate level rather than at the functional level of marketing management and it can be difficult to integrate public relations fully into the overall promotional plan. For many companies, public relations covers communication with investor and community groups, among others.

As an element within the promotion mix, public relations presents a number of valuable opportunities as well as problems. Some of its more important characteristics are described below:

- **Relatively low cost**: the major advantage of public relations is that it tends to be much cheaper in terms of cost per person reached than any other type of promotion. Apart from nominal production costs, much public relations activity can be carried out at almost no cost, in marked contrast to the high cost of buying space or time in the main media. To make the most use of this apparently free resource, many companies retain outside PR consultants who can prove themselves to be cost effective in developing these opportunities.

- **Can be targeted**: public relations activities can be targeted to a small specialized audience if the right media vehicle is used.

- **Credibility**: the results of PR activity often have a high degree of credibility, compared with other promotional sources such as advertising. This can occur because the audience may regard a message as coming from an apparently impartial and non-commercial source. Where information is presented as news, readers or viewers may be less critical of a message than if it was presented as a biased advertisement.

- **Controllability**: a company can exercise little direct control over how its public relations activity is subsequently handled and interpreted. If successful, a press release may be printed in full, although there can be no control over where or when it is printed. At worst, a press release can be misinterpreted and the result could be very unfavourable news coverage. This is in contrast to advertising, where an advertiser can exercise considerable control over the content, placing, and timing of an advert.

- **Saturation of effort**: the fact that many organizations compete for a finite amount of media attention puts pressure on the public relations effort to be better than that of competitors. There can be no guarantee that public relations activity will have any impact on the targets at whom it is aimed.

The most important thing that most companies have is their reputation. Many have gone to great lengths to protect their reputation when it has been under threat, as in the case of the Body Shop which vigorously defended itself against claims that it was exploiting workers in less developed countries, or Shell following the Brent Spar oil platform controversy. Should corporate reputation be regarded as a marketing task or something to be handled at a corporate level? Corporate reputation is a discipline with a lot of components, tied in with issues of brand development, crisis management, public affairs, and relations with the City. Many PR professionals see corporate reputation as a step to a more strategic role. Reporting to the chief executive is more rewarding than reporting to a brand manager.

No matter what audience a company wants to address, how that audience views it is very important, and will affect how successful it is in communicating its message. The memory of Gerard Ratner describing his cheap jewellery as 'crap' at an Institute of Directors speech still haunts many companies, fearful of being misrepresented. This applies to consumers as well as investor and politician publics. Maintaining corporate reputation has a particular bearing in the business-to-business arena, where it influences working relationships with other businesses, including suppliers, customers, and partners. High profile resignations of chief executives, succession vacuums, and aborted merger talks have put the value of corporate reputations into perspective. A company must communicate well beyond its customers to all stakeholders— employees, suppliers, financial backers, and the media.

One of the UK's leading PR companies, Shandwick, has worked with Professor Charles Fombrun of New York University, author of the book *Reputation*, in developing systems to offer strategic advice in the corporate reputation sector. Based on *Fortune's* annual list of the most-admired corporations, Professor Fombrun calculated that even a small percentage improvement in reputation can have a major impact on a company's stock market valuation.

The publics of public relations

Public relations can be distinguished from customer relations because its concerns go beyond the creation of mutually beneficial relationships with actual or potential customers. The following additional audiences for public relations can be identified:

■ **Employees**: public relations efforts aimed at employees assume great importance within the services sector where personnel become part of the service offer and it is important to raise the morale of employees. It may be important to communicate with employees on such issues as job security, working conditions, and the state of the market. Staff will inevitably hear things which may affect them from other sources, and PR can seek to provide an authoritative view on these issues, through the use of inhouse publications, newsletters, and employee recognition activities.

- **Suppliers**: these may need assurances that a company is a credible one to deal with and that contractual obligations will be met. Highlighting favourable annual reports and drawing attention to major new developments can help to raise the profile and credibility of a company in the eyes of its suppliers.

- **Intermediaries**: these may share many of the same concerns as customers and need reassurance about a supplier's capabilities. Are they showing commitment to a particular line of business?; are they financially sound?; what new product developments are being considered which may raise the morale of intermediaries?

- **Government**: in many cases, actions of government can significantly affect the fortunes of an organization and therefore relationships with government departments—at local, national, and supranational level—need to be carefully developed. This can include lobbying of Members of Parliament, and communicating the organization's views to government inquiries and civil servants.

- **Financial community**: this includes financial institutions that have supported, are currently supporting, or who may support the organization in the future. Shareholders—both private and institutional—form an important element of this community and must be reassured that the organization is going to achieve its stated objectives.

- **Local communities/pressure groups**: it is sometimes important for an organization to be seen as a 'good neighbour' in their local community. Therefore, the organization can enhance its image through the use of charitable contributions, sponsorship of local events, being seen to support the local environment, etc.

- **The media**: as important opinion formers, members of the media represent an important audience. Public relations activity seeks to create a favourable predisposition by this group, which is passed on to the other audiences identified above.

The tools of public relations

A WIDE range of tools is available to the PR practitioner, and the suitability of each tool is dependent upon the promotional objectives at which they are directed. In general, the tools of public relations are best suited to creating awareness of an organization or liking for its products and tend to be less effective in directly bringing about action in the form of purchase decisions. Some of the important elements which are used within the promotion mix are described below:

- **Press releases**: a press release can be defined as a communication which seeks to secure editorial space in the media, as distinct from paid-for advertising space.

Is the Internet a friend or enemy of the PR professional? Client companies have begun to appreciate the idea that a web site is a convenient way to disseminate information, or that news now crosses geographical frontiers quicker than you can blink. But against this is the realization that corporate reputations can be savaged as disgruntled customers and shareholders swap comments on the World Wide Web. Thorns in the side of PR people include the McSpotlight site (www.mcspotlight.org) which carries information critical of McDonald's restaurants and the Boycott Shell site (www.essential.org/action/shell). Such sites can be created without the companies' knowledge, if they are not monitoring, and contributing to, the forums and chat rooms. And it can end up as a damaging mix of rumour and untruths.

PR agencies that have the technical expertise have set up monitoring services. One PR consultancy, Edelman, monitors the Internet, checking on 33,000 user groups and bulletin boards and regularly prepares web pages for its clients in anticipation of crises. These are then 'hidden' on the web site, ready to be activated if needed.

PR professionals have had to face up to the new realities of the Internet. Response times need to be immediate, with no specific deadlines that are typical of conventional published media. But at the same time, activists are changing the nature of the game with which they have to deal. When environmental activists staged a sit-in at Shell's London offices in 1999, the group broadcast the protest live to the Internet and e-mailed the press using a digital camera, laptop computer and mobile phone.

Quite aside from the battle of technology is the fundamental question: why did a company allow itself to get into the position of exposing itself to criticism? Could this not have been foreseen? If there is little for people to campaign about, the dissident web sites would probably loose much of their support.

Because of its important contribution towards the promotion mix, this tool is considered in more detail below.

- **Lobbying**: professional lobbyists are often employed by a company in an effort to inform and hence influence those key decision-makers who may be critical to its success. Lobbying can take place at a local level (e.g. a fast food company seeking to convince members of a local authority about the benefits of allowing them to locate in a sensitive area); at a national level (e.g. the campaign mounted by the road haulage industry in 1999 seeking comparable taxation to its overseas competitors); and at a supranational level (e.g. the campaign by airlines and ferry companies which sought to prevent the abolition of duty-free sales within Europe).

- **Education and training**: in an effort to develop a better understanding—and hence liking—of an organization and its products, many organizations aim education and training programmes at important target groups. In this way, food manufacturers frequently supply schools and colleges with educational material which will predispose recipients of the material to their brand. Open days are another common method of educating the public by showing them the complex processes that occur 'behind the scene' in order to ensure a high quality of output to customers.

- **Exhibitions and shows**: most companies attend exhibitions not with the intention of making an immediate sale, but to create an awareness of their organization which will result in a sale over the longer term. Exhibitions offer the chance for potential customers to talk face to face with representatives of the organization and an opportunity to sample products. Exhibitions are used to target both consumer and commercial audiences. Many trade shows are important events in their respective business sectors, where a high proportion of key decision-makers are likely to be present. The annual World Travel Market in London, for example, is an ideal opportunity seized by many travel-related organizations to communicate with their key customers. The absence of a company at such key exhibitions may lead to concern among some visitors about why they have chosen not to be there.

- **In-house journals**: the number of in-house magazines produced by companies is now huge, with examples spanning sectors from airlines to banks and supermarkets. By adopting a news-based magazine format, the message becomes more credible than if it was presented as a pure advertisement. Often, outside advertisers contribute revenue which can make such journals self-financing. Travel operators often publish magazines which are read by a captive travelling public. The task of producing in-house journals is usually delegated to a specialist publishing company.

- **Sponsorship**: there is argument about whether this strictly forms part of the public relations portfolio of tools. It is, however, being increasingly used as an element of the promotion mix and is described in more detail later in this chapter.

Press relations

THE aim of press relations is to create a long-term sense of mutual understanding between an organization and the media. This understanding with the media is developed by means of:

- **Press releases**: this is the most frequent form of press relations activity and is commonly used to announce new product launches, new appointments, or significant achievements.

- **Press conferences**: these are used where a major event is to be announced and an opportunity for a two-way dialogue between the organization and the media is considered desirable.

- **Availability of specialist commentators**: faced with a news story which the media wishes to report on, a newspaper or radio station may seek specialists within an industrial sector who are knowledgeable on the issues involved. For example, a local tour operator may be asked by a local newspaper to comment upon the consequences of a natural disaster in an overseas resort. This helps both the reporter and the tour operator in question, whose representative is fielded as an expert.

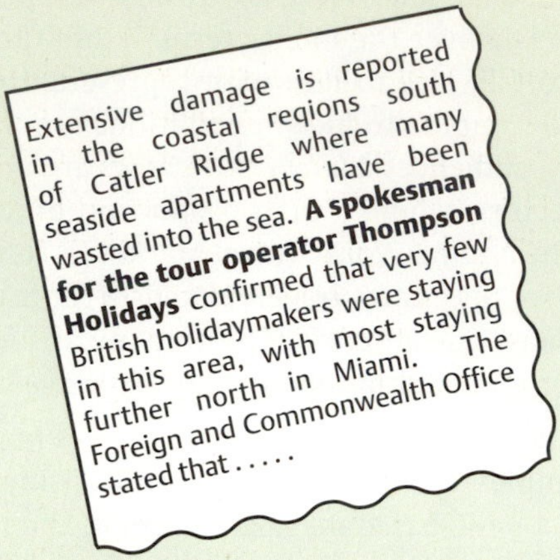
Extensive damage is reported in the coastal reqions south of Catler Ridge where many seaside apartments have been wasted into the sea. **A spokesman for the tour operator Thompson Holidays** confirmed that very few British holidaymakers were staying in this area, with most staying further north in Miami. The Foreign and Commonwealth Office stated that . . . . .

Figure 19.1 By fielding its representative as an expert, this tour company has helped develop relationships with the newspaper and raised awareness among the publics that it serves

Press relations activity has the advantage of being relatively inexpensive to use and can reach large audiences with a high degree of credibility. Against this, a major disadvantage is the lack of control which the generator of a press release has over how it is subsequently handled, in terms of appearance, timing, and content (it is likely to be edited). Because of the competition from other organizations for press coverage, there can be no guarantee that any particular item will actually be used. Indeed, it is often suggested that over 90 per cent of press releases sent to media editors end up in the bin without being used.

An important element of press relations is avoiding negative publicity. For highly variable goods and services (such as airline and train service), there is always the possibility that the media will pick up one bad incident and leave their audience thinking that this is the norm for a particular organization. This is particularly a problem for highly visible public or quasi-public services for which readers enjoy reading bad news stories to confirm their own prejudices. Media editors have a tendency to write stories that they believe their audience would like to hear, so if bad news stories about train companies can be assured of a sympathetic hearing they will most likely be run. It would take a great deal of effort by train operators to prove to editors that they are out of touch with the reality which faces their readers or viewers.

External events sometimes lead to bad publicity for an organization, as where increased air traffic congestion leads to stories of major delays for airline passengers. Sometimes the negative actions of other organizations within the same sector may lead to a generally poor reputation for the sector as a whole. In all situations, an organization needs to establish contingency plans to minimize any surprise and confusion resulting from such bad publicity. Bad publicity is more likely to be

It can be very easy to say that PR consultancies are experts at their job and that a company should give its PR work to just such a specialist. But how can the delicate relationship between client and consultancy be made to work? The advantage for a company of staying with a PR consultant over a long period of time is that the consultant can become part of the company's brand management team. But against this, change may be good in order to prevent complacency and stuffiness setting in. A number of points can facilitate the relationship between client and consultancy:

- It is essential to evaluate the agency's performance against previously agreed objectives (e.g. expressed in terms of media coverage, audience response).
- Regular performance reviews will prevent complacency setting in at the PR consultancy.
- PR works best when it takes a long-term view, for example it may take time to change the attitudes of the media and other key opinion formers. So it is important to undertake the selection and evaluation of a consultant with this longer-term perspective in mind.
- Honesty and openness is essential in dealings between client and consultant. Consultants should preserve confidentiality and avoid conflicts of interest with other clients.
- A balance should be struck between stability and new thinking—rapid turnover at a consultancy is bad, but so too is no new thinking.

effectively managed if an organization has invested time and effort in developing mutually supportive good relations with the media.

Preparing the press relations strategy

As with all aspects of the promotion mix, press relations will achieve maximum effectiveness if a plan is developed which begins with clearly formulated objectives, has a strategy which has been thoroughly thought through, a detailed implementation programme, and effective monitoring.

- Press relations objectives should state what end result is desired (e.g. the desire to raise awareness of a new product or to identify the organization with a desired image). Wherever possible, these should be quantified.
- Developing a strategy involves identifying items which should be brought to the attention of a wider audience by means of press relations and selecting the most appropriate media to target.
- Implementing the plan involves the development of a message, identification of specific media, and a time schedule for release. While the development of

objectives and strategy may typically be agreed jointly between a company and its PR agency, this stage is more likely to be dominated by the agency.

■ Evaluation is difficult as press relations is usually used in conjunction with other promotional tools. It is easier to evaluate if press relations is used before other tools are used. There are, however, a number of response measures that can be used, for example 'exposures' relate to the number of times news related to the company has been carried by the media. However, this does not give any indication of how many people actually saw or heard the information. Alternatively, surveys of awareness, comprehension, and attitudes before and after a press release could be undertaken and these may give some indication of the response to publicity. The most satisfactory measure of a successful contribution to promotional objectives is sales and profit contribution, but of course it is extremely difficult to isolate the effects of press relations activity.

Many people have traditionally argued that the results of public relations could not be measured. Furthermore, this did not really matter because PR was relatively inexpensive anyway and it was clearly a good thing to be doing. Such an attitude is now much less acceptable and there is growing demand for tools to measure and evaluate PR properly.

Media content analysis and press cuttings are the most commonly used evaluation technique but a range of confusing alternatives have appeared, including 'Advertising Value Equivalents' and 'Opportunities to See', all providing benchmarks by which the results of PR activities can be assessed. Innovations in computer software are providing new tools which can allow for rapid tracking of media coverage and calculation of the likely audience. In addition to measuring volume and circulation figures, national readership data are used to calculate reach and frequency, and occasionally gross rating points. While clients may wish to know that their money has been spent effectively, PR consultants are keen to show the high impact achieved by PR in comparison to a similar budget advertising campaign.

Another important aspect of PR evaluation is pre-testing of messages. According to the Institute of Public Relations, only 3 per cent of consultants have ever pre-tested their messages, despite opportunities for misinterpretation that may subsequently arise.

Who should do the PR evaluation? Many PR consultancies provide an evaluation service to their clients using agreed criteria. Meanwhile, many specialist evaluation companies have emerged who may be contracted directly by the client, or subcontracted by a consultant to provide detailed evaluation.

Sales promotion

SALES promotion involves those activities, other than advertising, personal selling, and public relations, that stimulate customer purchase and the effectiveness of intermediaries. The Institute of Sales Promotion defines sales promotions as

a range of tactical marketing techniques designed within a strategic marketing framework, to add value to a product or service in order to achieve a specific sales and marketing objective.

Although sales promotion activity can be used to create awareness, sales promotion is usually used for the later stages of the buying process, that is, to create interest, desire, and—in particular—to bring about action. Sales promotion can quite successfully complement other tools within the promotion mix, for example by reinforcing a particular image or identity developed through advertising.

Over the last few years there has been a rapid increase in the use of sales promotion, and a number of reasons can be identified for this trend:

■ There has been a greater acceptance of the use of sales promotion by top management and more people are now qualified to use it. In addition, there is greater pressure today to obtain a quick sales response, something that sales promotion can be good at achieving.

■ Markets have become increasingly competitive and there is evidence that customers have become less loyal to brands and are prepared to go for the best deal on offer. Sales promotion is often used to break brand loyalty.

■ As advertising channels proliferate, audiences have become saturated with messages and it has been argued that advertising efficiency is declining due to increasing costs and media clutter.

■ New technology in targeting has resulted in an increase in the efficiency and effectiveness of sales promotion.

Planning for sales promotion

EFFECTIVE sales promotion involves an ongoing process with a number of distinct stages:

■ **Establishment of objectives:** sales promotion objectives vary according to the target market. If the target is the customer, objectives could include the encouragement of increased usage or the building of trial among nonusers or other brand users. For intermediaries, objectives could be to encourage off-season sales, or offsetting competitive promotions.

■ **Planning the sales promotion programme**: the major decisions that need to be made when designing the sales promotion programme relate to the timing of the promotion and how long a tool is to be used for. Also important are the size of incentive, rules for entry, and the overall budget for the promotion.

■ **Selection of promotional tools**: promotional objectives form the basis for selecting the most appropriate sales promotion tools. The cost and effectiveness of each tool must be assessed with regard to achieving these objectives in respect of each target market. The tools available to the service marketer are described in more detail below.

■ **Pre-testing**: this should be undertaken in order to ensure that potentially expensive problems are discovered before the full launch of a promotion. Testing in selected market segments can highlight problems of ambiguity, response rates, and give an indication of cost effectiveness.

■ **Implementation**: the programme for implementation must include two important time factors. Firstly, it must indicate the 'lead time'—the time necessary to bring the programme up to the point where the incentive is to be made available to the public. Secondly, the 'sell in time', which is the period of time from the date of release to when approximately 90–5 per cent of incentive material has been received by potential customers.

■ **Evaluation**: the performance of the promotion needs to be assessed against the objectives set. If objectives are specific and quantifiable, measurement would seem to be easy. However, extraneous factors could account for the apparent success of many sales promotion activities, for example, competitive actions or seasonal variations may have influenced customers' decision-making. It can also be extremely difficult to separate out the effects of sales promotion activity from other promotional activity—or indeed from other marketing mix changes, such as a lower price. A further problem is that sales promotion activity may simply bring forward demand, resulting in buyers building up stockpiles which depresses demand for a product in future periods. This is especially true of products which are of low value and have a long shelf-life. This effect is illustrated in Fig. 19.2

Sales promotion objectives

Sales promotion contributes in a number of ways to achieving overall promotional objectives. While it can be used merely to gain attention for a product, it is more likely to be used as an incentive incorporating an offer which represents value to the target audience. It can also act as an invitation to make a purchase now rather than later. Sales promotion activity is often aimed at attracting brand switchers but is unlikely to turn them into loyal brand users without the use of other elements of the promotion mix. In fact, it is usually considered that sales promotion is used to break

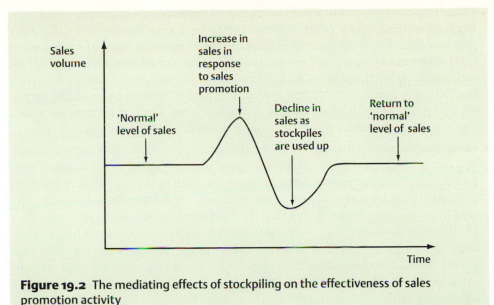

Figure 19.2 The mediating effects of stockpiling on the effectiveness of sales promotion activity

down brand loyalty, whereas advertising is used to build it up. Sales promotion can gain new users or encourage more frequent purchase but it cannot compensate for inadequate advertising, poor delivery, or poor product quality.

Sales promotion tools

A WIDE and ever increasing range of sales promotion tools are available to marketers. Some of the more commonly used tools aimed at the final consumer include the following:

- **Free samples/visits/consultations**: these encourage trial of a product and can be valuable where consumers are loyal to an existing supplier. They could, for example, be used by a breakfast cereal manufacturer to entice potential customers to try their brand. In the case of new products which are perceived as being expensive and of poor value to a consumer, they can encourage trial. This has been widely used by satellite television companies, for example, with free trial offers. For established products, the excessive offering of free samples can demean the value of the product on offer and buyers may become reluctant to pay for a product which they have seen being given away freely.

- **Money-off price incentives**: price incentives can be used tactically to try to counteract temporary increases in competitor activity. They can also be used to stimulate sales of a new product shortly after launch or to stimulate demand during slack periods where price is considered to be a key element in a customer's purchase decision. Price incentives tend to be an expensive form of sales promotion, as the incentive is given to customers regardless of its motivational effect on an individual. A restaurant reducing its prices for all customers is unable to extract the full price from those customers who may have otherwise been willing to pay the full price. There is also a danger that price incentives can become built into consumers' expectations and their removal result in a fall in business.

- **Coupons/vouchers**: these allow holders to obtain a discount off a future purchase and can be targeted at quite specific groups of users or potential users, often combined with the direct marketing techniques discussed in the following chapter. To encourage trial by potential new users, vouchers can be distributed to non-users who fit a specified profile. In this way, a manufacturer of cosmetics may provide a voucher with a women's magazine whose readership corresponds with the manufacturer's target market. To encourage repeat usage, vouchers can be given as a loyalty bonus. Voucher offers tend to be much more cost effective than straight price incentives because of their ability to segment markets. As an example, a tourist attraction can recognize that visitors from overseas might see the full price as being only a small part of their total holiday cost and representing good value, while a local family might need an incentive to make more frequent visits to the attraction.

- **Gift offers**: companies often provide the incentive of a gift to encourage short-term sales. Gifts can take many forms, such as a Marks & Spencer gift token or a T-shirt and can encourage immediate and/or repeated purchase. The gift can satisfy a number of objectives. In order to promote initial enquiry, many firms offer a gift for merely enquiring about their products. This provides an opportunity to submit, with the gift, samples and brochures of the firm's products. A gift can also be used to bring about immediate action—for example a free clock radio if a purchase is made within a specified period. For existing customers, gifts can be used to develop and reward loyalty. Many consumer goods companies encourage customers to collect tokens which can be redeemed against selected promotional merchandise.

  Sometimes, a company might charge for a gift. Not only could this make the gift be self-financing, but the gift could be inscribed with a message which will be seen by the user and others for some time to come. In this way, some petrol retailers and football clubs, among others, sell ranges of promotional clothing, often partly paid for by a combination of vouchers and cash. Some gifts are provided collaboratively between companies with quite different product ranges. As an example, a grocery retailer may give rewards of money-off vouchers at a chain of restaurants, satisfying the promotional criteria of the retailer (rewarding loyalty) and the restaurant (encouraging trial).

- **Competitions**: the offer of a competition adds to the value of the total offer. Instead of simply buying an insurance policy, a customer buys the policy plus a dream of winning a prize to which they attach significance. Competitions can be used both to create trial amongst non-users and to encourage loyalty among

FREE Parker Pen when you
call for a quote!

Find out how much you could save with The Insurance Shop. Call us now
for a free quote without obligation, and we'll send you a free Parker Pen
by way of a thank you.

FREE Up to £30 worth of Marks & Spencer Gift
Vouchers when you take out home insurance

That's right, just take out a building or contents insurance policy with
The Insurance Shop, and we'll send you Marks & Spencer Gift Vouchers
worth £15. Or £30 if you take out both.

the insurance shop

Figure 19.3 In many markets where products are perceived by buyers as being basically
similar, it may be necessary to offer an incentive in order to initiate a dialogue. Eager to
enter buyers' choice set, many insurance companies, such as this one, provide a token gift
in order to generate an initial response. Many companies offer further incentives that are
given following a completed purchase. Sales promotion activities of this type may be
particularly important where consumers' ability to differentiate between competing
products is low and an incentive offers a tangible basis for differentiation. (Reproduced
with permission of Lloyds TSB Insurance Services Ltd.)

existing customers (e.g. a competition for which a number of proofs of purchase are
necessary to enter).

Sales promotion activity aimed at intermediaries includes the following:

- **Short-term sales bonuses**: these can be used to stimulate sales during slack
  periods or to develop loyalty from intermediaries in the face of competitor activity.

Background music in retail stores may be dismissed by some as mere 'musac', while to others it may be deeply irritating. But does it make any difference in bringing about a sale?

Techniques to match music with retail environments are becoming increasingly sophisticated. AEI, a US-based company specializing in designing music for retailers has devised a system whereby tracks can be beamed into a store via satellite, allowing the selection of music to be controlled remotely. The company begins by analysing the environment of a store, including the demographics of customers, store layout, lighting, and the pattern of demand throughout the day. As an example of music selection, the company chose mellow jazz for the cosmopolitan and slightly off-beat coffee and sandwich shop, Pret à Manger. Contemporary jazz with hints of ethnicity were chosen for Habitat, supposedly to support traditional craft products.

We may not be aware of these assaults on our senses, but controlled experiments have shown that they can influence our buying behaviour. Using another of our senses, smell, the retailer Woolworth's has claimed that the smell of mulled wine increased its sales during the Christmas shopping period. Supermarkets routinely pump recirculated smells of bread and coffee through their stores, but exclude others such as fish and soap powder.

Gone are the days of a tape recorder under the manager's desk and the odd air freshener. To be effective, sales promotion techniques must gain a detailed understanding of what motivates a customer to buy. Very often, the most effective techniques are the ones that we are not even conscious of.

- **Competitions and gifts**: these can be aimed at sales personnel working for intermediaries and act to increase awareness of a brand, and, if entry to the competition is conditional upon achieving sales targets, encourage additional sales.

- **Point of purchase material**: to stimulate additional sales, a supplier can provide a range of incentives to help intermediaries. Many consumer goods suppliers offer retailers a range of eye-catching displays and field sales staff to demonstrate the benefits of their product at the point of purchase.

- **Co-operative advertising**: suppliers can agree to subscribe to local advertising by an intermediary, as where a car manufacturer promotes the location of its dealers as well as the core benefits of its cars. Co-operative advertising is often undertaken in conjunction with a significant event, for example, the opening of a new outlet by the intermediary, or the launch of a new product.

Sponsorship

SPONSORSHIP does not fit neatly into a categorization of the elements of the promotion mix. It essentially uses a combination of advertising, public relations, sales promotion, and direct marketing to associate a company's product or corporate image (which may be unknown or misunderstood) with the image of something which is well understood. As the general clutter of media advertising has increased in recent years, sponsorship has come to play an increasingly important role in the promotion mix. With consumers becoming increasingly critical of organizations' societal credentials, sponsorship has been seen by many organizations as a cost-effective means of enhancing their image.

Sponsorship involves investment in events or causes in order that an organization can achieve objectives such as increased awareness levels, enhanced reputation, etc. Sponsorship activities include such examples as a bank sponsoring cricket matches (e.g. the NatWest Trophy) and the sponsorship of specific television programmes (such as Cadbury's sponsorship of Coronation Street).

As with promotional planning in general, segmentation is crucial to successful sponsorship. A company must have a good definition of the audience to which it wishes to communicate its message, and then seek sponsorship vehicles whose audiences match the company's target market. This segmentation can be undertaken in

> Using celebrities to sponsor brands can work wonders. Walkers Crisps' use of Gary Lineker and Michael Owen proved particularly successful, with sales of 'Salt 'n' Lineker' branded crisps increasing by 60 per cent over their previous salt and vinegar equivalent. French Connection's sponsorship of Lennox Lewis exposed worldwide audiences to Lewis in the ring-side wearing a 'fcuk fear' hat for his World Championship fight against Evander Holyfield and was regarded as highly cost effective.
>
> Despite these successes, sponsors must be extremely careful about which celebrities they choose to sponsor. Relying on just one famous celebrity is a risk because there is always an element of the unknown. It is essential to analyse the qualities that an individual brings to a brand—merely having celebrity status is not on its own sufficient. There is a lengthy catalogue of celebrity sponsorships that have gone wrong. Pepsi aimed for maximum appeal among children by sponsoring Michael Jackson, until damaging allegations about his sex life were reported extensively in the media. Immediately prior to the 1998 World Cup, Adidas, who sponsored the England football team's David Beckham, proclaimed that 'After tonight, England v. Argentina will be remembered for what a player did with his feet', only to see the sad irony of the message when Beckham was sent off. And in 1999, Nike found that instead of sponsoring Lawrence Dallaglio as England rugby captain, he had instead become a suspected drug dealer.
>
> Another danger is that the sponsored celebrity doesn't truly believe in the product that they are endorsing, and makes this known to the public. Actress Helen Bonham-Carter might have appeared to be the ideal face to promote Yardley beauty products, but much of the benefit of her sponsorship was undone when she admitted to the media that she didn't wear make-up.
>
> How can a sponsor avoid such problems? Careful analysis of the risks beforehand is essential. Placing too much emphasis on just one celebrity can increase risks. Companies increasingly seek opt-out clauses in sponsorship contracts which allow them to pull out if a celebrity does anything which may harm the sponsor's brand.

Figure 19.4 Sponsorship of sporting events allows a company's brand name to be seen by viewers of the event and to associate the brand with the values of the sport concerned. Carlsberg-Tetley Brewing Company Ltd., owners of the Tetley's Bitter brand, were a sponsor of the 1999 Rugby World Cup. The logic of the sponsorship was based on the similarity between the profile of rugby spectators and the brand's target market. (Reproduced with permission of Carlsberg-Tetley Brewing Company Ltd.)

terms of socioeconomic, demographic, and geographic characteristics. As an example, the tour operator Kuoni's sponsorship of Classic FM programmes matches the former's target market with the latter's audience. Sponsorship often takes place at a local level, for example an estate agency moving into an area may seek to increase its awareness by sponsoring a school fête or a local theatrical group.

It is difficult to evaluate sponsorship activities because of the problem of isolating the effects of sponsorship from other elements of the promotion mix. Direct measurement is only likely to be possible if sponsorship is the predominant tool. Sponsorship should therefore be seen as a tool that complements other elements of the promotion mix.

Chapter summary and key linkages to other chapters

Public relations and sales promotions are both elements of the promotion mix that have seen considerable recent growth, partly because of the increasing saturation coverage of advertising. Public relations is often seen as a corporate-level rather than a marketing function activity and is essentially long term in its orientation. Sales promotion is essentially short term and seeks to bring about an immediate consumer response to a sales proposition. Whereas advertising helps to build strong brands, excessive sales promotion has often been accused of undermining them. Sponsorship combines elements of public relations, sales promotion, advertising, and direct marketing.

Public relations and sales promotion can be related to the following chapters in this book:

Chapter 1: What is marketing?: To many people, public relations is a gloss which is all about making excuses for bad service. Public relations can only succeed if an organization has fully embraced the marketing philosophy. Similarly, sales promotion will not be effective if the other elements of the marketing mix are not correct.

Chapter 2: The marketing environment: Public relations is essentially about maintaining mutual understanding with the multiple stakeholders who make up an organization's publics.

Chapter 3: Segmentation: Effective public relations and sales promotion depends crucially on an ability to segment audiences and develop a message which is most appropriate to each targeted segment.

Chapter 4: Branding: While advertising helps to build brands, sales promotion activity often undermines them. Public relations is often used to protect a brand when its image is under attack.

Chapter 5: Marketing and ethics: Public relations should anticipate problems likely to be caused by a firm's unethical behaviour and not just seek to make amends after damage has been done to an organization's reputation. Sales promotion practices have often been accused of being unethical (see Case Study).

Chapter 6: Marketing research: Marketing research is essential in order to identify and address target markets for sales promotion and for evaluating the effectiveness of promotional activity.

Chapter 7: Buyer behaviour: Public relations is generally aimed at the earlier buyer readiness states by encouraging awareness, whereas sales promotion is generally more effective at bringing about action.

Chapter 8: Buyer–seller relationships: Public relations activity can help preserve the image of a company in the eyes of its regular customers. Sponsored activities are often promoted to long-standing customers.

Chapter 9: The product: What are the unique benefits of a product that should be promoted to the target market?

Chapter 10: New product development and innovation: For radically innovative new products, public relations alone may be sufficient to launch a new product. For 'me-too' products launched into a competitive market, sales promotion efforts may be needed to encourage trial.

Chapter 11: Developing a sustainable competitive advantage: Public relations and sales promotion alone will not create and sustain a competitive advantage—the other elements of the marketing plan must also be correct.

Chapters 12/13: Pricing theory and applications: Sales promotion is often undertaken to fine-tune a company's prices. In a dynamic market characterized by falling prices, sales promotion incentives may be one way of gradually lowering prices.

Chapters 14/15: Intermediaries/logistics: Intermediaries are recipients of sales promotion activities, which may be necessary to encourage them to carry a manufacturer's stock. Public relations activity should also address intermediaries as important stakeholders.

Chapter 16: Principles of promotion planning: This chapter provided an overview of promotion planning and the communication process, of which public relations and sales promotion are interrelated components.

Chapter 17: Advertising: Sales promotion frequently undermines efforts to build strong brands through advertising. Public relations is less costly than advertising, but also less controllable.

Chapter 18: Selling and sales management: The task of personal selling can be facilitated by effective public relations and sales promotions.

Chapter 20: Direct marketing: Sales promotion activities are often executed through some form of direct marketing activity.

Chapter 21: Organizing for marketing: Public relations is often treated as a central corporate function, rather than a narrow marketing function.

Chapter 22: Services marketing: The intangibility of services often creates a perception of greater riskiness which public relations can seek to overcome.

Chapter 23: Global marketing: Public relations activity is frequently used to create awareness of a company when it enters an overseas market.

Case study

Free flights promotion ends in disaster

The Hoover company's attempts to sell more vacuum cleaners by offering an incentive of free flights has become a legendary disaster in the field of sales promotions. An examination of the case is useful for highlighting some of the problems of planning, implementing, and monitoring sales promotions.

During the early 1990s, Hoover was faced with a period of economic recession in which discretionary expenditure on consumer durables was held back. In these conditions, most vacuum sales were replacements for worn out machines or first-time buys for people setting up home. The challenge was to increase the sales of machines bought to upgrade existing equipment.

The company came up with the idea of offering free airline tickets to America for anybody buying one of its vacuum cleaners. For many people, a holiday in the USA may have been perceived as an unnecessary and unaffordable luxury during a period of recession, but one that might be justified if it came free with the purchase of an 'essential' vacuum cleaner.

The immediate result of the sales promotion was to boost the company's sales of vacuum cleaners to more than double the level of the previous year. So far so good, but then serious problems set in. The first problem occurred when Hoover could not satisfy demand for its vacuum cleaners and had to resort to paying its staff overtime rates of pay in order to increase supply. It should be remembered that the initial objective of the promotion was to utilize existing spare capacity rather than adding to that capacity. The company had carried out insufficient research prior to launching its incentive. Had it done so, it may have reached the conclusion that the incentive was too generous and likely to create more demand than the company could cope with.

A second problem occurred during subsequent periods when sales fell to below their pre-incentive levels. Many people had simply brought forward their purchase of a vacuum cleaner. Worse still, many people had bought their cleaner simply to get the free tickets, which at £70 for a cleaner with a free £250 ticket made sense. These people frequently disposed of their cleaner as they had no need for it. The classified ads of many local newspapers contained many adverts for 'nearly new, unused' vacuum cleaners at discounted prices and this further depressed sales of new machines once the sales promotion had come to an end.

A third and more serious problem occurred when large numbers of buyers tried to use their free flight vouchers. All sales promotions are based on an assumption of take-up rates, which can be as low as 5–10 per cent. Anything higher and the cost of the incentives actually given away can wipe out the benefits arising from increased sales. In this case, Hoover had carried out insufficient pre-testing of the sales promotion in order to assess the likely take-up rate and was surprised by the actual take-up which subsequently occurred. In an attempt to control costs, the company became notorious for its attempts to 'suppress' take-up of free flights. Many claimants complained that telephone lines were constantly busy and, when they did get through, they were offered the most unattractive flights possible. It was reported that claimants from the south-east of England were only offered flights departing from Scotland and those from Scotland only offered flights from London, done to reduce the attractiveness of the free offer. These activities attracted high levels of coverage in the media and left a once highly respected brand as one with a perception of mistrust. Five years after the initial débâcle, the Hoover Holiday Pressure Group continued to be an awkward reminder for the company.

The free flights promotion eventually cost Hoover a reported £37 million in redemption charges, without bringing about any long-term growth in sales. With appropriate pre-testing, these costs could have been foreseen. Worse still, the company's brand image had been tarnished in a way that would take many years—if ever—to recover from.

Case study review questions

1 What are the inherent problems for a company such as Hoover in assessing the effectiveness of sales promotion activity?

2 Identify a programme of research that Hoover could have undertaken in order to avoid the costly failure of its free flights promotion.

3 What alternative methods of promotion might have been more suitable to achieve Hoover's objective of utilizing spare capacity during a period of economic recession?

Chapter review questions

1 In what circumstances could a company be justified in relying on 'free' public relations activity in its promotional mix, rather than paid-for advertising?

2 How can a consumer goods manufacturer guard against the risk of a 'public relations disaster'?

3 Should a company handle its public relations internally or entrust the task to a

specialist PR agency? Weigh up the pros and cons for a consumer services organization.

4 What factors are critical to successful sales promotion activity?

5 To what extent is it still true to say that advertising builds brands, while sales promotion undermines them. Is there any overlap or convergence of the two functions?

6 Advise a company selling stairlifts for elderly and disabled people on the sponsorship opportunities that it may be able to exploit successfully.

Suggested further reading

The following provide a background to the theories and practices of public relations:

■ Gofton, K. (1999), 'PR Middle Ground Feels the Squeeze' (includes a listing of the top 150 public relation firms in the UK), *Marketing*, 27 May, pp. 37–44.

■ Gray, R. (1998), 'Keeping Connected', *Marketing*, 22 Oct., pp. 37–8.

■ Haywood, R. (1997), *Public Relations for Marketing Professionals* (Basingstoke: Macmillan).

■ Kitchen, P. (1997), *Public Relations Principles and Practice* (London: ITP).

■ L'Etang, J., and Pieckza, M. (1996), *Critical Perpectives in Public Relations* (London: ITP).

■ Seitel, F. (1998), *Practice of Public Relations* (Englewood Cliffs, NJ: Prentice Hall).

■ Summer, I. (1999), 'Web Site Novelties can Bring PR Opportunities', *Marketing*, 17 June, pp. 31–2.

The following provide a background to the theories and practices of sales promotion and sponsorship activities:

■ Acland, H. (1998), 'Do's and Don'ts of Sales Promotion', *Marketing*, 17 Sept., pp. 43–4.

■ Cummins, J. (1998), *Sales Promotion* (London: Kogan Page).

■ Donald, R., Lichtenstein, S. B., and Netemeyer, R. G. (1997), 'An Examination of Deal Proneness Across Sales Promotion Types: A Consumer Segmentation Perspective', *Journal of Retailing*, **73**, 2, pp. 283–97.

■ Gould, B. W. (1997), 'Consumer Promotion and Purchase Timing: the Case of Cheese', *Applied Economics*, **29**, 4, pp. 445–58.

■ Huff, L. C. (1998), 'An Investigation of Consumer Response to Sales Promotions in Developing Markets: A Three-Country Analysis', *Journal of Advertising Research*, **38**, 3, pp. 47–57.

■ Mela, C. F., Jedidi, K., and Bowman, D. (1998), 'The Long-Term Impact of Promotions on Consumer Stockpiling Behavior', *Journal of Marketing Research*, May, **35**, 2, pp. 250–62.

■ Schutz, D. E., Robinson, W. A., and Petrison, L. A. (1997), *Sales Promotion Essentials: The 10 Basic Sales Promotion Techniques . . . and How to Use Them* (NtC Business Books).

■ Shirley, I. (1997), 'Playing it Safe is a Serious Risk in Sales Promotion', *Marketing*, 9 Jan., p. 16.

Useful web links

Institute of Public Relations: http://www.ipr.org.uk/

Institute of Sales Promotion: http://isp.org.uk

The PR Network—an affiliation of communications experts who use this website to share information, promote their businesses, host their web sites, and enhance their professional development and employment opportunities: http://www.usprnet.com

Chapter 20
Direct Marketing

Chapter objectives

Many companies have sought to simplify their channels of promotion and distribution by adopting direct marketing techniques. This chapter explores the reasons why companies seek to deal directly with their customers rather than through intermediaries. As a strategy, direct marketing is often associated with efforts to develop relationship marketing. The methods of achieving this are discussed and the limitations of direct marketing noted.

Direct marketing and the evolution of marketing

DIRECT Marketing has become very important to marketing managers during the past couple of decades and there is every indication that it will continue to become increasingly significant in the future. Direct marketing is essentially about companies opening up a dialogue directly between themselves and the end consumers of their products, thereby avoiding the need to communicate through indirect media such as press and television advertising. Direct marketing can also allow a firm to communicate directly with its customers without the need to go through retail or wholesale intermediaries.

There is no universally agreed definition of what constitutes direct marketing, but we will begin with the definition used by the UK Direct Marketing Association. It defines direct marketing as:

Communications where data are used systematically to achieve quantifiable marketing objectives and where direct contact is invited or made between a company and its customers.

We will refine this definition of direct marketing a little later and explore the different ways in which organizations have interpreted the basic concept.

Direct marketing in its own right as an activity and as a business sector is growing very rapidly. This is indicated by expenditure on direct marketing activities, which in the UK grew by around 15 per cent a year during the late 1990s, reaching a total of £7.2 billion in 1997. As a further indicator of its significance to the marketing community, the Institute of Direct marketing has estimated that 10 per cent of all new graduates entering marketing careers begin in direct marketing.

Before discussing just what direct marketing involves, it is important to relate direct marketing to the evolution of the marketing concept. In tracing the evolution of direct marketing, many parallels can be observed with the evolution of relationship marketing (Chapter 8). There continues to be debate among academics and practitioners about what distinguishes the two concepts. To many, the two are indistinguishable. An alternative view, which is adopted here, is that relationship marketing should be seen as more embracing than direct marketing, often incorporating relationships between multiple levels of a supply/distribution chain. Viewed in this sense, direct marketing can be seen as a process of simplifying distribution and communication channels, whereas relationship marketing often involves structuring complex networks of interrelationships between organizations at different points in a value chain

In simple economies characterized by small-scale production and very local markets, most transactions between a company and its customers were conducted directly. There was only a very limited role for intermediaries and each producer could be said to have a one-to-one relationship with each of its customers. Consider the case of shoemaking. Each small community would have had its local cobbler who produced shoes to fit each individual customer uniquely. Through repeated dealings, the cobbler could come to learn the preferences of individuals and would also be able to assess their creditworthiness.

The industrial revolution of the nineteenth century meant that large factories could exploit economies of scale, thereby giving them a competitive advantage over small-scale craft-based producers. The village cobbler gave way to the centralized factory-based producer, who could use machinery to produce shoes more cheaply. However, the shoe factory had no means of keeping in touch with each of the customers who bought its shoes. It could only achieve large-scale output (and hence economies of scale) by selling its shoes in markets which were geographically removed from the point of production. Customers were too far away and too many in number to allow the company to enter into a dialogue with each of them. Instead, the company produced an 'average' shoe for the 'average' customer and relied on wholesalers and retailers to get its shoes to the final customers. Communication became impersonal and one way through the medium of advertising.

Over time, the shoe factory would probably have moved on from making shoes for the mass market. As its markets became more competitive, it would have identified market segments and targeted these with specially adapted product offers (e.g. by distinguishing between segments in terms of the importance attached to the appearance, fashionability, durability, and comfort of the shoes they buy). Many large shoe manufacturers developed distinctive brands to identify different levels of quality and fashionability (e.g. the former Sears subsidiary British Shoe Corporation effectively

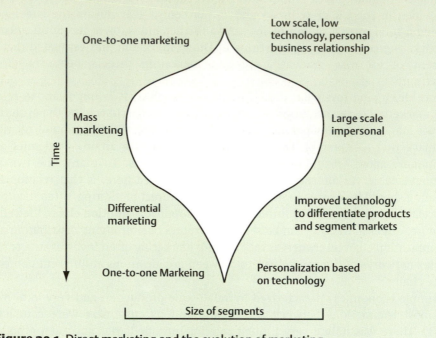

Figure 20.1 Direct marketing and the evolution of marketing

segmented the UK market with its Curtess, True Form, Freeman Hardy and Willis, and Saxone brands, among others).

Today, information technology is allowing many companies to go back to dealing with their customers on a one-to-one basis. Consider the factors that have helped to bring this about:

1. Modern databases can now allow a company to have immediate access to information about all of its customers. The small village cobbler had this ability of instant recall, but it became lost in the era of mass marketing when customer details would have been buried somewhere in a mountain of paper records, and probably only accessible to intermediaries and not the manufacturer. Some sellers of high value goods and services have always been able to keep records of each individual customer (e.g. banks and sellers of industrial capital equipment). Today, the opportunities for sellers of relatively low value, high volume goods to collect, store, analyse, and retrieve information about their customers is continually increasing.

2. Computer-assisted manufacturing systems are allowing products to be produced economically in very short runs, in some cases a run of one, tailored to the specific needs of individual customers. The services sector has led the way in being able to tailor products precisely to customers' needs (e.g. a tour itinerary packaged specifically by a tour company to meet the needs of one individual). Manufacturing companies are now catching up with flexible manufacturing systems.

3. The development of just-in-time production systems (JIT) is allowing companies to cater for small orders without needing to keep large stocks 'just-in-case' an order for an infrequently purchased variant of its product came in. Just-in-time systems require a company to design its whole supply chain so that it can fulfil customers' orders rapidly. Where they are working effectively, a company can offer guaranteed delivery of specialized products to its customers within a very short period of time (e.g., many suppliers of corporate workwear now compete on the basis of being able to meet customers' specific requests within one week of placing an order). Supply chain management is crucial to JIT production and demands high levels of co-operation and communication between chain members (refer back to Chapter 15 for further discussion).

4. Manufacturers' 'goods out' departments can become very busy places, even when they are only shipping a small number of large consignments of goods to a limited number of wholesalers and retailers. For the typical goods out department, the prospect of having to deliver single items to hundreds of thousands of individual final customers would have seemed impossible until recently. Yet automation of warehouses has been proceeding rapidly, with the development of automatic high speed picking systems and automatic routing to a dispatch bay. Many companies are now finding that their warehouses are able to handle very small orders much more effectively than ever before. Companies such as Next Direct and Lands' End have created very efficient systems for delivering unit sizes of one, direct to the final customer within a day or two of an order being placed.

5. Technology has also had effects in making final delivery systems more efficient, for example through computerized vehicle routing and tracking systems. However, advances in transport systems have not matched other aspects of distribution and manufacturing in their ability to cater for the specific needs of individual customers. Increasing real transport costs (as a result of real increases in the cost of labour, fuel, and taxes) and increasing levels of traffic congestion have inhibited delivery of goods direct to consumers' homes. Indeed, the tendency over recent years has been for home delivery of many goods to decline, as witnessed in the UK by the decline in home delivery of milk, bread, and meat.

The overall effect of the changes described above has been to allow firms to re-enter a direct dialogue with each of their customers. To stick with the example of shoes, this is beginning to happen, as companies such as Lands' End identify market segments that would prefer to deal direct rather than visit a traditional retail outlet. Some of the principal differences between traditional marketing and direct marketing are shown in Fig. 20.2.

Emphasis of traditional mass marketing	Emphasis of direct marketing
Average customer	Individual customer
Anonymous customers	Customer profiles
Standardized product offer	Customized product offer
Mass production	Customized production
Mass distribution	Individual distribution
Mass advertising	Individual dialogue
Mass promotion	Individual incentives
One–way messages	Interactive dialogue
Economies of scale	Economies of scope
All customers	Profitable customers
Customer attraction	Customer retention

Figure 20.2 Traditional mass marketing compared to direct marketing (based on Pepper and Rogers 1993)

Key features of direct marketing

THE terms used by industry and academics to define direct marketing remain fragmented. Direct response marketing (DRM) is a term which is now used to encompass marketing activities that are designed to induce a direct response from mail order, direct mail, direct response advertising, and telemarketing. These activities have developed rapidly since the 1980s and have been reliant on the production of mailing lists. As the use of computers has expanded so has the production, sale, and purchase of lists multiplied. Database marketing (DBM) is an interactive approach to customer contact management relying on the maintenance of accurate customer and prospective customer information, competitor information, and internal company information. The database is used to provide computer-aided sales support, for direct response marketing, and to support customer information and service systems (Hartley and Starkey 1996, p. 158).

The development of customer databases gives a company both direct market development benefits and cost reduction benefits. Market development benefits can be achieved in three principal ways:

1. establishing a database of current and potential customers;
2. delivering a differentiated message to these customers based upon their characteristics and preferences; and
3. tracking customer transactions to monitor the cost of acquiring particular types of customer and their lifetime value to the organization (Copulsky and Wolf 1990).

On the other side of the profit equation, many organizations see the development of databases as an opportunity to gain competitive advantage through cost cutting, where the use of databases reduces the cost of maintaining face-to-face dialogue through a sales force. Sellers of high value, low volume industrial products have been early users of database marketing. Within consumer markets, the use of database marketing has expanded from high value financial service sectors to low value fast moving consumer goods.

What is often referred to as computer-aided sales support (CASS) involves a company's field sales, sales support, and telemarketing teams having direct access to the organization's customer database via desktop or portable computers. Through this, they can access customer/prospective customer information, competitor information, and company information. When they are working effectively, such systems can allow a company's sales personnel to identify and pursue prospects in a much more coherent and targeted manner, compared with lone sales personnel whose information may be incomplete and out of date.

Finally, direct marketing is not just about recruiting new customers. It is concerned with creating loyalty among existing customers and retaining their business. So many companies include a customer information and service (CIS) system within their direct marketing efforts. Customer helplines are becoming an important feature of many companies in both the goods and services sectors. Databases and computerized telephone systems now provide the opportunity for companies to deal directly with their customers in a speedy and informed manner. There are many reasons why consumers may wish to contact the manufacturer or supplier of services direct, including enquiries about bills (e.g. public utilities); the amount outstanding on a loan (e.g. banks and finance companies); technical questions (e.g. electrical products); warranty cover (e.g. household products); product availability (e.g. mail order companies); schedules (e.g. airline and railway operators); or delivery (e.g. furniture retailers).

Customers increasingly expect a company to be able to answer their questions immediately and in a seamless manner which does not involve being transferred between numerous operators.

The development of customer databases

At the heart of companies' direct marketing efforts is a database identifying prospective customers, current customers, and lapsed customers. The effectiveness of direct marketing is critically dependent on the quality of customer details held on the database. To many people, direct marketing has become synonymous with 'junk mail'. Mail only becomes junk in the hands of the recipient if it has been poorly targeted so that it does not meet the needs of the person to whom it has been sent. Consider the following cases:

- a company selling bulbs and shrubs for domestic gardeners sent its catalogues to people living in upstairs flats in an inner-city area of London;

Airlines have always been at the cutting edge in terms of keeping information about their customers. The need to book seats in advance has meant that they have had to maintain some sort of reservation system. The fact that air tickets have tended to be high priced and infrequently purchased has made individual recording of all customers economically feasible. More recently, the need for high levels of security has sharpened airlines' attitudes towards the information they hold about their passengers' journeys. Recent competition and developments in telemarketing have seen a number of major initiatives by airlines. Some, such as the low cost, Luton-based EasyJet, have cut out the traditional travel agent completely and decided to deal directly with each of its customers. The company has used newspaper advertisements to promote its direct response telephone number. A customer service centre could then enter into a dialogue with each prospective customer to identify their needs and make the best reservation for them. Increasingly, the role of the telephone is being replaced by the Internet as a medium through which EasyJet communicates with its customers. It is not just small direct-sell airlines that have developed customer service centres. American Airlines is a major carrier within Europe and in the early 1990s was operating five reservation centres throughout Europe. In 1995 it decided to locate its new European reservation centre in Ireland, employing 220 multilingual staff and expecting to handle 2.5 million calls a year. The new centre gave a faster, twenty-four-hour service to customers and travel agents, and, by pooling resources into one central unit, saved an estimated £20 million a year in running costs.

- a bank which had just refused a loan to an individual shortly afterwards sent out a mailing to that same customer enclosing details of its loans and an application form;
- a company manufacturing baby nappies sent promotional material and a trial offer for its products to a resident of a retirement home.

In each of these cases, it is just possible that the companies concerned had carefully studied their target market and made a decision which successfully hit their target market, even though it seemed intuitively ridiculous (e.g. the firm supplying bulbs and shrubs may have identified a group of flat dwellers who went away to their country cottages at the weekend). However, the above examples serve only to show that the individual dialogue which is a defining characteristic of direct marketing cannot exist where a company is speaking to people who have no motivation whatsoever to enter into a dialogue.

So how does a company develop a database which at least allows it to enter into an appropriate dialogue with the right people? We will consider a number of aspects of database management: using all internal leads possible to build up a database of prospective customers; buying in mailing lists to supplement these sources; and updating the list so that it continues to be relevant to the needs of the company and its customers.

Developing a database from internal leads

Companies typically let a lot of information about prospective and actual customers pass them by, or at least they have it but do not make use of it. Consider the following sources of information to which companies typically have access, and which, with careful management, can be usefully added to a database:

- **Routine customer enquiries**: many companies have simply sent out sales literature in return for an enquirer giving their name and address. Increasingly, companies are taking the postcode element of an enquirer's address very seriously. By analysing postcodes using an approach such as ACORN, a lot can be learned about the background of an enquirer. At the very least, a careful analysis of postcodes tells the company something about the geographical spread of its enquiries, something that may be vital to planning future marketing efforts. It should also be able subsequently to identify which postcode areas result in the highest 'conversion' rate (that is, a sale is achieved). Companies often go beyond asking for an enquirer's name and address. Typical additional questions include: where did you see the advertisement? (helps monitor the effectiveness of the firm's advertising); when do you intend to buy? (helps the company follow up an enquiry at a later date if the purchase intention is not immediate); do you currently own a specified item? (can help to distinguish first-time purchasers from replacement purchasers who may approach the purchase decision in quite different ways); basic demographic details, such as age group and marital status (helps to develop a profile of an enquirer's needs specifically, and the profile of enquirers generally).

  Of course, companies can go too far in the information they collect from a casual enquiry and risk alienating the enquirer. There is also a danger that a firm's dealers may be suspicious of it opening a dialogue directly with what they regard as their own customers. Where a company intends retaining a dealer network to distribute its goods, a direct marketing approach can be of mutual benefit where the information captured is passed on to dealers so that they are better informed about prospects for the firm's products.

- **Customer orders**: an efficient company will capture information from enquirers, analyse it to create a profile of its prospects, and assess which sources of enquiry result in the most profitable business. Once a prospect has become an actual customer, a company can track their subsequent purchases, building up a more refined profile of the customer's needs. From this it should spot opportunities for opening a dialogue to sell related or replacement products.

GUARANTEE REGISTRATION CARD

Name   Mr/Miss/Mrs/Other _____ First Name _____ Surname _____

Address   _____

Postcode   _____

Model No. of product purchased   HN_____

Where did you buy this product?   _____

Which of the following best describes your reason for purchase?

Gift _____
Replacement for existing equipment _____
Purchase of addition equipment _____
First time purchase of this type of product _____

What is your age group?   Under 18 ☐   18–25 ☐   25–35 ☐

                                 36–45 ☐   46–55 ☐   56–65 ☐

                                 65+ ☐

Male or female?   Male ☐   Female ☐

Your occupation _____

PLease tell us whether you own, or are considering buying the following:

	Already own	Considering buying
Mobile telephone	☐	☐
Widescreen television	☐	☐
Home computer	☐	☐

Tick this box if you would NOT like to be informed from time to time of your new products and special offers. ☐

THANK YOU

Now return this card to the address shown overleaf.
You will also be entered in our monthly prize draw.

Figure 20.3 Gaurantee registration cards can say a lot about an individual. Cards such as this one offer consumers who complete them a number of benefits, such as priority attention in the event of a safety recall of the product and entry into a prize draw. But the main beneficiary is the manufacturer who gets to learn a lot about the profile of the buyer and their reason for buying its products

A supplier of domestic ride-on mowers to the UK market had traditionally used whole-page advertisements in Sunday magazines to promote its products. A considerable amount of the space in each advertisement was devoted to a list of dealers who held stocks of the firm's mowers. The company thought this approach would make it easy for customers to find their way to a distributor where they could see its products demonstrated. In fact, the company's magazine advertisements looked very cluttered and it knew very little about who was responding to them. So it had a rethink and decided to enter into a direct dialogue with its prospective customers. Out went the long list of dealers and in came a single freephone telephone number which callers could ring to find out the location of their nearest dealer. For the lawn mower manufacturer, there were numerous benefits. Firstly, space was freed up in its advertisement to feature the benefits of the mowers, providing greater impact than had been possible previously. Secondly, the company used the initial contact with its prospective customers to learn something more about where they had seen the advertisement and their future buying intention. Thirdly, the manufacturer worked closely with its dealers by passing on callers' information to the dealer who was best located to satisfy a particular caller. After a period of time, the dealer would give the enquirer a call to check that they had received the information requested and to help move them through the purchase process.

Buying in mailing lists

Very often a company will have few opportunities to build up its own database of prospective customers, or at least it would be extremely costly and time consuming. An alternative is to buy in an existing mailing list. Leasing mailing lists is becoming a major industry in its own right, with numerous organizations such as ICD and Experian offering mailing lists tailored to the needs of individual client companies. These list brokers gather information from multiple sources, including:

- the electoral register, to which everybody resident in the UK over the age of 18 must give their details;
- companies who have recently supplied particular categories of goods or services to their customers;
- directories, such as Yellow Pages;
- surveys specially commissioned by the list broker (e.g. ICD regularly distributes a questionnaire to households, asking the recipient to complete information about themselves and their buying habits, in return for an incentive reward);
- surveys bought in from other companies who had used the survey to research their own customers.

The extent to which companies can trade personal details of individuals is limited in the UK by the Data Protection Act 1998. In general, individuals have the right to prevent a company from passing on their details to organizations other than the one to which they initially gave the information. There has been debate about whether individuals should be presumed to have allowed disclosure unless they say otherwise, or whether they should be presumed to be against disclosure, unless they specifically authorize it.

Lists can become out of date very rapidly, so some mailing lists may be of dubious reliability. People moving house, deaths, and companies going out of business are typical reasons for a name on a mailing list not being a prospect at all. The better suppliers of mailing lists use multiple sources of information to confirm the existence of an individual on the list and to delete them if they have not had any recent positive confirmation of their existence. To illustrate the multiple sources of information which can be used to build a picture of an individual, ICD has estimated that for each person on its National Consumer Database, it has an average of seventy-two separate pieces of information.

Merging multiple lists can be a highly complex task, with electronically stored lists coming in a variety of formats. In many direct marketing organizations, individuals with a sound understanding of relational databases (that is, databases which relate to a number of sources of information) are a valuable resource in short supply.

Maintaining a database

Once a prospect has become an actual customer, a company can enter into a more personal dialogue than when dealing through the medium of bought-in lists. Companies should ensure that they collect information from customers which is relevant to understanding their needs and future purchase intentions. These are examples of simple questions that a company might ask its customers in order to obtain basic information about product requirements and delivery details:

- For what purpose are you buying this item (e.g. for gift or self-use)?
- How many of this type of product do you buy in a year (gives some indication of the purchasing potential of this customer)?
- How frequently do you buy a related product item (indicates opportunities for broadening the relationship between the company and its customers)?
- From which source do you normally obtain this type of product (can give an indication of the buying behaviour and socio-economic status of the customer, e.g. do they normally buy from upmarket specialist stores or general purpose stores?)?
- When do you intend to make your next purchase of this or a related product (allows the company to target the customer at a time when they are most receptive)?

In addition, the company should seek to fill in gaps in its knowledge abut the demographic and socio-economic profile of its customers. Of course, asking too many questions may be perceived as being too intrusive and a balance has to be struck between a company's need for information and customers' need for privacy.

If a company has maintained its database effectively, it should instantly be able to build up a picture of each of its customers. So when a customer calls in with an enquiry, any individual within the company taking the call should have available to them full details of their recent transactions, notes about their particular preferences, and any problems that they might have encountered in the past. Companies which have managed to make up-to-date information available to all of their front-line employees are recreating in these individuals the ability to have the one-to-one dialogue which the owner of a small business was able to have with each of the customers who was personally known to him. When systems are working well, customers can be awestruck with the attention to detail shown by the company and the feeling that the company has put them uniquely at the centre of all its attention. When companies fail to update their customer database, the results can be disastrous for developing ongoing relationships. Consider the following problems which customers frequently encounter:

- One employee alone does not have access to sufficient information to allow them to resolve an issue, so a customer is referred to numerous other employees, often having to explain afresh the problem that they are seeking to resolve.

- Data are incorrectly entered, resulting in incorrect records (e.g. the wrong telephone number is recorded for the customer).

- The company fails to note customers' preferences, resulting in goods and services being delivered which do not match their requirements, despite these preferences having been previously specified (e.g. a customer of a telephone company requests the option of monthly billing but instead is billed quarterly).

- The company does not record details of problems that the customer has had in their previous dealing, thereby preventing employees who have future contact with customer from being sensitive to the customer's perceptions of the company.

- Individuals are sent information which is completely irrelevant to their needs (e.g. a customer of a car manufacturer is sent promotional material for special offers on new cars for several months immediately after they have in fact bought a new car from the company).

Profiling and targeting

A PARTICULAR strength of direct marketing is its ability to understand its customers in great detail. Contrast this to companies who use more traditional indirect means of communication and distribution. Because they do not have an ongoing dialogue with their final customers, they can only really get to understand them through sample research. This can be costly, time consuming, and inaccurate if the sample is not representative of the company's customers at large.

With direct marketing, a company can use its database to develop a profile of who its best customers are. Consider the case of a direct response company advertising in the national press to promote a commemorative plate, a product which it has no previous experience in selling. It would probably have a reasonable idea of its target market from previous related experience, and select to advertise in national newspapers and magazines whose audience closely matches its own target market. Prospective customers would be invited to return a coupon or telephone for further information about the offer. In both cases, the company would obtain two vital pieces of information from the initial enquiry:

■ The postcode of the respondent, which can yield a lot of information about their demographic profile. Linked to an analysis programme such as MOSAIC, a company can learn a lot about the profile of individuals responding to its advertisements. Companies therefore go to great lengths to ensure that people disclose their postcode.

■ The source where the respondent saw the advertisement, which is vital for future campaign planning. Very often, codes are used in advertisements to identify an advertisement. At other times, more subtle efforts are made to identify the source, as where different response telephone numbers are given in different advertisements.

From its initial response, a company can get a reasonable idea of what type of person shows most interest in its commemorative plate. This is market potential, but the company needs to go one step further and analyse which of its callers is actually converted into a customer. Thus a further analysis of respondents is made to establish who are the most successful prospects in terms of conversion to paying customers. Very often a company may find that a high level of initial enquiry among one segment is matched by a below average level of conversions. Where this is the case, the company needs to examine the appeal of the offer to this segment. Was the product appropriately specified? Was it over-priced? Was it poorly packaged?

For the initial enquirers who were converted into customers, the company can seek to obtain further information at the time of ordering (e.g. the frequency with which they purchase this type of commemorative plate, purpose of purchase). If the company is offering credit facilities, this offers a further legitimate reason to collect more information to build up a profile of the customer.

Having started out with only a general idea about who constitutes its target market, the company now has a fairly detailed profile of who its customers are. If it is offering a range of plates, it would be able to identify who are the most profitable customers in terms of the total value of their orders. Armed with this more refined profile of its target market, the company can seek these out using direct methods of communication. Newspaper advertising may have been appropriate when the nature of its target market was poorly understood. It may also have had value in its own right for raising general levels of awareness of the company. But now it can look through its own customer records and pick out all of those customers who meet the profile of its most likely profitable customers. It can supplement this list by buying in lists based on the characteristics of prospects which it now knows are most likely to buy its commemorative plate.

The company can then go on to track the purchases of customers that it had attracted with its initial plate offer. It may find that some converts went on to become regular customers of not only its plates, but its related product offers. These represent particularly attractive prospects for the company, and it would seek to establish whether frequent buying is associated with any particular combination of an individual's demographic characteristics (e.g. age 65+, living in a better residential area, and reading the *Sunday Times*). The company may make particular efforts to obtain an initial purchase from this group, in the knowledge that there is a high probability of them going on to become regular, profitable customers. It may calculate that targeting this group with an introductory subsidized incentive offer may be justified in terms of the probable payback from future orders. Such an incentive may be unjustified when targeted at a segment for whom an analysis of buying behaviour showed that they only ever made one purchase from the company.

Finally, a profile analysis of an organization's customers may suggest that some are not at all profitable and unlikely to ever become profitable. Just as a company requires a means of adding new prospects to its database, it requires a means of 'exiting' those who have not responded profitably to its attempts to create a dialogue. Many companies determine a period of time after which a customer will be deleted from their active database if they have not placed an order. If a company has carried out a thorough profile analysis of its customers, it may decide that some groups should be given more latitude than others—analysis may suggest that although a particular customer has not placed an order for a considerable time, this category of customer has a tendency to place very profitable orders when it does eventually buy. Companies may adopt a graduated process of removing individuals from their active

SEND FOR OUR COLOUR BROCHURE !

To: GFI Direct, Dept ST2110 Freepost, 14 Swan Business Centre, Bristol BS99 1BR

Name _____

Address _____ Postcode _____

OR Telephone 0800 497812 and quote reference 470

Figure 20.4 Even a simple response form such as this one from a newspaper can give a company a lot of valuable information. A code helps to assess the effectiveness of specific media, while the respondent's postcode helps to build up a profile of enquirers and subsequent purchasers

How does a retailer strong on selling computer hardware overcome its poor showing at getting its customers to buy its software? The electrical retailer Comet claims to be one of the top three UK retailers of games console hardware. However, its out-of-town store format has appealed to people looking for special offers on its hardware but is not as well suited to competing with the major high street stores for follow-up software sales. Customers find browsing for a new game title easier in the high street, rather than making a special journey to one of Comet's out-of-town sites. The solution? Comet set to work building up a database of games console owners from its own sales records and bought-in lists. It then set about using this list to extend the relationship with its hardware customers. A direct marketing initiative featured new game show previews, competitions, in-store promotions, and money-off vouchers for games. By being seen to give special benefits to its hardware customers, it aimed to entice previous customers back and to extend its relationship with them in a cost-effective manner.

database. They may invite individuals to confirm that they want to continue mailings or reduce the frequency of mailings.

Direct marketing media

ONE of the problems in defining and quantifying direct marketing is that it uses a wide range of media. So advertising could be used as part of traditional mass marketing strategy, or it could be used to try and initiate a direct dialogue between a company and prospective customers. It is therefore difficult to get anything better than rough estimates of the spending by direct marketing on the various communication media.

The UK Direct Marketing Association regularly makes estimates of total expenditure by firms on direct marketing in the UK. Of the £7.2 billion estimated expenditure in 1997, the largest shares were accounted for by direct mail and telemarketing (Fig. 20.5). The main media used by direct marketers are described below.

Direct mail

To many people, direct mail and direct marketing are synonymous. In fact, the former is just one of numerous media used by companies to communicate directly with prospective and existing customers. Crucial to direct mail is a database which can be used by firms to initiate a dialogue with prospective customers, fulfil customers' orders, and tailor future communications based on previously expressed preferences and behaviour.

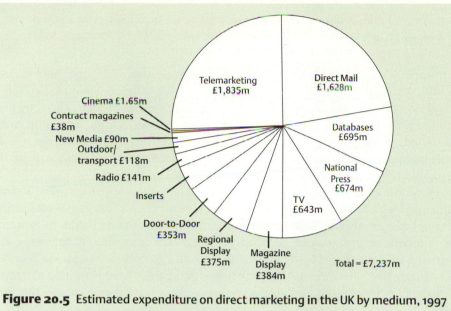

Figure 20.5 Estimated expenditure on direct marketing in the UK by medium, 1997

Source: Direct Marketing Association

Direct mail is able to communicate details of product features which would be difficult to achieve in a thirty-second television commercial, or even a whole-page newspaper advertisement. Many companies therefore use their mass media advertising to develop strong brand images, while direct mail is used to provide product particulars and a call to take immediate action. Within the financial services sector, companies have often used television advertising to present abstract images of themselves, while confining details of such things as interest rates, loan terms, and notice periods to direct mailshots. More recently, this tendency has spread to the fast moving consumer goods sector.

With the greater sophistication of databases, direct mail is gradually losing its image of junk mail. An item is only junk in the hands of the recipient if it is of no interest to the recipient. Many surveys have shown that most people actually like to receive direct mail. Among advertising agencies, direct mail is no longer seen as the cinderella which it once was, with greater creative effort being put into designing effective direct mail materials. Increasingly, advertising agencies are seeing direct mail and mass media advertising in terms of a single creative effort.

As direct mail continues to mature as a channel of communication, it faces new challenges from electronic media which are considered below.

Telemarketing

The telephone is increasingly being used as a communication tool throughout society generally. The cost of communicating by telephone has fallen relative to the cost of mail services, due to increasing competition and cost savings brought about by new technology. Furthermore, there is the suggestion that we are all becoming more accustomed to using the telephone, although differences do occur between individuals in how they relate to the telephone (e.g. it is suggested that females are better able to hold telephone conversations than their male counterparts).

Telemarketing can be divided into inbound and outbound operations. The former is concerned with handling incoming calls which result from a company's promotion of a telephone number for sales enquiries. With the use of mass media to promote such numbers, companies can be swamped with calls immediately following the advertising of a number. This is especially true of a freephone telephone number which is shown on television during peak times. Companies need to be able to handle such surges, otherwise the cost of generating leads is wasted and prospective customers who cannot get through may get such a bad impression of the company that they do not bother calling back. Large companies often use agencies to handle their incoming calls, and, using the latest switching technology, calls can be routed throughout the country to operators who are free. By staggering advertisements (e.g. by showing an advert in different television regions at different times of the day), problems created by surges in incoming calls can be reduced. Many inbound telemarketing agencies have begun using automated answering systems, in which callers give answers to a series of automated question prompts. Such systems can be very

Companies are taking unnecessary risks as they rush to cash in on a growing acceptance by the UK public of selling services over the phone. Eager to emulate the success of First Direct and Direct Line, companies have opened call centres and freephone helplines at a rapid rate. But some have learnt to their cost that failure to plan their telephone support accurately can actually lose business. Even Tesco came unstuck when its new banking operation was swamped by calls to its helpline and the company was forced to offer compensation to frustrated customers. The cause of the problem is difficulty or inexperience in predicting response rates and patterns to a company's marketing activities. Unfortunately, telephone selling often doesn't allow second chances. Research by the Henley Centre has shown that as a result of a single badly handled call 68 per cent of callers to a company would prefer not to do business with it again; 62 per cent said they would seek another company to buy from. There is debate about whether companies should handle large volumes of calls themselves, or contract out the task to a specialist call centre. While it may make sense to outsource large one-off campaigns, Thomas Cook is an example of a company that prefers handling calls internally in order to maintain one-to-one dialogue with its customers.

efficient at handling sudden surges in incoming calls and may be quite adequate for simple requests for brochures. However, many callers remain reluctant to use such systems and may become exasperated when the rigidity of a machine-based system does not allow for their specific needs to be addressed.

Outbound telemarketing involves a company using the telephone to contact potential or existing customers with a sales offer. Telephone selling has a very bad image in the UK, generating thoughts of poorly timed calls which disturb an individual with a sales offer which they have no interest in. As with direct mail, better targeting has reduced the nuisance value of receiving telephone calls which are of no interest to the receiver of the call. Companies have also learned to use outgoing calls more constructively, for example by calling to check on customer satisfaction with a previous sale, as a foundation for securing future sales. While outbound telemarketing is becoming reasonably well accepted in many business-to-business selling situations in the UK, its use remains limited in dealings with private consumers, especially in comparison to the extent of its use in the USA. The increasing number of private households who prefer to go 'ex-directory' poses further problems for outbound telemarketing.

Newspaper/magazine/television advertising

Very few brands have been built by relying solely on direct mail or telemarketing. Advertising remains an important contributor to direct marketing because it seeks to achieve two important aims:

1. It is often an efficient way of obtaining sales prospects. Where a company sells a fairly standard product to large numbers of buyers, mass communication via advertising may be a more cost-effective means of communicating details of the product offer than if it is done on a one-to-one basis via direct mail or telemarketing.
2. Advertising adds to the emotional appeal of a brand in a way which is difficult with direct mail. The fact that a product has been advertised through high profile channels can add to the credibility and desirability of a brand. In the case of items of ostentatious consumption (such as designer fashion clothing), advertising may be critical in developing brand values which are recognized by a person's peer group.

Sometimes an advertisement will place emphasis on just one of these aims (e.g. many financial services companies run television adverts to create awareness of the company's distinctive characteristics while using newspaper advertising to generate an immediate and direct response). Increasingly, firms are developing techniques to combine the two aims in one advertisement.

Where advertising is used to encourage an immediate and direct response, firms are able to monitor the effectiveness of individual advertisements. It was noted above that the use of codes can identify the level of new enquiries generated by each advertisement, and the proportion of these that went on to become actual customers. However, as with the assessment of all advertising effectiveness, it can be difficult to isolate completely the effects of extraneous factors. A direct response advertisement may only achieve a high level of response if potential customers see it in the context of the brand building advertising which has gone before it.

Door-to-door

The traditional mass media have developed methods of delivering their messages to progressively smaller audiences. Local editions of newspapers and cable television channels are evidence of this trend. A form of printed media which can deliver a message to a narrowly targeted audience is door-to-door leaflet distribution. Companies deliver promotional material to a block of addresses in a locality, either directly by themselves; through companies who specialize in door-to-door distribution of leaflets; through inserts in local newspapers; or through block distribution agreements with the Post Office. Door-to-door has traditionally been seen as the poor relation of the main advertising media, but has seen a resurgence in recent years. Developments in information technology are allowing the controlled distribution of promotional material to be undertaken more cost effectively. The method can also allow product samples to be delivered to selected households.

On-line marketing

There has been much debate about the potential for interactive electronic communication between a company and its customers. Interactive telecommunications systems are now firmly established with some buyers in some business sectors. Telephone banking, for example, has continued to gain in popularity with bank customers for whom the facility offers greater convenience and flexibility. Recent developments in technology are now allowing multi-media interactivity. Within the banking sector, many banks now offer services which link customers' computers to those of the bank.

Many people have laid great hope in the development of common, open access systems made possible through the Internet. Already, most major companies have developed their own home pages on the World Wide Web where the company can offer information about its goods and services. Increasingly, these sites are becoming interactive and able to process customers' orders. In theory, individuals can choose what information they wish to receive from companies and companies can develop the ability to tailor their messages to the information needs of particular individuals. Although the proportion of households with modem-linked PCs remains small, this is expected to rise rapidly in the first years of the twenty-first century, so that use of the Internet will become as commonplace as switching on the television. More encouragingly, those households who have innovated with Internet access tend to be the high income households which companies are particularly keen to target. The development of high capacity fibre optic lines will increase the amount of data which can be transmitted through the Internet, thereby reducing the problems of slow speed which have inhibited e-commerce.

On-line communication is particularly attractive for many services, such as travel and financial services where the costs of delivering bulky objects is not a major constraint. Already, many people buy these services by telephone and on-line services offer an opportunity to provide buyers with more information and a speedier response. It has been predicted that by 2010, the majority of package holidays will be bought through the Internet and high street travel agencies will serve only a small niche market. Many buyers retain doubts about the security of financial transactions carried out through the Internet, which has lagged behind the levels of security achieved by the banks' own closed Electronic Funds Transfer at Point of Purchase (EFTPOS) systems. Again, these problems are likely to be resolved over time, increasing the potential role of the Internet as a direct marketing medium.

Sceptics have argued that many of the hopes held out for the Internet are over-exaggerated. If use of the Internet increases significantly, it will eventually become cluttered and the advantages gained by pioneer users of the medium diluted. For many types of goods, customers may place great value on being able to inspect goods physically prior to purchase, something which will never be completely possible with 'virtual' representation of goods through electronic media. The very act of visiting stores brings significant social benefits to many personal buyers. Finally, as home delivery of many goods and services (such as bread and milk) declines due to rising costs, doubts have been raised about the economics of 'armchair shopping' in which goods ordered through a home terminal are delivered to the buyer's home.

Despite recent improvements, marketing managers remain dogged by old ghettos of 'above the line' and 'below the line' snobbery. Too few media decision-makers are familiar with the potential of direct mail as an acquisition and recruitment tool. While there is an upsurge in relationship building activity, acquisition remains the lifeblood of a competitive market-place. Tesco is a good example of the potential for direct marketing's ability to acquire customers. The store had set about positioning itself as the leading baby provisions expert to the market of expectant parents. The programme recruited nearly a quarter of a million members in just eight weeks from launch and a market share representing one-third of all UK births per year. The award-winning campaign involved six million mailings of letters, collectible magazines, and product coupons, targeting parents using advertising in media seen by expectant parents, as well as in-store recruitment. Once customers had been recruited, Tesco had a valuable basis for relationship development.

Limitations to the development of direct marketing

A<small>LTHOUGH</small> direct marketing has become an important part of many companies' marketing efforts, there are limits to its application. Here we summarize some of the more important constraints on direct marketing.

Direct marketing may not be cost effective

An important advantage of direct marketing is that it can target segments as small as one. This is fine for companies which produce high value goods and services which are tailored to the needs of specific customers. This helps to explain the popularity of direct marketing in such sectors as computer hardware and motor insurance. However, many goods and services are capable of appealing to large groups of customers in their 'standard' form without any attempt at differentiation. Where the value of the goods is low and volume sales high, the cost of attempting to communicate directly with each individual customer may appear prohibitive (see the Case Study below). Furthermore, the advantage of being able to tailor a product to customers' precise needs may be largely irrelevant where the product presents little opportunity for differentiation.

Sellers of fast-moving consumer goods have therefore tended to rely on traditional mass communication as a more cost-effective alternative than direct marketing. If a can of pasta sauce sells for only £1 and a mailing to promote the product costs 75p, how can the cost of individual communication be justified? How can the seller build on the opportunities to tailor the pasta sauce to the needs of individual customers? The answer is often with great difficulty and it is still too early to say whether direct marketing of low value fast-moving consumer goods will become widespread.

Legislative constraints

Effective direct marketing requires companies to handle large amounts of information about prospective, actual, and lapsed customers. The manner in which companies buy and sell information about individuals raises a number of ethical issues. Should a customer of a company have a right to consider the dialogue which they enter into with the company to be private between the two parties? Is it then unethical for the company to sell on information about its customers to third-party companies? How can an individual prevent damage being done to their reputation by incorrect information being distributed within and outside of a company? How can whole communities (e.g. in postcode areas with a poor credit rating) avoid being discriminated against?

Direct marketing has sought to put its own house in order with voluntary codes of conduct, in an attempt to deflect the call for greater legislation. In the UK, the Mailing Preference Service (which allows individuals to opt out of receiving direct mail) is an example of this approach. However, the direct marketing sector remains fragmented and it is very difficult to enforce a code of conduct which respects the concerns of society as a whole. Legislation has therefore been introduced to further safeguard ethical standards. In the UK the 1998 Data Protection Act (based on an EU directive) sets out rules by which companies can record and disseminate information about their customers.

Diminishing returns

New communication media have a tendency to go through a life cycle. This typically begins when a new medium appears, it is uncluttered, and users of it have relatively few other messages to compete against. Over time, the medium becomes more popular with advertisers, resulting in individual adverts having diminishing impact on their target audiences. This leads to an opportunity for new media to develop, offering innovative advertisers the chance to have maximum impact in an as yet uncluttered medium.

There is debate about where direct marketing currently is in its life cycle. The use of direct mail and telemarketing is certainly more mature in the USA than it is in Europe, with the result that many question its effectiveness in the USA. Even in the UK, there are signs that a direct approach might have limits within a company's marketing strategy. During the late 1990s, talk of 'disintermediation' turned to 're-intermediation' as a new breed of 'informediaries' emerged. Within the World Wide Web customers sought to simplify their choice through single websites which could offer choice rather than having a direct relationship with numerous suppliers. Many successful informediaries such as lastminute.com and QXL.com have emerged.

Chapter summary and key linkages to other chapters

Direct marketing has emerged as an important part of many companies' marketing plans. Rapid developments in information technology have helped companies to recreate the direct dealings they had when economies were relatively simple and the scale of production small. Rather than talk about mass marketing, or serving even small segments of the population, direct marketers talk about serving segments of one.

New developments such as the Internet are likely to present opportunities for further development of direct marketing, although this chapter has noted that there are limits on the extent to which direct marketing can replace traditional channels of communication.

The principles of direct marketing described in this chapter can be related to the following chapters in this book:

Chapter 1: What is marketing?: Marketing as a philosophy is customer focused and direct marketing puts individual customers at the centre of a firm's attention, rather than large groups of 'average' customers

Chapter 2: The marketing environment: Changes in customer expectations and developments in information technology have led to the modern development of direct marketing.

Chapter 3: Segmentation: Direct marketing ultimately seeks to address segments of one.

Chapter 4: Branding: Can strong brands be built solely by means of direct marketing?

Chapter 5: Marketing and ethics: To what extent should a company use information that customers have supplied in confidence to seek to sell further goods and services which were not originally envisaged by the customer?

Chapter 6: Marketing research: How do companies capitalize on the data which direct marketing can generate, to develop a better understanding of their customers' needs?

Chapter 7: Buyer behaviour: How do customers respond to direct marketing initiatives? To what extent do customers trust direct marketing sources? Can they reduce customers' perceptions of risk?

Chapters 9/10: Developing a product portfolio: How does a company develop a product portfolio with which it can profitably sell to meet the needs of customers on its database?

Chapter 11: Developing a sustainable competitive advantage: If implemented strategically, direct marketing can give a company a competitive advantage among key groups of customers. How can this be sustained?

Chapters 12/13: Pricing theory and applications: Because direct marketing has the capability to communicate with segments of one, prices charged by a company can be tailored to meet the product needs and price expectations of individuals.

Chapter 14: Intermediaries: Does direct marketing complement or compete with the functions of retailers and wholesalers in a channel of distribution?

Chapter 15: Logistics and physical distribution management: This chapter has stressed the importance of supply chain management in responding effectively and efficiently to individual orders placed by customers. When delivery is to consumers' front doors, logistical problems become more complex.

Chapters 16–19: Principles of promotion planning/advertising/sales promotion/personal selling: Direct marketing creates new media for communication, but traditional media remain important for initiating a dialogue.

Chapter 21: Organizing for marketing: Marketing information is at the core of direct marketing. How can a company ensure that information is effectively collected, analysed, and disseminated?

Chapter 22: Services marketing: The characteristic of intangibility makes services particularly suitable to a direct marketing approach. Direct marketing is itself a service sector which has grown rapidly in recent years.

Chapter 23: Global marketing: Will direct marketing strategies work in overseas markets where customers' expectations and the legislative framework may be quite different?

Case study

Beans by mail?

Is direct mail a sensible method by which fast-moving consumer goods (FMCG) manufacturers should keep in touch with their customers? Many eyebrows were raised in the advertising community in 1994 when the Heinz company announced that it was to cut its UK advertising budget and invest heavily in direct mail campaigns aimed at the end users of its products. The company had become only too aware of the power of the major retailers who had developed their own-brand ranges in direct competition with those of Heinz. The major retailers, it seemed, had become a major barrier to communication with its consumers. With increasing saturation of advertising, the company embarked on a two-pronged strategy. It would use a reduced advertising budget to promote the brand values of Heinz, stressing the heritage of the brand, without promoting any specific products. The second part of the strategy involved developing a database to communicate with consumers about the particular benefits of individual products. This potentially provided a wonderful opportunity for profiling customers individually and targeting them with offers (such as trial money-off vouchers) which took account of their preferences. The dialogue was also valuable for launching new products to identifiable targets. Heinz developed a database initially from bought-in lists, to which were added enquiries generated by the company. Consumers were targeted with a twice-yearly magazine which contained offers appropriate to the individual. The magazine aimed to encourage trial of products (facilitated by voucher offers) and loyalty (providing incentives for repeat purchase of designated products). To try to encourage the perception of Heinz as a friendly, trusted partner, the magazine included recipe suggestions and lifestyle articles.

At the outset, sceptics had doubted whether it was realistic to sell low value products such as baked beans by direct mail. Could it ever be cost effective? Wouldn't the cost of running the direct mail operation further undermine Heinz's price competitiveness in comparison to the retailers' own brands? By offering incentives through its magazines, wasn't it simply buying loyalty? And is it possible to maintain a brand, let alone create one, when the emphasis is on direct mail rather than advertising?

At the time of its launch, Heinz's venture was seen as an experiment into the unknown. Sceptics were partly vindicated in 1998 when the company quietly announced that it would run down its direct marketing efforts. Clearly, the cost effectiveness of talking to millions of people to promote low value products was poor in comparison to the benefits from mass media advertising.

Case study review questions

1 Critically assess the limitations of direct mail as a medium for promoting fast-moving consumer goods

2 Identify and critically assess the role which the Internet may play in Heinz's promotion and distribution strategy in the future.

3 Discuss possible bases that Heinz may have used to profile and target consumers of its products. To what extent is direct mail a suitable medium for understanding the attitudinal bases of consumer behaviour?

Chapter review questions

1 Critically evaluate the steps that companies can take to ensure that their direct mail does not become 'junk' mail.

2 It was observed in the late 1990s that companies often charged more for buying through their Internet site rather than through other channels. Why was this likely to occur? Is it a sustainable business practice?

3 Many companies talk about using direct marketing to enter into a dialogue with their customers. What evidence do you have that customers actually want a dialogue? Or is such dialogue almost doomed to an inevitable one-sidedness?

4 With the potential of so many direct marketing messages being targeted at individuals, their time budgets will be under pressure and confusion likely to increase. Discuss the view that these are ideal circumstances for the re-emergence of intermediaries.

5 Is there a role for mass media advertising in the new age of direct marketing? In what circumstances does advertising have a particular advantage over direct communication?

6 It is common to talk about 'below the line' and 'above the line' media. Is this distinction more apparent than real?

References

Copulsky, J. R., and Wolf, M. J. (1990), 'Relationship Marketing: Positioning for the Future', *Journal of Business Strategy*, July–Aug., pp. 16–20.

Direct Marketing Association (1999), *Census of the UK Direct Marketing Industry* (London: Direct Marketing Association).

Hartley, B., and Starkey, M. (1996), *The Management of Sales and Customer Relations: Book of Readings* (London: International Thompson Business Press).

Pepper, D., and Rogers, M. (1993), *The One to One Future: Building Relationships One Customer at a Time* (New York: Doubleday).

Suggested further reading

The literature on direct marketing is evolving very rapidly to match developments in current practices. The following provide a useful introduction to the principles of direct marketing:

- Bird, D. (1998), *Commonsense Direct Marketing*, 3rd edn. (London: Kogan Page).
- McCorkell, G. (1997), *Direct and Database Marketing* (London: Kogan Page).
- Tapp, A. (1998), *Principles of Direct and Database Marketing* (London: Financial Times Management).

The following provide a useful insight into aspects of profiling and targeting using direct marketing:

- Cobb, R. (1997), 'Finding the Right Doormat', *Marketing*, 25 Sept., pp. 14–16.
- Rosenspan, A. (1997), 'The Three Little Pigs: A Direct Marketing Fable' (targeting the right customers), *Direct Marketing*, **59**, 12, pp. 18–21.

The development of Internet marketing and electronic commerce is fast moving, and the following provide some pointers along this process of development:

- Fawcett, N. (1999), *Internet and Intranet Development for Business Advantage* (Oxford: Butterworth-Heinemann).
- Heilbrunn, H. (1998), 'Interactive Marketing in Europe', *Direct Marketing*, Mar., **60**, 11, pp. 56–9.
- Jerry, W. T. (1998), 'The Brave New World of Internet Marketing', *Direct Marketing*, **60**, 9, pp. 40–2.
- Sexton, C. (1999), *Commerce and Security* (Oxford: Butterworth-Heinemann).
- *The Economist* (1998), 'Brands Bite Back: Internet', 21 Mar., 346, 8060, pp. 78–80.
- Warner, M. (1998), 'Can Tupperware Keep a Lid on the Web?', *Fortune*, 137, 1, p. 144.

Useful web links

The UK-based Institute of Direct Marketing has developed a strong reputation for developing professional skills among staff employed in the sector: http://www.theidm.co.uk

UK body representing the direct marketing sector: http://www.dma.org.uk

Direct Marketing Association (USA) provides information and a market research database: http://www.the-dma.org

Links to direct marketing associations throughout the world: http://www.one1.com.sg/Resource/DMAssns.htm

Direct Mail Information Service—a UK site sponsored by Royal Mail providing detailed statistics about the UK and comparative European information: http://www.dmis.co.uk

Part IV

Bringing It Together

Chapter 21

Managing the Marketing Effort

Chapter objectives

This chapter brings together the theory of the previous chapters in a framework that can be implemented. Too many marketing plans fail to be implemented effectively and this chapter explores the bases for effective marketing management. Marketing management involves a never-ending process of analysis, planning, implementation, and control. Timely and relevant information, acted upon by appropriately structured and motivated management, is crucial to success.

Introduction

A FREQUENTLY heard comment about some aspects of marketing is that it is 'fine in theory, but doesn't work in practice'. This book has presented a lot of the theory that underlies marketing management decisions, but theory and good ideas alone will not create long-term profitability. Nor is it good enough just to have the right product at the right time. Good management is crucial to bringing about sustainable success.

Most people will have had experience of companies who do not appear to have the management capabilities for success. At the operational level, inadequate investment in staff training, and a distribution system that results in the wrong products being delivered late to the wrong place, are signs of bad management. At a strategic level, poor management can be seen by a preoccupation with declining products at the expense of new opportunities and a lack of information about current market conditions.

There is an ongoing debate about whether management is an art or a science. Those who advocate a scientific approach set great value in structured procedures, for example in the way that information is routinely collected and analysed. Rationality and safety underlies the scientific approach. Most of the top 100 UK companies have systematic procedures for management which make them a safe bet for investors, even if they lack the occasional sparkle of smaller and more volatile companies. The arts approach would argue that the business environment is changing rapidly and therefore a scientific framework which worked in the past may no longer be valid in the future. Furthermore, the scientific approach may take a long time in reaching a decision, putting a firm at a competitive disadvantage in a fast-moving market. By taking a scientific approach, managers often end up breaking a large problem down into component sub-problems, and fail to have a holistic overview. If all other firms are following a similar scientific approach, they may all end up with 'me-too' strategies. A more arts approach is more likely to encourage unique solutions which may either succeed spectacularly or fail miserably.

Information is a key element of the marketing management process. In large organizations, information is a medium for keeping in touch with customers, employees, suppliers, and intermediaries. Getting the right information to the right people at the right time is crucial if the management of a company is to be able to develop and implement a strategy. Without appropriate information, strategy formulation can become guesswork and the implementation of that strategy may be half-hearted. Inadequate monitoring may not warn of problems until it is too late to do anything about them.

The marketing management process

MARKETING management can be seen as a continual process. This section identifies the key elements of the process, although just who should be responsible for each element is a subject which will be returned to later in a discussion on marketing management organization.

There are five key stages in the marketing management process:

1. **'Where are we now?': analysis of the organization's current market position.** A vital starting-point for marketing planning is an analysis of a company's current marketing environment, often undertaken by means of a SWOT analysis or a marketing audit. A marketing audit is a relatively new concept and has been defined as:

   a systematical, critical and unbiased review and appraisal of the environment and of the company's operations. A marketing audit is part of the larger management audit and is concerned with the marketing environment and marketing operations. (McDonald 1995)

   A marketing audit typically includes analysis of the organization's current market share, the size and nature of its customer base, customer perceptions of the organization's output, and the internal strengths and weaknesses of the organization in terms of production, personnel, and financial resources. A marketing audit addresses these issues using both quantitative and qualitative methods where appropriate. But what information should be collected? A company's mission statement can provide a company's employees with guidance about what is relevant and irrelevant in analysing its current position.

How much analysis of the current situation should a company undertake? While it is nearly always true that a sound analysis of the current situation is an essential prerequisite to developing a marketing plan for the future, excessive preoccupation with the current situation can have its costs. Analysis on its own will not provide management decisions which are necessary for defining the future marketing plan. A 'paralysis by analysis' can occur in organizations which avoid making hard decisions about the future by continually seeking more information about the present. A plateau is usually reached at which little additional information becomes available which will improve the quality of marketing plan decisions. Worse still, in markets which are fast changing, excessive analysis of the current position can put a firm at a competitive disadvantage to firms who are more willing to take a risk and exploit a market opportunity ahead of its competitors.

2. **Where do we want to be?: setting marketing objectives.** Without clearly specified objectives, marketing management can drift aimlessly. Objectives have a number of functions within an organization:

- They add to the sense of purpose within the organization, without which there would be little focus for managers' efforts.

- They help to achieve consistency between decisions made at different points within the organization—for example it would be inconsistent if a production manager used a production objective which was unrelated to the marketing manager's sales objective.

- Objectives are used as motivational devices and can be used in a variety of formal and informal ways to stimulate increased performance by managers.

- Objectives allow for more effective control within an organization. Unless clear objectives have been set at the outset, it is very difficult to know whether the organization has achieved what it set out to achieve, and to take any corrective action if its efforts seem to be going adrift during the plan period.

To be effective, objectives must be capable of realistic achievement and accepted as such by the people responsible for acting on them. If objectives are set unattainably high, the whole process of planning could be brought into disrepute by staff in an organization. Wherever possible, objectives should be quantified and clearly specify the time period to which they relate (e.g. a firm may have an objective of achieving 15 per cent return on capital invested after three years, but may sacrifice this in the short term in return for achieving an objective of high market growth rate). Inconsistency between objectives should be avoided. This sometimes occurs, for example, where sales objectives can only be achieved by reducing selling prices, thereby making it impossible to achieve a profitability objective.

3. **How can we get there?: developing a marketing strategy.** There are usually many ways that marketing objectives can be achieved, for example a financial return objective could be satisfied equally well by a high sales volume/low price strategy or a low volume/high price strategy. Identifying the strategic alternatives open to an organization relies on interpreting data and evaluating a number of possible future scenarios. Within this evaluation, factors such as the likelihood of success, the level of downside risk, and the amount of resources required to implement a strategy need to be taken into consideration. What may be an appropriate strategy for one company may be quite inappropriate for another, on account of differences in financial resources, past history, and personnel strengths, among other things.

It often happens that the objectives set for the planning period are greater than what could be achieved if growth occurred at the historic trend rate. Where such a 'planning gap' exists, the aim of the planning process is to develop a strategy that will close this gap. This can be done either by reducing downward the original objective to a level that is more realistic, given the historical pattern, or, alternatively, action can be taken to accelerate the trend rate from its historical pattern to a higher level by means of marketing strategy. In practice, the planning gap is reduced by a combination of revising objectives and amending marketing strategies (Fig. 21.1).

There have been many prescriptions for developing a business strategy and some of these were discussed in Chapter 11 in the context of the development of a sustainable competitive advantage.

4. **How will we implement the strategy?:** having chosen a strategy, the next step is to implement this strategy. This is usually done through a twelve-month marketing plan which sets out programmes for, among other things, the timing and costing of promotional programmes, pricing plans, and how distributors are to be recruited and rewarded. These detailed programmes should flow directly from the marketing strategy, which itself starts from marketing objectives. Too many

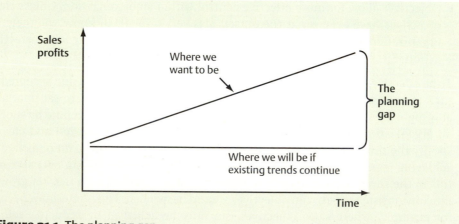

Figure 21.1 The planning gap

companies develop a strategy which sounds fine, but fail to think through fully the detail of implementation.

5. **Did we get there?: monitoring and controlling the marketing programme.** Marketing plans are of little value if they are only to be implemented half-heartedly. An ongoing part of the marketing management process is therefore to monitor the implementation of the plan and to seek an explanation of any deviation from the plan.

   Effective control systems demand timely, accurate, and relevant information about an organization's operations and environment. Control systems require three underlying components to be in place: setting of targets or standards of expected performance; measurement and evaluation of actual performance; and corrective action being taken where necessary.

   Many control systems fail because employees within an organization have been given inappropriate or unrealistic targets. Even where targets are set, and appropriate data are collected, control systems may still fail because of a failure by management to act on the information available. Control information should identify variances from target and should be able to indicate whether the variance is within or beyond the control of the person responsible for meeting the target. If it is beyond their control, the issue should become one of revising the target so that it becomes once more achievable. If the variance is the result of factors which are subject to a manager's control, a number of measures can be taken to try to revise their behaviour, including incentive schemes, training, and disciplinary action.

The elements of the strategic marketing management process can be summarized as analysis, planning, implementing, and controlling and are shown diagrammatically in Fig. 21.2. The marketing management process can be seen as a continuous circle. A periodic review of the marketing programme should be carried out, which may lead to a reassessment of strategy and revised marketing programmes.

Strategic, tactical, and contingency planning

From the above description, marketing planning is best viewed as a continuous process. However, it is necessary to produce periodic statements of a plan which all individuals in an organization can work towards. Three types of periodic plan can be identified: strategic plans, tactical plans, and contingency plans.

- The strategic element of a marketing plan focuses on the overriding direction which an organization's efforts will take in order to meet its objectives.
- The tactical element is more concerned with plans for implementing the detail of the strategic plan.

The division between the strategic and tactical elements of a marketing plan can sometimes be difficult to define. Typically, a strategic marketing plan is concerned with mapping out direction over a five-year planning period, whereas a tactical

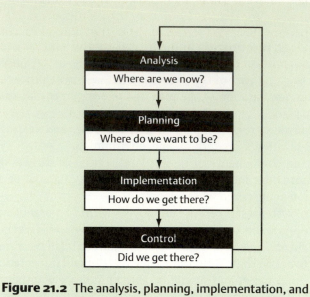

Figure 21.2 The analysis, planning, implementation, and control process

marketing plan is concerned with implementation during the next twelve months. Many business sectors view their strategic planning periods very differently, and in the case of large-scale infrastructure projects, such as airports or railways, the strategic planning period may be very long indeed. On the other hand, many small-scale, low technology businesses may find little need for a strategic plan beyond the immediate operational period.

■ A contingency plan seeks to identify scenarios where the assumptions of the position analysis on which strategic decisions were based turn out to be false. For example, a food manufacturer might have assumed that there would be no significant change in consumers' attitudes towards a particular category of food. However, the possibility of a food scare, such as those associated with salmonella in chickens and BSE in beef could seriously affect the implementation of a marketing plan. A contingency plan would allow a firm to react quickly to such a scenario, for example by increasing its promotional expenditure and cutting back on production capacity.

The dynamic marketing environment

In developing a marketing plan, it can be very easy to assume a stable market. In reality, most markets are dynamic and a marketing plan needs to take account not just of competitors' current strategies, but also their likely future strategies. If a market appears attractive to one organization, then it probably appears equally attractive to others as well. These may possess equal competitive advantage in addressing the market. If all such firms decide to enter the market, oversupply results, profit margins become squeezed, and the market becomes relatively unattractive. This could be observed in the semi-conductor market which in the mid-1990s looked highly attractive, with rapid growth in demand and a shortage of supply. This was the signal for many companies to enter the market, with the result that by the end of the 1990s, oversupply had resulted, the price of semi-conductors fell from over £4 to less than 50p, and many manufacturing operations became unprofitable.

Marketing planning and corporate planning

Marketing management is just one of the specialist management functions that can be identified within most commercial organizations. What is the relationship between marketing management and corporate management? At one extreme, the two are seen as synonymous. If an organization stands or falls primarily on its ability to satisfy customer needs, then it can be argued that marketing planning is so central to the organization's activities that it becomes corporate planning. The alternative view is that marketing is just one of the functions of an organization which affects its performance. Marketing takes its goals from corporate plans in just the same way as the personnel or production functions of the organization. In some business sectors where customers have relatively little choice and production capacity is limited, the significance of the marketing plan to the corporate plan will be less than for a generic product facing fierce competition. Many public sector-service organizations claim to go through the marketing planning process. In fact, the term marketing planning may be used in name but given much less significance than the development of production plans to serve a stable market.

The relationship between the processes of marketing and corporate planning can be two way, again reflecting the importance of marketing to the total planning process. Marketing information is fed into the corporate planning process for analysis and formulation of the corporate plan in a process sometimes referred to as 'bottom-up planning'. The corporate plan is developed and functional objectives specified for marketing in a 'top-down' process.

Planning as an inter-functional integrator

The marketing planning process helps to integrate the efforts of a diverse range of people throughout an organization. The plan allows everybody to 'sing from the same hymn sheet'. Without the plan, individuals may end up doing things that are in direct conflict with their colleagues.

Corporate and marketing planning processes act as integrators in horizontal and vertical dimensions (see Fig. 21.3):

■ In the horizontal dimension, the planning process brings together the plans of the specialized functions which are necessary to make the organization work. Marketing is just one function of an organization which generates its own planning process—other functional plans found in most organizations are financial plans, personnel plans, and production plans. The components of these functional plans must recognize interdependencies if they are to be effective, for example a car manufacturer's marketing strategic plan which anticipates a 20 per cent growth in sales of its cars over a five-year planning period should be reflected in a strategic production plan which allows for output to increase by a similar amount, a financial plan which identifies strategies for raising the required level of finance for new investment and work in progress, and a personnel plan for recruiting additional staff. Within the marketing department, a plan helps to ensure that the activities of advertising personnel are mutually supportive of the activities of sales and market research staff, for example.

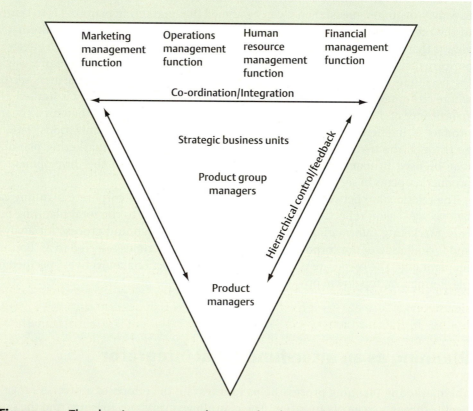

Figure 21.3 The planning process as a horizontal and vertical integrater within an organization

- In the vertical dimension, the planning process provides a framework for decisions to be made at different levels of the corporate hierarchy. Objectives can be specified in progressively more detail from the global objectives of the corporate plan, to the greater detail required to operationalize them at the level of individual operational units (or Strategic Business Units) and—in turn—for individual products.

The mission statement

A corporate mission statement provides a focal point for the marketing planning process. It can be likened to a hidden hand which guides all employees in an organization in developing and implementing marketing plans. Drucker (1973) identified a number of basic questions which management needs to ask in drawing up a mission statement:

- what is our business?
- who is the customer?
- what is value to the customer?
- what will our business be?
- what should our business be?

By forcing management to focus on the essential nature of the business which they are in and the nature of customer needs which they seek to satisfy, the problem of 'marketing myopia' advanced by Levitt (1960) can be avoided. Levitt argued that in order to avoid a narrow, short-sighted view of its business, managers should define their business in terms of the needs that they fulfil rather than the products they produce. In the classic example, railway operators had lost their way because they defined their output in terms of the technology of tracked vehicles, rather than in terms of the core benefit of movement which they provided. The Parker Pen company found itself in the gift business, rather than the more product-defined pen business.

The nature of an organization's mission statement is a reflection of a number of factors, including: the organization's ownership (e.g. contrast public-sector with private-sector statements); the previous history of the organization; resources available; and major opportunities and threats that the organization faces.

In services organizations where the interface between consumers and production personnel is often critical, communication of the values contained within the mission statement can be very important. The statement is frequently repeated by organizations in staff newsletters and in notices at their place of work. An example of a mission statement which is widely communicated to the workforce—as well as to customers—is shown in Fig. 21.4.

Statement of Purpose

We aim to be...
a world class energy company and the leading international gas business

by...

▶ running a professional gas business providing safe, secure and reliable supplies

▶ actively developing an international business in exploration and production of oil and gas

▶ making strategic investments in other energy-related projects and businesses world wide

▶ satisfying our customers' wishes for excellent quality of service and outstanding value

▶ constantly and energetically seeking to improve quality and productivity in all we do

▶ caring for the environment

▶ maintaining a high quality workforce with equal opportunities for all

▶ cultivating good relations with customers, employees, suppliers, shareholders and the communities we serve and thereby improving returns to shareholders.

British Gas

Figure 21.4 Many organizations use mission statements, such as this one of British Gas, to remind their employees and customers of the essential purpose of the organization. (Reproduced with permisson of British Gas plc)

Organizing the marketing management function

I T was noted earlier that the principles of marketing may be fine in theory, but less certain in practice. The same can be said for the process of marketing planning. The process may look fine in theory, but it needs people to implement the process and make it a success. There have been too many cases of marketing planners developing a marketing plan for which the operational implications have not been fully thought through and which therefore fails to deliver value to customers and profits to the company.

A frequent problem occurs where the marketing planning function becomes cut off from other functional departments. The whole issue of organizing a company so that it has a company-wide focus on marketing is considered in a later section. This section looks inwardly at the marketing department and asks how it can best be organized in order to meet corporate objectives.

Responsibilities given to the marketing department vary from one organization to another, reflecting the competitive nature of a company and also its traditions and organizational inertia. Within marketing departments, four basic approaches to allocating these responsibilities are identified here, although, in practice, most marketing departments show more than one approach. The four approaches allocate marketing responsibilities by: functions performed; geographical area covered; products or groups of products managed; market segments managed.

Organization based on functional responsibilities

A traditional and common basis of organizing a marketing department is to divide responsibilities into identifiable marketing functions. Typically, these functions may be advertising, sales, research and development, marketing research, customer services, etc. The precise division of the functional responsibilities will depend upon the nature of an organization. Buying and merchandising are likely to be an important feature in a retailing organization, while research and development will be important for electronics companies.

The main advantage of a functional organization lies in its administrative simplicity. Against this, there can be a tendency for policy responsibility on specific products or markets to become lost between numerous functional specialists. There is also the possibility of destructive rivalry between functional specialists for their share of marketing budgets—for example, rivalry between an advertising manager and a sales manager for a larger share of the promotional budget.

Organization based on geographical responsibilities

Organizations selling a product nationwide usually organize some of their marketing functions, especially the sales function, on a geographical basis. For companies operating internationally, there is usually some geographical basis to organization in the way that marketing activities are organized in individual national markets.

Management by product type

Where a company produces a variety of products, it is quite common to appoint a product manager to manage a particular product or product line. This form of organization does not replace the functional organization, but provides an additional layer of management which coordinates the functional activities. The product manager's role includes a number of key tasks:

- developing a long-range strategy and short-term annual plan for a product or group of products;

- working with internal and external functional specialists to develop and implement marketing programmes, for example in relation to advertising and sales promotion;

- monitoring the performance of their product and noting changes in the marketing environment which may pose opportunities or threats;

- a product manager can in theory react more quickly to changes in the product's marketing environment than would be the case if no-one had specific responsibility for the product.

Although product management structures can allow for a focused strategy to be developed in respect of individual products, there are nevertheless some short-comings. The most serious problem is where a product manager is given a lot of responsibility for ensuring that objectives for their product are met, but relatively little control over resource inputs which they have at their disposal. Product managers typically must rely on persuasion to get the co-operation of advertising, sales, and other functional specialist departments. Confusion can arise in the minds of staff within an organization as to whom they are accountable for their day-to-day actions—is it to the product manager, or a functional specialist such as a sales manager? Product management structures can lead to larger numbers of people being employed, resulting in a higher cost structure which may put the organization at a competitive disadvantage in price sensitive markets.

Market segment management

Many companies sell basically similar products to different types of customers who differ significantly in their needs. For example, an airline provides services targeted at leisure travellers, business travellers, tour operators, and freight forwarders, among others. Each of these groups has differing requirements in terms of speed, reliability, price, etc., and a market segment manager can become expert in understanding these needs and developing an appropriate product offer. Instead of being given specific financial targets for their products, market managers are usually given growth or market share targets. The main advantage of this form of organization is that it allows marketing activity to be focused on meeting the needs of distinct and identified groups of customers—something which should be at the heart of any truly marketing-oriented organization. It is also likely that new products are more likely to emerge within this structure than where an organization's response is confined within traditional product management boundaries. Market management structures are also arguably more conducive to the important task of developing relationships with customers, especially in business-to-business markets. Where an organization has a number of very important customers, it is common to find the appointment of key account managers to handle relationships with those clients in order to exploit marketing opportunities which are of mutual benefit to both (discussed in Chapter 18).

Many of the disadvantages of the product management organization are also shared by market-based structures. There can again be a conflict between responsibility and authority and this form of structure can also become expensive to operate.

The great diversity of organizational structures highlights the fact that there is not one unique structure which is appropriate to all firms, even within the same business sector. Overall, the organization of a marketing department must allow for a flexible and adaptable response to customers' needs within a changing environment, while aiming to reduce the level of confusion, ambiguity, and cost inherent in some structures. The organizational structures discussed above are shown diagrammatically in Fig. 21.5, with an airline being used as an illustrative example.

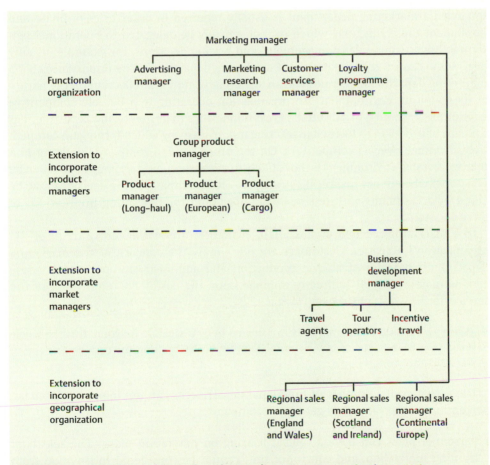

Figure 21.5 Alternative forms of marketing department organization structure, showing typical applications to an airline operator

Integrating marketing management with other management functions

SHOULD an organization actually have a marketing department? The idea is becoming increasingly popular that the existence of a separate marketing department may in fact hinder the development of a true customer-centred marketing orientation. By placing all marketing activity in a marketing department, non-marketing staff may consider that responsibility for getting new or repeat business is nothing to do with them, but should be left to the marketing department. While it is becoming fashionable to talk about everybody becoming a 'part-time marketer' (see Gummesson 1991) a marketing department is usually required in order to co-ordinate and implement those functions which cannot sensibly be delegated to operational personnel. Advertising, sales management, and pricing decisions, for example, usually need some central co-ordination by a marketing department. The importance that a marketing department assumes within any organization is a reflection on the nature of its operating environment. An organization operating in a fiercely competitive environment would typically attach great importance to its marketing department as a means of producing a focused marketing mix strategy by which it can gain competitive advantage over its competitors. On the other hand, a company operating in a relatively stable environment is more likely to allow strategic decisions to be taken by personnel who are not marketing strategists—for example, pricing decisions may be taken by accountants with less need to understand the marketing implications of price decisions.

In a marketing-oriented organization, customers are at the centre of all of the organization's activities. Customers are not simply the concern of the marketing department, but also of all the production and administrative personnel whose actions may directly or indirectly impinge upon the customers' enjoyment of the service. In the words of Drucker (1973);

Marketing is so basic that it cannot be considered to be a separate function. It is the whole business seen from the point of view of its final result, that is, from the customer's point of view.

The activities of a number of functional departments can impinge on customers' perceptions of the value they get from a company:

■ Personnel plans can have a crucial bearing on marketing plans. The selection, training motivation, and control of staff cannot be considered in isolation from marketing objectives and strategies. Possible conflict between the personnel and marketing functions may arise where—for example—marketing demands highly trained and motivated staff, but the personnel function pursues a policy which emphasizes cost reduction and uniform pay structures.

- Marketing managers may try to respond as closely as possible to customers' needs, but encounter opposition from production managers who argue that a product of the required standard cannot be achieved. A marketing manager may want large numbers of product variants in order to satisfy market niches, but a production manager may seek large production runs of standardized products.

- Ultimately, finance managers assume responsibility for the allocation of funds which are needed to implement a marketing plan. At a more operational level, finance managers' actions in respect of the level of credit offered to customers, or towards stockholdings can also significantly affect the quality of service and the volume of customers which the organization is able to serve.

The problem of how to bring people together in an organization to act collectively, while also being able to place responsibility on an individual, is one which continues to generate considerable discussion. Two recent developments in this debate are noted here: matrix organization structures and the idea of business process re-engineering.

Matrix approach to management

The essence of a matrix type of organization is to allow individuals to concentrate on a functional, product, or market specialization, and to bring them together in task force teams to solve problems taking an organizational view rather than their own narrow specialist view. Product managers can concentrate on excellence in production, while market managers focus on meeting consumer needs without any preference for a particular product (see Fig. 21.6).

The most important advantages of matrix structures are that they can allow organizations to respond rapidly to environmental change. Short-term project teams can be assembled and disbanded at short notice to meet changed needs. Project teams can bring together a wide variety of disciplines and can be used to evaluate new products before full-scale development is undertaken. A grocery retailer exploring the possibility of developing Internet-based home shopping might establish a team drawn from staff involved in distribution, advertising, market research, and technology-based research and development.

The flexibility of matrix structures can be increased by bringing temporary workers into the structure on a contract basis as and when needed. During the 1990s there has been a trend for many companies to lay off significant numbers of workers—including management—and to buy these back when needed. As well as cutting fixed costs, such 'modular' organizations have the potential to respond very rapidly to environmental change.

High levels of motivation can be present in effectively managed teams within matrix structures. Against this, matrix organizations can have a number of drawbacks. Most serious is the confused lines of authority which often result. Staff may not be clear about which superior he or she is responsible to for a particular aspect of

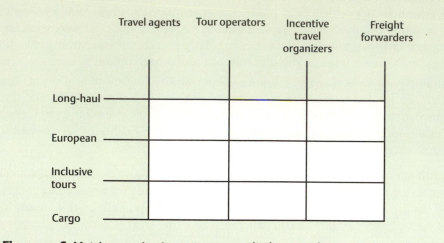

Figure 21.6 Matrix organization structure applied to an airline

their duties, resulting in possible stress and demotivation. Where a matrix structure is introduced into an organization with a history and culture of functional specialization, it can be very difficult to implement effectively. Staff may be reluctant to act outside a role which they have traditionally defined narrowly and guarded jealously. Finally, matrix structures invariably result in more managers being employed within an organization. At best this can result in a costly addition to the salary bill. At worst, the existence of additional managers can also slow down decision-making processes where the managers show a reluctance to act outside a narrow functional role.

Business process re-engineering

A more radical approach to integrating marketing with other functions is seen in what has come to be referred to as 'business process re-engineering'. The underlying principle of business process re-engineering is to design an organization around key value adding activities. Essentially, re-engineering is about *radically* redesigning the *processes* by which an organization does business in order that it can achieve major savings in cost, or improvements in output, or both. As such, the process begins with a clean sheet of paper. This is in contrast to traditional methods of organizational change where change is incremental and structures are often a poor compromise, influenced by historic factors and vested interests which are of no continuing relevance.

To be effective, re-engineering needs to be led by strong individuals who have authority to oversee implementation from beginning to end. They will need to overcome fear, resistance, and cynicism which will inevitably slow the task down. At first sight, though, this approach to reorganization would appear to be in conflict with participative approaches to management, such as total quality management that stress employee involvement in change. Successful companies therefore seek to involve their employees in the detail of implementation, even if the radical nature of the agenda is not negotiable.

Managing information

INFORMATION represents a bridge between an organization and its environment and is the means by which a picture of the changing environment is built up within the organization. Marketing management is responsible for turning information into specific marketing plans. The marketing management function of any organization requires a constant flow of information for two principal purposes:

- to provide information as an input to the planning of marketing activities;
- to monitor the implementation of marketing programmes and allow corrective action to be taken if performance diverges from target.

A timely supply of appropriate information provides feedback on an organization's performance, allowing actual performance to be compared with target performance. On the basis of this information, control measures can be applied which seek—where necessary—to put the organization back on its original targets. Organizations also learn from the past in order to understand better the future. For making longer-term planning decisions, historical information is supplemented by a variety of continuous and *ad hoc* studies, all designed to allow better informed decisions to be made. Marketing information cannot in itself produce decisions—it merely provides data which must be interpreted by marketing managers. As an inter-functional integrator, marketing information draws data from all functional areas of an organization, who in turn use data to focus on meeting customers' needs more effectively. Increasingly, information technology is allowing firms to deal with their customers on a one-to-one basis. Research involving employees, both as sources of information and recipients of research findings, assumes importance as an integrating device.

The use of information has been identified as a source of a firm's marketing orientation which allows it to obtain a sustainable competitive advantage (Kohli and Jaworski 1990). It has been argued that processing information should be regarded as the fifth 'P' of the marketing mix (Piercy 1985). As information collection, processing, transmission, and storage technologies improve, information is becoming more accessible not just to one particular organization, but also to its competitors. Attention is therefore moving away from how information is collected, to who is best able to make use of the information.

Recent technological innovations—for example Electronic Point of Sale (EPOS) systems—have enabled companies to improve greatly the quality and quantity of information available to them. Companies who have used this information to good effect have improved their operational efficiency and their effectiveness in delivering high quality goods and services which meet customers' expectations. At the same time, the increasing ease with which data can be collected and disseminated has made it easier for companies to manage quality by setting quantifiable objectives that can be effectively monitored.

Marketing information allows management to improve its strategic planning, tactical implementation of programmes, and its monitoring and control. A practical problem is that information is typically much more difficult to obtain to meet strategic planning needs than it is to meet operational and control needs. There can be a danger of marketing managers focusing too heavily on information which is easily available at the expense of that which is needed.

Marketing information systems

It was noted in Chapter 6 that information should be collected in a systematic manner. Many analyses of organizations' information collection and dissemination activities take a systems perspective in which the collection of marketing information is one sub-system of a much larger management information system. Other systems typically include production, financial, and human resource management systems. In a well-designed management information system, the barriers between these systems should be conceptual rather than real—for example, sales information is of value to all of these sub-systems to a greater or lesser extent (see Fig. 21.7).

A marketing information system has been defined by Kotler as a system that:

consists of people, equipment and procedures to gather, sort, analyse, evaluate and distribute needed, timely and accurate information to marketing decision-makers. (Kotler 1997)

In so far as a marketing information sub-system can be identified, it can conceptually be seen as comprising four principal components, although, in practice, they are operationally interrelated:

- Firms generate a lot of information internally, for example from invoices and sales enquiries. By carefully arranging its collection and dissemination, internal data can provide a constant and up to date flow of information at relatively little cost, useful for both planning and control functions.

- Marketing research is that part of the system concerned with the structured collection of marketing information and was discussed in Chapter 6. Marketing research can provide both routine information about marketing effectiveness—such as brand awareness levels or delivery performance—and one-off studies, such as changing attitudes towards diet or the pattern of income distribution.

- Marketing intelligence comprises the procedures and sources used by marketing management to obtain pertinent information about developments in their marketing environment. It complements the marketing research system, for whereas the latter tends to focus on structured and largely quantifiable data collection procedures, intelligence-gathering concentrates on picking up relatively intangible ideas and trends. Marketing management can gather this intelligence from a number of sources, such as newspapers, specialized cutting services, employees who are in regular contact with market developments, intermediaries, and suppliers to the company, as well as specialized consultants.

- Information alone is of little value if it is not used to improve the quality of decision-making by managers. Marketing decision support systems are developed in which information is both an input (because data are needed to calibrate a model) and an output (in that models provide information on which decisions can be based).

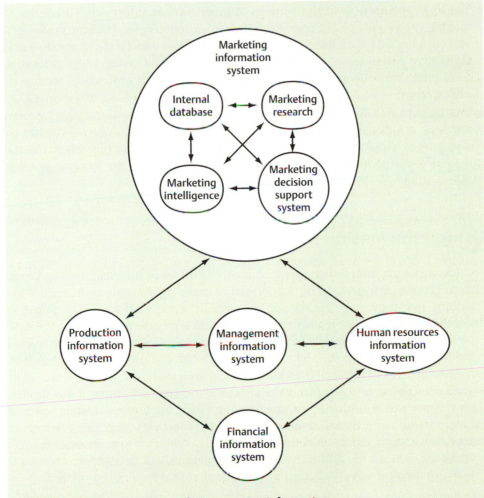

Figure 21.7 A systems approach to managing information

Marketing information systems vary in their complexity and effectiveness. A number of factors will determine their effectiveness:

- **The accuracy with which the information requirements have been defined**: it can be very difficult to identify what information should be of relevance in a company's information gathering activities and to separate relevance from irrelevance. This is a particular problem for large multi-output firms. The mission statement of an organization may give some indication of the boundaries for its information search.

- **The extensiveness of the search for information**: a balance has to be struck between the need for information and the cost of collecting it. The most critical elements of the marketing environment must be identified and the cost of collecting relevant information weighed against the cost which would result from a poorly informed management decision.

- **The appropriateness of the sources of information**: information for decision-making can usually be obtained from numerous sources, for example customers' attitudes towards a product can be measured using a variety of quantitative and qualitative techniques. Companies often rely on the former when more qualitative techniques are really called for. Successful companies use a variety of sources of information.

- **The speed of communication**: the marketing information system will only be effective if information is communicated quickly and to the people capable of acting on it. Deciding what information to withhold from an individual and the concise reporting of relevant information can be as important as deciding what information to include if information overload is to be avoided.

Using information for control

A good marketing information system can generate a lot of information. The key to effective control is to give the right information to the right people at the right time. Providing too much information can be costly in terms of the effort required to assemble and disseminate it and can also reduce effective control where the valuable information is hidden among information of secondary importance. Also, the level of reporting will be determined by the level of tolerance allowed for compliance to target. An analysis of variance from target should indicate if the variance is within or beyond the control of the person responsible for meeting the target. If it is beyond their control, the issue should become one of revising the target so that it becomes once more achievable. If the variance is the result of factors which are subject to an individual's control, a number of measures can be taken to try to revise behaviour.

These are some of the things that most organizations will need information on if they are to monitor adequately the implementation of their marketing plan:

- Financial targets—sales turnover/contribution/profit margin, disaggregated by product/business unit.

- Market analysis—e.g. market share.
- Effectiveness of communication—productivity of sales personnel, effectiveness of advertising, effectiveness of sales promotion.
- Pricing—level of discounts given, price position.
- Personnel—level of skills achieved by employees, survey of customer comments on staff performance.
- Quality levels achieved—e.g. reliability, complaint level.

Where performance is below target, the reasons may not be immediately obvious. A comprehensive marketing information system can allow an organization to analyse variance. A uniform fall in sales performance across the organization, combined with intelligence gained about the state of the market would suggest that remedial action aimed at improving the performance of individual sales personnel may not be as effective as a reassessment of targets or strategies in the light of the changed sales environment.

Successful control mechanisms require three underlying components to be in place:

- The setting of targets or standards of expected performance.
- The measurement and evaluation of actual performance.
- Taking corrective action where necessary.

During the 1990s governments sought to transform the UK's National Health Service from a slumbering, inwardly looking organization to one that is more focused on meeting patients' needs. In its attempts to become more professionally managed, governments increasingly set NHS managers performance targets. By publishing many of these targets in the Patients' Charter, users of the NHS should be able to expect a minimum level of service as specified. The idea of introducing targets which mainly relate to customer handling rather than clinical issues has been dismissed by many as mere window dressing. But even the meaning of these non-clinical statistics is open to doubt, as hospitals find ways of making their performance look good on paper, if not in practice. Accident and Emergency departments use triage nurses to assess new patients upon arrival, thereby keeping within their Patients' Charter target for the time taken to see a new patient first. However, Accident and Emergency departments may be slower to provide actual treatment, as subsequent waiting time was not recorded as a Patients' Charter performance indicator.

Even the whole value of publishing performance indicators for hospitals has been questioned by many. What does it mean if a consultant or a department has a long waiting time for appointments? Rather than being an indicator of inefficiency, could it be that a long waiting list is an indicator of a consultant who is very popular with patients?

Improving organizational effectiveness for marketing

WHAT makes some organizations more effective at marketing than others? And what practical steps can a company take to become one of the best at marketing?

The McKinsey 7S framework developed by Peters and Waterman (1982) identified seven essential elements for a successful business, based on a study of the most successful American companies. The elements are broken down into the hardware (Strategy, Structure, and Systems) and the software (Skills, Staff, Styles, and Shared values). Formalized strategies, structures, and systems on their own were not considered to be sufficient to bring about success—these could only be operationalized with appropriate intangible 'software'. In other words, the quality of management in terms of leadership and working with people to achieve stated goals is critical.

At a strategic level, companies have used a number of methods to try to develop a pervasive marketing orientation throughout their organization:

- In-house educational programmes can aim to train non-marketing employees to empathize with customers' expectations. Some organizations have tried 'job swops' in which backroom production people spend time at the sharp end of their business, in front of customers and learning about their needs.

- By appointing senior managers who have experience of marketing, marketing values may permeate throughout an organization in a top-down manner.

- The introduction of outside consultants is sometimes used as an external change agent. Consultants can impartially apply their previous experience of introducing a marketing culture to an organization.

- A commonly used method of making management think in marketing terms is to introduce a formal market-oriented planning system. When proposing any initiative, managers must work through a list of market-related headings, such as an analysis of the competitive environment and identification of market opportunities when developing their annual plans. This prevents a myopic focus on the product alone.

The overall result of these activities should be to develop a customer-focused marketing culture within an organization. Within many organizations, it has proved very difficult to change cultural attitudes when the nature of an organization's operating environment has significantly changed, rendering the established culture a liability in terms of strategic marketing management. As an example, the cultural values of UK clearing banks have for a long time continued to be dominated by prudence and caution when in some product areas, such as insurance sales, a more aggressive approach to marketing management is called for.

As an organization develops, it is essential that the dominant culture adapts. While a small business may quite successfully embrace a centralized power culture, continued growth may cause this culture to become a liability. There are many cases of businesses, such as the electronics company Amstrad, which have reportedly failed to make the cultural transition from small entrepreneur to large corporate entity. Similarly, the privatization of public utilities calls for a transformation from a bureaucratic role culture to a task-oriented culture (see Handy 1994).

Chapter summary and key linkages to other chapters

This chapter has provided a brief overview of marketing management. There are now many books which discuss how marketing management can be improved and this chapter has only been able to provide a summary of the main issues involved. Planning and control is central to marketing management. However, marketing plans do not develop by accident, so it is essential that an organization has a structure that facilitates the development of a strategy and its implementation. Marketing management cannot be separated from other business functions, especially finance, production management, and human resource management. Numerous approaches to improving the effectiveness of an organization's marketing implementation have been discussed and the importance stressed of focusing around key processes which create customer value.

The following key linkages to other chapters should be noted:

Chapter 1: What is marketing?: This chapter discussed the basic theories and tools of marketing, but these are of little value in an organization if they are not effectively managed.

Chapter 2: The marketing environment: The primary task of marketing management is to bring about internal adaptation in responses to changes in the external environment. Chapter 2 discussed a number of dimensions of the marketing environment which should be monitored and responded to.

Chapter 3: Market segmentation: Information can be used to generate seemingly endless market segments. However, it takes management decisions to prioritize these segments and identify the primary segments to target. It takes further management decisions to decide on strategies for developing each targeted segment.

Chapter 4: Branding: For many companies, brands are among their most valuable assets. Great brands take great management skills in nurturing and then maintaining in order to retain customer loyalty.

Chapter 5: Marketing and ethics: Buyers are increasingly judging the ethical standpoint of a company, which is very much based on the importance attached to ethical conduct by an organization's senior management.

Chapter 6: Marketing research: Successful companies have effective systems for collecting, analysing, disseminating, and acting on information. The role of management is increasingly being seen as one of information processor.

Chapters 7/8: Buyer behaviour and buyer–seller relationship development: Marketing management should never lose sight of its customers' needs. Processes by which customers buy must be understood carefully and management should design sale procedures around customers rather than their own organizational processes.

Chapters 9/10: Developing a product portfolio: With changes in customers' preferences and the development of new technologies, a company's portfolio of products could rapidly become unsuited to customers' needs. Marketing management should be proactive in updating the range of products offered to customers.

Chapter 11: Developing a sustainable competitive advantage: There is a very close link between this chapter and Chapter 11. Developing a truly sustainable competitive advantage is the mark of effective marketing management.

Chapters 12/13: Pricing theory and application: Developing a pricing strategy is a crucial part of marketing management. Pricing is the one element of the marketing mix that brings in revenue—the others are cost items.

Chapter 14: Intermediaries: Strategic decisions need to be made about the structure of distribution channels. Intermediaries need to be recruited, motivated, and controlled if they are to work towards meeting a company's marketing objectives.

Chapters 16–20: Principles of promotion planning/advertising/sales promotion/ personal selling/direct marketing: How much should be spent on promotion? What promotional position should be adopted? How should promotional decisions be related to price and distribution decisions? It is the task of marketing management to integrate these issues.

Chapter 22: Services marketing: In services organizations, the management of the marketing effort cannot be as easily separated from operations management and human resource management, compared with goods manufacturers.

Chapter 23: Global marketing: The tasks of marketing management in overseas markets are in principle similar to those in the domestic market. However, risks are likely to be greater in view of the uncertainty of the overseas business environment.

Case study

How well is marketing performing?

An important theme of this book has been the need to evaluate the results of marketing activities. Various forms of evaluation have been discussed, combining objective measures with more holistic subjective ones. While marketers might be good at measuring certain key indicators, how can you measure the effectiveness of an organization's marketing function?

The Marketing Metrics research project, sponsored among other organizations by the Chartered Institute of Marketing, set out in 1997 to look at real-world marketing performance assessment. It found that only a small minority of UK firms fully assess their marketing performance, despite most thinking that they do so adequately. Nearly all firms compare actual sales with sales targets and there is an increasing focus on shareholder value, but relatively few measure customer value. It seems that few firms assess their total marketing effort. Why don't firms measure performance? Does it matter?

If marketers have been telling their board of directors that marketing expenditure is an investment, not a cost, the board is entitled to see the resulting asset and its valuation. The asset created by effective marketing has often been referred to as 'brand equity'. The Marketing Metrics research found that about one-third of UK companies had no language for this concept. Of those who did, about half regularly quantify brand equity.

The 1999 Marketing Forum, comprising leading UK marketers, found that those claiming to measure marketing expenditure effectiveness grew from 75 per cent to 83 per cent between 1995–7, but of those, only 14 per cent, growing to 21 per cent, had measures of brand equity. Part of the problem here is language: some measure brand equity but do not call it that. Some companies may have systems for major brands but not for minor ones. Measuring the concept can be expensive, especially where a firm operates globally.

A number of reasons can be identified why firms may be unwilling or unable to measure their marketing effectiveness:

1. The board is not marketing or customer oriented, with no senior marketing representation on it. Little board agenda time is made available to discuss marketing issues.
2. Determination and effort may be considered more important than objectivity. To use an analogy, the First World War would never have been won if the soldiers had known the score—it was won by sheer determination.
3. Some company boards believe that accountants should be responsible for accounting for all that matters. Internal measures are interpreted as navel gazing, and are no substitute for measuring sales and market share.
4. Marketers may argue against having their effectiveness measured too closely by pointing out that marketing is the business of the whole company, and so they cannot be held specifically accountable.
5. Marketers are often too busy fighting the next battle and this should take priority over worrying about the last one. Most promotions, for example, have pre-set targets but only a minority of those are formally compared with results.
6. In reality, the status of a marketer is determined by the size of his/her marketing budget. Size of budget, which can be measured, looks more credible on a CV than subjective outcomes.
7. Marketing effectiveness may be perceived as something essentially unmeasurable and that should be assessed by more subjective 'feel good' or 'good news' aspects.
8. Marketers may argue that past experience has shown that marketing expenditure cannot be related to sales and profits, i.e. profit and loss account measures do not work.
9. The environment changes too fast, so results need to be judged by the new realities, not those expected when the plan was drawn up.
10. Creating new measurement systems takes too long. The current marketing team will have moved on by the time it reports.

It is important to note that measuring overall marketing performance is not the same as measuring marketing expenditure effectiveness. Some marketing-led organizations, such as Marks & Spencer, have managed with only minimal marketing expenditure budgets. More importantly, the effectiveness of the marketing expenditure budget cannot be assessed without measuring the change in the asset of brand equity.

Brand equity is fundamental to assessment. The results of marketers' actions should live on after the current financial period. Costs today may pay back next year or the year after. Good marketing may or may not affect sales, but it always increases brand equity. There is plenty of evidence of organizations whose marketing is ineffective and who have seen their brand equity diminish. Banks who were once trusted institutions have caused anger among many of their customers through perceptions of overcharging, incorrect debits, and poor communication. One result has been that many customers have shifted their bank accounts and credit cards to supermarkets and other rivals to banks who have achieved high levels of brand equity. Many of these misgivings about banks can be attributed to operational functions, but this only serves to emphasize the point that marketing should be a company-wide integrator. Customers may not care who in the bank is the source of their grievance, but the result is the same—the value they place on a bank's brand is lower than it was before.

A diminution of brand equity has wide-ranging consequences for an organization and can affect its ability to charge a price premium (e.g. the premium charged for Coca-Cola compared to Sainsbury's own-label cola) and reinforces consumers' buying habits.

Building brand equity is the primary marketing function and is likely to be developed by the following:

- Getting top management to empathize with customers, to understand what they value in a brand.
- Having a shared language internally and with advertising and other marketing service agencies.
- Developing a more realistic set of targets than sales.
- Using brand equity as a basis for rewarding managers.

If the maintenance of brand equity is a crucial measure of marketing effectiveness, it might be expected that marketing managers' pay would be related to changes in brand equity. Yet there is little evidence that this takes precedence over more conventional reward systems based on sales and profitability.

Adapted from Tim Ambler, 'Why is Marketing not Measuring Up?', *Marketing*, 24 Sept. 1998, pp. 24–5.

Case study review questions

1 Given the importance of measuring marketing effectiveness, how do you explain the success of apparently intuitive marketers such as Richard Branson?

2 What is the difference between marketing efficiency and marketing effectiveness?

3 To what extent is it desirable, or feasible, to use brand equity as a measure of marketing effectiveness?

Chapter review questions

1 What is the difference between marketing planning and corporate planning? Should they be considered synonymous?

2 'Mission statements are the result of senior managers undertaking management

development courses. They may have the language, but mission statements are invariably ignored by the very people who they are aimed at'. Is this a fair statement?

3 Do you agree with the notion that a marketing department can actually be a barrier to the successful development of a marketing orientation? Give examples.

4 What is the value of contingency planning? Identify one sector where the production of contingency plans is likely to have significant marketing benefits, and the factors which need to be taken into account.

5 Every now and again management gurus develop new ideas for managing organizations, such as business process re-engineering. Is there too much hype in such prescriptions?

6 What are the main differences in implementing a market-oriented management structure within the public as opposed to the private service sector?

References

Drucker, P. (1973), *Management: Tasks, Responsibilities and Practices* (New York: Harper & Row).

Gummesson, E. (1991), 'Marketing-Orientation Revisited: The Crucial Role of the Part-Time Marketer', *European Journal of Marketing*, **25**, 2, pp. 60–75.

Handy, C. (1994), *Understanding Organizations*, 4th edn. (Harmondsworth: Penguin).

Kohli, A. K., and Jaworski, B. J. (1990), 'Market Orientation: The Construct, Research Propositions and Management Implications', *Journal of Marketing*, **54**, pp. 1–18.

Kotler, P. (1997), *Marketing Management: Analysis, Planning, Implementation and Control*, 9th edn. (Englewood Cliffs, NJ: Prentice Hall).

Levitt, T. (1960), 'Marketing Myopia', *Harvard Business Review*, **38**, 4, pp. 45–56.

McDonald, M. (1995), *Marketing Plans, How to Prepare Them: How to Use Them*, 3rd edn. (Oxford: Butterworth-Heinemann).

Piercy, N. (1985), *Marketing Organisation: An Analysis of Information Processing, Power and Politics* (London: Allen and Unwin).

Peters, T. J., and Waterman, R. H. (1982), *In Search of Excellence: Lessons from America's Best Run Companies* (New York: Harper & Row).

Suggested further reading

There are many texts on the subject of marketing management which focus on how an organization can implement measures to respond to a changing external environment. The following are useful:

■ Baker, M. J. (1999), *Marketing Strategy and Management*, 3rd edn. (Basingstoke: Macmillan).

- Doyle, P. (1994), *Marketing Management and Strategy* (Englewood Cliffs, NJ: Prentice Hall).
- Fifield, P. (1998), *Marketing Strategy*, 2nd edn. (Oxford: Butterworth-Heinemann).
- Gilligan, C., and Wilson, R. (1997), *Strategic Marketing Management*, 2nd edn. (Oxford: Butterworth-Heinemann).
- Kotler, P. (1997), *Marketing Management: Analysis, Planning, Implementation and Control*, 9th edn. (Englewood Cliffs, NJ: Prentice-Hall).
- Mintzberg, H. (1993), *The Rise and Fall of Strategic Planning* (New York: The Free Press).
- Piercy, N. (1998), *Market-Led Strategic Change*, 2nd edn. (Oxford: Butterworth-Heinemann).

The following useful references for the development of a marketing plan:

- Dibb, S., Simkin, L., and Bradley, J. (1996), *The Marketing Planning Workbook: Effective Marketing for Marketing Managers* (London: International Thomson Business Press).
- Keegan, W., and McDonald, M. (1997), *Marketing Plans that work; Targeting Growth and Profitability* (Oxford: Butterworth-Heinemann).
- McDonald, M. (1995), *Marketing Plans: How to Prepare Them: How to Use Them*, 3rd edn. (Oxford: Butterworth-Heinemann).
- —— (1999), *Marketing Plans* (Oxford: Butterworth-Heinemann).
- Westwood, J. (1998), *The Marketing Plan: A Practitioners Guide* (London: Kogan Page).

The following references discuss issues of implementing marketing plans:

- Hardy, K. (1991), 'Implemeting Marketing Strategy', *Business Quarterly*, **55**, 3, pp. 33–6.
- Harris, L. (1996), 'The Application of Piercy and Morgan's Dimensions of Marketing Planning', *Management Decision*, **34**, 3, pp. 35–41.
- Lancaster, G., and Waddelow, I. (1998), 'An Empirical Investigation into the Process of Strategic Marketing Planning in SME's: Its Attendant Problems and Proposals Towards New Practical Paradigm', *Journal of Marketing Management*, **14**, pp. 853–78.

The effects of organizational structure and culture on marketing planning are discussed in the following:

- Gummesson, E. (1990), 'Organizing for Marketing and Marketing Organizations', in C. A. Congram and M. L. Friedman (eds.), *Handbook of Services Marketing* (New York: Amacon).
- Handy, C. (1994), *Understanding Organizations*, 4th edn. (Harmondsworth: Penguin).
- Hogg, G., Carter, S., and Dunne, A. (1998), 'Investing in People: Internal Marketing and Corporate Culture', *Journal of Marketing Management*, **14**, pp. 879–95.
- Simkin, L. (1996), 'Addressing Organisational Prerequisites in Marketing Planning Programmes', *Marketing Intelligence and Planning*, **14**, 5, pp. 39–47.

The important role played by information in marketing planning is discussed in the following:

- Galliers, R. D., and Baker, B. (1998), *Strategic Information Management*, 2nd edn. (Oxford: Butterworth-Heinemann).
- Piercy, N. (1985), *Marketing Organization: An Analysis of Information Processing, Power and Politics* (London: Allen & Unwin).
- Porter, M., and Millar, V. (1985), 'How Information Gives You Competitive Advantage', *Harvard Business Review*, **85**, pp. 149–60.

Useful web links

Chartered Institute of Marketing: http://www.cim.co.uk/

British Institute of Management: http://www.inst-mgt.org.uk

Institute of Management and Administration (US source of business and management information): http://www.ioma.com/

Inc. magazine Small Business Resource Index: http://www.inc.com/idx/idx_t_Sb.html

Strategy & Business Articles, book reviews, and special features for business leaders (sponsored by Booz Allen and Hamilton): http://www.strategy-business.com/

Manager's Daily: news and reports for management: http://www.dma.net/managers/

A discussion group for academics engaged in research into what constitutes organizational effectiveness and how this may be achieved and maintained in contemporary business: http//www.mailbase.ac.uk.lists.org-effectiveness/

Chapter 22

The Marketing of Services

Chapter objectives

Services now form the dominant sector of most western economies, yet marketing theory still tends to be oriented towards the goods sector. This chapter sets out to identify the distinguishing characteristics of services and the effects these have on marketing. Key topics of intangibility, inseparability, variability, and perishability are introduced. It is noted that it may be more appropriate to talk about a goods–service continuum rather than a clear distinction between the two. An extended marketing mix is developed, in which the importance of people management is emphasized.

Introduction

THE literature on marketing theory and applications has been dominated by the manufactured goods sector. This is probably not surprising, because marketing in its modern form first took root in those manufacturing sectors that faced the greatest competition from the 1930s onwards. However, the services sector has continued to grow in industrialized economies where it now forms the dominant part of many national economies. In growing, the services sector has become more competitive and taken on board the principles of marketing. Deregulation of many services and rising expectations of consumers have had a dramatic effect on marketing activities within the sector.

But can we simply apply the established body of marketing knowledge, which is based on manufactured goods, to the services sector? Is the marketing of services fundamentally different from the marketing of goods? Or is services marketing just a special case of general marketing theory?

This chapter discusses the distinctive characteristics of services and the extent to which these call for a revision to the general principles of marketing. While many of the general principles can be applied to services, there are areas where a new set of tools need to be developed. Of particular importance are the effects of service intangibility on buyers' decision-making processes; the effects of producing services 'live' in the presence of the consumer; and the crucial role played by an organization's employees in the total product offer.

The importance of the services sector

ALTHOUGH we have seen recent rapid growth in the services sector, the sector itself is not new. Even the so-called 'Industrial Revolution' can be more accurately described as a service revolution. The industrial revolution could not have happened without the services sector. The period saw the development of many services whose presence was vital to economic development. Without the development of railways, goods would not have been distributed from centralized factories to geographically dispersed consumers and many people would not have been able to get to work. Investment in new factories called for a banking system that could circulate funds at a national rather than a purely local level. A service sector emerged to meet the needs of manufacturing, including intermediaries who were essential to get manufacturers' goods to increasingly dispersed markets. Today, we continue to rely on services to exploit developments in the manufacturing sector.

There is little doubt that the services sector has become a dominant force in developed economies, accounting for about three-quarters of all employment in the USA, UK, Canada, and Australia. Between 1980 and 1992, it is reported that the EU created almost 1.3 million new jobs per year in the services sectors—twice the average for the rest of the economy (Eurostat 1995). There appears to be a close correlation between the level of economic development in an economy (as expressed by its GDP per capita) and the strength of its service sector, although whether a strong service sector leads to economic growth or results from it is debatable.

Services have had a major impact on national economies and many service industries have facilitated improved productivity elsewhere in the manufacturing and agricultural sectors. As an example, transport and distribution services have often had the effect of stimulating economic development at local and national levels (e.g. following the improvement of rail or road services). One reason for Russian agriculture not having been fully exploited has been the ineffective distribution system available to food producers.

What are services?

I͏T can be difficult to define just what is meant by a service because most products we buy contain a mixture of goods elements and service elements. A meal in a restaurant contains a combination of goods elements (the food) and service elements (the manner in which the food is served). Even apparently 'pure' goods such as timber often contain service elements, such as the service required in transporting timber from where it was produced to where a customer requires it.

Modern definitions of services focus on the fact that a service in itself produces no tangible output, although it may be instrumental in producing some tangible output. A contemporary definition is provided by Kotler *et al.* (1996):

A service is any activity or benefit that one party can offer to another which is essentially intangible and does not result in the ownership of anything. Its production may or may not be tied to a physical product.

In a more tongue-in-cheek manner, services have been described as 'anything which cannot be dropped on your foot'.

'Pure' services have a number of distinctive characteristics that differentiate them from goods and have implications for the way in which they are marketed. These characteristics are often described as intangibility, inseparability, variability, perishability and the inability to own a service.

Intangibility

A pure service cannot be assessed using any of the physical senses—it is an abstraction which cannot be directly examined before it is purchased. A prospective purchaser of most goods is able to examine the goods for physical integrity, aesthetic appearance, taste, smell, etc. Many advertising claims relating to these tangible properties can be verified by inspection prior to purchase. By contrast, pure services have no tangible properties which can be used by consumers to verify advertising claims before the purchase is made. The intangible process characteristics which define services, such as reliability, personal care, attentiveness of staff, their friendliness, etc., can only be verified once a service has been purchased and consumed.

Measuring quality for services can be very different compared with goods. Goods generally have tangible benchmarks against which quality can be assessed (e.g. durability, reliability, taste). In the case of services, these benchmarks can often only be defined in the minds of consumers. So while there may be little doubt that a car which does 40 miles per gallon of fuel is better than one which only does 30, the same quality judgement cannot be made between, say, a restaurant meal that takes one hour and another that takes two hours. In the latter case, the expectations of diners are crucial to an understanding of their perceptions of service quality, which may not be the same as the judgements of an outside observer.

Where goods form an important component of a service offer, many of the practices associated with conventional goods marketing can be applied to this part of the service offer. Restaurants represent a mix of tangibles and intangibles and, in respect of the food element, few of the particular characteristics of services marketing are encountered. The presence of a tangible component gives customers a visible basis on which to judge quality. While some services (such as restaurants) are rich in such tangible cues, other services provide relatively little tangible evidence (e.g. life insurance).

Intangibility has a number of important marketing implications. The lack of physical evidence which intangibility implies increases the level of uncertainty that a consumer faces when choosing between competing services. An important part of a services marketing programme will therefore involve reducing consumer uncertainty by such means as adding physical evidence and the development of strong brands. It is interesting to note that pure goods and pure services tend to move in opposite directions in terms of their general approach to the issue of tangibility. While service marketers seek to add tangible evidence to their product, pure goods marketers often seek to augment their products by adding intangible elements such as after-sales service and improved distribution.

Inseparability

The production and consumption of a tangible good are two separate activities. Companies usually produce goods in one central location and then transport them to the place where customers most want to buy them. In this way, manufacturing companies can achieve economies of scale through centralized production and have centralized quality control checks. The manufacturer is also able to make goods at a time that is convenient to itself, then make them available to customers at times which are convenient to customers. Production and consumption are said to be separable. On the other hand, the consumption of a service is said to be inseparable from its means of production. Producer and consumer must interact in order for the benefits of the service to be realized. Both must normally meet at a time and a place that is mutually convenient in order that the producer can directly pass on service benefits. In the extreme case of personal care services, the customer must be present during the entire production process. A surgeon, for example, cannot provide a service without the involvement of a patient. For services, marketing becomes a means of facilitating complex producer–consumer interaction, rather than being merely an exchange medium.

Inseparability occurs whether the producer is human—as in the case of healthcare services—or a machine (e.g. a bank ATM machine). The service of the ATM machine can only be realized if the producer and consumer interact. In some cases, it has been possible geographically to separate service production and consumption, especially where there is a low level of personal contact. This has happened, for example, in the banking sector where many banks have replaced local branches (where there is face-to-face interaction between producer and consumer) with centralized telephone call centres (where interaction takes place through the medium of the telephone).

Inseparability has a number of important marketing implications for services. Firstly, whereas goods are generally first produced, then offered for sale, and finally sold and consumed, inseparability causes this process to be modified for services. They are generally sold first, then produced and consumed simultaneously. Secondly, while the method of goods production is to a large extent (though by no means always) of little importance to the consumer, production processes are critical to the enjoyment of services.

In the case of goods, the consumer is not a part of the process of production and, in general, so long as the product which they receive meets their expectations, they are satisfied (although there are exceptions, for example where the ethics of production methods cause concern, or where quality can only be assessed with a knowledge of production stages that are hidden from the consumer's view). With services, the active participation of the customer in the production process makes the process as important as the end benefit. In some cases, an apparently slight change in service production methods may totally destroy the value of the service being provided. A person buying a ticket for a concert by the Bee Gees may derive no benefit at all from the concert if it is subsequently performed by Oasis instead.

Variability

Most manufactured goods can now be produced with high standards of consistency. However, when asked about the consistency of services such as railway journeys, restaurant meals, or legal advice, most people would probably have experienced high levels of variability. For services, variability impacts upon customers not just in terms of outcomes but also in terms of processes of production. It is the latter point that causes variability to pose a much greater problem for services, compared to goods. Because the customer is usually involved in the production process for a service at the same time as they consume it, it can be difficult to carry out monitoring and control to ensure consistent standards. The opportunity for pre-delivery inspection and rejection which is open to the goods manufacturer is not normally possible with services.

Variability in production standards is of greatest concern to services organizations where customers are highly involved in the production process, especially where production methods make it impractical to monitor service production. This is true of many labour-intensive personal services provided in a one-to-one situation, such as personal healthcare. Some services allow greater scope for quality control checks to be undertaken during the production process, allowing an organization to provide a consistently high level of service. This is especially true of machine-based services, for example telecommunication services can typically operate with very low failure rates.

The tendency today is for equipment-based services to be regarded as less variable than those which involve a high degree of personal intervention in the production process. Many services organizations have sought to reduce variability—and hence to build strong brands—by adopting equipment-based production methods. Replacing human telephone operators with computerized voice systems and the automation of many banking services are typical of this trend. Sometimes reduced personnel variability has been achieved by passing on part of the production process to consumers, in the way that self-service petrol filling stations are no longer dependent on the variability of forecourt serving staff.

The variability of service output can pose problems for brand building in services compared to tangible goods. For the latter it is usually relatively easy to incorporate monitoring and quality control procedures into production processes in order to ensure that a brand stands for a consistency of output. The service sector's attempts to reduce variability concentrate on methods used to select, train, motivate, and control personnel. In some cases, service offers have been simplified, jobs have been 'deskilled', and personnel replaced with machines in order to reduce human variability.

Perishability

Unlike most goods, services cannot be stored. Most manufactures of goods who are unable to sell their current output can carry forward stocks for future sale. The only significant costs are storage costs, financing costs, and the possibility of loss through wastage or obsolescence. By contrast, the producer of a service which cannot sell all of its output produced in the current period gets no chance to carry it forward for sale in a subsequent period. A train operator which offers seats on the 8.10 a.m. train from Leeds to Bradford cannot sell any empty seats once the train has departed. The service offer disappears and spare seats cannot be stored to meet a surge in demand which may occur later in the day.

Very few services face a constant pattern of demand through time. Many show considerable variation, which could follow a daily pattern (e.g. city centre sandwich bars at lunchtime), weekly (the Friday evening peak in demand for railway travel), seasonal (shops at Christmas time), cyclical (mortgages), or an unpredictable pattern of demand (emergency building repair services following heavy storms).

The perishability of services results in greater attention having to be paid to the management of demand by evening out peaks and troughs in demand and in scheduling service production to follow this pattern as far as possible. It is not good enough to ensure that supply and demand are matched overall in the long term. They must match for each minute and for each place that service is offered. Pricing and promotion are two of the tools commonly adopted to resolve demand and supply imbalances.

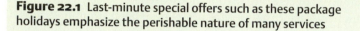

WHITEHEAD TRAVEL

LATE AVAILABILTY OFFERS

21 June	Gran Canaria	14 nights H/B	£259
21 June	Crete	7 nights B/B	£159
22 June	Palma	7 nights B/B	£139
24 June	Orlando Fly/Drive	14 nights	£339

All flights from Gatwick

Figure 22.1 Last-minute special offers such as these package holidays emphasize the perishable nature of many services

Inability to own services

The inability to own a service is related to the characteristics of intangibility and perishability. In purchasing goods, buyers generally acquire title to the goods in question and can subsequently do as they wish with them. On the other hand, when a service is performed, no ownership is transferred from the seller to the buyer. The buyer is merely buying the right to a service process such as the use of a car park or an accountant's time. A distinction should be drawn between the inability to own the service act, and the rights which a buyer may acquire to have a service carried out at some time in the future (a theatre gift voucher for example).

The inability to own a service has implications for the design of distribution channels, so a wholesaler or retailer cannot take title, as is the case with goods. Instead, direct distribution methods are more common and, where intermediaries are used, they generally act as a co-producer with the service provider.

Goods and services compared

I was noted earlier that most products are a combination of goods and services. This has led some people to argue that we do not really need a separate theory of marketing for services. In the words of Theodore Levitt:

there is no such thing as service industries. There are only industries where service components are greater or less than those of other industries. (Levitt 1972)

Others have pointed to the distinctiveness of services which makes the application of traditional marketing principles inappropriate. Examples of early work which sought to define the nature of services is provided by Gronroos (1978), Lovelock (1981), and Shostack (1977).

Most products which we buy are a combination of goods and services. In this way, cars have traditionally been considered examples of pure goods. However, today, most cars are sold with considerable service benefits, such as an extended warranty, a maintenance contract, or a financing facility. In fact, many car manufacturers now see themselves as service providers in which a lease contract provides all the services necessary to keep a car maintained, insured, financed, and replaced. The idea of a manufacturer selling a tangible item (the car) and then not having any dealings with the customer until they are ready to replace the car is a rapidly disappearing goods approach to the marketing of cars (see Case Study).

Just as many pure goods may in reality be quite service like, so many apparently pure services contain substantial goods elements. A package holiday may seem like a pure service, but it includes tangible elements in the form of the airplane, the hotel room, and transfer coach, for example.

Pure goods and pure services are hypothetical extremes, but they are nevertheless important to note because they help to define the distinctive characteristics of goods and services marketing. In between the extremes is a wide range of products which are a combination of tangible goods elements and intangible service elements. It is therefore common to talk about a goods–services continuum along which all products can be placed by reference to their service or goods dominance (see Fig. 22.2).

The five characteristics of intangibility, inseparability, perishability, variability, and lack of ownership are not entirely exclusive to services, as they are shared by

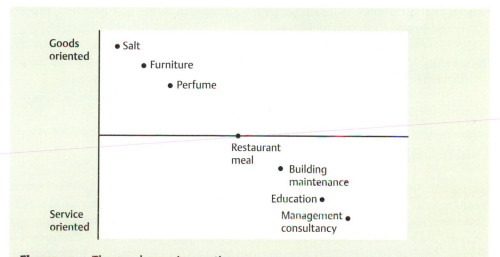

Figure 22.2 The goods–service continuum

many manufactured goods. For example, on the subject of variability, there are some non-service industries—such as tropical fruits that have difficulty in achieving high levels of consistent output, whereas some service industries such as car parks can achieve a consistent standard of service in terms of availability and cleanliness, etc. Similarly, many tangible goods share the problem of intangible services in being incapable of full examination before consumption. It is not normally possible, for instance, to judge the taste of a bottle of wine in a supermarket before it has been purchased and (at least partially) consumed. Fig. 22.3 illustrates the points of convergence between goods and services.

Classifying services

BECAUSE the services sector accounts for about three-quarters of economic activity in developed countries, it is unlikely that one body of marketing theory will be applicable to all services, from a jobbing electrician to a multinational airline.

The goods sector has traditionally developed classifications to describe the marketing needs of different groups of goods. Terms such as fast-moving consumer goods, shopping goods, speciality goods, white goods, brown goods, etc., are widely used and convey a lot of information about the marketing requirements of products within a category, for example with respect to buying processes, methods of promotion, and distribution. Something similar is needed for the service sector.

Traditional production-based methods of classifying services are not particularly useful for marketers. Small guest houses and international hotels may fall within the same sector, but their marketing needs are very different. The international hotel may in fact share more in common with an airline in terms of customers' expectations and a peaked pattern of demand.

The following sections identify some of the more commonly used bases for classifying services. It should be noted that many of these bases derive from the five fundamental characteristics of services which were noted earlier.

Degree of intangibility

Intangibility goes to the heart of most definitions of services. It was noted earlier that intangibility has consequences for the way in which buyers perceive risk in a purchase decision. The task of providing evidence that a service will deliver its promises becomes more difficult where the service is highly intangible. As a classification device, degree of intangibility has many uses and this will be returned to later in the context of the management of the marketing mix.

Intangibility	Goods are increasingly augmented with intangible services (e.g. insurance, credit facilities) Services are augmented with tangibles (e.g. staff uniforms, brochures)
Inseparability	Goods are increasingly produced in the presence of customers (e.g. while you wait tailoring) Service consumption is increasingly separated from production (e.g. telephone banking)
Perishability	Goods are now more likely to be supplied using 'just-in-time' principles of the service sector Tangible components of the service offer can be stored. Improved management of supply and demand patterns reduces problem of perishability.
Variability	Industrialization of services allows levels of reliability to be achieved that match those of goods
Lack of ownership	Goods increasingly comprise service elements which cannot be owned Services companies aften comprise tangible elements that can be owned (e.g. a telephone 'calling card')

Figure 22.3 Points of convergence between the goods and services sectors

Producer v. consumer services

Consumer services are provided for individuals who use up the service for their own enjoyment or benefit. No further economic benefit results from the consumption of the service. By contrast, producer services are bought by a business in order that it can produce something else of economic benefit. An industrial cleaning company may sell cleaning services to an airport operator in order that the latter can sell the services of clean terminal buildings to airline operators and their customers.

The status of the service within the total product offer

Many services exist to add value to the total product offer, as where a goods manufacturer augments its core tangible product with additional service benefits, such as after-sales warranties. At other times, the service is sold as a separate product that customers purchase to add value to their own goods (e.g. a car valeting service is purchased to add to the resale value of a used car). A further group of services may add value to a product more fundamentally by making it available in the first place (e.g. distribution and financing services).

Extent of inseparability

Some services can only be provided in the presence of customers, for example the production of personal care services, almost by definition, cannot be separated from their consumption. Other services are more able to separate production from consumption, for example a listener to a radio station does not need to interact with the staff of the radio station. Customer involvement in production processes is generally lower where the service is carried out on their possessions, rather than on their mind or body directly.

The marketing of highly inseparable services calls for great attention to the processes of production with fewer opportunities for 'back-room' quality control checks before service delivery takes place.

The pattern of service delivery

At one extreme, some services are purchased only when they are needed as a series of one-off transactions. This is typical of low value, undifferentiated services which may be bought on impulse or with little conscious search activity (e.g. taxis and snacks in cafes). It can also be true of specialized, high value services that are purchased only as required (e.g. funeral services are generally bought casually only when needed).

By contrast, other services can be identified where it is impractical to supply the service casually. This can occur where production methods make it difficult to supply a service only when it is needed (e.g. it is impractical to provide a telephone line to a house only when it is needed—the line itself is therefore supplied continuously) or where the benefits of a service are required continuously (e.g. insurance policies).

Extent of people orientation

For some services, by far the most important means by which consumers evaluate a service is the quality of the front-line staff who serve them (this is important for sectors as diverse as hairdressing, accountancy, and law). At the other extreme, many services can be delivered with very little human involvement—a pay and display car park involves minimal human input in the form of checking tickets and keeping the car park clean. The management and marketing of people-based services can be very different from those based on equipment.

The significance of the service to the purchaser

Some services are purchased frequently, are of low value, are consumed very rapidly, and are likely to be purchased on impulse with very little pre-purchase activity. Such services may represent a very small proportion of the purchaser's total expenditure and correspond to the goods marketer's definition of fast-moving consumer goods (FMCGs). The casual purchase of a lottery ticket would fit into this category. At the other end of the scale, long-lasting services may be purchased infrequently and, when they are, the decision-making process takes longer and involves more people. Life insurance and package holidays fit into this category.

Marketable v. unmarketable services

Finally, it should be remembered that many services are still considered by some cultures to be unmarketable. Many government services are provided for the public benefit and no attempt has been made to charge users of the service. This can arise where it is impossible to exclude individuals or groups of individuals from benefiting from a service (e.g. it is not possible in practice for a local authority to charge individuals for the use of local footpaths). Many services provided within private households (e.g. childcare) are considered by many cultures to be unmarketable.

Multiple classifications

The great diversity of services have now been classified in a way which focuses on their marketing needs rather than their dominant methods of production. It will be apparent that, within any sector, there are likely to be major subcategories of services which have distinctive marketing needs, and which may share a lot with other sectors. This commonality of marketing needs has provided great opportunities for companies who have extended their product range into services which are basically similar in their marketing needs if not in their production methods. Many of the UK grocery retailers have considered that the way people open savings accounts is similar to the way that they select groceries, so have extended their marketing expertise by applying it to the savings and investment market.

Although a number of bases for classifying services have been presented in isolation, services are in practice, like goods, classified by a number of criteria simultaneously. There have been a number of attempts to develop multidimensional approaches for identifying clusters of similar services (e.g. see Solomon and Gould (1991) who researched consumers' perceptions of sixteen different personal and household services).

An extended marketing mix for services

THE marketing mix is not based on any theory, but on the need for marketing managers to break down their decision-making into a number of identifiable and actionable headings. The familiar 4Ps marketing mix is very much based on the needs of the manufactured goods sector and has given us the four familiar Ps of Product, Price, Promotion, and Place. These 4Ps have been found to be too limited in their application to services. Particular problems which limit their usefulness to services are:

■ The intangible nature of services is overlooked in most analyses of the mix—for example, the product mix is frequently analysed in terms of tangible design properties which may not be relevant to a service. Similarly, physical distribution management may not be an important element of place mix decisions.

■ The promotion mix of the traditional 4Ps fails to recognize the promotion of services which takes place at the point of consumption by the production personnel, unlike the situation with most goods which are normally produced away from the consumer and therefore the producer has no direct involvement in promotion to the final consumer. For a bank clerk, hairdresser, or singer, the manner in which the service is produced is an essential element of the total promotion of the service.

■ The price element overlooks the fact that many services are produced by the public sector without a price being charged to the final consumer.

The basic list of 4Ps also fails to recognize a number of key factors which marketing managers in the service sector use to design their service output. Particular problems focus on:

- the importance of people as an element of the service product, both as producers and co-consumers;
- the oversimplification of the elements of distribution which are of relevance to intangible services;

- definition of the concept of quality for intangible services, and identification and measurement of the mix elements that can be managed in order to create a quality service.

These weaknesses have resulted in a number of attempts to redefine a marketing mix for the services sector. The expansion by Booms and Bitner (1981) provides a useful framework for the services sector. It should be stressed that this is not an empirically proven theory of services marketing, but an analysis of the decisions that services marketers take in developing services to satisfy customers' needs. In addition to the four traditional elements of the marketing mix, it is common to recognize the importance of People and Processes as additional elements. Booms and Bitner also talk about Physical evidence making up a seventh P.

Decisions on one element of the extended marketing mix can only be made by reference to other elements of the mix in order to give a sustainable product positioning. The importance attached to each element of the extended marketing mix will vary between services. In a highly automated service such as vending machine dispensing, the people element will be a less important element of the mix than a people intensive business such as a restaurant.

A brief overview of the extended services marketing mix elements is given below. In the case of the four traditional Ps, emphasis will be given to distinguishing their application in a services rather than a goods context.

Products

Marketing mix management must recognize a number of significant differences between goods and services. In Chapter 10, a model was described comprising various levels of product definition. The model developed starts from the 'core' level (defining the basic needs which are satisfied by the product), through a 'tangible' level (the tangible manifestation of the product), through to an 'augmented' level (the additional services which are added to the product). While this analysis is held to be true of products in general, doubts have been expressed about whether it can be applied to the service offer.

Most analyses of the service offer recognize that the problems of inseparability and intangibility make application of the three generic levels of product offer less meaningful to the service offer. Instead, the product offer in respect of services can be more usefully analysed in terms of two components:

- the core service which represents the core benefit;

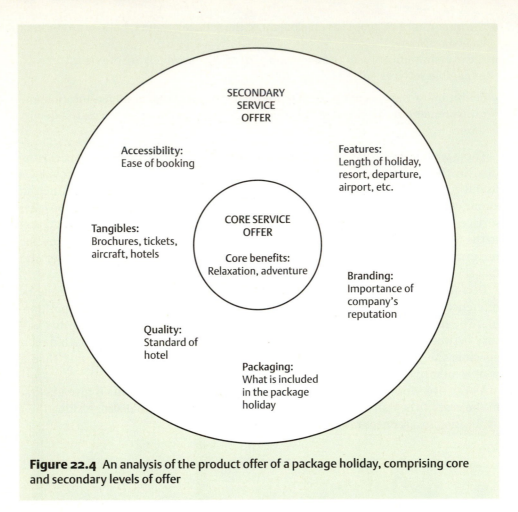

Figure 22.4 An analysis of the product offer of a package holiday, comprising core and secondary levels of offer

- the secondary service which represents both the tangible and augmented product levels (Fig. 22.4).

The secondary service can be best understood in terms of the manner in which a service is delivered. For example, Little Chef and Brewers Fayre restaurants both satisfy the same basic need for fast, economical, hygienic food, but they do so in differing ways. This is reflected in different procedures for taking and delivering orders, differences in menus and in the ambience of the restaurants.

Services tend to be relatively easy to copy and cannot generally benefit from patent protection, as is often the case with goods. New product development often occurs in an incremental fashion, with a lot of variants of a basic service. The proliferation of mortgage products by a building society, all with slightly differing terms and conditions, but basically similar in their function, is an example of this.

Pricing

A number of points of difference with respect to services pricing are noted here:

- The inseparable nature of services makes the possibilities for price discrimination between different groups of users much greater than is usually the case with manufactured goods. Goods can easily be purchased by one person, stored, and sold to another person.

- A second major difference between goods and services pricing is based on the high level of fixed costs that many service providers experience. The marginal cost of one additional telephone call, one additional seat on an airplane, or one additional place in a cinema is often very low. This can give service suppliers a lot of scope for charging different prices for what is basically the same product offer.

- Services are more likely than goods to be made available in distorted markets, or in circumstances where no market exists at all. Public services such as museums and schools that have sought to adopt marketing principles often do not have any control over the price element of the marketing mix. The reward for attracting more visitors to a museum or pupils to a school may be additional centrally derived grants, rather than income received directly from the users of the service.

Promotion

Although the principles of communication discussed in Chapter 16 are similar for goods and services, a number of distinctive promotional needs of services can be identified, deriving from the distinguishing characteristics of services. The following are particularly important:

- The intangible nature of the service offer often results in consumers perceiving a high level of risk in the buying process, which promotion must seek to overcome. A number of methods are commonly used to remedy this, including the development of strong brands; encouragement of word-of-mouth recommendation; promotion of trial usage of a service; and the use of credible message sources in promotion (especially through public relations activity).

- Promotion of a service offer cannot generally be isolated from promotion of the service provider. Customers cannot sensibly evaluate many intangible, high perceived risk services, such as pensions and insurance policies, without knowing the identity of the service provider. In many cases, the service may be difficult to comprehend in any case (this is certainly true of pensions for most people), so promotion of the service provider becomes far more important than promotion of individual service offers.

- Visible production processes, especially service personnel, become an important element of the promotion effort. Where service production processes are inseparable from their consumption, new opportunities are provided for promoting a service. Front-line staff can become sales people for an organization. The service outlet can become a billboard which people see as they pass by.

- The intangible nature of services and the heightened possibilities for fraud result in their promotion being generally more constrained by legal and voluntary controls than is the case with goods. Financial services and overseas holidays are two examples of service industries with extensive voluntary and statutory limitations on promotion.

Place

Place decisions refer to the ease of access which potential customers have to a service. For services, it is more appropriate to talk about accessibility as a mix element, rather than place.

The inseparability of services makes the task of passing on service benefits much more complex than is the case with manufactured goods. Inseparability implies that services are consumed at the point of production, in other words, a service cannot be produced by one person in one place and handled by other people to make it available to customers in other places. A service cannot therefore be produced where costs are lowest and sold where demand is greatest—customer accessibility must be designed into the service production system.

Place decisions can involve physical location decisions (as in deciding where to place a hotel), decisions about which intermediaries to use in making a service accessible to a consumer (e.g. whether a tour operator uses travel agents or sells its holidays direct to customers), and non-locational decisions which are used to make services available (e.g. the use of telephone delivery systems). For pure services, decisions about how physically to move a good are of little strategic relevance. However, most services involve movement of goods of some form. These can either be materials necessary to produce a service (such as travel brochures and fast food packaging material) or the service can have as its whole purpose the movement of goods (e.g. road haulage, plant hire).

People

For most services, people are a vital element of the marketing mix. It can be almost a cliché to say that for some businesses, the employees are the business—if these are taken away, the organization is left with very few assets with which it can seek to gain competitive advantage in meeting customers' needs. For some organizations, the management of personnel can be seen as just one other asset to be managed. For others, human resource management is so central to the activities of the organization that it cannot be seen as a separate activity.

Where production can be separated from consumption—as is the case with most manufactured goods—management can usually take measures to reduce the direct effect of people on the final output as received by customers. In service industries, all employees are what Gummeson (1991) has called 'part time marketers' in that their actions have a much more direct effect on the output received by customers.

People planning in its widest sense has impacts on a firm's service offer in three main ways:

- Most service production processes require the service organization's own person-nel to provide significant inputs to the service production process, both at the front-line point of delivery and in those parts of the production process which are relatively removed from the final consumer. In the case of many one-to-one personal services, the service provider's own personnel constitute by far the most important element of the total service offering.

- Many service processes require the active involvement of consumers of the service and consumers therefore become involved as a co-producer of the service. At its simplest, this can involve the consumer in merely presenting themselves or their objects to the service provider in order for the service to be provided—for example, a customer might deliver their car to the garage rather than have it collected by the garage. In the case of services performed on the body or mind, the consumer must necessarily be designed into the production process.

- Other people who simultaneously consume a mass produced service can affect the benefits which an individual receives from the service in a number of ways. Firstly, the characteristics of other users of a service can affect the image of the service, in much the same way as owners of certain brands of goods can lend them some degree of 'snob' appeal. In this way, a nightclub can build up an exclusive image on account of the high spending, high profile users who patronize it. Secondly, the presence of other consumers in the service production-delivery process means that the final quality of the service which any customer receives is dependent on the performance of other consumers. They in effect become co-producers of the service offering. Often fellow consumers have an important role to play in enhancing the quality of the service offering, as where a full house in a theatre creates an ambience for all customers to enjoy. On other occasions, fellow consumers can contribute negatively to the service production process, as where rowdy behaviour in a pub or smoking in a restaurant detracts from the enjoyment of an event for other customers.

We're not the
best airline
because of our awards.
We're the best
airline because of
our people.

Thanks to everyone who
works for British Airways,
we've been voted 'Best
Airline of the Year' for the
10th year running by
the readers of Business
Traveller Magazine.

BRITISH AIRWAYS
The world's favourite airline

Figure 22.5 In this advertisement, British Airways stresses the importance of the 'people' element of its marketing mix in giving it a competitive advantage. (Reproduced with permission of British Airways plc)

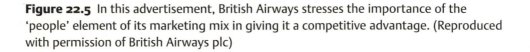

Processes

Production processes are usually of little concern to consumers of manufactured goods, but can be of critical concern to consumers of 'high contact' services where the consumer can be seen as a co-producer of the service. A customer of a restaurant is deeply affected by the manner in which staff serve them and the amount of waiting which is involved during the production process. Issues arise as to the boundary between the producer and consumer in terms of the allocation of production functions—for example, a restaurant might require a customer to collect their meal from a counter, or to deposit their own rubbish. With services, a clear distinction cannot be made between marketing and operations management.

A lot of attention has gone into the study of 'service encounters', defined by Shostack (1985) as 'a period of time during which a consumer directly interacts with a service'. Among the multiplicity of service encounters, some will be crucial to successful completion of the service delivery process. These are often referred to as critical incidents and have been defined by Bitner, Booms, and Tetreault (1990) as ' . . . specific interactions between customers and service firm employees that are especially satisfying or especially dissatisfying'. While their definition focuses on the role of personnel in critical incidents, they can arise also as a result of interaction with the service provider's equipment.

Where service production processes are complex and involve multiple service encounters, it is important for an organization to gain a holistic view of how the elements of the service relate to each other. 'Blueprinting' is a graphical approach proposed by Shostack (1984), designed to overcome problems which occur where a new service is launched without adequate identification of the necessary support functions. A customer blueprint has three main elements:

- All of the principal functions required to make and distribute a service are identified, along with the responsible company unit or personnel.
- Timing and sequencing relationships among the functions are depicted graphically.
- For each function, acceptable tolerances are identified in terms of the variation from standard which can be tolerated without adversely affecting customers' perception of quality.

Services are, in general, very labour intensive and have not witnessed the major productivity increases seen in many manufacturing industries. Sometimes, service processes have been 'industrialized' and deskilled by simplifying employees' tasks and reducing their scope for judgement and error.

As real labour costs have increased and service markets become more competitive, many service organizations have sought to pass on a greater part of the production process to their customers in order to try to retain price competitiveness. At first, customers' expectations may hinder this process, but productivity savings often result from one segment taking on additional responsibilities in return for lower prices. This then becomes the norm for other follower segments. Examples where the boundary has been redefined to include greater production by the customer include supermarkets who have replaced checkout operators with customer-operated scanners and restaurants which replace waiter service with a self-service buffet.

While service production boundaries have generally been pushed out to involve consumers more fully in the production process, some services organizations have identified segments who are prepared to pay higher prices in order to relieve themselves of parts of their co-production responsibilities. Examples include car repairers who collect and deliver cars to the owner's home and fast food firms who avoid the need for customers to come to their outlet by offering a delivery service.

Physical evidence

The intangible nature of a service means that potential customers are unable to judge a service before it is consumed, increasing the riskiness inherent in a purchase decision. An important element of marketing planning is therefore to reduce this level of risk by offering tangible evidence of the promised service delivery. This evidence can take a number of forms. At its simplest, a brochure can describe and give pictures of important elements of the service product—a holiday brochure gives pictorial evidence of hotels and resorts for this purpose. The appearance of staff can give evidence about the nature of a service—a tidily dressed ticket clerk for an airline gives some evidence that the airline operation as a whole is run with care and attention. Buildings are frequently used to give evidence of service characteristics. Fast food and photo processing outlets often use red and yellow colour schemes to convey an image of speedy service.

Chapter summary and key linkages to other chapters

The services sector is now a dominant part of the economies of most developed countries. However, defining just what is meant by a service has caused some debate and this chapter has reviewed some of the bases for classifying services into categories that are useful for the purposes of marketing management. Pure services are distinguished by the characteristics of intangibility, inseparability, perishability, variability, and a lack of ownership. Increasingly, however, goods and services are converging in terms of these characteristics. Few products can be described as pure goods or pure services—most are a combination of the two. There has been considerable debate about whether a new set of principles of marketing is required to understand services, or whether the established basic principles merely need adapting to the needs of services. The traditional marketing mix of the 4Ps has been found to be inadequate for managers in the services sector and this chapter has discussed an alternative extended marketing mix of 7Ps which recognizes the distinctive characteristics of services.

The following linkages to other chapters should be noted:

Chapter 1: What is marketing?: Even for goods manufacturers, providing added services can be crucial to meeting customers' needs.

Chapter 2: The marketing environment: Changes in the economic, social, and technological environments have contributed to a growth in the services sector. As countries get stronger, their service sectors tend to grow.

Chapter 3: Market segmentation: Services industries are becoming increasingly sophisticated in the methods used to segment markets. Because services are personal to individuals, segmentation methods can be more specifically targeted.

Chapter 4: Branding: Service purchases can be potentially very risky, and a strong brand is used by services organizations as a method of reducing buyers' perceived risk.

Chapter 5: Marketing and ethics: Most concern about ethics has focused on manufacturing industries, but there have now been many cases of consumer action against bad practice by services companies.

Chapter 6: Marketing research: Successful services companies have effective systems for collecting, analysing, disseminating, and acting on information, for planning and control purposes. Employees play an important role in information gathering within services companies because they are close to customers.

Chapter 7: Buyer behaviour: Because intangible services cannot be inspected before consumption, purchases are inherently more risky than for manufactured goods. Buying processes may therefore rely heavily on word-of-mouth recommendation and seek to minimize exposure to risk.

Chapter 8: Buyer–seller relationship development: For manufacturers and services companies alike, providing an ongoing relationship is often seen as an added service feature that differentiates one company's product offer from its competitors'.

Chapter 9: Developing a product portfolio: It is now common to talk about services as 'products', although their intangibility and inseparability have implications for the analysis of the product offer.

Chapter 10: Innovation and new product development: Most new services are modifications of existing services. The inseparability of services results in front-line employees being important sources of ideas for new service development.

Chapter 11: Developing a sustainable competitive advantage: For many companies, the quality of service is an important differentiating feature that gives a competitive advantage. However, customers' expectations rise and the quality of service must rise in line with these expectations.

Chapters 12/13: Pricing theory and application: The inseparable nature of services can make price discrimination more effective than for goods. The lack of physical evidence means that price may be perceived as an important indicator of quality. Many public services are provided at no price or a price that does not reflect market forces.

Chapter 14: Intermediaries: Services cannot be handled through a channel of distribution in the conventional sense. Because of their inseparability, intermediaries become involved as co-producers of a service.

Chapter 15: Logistics: Pure services do not require any physical distribution effort, but most services in fact have associated tangibles which must be distributed effectively and efficiently.

Chapters 16–20: Principles of promotion planning/advertising/ sales promotion/personal selling/direct marketing: Promotion should seek to reduce the perceived riskiness of many services purchases. An extended marketing mix for services incorporates the promotional role of front-line employees and service outlets.

Chapter 21: Managing the marketing effort: In services marketing, the need to integrate marketing, human resource management, and operations management is particularly important.

Chapter 23: Global marketing: The tasks of marketing services in overseas markets are in principle similar to those in the domestic market. However, risks are likely to be greater in view of the uncertainty of the overseas business environment.

Case study

Ford cars go in for a service

To many people, cars come pretty close to the goods-dominant extreme of a goods–services continuum. They are produced in factories from the combination of thousands of components, and to most people the physical properties of a car can readily be assessed. But recent experience from the car sector suggests that car manufacturers may be rather more enthusiastic to describe themselves as service-oriented companies.

The days are long gone when a car manufacturer would sell a car on the strength of its design features, and then forget about the customer until the time came to replace the car three years later. Car manufacturers realized that car buyers sought more than the tangible offering—important though that was. Over time, they have moved increasingly into the services sector in an attempt to gain a larger share of car buyers' wallets.

In the UK, Ford has led the way in many aspects of this increasing service orientation. It saw an opportunity in the 1970s with the liberalization of consumer credit regulations to offer car buyers loan facilities with which to make their car purchase. Not only did this make it easier for middle-income groups to buy its cars, it also allowed Ford to retain the margins which would otherwise have gone to banks who were the main alternative source of car loan finance. Ford Motor Credit has become a licensed credit broker and a major profit centre within the company.

The next major attempt to gain a greater share of car buyers' wallets came through offering extended warranties on the cars it sold. Traditionally, new cars had come with just twelve months warranty, but Ford realized that many buyers wanted to buy peace of mind that they were not going to face unexpected repair bills after their initial warranty had expired. Increased competition from Japanese importers, and the improving reliability of its new cars encouraged this development.

By the mid-1990s, Ford came round to the view that many of its customers were buying transport solutions, rather than a car *per se*. So it came up with schemes where customers paid a small deposit, followed by a fixed amount per month, in return for which they received comprehensive finance and warranty facilities. In addition, it promised that the company would take back the car after three years and replace it with a new one. Marketed under the 'Options' brand name, Ford was soon selling nearly half of its new cars to private buyers using this method. Over time the scheme was developed to include facilities for maintaining and insuring the car.

Repairs and maintenance have always been important in the car sector, but manufacturers tended to lose out on much of the benefits of this to a fragmented dealership network. Separate customer databases for maintenance and new car sales often did not meet and Ford found that it had very little direct communication with the people who bought its cars. By the 1990s, the dealership network was becoming more closely integrated with Ford's operations and new opportunities were seized for keeping new car buyers within the system. Recent buyers could be alerted to new services available at local dealers, using a database managed centrally by Ford. Numerous initiatives were launched, such as Ford's own mobile phone service. Ford sought to make it easy for customers to get back on the road when their own car was taken in for servicing, so the provision of car hire facilities contributed to the service ethos. In 1996 the company linked up with Barclaycard to offer a Ford branded credit card, so Ford found itself providing a service to its customers which was quite removed from the tangible cars that it sold (although points accrued using the card could be used to reduce the price of a new Ford car).

By 2000, volume car manufacturers had ceased to make big profits in the UK. Ford, with 18 per cent of the market in 1998 lost money on its European operations. Falling profit margins on selling new cars were partly offset by profits made on service-based activities. For the future, Ford is increasingly positioning itself as a service provider offering transport solutions. In 1998 it sought to acquire the RAC's breakdown service operation when it came up for sale. It lost out on that occasion to Lex Services, but later went on to acquire Kwik Fit, a leading UK car servicing and repair business, which had itself expanded into the car insurance market.

Case study review questions

1 Given the evidence of Ford, is it still appropriate to talk about the goods and services sectors being quite distinctive?

2 What business is Ford in? What business should it be in?

3 Discuss the view that Ford should do what it is good at—designing cars—and leave services to other companies.

Chapter review questions

1 With the service sector now accounting for over three-quarters of GDP in western countries, is it still sensible to talk about services as a special case of marketing, rather than treating goods as the special case?

2 Critically assess the effects of service inseparability on marketing management.

3 How can you explain the fact that some countries (e.g. the USA) seem to be particularly good at producing services, whereas others with a similar level of education and GDP (e.g. Germany) are viewed as relatively inferior. Does national culture affect the performance of services organizations?

4 Many in the UK have associated service with servitude. Is there any continuing basis for this description?

5 Critically examine the advantages and disadvantages to a company producing packaging machinery for the food industry of recruiting a marketing manager whose experience has been in service sector companies.

6 Discuss the view that the extended marketing mix of seven 'P's may go some way to overcome shortcomings of the traditional marketing mix, but is still unsuitable compared to a relational approach which starts from the needs of the customer, rather than the marketing agenda of the supplier.

References

Bitner, M. J., Booms, B. H., and Tetreault, M. S. (1990), 'The Service Encounter: Diagnosing Favorable and Unfavorable Incidents', *Journal of Marketing*, **54**, Jan., pp. 71–84.

Booms, B. H., and Bitner, M. J. (1981), 'Marketing Strategies and Organization Structures for Service Firms', in J. H. Donnelly and W. R. George (eds.), *Marketing of Services* (Chicago: American Marketing Association), pp. 51–67.

Eurostat (1995), *Europe in Figures* (Luxembourg: Office for Official Publications of the European Communities).

Gronroos, C. (1978), 'A Service Oriented Approach to Marketing of Services', *European Journal of Marketing*, **12**, 8, pp. 588–601.

Gummeson, E. (1991), 'Marketing-Orientation Revisited: The Crucial Role of the Part-time Marketer', *European Journal of Marketing*, **25**, 2, pp. 60–75.

Kotler, P., Armstrong, G., Saunders, J., and Wong, V. (1996), *Principles of Marketing*, European edn. (London: Prentice Hall).

Levitt, T. (1972), 'Production Line Approach to Service', *Harvard Business Review*, **50**, Sept.–Oct., pp. 41–52.

Lovelock, C. (1981), 'Why Marketing Needs to be Different for Services', in J. H. Donnelly and W. R. George (eds.), *Marketing of Services* (Chicago: American Marketing Association).

Sasser W. E., Olsen, R. P., and Wyckoff, D. D. (1978), *Management of Service Operations: Texts, Cases, Readings* (Boston: Allyn and Bacon).

Shostack, G. L. (1977), 'Breaking Free From Product Marketing', *Journal of Marketing*, **41**, pp. 73–80.

—— (1984), 'Designing Services that Deliver', Harvard Business Review, Jan.–Feb., pp. 133–9.

—— (1985), 'Planning the Service Encounter', in J. A. Czepiel, M. R. Solomon, and C. F. Suprenant (eds.), *The Service Encounter* (Lexington, Mass.: Lexington Books), pp. 243–54.

Smith, A. (1977), *The Wealth of Nations* (Harmondsworth: Penguin) [first published 1776].

Solomon, M. R., and Gould, S. J. (1991), 'Benefitting From Structural Similarities Among Personal Services', *Journal of Services Marketing*, **5**, 2, pp. 23–32.

Wind, Y. (1986), 'Models for Marketing Planning and Decision Making', in V. P. Buell (ed.), *Handbook of Modern Marketing*, 2nd edn. (New York: McGraw-Hill), pp. 49.1–49.12

Suggested further reading

There are now numerous texts which deal specifically with the marketing of services and the following are among recent works which provide a comprehensive coverage.

■ Hoffman, K. D., and Bateson, J. (1997), *Essentials of Services Marketing* (Fort Worth: Dryden Press).

■ Lovelock, C., Lewis, B., and Vandermerwe, S. (1999), *Services Marketing* (Hemel Hempstead: Prentice-Hall).

■ Mudie, P., and Cottam, A. (1994), *The Management and Marketing of Services* (London: Heinemann).

- Palmer, A. (1998), Principles of Services Marketing, 2nd edn. (Maidenhead: McGraw-Hill).

- Zeithamal, V., and Bitner, J. (1996), *Services Marketing* (New York: McGraw-Hill).

The literature on services marketing has grown significantly during the past couple of decades, reflecting the growing importance of the services sector. The following article discusses the development of the literature:

- Fisk, R. P., Brown, S. W., and Bitner, M. J. (1993), 'Tracking the Evolution of the Services Marketing Literature', *Journal of Retailing*, **69**, 1, pp. 61–103.

A number of articles appeared towards the end of the 1970s seeking to identify the nature of services and their distinctive marketing needs. The articles by Lovelock (1981); Sasser, Olsen, and Wyckoff (1978), and Shostack (1977) referred to above are worth revisiting. In addition, the following are still worth reading because they establish many of the basic principles of services marketing:

- Bateson, J. (1977), 'Do We Need Service Marketing?', in *Marketing Consumer Services: New Insights, Report 77–115* (Boston: Marketing Science Institute).

- Berry, L. L. (1980), 'Service Marketing is Different', *Business*, **30**, 3, pp. 24–29.

- Eiglier, P., and Langeard E. (1977), 'A New Approach To Service Marketing', in *Marketing Consumer Services: New Insights, Report 77–115* (Boston: Marketing Science Institute).

- Levitt, T. (1981), 'Marketing Intangible Products and Product Intangibles', *Harvard Business Review*, **59**, pp. 95–102.

- Zeithamal, V. A. (1981), 'How Consumers Evaluation Processes Differ Between Goods and Services', in J. H. Donnelly and W. R. George (eds.), *Marketing of Services* (Chicago: American Marketing Association), pp. 186–90.

For a good selection of classic articles covering the breadth of services marketing issues, the following readers are useful:

- Carson, D., and Gilmore, A. (1997), *Services Marketing: Text and London Readings* (London: Paul Chapman).

- Gabbott, M., and Hogg, G. (1997), *Contemporary Services Marketing Management: A Reader* (London: Dryden Press).

Useful web link

A forum to discuss research, trends, and best practices for excellence in customer service. List members are encouraged to discuss practical business issues as well as academic research: http://www.mailbase.ac.uk/lists/customer-service/

Chapter 23
Global Marketing

Chapter Objectives

Markets are becoming increasingly global and the aim of this chapter is to understand the main challenges facing a company setting out to develop foreign markets. The chapter begins by discussing in general terms the reasons why international trade takes place. For a company that has decided to expand overseas, careful market analysis is necessary to avoid failure. A product may need to be adapted to suit the needs of a local market. Distribution is crucial and this chapter discusses alternative approaches to gaining access to customers in foreign markets.

Introduction

FEW firms can afford to think of their markets purely in terms of their domestic market. To survive and prosper, they must increasingly look to the world as their market. Foreign countries pose opportunities as well as threats. The opportunities for a firm come from being able to sell its products in a market where it may have a competitive advantage relative to domestic producers. The problems arise where those foreign producers themselves possess competitive advantages which challenge a firm in its own domestic market.

The global marketing environment is changing rapidly and understanding that environment calls for a great amount of research. The impact of improving international communications and cultural convergence are just two dynamic factors at work to shape the global marketing environment. A failure to understand these dynamic forces has resulted in many failures by companies seeking to exploit foreign markets, including the following examples:

- British Airways failed in its attempts to enter the North American market through its investment in the ailing airline USAir. BA had difficulties in overcoming trade union objections to changes in working practices among other things, which led the company eventually to pull out of its involvement with USAir.

- The UK retailer Sock Shop expanded rapidly in the USA during the 1980s, but its failure to appreciate the tough operating environment was a contributory factor to the company's financial failure.

- Even the fast food retailer McDonald's initially failed to make profits when it entered the UK market in the 1970s and had to adjust its format rapidly in order to achieve profitability.

For firms that persevere, the benefits of developing international markets can be quite significant to a company's overall profitability. Consider the following cases:

- Although McDonald's may have had difficulties in the early stages of developing many of its foreign markets, they now account for the bulk of the company's sales turnover and profits. Had it confined itself to its domestic American market, saturation and increased levels of competition within that market would have severely limited its future profit growth.

- The German yoghurt brand Müller was little known in the UK a decade ago, but by successfully exploiting a market niche and rapidly developing its product portfolio, it has become a leading yoghurt brand in the UK.

- The retailer Marks & Spencer has reduced its dependence on the UK market by expansion throughout Europe, North America, and the Far East. The company has used a combination of direct investment and franchising, and with the exception of a few local difficulties has been successful. In developing foreign branches the company has been careful to adapt its format, so in Indonesia, for example, it has developed an exclusive, small shop format.

Fundamentally, the task of marketing management in foreign markets is similar to the task in domestic markets. Customers' needs remain the driving force of marketing efforts and a company promotes the benefits to customers of buying its products, which are produced as efficiently as possible, distributed through the most appropriate channels, and priced according to local market conditions. The major challenge to exporting companies lies in sensitively adapting marketing strategies which have worked at home to the needs of foreign markets whose environments may be totally different from anything previously experienced. 'Global strength and local adaptability' form the basis of many firms' mission statement in relation to foreign markets.

This chapter begins by exploring the reasons why firms should seek to develop foreign markets in the first place. Once a firm has decided to operate at an international rather than a local level, it must go about assessing possible markets, and the bases for such assessments are discussed. If it decides to enter a market, a firm must consider how its product offer might need to be adapted to meet local sensitivities. Most firms enter international markets with the help of partners of some kind, and this chapter concludes with a discussion of market entry strategies.

Why export?

THERE is clear evidence that the volume and value of international trade has been rising significantly in recent years. Taking the UK as an example, the percentage of GDP accounted for by exports increased to 6.3 per cent in 1996–7 from 5.9 per cent in 1995–6. This growth can be understood from two perspectives: from the perspective of national economies, and from that of individual trading organizations.

From the perspective of national economies, there are many reasons for the increasing importance of international trade:

■ Goods and services are traded between economies in order to exploit comparative cost advantages. This means that an economy will export those goods and services that it is particularly well suited to producing, and import those where another country has an advantage. A simple example can illustrate this point. Imagine two countries, country A which had ideal conditions for mining of minerals but a climate that is inhospitable to agriculture, and country B that is ideally suited for agriculture, but has mineral resources which are expensive to exploit. It would make little economic sense for country A to try to develop its agricultural sector when its output would be much more expensive than buying from country B. Likewise, it may be uneconomic for country B to develop its mining industry. In both cases, it would almost certainly be better for each country to concentrate on what it is good at producing, and export the surplus in exchange for goods and services which other countries can produce more cost effectively.

■ Although the theory of comparative cost advantage sounds fine in principle, many countries try to protect their own industries against foreign competition, however inefficient they are, with tariff barriers. The removal of many restrictions on international trade (such as the creation of the Single European Market) has allowed countries to exploit their comparative cost advantages. Nevertheless, many distortions to international trade remain, especially those affecting agricultural products.

■ Rising disposable incomes have resulted in greater consumption of many types of goods and services which can only be provided by foreign suppliers, for example foreign tourism and the consumption of exotic fruit and vegetables (although, on the other hand, many developing economies which previously imported specialist goods and services can now produce these items domestically).

■ Homogenization of international market segments has resulted from cultural convergence, which itself has been encouraged by improved communications and increasing levels of overseas travel. Combined with the decline in trade barriers, convergence of cultural attitudes towards many products has allowed many companies to regard parts of their foreign markets as though they are part of their domestic market.

For an individual company, development of foreign markets can be attractive for a number of reasons. These can be analysed in terms of 'pull' factors, based on the attractiveness of a potential foreign market and 'push' factors which make an organization's domestic market appear less attractive.

- Foreign markets represent new market segments which a firm may be able to serve with its existing range of products. In this way, a company can stick to making products that it is good at.

- By expanding overseas, a company that has developed a strong brand can stretch the coverage of that brand. By developing in a foreign market, the company will start with the advantage that some visitors from its domestic market will already understand what the brand stands for. Similarly, for residents of the new market, many may have already become familiar with the brand during visits to the manufacturer's home market. In short, there are economies of scale in promoting a brand in multiple markets simultaneously.

- Saturation of its domestic market can force a company to seek foreign markets. Saturation can come about where a product reaches the maturity stage of its life cycle in the domestic market, while being at a much earlier stage of the cycle in less developed foreign markets. As an example of this, the market for fast food restaurants is approaching saturation in a number of western markets—especially the USA—but fast food represents a new opportunity in the early stages of development in many eastern European countries.

- Spreading risk is an important motivation for foreign expansion, and can allow a company to reduce its dependence on one geographical market.

- The nature of a product may require an organization to become active in a foreign market. In the case of scheduled international air services, an airline flying an overseas route will inevitably become involved in marketing at the foreign end of its routes.

- Some companies supply goods and services to business buyers who themselves operate internationally. Such large customers may demand that one single supplier is able to meet their needs in all of the international markets in which they operate. This means that a supplying company has to become involved in international trade. As an example, many multinational businesses seek to engage an advertising agency that can organize a global campaign to implement in all of their markets.

- There are also many cases where private consumers demand that goods and services are internationally available. An example is the car hire business where customers often need to be able to book a hire car in one country for collection and use in another. To succeed in attracting these customers, car hire companies need to operate internationally.

- Some products are highly specialized and the domestic market is too small to allow economies of scale to be exploited. Foreign markets must be exploited in order to achieve a critical mass which allows a competitive market positioning. Aircraft engine maintenance and oil exploration services fall into this category.

- A company may have developed a product that is not suited to its domestic market, and therefore exporting is the only option for exploiting the product. As an example, domestic legislation may make the market for drugs, alcohol, or tobacco related products less attractive than foreign markets where more liberal legislation exists.

A note on exporting of services

Export of manufactured goods can be represented by stocks of goods moving in one direction, and payment (in cash or in goods) in the other. However, the intangible nature of most services gives a different meaning to the export of services. Any analysis of international trade in services is complicated by the diverse nature of producer–supplier interaction, stemming from the inseparability of service production/consumption processes.

International trade statistics for services hide the fact that trade can take a number of forms. Sometimes, credits (or 'exports') are earned by customers from overseas travelling to an organization's domestic market in order to consume a service (e.g. a foreign patient visiting a doctor in the UK). On other occasions, credits are earned by domestic producers taking their production processes to customers in foreign markets (e.g. a builder travelling to do a job in a foreign country). Sometimes, production and consumption of services can be separated, as in the case of electronic information services, avoiding the need for buyer and seller to meet in order for international trade to occur.

Analysing foreign marketing opportunities

FOREIGN markets can present very different opportunities and threats compared to those which a company has been used to in its domestic market. Before a detailed market analysis is undertaken, a company should consider in general terms whether the environment of a market is likely to be attractive. By considering in general terms such matters as political stability or cultural attitudes, the company may screen out potential markets for which it considers further analysis cannot be justified by the likelihood of success.

The PEST framework is useful for analysing foreign marketing opportunities.

Political factors

Government and quasi-government organizations influence the legislative and economic frameworks within which organizations trade.

At a national level, individual governments can influence marketing opportunities in a country in a number of ways:

- Unstable political systems are often very unattractive to companies considering foreign expansion. For example, the instability of many eastern European governments has posed unacceptable risks for firms considering committing resources to a market.
- Regulations governing product standards may require an exporter to reconfigure its products expensively for a foreign market. Sometimes this may be done covertly to protect domestic producers.
- Legislation may be used by governments to try to protect domestic producers against foreign competition. Sometimes, governments impose import controls or simply make the task of getting clearance for imports very difficult.
- Where a company is planning to set up a production facility overseas, legislation on health and safety standards as well as minimum wages and welfare provision may add to a firm's costs.
- Restrictions on currency movements may make it difficult to repatriate profits earned from a foreign operation.
- Legislation protecting trade marks varies between companies—in some countries, such as Thailand, trade mark owners may find it very hard to protect itself legally from imitators.

Exporters also need to consider the political significance of regional trading blocs. The European Union (EU) is an example of a trading bloc which seeks to create favourable trading conditions for companies located within the bloc regardless of the existence of national borders within the bloc. For companies seeking to develop within one of those countries, the creation of trading blocs creates problems and opportunities. The problems occasionally arise where tariffs or other restrictions are placed on goods and services imported from outside the bloc. The biggest opportunity is that once an exporter is inside one member country, the process of expansion to other bloc member counties can be made very much easier through the harmonization of standards and dismantling of internal borders. Within the EU, monetary union has also reduced obstacles to international trade posed by the volatility in exchange rates, alleviating the problem of fluctuating exchange rates. These make it difficult for sellers to predict the value of their future foreign sales in terms of their own domestic currency.

The development of the EU has been paralleled by the development of a number of other regional trading blocs, most notably the ASEAN group of South-East Asian countries and the NAFTA grouping of the USA, Canada, and Mexico.

There have been many attempts to liberalize world trade. Members of the World Trade Organization seek greater international economic prosperity by exploiting fully the comparative cost advantages of nations by reducing the barriers which inhibit international trade. Members agree not to increase tariffs or quotas on imports, except in permitted circumstances.

Economic factors

All other things being equal, an exporter would target prosperous foreign markets. A generally accepted measure of the economic attractiveness of a foreign market is the level of GDP per capita. The demand for most goods and services increases as this figure increases (Fig. 23.1). However, intending exporters should also consider the distribution of income within a country which may identify valuable niche markets. As an example, Indonesia has a relatively low GDP per head, but this still allows for a small but wealthy segment of society which has the desire and ability to pay for luxury western goods.

An exporter should not only consider economic prosperity as it is today, but how it is likely to develop in the future. While the market for some goods and services in the West may be saturated, they may be at the start of a growth phase in less developed economies. The level of competitive pressure within the economy must also be considered, again, not just as it is now, but how it is likely to be in the future.

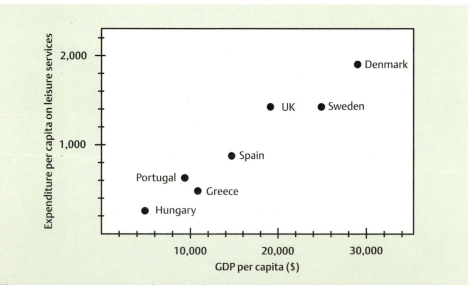

Figure 23.1 A comparison of GDP per head and consumption of leisure services (based on National Statistical Offices/Keynote data for 1997 or nearest available year)

The chairman of Bata, the shoe manufacturer, is famously quoted for his analysis of a foreign market for his firm's shoes. Two people were dispatched to a potential market in Africa and noticed that very few people were wearing shoes. 'No hope here—the people don't wear shoes' was the response of one. But the other saw it quite differently 'What an opportunity—just think what this market will be worth when these people start wearing shoes!'

Social factors

An understanding of a society's cultural values is crucial for an exporter. Individuals from different cultures not only buy different products, but may also respond in different ways to the same product. Examples of differing cultural attitudes and their effects on international trade include the following:

- Some goods and services may be rendered obsolete by different types of social structure. As an example, extended family structures common in some countries have the ability to produce a wide range of services within the family unit, including caring for children and elderly members.
- A product that is taken for granted in the domestic market may be seen as socially unacceptable in a foreign market.
- Buying processes vary between different cultures—for example, the role of women in shopping for certain types of products may differ in foreign markets compared to the domestic market.

It is also important to consider the demographic structure of a foreign market.

Within the EU countries, the total population in recent times has increased at a natural rate of about 1.0 per 1,000 population (that is, for every 1,000 deaths, there are 1,001 births). However, this hides a range of rates of increase, with, at each extreme, Ireland having a particularly high birth rate and Germany a particularly low one. Much faster population growth has occurred outside Europe. Between 1960 and 1994, the population of Africa rose by 150 per cent and Latin America by 100 per cent, compared to just 17 per cent in EU countries. More importantly, these trends seem set to continue.

Within the population total for any country, structures can differ significantly. To illustrate this, there are significant differences within the EU in the proportion of the population which is either young or elderly, with implications for the demand for age-related products. As an example, Ireland has a very low proportion of the population aged 60 and above, but a very high proportion aged under 20. This situation is reversed in Germany.

Technological factors

An analysis of the technological environment of potential foreign markets is important for companies who require the use of a well-developed technical infrastructure. Communications are an important element of the technological infrastructure. Poorly developed telephone and postal communications may, for example, inhibit attempts to respond rapidly to customers' requests. Where there is only a low level of skills among the population, the ability to produce goods and services in the local market, or to offer back-up support, may be limited.

A more detailed analysis of potential markets

A ROUGH environmental analysis along the lines discussed above would have reduced the number of possible foreign markets. At this stage, the method of analysis is very qualitative and is often based on the 'gut feeling' of a company's senior management. Very often, the list of potential markets is reduced through idiosyncratic factors, such as personal links between senior management and their friends and family in a country. Senior management have been known to target a market for apparently selfish reasons, such as the opportunity to get away to enjoy good golf courses. Where the business potential of potential markets is otherwise fairly indistinguishable, such personal factors may sway the final choice. However, if they are a starting-point for a decision, without being based on an underlying business assessment, a foreign venture could be doomed.

Once a company has developed a shortlist of foreign markets, it can set about the task of collecting more detailed information about it. The methods used to research a potential foreign market are in principle similar to those used to research the domestic market. Research would normally begin by using secondary data about the potential foreign market which are available at home. Sources which are readily available through specialized libraries, government organizations, and specialist research organizations include Department of Trade and Industry information for exporters, reports of international agencies such as the Organization for Economic Cooperation and Development (OECD), Chambers of Commerce, and private sources of information such as that provided by banks. Details of some specific sources are shown in Fig. 23.2.

Secondary research at home will often be followed up with further desk research of materials available locally within the shortlisted markets. This is most likely to be carried out be appointing a local research agency. Their brief may include a review of reports published by the target market's own government and specialist locally based market research agencies.

Secondary data have their limitations in assessing the attractiveness of a foreign market. Problems are compounded by the greater difficulty in gaining access to data, possible language differences, and problems of definition.

Primary research would be undertaken in a foreign market when a company has become happy about the general potential of a market, but is unsure about a number of issues which would be critical for success. These might include whether inter-mediaries would be willing and able to handle their product, or whether traditional cultural attitudes will prevent widespread adoption of it. Prior to commissioning its own specific research, a company may go for the lower cost, but less specific route of undertaking research through an omnibus survey. These are surveys regularly

Government agencies
    Department of Trade and Industry market reports
    Foreign governments—e.g. USA
      Department of Commerce
    Foreign national and local development agencies

International agencies
    European Community (Eurostat, etc.)
    Organization for Economic Co-operation and
      Development
(OECD)
    World Trade Organization
    United Nations
    World Bank
    International Monetary Fund
    World Health Organization

Research organizations
    Economist Intelligence Unit
    Dun and Bradstreet International
    Market research firms

Publications
    Financial Times country surveys
    Business International
    International Trade Reporter
    Banks' export reviews

Trade associations
    Chambers of trade and commerce
    Industry specific associations

Figure 23.2 Sources of secondary information on foreign markets

undertaken among a panel of consumers in foreign markets (e.g. the Gallup European Omnibus) which carry questions on behalf of a number of sponsors.

A local agency would better understand attitudes towards privacy and the level of literacy that might affect response rates for different forms of research. Language barriers would be reduced, but not eliminated, as the problem of comparability between markets remains. For example, when an American respondent claims to 'really like' a product, the meaning may be comparable to a German consumer who claims to 'quite like' the product. It would be wrong to assume on the basis of this research that the product is better liked by American than German consumers.

Adapting the product offer to foreign markets

'GLOBAL strength and local adaptability' are the stated aims of many successful companies that operate in international markets. But how can such local adaptability be achieved? And how can a company ensure that the benefits of economies of scale which derive from global size are not undermined by the cost of adapting to each individual market? Too many companies have failed overseas because they did not fully take into account local sensitivities to their products. For example, attitudes towards promotional programmes differ between cultures. The choice of colours in advertising or sales outlets needs to be made with care because of symbolic associations (e.g. the colour associated with mourning/bereavement varies across cultures). Also, what is considered to be an acceptable method of procuring a sale varies between cultures. In Middle Eastern markets, for example, a bribe to a public official may be considered essential, whereas it is unacceptable in most western countries.

A crucial task of overseas marketing management is the design of a marketing programme which is sensitive to local needs. The following sections examine the extent to which adaptation of the marketing mix to local needs is either desirable or possible. In particular, should a company seek to develop one globally uniform product offer, or make it different in each of the foreign markets which it serves? Sometimes, a company may simply change the promotion of its product, while keeping the product itself the same in all markets. Five types of strategy can be identified, based on the extent to which product and promotion decisions vary from the global norm:

Maintain a uniform product and promotion worldwide

This approach develops a global marketing strategy as though the world was a single market. The benefits of this approach are numerous. Customers travelling from one market to another can immediately recognize a brand and the values which it stands for. If, on the other hand, the product was different in a foreign market, a traveller purchasing a brand overseas may come away confused about the qualities of the brand. If Coca-Cola tasted too different in foreign countries, could this detract from an individual's perceived value of the brand when they get back home?

Product standardization can also yield benefits of economies of scale. As well as lowering the unit costs of production, economies can extend to the collection of market research, the design of buildings and uniforms, etc. The use of a common brand name in foreign markets also benefits from economies of scale. Travellers to foreign markets will already be familiar with the brand's values as a result of promotion in the domestic market. However, care must be taken in selecting a brand name which will have no unfortunate connotations in foreign markets. There are many legendary cases of brand names which have not worked in foreign markets, for example Opel's Corsa car translated into 'won't go' in Spain and many English speaking people are left wondering about the likely taste of 'Bum' crisps or 'Pschitt' soft drinks. There can also be problems where legislation prevents an international slogan being used. In Quebec, for example, companies have been fined for using standard Anglicized advertising material without changing it to French as required by the Province's legislation.

Retain a uniform service formulation, but adapt promotion

This strategy produces an essentially uniform global product, but adapts the promotional programme to local markets. The manner in which brand values are communicated in advertisements is a reflection of the cultural values of a society. For this reason, a snack foods manufacturer may use a straightforward, brash hard sell approach in its American market, a humorous approach in its British market, and a seductive approach in its French market, even though the product offer is essentially identical in each market. Some images and symbols used to promote a product in the domestic market might fail in a foreign market. Animals, which are often used in Britain to promote a range of home-based goods and services present a caring and comfortable image, but in some markets such as Japan, animals are seen as unclean, disgusting objects.

How do you promote the image of a holiday destination in foreign markets? The destination itself cannot be adapted to suit the needs of individual markets. The Tower of London will always be the same for tourists whether they are from Manchester, Madras, or Melbourne. But the promotional message can be fine-tuned to stress the aspects on which different markets place high value. Take the case of the Brand Ireland campaign, a joint effort by the Northern Ireland Tourist Board and Bord Failte to increase the number of visitors to Ireland, north and south. A thirty-second television commercial was recut several times, with the German cut stressing the wild, rugged nature of the country, the Italian cut stressing the romance of the island, the American cut stressing its history, and the English cut stressing that Ireland is so close, but so different. The strap line 'Live a different life' worked well in most markets, but had to be changed in the USA where it had unfortunate associations with cross-dressing.

Adapt the product offer only

This may be done in order to meet specific local needs or legislation, while retaining the benefits of a global image. For example, flavourings and colourings used in some confectionery may be illegal in some foreign markets, requiring reformulation of the product.

Adapt both product and promotion

In practice, most companies undertake a combination of product and promotion modification in order to meet local market needs, while still trying to stay true to their global brand values and worldwide economies of scale.

Develop new products

Sometimes, markets emerge for which a company has no product offering which can be easily adapted. In order to gain access to a foreign market, it may be necessary to develop new products. This option compounds the risk of a new market with the risk of a new product.

Pricing in foreign markets

THE issue of whether to globalize or adapt to local conditions arises again in respect of pricing decisions. On the one hand, it might be appealing to customers if a company offered a standard charge for a product regardless of where in the world it is purchased. This way, customers will immediately have an idea of how much a product will cost and this helps to develop a long-term relationship between the company and its customers. However, the reality is that a variety of factors cause global companies to charge different prices in the different markets in which they operate. There are many reasons why pricing should differ between foreign markets:

- A brand which is highly valued at home may be unheard of in a foreign market, and therefore unable to command its accustomed price premium.

- Competitive pressure varies between markets, reflecting the stage of market development that a product has reached and the impact of regulations against anti-competitive practices.

- Where it is difficult to make a product at home and export it to the foreign market, a company will face cost levels which may be significantly different compared with the domestic market. For services which use people-intensive production methods, and which cannot be 'exported' from a company's domestic base, variations in wage levels between countries will have a significant effect on total costs, and hence influence pricing. Personnel costs may also be affected by differences in welfare provisions which employers are required to pay for. Other significant cost elements which often vary between markets include the level of property prices or rental costs.

- Taxes vary between different markets—for example, the rate of value added tax (or its equivalent sales tax) can be as high as 38 per cent in Italy compared to $17\frac{1}{2}$ per cent in the UK. There are also differences between markets in the manner in which sales taxes are expressed. In many markets, taxes are fully incorporated into price schedules, although on other occasions (such as in the USA) it is more usual to price a service exclusive of taxes.

- Local customs influence customers' expectations of the way in which a product is priced. While customers in the domestic market might expect to pay for bundles of products, in a foreign market consumers might expect to pay a separate price for each component of the bundle, or vice versa. It has been noted, for example, that UK car buyers prefer to pay an all-inclusive price for new cars, while buyers in continental Europe prefer a low base price, but to be able to add features to their own specification.

- Formal price lists for a product may be expected in some markets, but, in others, individual bartering may the norm. Having a published price list which it sticks to may put a firm at a competitive disadvantage.

■ Government regulations can limit price freedom in foreign markets. In addition to controls over prices charged by public utilities, many governments require 'fair' prices to be charged in a wide range of goods and services—e.g. tourism-related services—and for the prices charged to be clearly publicized.

If wide differences in the pre-tax price of goods emerge between countries, it is open to entrepreneurs to buy goods in the lower priced market and sell them in the higher priced market. The 'grey' market in perfume imported from the Far East to western Europe is evidence of this. Because of their inseparability, it is much more difficult, or impossible, to transfer a service from a low priced market to a high priced one.

Distributing goods and services in foreign markets

GETTING distribution strategy right is crucial to success in foreign markets. The cost of making goods and services readily available to consumers can be quite daunting and, for this reason, many exporters choose to go into partnership with companies who are already established in a market. The whole issue of market entry strategy is considered in more detail later in this chapter. Many exporters have failed because they did not fully think through the costs and barriers of getting their products to the final consumer.

Although the principles of distribution planning are similar in foreign markets as for the domestic market, the following potential differences should be noted and accommodated:

■ Consumer behaviour may differ significantly in foreign markets. What is a widely accepted outlet in one country may be regarded with suspicion in another. For example, buying cosmetics in a supermarket is now accepted as normal in the UK, but may meet resistance in some countries.

■ Consumers vary in the extent to which they are prepared to travel to obtain a product. In less developed economies where transport and refrigeration equipment are less readily available, consumers may seek very local access to intermediaries to replenish their stocks of perishable products. In car-based economies such as the USA, intermediaries may be selected by consumers on the basis of their range of choice and easy access by car.

■ Differences in the social, economic, and technical environments of a market can result in the existence of different patterns of intermediaries. As an example, the interrelatedness of wholesalers and retailers in Japan can make it much more difficult for a foreign retailer to get into that market compared to other foreign opportunities. In some markets, there may be no direct equivalent of a type of intermediary found in the domestic market (e.g. estate agents on the UK model are often not available in many foreign markets).

- The law of a country can restrict the use of intermediaries which would be commonplace in the domestic market. Governments of many countries restrict the sale of alcohol, financial services, and gambling services—among others—to a much narrower set of possible intermediaries than is the case in the domestic market.

People decisions

SHOULD a company employ local or expatriate staff? The latter may be preferable where a company is providing a highly specialized product and may be useful in adding to the global uniformity of the product offer. In some service industries, the presence of front-line expatriate serving staff can add to the appeal of a service, for example a chain of traditional Irish pubs established in mainland Europe may add to their appeal by employing authentic Irish staff.

For relatively straightforward goods and services, a large proportion of staff is likely to be recruited locally, leaving just senior management posts filled by expatriates. Sometimes, an extensive staff development programme may be required to ensure that locally recruited staff perform in a manner which is consistent with the company's global image. This can often be quite a difficult task. A company moving into a previously centrally planned economy may have difficulty developing values of customer focus among staff who have been accustomed to taking instructions from above.

Market entry strategies

ALTHOUGH new foreign markets provide a company with opportunities, they can also present high levels of risk. A company's market entry strategy should aim to balance the opportunities with the risks involved.

The main issues here are:

- how rapidly should a company commit itself to a foreign market?
- who, if anybody, should the company work with in developing a foreign market?

Time-scale for foreign market development

Should a company move as quickly as possible to develop a foreign market when the opportunity arises? This approach may have some merit, as being first can give long-term advantages. The market leader's product could become the benchmark by which consumers subsequently judge all products within its class. An early developer could also tie up key distribution outlets, making it difficult for a subsequent competitor to move into the market.

While there may be long-term benefits from being the first company to develop a new category of product in a foreign market, there are also risks. If development is hurried and a product launched before quality can be guaranteed to live up to an organization's international standards, the company's long-term image can be damaged, both in the new foreign market and in its wider world market. In the turbulent marketing environment of eastern Europe in the late 1980s, two of the world's principal fast food retailers—McDonald's and Burger King—pursued quite different strategies. McDonalds waited until political, economic, social, and technological conditions allowed it to launch a restaurant which could meet its global standards. However, Burger King, in its desire to be first in the market, could only offer a sub-standard service giving it an image from which it subsequently struggled to recover.

Risk can be minimized by gradually committing more resources to a market, based on experience to date. Temporary facilities could be established which have low start-up and close-down costs and where the principal physical and human assets can be transferred to another location. Rather than setting up its own distribution system, a company can buy in distribution services from another company, with relatively low close-down costs should the venture fail.

A good example of risk reduction through the use of temporary facilities was found in the pattern of retail development throughout eastern Germany following reunification. Foreign companies were initially reluctant to commit themselves to building stores in specific locations in a part of the country which was still economically unstable and where patterns of land use were rapidly changing. The solution adopted by many companies was to set up branches in temporary marquees or mobile vehicles. These could move in response to the changing pattern of demand. While the location of retail outlets remained risky, this did not prevent retailers from establishing their networks of distribution warehouses which could respond more flexibly to the changing pattern of retail location.

Who should be involved in foreign market development?

An assessment of risk is required in deciding whether an organization should enter a foreign market on its own, or in association with another organization. Going in alone increases the strategic and operational control which the organization has over its foreign operations. However, it exposes it to the greatest risk where the foreign market is relatively poorly understood. A range of entry possibilities are considered below.

Exporting directly to customers overseas

This involves producing goods at a firm's domestic production facilities and shipping them to the foreign market. Choosing to sell directly to customers can be an extremely expensive task where the product in question is low in value and high in volume. Direct exporting is therefore limited to companies who sell specialized, high value products.

Exporting through an export/import agent

Because of the difficulty in obtaining access to foreign customers, many first-time exporters would choose to use an import or export agent. In return for a fee or commission, the agent will use its contacts to exploit distribution opportunities in a foreign market. Agency agreements vary in their time-scale and responsibilities. At one extreme, an agent can be casually recruited to sell a batch of items on a no sale, no fee basis. At the other extreme, an agent may agree to develop a market and be given sole rights to sell the company's product in that market for a number of years.

Direct investment in a foreign subsidiary

Very often it is difficult for an exporter to serve a market from its home base. The cost of transporting goods to foreign markets may put it at a competitive disadvantage. It may even face tariff barriers levied on imported goods. The use of an import or export agent can leave an exporter with very little control over its foreign market.

Direct investment in a foreign subsidiary gives a company maximum control over its foreign operations, but can expose it to a high level of risk where it has only a poor understanding of the foreign market. A company can either set up its own foreign subsidiary from scratch (as many UK hotel companies have done to develop hotels in foreign markets), or it can acquire control of a company which is already trading.

Where the nature of the product offer differs very little between national markets, or where it appeals to an international market (e.g. hotels), the risks from creating a new subsidiary are reduced. Where there are barriers to entry and the product is aimed at a distinctly different local market with its own preferences, the acquisition of an established subsidiary may be preferred. Even the latter course of action is not risk free, as was illustrated by the problems encountered by British Airways following its acquisition of a substantial share in the American airline USAir, which it eventually sold in 1997 following operating losses.

Direct investment in a foreign subsidiary may also be made difficult by legislation restricting ownership of certain services by foreigners. Many developing countries have complex requirements which only allow a foreign investor to acquire a minority stake.

Licensing/Franchising

Rather than setting up its own operations in a foreign market, a company can license a local company to provide a product. A licence allows the local licensee to manufacture and sell the product as if it was made by the licensor itself. The licensee agrees to pay an agreed amount to the licensor for the right to sell its products (usually on the basis of turnover or volume of sales) and agrees to maintain specified quality standards. Licensing is widely used for low value, high volume products such as soft drinks. The Coca-Cola company licenses local bottlers around the world to produce and sell its drinks.

In the case of services, it is necessary for a licensor to retain greater control over the processes of production, and not just the tangible outcome. Licensing, or franchising in a foreign market can take a number of forms. Sometimes, the franchisor would enter into a direct franchising relationship with each individual franchisee. The difficulty in this approach lies in monitoring and controlling a possibly large number of franchisees in a country far from home. To overcome some of these problems, the franchisor would normally establish its own subsidiary in the foreign territory which would negotiate and monitor franchisees locally. Alternatively, it could grant a master franchise for an area to a franchisee where the latter effectively becomes the franchisor in the foreign country.

Franchising can allow an organization to expand rapidly overseas with relatively low capital requirements. However, it is subject to the same issues of control which affect domestic franchise agreements and which were discussed in Chapter 14.

Joint ventures

International joint ventures involve two or more firms sharing their competencies to develop a market. Usually, one of the partners will be a local company in the target market who has detailed knowledge of that market, while another will be a company back home who has technical and/or financial competencies, but little knowledge of foreign markets. Joint ventures can balance a company's desire for control with risk minimization. They can take a number of forms and are particularly attractive to a domestic firm seeking entry to a foreign market in many situations:

■ A joint venture with an organization already based in the proposed foreign market makes the task of collecting information about a market, and responding sensitively to it, relatively easy.

■ A joint venture can spread risk where the initial capital requirement threshold is high.

■ Where foreign governments restrict the rights of foreign companies to set up business on their account, a partnership with a local company—possibly involving a minority shareholding—may be the only means of entering the market.

■ There may be significant barriers to entry which a company already based in the foreign market could help to overcome. A common barrier to entry is access to a comprehensive network of intermediaries.

■ There may be reluctance of consumers to deal with what appears to be a foreign company. A joint venture can allow the operation to be fronted by a domestic producer with whom customers can be familiar, while allowing the foreign partner to provide capital and management expertise.

■ Taxation of company profits may favour a joint venture rather than owning a foreign subsidiary outright.

Joint ventures are an important feature of many business sectors where the benefits listed above can be achieved. They have assumed particular importance in the car manufacturing, airline, and financial services sectors—some recent examples in the latter are shown in Fig. 23.3.

Strategic alliances

Strategic alliances have become an important form of joint venture in international business. They comprise agreements between two or more organizations where each partner seeks to add to its competencies by combining its resources with those of a partner. A strategic alliance generally involves cooperation between partners rather than joint ownership of a subsidiary set up for a specific purpose, although it may include agreement for collaborators to purchase shares in the businesses of other members of the alliance.

Strategic alliances allow individual companies to build upon the relationship which they have developed with their clients by allowing them to sell on services which they do not produce themselves, but are produced by another member of the alliance. This arrangement is reciprocated between members of the alliance. Strategic alliances have become important within the airline industry, where operators share their route networks through 'code-sharing', thereby increasing the range of

Venture Partners	% holding	Subsidiary/Purpose
British Energy PECO Energy	50 50	Creation of new company Amergen to acquire nuclear power stations in USA
British Telecom NS Dutch Railways	50 50	Development of Telfort mobile telephone service in the Netherlands
Siemens AG 3M Corp	50 50	Creation of enterprise to deliver converged voice and data products to enterprise
Shell Texaco	88 12	An opportunity for Shell and Texaco to gain ground in the markets where the joint venture is weak by swapping assets with other players

Figure 23.3 Examples of joint ventures

An introduction to **one**world
The alliance that revolves around you

AmericanAirlines

BRITISH AIRWAYS

Canadian Airlines

CATHAY PACIFIC

QANTAS

Figure 23.4 With the globalization of markets, strategic alliances are becoming increasingly crucial in order to facilitate overseas growth. In the airline sector, an alliance such as the One World alliance allows one airline's services to be marketed by all other alliance members. To its customers, British Airways is able to offer 'seamless' travel around the globe on services of fellow alliance members. For the company, there are opportunities to rationalize operations in foreign countries. (Reproduced with permission of Oneworld Alliance)

origin–destination opportunities which can be provided with a through ticket. Some strategic alliances of airlines, such as the 'One World' alliance comprising British Airways, Quantas, Cathay Pacific, American Airlines, and Canadian Airlines, allow an extensive range of 'seamless' travel possibilities, to the mutual advantage of all members of the alliance.

Global e-commerce

The Internet is changing the landscape of global competition. In theory, a company can use its website to promote its products around the world very cost effectively. A buyer in one country can, in theory, surf the World Wide Web to find the best combination of product and price available to them, regardless of the country in which a supplier is based. The transparency of prices and apparent easy availability of products from overseas suppliers has forced many organizations to see their markets at a global rather than a purely local level.

Although e-commerce has created a lot of interest as a means of opening up world trade, its limitations must be noted. Buyers are just as likely to be cautious about dealing with a foreign company that they have not heard of. If it is difficult enough for a foreign supplier of television sets to establish itself in the UK market when it has real products available for inspection in local shops, how much harder is it going to be for a foreign based Internet Company? Can the buyer trust an unknown brand to perform as promised. What will happen about after sales service? Who can the buyer complain to if things go wrong? There is also the question of actually distributing the product. This has been overcome with some services (for example electronic ticketing has created more efficient and effective competition between airlines). For bulky goods, the sometimes difficult reality of global physical distribution has to be balanced against the simplicity of global promotion through a website.

The Internet is undoubtedly offering new opportunities for firms to enter foreign markets. However, basic rules of foreign market entry still apply and many of the successful uses of global e-commerce have involved more traditional approaches based on joint ventures and strategic alliances. A number of global Internet intermediaries (or informediaries), such as Amazon.com and Yahoo! have emerged as internationally respected brands. For many suppliers entering a foreign market it may be safer and more cost effective to work through these, rather than acting alone.

Chapter summary and key linkages to other chapters

Few firms can afford to define their marketing environment only at the national level. Markets are becoming increasingly global in their nature, presenting opportunities for expansion overseas, but also the threat of new entrants in the domestic market appearing from overseas. Many foreign ventures undertaken by firms fail, suggesting the need for a rigorous appraisal of potential new markets. If a decision is made to enter a foreign market, care must be taken to be sensitive to local needs, while still maintaining the strength and economies of scale of a global brand. Entering a new market involves a high level of risk, and firms often seek to minimize this by sharing risk with other companies, although this can result in a loss of control.

The following key linkages to other chapters should be noted:

Chapter 1: What is marketing?: Companies fail at home because they fail to recognize the basic principles of marketing. In foreign markets, the process of marketing orientation is the same, even if the marketing environment is very different.

Chapter 2: The marketing environment: A thorough analysis of the foreign market environment is crucial. PEST analysis is a useful framework for analysing domestic and foreign markets. Very often, assumptions made about the domestic environment can be very different from those applying overseas.

Chapter 3: Market segmentation: Domestic markets are not homogeneous in their buying behaviour. This applies equally to foreign markets, although the bases for segmentation may differ.

Chapter 4: Branding: A major reason for firms seeking foreign expansion is to exploit a strong brand in as many markets as can be profitably achieved.

Chapter 5: Marketing and ethics: International marketing can raise many ethical issues, for example whether it is right to market a product overseas (such as tobacco) which is severely curtailed at home. Ways of doing business overseas (e.g. through bribes) may conflict with a company's domestic ethical policy.

Chapter 6: Marketing research: The processes of market research are similar to those applying in the domestic market. Problems arise in accessing foreign data and in interpreting results.

Chapter 7: Buyer behaviour: Many foreign ventures have failed because companies have failed to understand how buying processes differ from those in the domestic market (e.g. in respect of the make-up of the decision-making unit).

Chapter 8: Buyer–seller relationship development: Ongoing buyer–seller relationships are a fundamental part of the way many cultures do business. How does a company's relationship marketing strategy adapt to cultural norms?

Chapters 9/10: Developing a product portfolio: Are there any opportunities for new product development in a foreign market which are not evident at home? Should the product portfolio differ between home and foreign markets?

Chapter 11: Developing a sustainable competitive advantage: Many companies have launched successfully in a foreign market, with high levels of support from the parent company back home. But how can a high initial uptake be converted into profitable and sustainable long-term business?

Chapters 12/13: Pricing: Should a company adopt a uniform or local approach to pricing? How effective is price discrimination between markets? How should pricing strategy be developed in each market?

Chapters 14/15: Intermediaries: Which intermediaries are most appropriate to a foreign market? How are intermediaries selected, motivated, and controlled? What opportunities and constraints for physical distribution management are present in the foreign market?

Chapters 16–20: Principles of promotion planning/advertising/sales promotion/ personal selling/direct marketing: How does the company build up a strong global brand image? To what extent should it adapt its promotion to local circumstances?

Chapter 21: Organizing for marketing: How does a company control an operation in an environment which may be a long way from base and culturally quite different? Should it rely on locally recruited employees or use expatriates?

Chapter 22: Services marketing: Services are increasingly entering international trade, but because of the inseparability of services, direct export is generally not a possibility. Service companies must either go to their customers, or customers must come to the company.

Case study

Bass exploits fragmented Czech beer sector

Why should one of the UK's leading brewers choose to develop the market for beer in a country which is already saturated with famous beers at rock bottom prices? To lovers of real ale, the Czech Republic is probably a heaven. But to Bass Breweries, the Czech market represented an opportunity waiting to be developed.

Eastern Europe, and the Czech Republic in particular, has one of the world's highest rates of per capita consumption of beer, which in 1997 stood at 160 litres per person, double the rate of most western European countries. The Czech Republic has a long tradition of brewing, with some of the world's oldest and most respected beers, including the Staropramen, Ostravar, and Vratislav brands. One of the reasons for the high consumption of beer has been its high quality and low price. The price of a litre of beer in 1997 was typically less than a quarter of what a comparable litre would have cost in the UK, the low price reflecting low taxes and low margins for producers.

So in a country of high quality beers and low prices, what possibly could Bass hope to add to the market? When it first looked at the beer market in the Czech Republic, it saw a fragmented market where marketing was just emerging after decades of centralized planning. Beer drinkers had become used to a mentality of taking what was available, rather than seeking the best product to suit their needs. Bass saw that the fragmented market was ripe for consolidation. In 1997, the three largest breweries held only 55 per cent of the market, with another 25 per cent being made up of small regional brewers, none of whom had a national market share of over 3 per cent. Even Budwar, possibly the best known Czech beer in the UK, accounted for just 3 per cent of the domestic market. Many of the Czech Republic's near neighbours had similar structural problems and opportunities in their beer sector and, like other western investors, Bass saw the country as a platform for expansion into the rest of eastern Europe.

In addition to exploiting the Czech market, Bass also saw an opportunity to develop global markets for the high quality beers which were currently confined to the domestic Czech market. Bass could use its global distribution network to exploit the brands in a way that would have been impossible to domestic companies.

Bass first invested in the Czech Republic in 1994, with a 34 per cent stake in Prague Breweries, later increasing this to 46 per cent. This brought Bass three Prague-based breweries which would have seemed quite small and unsophisticated by UK standards. In 1995 it bought 78 per cent of Vratislavice nad Nisou (with two breweries in North Boherrda) and 51 per cent of Ostravar, a brewery in North Moravia. In 1996 Bass acquired a controlling interest in Prague Breweries when it increased its stake to 51 per cent. In 1997, the three companies in which it had invested were merged under the name Prague Breweries, in which Bass has a 55 per cent stake. This made Prague Breweries the second-biggest brewer in the Czech Republic, but it still only had a 14 per cent market share. The market leader, Prazdroj, had 27 per cent. Bass had started the process of consolidation in the industry, but it still had a long way to go if it was to match progress in western Europe.

The merger of the three breweries started the process of reducing competition in the sector. It also gave an opportunity to begin cutting costs, by disposing of three of its six breweries. It decided early on that its core business was brewing and subsequently sold on its acquired soft drinks businesses to Corona.

A further approach to making the Czech market profitable was the development of strong brands which could be sold at decent margins. By 1997 Bass had four national and three regional brands, but took a pragmatic approach to retaining the long-established regional brands—they would be retained as long as people continued to buy them. Doubtless Bass was mindful of the shortsightedness of UK brewers' attempts to suppress regional brands a couple of decades earlier, only to see them find a valuable role a few years later. Its first new product development in the country was a premium lager called Velvet, developed and brewed in the Czech Republic, but with the help of Bass in the UK. From the beginning, Bass sought to position Velvet as something quite different from commodity beers. It had a distinctive smooth, creamy head and Bass commissioned special glasses for it to be served in. To add to its differentiation, Bass provided training for bar staff on how to pour and serve it. Velvet was aimed at high-income consumers and promoted through bars and restaurants with targeted tastings. Promotional support was provided by advertising in *Elle*, *Harper's Bazaar*, and *Esquire*, and by a dedicated sales team. Despite the conservatism of Czech drinkers, Bass had successfully found a niche market—the emerging middle classes in stylish bars. Bass's strategy has been to invest heavily in brands for the long term. In developing a brand, the company has started with a research programme among consumers to learn more about their beer needs, followed with research on respondents' perceptions of competing brands. It then undertook lifestyle segmentation, something previously unheard of.

Another strength of Bass in its home market is distribution and this represented another opportunity in the Czech market. By the end of 1997, a new sales, marketing, and distribution structure was in place, making it possible to distribute national brands efficiently and effectively. The structure included national marketing, key account, and business development teams, along with a unified sales force and distribution network. In three years, one result of this reorganization had been to increase penetration of the company's products from 50 to 80 per cent of all retail outlets in the country.

Overcoming cultural barriers of the Czech people proved to be one of the biggest challenges for Bass. It seemed that many people found change to a market-based system difficult to cope with, after 40 years of centralized planning. The whole idea of customer focus seemed to lack credibility among employees who had been used to customers having no choice. While Bass might have been expert at brewing, branding, and distribution issues, it underestimated how much time it would have to spend to change management issues and instilling western values into staff. Problems were found in getting people to make decisions, motivating them to act on their decision, and then having to check that agreed actions were actually being undertaken. Recruitment, appraisal, and reward increasingly stressed a number of key attitudes of mind: being customer focused, results driven, and innovative, behaving with integrity, treating people with respect, and showing respect for the community. As an example of the problems that had to be overcome, salesmen had a pride that prevented them from listening to retailers, fostered by years of production orientation.

Based on 'Brewing Up', *Marketing Business*, December 1998, pp. 26–30.

Case study review questions

1 Review the alternative market entry strategies that were open to Bass in 1994 and assess each for its level of risk.

2 Identify the principal barriers Bass faces in developing a marketing culture in its Czech operations. How can it overcome these barriers?

3 Critically assess the problems and opportunities for Bass's investment in the Czech Republic arising from further integration of the country into the European Union.

Chapter review questions

1 Examine the reasons why a UK-based furniture retailer should seek to expand into continental Europe

2 What cultural differences might cause problems for a fast food chain developing outlets in India?

3 How might a UK clothing manufacturer go about researching market potential for its products in Germany?

4 In what circumstances is a global, rather than a localized, marketing strategy likely to be successful?

5 Suggest methods by which a firm of building contractors can minimize the risk of proposed foreign expansion.

6 What is meant by a strategic alliance and why are they of importance to the services sector? Give examples of strategic alliances.

Suggested further reading

The following references offer a general review of the factors that influence firms' foreign expansion decisions.

■ Cateora, G. (1996), *International Marketing*, 9th edn. (New York: McGraw-Hill).

■ Chee, H., and Harris, R. (1998), *Global Marketing Strategy* (London: Pitman).

■ Paliwoda, S. J. (1998), *International Marketing*, 3rd edn. (Oxford: Butterworth-Heinemann).

■ Spencer, J. (1994), *Principles of International Marketing* (Oxford: Blackwell).

■ Walsh, L. S. (1995), *International Marketing*, 3rd edn. (London: Pitman).

For a general overview of trends in international business, consult the following:

■ Czinkota, M. R., and Kotabe, M. (1997), *Trends in International Business* (Oxford: Blackwell).

- 'Overseas Trade', a DTI-FCO magazine for exporters published ten times per year by Brass Tacks Publishing Co., London.

- World Trade Organization, *Annual Report*, published annually.

- ——— *Trade Policy Review* (serial).

For statistics on the changing pattern of UK trade, the following regularly updated publications of the Office for National Statistics provide good coverage:

- Economic Trends: a monthly publication which includes statistics relating to international trade performance.

- Overseas Direct Investment: detailed breakdown of UK overseas direct investment activity, outward and inward, by component, country, and industry.

The homogenization of world markets and the development of global brands is covered in the following:

- Ritzer, G. (1995), *The MacDonaldization of Society* (Pine Forge Press).

- Samiee, S., and Roth, K. (1992), 'The Influence of Global Marketing on Performance', *Journal of Marketing*, **56**, 2, pp. 1–17.

- Simms, J. (1998), 'Global Branding: Do the Right Thing', *Marketing Business*, Apr., pp. 24–29.

For a review of the development of the European Economic Area, the following are useful:

- EU Sources:
  Bulletin
  European Voice
  Frontier-Free Europe
  European Business Journal
  Bulletin of the European Community

- Mayes, D. G. (ed.) (1995), *The European Challenge: Industry's Response to the 1992 Programme* (London: Harvester Wheatsheaf).

- McDonald, F., and Dearden, S. (eds) (1998), *European Economic Integration* (Harlow: Longman).

- Perry, K. (1994), *Business and the European Community* (Oxford: Butterworth-Heinemann).

Strategic alliances are becoming increasingly important and the following references provide greater insight into their operation:

- Meyer, H. (1998), 'My Enemy, My Friend', *Journal of Business Strategy*, **19**, 5, pp. 42–6.

- Ohmae, K. (1989), 'The Global Logic of Strategic Alliances', *Harvard Business Review*, Mar.-Apr., pp. 143–54.

Useful web links

Overseas Trade Statistics: http://www.ons.gov.uk

EmuNet: The on-line gateway to Europe: http://www.euro-emu.co.uk/

OECD International Trade:—Statistics on International transactions: http://www.oecd.org/std/serint.htm

U.S. International Trade Statistics: http://www.census.gov/ftp/pub/foreign-trade/www/

International Business Resources on the WWW: Statistical Data and Information Resources: http://www.ciber.msu.edu/busres/statinfo.htm

University of Massachusettes database of international business periodicals, economic surveys, country factbooks, export/import information, statistical compilations and guides to government contacts and trade associations: http://www.lib.umb.edu/reference/int_buss.html

Glossary

ACORN ('A Classification of Residential Neighbourhood') A widely used geodemographic database of residential locality types.

Adoption Rate at which individuals start buying a product.

Advertising The process by which an advertiser communicates with target audiences through paid-for messages.

Advertising agency An organization which specializes in communication on behalf of clients.

Advertising campaign A coherent and planned approach to communication over a specified period of time.

Advertising media Communication channels such as radio, television, and newspapers.

Agent An individual or company acting in a capacity on behalf of a principal (e.g. a sales agent). An agent does not take ownership or handle goods.

AIDA model (Attention, Interest, Desire, Action) A mnemonic used to describe the process of communicating a message.

Augmented product The core product offer with the addition of differentiating benefits, e.g. additional services.

Awareness The proportion of a target audience who have heard of a particular product or service (either 'prompted' or 'unprompted').

Below the line Expenditure on promotional activities which involves non-commission paying media.

Benchmarking Setting performance goals for an organization based on those achieved by its competitiors.

Branding The process of creating a distinctive identity for a product which differentiates it from its competitors.

Budget The amount of money scheduled to be spent and received in future periods.

Business cycle Fluctuations in the level of activity in an economy, commonly measured by employment levels and aggregate demand.

Buying behaviour The way in which customers act, and the processes involved in making a purchase decision.

Cannibalization Occurs where one product within a company's range reduces sales of other products in its range.

Cartel An association of suppliers which seeks to restrict costly competition between its members.

Communication mix The various media and messages which are used to communicate with a target audience.

Competitive advantage A firm has a marketing mix that the target market sees as meeting its needs better than the mix of competing firms.

Consumer The final user of a good or a service.

Consumer goods Goods or services which are targeted at private individuals, rather than at organizations.

Consumer panel Research involving a group of consumers who continuously report on their purchases over a period of time.

Consumerism Actions taken to promote change by organizations which protects the interests of consumers.

Contingency planning An alternative

plan which can be rapidly implemented if the assumptions underlying the original plan turn out to be false.

Core product The essential benefit provided by a good or service.

Corporate planning Planning which involves all functions within an organization.

Cost per thousand Used in advertising as a measure of cost per thousand people viewing or reading the advertisement.

Cost plus pricing A pricing method in which a percentage 'mark-up' is added to the costs of a product.

Coverage The percentage of a targeted audience that have an opportunity to see a particular advertisement.

Culture The whole set of beliefs, attitudes, and ways of behaving shared by a group of people.

Customer People who buy a firm's products (although customers may not be the actual consumers of the product).

DAGMAR model (Defining Advertising Goals for Measured Advertising Results) An acronym for a model of the communication process.

Database marketing (DBM) The use of a list of customers (potential and actual) which drives communication between an organization and its customers.

Decision-making unit (DMU) The group of individuals who are involved in making a purchase decision.

Decision-support system Models which are used to inform management decisions on the bases of available data.

Demand The willingness and ability of buyers to buy a particular product at a particular time.

Demography The study of population characteristics, e.g. relating to broad population statistics, such as age, sex.

Desk research Research which uses existing (secondary) sources of information.

Differentiation Creating a product which is different in some way from its main competitors, in the eyes of the target market.

Diffusion The rate at which new products are adopted by different adoption categories.

Direct mail A form of below-the-line advertising which uses personalized communication sent directly from the advertiser through the post to potential customers.

Direct marketing Direct communication between a seller and individual customers using a promotion method other than face-to-face selling.

Discriminatory pricing Selling a product at two or more prices, where the difference in prices is not based on differences in costs.

Distributor A person or organization who assists in the task of maketing goods and services available to end users. Distributors take ownership of goods from suppliers and are responsible for collecting payments.

Diversification Broadening the spread of markets served and/or products supplied by a business.

Economies of scale Costs per unit fall as total output increases.

Elasticity Responsiveness of customer demand to changes in price.

Entrepreneur An individual who takes risks to profitably exploit business opportunities.

Environmental set The elements within an organization' s environment which are currently of major concern to it.

Environment Everything that exists outside the boundaries of a system.

Ethics Statements of what is right and wrong.

Exchange rate The price of one currency expressed in terms of another currency.

Experimental research A research

approach which evaluates alternatives within a controlled framework.

Exploratory research Initial marketing research used to review a problem in general before committing larger expenditure to as study.

External benefits Product benefits for which the producer cannot appropriate value from recipients.

External costs Production costs which are borne by individuals or firms who are not compensated for the costs they incur.

Fast-moving consumer goods (FMCGs) Frequently purchased products, usually of low value.

Field research Primary research, not using existing published sources.

Fixed costs Costs that do not increase as total output increases.

Focus group A qualitative research technique in which groups of consumers are brought together to discuss their views and attitudes to a specific topic.

Franchising An agreement where a franchisor develops a product format and marketing strategy and sells the right for other individuals or organizations ('franchisees') to use that format.

Gatekeepers Members of a decision-making unit who control access to information about available choices.

Geodemographic analysis The analysis of markets using a combination of geographic and demographic information.

Global brands Goods and services which can have universal appeal and are marketed in numerous countries with little modification to product or image.

Hierarchy of needs A model of consumer behaviour proposed by A. Maslow.

Horizontal integration Merging of firms' activities at a similar point in a value chain.

Image The perceptions of a product, brand, or company.

Industrial goods Goods which are bought by industrial organizations.

Imperfect market A market in which the assumptions of perfect competition are violated.

Income elasticity of demand A measure of the responsiveness of demand for a product to changes in household incomes.

Industrialization of services The process of standardizing and mass producing services.

Inseparability The inability to separate consumption of a service from its production.

Intangibility The inability to assess a service using any tangible evidence.

Intermediaries Individuals or organizations involved in transferring goods and services from the producer to the final consumer.

Internal marketing The application of the principles and practices of marketing to an organization's dealings with its employees.

Joint venture An agreement between two or more firms to exploit a business opportunity, in which capital funding, profits, risk, and core competencies are shared.

Just-in-time production Reliably producing goods and getting them to customers just before customers need them.

Key client A customer who is particularly important to an organization.

Ladder of loyalty A representation of the stages a buyer goes through in the process of becoming a committed and loyal customer of a supplier.

Life cycle A phenomenon that exhibits cyclical patterns (e.g. in respect of products, markets, and buyer–seller relationships).

Loyalty Non-random repeat purchasing from a seller, with behavioural and attitudinal dimensions.

Macro-environment The general external

business environment in which a firm operates.

Marginal cost The addition to total cost resulting from the production of one additional unit of output.

Market A group of potential customers with similar needs who are willing to exchange something of value with sellers offering products that satisfy their needs.

Market development A strategy used by an organization to increase sales by offering their existing product in new markets.

Market leader The organization which has the greatest share of sales in a given market.

Market penetration A strategy used by an organization to increase sales by offering more of their existing products to their existing markets.

Market research Activity to acquire knowledge of external factors relating to an organization's market-place.

Market research agencies Organizations employed by client companies to collect information about the client company's market-place (although market research agencies do not strictly act in an 'agency' capacity).

Market segmentation A process of identifying groups of customers within a broad product market who share similar needs and respond similarly to a given marketing mix formulation.

Market share One company's sales value (or volume) as a proportion of the total sales (or volume) for that market.

Marketing The management process which identifies, anticipates, and supplies customer requirements efficiently and profitably (CIM definition).

Marketing audit A systematic review of a company's marketing activities and of its marketing environment.

Marketing environment The social, economical, legal, political, cultural, and technological factors, external to an organization which affect its actions.

Marketing information system A systematic way of collecting, analysing, and disseminating information which is relevant to the company's marketing.

Marketing intelligence Relatively unstructured information about trends and events in a company's marketing environment.

Marketing mix A series of convenient headings for decisions to be made by marketing managers in eliciting a profitable consumer response.

Marketing planning A systematic process of analysing a company's environment, then developing objectives, strategies, and action which are appropriate to the company's resources.

Marketing research Distinguished from market research because marketing research is concerned with research into all of a company's marketing functions (e.g. research into pricing and distribution effectiveness).

Mark-up Selling price based on production costs, plus a margin for profit.

Matrix organization structure An organization structure which relies on co-ordination of management through cross-functional group leaders.

Media Channels of communication, e.g. television, radio, newspapers, etc.

Mission statement A means of reminding everyone within an organization of the essential purpose of the organization.

Model of buyer behaviour A simplified representation of the processes that buyers go through in making a purchase decision.

Monopoly A market in which there is only one supplier. Rarely achieved in practice, as most products have some form of substitute.

Mystery shoppers An observational form of marketing research.

Needs The underlying forces that drive an individual to make a purchase which will remove the feeling of deprivation.

New product development The process of identifying, developing, and evaluating new product offers.

Niche A small sub-segment of a market which can be targeted with a distinct marketing strategy.

Noise Factors that distort the flow of communication between sender and receiver.

Non-price competition Non-price benefits such as warranties or additional features or merchandising which can give a company's product a competitive advantage.

Objective A target to be achieved.

Observational research Research which studies customers' reactions and behaviour without any direct interaction.

Oligopoly A market dominated by a few interdependent suppliers.

Omnibus survey A regular questionnaire undertaken on behalf of multiple clients, usually involving very large samples.

Organic growth A 'natural' form of growth in which a company's growth rate is influenced by its previous success rate.

OTS (opportunities to see) The average number of viewing occasions for a particular advertisement.

Perfect competition A market in which there are no barriers to entry, no one firm can dominate the market, there is full information available to all buyers and sellers, and all sellers sell an undifferentiated product.

Perishability Services perish instantly, as the service offer cannot be stored for sale at a future time.

Personal selling A face-to-face communication between an organization and its customers, with a view to achieving a sale.

PEST analysis (or 'STEP') Elements of the macro-marketing environment, comprising political / legal, economic, social / cultural and technological environments.

Physical distribution management The process of ensuring that the right goods get to the right place at the right time, cost effectively.

Place The point where a product is to be made available to consumers.

Point of sale (or Point of purchase) In retail, the area where customers make their final decision to buy.

Positioning A marketing mix which gives an organization a competitive advantage within its chosen target market.

Press release News story written for, and distributed to, the news media with a view to inclusion in media editorial.

Pressure group A group which is formed to promote a particular cause.

Price elasticity of demand A measure of the responsiveness of demand for a product to change in the price of the product.

Primary data Original data obtained from field research.

Product life cycle The different stages through which a product develops over time, reflecting different needs, sales levels, and profitability.

Product line A number of related products offered by a supplier, which often covers a broadly similar type of need.

Product mix The total range of goods and services offered by an organization.

Production orientation Where the focus of an organization is on production capability rather than consumers' needs.

Productivity The efficiency with which inputs are turned into outputs.

Profit The excess of revenue over costs (although it can be difficult to calculate costs, and therefore profit).

Promotion mix The combination of media and messages which a company uses to communicate with actual and potential customers.

Prospecting A technique to identify potential new customers.

Psychographics A basis for segmentation derived from attitudinal and behavioural variables.

Public relations A deliberate and planned effort to create mutual understanding between an organization and its various publics.

Pull strategy A marketing strategy in which the manufacturer promotes directly to the final customers, who then demand products from intermediaries, who in turn 'pull' goods from the manufacturer.

Push strategy A marketing strategy in which the manufacturer promotes primarily to intermediaries, relying on them to promote to their customers.

Quality The standard of delivery of goods or services, often expressed in terms of the extent to which they meet customers' expectations.

Qualitative research Research which produces essentially attitudinal, non-numerical data.

Quantitative research Research based on large samples, but which may be lacking in interpretation. Sometimes called 'hard data'.

Questionnaire A set of questions used to obtain information from a respondent.

Quota sample A sampling method where those questioned are numerically in proportion to pre-defined characteristics, e.g. sex, age, occupation.

Random sample A sampling method where everyone in the population has an equal chance of being included in the sample.

Relationship marketing A means by which an organization seeks to maintain an ongoing relationship between itself and its

customers, based on continuous patterns of service delivery, rather than isolated and discrete transactions.

Repositioning The development of a new marketing mix relative to that of competitors, to replace the existing mix.

Sales orientation The focus of an organization is on selling its products more aggressively, while probably not fully understanding the needs of customers and the types of products they would prefer to buy.

Sales promotion Techniques and incentives used to increase short-term sales.

Scientific approach Using the rules of scientific procedure in order to ensure objectivity and repeatability.

Sealed bid pricing Submission of a price quotation for supplying goods or services, in which the identity or price of competitng bids is not known.

Secondary research Using previously conducted research.

Segment A grouping of customers who have similar needs and respond in a similar way to a given marketing stimulus.

Services Products which are essentially intangible and cannot be owned.

Social responsibility Accepting corporate responsibilities to customers and non-customers which go beyond legal or contractual requirements.

Societal marketing Marketing which attempts to improve social benefits.

Socio-economic groups A grouping of the population based on occupation.

Speciality goods Consumer goods for which buyers are prepared or make an effort to acquire.

Sponsorship Payment by a company to be associated with a particular event or activity.

Stakeholder Any person with an interest in the activities of an organization (e.g.

customers, employees, government agencies, and local communities).

Stimulus A trigger that starts a purchasing process.

Strategic alliances Agreements between organizations which are based on a long-term recognition that they could each benefit by co-operating on some aspect of their marketing.

Strategy The overall, long-term direction or approach which a company aims to follow, in order to achieve its objectives.

SWOT analysis An acronym for strengths and weaknesses, opportunities and threats and used to assess the internal strengths and weaknesses of an organization against its external threats and opportunities.

Tactics operational activities that put into effect a company's marketing strategy.

Target market The segment of a market at which a marketing mix is aimed.

Test marketing A trial launch of a product into a limited area to test its marketing mix prior to a full national launch.

Telemarketing Sales activity which focuses on the use of the telephone to enter into a two-way dialogue with present and potential customers.

Unique selling proposition (USP) A selling claim based on a differentiated product feature or unique element of the marketing mix.

Value chain The sequence of activities and organizations involved in transforming a product from one which is of low value to one that is of high value.

Vertical integration The extension of a firm's activities to previous or subsequent points in a value chain.

Vertical marketing systems (VMS) The integration of intermediaries at different levels of a distribution chain to improve efficiency and effectiveness of the chain as a whole.

Wholesaler An intermediary which buys products in bulk and resells them in smaller quantities to retailers.

Word-of-mouth promotion The act of recommendation by exisiting customers to their friends.

Subject Index

Index of Authors Cited in Text

Index of Organizations and Brands Cited in Text